been the subject of substantial debate in recent years. While caricatures are not always helpful, it is broadly true to say that German scholarship has advocated the model of peaceful infiltration while American scholarship has posited that of violent conquest. A *via media* emerged in the 1960s when the Settlement was explained in terms of social revolution. In the last 25 years, attention has focused on the internal dynamics of Canaan which led to the emergence of the Israelite nation.[4]

Before reviewing these different theories, it will be helpful to consider an article by Neil Asher Silberman which helpfully observes (and by no means self-evidently) that the description of the Israelite Settlement process by scholars of different generations reflects the interests and outlook of the scholar and generation in question.[5] This is the methodological observation that the interpretation of uncertain evidence is not free from the interpretive bias of the reader; and that each act of interpretation utilizes the previous experiences and beliefs of the interpreter, so that the act of reading is far from an innocent one.

The notion of a gradual and peaceful infiltration into Canaan by the Israelites was proposed by Albrecht Alt.[6] More recent supporters of this theory include such influential figures as Martin Noth, Alberto Soggin and Yohanan Aharoni.[7] This theory was, however, challenged by American and Israeli scholars who maintained that the Settlement was in fact a conquest: an organized and systematic military invasion by Joshua and his supporters. Scholars who incline to this view include William Foxwell Albright, John Bright and Yigael Yadin.[8]

The *via media* emerged during the 1960s under the influence of George Mendenhall and Norman Gottwald.[9] This so-called 'internal revolution hypothesis' takes the view that poor Canaanites oppressed by demands for taxation from Egypt burned their cities in revolt and fled to the highlands in an effective process of retribalization. Mendenhall thinks that a number of Yahweh worshippers from Egypt crystallized this revolt. Gottwald argues against any outside group, seeing the internal struggle in the Canaanite cities in Marxist categories as an act of peasant rebellion.

None of these models has escaped criticism from the scholarly guild. The chief weakness of the peaceful infiltration theory is its inability to prove that a large number of Israelites came from outside Palestine.[10] Moreover, Alt has been criticized for an inadequate understanding of nomadism and for ignoring the plain statement of the Pentateuch that the Israelites initially saw the promised land as a hostile environment.[11] The violent conquest model has received much fiercer criticism.[12] Its supporters were censured for their naive assumption that archaeology necessarily verifies biblical texts.[13] Moreover, the destroyed cities in Canaan fell at different times and were probably attacked by the Egyptians in military campaigns. Ahlström argues further that the continuity of material culture between the Canaanites and the Israelites speaks against the idea of an external origin for the Settlement.[14] Gottwald's articulation of the 'revolutionary' hypothesis has been criticized over the lack of any evidence for a peasants' revolt in Israel;[15] while both Gottwald and Mendenhall have been censured for relying too heavily on cultural evolution theories which reflect little knowledge of nomadic societies, as well as for the trust they place in the notion of an early covenant and amphictyonic league in Israel.

This criticism has led to the emergence of the fourth or 'new' model, according to which the Israelite community arose peacefully and internally in the highlands of Palestine.[16] This new model itself takes two forms: the 'frontier society' model of Joseph Callaway and the symbiosis or internal nomadic model of Volkmar Fritz and Israel Finkelstein.[17] Callaway laid the ground for this theory with his excavations at Ai and Raddana.[18] These disclosed that the inhabitants of these, presumably Israelite, sites had much the same skills as the Canaanites of the lowlands. Callaway thinks that people simply retreated to the highlands because they were less congested than the lowlands. This is the 'frontier society' view, according to which people withdraw to a previous undeveloped frontier to find an effective mode of subsistence.

Fritz also excavated in the Negev and uncovered evidence of continuity between Israelite and Canaanite culture.[19] Fritz believed that the occupants of the highland villages could not have come from the cities. He suggested they migrated into the land in the fifteenth or fourteenth century BCE; and that the collapse of the Canaanite urban centres between 1225 and 1175 BCE encouraged them to expand and engage in farming.[20] Finkelstein thinks that these people lived in Israel throughout the Late Bronze Age (1550–1200 BCE) and that when the Canaanite cities declined, they had to engage in agriculture to compensate for the goods which they could no longer obtain from the cities.

This brief discussion shows that our understanding of biblical history is in continual process of assessment. The most recent theory of the Settlement is the model of 'peaceful transition', according to which the emergence of highland Israel was due to the synthesis or amalgamation of several different peoples. The answers are by no means clear in the Bible. The Bible must be read in the light of scholarship, and scholarship tested in the light of the Bible. In another context, this is true also of the rise and development of monotheistic faith in Israel.[21]

The Monarchy

The next significant phase in the emergence of the Jewish nation-state was the development of a centralized bureaucracy which provided order for a previously disparate people. This happened over a gradual period. The Israelites lived in Canaan without a monarchy for two centuries following the original settlement. The military threats posed by the inhabitants of Hazor (Judges 4–5) and the Midianites (Judges 6–8) threw up individual and evidently impromptu military leaders. Only later (1 Samuel 8–10) was it recognized that such crises could be better addressed through centralization.[22]

The crucial stage was Gideon's victory over the Midianites described in Judges 8. Gideon was offered and declined the kingship (Judg. 8.22-3). His son Abimelech had no such reserve, but this early experiment at monarchy proved unsuccessful (Judges 9). There were further moves in this direction in the eleventh century when the Israelite tribes began to expand beyond the highlands of Canaan. This brought them into conflict with other peoples. Saul's initial success with the Ammonites (1 Samuel 11) and Philistines (1 Samuel 13–14) led to his election as king.[23] After Saul's death in battle (1 Samuel 31), David was anointed king (2 Samuel 7). David founded a small nation-state based on Jerusalem which was placed on a surer footing by his son, Solomon. It was Solomon who established a bureaucracy and consolidated his father's advances (1 Kgs 4.1-6), enlarging Jerusalem and building the first temple.

Problems, however, set in on Solomon's death. Rehoboam was pronounced king in Jerusalem (1 Kgs 11.43b), but he was rejected in the northern outpost of Shechem where people had grievances inherited from Solomon's day, principally concerning the issue of taxation. They offered the kingship to Jeroboam who established a new state based in Shechem (1 Kgs 12.25). The strong implication of this division is that a 'united kingdom' never substantially existed. The (probably superficial) unity achieved by David and Solomon was set aside almost immediately afterwards. This led to the emergence of two separate kingdoms which lasted for two centuries: the northern kingdom of Israel (or Ephraim) and the southern kingdom of Judah.[24]

Following some successes, notably during the reign of Jeroboam II (786–746 BCE), the northern kingdom fell under the shadow of the Assyrians. Internal strife led to Menahem (745–737 BCE) becoming a vassal of the Assyrians to whom he was required to pay tribute (2 Kgs 15.19-20). This policy was continued by his son Pekahiah (737–736 BCE), but it changed when Pekahiah was assassinated by Pekah. Pekah joined Aram in an anti-Assyrian coalition and was firmly put down by his masters. The result was a rump state ruled by Hoshea (732–724 BCE). Foolishly, Hoshea negotiated with Egypt in 724 BCE and the Israelite army was crushed by Shalmaneser V. Samaria was besieged and finally captured. Samaria became an Assyrian province and was repopulated. This was the origin of the Samaritan schism which is reflected in more than one place in the New Testament.[25]

Judah fared no better at the hands of foreign overlords. Hezekiah (715–687 BCE) also moved against Assyrian occupation, as a result of which the Assyrians marched through the land in 701 and captured 46 cities before laying siege to Jerusalem. The city was saved only when the

Assyrians suddenly broke off the siege. Hezekiah had to pay substantially increased tribute in consequence. Manasseh (687–642 BCE) remained compliant to Assyria. Amon (642–640 BCE) was assassinated by anti-Assyrian factionaries. Josiah (640–609 BCE) is credited with his eponymous 'reforms' which have been described both as a cultural revolution and as an attempt at national liberation rather than religious reform as such.[26] He was killed by the Egyptians at Megiddo in 609 BCE.

There was a further change in fortune when the Babylonian Nebuchadnezzar defeated the Egyptians at Carchemish in 605 BCE. Jehoiakim, the king of Judah, rebelled in 598 BCE and Jerusalem was captured in 597 BCE. Zedekiah was appointed king and initially paid tribute to the new overlords. This changed, however, in 591 BCE when with Egyptian support he decided to withold the required payment.

The Exile

Nebuchadnezzar was not amused by this change in policy. Zedekiah was captured and exiled (2 Kgs 25.5–7). The Babylonians destroyed the temple and royal palace in Jerusalem, executing or exiling the leading people in 587 BCE. This was the event known as 'the exile' to which the prophecies of Ezekiel, Jeremiah and Deutero-Isaiah are variously addressed.[27]

The Babylonians did not react as the Assyrians had done with Israel. They did not import outsiders. Nebuchadnezzar appointed Gedaliah as governor (2 Kgs 25.22-4). Gedaliah was subsequently murdered. This led to the flight of Jeremiah and others to Egypt (Jer. 41.17–43.7). That was effectively the end of the monarchical period in Israel.

Jeremiah prophesied that the exile would last seventy years (Jer. 25.11). It was in fact shorter than this. The return was effected by the demise of the Babylonian empire and the emergence of Cyrus the Persian. This is why Isa. 45.1 calls Cyrus God's 'anointed'. In 539 BCE Babylon fell to the Persians. In 538 BCE Cyrus issued a decree ordering the restoration of the Jewish community in Palestine (Ezra 1.2–4; 6.3–5). We know from non-biblical sources that many Jews chose not to return to their homeland.[28] In the words of John Bright, 'it is probable that only a few of the boldest and most dedicated spirits were willing to accompany Shesh-bazzar' as he set out for Jerusalem (Ezra 1.5).[29] The foundations of the temple were relaid almost immediately (Ezra 5.16; cf. Zech. 4.9). Yet we know from Haggai and Zechariah that the reconstruction of the post-exilic community, with temple worship at its centre, was a slow and painful business.[30] Zech. 4.10 calls this time 'the day of small things'. This period is chronicled also by Isaiah 56–66. Economic and social tensions were prevalent. The temple was only completed some 22 years after the return from Babylon. This second temple lasted until the days of Herod the Great.

The post-exilic community was the social location for the redaction

of the Pentateuch.[31] The religious situation at this time is documented
by Ezra and Nehemiah. Both the rebuilding of the temple and the establishment of the law in the restored Israel are presented as significant
religious enterprises. Ezra 9 hopes for the removal of the Persian yoke
and criticizes the practice of intermarriage.

The Antiochian Crisis

We now leap forward to the post-biblical period. In order to understand
this period of history, we need briefly to know something about the
third century BCE.[32] This was the age of Alexander the Great (336–323
BCE).[33] Alexander's untimely death at the age of 33 led to factions among
his former generals, the two most important of whom for our purposes
were Ptolemy (Lagi) and Seleucus (I). The former seized control of Egypt,
establishing his capital at Alexandria. The latter inherited Babylonia.
Both men desired Palestine and Phoenicia; Ptolemy got control of this
region in 301 BCE. Palestine during the third century was ruled by the
Ptolemaic dynasty.

Throughout this was a time of relative prosperity, the contours of which have been
eloquently described by Martin Hengel in his *Judaism and Hellenism*.[34]
Hengel shows that the Palestinian harbours were important strategically
and commercially. The Zeno papyrus discloses something of the economic resources of the region during this period. The slave trade was
especially profitable. Palestine also exported grain to Egypt and olive
oil to Greece. Finds of coins support this commercial boom. Hengel's
conclusion is that 'by and large it may be assumed that in Palestine,
as in Egypt, agricultural and commercial production was considerably
increased, leading not only to a substantial increase in the revenue from
taxes but also to an increase in the population itself'.[35]

Things changed, however, at the beginning of the second century BCE.
The initial event in this was the accession of Antiochus III (the Great) in
223 BCE. In 198 BCE Antiochus defeated the army of the child Ptolemy
IV Philopator at Panium. Josephus says that the Jews received the news of
this event with joy (*Ant.* 12.3). Antiochus showed the Jews great consideration. He ordered the return of Jewish refugees and remitted taxes
for three years. Ominously, though, the legacy of Alexander the Great
had created the possibility for a much more uniform or widespread
cultural understanding in the Near East than had pertained previously.
Palestine was not innocent of this cultural shift, which brought with it
a marked division of opinion among the different parties involved.
Antiochus III died in 187 BCE and was succeeded by Seleucus IV in 187
BCE, then by Antiochus IV (Epiphanes) in 175 BCE. This last date is a
crucial one for all students of post-biblical Judaism.

The situation in Jerusalem at this time was a complicated one.[36] The
hereditary high priesthood was held by Onias III whom 2 Macc. 4.2 calls

'a zealot for the laws'. Yet Jerusalem was by no means full of people who agreed with this position. Judaea was encircled by Greek towns. It was inevitable that Greek culture should and did permeate inwards under this influence. 1 Macc. 2.42; 7.13 speaks of two opposing factions in Jerusalem, the Hellenists and the Devout. The Hellenists welcomed contact with Greek culture. The Devout by and large opposed it.

The pro-Greek faction in Jerusalem was led by Onias' own brother, Jason. Jason promised Antiochus a large sum of money if he would transfer the high priesthood to himself and establish a gymnasium in Jerusalem, among other things. The significance of this last point should not be neglected. Jason was no mere lover of physical prowess. What he wanted was to transform Jerusalem into a Hellenistic *polis* or city-state. That would bring it into line with the surrounding Hellenistic cities. In the eyes of the Devout, however, it would destroy the traditional character of Jerusalem and Judaism as distinct within ancient civilization.[37]

Antiochus readily acceded to Jason's request. Onias was deposed and Jason appointed as high priest. 2 Maccabees says (only) of this period that 'new usages contrary to the Law' were introduced (4.11). A gymnasium was established, attracting even the priests. Many people tried to remove the marks of their circumcision (1 Macc. 1.15). Jason himself sent money to pay for sacrifices to Heracles at the games in Tyre (2 Macc. 4.19–20).

Jason held office for three years until he was deposed by Menelaus, who secured office by the same means that Jason himself had done. Jason aroused controversy by abusing the temple vessels and by instigating the murder, probably in 170 BCE, of the high priest Onias III who had taken refuge in Egypt. Jason took revenge on Menelaus and laid siege to him in the citadel. The author of 2 Maccabees (5.5-14) says that this is why Antiochus Epiphanes intervened directly in Jerusalem, which he did in 169 BCE.

Antiochus conducted a massacre in Jerusalem and looted the temple; evidently with the help of Menelaus himself. The following year Antiochus was prevented by the Romans from campaigning against Egypt. Dan. 11.30 implies this is why Antiochus turned his attentions once again to Jerusalem. In 167 BCE Antiochus sent his chief tax-collector (whom 2 Macc. 5.24 names as Apollonius) to the city. This man began a campaign of terror in Jerusalem. The precise chain of events is disputed, but the parameters of the crisis for Judaism are not left in doubt by the ancient sources. Those who refused to acquiesce with Apollonius were killed or enslaved. Many left the city. Its walls were torn down. The old Davidic stronghold was converted into a fortress known as the 'Akra'. A Seleucid garrison was stationed there (Dan. 11.39). This garrison remained on site for a substantial time, despite the territorial successes of the Maccabee (later known as the Hasmonean) dynasty. It was finally removed only by Simon in 142 BCE, some 26 years later.

A new phase in this hostile challenge to Jerusalem was marked by the arrival of instructions from Antiochus to abolish the Jewish cult and law.[38] Sabbath observance and circumcision were proscribed on pain of death. Sacrifice was ordered to the pagan gods. The Jerusalem sanctuary was turned over to a shrine of Zeus Olympios (see 1 Macc. 1.54, 59; Dan. 11.31; 12.11).

This is the situation that Daniel addresses.[39] My short description shows how critical this time was for Judaism. The dimensions of the crisis are given by the formal ban placed on distinctive Jewish practices. It is documented also by the two books of the Maccabees in the Apocrypha. We know from 2 Maccabees 7 that some if not many people met their deaths in the Antiochian pogrom.[40] It must have seemed a life-or-death situation so far as the Jewish religion was concerned.

The response to the crisis was initially organized by the Maccabee dynasty. A priest called Mattathias of Modein, together with his five sons who included Judas Maccabaeus, rose in open revolt against the ban on Judaism. Following the death of Mattathias in 166 BCE, Judas succeeded to the leadership of this, initially guerrilla, movement. In 165 BCE Judas defeated the Syrian army at Beth-zur, south of Jerusalem. Judas then retook Jerusalem and restored the temple cult. 1 Macc. 4.52 states that the restored temple was rededicated in December 164 BCE.

The Roman Period

The history told here is inevitably a selective one. I have made no attempt at completeness, and simply refer my reader to the standard literature on the subject.[41] From the Antiochian crisis we move to the Roman period in which Jesus himself was born. The crucial date here is the surrender of Jerusalem to the Roman general Pompey in 63 BCE. Pompey rashly entered the Holy of Holies, the sacred part of the Jerusalem temple to which even the high priest was allowed to go only once a year. He left the sanctuary untouched, but caused considerable devastation in the remaining parts of the city. From then on, and until 70 CE, Palestine was subject to the supervision of the Roman governor of Syria.

In this period, Herod the Great enters the scene.[42] Herod was the governor of Judea in 47 BCE. He was designated tetrarch by Mark Antony. Herod was crowned king of Judaea in Rome, returning to his territory in 39 BCE. In 37 BCE Herod captured Jerusalem and began to consolidate his rule there. Herod is best remembered for his vanity, his ambition and his grandiose building projects.[43] He constructed a theatre in Jerusalem and an amphitheatre just outside it. In 24 BCE he built himself a splendid palace in Jerusalem. The most ambitious of his projects, however, was the rebuilding of the temple in Jerusalem.[44] This was begun in 20 BCE; Jn 2.20 states that the project took 46 years to complete. Herod decided, on the basis of the Hebrew Bible, that the

temple building must have the same dimensions as its predecessor; but he
decided to raise the platform to create an immense edifice that dwarfed
what had stood there previously.[45] Herod's grand design was finished
barely years before the public ministry of Jesus; Herod did not live to
see it finished. Its construction would have been a familiar sight to
everyone who journeyed to Jerusalem on pilgrim festivals, as Jesus did. It
was funded by a substantial burden of taxation (see Josephus, *Ant.* 17.205;
317–21). Herod even plundered David's tomb and stole 3,000 talents to
build it (Josephus, *Ant.* 16.179–82).

Jesus was born in the period of the Roman occupation. The greater
part of his life was spent under the jurisdiction of the Jewish tetrarch Herod
Antipas who reigned from 4 BCE to 39 CE (and is *not* to be confused with
Herod the Great).[46] We know from the Gospels (and other literature)
that the Romans maintained a significant presence in Jerusalem during
this time. We cannot begin to understand the story of Jesus without
recognizing the importance of the Romans and their place within that
story.

The First Jewish Revolt

One more thing may be said about Jewish history in the first century CE.
This is that the seventh decade witnessed the First Jewish Revolt against
Rome (66–73 CE), which reached its zenith in the Roman destruction of
Jerusalem (70 CE).[47] The second century saw a further revolt (132–35 CE)
which was even more disastrous in its consequences for Judaism.[48]
Although it has been disputed to what extent the destruction of Jerusalem
was a significant factor for Christian people,[49] and although again
the extent of the revolutionary instinct in Judaism should not be over-
estimated, this period of history demands brief attention because of its
importance for Judaism.

The history of the First Jewish Revolt against Rome, like the analysis
of its causes, is a complex matter which is difficult if not impossible to
reduce to a few lines.[50] Suffice it to say that there were sporadic outbursts
of anti-Roman feeling on the part of Jewish people at various points in
the first century CE. None of this, however, is to be confused with the
war against Rome which broke out in 66 CE. The initial cause of this
conflict was a quarrel about civil rights in Caesarea which had raged on
and off for almost a decade.[51] The Jews had apparently grown as numerous as the Greeks (cf. Josephus, *War* 2.457) and wanted the same civic
rights. After instances of street-fighting, the procurator Felix referred the
matter to Nero in Rome. Nero decided to favour the Greeks. This
created further tension which came to a head when a Greek regrettably
parodied a Jewish sacrifice outside the synagogue and prompted a full-
scale riot.

Gessius Florus became procurator of Judaea in 64 CE. Not long after the riot in Caesarea he sent for 17 talents from the temple in Jerusalem. This annoyed the Jews, who responded by holding a mock street-collection on behalf of the impoverished official. Florus lost his temper and told his soldiers to attack the upper city in Jerusalem. These soldiers exceeded their authority and executed a massacre. Some of those who survived the massacre were subsequently crucified, including Jews who were Roman citizens. Not much later there was another massacre in Jerusalem. The scene was set for full-scale confrontation in which Jewish dislike of Gessius Florus was the determining factor.

'Judea took no sudden and dramatic plunge into war' is one commentator's verdict on the crisis that ensued.[52] The early months of the conflict, and indeed its eventual resolution, were marked by internal Jewish conflict in which one Jewish faction was set against another. The conflict centred inevitably on Jerusalem, which was besieged by Titus in 70 CE. Josephus was employed as a mediator to persuade the factions to surrender, in the hope of preventing the destruction of the temple; but in vain. The end was as dramatic as it was inevitable. The temple was burned, having been looted of its sacred treasures by Titus' men.

One further event deserves to be mentioned. This is the fate of the so-called Zealots in Herod's former stronghold of Masada.[53] The tale is a simple but moving one of Jewish heroism and resistance. When the Romans stormed Masada in 74 CE, they found nothing but a pile of bodies. The Jewish revolutionaries had committed mass suicide rather than be captured by the hated enemy. One is reminded here of the days of the Maccabees, except in this instance the Jews were the victims rather than the victors in a conflict with a greater power. The eerie silence of Masada testifies to the indomitable Jewish mindset in its refusal to abandon ancestral traditions.

THE GOD OF ANCIENT ISRAEL

We turn now to examine the nature of Jewish religion in the period under discussion.[1] By and large, this was determined by belief in the one God and the historical and theological conviction that this God had made a covenant with Israel, his chosen people. Any treatment of Jewish religion should begin by examining the Israelite understanding of God and consider the significance of the covenant in the religious understanding of the Jewish people.

Monotheism and the Hebrew Bible

The history of monotheism in Israel is not as straightforward as might appear.[2] Christians today are accustomed to belief in one God, albeit through the distinctive lens of Trinitarianism.[3] The Jewish daily prayer the *Shema*, which draws on the three passages Deut. 6.4-9, Deut. 11.13-21 and Num. 15.37-41, begins with the words, 'Hear, O Israel, the Lord is our God, the Lord is One.' This looks like, and indeed is, a declaration of belief in only one God. In evaluating the religion of ancient Israel, however, we shall consider the likelihood that this monotheistic understanding resulted from a process of evolution or development. There is no detailed *philosophical* defence of monotheism in the Hebrew Bible. These observations demand some preliminary study to discern how monotheism emerged in Israel.[4]

The study by Gnuse I drew on in Chapter 3 appropriately links the subject of emergent monotheism in Israel with discussion of the 'Settlement' process.[5] Gnuse shows on the basis of archaeological and other evidence that the Israelites were not necessarily immigrants who were radically discontinuous with the Canaanites in terms of their religious understanding and ideas.[6] He concludes that Israel emerged in the highlands of Palestine in Iron Age I in a peaceful and internal process which took centuries to accomplish. This conclusion has clear implications for the study of Israelite monotheism. Canaanite religion was polytheistic in character, as revealed by the Ugaritic texts from Ras Shamra.[7] There are places in the Hebrew Bible where a polytheistic understanding seems to surface, most notably perhaps in the notion of the divine council in Ps. 82.1 and the night-time vision of Dan. 7.9-14.[8]

If it is true that the Settlement was not accomplished by absolute immigration, we need to reckon with a likely polytheistic basis to Israelite religion that was only gradually displaced by emerging notions of monotheism. To be sure, there were a variety of monotheistic understandings in the Ancient Near Eastern world of the second millennium

BCE. These have been characterized by Denis Baly under the headings 'primitive monotheism', 'proto-monotheism', 'pseudo-monotheism' and 'absolute or transcendent monotheism'.[9] Interestingly, Baly argues that monotheism did not emerge in the desert but in urban areas where intellectual struggles provided a critical ferment. 'Primitive monotheism' occurs among primitive agrarian societies where one god is elevated above the hierarchy of others. 'Proto-monotheism' is the prerogative of more developed religions and depends on political or cultural expansion when the dominant group synthesizes native deities under a national god. 'Pseudo-monotheism' occurs when a strong ruler tries to impose monotheism on his subjects for cultural solidarity. In applying these categories to ancient Israel, it seems that the Israelites acquired 'absolute or transcendent monotheism' only in the period of the Babylonian exile and beyond.

Baly argues that the Sinai theophany (Exodus 24) prepared the ground for this post-exilic development. Sinai rejected the natural world as providing the framework of reality and meaning, emphasizing the absolute power and jealousy of Yahweh as sovereign. Baly comments effectively on the socio-economic situation of Palestine after the Settlement: 'It was the tragedy of these small Levantine states that the peace their people so much desired proved to be their enemy, for the land could not long support an expanding population, unrestrained by the savagery of war.'[10] A way forward had to be found given the failure of the Israelites on several occasions to become a great commercial power. It was the achievement of Amos to recognize that the concept of the covenant might cross national boundaries and involve Israel's neighbours in the scheme of election. Subsequent prophets developed this idea, notably Deutero-Isaiah in the period of the Babylonian exile.

The development of monotheism in Israel was thus an exilic and post-exilic phenomenon.[11] Besides Deutero-Isaiah, who argues strongly for the uniqueness of Yahweh, monotheism is most clearly articulated in the younger strata of the Hebrew Bible, including the final redaction of the Pentateuch which was completed only by the fourth century BCE. It is now becoming increasingly common among scholars to speak of a distinction between the 'official' representatives of Israel – the priests and the prophets who formed a minority in the nation – and the religion of the ordinary people which is much more truly demonstrated by the folk-religion of the historical books and the prohibitions on sorcery of Deuteronomy 18 and elsewhere. As Baly himself notes,[12] the frequent appearance of polytheism in the sanctuaries dedicated to Yahweh shows that sometimes even the religious leaders (or at least some of them) found nothing incompatible in the joint worship of Yahweh with other gods. This is a sobering reminder of the actual nature of religious life in ancient Israel.

The Divine Covenant

If monotheism was an emergent understanding in Israel and not a fixed concept from the beginning, we shall need to consider the parallel concept of the covenant to evaluate the distinctive self-understanding of the Israelite people. A 'covenant' may be defined as an agreement between two parties in which both undertake on oath to perform mutually beneficent activities.

The Bible knows of several covenants between God and the people of Israel.[13] The book of Genesis mentions two such covenants, both of which are transmitted in more than one form. The first is the covenant between God and Noah which is described in Gen. 6.18 and 9.8-17. The covenant with Abraham is introduced in both Genesis 15 and 17, promising the multiplication of Abraham's offspring in exchange for faithful obedience symbolized by the rite of circumcision. In Exodus we find a third and, sociologically and historically, more important covenant. This is the covenant between God and Moses on Mount Sinai when the Ten Commandments (otherwise known as the Decalogue) were imparted.

Scholars are divided about whether the Sinai covenant was an actual event of the pre-monarchical period (*c*.1200–1000 BCE) or merely a pious invention of a later period which the Pentateuch transmits as authentic. Although there has been no full agreement on this issue, historical investigation has compared the Sinai covenant with other known covenants from the Late Bronze Age.[14] This has led to the conclusion that the Sinai covenant, if it was authentic, was a 'suzerainty treaty' between Yahweh and Israel in which Yahweh was the king and Israel the vassal.[15] Parallels for this type of understanding are provided by the treaties recorded in the Ebla cuneiform texts from the third millennium BCE.[16]

Scholars have also debated the form and function of the Ten Commandments. There is by now general agreement that they constitute 'apodictic' as opposed to 'casuistic' biblical law. This theory goes back to Albrecht Alt in 1934.[17] Alt defined casuistic law as that which is defined in the conditional form with a protasis and apodasis (e.g. Exod. 21.18-19). Apodictic law, by contrast, is terse and unconditional. Of the Decalogue Alt observed that 'the categorical negative is the strongest unifying element in the whole list'. It is law provided for all peoples and all times, enshrined in the divine revelation to Israel.

In the narrative of Israel's history, the Sinai covenant is later than the covenant with Abraham but it features in earlier sources. The tradition of the Abrahamic covenant stems only from the period of the united monarchy. It so closely resembles the traditions about the Davidic covenant, including the promise of Davidic succession, that many scholars think that both traditions stemmed from the same source.[18] This source was probably the old Canaanite traditions of Jebusite Jerusalem, although admittedly that tradition had a long and complex pre-literary form. Mendenhall has shown more recently that the Abrahamic covenant went through three probable recensions.[19] We cannot therefore take Genesis 17 as necessarily the oldest covenantal tradition in Israel, however tempting it is to do so.

Being Jewish in the First Century CE

This brings us to a yet more basic question. This is the question of what it meant to be Jewish in the first century CE. Although more remains to be said on this subject, we shall proceed by further considering the role of monotheism and covenant observance in the religious understanding of the period.

The daily recitation of the *Shema* with its monotheistic requirement is an indication of what those who compiled the *Shema* wanted people to believe; and probably also of what many of those who recited the *Shema* themselves believed.[20] In saying this, we should beware of the conclusion that such belief was a matter of abstract or speculative theology alone. Besides their declaration of belief and trust in God, Jews in the first century held to certain hopes, on biblical authority, about the election of Israel and the future introduction of freedom by God. Beliefs about God are intrinsically related to beliefs about election and the covenant and cannot be considered apart from these issues.

This brings us to the area of research made his own by Ed Sanders. Sanders has written a significant tome on the nature of Jewish praxis and belief in the years between 63 BCE and 66 CE.[21] This book includes a chapter entitled 'common theology' (chapter 13) in which he examines the generic Jewish beliefs of the period. Sanders observes that belief that their God was the only true God, that he had chosen them and given them his law which they were required to obey were the basic features of all Jewish religion of this time. They held all the different varieties of Judaism together.

Worship of the one true God was enjoined on all Jewish people in the first century CE. One of the ways in which this commandment found expression was in the Jewish horror of what have come to be known, in the words of the Authorized Version of the Bible, as 'graven images'. Sanders notes a particular sensitivity in this area concerning Jerusalem and the temple.[22] While Jews were generally tolerant of religious images in other parts of the world, they did not bend their scruples when it came to the holy city. When Pilate introduced Roman standards into Jerusalem, there was an immediate riot (Josephus, *War* 2.169–74). It seems that this was very much a question of degree concerning public perception of what was permissible. Coinage, for instance, bearing images of more than one kind, circulated in Palestine in the first century and that did not provoke a riot. Even the synagogue excavated at Hammath had as its main decoration the signs of the zodiac in a circle.[23] We should not conclude that all 'graven images' provoked offence. We should, however, note the significant and quite public exceptions which were matters of judgment concerning what was acceptable.

This true and unique God was regarded as the creator of the physical universe. Both Philo and Josephus include passages explaining that the law contains everything necessary for human life, including what we now term ecological issues as well as the basic question of rest on the sabbath. Josephus claims that Jews 'would rather give up their lives than the worship which they are accustomed to offer God' (*Ant.* 15.248); Philo, speaking of ecology and animal rights, that 'great is the law which ordains them and ever watchful is the care which it demands' (*Hypothetica* 7.9). While we must not neglect the cosmic and even the mystical understanding which stemmed from this conviction (not least in Philo's mind), the fact remains that much of the legislation the Torah produced was very much down to earth, covering such issues as the care of cattle and basic social concerns.

Inherited in part from the apocalyptic tradition, but by no means always deterministic in its outlook, was the belief that God controlled human history. The Qumran community, for instance, had an eschatology in which the children of light were expected to prove victorious in the final battle against the children of darkness (1QM).[24] This expectation was held in less intense form by others in first century Judaism. It issued in the different forms of eschatology we shall consider in Chapter 10. Most if not all Jewish theology of the period is eschatological in orientation once the term 'eschatology' is set in broad perspective as an expression of hope which is susceptible to a variety of different outcomes.

Sanders goes on to discuss the theology of the various sacrifices and offerings which were presented in the temple in Jerusalem.[25] There is a tendency among modern readers to assume that the ancient Jewish sacrificial system was mechanistic in its intention, but this is not a fair interpretation of the issue. While no doubt some sacrifices were presented in an unthoughtful way, we should not debase the integrity of ancient Judaism by implying that this was always or indeed often the case. The essential understanding of the sacrifice was that it atoned for sins. This depended on the ancient and widespread notion that atonement and purification – the means of redressing a sin – required the shedding of blood. Philo's understanding of what occurred in a sacrifice is certainly broader than his own system alone. He acknowledges that atonement requires 'prayers and sacrifices to propitiate the deity' (*Moses* 2.147); and that those who participate are thereby 'changing their way for the better' (*Spec. Leg.* 1.227). This links the ceremonial offering to the realm of moral improvement in a way which doubtless other Jews accepted.

Sanders further mentions the summary or epitome of the law as a convenient way of teaching covenant obedience to the people at large.[26] Hillel is recorded in the Talmud as having summarized the law in a sentence with the words, 'What is hateful to you, do not do to your neighbour' (*b. Sab.* 31a). A similar understanding is found in Philo, who observed, with equal brevity, that the Jewish 'philosophy' had two branches, duty to God and duty to other people (*Spec. Leg.* 2.63). All of this was incorporated in the daily Jewish prayers which asked God to act in a providential and hopeful way.

Covenantal Nomism

Sanders coined the phrase 'covenantal nomism' to describe the piety that pertained in mainstream Judaism in the period under discussion.[27] This phrase designates the two halves of the covenant relationship. God was the creator of the universe and the elector of Israel. His election of the Jewish nation was a matter of grace; God's free choice alone. Staying within the covenant meant a matter of continual obedience on the part of the Jewish people.

At the heart of covenantal nomism stood the belief that such obedience meant keeping the law. That Israel had entered into covenant relationship with God is stated in a whole variety of texts, including texts produced by sectarian groups like the Qumran community and the early Christians. Nowhere is the gift of the law more clearly stated than in the words of Pseudo-Philo, 'I have given an everlasting Law into your hands and by this I will judge the whole world' (*LAB* 11.2). Side by side with this conviction stood belief in the fundamental justice of God and the expectation that God would judge the universe he had created. This is no doubt why Philo wrote an entire text on the subject of *Rewards and Punishments*.

Christian readers will be familiar with an element of ambiguity concerning the concepts of divine grace and punishment. The God who graciously elects in biblical theology is the just God who righteously punishes. The roots of this ambiguity lie in the system of covenantal nomism Sanders discerns. Since God is merciful, sinners may always repent and, through proper use and understanding of the sacrificial system, find forgiveness for their sins. Conversely, those who refuse to repent bring wrath upon themselves and in this sense, it might be said, are responsible for their own punishment. This tension is a delicate one between divine grace and human responsibility.

Sanders criticizes earlier scholarship on Judaism – particularly Christian scholarship – for its presentation of that religion as dominated by the perennial balance between sins and merits.[28] Sanders shows this is a gross misunderstanding of the first-century evidence. For one thing, it imposes a Christian eschatological understanding on material which, in general, neither deserves nor supports that imposition. Most Jewish discussion of the balance between sins and merits has the present life in view and takes little interest in a possible life to come. In those places where a *post-mortem* interest does emerge, a mechanistic computation of the two forms of life and their moral value is by no means evident. *T.Qidd.* 1.15–16 probably speaks for a wider understanding when it says that even a person who is completely wicked can repent at the end and be saved.

The questions of Jewish belief in God and the covenant, then, raise a variety of issues. What emerges most obviously is the centrality of the covenant in the Jewish mindset and the need to evaluate this understanding in positive terms, not patronizingly. We shall also consider the centrality of divine grace and providence in Jewish theology. Such an approach constitutes a helpful introduction to post-biblical Judaism.

THE INTERPRETATION OF SCRIPTURE

Ancient Judaism is often described, and by no means inaccurately, as 'a religion of the book'. Having seen something of the Jewish understanding of God, we shall now investigate the centrality of the Bible in Judaism as a further means of investigating the Jewish religious outlook. I shall begin by summarizing what we have seen so far.

The Canonicity of Scripture

The Hebrew Bible ('The Old Testament') is the product of several centuries of writing.[1] Some of the key texts, like the Pentateuch, went through more than one stage of development. We saw that the Hebrew Bible divides into three parts, generally called the Law (the Torah), the Prophets and the Writings. These three parts were recognized as canonical at different times in the history of the nation concerned.[2] The way in which the biblical canon developed requires a little explanation.[3]

The first division of the Hebrew Bible is called the Torah or the Law, generally held to be the five books of Moses (Genesis, Exodus, Leviticus, Numbers and Deuteronomy). The Torah as such narrates the period from the creation to the time when Israel was on the point of entering the promised land of Canaan. The early chapters narrow their scope from the creation of Adam and Eve as the first human beings to the family of Abraham, with whom God made the covenant in Genesis 17. The farewell of Moses, the person who led the Israelites out of Egypt, occupies the whole of Deuteronomy.

Although traditionally held to be the work of Moses himself, critical scholarship has established beyond doubt that the Torah was the result of lengthy redaction and drew on several sources. The classical theory is that there were four such sources, generally called J, E, D and P. These sources were redacted over a lengthy period to yield the present form of text by the fourth century BCE.

Critical study of the Torah is a modern phenomenon, however.[4] In the New Testament we find Moses himself commonly regarded as the author of the Torah. The phrase 'the law and the prophets' is a frequent designation of the scriptural understanding of the period (see e.g. Mt. 11.13). We do not know whether or how many people paused to consider whether Moses could really have been the author of a body of literature that describes his own death (Deut. 34.7–8). We can at least say that some views about the origin of the Torah did not encourage such reflection. Thus *Jubilees* asserts in many places that the present Torah is merely a copy of the heavenly original (e.g. *Jub.* 3.10; 33.10). A similar view is expressed in the Mishnah (*m.Sanh.* 10.1). A culture that viewed the Pentateuch as dictated by God (or the Angel of the Presence) doubtless tended away from the need for critical investigation of its literary origins. The climax of this view is the suggestion, found in later rabbinic literature, that the entire book was handed to Moses already completed, the only pertinent question being whether Moses received it all at once or merely scroll by scroll (*b.Git.* 60a).

That the five books of Moses were regarded as authoritative by the first century CE is certain.[5] In the book of Nehemiah (fourth century BCE) we find a passage which describes how Ezra read the Torah to the people and how the people pledged themselves to obey it (Nehemiah 8–10). While it remains uncertain whether the material in question was the whole Torah or merely the so-called 'Priestly Code', this does not affect the fact that the literature associated with Moses was felt to constitute a binding rule of life. This passage from Nehemiah is rightly regarded as an important one so far as the issue of biblical canonicity is concerned.

The Prophets are not as old as Moses, who was a figure of the second millennium BCE. The earliest prophets, Amos and Hosea, did not write until the eighth century BCE. The prophets are a varied bunch, loosely held together by the belief that each had been called by God to address the Jewish nation in a particular way. The prophets developed the Jewish messianic hope and often include a very prominent eschatology. It seems that the corpus of prophetic writings was regarded as canonical in the first century CE.

The third division of the Hebrew Bible is known as 'the Writings'. The Writings in the Hebrew Bible include the youngest text of all, the book of Daniel, which was written in the second century BCE and is included among the Prophets in English Bible translations. Sirach in the second century BCE refers to the tripartite division of Jewish authoritative writings in its Prologue, but we do not know the precise extent of the third division at this time nor the general regard in which it was held. The two-membered formula of Mt. 11.13 ('the law and the prophets') is characteristic of the first century CE, but this does not mean that the third division did not exist at this time or even necessarily that it was marginalized then. Given that Daniel was able to enter the Writings in the second century BCE, this part of the Bible must have been sufficiently flexible then to permit such an inclusion.

The earliest evidence for our present version of the Hebrew canon comes from Josephus, who states that the Jews hold 22 writings as authoritative (*Apion* 1.8). At the Jamnian Academy which convened after the Fall of Jerusalem (70 CE) doubts were raised about a surprisingly small number of books. The Song of Solomon and Ecclesiastes were the principal texts to be questioned on this occasion.[6] In the case of both, however, authorities were found who declared that they 'rendered the hands unclean', which is a technical term for authoritative or canonical status (*m. Yad.* 3.5).

None of this alters the fact that the Torah was given precedence over the other two divisions of the Hebrew Bible, which were regarded in one sense as commentary on the Torah. Such a view was aided by belief in the heavenly origin of the Torah. For this reason the Prophets and the Writings are often referred to as 'tradition' in rabbinic literature (*m. Taan.* 2.1; *j. Hal.* 57b).

Interpreters of the Law

The status of Judaism as a religion of the book gave rise at an early stage to the need for a professional class of people who were skilled and competent interpreters of the Bible. In the period of Ezra and Nehemiah this task was principally allocated to the priests.[7] Ezra himself discharged the double role of priest and scribe. In later Judaism – and certainly before the period of Christian origins – these roles became distinguished. In the period of Judaism with which we are concerned, the priests operated in the temple and were concerned with sacrifices. The scribes were associated with the synagogues and were first and foremost teachers of the Law.

The rise of the scribal class as a distinguishable entity in post-biblical Judaism reflects the importance attached to the Law after the Exile.[8] We can discern something of the status that the scribes had acquired by considering a passage from Ecclesiasticus (Sirach) which was written even before the book of Daniel. According to Ecclus 38.24–39.11 the scribes have a prominent position in assemblies of the people (which probably means in synagogues).[9] They know the wisdom of the ancients and are regarded as judges and legal experts. My reference to Daniel is by no means out of place in this context. During the Antiochian crisis, when many of the priests adopted the values of Hellenism, the scribes steered a different course. They were the people who upheld the traditional values enshrined in the Law, even if the precise history of the so-called 'wise men' in Judaism of the second century BCE is a little difficult to unravel. From the second century onwards the scribes established themselves as a recognizable class in Judaism, distinct from the priests. The Antiochian crisis exacerbated this development, but it cannot be regarded as wholly responsible for it.

The early Enochic literature is often thought to have stemmed from scribal circles.[10] This is a significant insight given that more than one strand of the apocalypse known as *1 Enoch* comes from the period before the Antiochian crisis, even from the third century BCE. In *1 En.* 12.3-4 and 15.1 Enoch is called 'scribe of righteousness'. Enoch appears in similar guise at the beginning of the *Epistle of Enoch* (*1 En.* 92.1).

Although there is occasional (and in places unwarranted) criticism of the scribal tradition in the Gospels, the dominance of the scribes in Judaism during the early Common Era is certainly not an exaggeration as the Gospels record it. There are various titles for the scribes in the New Testament, but we probably do right to conclude that research in the law and teaching of the law were not unrelated activities, as in the modern university setting. Scribes are addressed in the New Testament by reverential titles which confirm their respected status. Rabbi, for instance, means 'my lord' even though it is more commonly translated as 'my teacher'. The rabbis were greeted and honoured wherever they went, as more than one New Testament passage records ironically (see e.g. Mt. 23.6-7). It is, however, probably true to say that the New Testament tends to present the scribal body as more monolithic than it actually was.

There are obvious parallels with the contemporary judicial system, but these must not be pressed further than the evidence allows. The most obvious difference is that the Jewish scribes were unpaid rather than well paid.[11] Those scribes without private means had to work for a living to support their scriptural activity. The Mishnah puts the matter bluntly: the judge who takes money for a legal decision has his decision annulled (*m.Bek.* 4.6). Although the realities of the situation are mostly lost to us, it is possible that the scribes were remunerated to some extent for their educational work (as opposed to their legal judgments). The criticism of greedy Pharisees in the Gospels is meaningless otherwise (Mk 12.40). These legal experts defined legal principles related to the Torah, taught them to their pupils (evidently in the form of rabbinic 'schools') and administered the judicial system.

Halakah and Haggadah

The tripartite division of the Hebrew Bible means that the raw material on which the scribes worked occupied more than one literary form. Not even the Pentateuch is monolithic in genre, containing both legal and narrative material. This distinction led to more than one form of exegesis in post-biblical Judaism. Legal elaboration was known as halakah; narrative expansion as haggadah. Both categories of exegesis were important in the period under discussion.[12]

The basis of halakah was the need to apply biblical law to the constantly changing practicalities of everyday life. This led to elaborate systems of casuistry: the division and application of the different categories of law to ensure their precise fulfilment. One of the problems this approach was designed to overcome was the fact that in places the Law seemed incomplete or even outdated to deal with a particular situation. The scribes tried to show that the Law did indeed apply to everyday life by giving it contemporary relevance.

They were aided in this by a second stream of material which came to be regarded as authoritative over a period of time.[13] There were inevitably areas of life that were not directly determined by the Torah, thrown up largely by the process of social change. Mt. 15.2 refers to 'the traditions of the elders'. This was essentially the fund of Jewish common law: what had been done since ancient times, even though not directly determined by the Torah, and which had acquired authoritative status for that reason. Halakah covered both kinds of material. It led to the emergence of three different categories of halakah: (1) individual statutes that could be traced back directly to Moses; (2) the general corpus of halakah; and (3) the so-called 'ordinances of the scribes' which I have defined here as common law. These three types of halakah held descending grades of authority. Curiously, the fiction that all halakah derived from the law was rigorously maintained.

The continuing process of halakah supplied a set of rules for scriptural interpretation. Among the more prominent we may mention the argument *a minori ad maius* – what applies in a lesser situation will apply also in a more important one; and a proposition based on two scriptural passages, including the principle of *gezerah shawah* where the same words are applied to two separate cases. These rules for scriptural interpretation were originally six in number, but they were later expanded to thirteen.

Haggadah

In parallel with halakah we can consider haggadah.[14] If halakah was the exegesis of the legal precepts of the Bible, haggadah constituted exegesis of its narrative portions. We even have an example of one form of haggadah within the Bible itself in the form of the books of Chronicles.[15] Comparison of the books of Chronicles with the earlier books of Samuel and Kings shows that the Chronicler has introduced a variety of new material which reflects his own interests and convictions. A significant factor is that the Chronicler reads back post-exilic institutions to the period of the monarchy.

This was not so much dishonesty as an example of the attempt to write history in a way which claims an earlier period of history as fully in agreement with the ideological convictions of the present. The rationale of haggadah was similar to that of halakah. It was to make the biblical text relevant, smoothing out inconsistencies in the narrative and explaining points of detail. The stories of many biblical figures were embellished in this way including Adam, Enoch, Abraham and Moses. Besides the book of *Jubilees* which has been mentioned already, the most striking example of haggadah from the annals of post-biblical Judaism was the *Genesis Apocryphon* produced by the Qumran community.

The *Genesis Apocryphon* is an incomplete manuscript comprising 22 surviving columns of Aramaic text which comes from the second century BCE.[16] It sets out to retell certain parts of the Genesis story, narrating the marriage that resulted in the birth of Noah. Noah is presented as such a wonderful child that his father suspected his mother of having intercourse with the angels. There are parallels for this story in *1 Enoch* 106. The text then retells the Genesis story up to the story of Abraham in Genesis 15. We have no way of telling how long the *Genesis Apocryphon* was originally, but presumably it was longer than the stories that are currently recorded there.[17]

In these various ways, Jews of the early Common Era tried to make scripture relevant for changing times and circumstances. Such procedures draw attention to the centrality of the Bible within Judaism. This centrality became more obvious with the cessation of the Jewish sacrificial system in the period following the abortive Bar Kochbah revolt (132–5 CE). The central place of the Bible in Judaism is an indispensable observation when we come to study Christian origins.

THE SYNAGOGUE

The synagogue was the home of the scriptural scholars in post-biblical Judaism.[1] Josephus records Moses as teaching that all Jewish boys should learn the law (*Ant.* 4.8). In another passage he commends elementary education involving the basics of reading and writing (*Apion* 2.25). Although the evidence for such education is rather patchy, it seems that by the time of Jesus elementary schools had been established in Palestine for this purpose.[2] These schools were connected with the synagogue and offered a syllabus that was biblically based. That people did indeed study the Bible privately before the period of Christian origins is indicated by 1 Macc. 1.56-7.

The synagogue was a place for adult scriptural reading and exposition. It thus differed from the modern Christian understanding of church-going where worship is the primary focus. This is not to suggest that the ancient Jewish synagogues lacked reverence or a sense of worship; but that they conceived these ideas differently from Christians today. Given that the Law was believed to embody the totality of God's will for Israel, it was thought necessary to study the Bible and to teach its principles and deductions to the people. Josephus is doubtless to be believed when he states that, in a tradition deriving from Moses himself (by which he means the Torah), every week the Jewish people must leave their normal occupation and gather together to study the Law (*Apion* 2.17). The very important Theodotus inscription which was discovered in Jerusalem in 1913 describes the synagogue that Theodotus founded as a place for 'the reading of the Law and the teaching of the precepts'.[3]

The earliest synagogues of which we know are found in Egypt and come from the third century BCE. We have inscriptions and papyri from Egypt dating to the reign of Ptolemy III (Euergetes) and also from Delos in Greece from the first century BCE. It has been suggested that the origins of the synagogue go back to the time of Ezra in the fourth century BCE or even to the exile in the sixth century BCE. The former suggestion seems quite plausible given what we saw about the status of the Law in Ezra-Nehemiah. Many scholars think that both Ezek. 11.16 and Jer. 39.8 bear on this historical problem. The theory that the Babylonian exile, which involved the loss of the national sanctuary, was responsible for this development seems a plausible one.

One of the oddities of this area is that, despite the obvious importance of synagogues in Jewish life, only three synagogues from the Second Temple period have been excavated in Palestine, including one at Masada.[4] The most obvious explanation of this evidence is that 'syna-gogue' as the name for a Jewish religious community denoted the convocation of the community and not exclusively the building where the community met. Presumably, large houses were used for meetings, as we know from the New Testament they were in the early Christian world.[5] It was perhaps as much as a hundred years after the destruction of the temple that formal synagogue buildings were constructed on a widespread basis.

Jesus himself was no stranger to the synagogue. According to the Gospels he visited the synagogue on the sabbath and taught there (Mk 1.21). The synagogues were one of the primary locations for the earliest spread of Christianity. This situation persisted until the closing decades of the first century CE when the Eighteen Benedictions were reformulated to exclude 'the heretics' from the synagogue.[6] Although it is not certain that this term applied exclusively to the Christians, it seems likely that the Christians featured among the undesirable people identified in that way. The situation of the followers of Jesus as excluded from the synagogue is evidently reflected in the story of the man born blind (Jn 9.22).

The last point can be illustrated from wider literature. The synagogue was governed by a council of elders who may or may not also have been civic leaders, depending on the particular locality. The phenomenon of expulsion is found also in the Qumran scrolls (see also Josephus, *War* 2.8). 1QS 6–7 prescribes penalties for different offences including both temporary and permanent expulsion from the community. The latter was demanded in the case of uttering the name of God, slandering the congregation and several other offences. It is likely that, with appropriate sectarian variation, these penalties reflect those that applied in the synagogue and which the New Testament and the Eighteen Benedictions also illustrate.

The Synagogue Service

The nature of the synagogue service at the time of Jesus may be discerned relatively easily.[7] The seating was arranged on a hierarchical principle as we know from Mt. 23.6 and other passages in the New Testament. Men and women were probably segregated, as they are in Jewish synagogues today. *M.Neg.* 13.12 states even that a leper had to be separated from the rest of the congregation on the grounds of his affliction.

The same tractate from the Mishnah gives us an insight into the synagogue service. It mentions the public praying of the *Shema*, prayer, the reading of the Torah and the prophets. This was accompanied by the reading of the scriptures in the local language which we saw in Chapter 2 to be the origins of the Targumic tradition. Philo also has three summaries of the synagogue meeting from which a roughly similar order of service emerges. The Torah was read apparently on a three-year cycle.

There were various divisions of the Bible for lectionary purposes, as if local customs prevailed on this issue.

The reading from the Bible and the local paraphrase was followed by what we would call a sermon. The best-known example of such a sermon is Jesus' homily in the Nazareth synagogue recorded in Luke 4. Philo implies that the sermon could be given by any member of the congregation. If a priest was present, the service concluded with the priestly blessing.

Synagogue Personnel

The emergence of the synagogue as a Jewish religious institution presupposes a community organization which we shall also consider.[8]

The organization of the Jewish communities in the various provinces of the Roman empire was not done according to a uniform pattern. There was more than one potential form of enfranchisement for people of Jewish origin. In those places where the population was predominantly Jewish (notably of course Jerusalem) the synagogues were probably governed by the civic authorities. In predominantly Greek or Roman cities, and especially where Jews were excluded from civic rights, the synagogues were independent bodies more often than not protected by law or by local custom and with their own circle of elders. The Mishnah, whose interests of course are exclusively Jewish, regards the synagogue and its artefacts as public property (m.Meg. 3.1). This ideal is likely to have been fulfilled in predominantly Jewish areas but less likely elsewhere.

Besides the council of elders, officers were appointed to discharge specific functions. There was, however, no 'minister' in the sense of a regular leader of worship. The president of the synagogue was known in Greek as archisynagogos. It was his task to choose the Bible reader and preacher and to care for the building if there was one. There was also a receiver of alms and a lesser figure called the 'minister', who in modern Christian terms was more of a verger than a minister as such. He put out the books for the service and apparently taught the children to read (m.Sab. 1.3).

THE TEMPLE

The next Jewish institution to be considered is the temple. This topic involves consideration of the priesthood and the different sacrifices that were offered in the temple.

The Temple in Jerusalem

The temple which stood in Jerusalem when Jesus was born had undergone, and was still undergoing, considerable renovation work in a project inaugurated by Herod the Great who died in 4 BCE.[1] Herod was an energetic figure with high if not megalomaniac aspirations. He built a theatre, an amphitheatre and a royal palace in Jerusalem.[2] In 20 BCE he set about the task of rebuilding the temple.[3] This project retained the biblically determined proportions of the sanctuary but substantially increased the plinth and environs of the temple.[4] Jn 2.20 states that the Herodian temple took 46 years to construct. This means it was not finished until after Herod's death, not long before the death of Jesus himself. It bore testimony, both to the importance of the national sanctuary in the Jewish mindset but also to Herod's high opinion of himself and the burden of taxation that was imposed to fund its construction.[5]

The result of Herod's endeavours was a building which stood justifiable comparison with all other religious buildings in the ancient world, including the Parthenon in Athens. The temple proper was relatively small when compared with the courts and gates by which it was surrounded.[6] All significant cultic activities took place in the inner forecourt, which was divided by a wall into two different halves. The eastern part was called the 'court of the women', which was as far as women were allowed to go (Josephus, *War* 5.199; cf. *m.Mid.* 2.5). This forecourt was accessed by the so-called Beautiful Gate (Acts 3.2). The temple as such had but two rooms. There was an ante-chamber and a much smaller further chamber. The latter was the 'Holy of Holies' into which only the high priest was allowed to go, and he only once a year on the Day of Atonement. The ante-chamber contained the altar of incense, the seven-branched candelabrum and the table of the shewbread. The outer wall enclosed the so-called 'court of the Gentiles' into which anyone could go except for women who were ritually impure (Josephus, *Apion* 2.102–5).

In front of the temple, and to be distinguished from the internal altar of incense, was the much larger altar of sacrifice on which all sacrificial activity was conducted. According to the descriptions provided by *m.Mid.* 3.1–4 and Josephus (*War* 5.5), this altar was 32 cubits square at its base and 24 cubits square on the upper level. Near the altar was a bronze basin in which the priests purified themselves before offering the daily sacrifices. North of the altar was the slaughter area, which must have resembled a butcher's shop.

Before the cessation of the temple cult under Roman instructions, Jewish religion was essentially sacrificial in nature.[7] Generically, it was not much different from religion in the ancient world but there were at least two distinctive features.[8] In the first place, sacrificial worship was formally confined to the temple in Jerusalem and not distributed among a number of autonomous temples. Secondly, the temple establishment in Jerusalem supported a large number of hereditary priests for which those who were not priests were expected to pay. Sanders notes that this and the practice of 'whole burnt-offerings' twice a day made the Jewish religion more expensive for its participants than other cults in the Graeco-Roman world.[9] This offering was funded by the kings in the period before the exile, but it had become the responsibility of the Jewish people by the time of Christian origins. The Pentateuch prescribes that a year-old unblemished lamb was to be offered, accompanied by a grain-offering and a drink-offering (Exod. 29.38-42; Num. 15.1-16; 28.3-8). Besides the duty of supervising the slaughter and burning of the animals, the priests had also to service the candelabrum and altar of incense in the inner temple. When the burnt-offering was made, the Levites sang and played stringed instruments and two priests blew silver trumpets (Num. 10.1-2, 10; 2 Chron. 29.26-8). A different psalm was recited on each day of the week.

The general impression gained from ancient literature is that most Jews were faithful in their required duty to support the temple and its cult financially. Philo's *Embassy* (156) states that money was sent to Jerusalem for this purpose from all over the Roman empire. Josephus adds that priestly purity was regarded as a significant thing, even in the Jewish Diaspora (*Apion* 1.32). The story of Mary and Joseph in the temple (Lk. 2.22-35) shows the nature of Jewish attitudes towards the temple in the first century CE. The parents of Jesus come to make the required offering after their son's birth; Anna and Simeon come there to worship. The buying and selling of sacrificial animals was probably conducted beyond the outer wall, not inside the temple as is implied by some passages in the Gospels.[10] A whole variety of sacrifices was offered in addition to the daily and annual liturgical ritual.

The calculation of Jeremias and Sanders is that there were about 20,000 priests and Levites in the first century.[11] This marked a sharp decline from the number of 38,000 officials mentioned by 1 Chron. 23.3. The figure of 20,000 is given by Josephus in his *Apion* 2.108. These priests were divided into 24 'courses' (*m.Sukk.* 5.6), each of whom served a week at a time. These courses were further divided into 'houses' which served a day at a time. Their ministry would have accelerated at the regular pilgrim festivals. The priests were rewarded with a share of the meat that they sacrificed. The Levites were lesser officials, performing such functions as gatekeepers and musicians.

The Pilgrim Festivals

Large crowds flocked to Jerusalem for the three pilgrim festivals: Passover, Weeks and Booths. (The Day of Atonement was not, as is sometimes supposed, a pilgrim festival.) According to Exod. 23.17 and Deut. 16.16 all adult males were required to attend these festivals. Sanders offers an educated guess that a Palestinian family might attend one of these festivals annually and that Diaspora Jews did so perhaps once in a lifetime. Simply put, there just was not enough room in Jerusalem to accommodate all the people who might otherwise attend. 'The spread of the Jewish population throughout Palestine', Sanders drily observes, 'required a certain amount of benign neglect of the festival laws.'[12]

Of the three festivals mentioned here, Passover is the most important.[13] Composed originally of two festivals, Passover and Unleavened Bread, it celebrates the deliverance of the Israelite people from Egypt. The Passover lamb was supposed to be slaughtered on 14 Nisan (our April). Although the sacrifice was required to be undertaken in Jerusalem, there is some evidence that the rules were bent and that sacrifices took place in the Diaspora.[14] The sacrifice itself was preceded by a period of preparation. First of all corpse-impurity and other defilements had to be removed. The people went up to Jerusalem, ritually bathed on the night before the festival and abstained from sexual activity. They purchased the requisite sacrifices and passed beyond the Levite checkpoint to the main sacrificial area. Only the men were allowed to enter this; the women remained in the court of the women. The man sacrificed his animal with the help of a priest. At the conclusion of the ritual, once the priest had been given his share of the meat, the family took the cooked animal back to where they were staying and feasted on the meat with their friends.[15]

JEWISH PARTIES

So far, we have considered the nature of Jewish religious life in the period of Christian origins. The discussion has of course been a restricted one. Nothing has been said about social and economic conditions, which would demand a much larger tome and require the study of individual people and places.[1] I shall say something along these lines when it becomes necessary to do so in Parts II to IV of this book. Now that the essence of first-century Judaism has been introduced, it is appropriate to consider something of the different varieties of Judaism in the world where Jesus was born. This immediately brings us to an important statement by Josephus.

In *Ant.* 13.171 and *War* 2.119–66 Josephus mentions three Jewish 'parties' or 'philosophical schools': Pharisees, Sadducees and Essenes.[2] In *Ant.* 18.23 he refers to a so-called 'fourth philosophy' with revolutionary tendencies which he associates with the figure of Judas the Galilean. This 'fourth philosophy' is often identified with the Zealots; but that identification raises a difficult question of the division of Jewish revolutionary groups at the time of the First Revolt which we shall consider in a moment. The crucial point is that Josephus himself states – and there is no reason for disbelieving him – that the Judaism of his day had several different parties. We shall examine each of these in turn.

The Pharisees

The Pharisees and Sadducees are the two best-known Jewish groups, if only because of the heavy and in places unflattering press they receive in the New Testament. Readers of the New Testament are left with the caricature that the Sadducees did not believe in the resurrection (Acts 23.7) and that the Pharisees were religious timeservers who had no real concern for true religion (e.g. Mt. 23.14). This is in fact a dangerous impression so far as both groups are concerned.

The first point to make is that the Pharisees can formally be distinguished from the scribes whom we considered in Chapter 5.[3] The Pharisees were not professional scripture interpreters. Likewise, not all scribes were Pharisaic in their outlook. Jesus ben Sirach, for instance, agreed with the Sadducean understanding of the scriptures (cf. *Ecclus.* 50.1–21). The reference in Mk 2.16 to 'the scribes of the Pharisees' is no doubt historically accurate. It shows that the scribes were affiliated to various Jewish parties and thus had exclusive links with none in particular.

The origins of Pharisaism lie in the second century BCE in the reign of

Jonathan Maccabee (see Josephus, *Ant.* 13.171). The Pharisees enjoyed significant power in the reign of Salome Alexandra (76–67 BCE) when Josephus says that they 'became at length the real administrators of the state' (*War* 1.111), having previously been victimized in the reign of Alexander Jannaeus (103–76 BCE). In the changed circumstances which followed the Roman occupation of 63 BCE, the Pharisees lost some of their power. At the end of Herod's reign Josephus reports that two 'teachers', Judas and Matthias, encouraged their supporters to pull down the golden eagle which Herod had erected over the temple (*Ant.* 17.149–67). Many scholars think these 'teachers' were Pharisees. Josephus states that in 6 CE the revolt of Judas the Galilean was aided by a Pharisee named Zadok (*Ant.* 18.4). The Pharisees thereafter vanish from Josephus until the time of the First Revolt. During the Revolt, in a desperate attempt to prevent insurrection, the chief priests consult the 'leading Pharisees' (*War* 2.411) about what is to be done in Jerusalem. The Pharisees took an active part in the Revolt. When it failed, they led the rabbinic movement which emerged from the Jamnian Academy and became the dominant intellectual force in Judaism.

The history of the Pharisees reveals a somewhat complex situation in terms of their public perception. Sanders notes their lack of institutional authority but at the same time their ability to exercise influence among the ordinary people which he terms their 'indirect power'.[4] This ambivalence has led to a variety of scholarly assessments of the Pharisees. We shall begin by considering the nature of their activity in Jewish society.

Josephus says of the Pharisees that 'they are reckoned to interpret the laws exactly' (*War* 2.162).[5] We have seen this does not necessarily mean that the Pharisees were scribes in the sense of professional scriptural interpreters. Although Josephus adds that 'the Pharisees have imposed on the people many laws from the tradition of the fathers not written in the Law of Moses' (*Ant.* 13.297), this statement must be interpreted with regard to their particular understanding of holiness. Their view was that they emulated priestly standards of holiness and that, while they did not think the ordinary people lacked the potential for holiness, they regarded themselves as just below the priests in terms of how holiness was to be lived and demonstrated. This self-understanding reflects the Pharisees' status as a lay movement who formed a 'brotherhood' (their own title for themselves) and who separated themselves from other people at least to some extent (hence the name 'Pharisee', which apparently means 'separated one').

Josephus' comment about the 'tradition of the fathers' in respect of the Pharisees is confirmed by numerous passages from the Gospels.[6] It brings us straight to the Pharisaic understanding of purity. This was based on a high view of the priestly office as revealed by the Mosaic Torah. Negatively, there are no passages in the earliest rabbinic literature which come out firmly in opposition to the priesthood. Positively, Pharisaic traditions about purity generally support the priesthood. Sanders shows this quite categorically in his *Jewish Law*. He argues that the Pharisees did not necessarily see their own food as holy, but that they were scrupulous in interpreting the rules which dictated what the priests might eat. The critical thing for them was to keep impurity away from the priests' food. This meant they were scrupulous about *their own* purity when it came to such actions as tithing and offering sacrifices in the temple.

The common assumption that the Pharisees arrogated priestly purity *absolutely* to themselves falls down on evidence that argues to the contrary.[7] Lev. 21.1-3 orders priests to avoid corpse impurity entirely. Not only did the Pharisees not observe this rule but the Talmud enjoins participation in burial rites as an obligation (see *b.Ber.* 18a; cf. Josephus, *Apion* 2.205). Sanders shows further that rabbinic literature completely lacks the rules that living like priests would require. The constant discussions of minor impurities in the Mishnah presuppose that these could be acquired at home. That was precisely what the priests were not allowed to do. Sanders' conclusion is that 'the Pharisees were what they appear in Josephus to be: a group of mostly lay people who were constantly concerned to study, interpret and apply the biblical law, and who did not fear to go beyond it . . . Their close attention to law and tradition made them stand out, not only because they cared for the law, but because they were so exact and because they applied law and tradition to even more areas of life than did most Jews.'[8]

The Sadducees

The Sadducees are the second Jewish party mentioned by Josephus.[9] The Sadducees have traditionally been regarded as an aristocratic section of the Jewish populace. To a large extent, this assessment is correct. The etymology of their name, however, reminds us that they were also a priestly faction. The name suggests affinity to Zadok, meaning 'Righteous One', the legendary priest in the days of David and Solomon. We shall consider both aspects of their identity.

Before the Hasmonean period, Jewish government was vested in the hands of the high priest assisted by a 'council of elders'. There was a fundamental change in this policy, at least so far as the identity of the high priest was concerned, when Jonathan Maccabee accepted the high priesthood from Alexander Balas in 152 BCE, even though he was not qualified to do so in terms of his descent. This effectively subordinated the role of high priesthood to that of military leader, although the high priestly title was retained. This situation persisted in Jerusalem until the time of Herod the Great. Herod executed the high priest Antigonus whom he found in office when he conquered Jerusalem and appointed a man called Ananel, whom Josephus says was from Babylon and came from 'a high-priestly family' (*Ant.* 15.39–41). This reversed the policy inaugurated by Jonathan and instituted somebody with pre-Maccabean claims to hold the office. Ananel was reappointed to this office some years later, having briefly been deposed in favour of Aristobulus III, whose suspicious death marked the end of the Hasmonean dynasty.

The status of the high priests in Judaism after 63 BCE was muted when compared with what had pertained previously. Nevertheless, even though the Romans were the dominant power, it is clear (not least from the reports of the trial of Jesus) that the high priests retained considerable power and influence in the eyes of the Jewish people. The high priest seems to have functioned effectively as a mediator between the overlords and the people. High priests changed frequently, being appointed and dismissed according to the whims of whoever was in power.

Subordinate to the high priest were what Josephus and the Gospels call 'the chief priests'.[10] Unlike the high priestly office, this seems not to have been a matter of appointment and thus of potential dismissal. Two proposals have been made to explain the identity of these 'chief priests'. It has been suggested, both that they were people from the four or five wealthy families from whom the high priests were drawn; and alternatively that they were holders of special office in the Jerusalem religious establishment. The conclusion of such reputable scholars as Vermes, Goodman and Sanders is that the former interpretation has more to commend it.[11] This must mean there were quite a number of 'chief priests' in the early Common Era, though whether age alone determined precedence among them is uncertain. In addition, there were other aristocratic figures whom Josephus calls variously 'the powerful' and 'the best known'. The somewhat confused history of the First Revolt, in which apparently not even the priests were united on which course of action to follow, shows the difficulty of discriminating precisely between these different figures.

For this reason one cannot, as Sanders notes, assume that all aristocrats were Sadducees but it is nonetheless a reasonable assumption that all Sadducees were aristocrats. Two issues distinguished the Sadducees from other kinds of Jews, and from Pharisees in particular. They accepted only the written law, not the 'tradition of the fathers', and they did not believe in resurrection. Josephus states additionally that they believed in free will (*War* 2.164f.; *Ant.* 13.173). It has sometimes been thought that their mistrust of the resurrection hope was because that doctrine is only dimly articulated in the Hebrew Bible, but this argument is not necessarily conclusive once one accepts the force of Dan. 12.1-2 that resurrection was a feature of at least the Writings of the Hebrew Bible. It seems likely that their rejection of non-biblical traditions was connected with their desire to distinguish themselves from other Jewish parties, notably the Pharisees and Essenes, and that their dislike of resurrection was related to this differential. For a similar reason (and not least because of the popularity of the crucified Jesus) the Sadducees are also recorded as having persecuted the Christians in the early chapters of Acts.

The Essenes

Josephus' third party is the Essenes.[12] We have met the Essenes already when considering the Dead Sea scrolls. Although the opinion is occasionally voiced that the Dead Sea community were not Essenes, the majority opinion is that they were.[13]

The precise origin of the Essenes is disputed and is probably now lost to history given the difficulties of discerning exactly what went on in Jerusalem during and after the Antiochian crisis.[14] The origin of the Qumran community is documented in codified form by their *Damascus Document*, which states that 'in the age of wrath, three hundred and ninety years after He had given them into the hand of King Nebuchadnezzar from Babylon, He visited them, and He caused a plant root to spring from Israel and Aaron to inherit His Land and to prosper on the good things of His earth' (CD 1.6–9).[15] It is not certain whether this passage describes the formation of the Qumran community as such or merely the group of people who would later secede to form that community; the latter hypothesis seems more likely. CD goes on to describe the advent of the sect's inspired teacher: 'And God observed their deeds, that they sought Him with a whole heart, and He raised for them a Teacher of Righteousness to guide them in the way of his heart' (CD 1.11–12). Even though these passages from CD cause problems of chronological calculation, for the numbers seem symbolic rather than necessarily precise, the scene is set for the formation of a new and self-consciously 'different' party in the aftermath of the Antiochian crisis.[16] This new community had both a town branch – evidently in Jerusalem – and a desert retreat which the excavations at Qumran have unearthed.[17]

The Qumran community was a small one, composed of no more than a few hundred people. Philo (*Good Man* 75) and Josephus (*Ant.* 18.20) tell us that the Essenes were 4,000 in number.[18] If this figure is correct, it surely indicates that the Qumran branch, although the spiritual centre of the movement, was not its dominant form of expression, at least in terms of numbers. Although the Essenes had ordinary occupations, Philo says they had a common purse (*Hypothetica* 11.10–12; *Good Man* 86–7) from which all corporate needs were supplied. *Hypothetica* 11.5 states that a common meal formed the centre of their community life.

This common organization is reflected in the sectarian documents unearthed at Qumran. The *Community Rule* (1QS) deals with the matter of private property, among other things. If a person was accepted into the community, his money and property were put on trust for a year and then merged into the common fund, at which point the initiate was admitted to the common meal (1QS 6.18–23). Lying about property was a serious matter for this reason, potentially punishable by expulsion from the community. Something of this understanding lies behind the story of Ananias and Sapphira in Acts 5.[19] Joining the community was seen as entry into a new covenant. The sect was critical of the current organization of the temple in Jerusalem. It believed that in worship it joined with the heavenly host in gaining authentic access to God's presence.[20]

A particular feature of Essene belief was their use of the solar calendar as opposed to the lunar calendar which prevailed in mainstream Judaism.[21] This inevitably led to festivals being celebrated on different days from other Jews. This is reflected in a notorious passage from the scrolls when a figure called 'the wicked priest' (probably Jonathan Maccabee) harassed the community on their Day of Atonement (1QpHab 2.15). The solar calendar features elsewhere in Jewish literature, notably in *1 Enoch* and *Jubilees*.

The significance of the Essenes for the study of Christian origins lies in the fact that they represent a Jewish sectarian community in the early Common Era who were not themselves influenced by Christianity but who nevertheless illustrate certain trends among the earliest followers of Jesus.[22] While we should rightly hesitate to speak glibly in terms of 'parallels', the Essenes show that the Christians were not the only Jewish sectarians to be held in suspicion by other Jews during the period under discussion. It seems that Judaism before 70 CE was sufficiently diverse to accommodate a broad mainstream and more than one deviationist movement. This is an important indicator of the religious and intellectual climate which prevailed at that time.

Josephus' 'Fourth Philosophy'

Josephus' 'fourth philosophy' is a little more difficult to explain because of the complexities of the Jewish parties at the time of the First Revolt. This 'fourth philosophy' is commonly assumed to be the Zealots. Yet the use of the term 'Zealot' raises considerable problems.[23]

The essential problem is deciding whether the title 'Zealot' properly belonged to all the Jewish parties at the time of the Revolt or merely to one group in a wider spectrum of others. This problem focuses in no small measure on the interpretation of the writings of Josephus.[24] Josephus was in some senses an agent of the Roman government, having been taken by Titus to Rome after the destruction of Jerusalem and provided with an official house and pension in exchange for his services. So far as Josephus' portrait of the Zealots is concerned, there is disagreement about his portrait of Judas the Galilean and the activity of this figure in 6 CE; specifically, whether this Judas merely called for non-cooperation in the census that was imposed at that time or actually incited rebellion against Rome. Many commentators now take the second view. Josephus shows that rebellion became something of a family business for the descendants of Judas the Galilean. His sons James and Simon were executed under Tiberius Alexander (*Ant.* 20.102). His grandson Menahem was killed by fellow revolutionaries in 66 CE (*War* 2.448).

Josephus insists this Judas was the founder with Zadok the Pharisee of the 'fourth philosophy', which closely resembled the Pharisees save for the principle of 'no lord but God' (*Ant.* 18.23). Scholars such as Brandon and Hengel assume that Josephus is correct in his report and that these two figures inaugurated a revolutionary movement whose activity was clearly discernible some sixty years later during the First Revolt.[25] More recent scholars, typified by David Rhoads, argue for a less monolithic picture which acknowledges the diversity of Jewish revolutionary groups at the time of the First Revolt.[26] Not the least important reason for this revised opinion is the recognition that Josephus probably exaggerated the importance of Judas' group in the apologetic interests of blaming the cause of the Revolt in part on a small number of insurrectionaries. Rhoads points to such disparate groups as the *Sicarii*, the followers of John of Gischala and those of Simon bar Giora as well as the Zealots as significant parties during the First Revolt against Rome. The recognition of such diversity is a significant feature of research into Jewish history in the period of Christian origins. It must be allowed to qualify the portrait of a substantially united Judaism.

The upshot of this research is the probable conclusion that we can speak of four Jewish 'parties' only in an attenuated form given the problems with the so-called 'fourth philosophy'. This does not necessarily detract from Josephus' analysis of the situation. It simply demonstrates the diversity that pertained in the Judaism of the first century CE. This should constantly be borne in mind by all who would understand the path of Christian origins.

Common Theology

In saying this, we remind ourselves of what it was that held these disparate groups together within a single and unified religion. This was the common theology or covenantal nomism we considered in Chapter 4.

Sanders has argued persuasively that this concept centred around the conviction that the true God had given his people his law which they were required to obey in all its various ordinances.[27] This involved the performance of regular sacrifices, which again we saw were offered from a position of religious integrity and not blindly on an *ex opere operando* basis. It was this sense of being Jewish and of performing these distinctive Jewish activities, which had relevance within a specifically

Jewish framework of belief, that bound the various Jewish groups together. This is said without prejudice to the certainty that the different Jewish groups did things in different ways. Such diversity permitted the Christian religion to emerge initially as a messianic sect within Judaism. Diversity within a common outlook is the key to understanding what was in fact a very complex religion operating within a difficult political climate.

DIASPORA JUDAISM

Our penultimate question is how different Judaism was outside the land of Israel.[1] The origins of the Jewish Diaspora ('Dispersion') lie in the Babylonian exile of the sixth century BCE. Not all of those who travelled to Babylon in 587 BCE chose to return to Palestine in 537 BCE.[2] By the early Common Era, and not least through trading relations, Jews were scattered throughout the mediterranean world.[3] The presence of Jewish communities in many cities of the mediterranean world was one of the principal reasons for the first initial (and successful) spread of Christianity.

Study of the Jewish Diaspora must take account of John Barclay's book on this topic published in 1996.[4] Barclay studies this matter from a variety of perspectives, not the least important of which is the question of cultural assimilation which we know from the book of Revelation was a subject of concern for developing Christianity also.[5] In his chapter on the Egyptian Diaspora, Barclay notes varying levels of cultural assimilation and convergence. It is not surprising to learn that there were Jews in Alexandria who exhibited a low level of assimilation to the surrounding environment. The Delta quarter of Alexandria was a Jewish residential district; Philo mentions a Jewish sectarian group known as the Therapeutae (*Vit. Cont.* 24–34). What is perhaps more surprising to discover is that there were Jews who had a high level of assimilation. One such was Dositheos, son of Drimylos, who appears in a number of papyri (e.g. CPJ 127) as the scribe of Ptolemy Euergetes I and even as 'priest of Alexander and the Gods Adelphoi and the Gods Euergetai'. This undoubtedly implies a renunciation of Dositheos' ancestral religion. His service at a foreign altar is a striking indication of the length to which some Jews were prepared to go in the service of their careers.

Jewish literature produced in Egypt shows evidence of both cultural convergence and antagonism. In terms of convergence, the *Exagoge* of Ezekiel the Tragedian reveals a measured adoption of the Greek literary tradition in which Jewish history (including the divinization of Moses) is retold in Hellenistic guise. The *Exagoge*, however, is not the only kind of text produced by Alexandrian Judaism. To find an example of cultural antagonism we need turn no further than the Wisdom of Solomon, which Barclay interprets as 'an educated and deeply Hellenized exercise in cultural aggression'.[6] Thus the author of Wisdom powerfully criticizes idolatry (Wis. 13.10–15.17) and extols the election of the Jewish people by God together with his providential care for them (e.g. Wis. 19.22).

Barclay's book repays careful study for its meticulous assessment of what remains a multi-faceted problem. I can but cite his major conclusions here. Barclay argues broadly (and against earlier commentators) that social, economic and cultural factors all influenced the fortunes of Diaspora Jews at various times and in different places. This is not perhaps so very different from the fate of people in the Jewish homeland; but the position of Jews in the Diaspora was much more directly influenced by the experience of living in an alien environment. The wide scope of Barclay's study confirms it is difficult to generalize about individual Jewish reactions to the Diaspora environment. These had a considerable variety which up to a point was circumstantially determined.

Nevertheless, Barclay feels able and even obliged to offer an explanation of how Jewish communities survived as coherent and enduring realities.[7] This raises a hermeneutical problem. There are at least three levels on which this issue can be assessed: how Jews viewed themselves, how they were viewed by other Jews and how they were viewed by those outside the Jewish community. The most promising conclusions, Barclay argues, can be drawn in those areas where these three levels converge and where perceptions are the same whether one looks at insider or outsider opinion concerning what it meant to be Jewish. Several issues should be considered when making this assessment.

Almost all the literature from the Diaspora indicates the significance of the 'nation' as a central concept in what it meant to be Jewish.[8] In *3 Maccabees*, which generally exhibits cultural antagonism, there are significant references to the Jewish 'nation', 'race' and 'people'. Even Aristobulus, whom Barclay presents under the heading of 'cultural convergence', presents Solomon as 'one of our ancestors' (12.11). This Jewish consciousness is matched by the way in which outsiders perceived the Diaspora Jewish communities. Strabo (according to Josephus, *Ant.* 14.115) refers to the Jewish 'tribe'; Cicero (*De Provinciis Consularibus* 5.10) to the Jewish 'nation'; and Tacitus (*Hist.* 5.4.1) to the Jewish 'people'. In the third century CE Dio Cassius was still insisting that Jewish customs were an ethnic, not a religious peculiarity (37.17.1–2).

This ethnic pride was fuelled by links with Jerusalem and the land of Israel. Symbolically, this link found expression in the collection of temple dues among the Jewish communities which clearly resourced their sense of self-identity.[9] This piety was noticed even by the Roman historian Tacitus (*Hist.* 5.5.1). Closely associated with the temple dues were the pilgrim festivals to Jerusalem which, as we said in Chapter 7, a Diaspora Jew might make perhaps once in his or her lifetime. The very irregularity with which such visits were made reinforced the iconic significance of Jerusalem in the mind of scattered Judaism, not unlike the role that Mecca holds for Muslims today. In speaking of links with the Jewish homeland, we must not ignore the importance of trade as a means of establishing such cosmopolitan contact.[10] Palestinian Jews, for instance, were regularly taken to Rome as slaves; and, although this was no doubt a doleful passage, it shows the cross-border transport by which ethnic pride and awareness was retained. The situation of slaves transported to Europe and North America at a later period is in every sense an appropriate analogy.

Beside the figure of Moses who was revered as the Jewish lawgiver, the law or Torah stood as a prominent symbol of Jewish distinctiveness.[11] In Alexandria there was an annual festival to celebrate the translation of the Septuagint. Diaspora communities gathered weekly in their synagogues much like the Jews of Palestine. The allegorical tradition which stemmed from Aristobulus (second century BCE) to Philo (first century CE) had as its rationale the supreme authority of the Torah in all matters of faith and conduct.

This sense of Jewish self-identity was reinforced by elements of practical religious distinctiveness. These included the refusal to worship any deity but the God of Israel, separation at meals, circumcision and sabbath observance. Such factors helped Diaspora Jews to retain their ethnic and religious individuality in the face of a variety of social alternatives if not pressures. The weekly gathering of the Jewish community in the synagogue was a powerful reminder that this was indeed a 'peculiar people'. It is a testimony to the Jewish spirit that such practices were sustained over the whole of the period we are examining; sometimes in the face of fierce opposition.

JEWISH ESCHATOLOGICAL HOPE

The final matter to be considered in this Part of the book is the nature of Jewish eschatological hope. Since this bears quite directly on the topic of Christian origins, we shall need to examine it in some detail.

The term 'eschatology' is a nuanced one. It derives from the two Greek words *eschatos* and *logos* which, put together in this form, literally mean 'talk about the last things'. This term is not used in any Jewish and Christian writing of the period under review. It was first used by the Lutheran theologian Abraham Calov in 1677 as the title for the last section of his work on dogmatics, which dealt with the issues of death and eternal life.[1] The Christian nuance post-Calov has been that ultimate hope lies beyond the grave rather than in this world.[2]

Problematically, this is not the orientation that future hope takes in the Hebrew Bible; nor indeed in first-century Judaism. There is only a faint resurrectional hope in the Jewish scriptures. The dead have but a shadowy existence in Sheol in most Hebrew Bible writings.[3] A more prominent hope is for the Messiah and for Israel's dominance, of a kind that will transform its fortunes in respect of the surrounding nations.[4] Often, this is linked to the concepts of monotheism and covenant obedience which we have mentioned already in this book. In the later biblical literature, apocalypticism emerges as a significant factor. This is obvious especially in Deutero-Zechariah, whose author anticipates God's appearance in the arena of human history, as it were from without (Zech. 14.5); and of course in the book of Daniel. Despite this apocalypticism, the future hope found in the Hebrew Bible is very different from the understanding of 'eschatology' that pertains in Christianity today where the *post-mortem* aspect is dominant.

The question therefore arises of whether the biblical perspective can be called 'eschatological' at all. The answer is that, in the broadest sense, it probably can. Given that 'eschatology' means 'the doctrine of the last things', this term can be applied to the better future of the Jewish nation if that is judged to constitute 'the last things' (or ideal state) in terms of the Hebrew writers' ultimate perspective on human history. In saying this, we must be careful to note the differences between ancient Judaism and modern Christianity and not to impose the younger understanding arbitrarily on older and quite different texts. This is to call for sensitivity in interpretation which allows the ancient texts to speak for themselves and not through a Christian matrix. Christian readers should recognize their natural bias in this respect.

Eschatology in the Hebrew Bible

David L. Petersen identifies three separate sources for the future hope in the Hebrew Bible.[5] These are the patriarchal promise tradition, the David–Zion tradition and the Sinai covenant tradition. Each of these contributes in different ways to the development of the biblical perspective.

The patriarchal promise tradition derives from the Pentateuch, but reflects the understanding superimposed on the patriarchal age in the period of the monarchy. Gen. 15.18-20 has been identified as describing the land that Israel controlled during this time, projected back anachronistically onto the earlier period. The David–Zion tradition looks back to the promise of 2 Samuel 7 that one of David's descendants would always occupy the throne of Israel. This not only involved Zion or Jerusalem as the geographical centre of the royal domain; it also imported wider Ancient Near Eastern hopes which expected peace and fertility to emerge when a new king acceded. Petersen relates the 'day of the Lord' motif (found e.g. in Amos 5.18–20) to this strand of belief on the grounds that it anticipates Yahweh's enthronement as king following his victory in battle. The Sinai covenant tradition is different again. It involves the idea of a contract between Israel and God in which distinctive things are promised on either side. Success or failure in keeping the covenant is characteristically expressed in Deuteronomy in terms of blessing or curse, both of which are held to affect Israel's future for better or for worse.

It has become customary in scholarly literature to distinguish between prophetic and apocalyptic eschatology, particularly in discussion of post-exilic Israel.[6] That convention will be followed here, with the proviso that the distinction cannot be made in absolute terms. In the prophetic writings, broadly speaking, the future breaks out of the present when a symbol of hope such as the Messiah appears from within the historical process. In the apocalyptic writings, by contrast, the future breaks into the present as it were from outside in the form of a supernatural intervention. This shift in eschatological understanding took place in the period following the exile, and especially in literature from the third century BCE onwards. The contrast between these two forms of eschatology can be seen when Isaiah 11 is compared with Zechariah 14. Isaiah 11 predicts that 'a shoot shall come out from the stock of Jesse, and a branch shall grow out of his roots' (Isa. 11.1). This is a reference to the birth of a future monarch. Zechariah 14, by contrast, expects the personal appearance of God within the arena of human history, especially in 14.5 ('Then the LORD my God will come, and all the holy ones with him'). The difference between these two passages lies in their attitude to the historical process. H.H. Rowley commented famously on this distinction, 'The prophets foretold the future that should arise out of the present, while the apocalyptists foretold the future that should break into the present . . . The apocalyptists had little faith in the present to beget the future.'[7] Apocalyptic eschatology looks for supernatural intervention in a situation which we know from writings such as Daniel often seemed desperate to the individual concerned.

Eschatology in Post-biblical Literature

As in the Hebrew Bible, we find a variety of eschatological hopes in the literature of post-biblical Judaism. I shall present a broad overview of the material before proceeding to distinctive themes such as the messianic hope and questions of resurrection and immortality.[8]

The earliest apocalyptic literature stems from the third century BCE and is represented by *1 Enoch* 1–36 and 72–82.[9] The authors(s) of this early Enochic material were much preoccupied with the theme of judgment. They saw the prophetic writings as containing material which had yet to be accomplished. *1 Enoch* 6–11 weaves together traditions from more than one source to link the present generation, on the authority of heavenly revelation, with the antediluvian generation, in the expectation that widespread destruction will once again affect the earth.[10] In the new creation, the author expects all humankind (including the Gentiles) to turn to God so that evil will be banished forever.

In the so-called *Dream Visions* (*1 Enoch* 83–90), the *Animal Apocalypse* exemplifies the periodization of history in a way that was to become significant for the later apocalyptic tradition.[11] The author of this part of *1 Enoch* sees the seventy shepherds of Jer. 50.6 and Ezekiel 34 as wicked. He anticipates the construction of a new temple to which the Gentiles will come and be made subject to the Jews.

The notion that history is predetermined, with its consequences for eschatology, features in both the *Testament of Moses* and the book of Daniel. Two passages in the *Testament of Moses* (1.13–14; 12.4–5) explain that the whole of human history was known to God before the creation of the earth.[12] The testamentary form allows the eponymous patriarch to make a dying declaration which sets the events of the Antiochian crisis in eschatological perspective and identifies them as the end of history. A particular feature of this text is the superimposition of a mythical resolution onto the historical drama. Although there is no messianic hope in the technical sense, judgment is assigned to God and his chief angel. The author anticipates the appearance of the divine kingdom and the destruction of the Gentiles, after which Israel will be lifted up to the stars in a form of astral immortality (10.9–10). This includes a spatial dualism in which heaven is made the place of salvation and earth the place of punishment.

Daniel is divided into two halves. Chapters 1–6 tell stories about the life of Jewish exiles in the Babylonian court. Chapters 7–11 present the author's own visionary experience.[13] Chapter 7 is rightly regarded as a pivotal passage in the Daniel apocalypse.[14] Where chapters 1–6 hint (on occasion, more than broadly) at the future supremacy of the Jewish people, chapter 7 links the triumph of Israel with the presentation of a quasi-angelic figure in the heavenly court and his investiture with authority there. The longest vision is found in chapters 10–12 of the work. Here, the author describes in scarcely veiled detail the course of the Antiochian crisis. At the beginning of chapter 12, he promises the intervention of Michael and the subsequent provision of resurrection and astral immortality for those who have been faithful in the conflict.[15]

The different texts that make up *1 Enoch* were written between the third century BCE and the first century CE. The youngest text is called the *Similitudes of Enoch*.[16] The author of the *Similitudes* describes the enthronement of a heavenly mediator called variously the Son of Man and the Chosen One who is held to discharge judgment over those who have worked tyranny on the earth. In *1 En.* 48.10 and 52.4 this mediator is identified as the Messiah.

Two apocalypses written after the destruction of Jerusalem show the regret felt by Jewish people over that event. *4 Ezra* poses a series of questions about the disaster in which eschatology is one of the topics the seer puts forward for consideration.[17] The messianism of *4 Ezra* has more than one facet.[18] In chapter 7 the Messiah is a human figure who reigns for 400 years but dies before the general resurrection. In chapter 13, however, the Messiah is a mythical or supernatural figure who comes up from the sea and reigns on Mount Zion.

The latter passage represents a point of contact with *2 Baruch*, otherwise known as *Syriac Baruch*, which was also written in the aftermath of the destruction of Jerusalem.[19] The author of *2 Baruch* looks beyond this disaster to the time of the eschatological climax. He interprets the disaster as a punishment for the sins of Israel, but promises that divine wrath will be averted and that resurrection will yield a form of heavenly immortality for the righteous (*2 Bar.* 49–52). There is a fascinating antithesis between the doleful effects of Adam's transgression and the peace and incorruptibility of the eschatological age in chapters 55–74 of this text.

Although one should beware of artificial distinctions between genres of literature, it is probably helpful to separate the wisdom from the apocalyptic literature in discussion of the Jewish eschatological hope. The essence of apocalypticism is the revelation of heavenly secrets; of apocalyptic eschatology, the transcendental in-breaking of the future into the present through supernatural intervention. The wisdom literature, by and large, lacks these characteristics. In the main, it draws on the stream of 'prophetic' eschatology. In Tobit, for instance, the essence of future hope lies in the salvation which the prophets predicted (14.5). Interestingly, however, there is a form of determinism in Tob. 14.4-7. This work's eschatology climaxes in the hope for the restoration of Jerusalem and the temple.

Sirach also looks back to the prophets, claiming that Isaiah saw 'the hidden things before they came to be' (Ecclus 48.25). In chapter 36, Sirach laments the subordination of the Jews to the Gentiles and hopes for the restoration of the divine glory. In chapter 45, he follows the thought of the early chapters of Zechariah (esp. Zech. 4.14) by associating the priest and the king in an interesting anticipation of the eschatological view that would later come to be prominent in the Qumran community.

The Eschatology of the Qumran Community

The eschatology of the Qumran community deserves to be treated separately.[20] We saw in Chapter 8 that the Qumran community are probably to be identified with the Essenes and that they were one of the four Jewish 'parties' of whom Josephus speaks. We would describe them as a 'sect', in the sense that they were conscious of an ideological distance from mainstream Judaism; not least so far as the temple was concerned.[21]

The essence of the Qumran ideology was belief in the election of the community as such. This was set against a background, inherited from apocalyptic circles, in which the whole of human history was held predetermined by God (1QS 3–4; CD 2.3–10; 1QH 1.7–8; 4Q180 1; 1QpHab 7). This is a way, which includes a prominent psychological dimension, of legitimating the present position of the sect as effectively exiles within Israel at large. The Qumran community believed that the worship of the temple in Jerusalem was defiled and that they alone remained true to the covenant which God had made with Israel. The similarity of Qumran eschatology to the eschatology of works such as *1 Enoch* and Daniel is to be explained by the historical origins of the movement which, although difficult to unravel and notoriously contentious in the annals of scholarship, demonstrated unease with the situation that developed after the Antiochian crisis.

As a sect, the Qumran community produced an eschatological view in which its own life featured prominently.[22] The story of the community's formation is told in the early columns of the *Damascus Document*. In codified language CD 1 mentions 'the age of wrath, three hundred years after He [i.e. God] delivered' Israel into the hands of the Babylonians at the time of the exile. The same reference describes how, twenty years later, God sent the Teacher of Righteousness to lead the community into its sectarian existence.

The 'charter' of the community is provided by the *Community Rule*. 1QS 8.1–9.11 states that the community constituted the true temple and that they atoned for the land of Israel. This is why (the literature claims) they had separated themselves from 'the wicked' (i.e. the rest of Israel) to devote themselves to scriptural study until the eschatological age. This passage provides a direct transition to messianic hope. 1QS 9.11 says that this state of alertness will continue 'until there shall come the prophet and the anointed ones of Aaron and Israel'.[23] This takes us back to the thought of Zech. 4.14 and of Sirach after him to establish a double messianism (i.e. the hope for a royal *and* a priestly figure) which was the distinctive feature of the Essene hope.

Having said this, we can immediately note that Essene messianism is frustratingly unsystematic and that the *Testimonium* (4Q175) anticipates *three* eschatological figures, the anointed ones of Aaron and Israel and 'the prophet', the latter evidently based on the hope for the prophet like Moses in Deuteronomy 18. The *Damascus Document* introduces a further note of uncertainty when it refers in the singular to the 'anointed one' of Aaron and Israel (co 12.23–13.1; 14.19; 19.10 cf. 20.1).

One wonders what to make of all this evidence. In all probability, we should not press the distinctions between the different texts too closely; still less run the risk of assuming that the differentiation corresponds to a strictly chronological development of the messianic scheme in question. Some texts describe what the eschatological figures will do. Others significantly do not. This is in line with many wider expressions of eschatological hope, especially those which come from sectarian or so-called 'millenarian' communities, where the promise *that* salvation will come is often more important than a precise description of *what* salvation will be like.

The Jewish Messianic Hope

This leads me now to examine the nature of the messianic hope in Judaism.[24] The term 'Messiah' derives from a Hebrew word meaning 'anointed one'. In the Hebrew Bible, this term never designates a future redeemer, for it is clear that even in Dan. 9.25-6 past figures are meant once Daniel's pseudepigraphy is acknowledged.[25] The figure it designates is often, but by no means always, the Jewish king. Three categories of people are said to be 'anointed' in the Hebrew Bible.[26] These are kings (often), priests (less often but including Daniel 9) and prophets (Elisha alone). The kingly strand particularly concerns us here. In 2 Sam. 2.4-7 David is anointed king over Judah; 1 Sam. 16.6 calls David 'the Lord's anointed'. This title is used also for Saul in 1 Sam. 12.3, 5. It has sometimes been questioned how accurately the historical books reflect the circumstances of the monarchical period; but the crucial point is that this is what was believed to have happened when the books in question were compiled. They emphasize the concept of anointing to designate God's choice of the king in question.

Post-biblical literature reveals a more developed understanding. There, in a variety of sources, '(the) Messiah' appears as the title for a future figure (or figures) who will function as an eschatological redeemer in the sense that he (they) will introduce a new era in the experience of the people of Israel. To speak of 'the messianic hope' in Judaism is thus to mention the hope for a future redeemer who will act in an eschatological way. Horbury distinguishes between 'the kingship ideology' of the Hebrew Bible and Jewish 'messianic hope, the latter in the sense of the expectation of an eschatological ruler and Saviour'.[27] He also shows that 'the Messiah' was current as a title in Judaism from at least the second century BCE.[28] This marks a difference from the Hebrew Bible usage.

The question of what place messianism occupies in Hebrew Bible *theology* lies beyond the scope of this study, but doubtless one would point to passages such as Jer. 23.5 and Isaiah 9 and 11 in trying to answer it; not to mention the more apocalyptically oriented hope for future change that is found in texts such as Daniel 10–12 and Zechariah 9–14.[29] These passages show that the hope for a king is prominent in the biblical mindset and that this is bound up with the hope for deliverance from enemies.[30] The so-called Royal Psalms (Pss 2; 18; 20; 21; 45; 72; 89; 101; 132 and 144.1-11) are overtly messianic and, if A.R. Johnson is to be believed, were used in the enthronement festival and implied a future ideal ruler even when the reigning monarch was present at the ceremony.[31] The understanding of kingship in ancient Israel was significantly illuminated by the discovery of the Ras Shamra texts in 1929.[32] These texts identify the monarch as the focal link between the cult and the expression of future hope within a mythological ambience.

A variety of material anticipates the advent of a king analogous to David. The *locus classicus* of this view is 2 Samuel 7, where David is promised that 'your throne shall be established for ever' (2 Sam. 7.16). In Isaiah 7, the birth of a child (evidently Hezekiah) is promised in the context of an address to 'the house of David'. Isa. 9.2-7 anticipates the birth of a Davidic king who will usher in a new era of peace and justice. This figure is not named but he is explicitly identified as a ruler. Isa. 9.7 states that:

His authority shall grow continually and there shall be endless peace for the throne of David and his kingdom. He will establish and uphold it with justice and with righteousness from this time onwards and for evermore.

Similarly, Isa. 11.1-9 predicts that 'a shoot shall come out from the stock of Jesse, and a branch shall grow out of his roots'. Since Jesse was the father of David, the promise of Davidic succession is again implied. There is relevant material also in Jer. 23.1-8 and Ezek. 17.22-4, not to mention Hag. 2.20-3 and Zechariah 12.

Horbury's Theory

William Horbury's assertion that 'the word Messiah itself attests a special accepted notion at the end of the Old Testament period, in the second century BC and later' is based on a variety of evidence.[33] Horbury argues that the Hebrew Bible phrase 'the Lord's Anointed', familiar from such passages as 2 Sam. 2.4 and 23.2, had been abbreviated to *(ha-) mashiah*, 'the Anointed', in the period under discussion. Important evidence for this is found in the twice-mentioned noun *ho messias* in the Fourth Gospel (Jn 1.41; 4.25). This is an apparently deliberate alternative to the more familiar *ho christos* which occurs many times in the New Testament and elsewhere. *Ho messias* is a direct translation of the Aramaic *mᵉshiha*, 'the Anointed'. It shows that that term was not just preserved but brought into contemporary usage through the device of transliteration. That suggests a familiar appeal and understanding.

Horbury turns next to the book of Daniel from the second century BCE. The term 'anointed one' occurs twice in Dan. 9.25-6 in connection with priestly figures. In both references, the noun is used without the definite article, showing that it is a technical term and not just discrete local usage. Although the high priest is designated here and not the king, the anarthrous use of this title is a significant milestone in the historical development of 'the Messiah' as a specified figure in Judaism.

This use of 'Messiah' as a technical term is supported by Jewish literature from either side of the beginning of the Common Era, including rabbinic sources.[34] The double messianism of the Qumran community deserves attention for its precise use of language. In both 1 QS 9.11 ('until there shall come the prophet and the messiahs of Aaron and Israel') and CD 12.23–13.1 ('until there shall arise the messiah of Aaron and Israel') a specific figure or figures is intended. The same is evidently true of Jewish literature found now in translation. Thus *2 Bar.* 29.3 predicts that 'the Anointed One will begin to be revealed'; and 2 Esd. 12.32 mentions 'the Messiah, whom the Most High has kept until the end of days'. Both Talmuds know this titular usage: 'So, when messiah comes, I shall be ready' (*j.Kil.* 32b); and 'for it is taught, Three come unexpectedly: messiah, a discovery, and a scorpion' (*b.Sanh.* 97a). So also do the Targums. In Targum Onkelos to Gen. 49.10 we find the phrase 'until messiah comes'. The Targum to Isa. 52.13 reads, 'my servant messiah shall prosper'; and to Zech. 6.12, 'a man whose name is messiah'.

This evidence is not extensive, but it occurs quite strikingly across a range of literature. This makes the strength of Horbury's conclusion difficult to resist. It seems that 'Messiah' was used as a technical term in Judaism before the birth of Christianity. The Septuagint (LXX), apocrypha and pseudepigrapha all support this conclusion. In Num. 24.7, for instance, in the prophecy of a star emerging from Jacob, the translation interprets the more ambiguous 'star' and 'sceptre' of the Hebrew original as a specific person, although the title *ho christos* is not used for him. Elsewhere, both Abraham (Gen. 23.6 LXX) and Moses (Exod. 4.20 LXX) are described as 'king'. The Apocrypha mentions the hope that God will regather the dispersed tribes (2 Macc. 2.18; Bar. 2.27–35) and that the Jewish nation will be established for ever (2 Macc. 14.15).[35] The *Sibylline Oracles* (mid-second century BCE), especially 3.652–795, have substantial and significant messianic content.[36] This passage opens with the statement that God will send a king from the East who will end all the wars on earth. The Gentiles, gathered against Jerusalem, will perish and the children of God live in peace and tranquillity, guided by the divinely revealed law. God himself will dwell in Zion and peace will prevail on the earth. From a somewhat later period – evidently the time of Antony and Cleopatra – *Sib. Or.* 3.46–50 voices the hope that 'a holy prince will come to gain sway over the scepters of the earth'.

Similar sentiments are expressed in *1 En.* 90.16–38, whose author expects a throne to be erected and God to sit in judgment following the eschatological assault of the Gentiles. The Messiah appears here under the symbol of a white bullock after the renewal of Jerusalem. The Gentiles will then be converted. This hope was continued in the first century BCE by the author of the *Psalms of Solomon* (63–48 BCE). *Pss. Sol.* 17 directly illustrates the Jewish messianic hope.[37] It juxtaposes the belief in God as king (17.1) with the theme of the election of David (17.4) and the hope for a future Davidic ruler who will remove the Gentile usurpers (17.21–2).

In the first century CE we have evidence for messianism in a number of different writings.[38] Josephus (*Ant.* 17.45) narrates an incident in which a eunuch named Bagoas is promised that the future king – evidently the Messiah – will grant him the ability to marry and father children. Two generations later, in the moves which led to the First Jewish Revolt against Rome, messianism played a crucial part in the coalescence of Jewish revolutionary hope as we know from a variety of writings. Later, during the Second Revolt, Rabbi Akibah proclaimed the rebel leader bar Kochbah as the Messiah. Significantly, in the *Similitudes of Enoch* (*1 Enoch* 37–71) the heavenly mediator reinterpreted there from Daniel 7 is identified as the Messiah (*1 En.* 48.10; 52.4).[39]

The Resurrectional Hope in Judaism

The hope for the resurrection in Judaism is essentially a post-biblical development from biblical roots.[40] In this case, the biblical roots are rather more slender than in the case of messianism. We have seen that there is very little 'resurrectional' understanding in the Hebrew Bible. What material there is is confined to one, possibly two passages. These are Isa. 26.19 and Dan 12.2, the latter significantly from the apocalyptic genre.

The Hebrew Bible places greater store on the present life than on the afterlife.[41] At the heart of the Israelite view of prosperity stands the idea of the covenant. The promise to Abraham in Genesis 17 is relevant here. God promised Abraham, 'I will make nations of you, and kings shall come from you' (Gen. 17.6). The Jewish hope was thereafter a hope for longevity and prosperity. Premature death was regarded as misfortune. Isa. 38.10 vividly records Hezekiah's lament when told of his impending death that 'in the noontide of my days I must depart'. Exceptionally poignant was the death of an only son (Amos 8.10; cf. Jer. 6.26). The levirate law was introduced to deal with the problem of what happened when a man died childless leaving a widow (see Deut. 25.5–10).

Israel did, however, share with other Ancient Near Eastern cultures belief in the shadowy world of the dead, known in Hebrew as Sheol. Sheol was understood as a vast subterranean region populated by shades. It should not be assumed that this was an 'intermediate' state anticipating future resurrection and judgment, which is how much post-biblical literature describes the fate of the departed. Eccles. 9.5–10 offers a *post-mortem* view which stands at variance with the later hope: 'The dead know nothing; they have no more reward, and even the memory of them is lost.' One consequence of this view is that the dead have no contact with God (see Ps. 88.10-12). This does not, however, deny that God can perceive Sheol himself (see Prov. 15.11).

Some, but not all, scholars think that the Jewish resurrectional hope is articulated in Isa. 26.19: 'your dead shall live, their corpses shall rise'. The problem with this passage is that it comes from the so-called 'Isaiah apocalypse' (Isaiah 24–7), which many scholars date long after the original Isaiah; some as late as the second century BCE.[42] The evaluation of Isa. 26.19 must therefore proceed with caution so far as its date is concerned. Moreover, it is not certain to what extent the language used is metaphorical. Isa. 26.19 might for instance testify (only) to the same hope for national restoration that can be discerned in Ezekiel 37 (the passage describing the Valley of Dry Bones). The resurrectional force of Isa. 26.19 should thus be left an 'open question'; albeit with the proviso that, the later the passage is set chronologically, no doubt the more plausibly it does attest the hope for resurrection.

This brings us to Dan. 12.1-3 as the only certain articulation of the resurrection hope in the Hebrew Bible.[43] Dan. 12.1-3 comes in the context of the long eschatological prophecy which makes up the bulk of Daniel 10–12. In terms of the eschatological timescale outlined by that passage, Dan. 12.1-3 describes what will happen once the tyrant Antiochus Epiphanes has been removed from the scene. The hope in this passage is for the 'arising' of Michael followed by the selective resurrection of some to reward and others to punishment. The resurrection anticipated here is a bodily one, and to a form of astral immortality

(12.3) in which the righteous acquire what appears to be angelomorphic existence in the heavenly world.

Post-biblical Literature

Dan. 12.1-3, however, is not the first articulation of the resurrection hope in Jewish literature. Ever since Milik published the Aramaic fragments of *1 Enoch* in 1976, it has been recognized that parts of *1 Enoch* come from the third century BCE and are a generation older than Daniel. *1 Enoch* 22 offers the first certain statement of the Jewish resurrection hope. The material in question comes from the *Book of Watchers* (*1 Enoch* 1–36). *1 Enoch* 22–7 is part of the longer section *1 Enoch* 17–36 which recounts Enoch's journey through the universe. In this part of the travelogue, Enoch sees the distant place of punishment. In *1 Enoch* 22 the dead are separated into three chambers. In the first chamber, the spirits of the righteous enjoy a spring of water (*1 En.* 22.9). The second chamber contains sinners subjected to punishment for their misdeeds. In the third, the spirits of the assassinated plead to God for vengeance. There is some confusion here.[44] The most obvious interpretation of *1 En.* 22.9 is that the righteous receive their reward immediately after death, consisting of the pleasant spring. Yet Nickelsburg thinks that future resurrection is also intended by this passage. On this view, *1 Enoch* 22 describes a place of preliminary confinement which is characterized by different categories of recompense and which looks forward to a future blessed state.

One can hardly over-estimate the significance of this passage in the history of Jewish thought. Where Isa. 26.19, which may not be much earlier than *1 Enoch* 22, alludes only in passing to the hope for resurrection, *1 Enoch* 22 offers a (relatively) detailed description of the intermediate state which, like the later Dan. 12.1-3, knows of more than one possible outcome. It is doubtless right to identify Babylonian influence on this passage; but that does not obscure the novelty of this chapter in Jewish tradition, nor its significance as found there. *1 Enoch* 22 may be presented as the *Ursprung* of the Jewish resurrectional hope given the difficulties with Isa. 26.19. Further Enochic material from the second century BCE (notably *1 En.* 90.33; 103.4) develops the resurrectional hope in this strand of apocalyptic literature.[45]

Also from the second century BCE is the book of *Jubilees*.[46] In chapter 23, the author implies that sin resulted in decreased human longevity. He promises that this will be overcome when people begin to study the law (23.26). The conclusion of *Jubilees* 23 introduces the hope for immortality in a paradisiacal context: 'And their bones will rest in the earth, and their spirits will increase joy' (23.31). This is not the hope for resurrection as such, but for a form of immortality akin perhaps to the hope for angelomorphic existence found in Daniel 12 and elsewhere.

The Antiochian crisis remained an indelible memory for Jewish people.

The somewhat later 2 Maccabees 7 tells the story of the crisis from the vantage-point of the subsequent Maccabean victory. Chapter 7 narrates the famous story of the mother and the seven sons who choose death rather than neglect of their ancestral traditions. This story redounds with resurrectional hope. As the first brother is being tortured he tells his persecutor, 'You accursed wretch, you dismiss us from this present life, but the King of the universe will raise us up to an everlasting renewal of life, because we have died for his laws' (7.9). The six other brothers perish in a similar way. The mother encourages her sons, saying to them: 'The Creator of the world, who shaped the beginning of humankind and devised the origin of all things, will in his mercy give life and breath back to you again, since you now forget yourselves for the sake of his laws' (7.23). Nickelsburg has shown that, in a tradition stemming from Deutero-Isaiah, the author presents the brothers as the suffering and vindicated servants of Yahweh and the mother as a personification of Zion who anticipates the return of her children, dispersed in death.[47]

From the turn of the eras comes the Wisdom of Solomon.[48] Chapters 1–6 present a treatise on immortality which asserts, against the mocking of the wicked, that 'the souls of the righteous are in the hand of God' (3.1) and that 'their hope is full of immortality' (3.4); 4.16 promises that the 'righteous who have died will condemn the ungodly who are living'. The theme of this writing is that immortality is God's gift to the righteous person and not a human birthright. The somewhat later *4 Maccabees* takes up the Jewish folk-tales found in 2 Maccabees and gives them Hellenistic orientation.[49] Chapters 8–17 retell the story of the mother and the seven brothers, replacing the hope for resurrection with that of immortality of the soul. Thus 14.5 says of them that 'as though running on the highway to immortality, [they] hurried on to death by torture'; and 16.13, of the mother, that 'as though she had a mind of adamant and were this time bringing her brood of sons of birth into immortal life, she encouraged and pled with them to die for pity's sake'. The author here presents 'immortal life' as the fruit of obedience to Jewish traditions which the entire family exemplify.

The Period of Christian Origins

Round about the time that Jesus was born, the Egyptian author of *Joseph and Asenath* described how Asenath was invested with immortality by an angel:

For behold, your name was written in the book of the living in heaven; in the beginning of the book, as the very first of all, your name was written by my finger, and it will not be erased forever. Behold, from today, you will be renewed and formed anew and made alive again, and you will eat blessed bread of life, and drink a blessed cup of immortality, and anoint yourself with blessed ointment of incorruptibility.' (15.5–6)[50]

This is the promise (strikingly similar to later Christian belief) of eternal life which begins now and never ceases; but there is no mention of resurrection as such.

Josephus offers a little information about the nature of Jewish eschatological belief in the first century CE (*War* 2.8.154; *Ant.* 18.14).[51] He states that the Essenes hold a belief analogous to the immortality of the soul, and that the Pharisees anticipate the resurrection of the body. He also states that the Sadducees do not believe in any kind of *post-mortem* reward or punishment; a view corroborated by Acts 23.7.

The two apocalypses from after the Roman destruction of Jerusalem, *2 Baruch* and *4 Ezra*, contain important material.[52] The author of *2 Baruch* picks up the dualism of the apocalyptic tradition and discusses the resurrection in this context (49–51). He opens with the striking hope for resurrection in unaltered form (50.2), continuing with the hope for transformation 'into the splendor of angels' (51.5), while the wicked experience torment. The author of *4 Ezra* (7.75–101) describes the intermediate place of the dead in advance of the final judgment (cf. the much earlier *1 Enoch* 22). The godly are said to be 'gathered into their chambers and guarded by angels in profound quiet' (7.95). They will receive glory when the judgment has occurred.

Conclusion

This material shows some of the ways in which ideas about resurrection and immortality flourished in post-biblical Judaism, from what I have shown are slender biblical roots. No survey of this material can afford to ignore Nickelsburg's work.[53] Nickelsburg argues that, in intertestamental Jewish theology, ideas about resurrection, immortality and eternal life were carried in three distinct forms: the story of the Righteous Man and the Isaianic Exaltation Tradition; the Judgment Scene; and the Two-Way Theology. In the first of these, the protagonist is a wise man in the royal court. He is falsely accused of law-breaking and sentenced to death. He is rescued at the point of death, and his enemies suitably punished. The second form is self-explanatory. In the third, good and bad and the reward that they bring are juxtaposed.

Nickelsburg argues that all three forms share the common motif of judgment, and that there is a definite movement towards *the resurrection of the body* as the standard mode of judgment in Jewish literature. Even though the tradition shows developmental tendencies, notably the flattening or even the complete removal of certain elements, it retains a certain conservatism. This is most obvious in the return to or retention of the idea of this-worldly reward and punishment, with which the notion of *post-mortem* judgment conflicts to some degree. This evidence confirms that pre-Christian Judaism (no doubt under Hellenistic influence) was capable of thinking in terms of resurrection *and* immortality simultaneously. Nickelsburg thereby disagrees with Oscar Cullmann, who drove a wedge between these two strands of thought in Judaism.[54]

It need hardly be said that ideas about messianism and resurrection formed the seed-bed of nascent Christianity. Jesus evidently believed himself to be the Messiah. The religion which emerged after his death presented his resurrection as the decisive eschatological event, through which Jesus was revealed as divine and God's kingdom as an eschatological reality. None of this would have been possible without the developments in post-biblical Judaism we have considered here. This is not to say that Christianity represented a simple continuation of what had been believed previously; it was rather a religious innovation which drew on these very fertile strands represented especially by the Jewish apocalyptic heritage.

PART II

JESUS AND HIS MISSION

AN APPROACH TO JESUS

The study of Christian origins begins with Jesus himself. The question of
how we approach Jesus is by no means a straightforward one: Jesus has
been viewed through a variety of lenses in the history of theological
research. The quest for the historical Jesus continues apace at the start
of the third millennium, much as it did throughout the twentieth century, and there are no signs that it will abate in the foreseeable future. It
is important to make the point that no work on Jesus can be done in
a vacuum. We begin this Part of the book with a study of what previous researchers have thought about Jesus. This is an essential means of
approaching the subject-matter, which depends on the interpretation of
ancient texts and is thus quite a contested phenomenon.

The Nature of the Sources

In part, this approach is made necessary by the *nature* of the ancient
sources. Our primary material about Jesus is confined almost entirely to
the Gospels.[1] The Gospels were written at least forty years after his
death. They offer a truncated sequence of information about Jesus,
including on occasion conflicting reports; they have substantial lacunae
to the eye of the modern historian.[2] This raises the question of what
value the Gospels have as historical sources. A second reason for this
approach was stated by Albert Schweitzer at the beginning of the last
century.[3] This is that Jesus inhabited a world in many ways so very
different from our own that those who quest after Jesus often (if not
generally) discover the Jesus they would *like* to find in the ancient
sources.[4] There is no clearly defined and objective 'Jesus of history'. The
sources themselves prevent such a reconstruction. The quest for the
historical Jesus reveals as much about the presuppositions and interests
of the questors as it does about the figure of Jesus himself. That is why
the quest continues, and must continue, in every generation, our own
included. Continuing research sheds new light in different areas, and
prompts the researchers to think again on crucial points.[5]

The Gospels as Sources

So we begin by considering the nature of the sources about Jesus. A
Gospel is a written record of the life of Jesus. It tells the story of his
adult ministry (or at least of what were considered to be the significant
parts of it) and concludes with his death and resurrection (uniquely in
Luke with the ascension of Jesus to heaven). Matthew and Luke describe

the birth of Jesus. All the Gospels omit the substantial details of his childhood (apart from one sparse Lucan anecdote). This is, to say the least, restricted information which has been written from the perspective of four quite different interpreters.

The four Gospels in the New Testament ('the canonical Gospels') need to be distinguished, in form and in content, from the other so-called 'Gospels' which lie beyond the New Testament canon.[6] These non-canonical Gospels were written later than the canonical Gospels. They lack the narrative structure which gives the canonical Gospels their character. In any analysis of genre, the observation that the New Testament Gospels have a narrative structure – that they 'tell a story' – is an important one.

Mark was the first Gospel to be written. People now think that Mark was written in the decade 70–80 CE and not earlier than this.[7] Matthew was written 80–90 CE, Luke 90–100 CE and John round about 100 CE.[8] This rough calculation shows that a considerable period elapsed between the death of Jesus and the writing of the first Christian Gospel. This observation raises acutely the questions of what sources were used by Mark as the first Gospel writer, and whether those sources can be trusted given the long period over which they were transmitted.

It is certain that Mark used sources. His is not a haphazard arrangement of material but a description of the life of Jesus that owed much to the reflection about Jesus which had flowed in Christian circles for two generations before Mark wrote. Some (but not all) scholars think that Mark had access to an oral source called Q, which was essentially a collection of sayings of Jesus.[9] Whatever the truth of this hypothesis – and a prominent group of British scholars vociferously challenges Q's existence – we should neither ignore the use that Mark made of existing material nor obscure his creativity as a Gospel writer.

The Gospels and the Lives

The Gospel genre was an innovation in first-century Christianity; but it is broadly related to other ancient literary types, including the so-called Hellenistic 'Lives' of famous people. Richard Burridge has examined five such 'Lives' which were written before Mark.[10] Burridge shows that all exhibit a similar range of features within a flexible pattern, and he mentions the following points of comparison. Their flexibility operates within perceptible boundaries. The 'Lives' are generally called by their subject's name (cf. Mk 1.1), and their subject dominates the narrative. The way the story is told varies from example to example: some texts adopt a strict chronological sequence, while others mix this with topical analysis. Their scale is limited to the subject's life, deeds and character. The anecdote ('a brief biographical narrative that relates a striking or unusual feature of the hero's character') plays a significant role in all of them. Many such works conclude with the story of the hero's death. Its cause is sometimes described in detail. Burridge discerns a variety of reasons for the writing of these Lives, including the need to preserve the hero's memory and to pass on his teaching. He shows that they were read at public occasions such as festivals. They were thus not originally intended for private consumption, but for public edification.

These points of comparison are instructive; but we should not ignore some significant differences between the Gospels and the Lives. Graham Stanton observes that only a small number of the features of Mark can be found either in any one ancient biography, or in any single type of biography.[11] Moreover, many features of Mark would have puzzled the readers of ancient biography. These include the evangelist's concentration on the death of Jesus, his seemingly abrupt ending and his evident dislike of anecdotes. The later Gospels offer something more than the life of Jesus *tout court*, for they begin with the birth of John the Baptist (Luke) and with the creation itself (John). Luke adds a second volume, the Acts of the Apostles, which describes certain key events in the life of the primitive church, evidently as the sequel to the ministry of Jesus.

Probably the most important difference between the Gospels and the Lives is the status accorded the heroes in the two strands of literature. For the first readers of the Gospels, Jesus was not a dead hero but the heavenly Lord whose presence was experienced whenever they met for worship. There was thus a dialectical relationship between the story of the historical Jesus and the liturgical experience of being a Christian which was essentially lacking for readers of the Lives. It would be foolish to pretend that this dialectic did not shape the Gospels, or that it failed to determine the way they were read in early Christian communities.

Nor should the comparison between the Gospels and the Lives be allowed to yield the conclusion that the Gospels are biographies as we understand that term today. Biographies are two-a-penny at the moment. They fall into different forms ranging from serious historical scholarship to romantic or fictional reconstruction. Those who look to the Gospels to provide a full-blown life of Jesus will be sadly disappointed.[12] Much of the crucial information is missing: what Jesus' parents did, what were the formative influences on his life and so on. Moreover, some of the information that is included is unconvincing. It is incredible that Jesus should have predicted his fate in the terms suggested by Lk. 9.22 (although Lk. 9.44 seems a more convincing prediction). The discrepancies between the Gospels, notably in the trial narrative, pose a serious problem for historians which cannot be ignored.[13] All of this warns us that the Gospels must be read on their terms and not on ours. When this point is acknowledged, it is possible to make tentative snatches at the elusive Jesus of history; even to reconstruct an outline of his career. But

there is much that we cannot say from a reading of the Gospels; and
perhaps even some that we might not want to say (notably Jesus' attitude
towards his own family).[14] This problem of information is created by the
Gospels themselves.

In his review of my book on Jesus, Anthony Harvey rightly criticized
me for failing to include a detailed discussion of the relationship between
the four Gospels as the key to discerning the authentic Jesus of history.[15]
While I would not want study of Jesus to be bogged down unduly by
what has come to be known as 'The Synoptic Problem', I agree it is
essential to consider the relationship between the ancient sources as a
means of approaching their central character. For this reason, I have
included an Appendix at the end of this book on the relationship
between the Gospels to provide my readers with a guide to how this
issue has been understood in twentieth-century scholarship. This is not
ancillary to the subject matter of this Part of the book; but it constitutes
an attempt to let my narrative unfold here, and to provide a subsequent
explanation of my major principles of interpretation, to answer questions
that may have been formed in the course of reading. The question of
Gospel priority is an important one; but it is also helpful to consider the
Gospels as individual sources in their own right, and to ponder their
value when this is done.

What Kind of Jesus Are We Looking For?

The next question to ponder is the question of the kind of Jesus we
are looking for. This may seem a strange question; but it is necessary
because researchers have found quite a number of different Jesuses since
the nineteenth century. We can speak of at least four phases of research
over the last one hundred years.

In the Germany of the nineteenth century, there was a strongly
held connection between Christian profession and ethical action. In
the wake of Friedrich Schleiermacher (1768–1834), it came increasingly to be accepted that Christianity had to do with religious *experience*,
which Schleiermacher held that Jesus himself reflected to a unique
degree.[16] Thus a prominent scholar such as Adolf von Harnack (1851–
1930) interpreted 'the kingdom of God' as the rule of God in human
hearts.[17] The great exponent of the 'Social Gospel' in America, Walter
Rauschenbusch (1861–1918), understood the Kingdom as the exercise of the moral life in society.[18] Both scholars are typical of their
generation. They set the agenda with which 'life of Jesus' researchers in
the first half of the twentieth century profoundly and quite vociferously
disagreed.

Phase One

Johannes Weiss

The first critical figure in this disagreement was Johannes Weiss (1863–1914). In a short but succinct publication, Weiss challenged the existing understanding of Jesus' preaching:

> The Kingdom of God as Jesus thought of it is never something subjective, inward or spiritual, but is always the objective messianic kingdom, which usually is pictured as a territory into which one enters, or as a land in which one has a share, or as a treasure which comes down from heaven.[19]

Weiss thereby introduced an eschatological Jesus who was motivated by apocalyptic concerns. This Jesus proclaimed the dawn of God's kingdom as an external and imminent reality. Where Weiss's own father-in-law Albrecht Ritschl had said, 'Those who believe in Christ are the kingdom of God insofar as they . . . act reciprocally out of love',[20] Weiss retorted (but only after Ritschl's death), that 'He (Jesus) has nothing in common with this world; he stands with one foot already in the future world.'[21] Weiss thereby drew attention to the futurist and unfulfilled aspect of Jesus' eschatology which he regarded as a crucial feature of the Galilean's preaching.

Weiss provided a double answer to the question of when Jesus thought that the end of the world would come. At first, he argued, Jesus expected God's kingdom to come immediately. Later, however, Jesus changed his mind on this matter.[22] This was because, although Jesus had preached a call to repentance, people had not responded as he hoped that they would. Jesus therefore began to think that the kingdom would not come before his own death; and even that his death would play a crucial role in its coming. The idea seized Weiss's Jesus that his own death would be the ransom for the Jews who were otherwise destined to destruction (cf. Mk 10.45).[23] This represented a definite theology of atonement. It stood in an existing tradition of martyrdom.

At the same time, Weiss recognized that no human action as such – not even action on the part of Jesus himself – was sufficient to bring in the kingdom unaided. Weiss's Jesus understood this as a divine task which God alone could accomplish. That attitude determined Jesus' ethic in respect of the coming kingdom. This was an ascetic, even a penitential ethic in which people must live out the statement that the kingdom was coming and where only those who gave up worldly ties and treasures were fit to receive the kingdom when it came.[24] For this reason, Weiss declined to identify the kingdom with Jesus' own circle of disciples; although he did acknowledge that Jesus and the twelve would rule over the restored Israel.

Albert Schweitzer

Johaness Weiss quite literally changed the face of Jesus studies.[25] He diverted study of Jesus away from ethics and towards eschatology, with a strong orientation towards apocalypticism. This was the direction in which later interpreters travelled. Albert Schweitzer (1875–1965) was prominent among them.

Schweitzer is a fascinating subject of study in his own right.[26] Born in Alsace, he showed early promise as a student of theology but turned from theology to medicine. In 1913 he journeyed to the Gabon (then French Equatorial Africa) to work as a missionary doctor. In 1901 Schweitzer published his *Das Messianitäts- und Leidensgeheimnis* (ET, *The Mystery of the Kingdom of God*, 1914) in which he argued that the teaching of Jesus centred around his hope for the imminent end of the world. This book was followed in 1906 by *Von Reimarus zu Wrede* (ET, *The Quest of the Historical Jesus*, 1910) where Schweitzer developed his argument that Jesus expected the imminent end of the world and that, when this hope proved mistaken, Jesus concluded he must suffer in his own person to save his followers from eschatological tribulation. Posthumously published but also important is Schweitzer's *Reich Gottes und Christentum* (1967; ET, *The Kingdom of God and Primitive Christianity*, 1968), which in many ways represents the clearest exposition of Schweitzer's understanding of Jesus.

Schweitzer's portrait begins with John the Baptist. Schweitzer presents John as one who bore 'emphatic witness to the nearness of the kingdom and the coming of the mighty messianic forerunner'.[27] He thought that Jesus identified John with Elijah (Mt. 11.14). Schweitzer drew attention to Jesus' baptism as a significant moment in his perception of his own religious significance. This was the time when God disclosed to him his unique status as the Messiah.[28] Due to the conventions of Jewish apocalypticism, however, Schweitzer's Jesus regarded both his messiahship and his perception of future suffering as secrets to be kept until his affliction was over.

Jesus did, however, reveal the secret of his identity to his innermost circle of disciples. This is where the so-called 'Son of Man' title finds its meaning. Although to outsiders 'Jesus spoke of the Messiah in the third person and as a character of the future',[29] his disciples used 'Son of Man' as a kind of code-name for 'Messiah'. Schweitzer thought that this title designated Jesus' future dignity as a heavenly being. It thereby conveyed meaning among some but distanced understanding among the majority by the use of a striking phrase.

At the centre of Schweitzer's canvas stood the proposed connection between eschatology and ethics in the mind of Jesus. Schweitzer found this disclosed more than anywhere else in the parables. The parables were signs of the kingdom; they encouraged 'moral renewal' which Schweitzer saw as the key to the eschatological climax. This was not simply a flashback to the ethical Jesus of nineteenth-century Germany, but the construction of a Jesus whose ethics had a strong eschatological base. Repentance for Schweitzer meant not just moral recovery but 'moral renewal in prospect of the accomplishment of universal perfection in the future'.[30] Jesus' view of the kingdom and of himself were linked through his conviction that the kingdom's arrival and his own revelation as Messiah were entirely future events. Schweitzer thought that Jesus and his disciples must undergo a period of suffering while the kingdom gestated. This was their view of what post-biblical Judaism knew as the 'messianic woes'.

Convinced by his identification of John with Elijah, Schweitzer's Jesus thought the kingdom almost immediately to hand. The sending of the Twelve was initially his last effort for bringing in the kingdom.[31] He even doubted whether they would return before it came. When the kingdom failed to come as he had anticipated, however, Jesus changed his mind on an important issue. Jesus thereafter held that God would bring in the kingdom *without* the general affliction he had previously posited.[32] From then on, Schweitzer's Jesus began to believe he would atone for the many in his own person. Schweitzer thought that Jesus came to this belief through meditation on Isaiah 53 and other passages and that herein lay the origin of his last journey to Jerusalem. Schweitzer described this journey with characteristic pith as a 'funeral march to victory' in which Jesus expected to die and yet simultaneously to be revealed as Messiah.[33]

Schweitzer offered an important theory about what Judas did when 'betraying' Jesus. Judas, Schweitzer believed, broke rank over the issue of the messianic secret and told the Jewish authorities that Jesus and the disciples thought about him as Messiah.[34] This is what led to the arrest and investigation of Jesus. Judas' betrayal assisted the high priest in his questioning of Jesus which resulted in the most public acknowledgment of Jesus' messiahship (Mk 14.62). Jesus died on the cross as Messiah, and having been identified as Messiah, with all the ironies that the trial threw up. The greatest of these ironies was that people only realized that Jesus was Messiah after his death.

Phase Two

C.H. Dodd

This apocalyptic view of Jesus dominated scholarship up to the time of the Second World War without serious challenge. The orientation of Jesus' eschatology was initially reconsidered by C.H. Dodd (1884–1973).[35] Dodd was a Congregationalist minister who became Norris-Hulse Professor of Divinity at the University of Cambridge.

Dodd reacted (though without always saying so) against the view of Jesus as eschatological prophet proposed by Weiss and Schweitzer. He argued that Jesus was indeed a prophet; but that Jesus thought his eschatological message had been fulfilled in his own preaching and person. Dodd observed, in deference to nineteenth-century German liberalism, that 'the kingdom of God means God reigning, reigning in the hearts of men.'[36]

Dodd came to this distinctive view through ethical considerations. The problem as he expounded it in *The Parables of the Kingdom* was that, if Jesus really did expect the kingdom in the near future, this would allow for a theory of merely 'interim ethics' which Dodd held problematic for the subsequent development of Christianity. The problem in this case would be that the ethical basis of the religion was suspended 'in the air' without the support of a visible foundation. Dodd devised his theory of 'realized eschatology' to deal with this problem. He posited that Jesus thought the kingdom of God, the Son of Man, the judgment and utopian bliss were *already present* in his own ministry. They needed no future realization. Dodd argued that for this reason Jesus was not mistaken about the coming of the kingdom and that the kingdom had been effectively present since his first preaching of it in Galilee.

Phase Three

Werner Georg Kümmel
Werner Georg Kümmel, who was Professor of New Testament in the University of Marburg, fused together these two conflicting approaches to the eschatology of Jesus.[37] Kümmel argued that Jesus made both present *and* future statements about the kingdom of God. He thought that Jesus made his own person the basis of continuity between these two different periods, arguing that Jesus reckoned with only a short time between his death and the projected coming of the kingdom. This third phase continues today in the debate about eschatology and apocalypticism in the preaching of Jesus.

Ed Sanders
The third phase is well explained by E.P. (Ed) Sanders. Two books by Sanders are relevant: *Jesus and Judaism* (1985) and *The Historical Figure of Jesus* (1993).

Sanders begins with the question of method, asking how we know what we claim to know about Jesus. In this context, Sanders criticizes the received portrait of Jesus as first and foremost a *teacher of theology* and the resulting interest in the content of his message which had dominated the earlier agenda.[38] Sanders begins with the *facts* about Jesus, acknowledging eight indisputable (or nearly indisputable) things about him.[39] These are (1) that Jesus was baptized by John the Baptist; (2) that Jesus was a Galilean who preached and healed; (3) that Jesus called disciples and spoke of there being twelve such people; (4) that Jesus confined his activity to Israel; (5) that Jesus engaged in a controversy about the temple; (6) that Jesus was crucified outside Jerusalem by the Roman authorities; (7) that, after his death, the followers of Jesus continued as an identifiable movement; and (8) that at least some Jews persecuted parts of the newly emerged Christian movement.

Of these eight facts, Sanders names (5) – Jesus' controversy about the temple – as the starting-point for his own investigation. It leads him to a close examination of 'the cleansing of the temple' (Mk 11.15-18 and parallels), from which he concludes that 'Jesus predicted (or threatened) the destruction of the temple and carried out an action symbolic of its destruction by demonstrating against the performance of the sacrifices . . . He intended . . . to indicate that the end was at hand and that the temple would be destroyed, so that the new and perfect temple might arise.'[40] This assessment makes the 'cleansing of the temple' a prophet's eschatological sign and a positive, not a negative prediction. Sanders cites a variety of Jewish literature (from within and beyond the Hebrew Bible) to set Jesus' words within the context of what he calls 'Jewish restoration eschatology'.[41] In Isa. 44.28, *1 En.* 90.28–9 and 11QTemple 29.8–10, for instance, God promises to provide a new temple. Sanders argues from this evidence that Jesus stood in the hopeful tradition of Jewish eschatology, believing that God would restore the fortunes of Israel and renew the temple in the eschatological age.

Sanders finds further evidence for this 'restoration eschatology' in the Jesus tradition.[42] He notes that the hope for the restoration of the twelve tribes is frequently found in Jewish literature. Sanders links this to the (almost) indisputable fact that Jesus was attended by twelve disciples. He thinks that Jesus introduced this number for symbolic reasons and that it was related to his belief that he was engaged in a task which involved the eschatological restoration of Israel.[43] This is the context in which Sanders discusses the phrase 'the kingdom of God'. Sanders notes (in the tradition of Kümmel) that Jesus used this phrase in both a present and a future sense, interpreting this information to imply that Jesus understood the kingdom as what he calls 'immediately future'.[44] When he preached, Jesus demonstrated God's kingly power. When the kingdom came, Sanders' Jesus believed it would have some unlikely features. Jesus' preaching singled out individuals, 'sinners' and 'Gentiles' prominent among them. These would find their own special place in the restored Israel.

Sanders doubts whether Jesus had a *fully-developed* plan for Israel's restoration. He thinks that Jesus believed John the Baptist had sufficiently articulated the message of repentance to obviate the need for him to do so himself.[45] So far as the *nature* of the kingdom was concerned, Sanders thinks that Jesus and his followers expected a renewal reminiscent in some respects of the *War Scroll* and the *Temple Scroll* from Qumran. Such renewal included the transformation of familiar social elements and institutions, but it could not be achieved without the direct intervention of God.

Phase Four

John Dominic Crossan

This portrait of the eschatological Jesus, revised by Sanders *pace* Schweitzer and set against Dodd, has in turn been challenged in North American scholarship in the work of John Dominic Crossan and Marcus J. Borg.[46] Crossan portrays Jesus as a Jewish representative of the widespread Cynic movement.[47]

Cynicism derived from one Diogenes of Sinope (Greece) who lived in the fourth century BCE. Diogenes pursued a manner of life that was closely akin to the primitive. His lifestyle demanded the minimum of possessions, a coarse view of social graces and the renunciation of conventional values. He rejected all forms of culture and education as irrelevant to the happy life. Cynicism was not a formal philosophical school such as Pythagoreanism or Epicureanism, but a way of life that followed these anarchic principles. The Cynics wrote widely and influenced others. Not without reason did Diogenes acquire the nickname 'the dog' on account of his shameless behaviour.

Crossan presents Jesus as what he calls a 'peasant Jewish cynic'. He uses Bryan Wilson's well-known typology of sects to investigate what people could do to withdraw from Graeco-Roman civilization in the period under discussion.[48] Crossan's Jesus 'sought to rebuild society upwards from its grass roots but on principles of religious and economic egalitarianism'.[49] Crossan thinks that Jesus attempted a social revolution in which dominant distinctions were set aside. This Jesus symbolically destroyed the 'brokerage function' of the temple and the priesthood, refusing any special role for himself in the kingdom he announced.

Crossan's Jesus was an essentially non-apocalyptic Jesus. Crossan argues that 'the kingdom of God' was understood in a sapiental (i.e. wisdom) sense in Jewish literature of the period. He cites Philo, the Wisdom of Solomon and the *Sentences of Sextus* to support this interpretation.[50] This evidence allows him to construct a fourfold typology of 'the kingdom of God' in contemporary Jewish usage. He does this by crossing what he calls the thematic distinction of the apocalyptic and the sapiental with the class distinction of retainers and peasants.[51] Applied to Jesus, this fourfold matrix yields the suggestion that Jesus should be located within the quadrant formed by the sapiental and the peasant. Jesus for Crossan was a peasant Jewish Cynic who announced that neither broker nor mediator should exist between humanity and divinity. This explains Crossan's much-cited references to 'the brokerless kingdom of God'.[52]

Although I cannot evaluate Crossan's argument in full detail, I note that the Cynic hypothesis has not met with full acceptance from scholars.

Writing in criticism of F. Gerald Downing, who argues a case similar to Crossan's, W.H.C. Frend observes there is no evidence for the presence of Cynic philosophers in the villages of southern Galilee at the time of Jesus' ministry, even though the Cynics had a foothold at Gadara in the Decapolis; nor do the earliest pagan authorities, Tacitus, Suetonius and Pliny, associate the two groups.[53] Allegedly cynical aspects of Jesus' preaching find more convincing analogies in contemporary Judaism, as for instance in the asceticism of Qumran and the developing martyro-logical tradition represented by *4 Maccabees*. Frend argues that it was only when Christianity moved to Asia Minor that the Cynic influence became stronger. By the third century, the Christians had effectively taken on the mantle of the Cynics. Henry Chadwick adds that Downing underweighs texts which presuppose dissimilarity between the two different movements.[54] We do not, for instance, hear of missionaries copulating in the streets! Many people in late antiquity resembled the Cynics without being Cynics. One cannot formally conclude that Jesus was a Cynic on the basis of allegedly cumulative parallels.

Further criticism comes from Tom Wright.[55] Wright denies that the Wisdom of Solomon (on which Crossan leans heavily) attests a non-apocalyptic understanding of the kingdom of God. Although Wis. 6.3-4 superficially discloses this view, it is flanked by other passages which are unhesitatingly apocalyptic in their outlook. It is certain, on reading the Wisdom of Solomon as a whole, that notions of judgment and divine intervention feature strongly in that text (e.g. 'he will come upon you terribly and swiftly', Wis. 6.5). This means that Crossan's list of parallels for his proposed portrait of Jesus as a 'peasant Jewish Cynic' are confined to Philo, the *Sentences of Sextus* and popular philosophical texts. These sources are far too strikingly and implausibly distant from the ambience of the Galilean peasantry to connect them with Jesus. One therefore wonders how convincingly (if at all) Crossan's portrait of the Cynic and non-eschatological Jesus is founded in the ancient sources.

Other Contributors

Geza Vermes

Two further scholars have made important contributions. Geza Vermes is first and foremost a scholar of the Dead Sea scrolls. He has written several books about Jesus in which an influential thesis is articulated.[56] This is that Jesus is best considered a representative of what Vermes calls 'charismatic Judaism' insofar as Jesus is reported to have healed the sick, exorcized the possessed and dispensed forgiveness. Vermes draws atten-tion to other figures in contemporary Judaism who acted in the same or in similar ways.[57] The two most important are Honi the Circle-Drawer (called Onias the Righteous by Josephus) and Hanina ben Dosa.[58] Honi is reported by *m. Taan.* 3.8 to have forced God's hand into providing rain in the first century BCE (cf. Josephus, *Ant.* 14.22–4). Hanina was a Galilean of the first century CE who was accredited with healing powers.[59] It was apocryphally reported that not even reptiles could interrupt his time of prayer. A snake which tried to do this and bit him itself died (*j. Ber.* 9a; *t. Ber.* 2.20; *b. Ber.* 33a). Hanina is also credited with having successfully prayed for the recovery of the son of R. Johanan ben Zakkai (*b. Ber.* 33b).

Vermes argues that

a distinctive trend of charismatic Judaism existed during the last couple of centuries of the Second Temple . . . These holy men were treated as the willing or unsuspecting heirs to an ancient prophetic tradition. Their supernatural powers were attributed to their immediate relation to God. They were venerated as a link between heaven and earth independent of any institutional mediation.[60]

Vermes locates Jesus within this tradition he establishes. His book *The Religion of Jesus the Jew* includes a section outlining the 'charismatic authority' of Jesus in which he cites popular belief in the heavenly origin of Jesus' preaching, together with his mastery over bodily and mental affliction, as the reason why Jesus was revered in his own time.[61]

This approach cannot be accepted without noting some differences between Jesus and the two figures Vermes cites, however. Theissen and Merz observe that they were primarily active through prayer.[62] They do not work eschatological miracles as Jesus is reported to have done. Yet, despite this, the material certainly does bear comparison with the Gospels. It does much to set Jesus in his wider context of a broadly based Judaism where interest in the supernatural was a prominent feature.

Richard Horsley

The notion of Jesus as a 'charismatic' or prophet is developed in the work of Richard Horsley.[63] Horsley presents the Jesus movement as initially based on the villages and towns of Jewish Palestine. He thinks it included Gentiles because of the ordinary (that is, non-establishment) nature of the movement. Although people of modest means were not excluded, the bulk of its members came from the ranks of the poor. These would have been marginalized economically, and either in debt or else perpetually liable to fall into debt. On Horsley's view, the communities of the Jesus movement thought about themselves as a new social order.[64] The concept of the 'kingdom of God' referred both to God's ruling and redeeming activity, and also to the renewal of society that stemmed from divine activity.

In terms of their status as local communities, the most significant feature of the Jesus movement was the emergence within it of a new understanding of 'family'.[65] Given that the traditional patriarchal unit had been heavily undermined by economic pressures in first-century Palestine, the Synoptic understanding of 'family' sharply criticizes patriarchal norms. Doing the will of God counted for more than family ties (Mk 3.35). The new communities of the Jesus movement were composed entirely of equals (Mt. 23.8). This implies an alternative system of justice (see Lk. 12.58-9/Mt. 5.25-6). Horsley's conclusion is that 'the Jesus movement was attempting to restore the typical peasant practices of reciprocal generosity between households. Specifically called for were cancellations of debts and mutual sharing, forms of cooperation that had likely been disintegrating under the prevailing conditions of heavy taxation, indebtedness, and even hunger, which left people unable or unwilling to respond to each others' needs and turned "neighbours" into "enemies." '[66]

This response to endemic problems inevitably brought the Jesus movement into conflict with the rulers.[67] Horsley thinks that the movement rejected the rulers, who responded with a certain degree of repression. The kingdom that Jesus envisaged had no need of a mediating hierocracy or a temple system. Such a view explains the material in the Gospels which presents Jesus as hostile both to the religious authorities (Mk 12.1-9) and to the temple (Mk 11.15-17; 13.2; 14.58; 15.29-30). Horsley takes Mt. 17.24-7 to imply that the followers of Jesus exempted themselves from paying the temple tax. Hostility towards the followers of Jesus continued after the death of the founder; Horsley thinks that the post-Easter movement came into sharper conflict with the Pharisees than Jesus himself had done.

Who Is the Real Jesus?

This review of scholarship inevitably poses the question of which of these Jesuses is the real Jesus. The answer is that all of the scholars mentioned have brought valuable insights to the problem. The disagreements between them draw attention to the need to examine the primary sources – including the question of their dates – and to adopt an optimistic pessimism about the possibility of reaching final certainty over disputed matters. The extent to which this can be done depends on the interpretation of complex and sometimes conflicting material; and that is never going to be an easy task.[68]

This notwithstanding, the basic question posed by Jesus researchers in the twentieth century was the extent to which Jesus was or was not an apocalyptic figure. This embodies the related questions of whether Jesus preached an 'apocalyptic eschatology'; and whether he anticipated any form of divine intervention from outside the historical process. It will be clear that I personally have more sympathy with the portrait of an eschatological Jesus who preached from an apocalyptic base than I do with the Cynic hypothesis of Crossan and its essentially non-apocalyptic foundation. I think that Jesus inherited and developed an apocalyptic world-view and that his own view of the Jewish nation and its traditions led him to suppose the present was the time when God would finally act to bring in his kingdom, effecting the decisive status of Israel that had been promised in the Hebrew Bible This explains the urgency of Jesus' preaching campaign and, I think, the importance of his journey to Jerusalem.

In saying this, I do not want to lose sight of what Crossan has emphasized about the distinctive nature of Jesus' preaching with its love of witty aphorisms and contrasts. He provides a necessary reminder of the *forms* in which Jesus' preaching was set. A witty and sophistic Jesus, however, can also have been an apocalyptic and eschatological Jesus. This is the portrait of Jesus I want to explore in the following chapters.

A BRIEF HISTORY OF JESUS

Having identified the difficulties of writing about the founder of Christianity, the next step is to consider what we actually know about Jesus.[1]

The Limitations of the Sources

Frustratingly, this is one of the areas where the relative paucity of the sources exercises its maximum inconvenience. We saw that the Gospels offer only selective information about Jesus in which much-needed and crucial evidence is missing. Although we have non-canonical sources which do give more information (such as the infancy narrative known as the *Protevangelium of James*),[2] the historical reliability of these sources is often (if not always) suspect. The Jesus researcher is bound to acknowledge we will never possess the full picture that is offered by the biography of a modern figure. It is worth observing, however, that this sketchiness about Jesus is not much different from the sketchiness that surrounds many other ancient figures, including such well known people as Julius Caesar. The paucity of information, mercifully, is relative and not absolute.

The Birth of Jesus

With this *caveat* we may begin at the beginning. The story of Jesus' birth is well known from Christian hagiography. According to the Gospels, Jesus was born in Bethlehem, a small and somewhat insignificant village not far from Jerusalem.[3] The family of Jesus consisted of a birth mother and an adoptive father if the tradition of the virginal conception is accepted.[4] After the birth of Jesus his family settled in Nazareth, a small and even less significant village in Galilee. The story of Jesus' birth, it must be said, has been questioned on more than one front. It will be wise to examine the disputed areas to see what can be said about this matter.

The first question to consider is whether Jesus was born in Bethlehem.[5] The Gospels insist that he was (Mt. 2.1; Lk. 2.4-7). Doubt has arisen on this point due to the fact that Bethlehem was King David's home village and the observation that the Gospels have a demonstrated interest in presenting Jesus as the Jewish Messiah, a descendant of David. Given the words of Mic. 5.2 ('But you, O Bethlehem . . . from you shall come forth for me one who is to rule in Israel'), where else, we might ask, should the Messiah be born but in Bethlehem? A second source of doubt is introduced by Luke. Luke 2 describes a universal census when Quirinius was governor of Syria. This information cannot be corroborated by any external report of a census at this time. A related problem is that Quirinius did not become governor of Syria until 6 CE; but that Luke also states the angelic announcement of John the Baptist's birth occurred in the reign of Herod the Great (Lk. 1.5), who died in 4 BCE.[6] There is no possible way of reconciling these chronologies. Added to this is the improbability that a Roman census would have recalled people to their ancestral homes for enrolment. The normal practice was to enrol people where they lived.[7]

There are two possible reconciliations of this dilemma. Either Jesus really was born in Bethlehem and Luke has got his chronology wrong (or at least conflated more than one event); or we have grounds for disputing the tradition of the birth in Bethlehem in terms of historical probability. Readers of this book must make up their own minds on this matter. The tradition of the birth at Bethlehem is supported by some later Christian evidence, but its date again poses questions of reliability.[8] If we acknowledge that the story of the shepherds and the wise men is potentially fictitious, that would raise the question of how much else of the birth story is historically verifiable.[9] A related question is of course how much this uncertainty actually *matters* when considering the total impact of Jesus' life and preaching. There are real grounds for supposing that uncertainty about his birth, while no doubt frustrating, does not of itself greatly affect the attempt to evaluate the significance of his message, which is the really important aspect of interpreting Jesus.

The date of Jesus' birth is also problematic. Jesus *ought* to have been born at the intersection of the ages denoted by the abbreviations 'BC' and 'AD' on the common understanding of these terms. We must note, however, an historical problem of calculation. In the sixth century CE a monk called Dionysius Exiguus miscalculated the date of the incarnation when he made the 248th year from the accession of Diocletian (284 CE) the year 532 CE.[10] This explains the otherwise odd conclusion that Jesus was born in 4 BCE on the conventional dating of the death of Herod the Great.

Things are thus not what they seem when evaluating the birth of Jesus. Neither the original sources nor subsequent Christian interpretation are necessarily accurate accounts of the matter. I ask my reader to consider what is actually lost to the story of Jesus when the ambiguities are accepted. Too great a concentration on the events of his birth tends to detract from the striking impact of his preaching (let alone the interpretation of his death). An open mind, a critical view of the sources and the willingness to ask uncomfortable questions are key tools when evaluating the traditions about Jesus.

The Baptism of Jesus

The next thing we know about Jesus (apart from one sparse Lucan anecdote)[11] is that he was baptized by John the Baptist in the River

Jordan. This event was allegedly followed by an apocalyptic experience in which Jesus heard a heavenly voice identify him as the Messiah and saw the Holy Spirit settle on him in the form of a dove. In order to evaluate this story, we shall look briefly at the figure of John the Baptist.[12]

John the Baptist

The Gospels present John the Baptist as the leader of a Jewish sectarian movement with an eschatological basis. His distinctive feature was his rite of baptism which the Gospels (Mk 1.4 and parallels) say was 'for the forgiveness of sins'. There is further information about John in Josephus (*Ant.* 18.116–19). Josephus calls John 'a good man', stating that he 'had exhorted the Jews to lead righteous lives, to practise justice towards their fellows and piety towards God, and so doing to join in baptism'. Josephus advocates a different understanding of John's baptism from that found in the Gospels. He states that '[the Jews] must not employ it to gain pardon for whatever sins they committed, but as a consecration of the body implying that the soul was already thoroughly cleansed by right behaviour'. It has occasionally been suggested that this report is a Christian interpolation in Josephus.[13] Such a view is very unconvincing. The text as translated here is found in all the extant manuscripts of the *Antiquities*; and it contains sufficient differences from the Gospels to raise the question of whether a Christian author would have written about the Baptist in that way. Moreover, Josephus' report is mentioned by Origen in the third century CE.[14] The two different strands let us draw some conclusions about John the Baptist.

Josephus is silent about the background and religious development of the Baptist.[15] Luke 1 mentions John's priestly ancestry, calling him a cousin of Jesus. The Baptist's priestly origins are mentioned also by the *Gospel of the Ebionites*; fragment 33.[16] While this ancestry is by no means implausible, it is clear that at our distance we have no possible means of checking the information. It has often been suggested that John had a link with the Essenes, the Jewish sectarian group who lived at Qumran and produced the Dead Sea scrolls.[17] This suggestion gains a superficial plausibility from observing the nature of the baptismal practices adopted by John and the Qumran community. Ritual washing was a familiar feature of life at Qumran, undertaken before the communal meal. 1QS 3.6–9 speaks also of an initiatory immersion that has certain parallels with John the Baptist's practice.

On the other hand, some key differences between John and Qumran have been noted by Robert Webb.[18] The Qumran text relates immersion to atonement; John related it to forgiveness. At Qumran, a person turned from sin to Torah-obedience, which was demonstrated by appropriate behaviour and a commitment to enter the community. Such repentance atoned for past sin and made the immersion effective. With John, however, a person turned from sin in a repentance that was symbolized by baptism to which God responded by forgiving the sin. Another reason why John has been compared with the Essenes is because of his ascetic lifestyle. Yet these parallels are superficial rather than developed and really convincing. There is no concrete evidence to link John with Qumran. Any such link remains conjectural. The tendency of recent scholarship is to deny any connecting link at all.[19]

This is not to deny that John the Baptist was the leader of a Jewish sectarian movement with distinctive baptismal practices.[20] We should adopt firm critical standards when approaching both strands of evidence concerning John. It is possible that Josephus' insistence on the ethical orientation of John's baptism represents a suspicion of eschatological hopes in the wake of the abortive First Jewish Revolt against Rome. Equally, the Gospels may have suppressed the ethical side of John's message in the interests of demonstrating the eschatological continuity between John the Baptist and Jesus. Whatever the resolution of these problems, it is certain that John the Baptist was an historical figure and that he made a real impact on Judaea at the time when Jesus was growing towards his public ministry.

The Baptism of Jesus

We need not doubt that Jesus was baptized by John.[21] The Synoptic Gospels include this fact when the reserve shown by Matthew (and the silence of John's Gospel) show that it was found increasingly embarrassing as early Christian narrative developed.[22] The crucial question to consider is why Jesus was baptized by John. This includes the question of whether that implied an understanding of his own sinfulness on the part of Jesus himself.

Most readers of this book will approach this question through the lens of Christian theology where Jesus is dogmatically proclaimed as the sinless Christ who reconciled humankind to God. It goes against the grain to consider the possibility that Jesus contemplated his own sinfulness.[23] The answer to this conundrum lies in differentiating modern and inherently Western ideas about sinfulness from the corporate and indeed corporeal understanding that pertained in first-century Judaism.[24] We saw when discussing the Jewish sacrificial system that virtually any defilement could be purified by some form of offering. The sins that were dealt with in this way were particular to the person in question, but also all well-established actions of the human race, identified as such in the Torah. We need not suppose that Jesus came for baptism by John because he regarded himself as an exceptionally sinful person; still less that he did so in the modern Western sense. He rather came through *solidarity* with the Jewish people as the nation stood before God, identifying himself with John's new start and pledging himself to covenant obedience towards God.

It was only later, and possibly gradually, that he realized he was called to lead a different kind of religious movement, one which had a heightened eschatology and definite messianic convictions. Jesus thereafter separated himself from John the Baptist; but this does not detract from the significance of his baptism by John through which his public ministry began. His baptism reflects solidarity rather than sinfulness as such. One can acknowledge a certain tension between the modern doctrinal conviction that Jesus is the sinless Christ and the Gospels' statement that he underwent a rite which was for 'the forgiveness of sins'.

The Apocalyptic Vision

Mark, followed by Matthew and Luke, makes his baptism the moment when Jesus became aware of his special destiny on the basis of the heavenly revelation which accompanied it. Mark states that, following his baptism, Jesus came up from the Jordan and saw the heavens opened. He witnessed the descent of the Holy Spirit upon him and heard a heavenly voice which acclaimed him as God's own Son (Mk 1.9-11). One wonders what kind of religious experience lies behind this report; and, again, whether Mark's connection of the revelatory experience is an accurate historical record.

There seems to be no necessary connection between the baptism and the revelation beyond Mark's adverb 'immediately' (1.10), which links the two events. The revelation itself falls into two parts. The first part is Jesus' vision of a dove, which the words 'he saw the heavens opened' formally connect with the Jewish apocalyptic tradition.[25] The second is the heavenly voice which identifies Jesus as Messiah in the form of a scripture medley.[26] In Mark's account, which is followed by Matthew and less obviously by Luke, this vision is a private one in which Jesus alone is told his true significance and hears the heavenly voice. This observation raises problems of verification which suggest we must assume that the event, if original, was reported by Jesus to his disciples at some later point.

The content of the vision has long been the subject of interest among commentators. Joel Marcus believes that here we have only one part of an originally longer vision, the rest of which is given by Lk. 10.18.[27] In that passage Jesus reports another vision in which he saw Satan falling like lightning from heaven. If Marcus' theory is accepted, it would imply Jesus' belief that Satan's kingdom was ending with the identification of himself as the Messiah, the person possessed by the Spirit. In the case of the heavenly words, it has been observed that they represent a fusion of the biblical texts Ps. 2.7 and Isa. 42.1. This obviously biblical background problematizes the authenticity of the heavenly address. There is a possibility – perhaps even a suspicion – that the words in their present form were the work of the early church and read back into the story of Jesus to establish his messianic credentials from the very beginning.[28] But this is not to say that the incident itself was invented, or that it lacked a meaning for the historical Jesus. We must simply wrestle with the evidence as we have it; and acknowledge that the Gospels present the baptism as a watershed in the life of Jesus, after which he became conscious of a unique destiny.

One can see that it was easier for the Gospel writers to describe a Jesus who was conscious of his vocation from the very beginning than a Jesus who came to his self-understanding only gradually. Many have fought shy of the suggestion, found prominently in Weiss and in Schweitzer, that Jesus was so uncertain about things as to change his mind in the period before his journey to Jerusalem. There is an innate tendency for the Jesus of the Gospels to resemble the Jesus of early Christian belief, whose messianic status and heavenly connections were unimpeachable and his self-understanding complete.[29] A Jesus who came to his vocation only gradually, however, is not incompatible with the Son of God whom the Christian creeds proclaim. We shall remain open-minded about the content of Jesus' post-baptismal experience, and try and relate it to his ministry which followed.

The Public Ministry

The baptism of Jesus leads to his public ministry in the Gospel sequence. We do not know how long this ministry lasted. The traditional scheme of three years is derived (only) from John's Gospel which mentions three Passover journeys of Jesus to Jerusalem. Given the symbolism that is prominent in John, once again we cannot be sure that this is an accurate record.

The ministry of Jesus was initially an itinerant one in the region of Galilee. It centred in the village of Capernaum (not Nazareth).[30] Jesus was not a rabbi in the technical sense, still less a settled figure confined to one particular place. Jesus travelled round the villages of Galilee, as Mark's Gospel puts it 'proclaiming the good news of God' and preaching that God's kingdom was at hand (Mk 1.15). He was remembered as the worker of miracles, and his ministry brought him to public attention in Galilee. We note, however, that when Jesus made his last appearance in Jerusalem he seems to have been an unknown figure in the Jewish capital. The temple authorities had to bribe Judas to discover the secret of the Jesus movement. This suggests that Jesus exercised a mainly local impact in the Galilean region before his decisive journey southwards.

The Miracles of Jesus

We shall consider the content of Jesus' preaching in the next chapter. We now briefly examine his miracles.[31] Jesus was not the only wonder-worker in the Jewish world, still less the ancient world. We have mentioned Honi the Circle-Drawer and Hanina ben Dosa already. In Graeco-Roman culture, Apollonius of Tyana was famed as a miracle-worker.[32] The miracles of Jesus have wider parallels. How we view his miracles naturally depends on how we view miracles more generally. A miracle is an exceptional setting-aside of the rules of nature in which something that is ordinarily impossible allegedly occurs. We stand at too great a distance to answer the question of which of the miracles of Jesus actually 'happened'. Nor should we assume that modern criteria for evaluating miracles, which consist of careful examination under research conditions, pertained in the ancient world. The critical question is whether Jesus was fêted as a miracle-worker by his contemporaries; or whether this view was superimposed on the Gospels by the early church.

That Jesus performed miracles is a consistent feature of the Gospel tradition. It strains the evidence to suggest that this tradition was entirely invented by post-Easter Christianity. It is frankly impossible to delete all the miracles of the Gospels, whether by rationalizing exegesis or simple dislike of them. Equally, it will not do to say that Jesus necessarily worked *all* the miracles attributed to him by using the unexamined argument that what the Bible says is always true. Among the recent treatments of the issue, the balanced conclusion of John P. Meier that some but not all of the miracles happened seems reasonable.[33] We cannot and must not delete the miracle tradition in its entirety; but this does not mean that we have to accept every miracle story as absolute and historical truth in its present form. The very fact that we cannot delete the miracle tradition by using critical reason is a powerful testament to this aspect of what was remembered about Jesus.

The miracles themselves fall into more than one category. Important research in this area was undertaken here by Gerd Theissen in his *Miracle Stories of the Early Christian Tradition*. Theissen builds on the work of Dibelius and Schille to draw up a list of miracle categories.[34] He finds six categories of miracle attributed to Jesus: exorcisms, healings, epiphanies, rescue miracles, gift miracles and rule miracles. Some of these require explanation. Epiphanies 'occur when the divinity of a person becomes apparent not merely in the effects of his actions or in attendant phenomena, but in the person himself'.[35] Theissen further divides this category into theophanies, christophanies, angelophanies and pneumatophanies.[36] Rescue miracles include both stories of rescue at sea and the freeing of prisoners.[37] The characteristic feature of a gift miracle is that it makes material goods available in surprising ways.[38] Rule miracles seek to reinforce sacred prescriptions.[39] These different miracles combine to make up the portrait of Jesus as the miracle-worker for which he was widely known in ancient Galilee.

Theissen concludes that only the exorcisms and healings formed authentic parts of the Jesus miracle tradition. The rest of the tradition, he thinks, was shaped at some distance from the historical Jesus and cannot necessarily be considered authentic. This brings us back to Meier's conclusion that some but not all the reported miracles of Jesus are historical. The interpreter's judgment must not be suspended in this aspect of Jesus studies. While there has undoubtedly been a process of development behind and within the Gospel tradition, the perception that Jesus was the worker of miracles is found in the oldest layer.[40] It cannot be set aside for that reason.

The Journey to Jerusalem

At some point Jesus decided to go to Jerusalem. The Gospels make this decision a watershed in his ministry. It is described with great clarity by passages such as Mk 10.33 and Lk. 9.51. Whether or not Jesus knew he would die at the conclusion of this visit is difficult to say; but we may presume that the so-called 'passion predictions' in the Gospels (Mk 8.31; 9.31; 10.33 and parallels) were not created out of nothing, even if they were potentially embellished in the course of retelling. Jesus led his band of disciples to Jerusalem at the time of the Passover (probably in 30 CE). It appears from what he did there that Jesus had a particular purpose for this visit.[41]

Neither the triumphal entry nor the cleansing of the temple were innocent events. Their meaning has been much discussed by scholars; but it seems likely that they were eschatological symbols which Jesus and the disciples connected with the imminent coming of God's kingdom.[42] Thus the triumphal entry possibly symbolized the return of the twelve tribes to Jerusalem, and the 'cleansing' the purification of the temple by God. It is impossible to be sure what ideas ran through Jesus' mind at this time, as with other matters; but I shall argue in the next chapter it is a reasonable deduction that Jesus' last days in Jerusalem were sustained by eschatological convictions. I think it likely that Jesus expected God's kingdom to appear with the fulfilment of his circle's eschatological activity in Jerusalem, so that their history was profoundly related to the wider status of the Jewish nation before God.

The Trial and Death of Jesus

The trial of Jesus poses notorious problems; I shall consider them in Chapter 15. I note here only that the Gospels make the charge of blasphemy the reason that Jesus was brought before Pilate, but that the charge of potential sedition seems the more convincing reason for his execution. It is certain that Jesus was put to death by the Romans, not the Jews. Jn 18.31 makes the Jews remind Pilate that they no longer had the power to carry out capital sentences. This statement is accepted as historical by the vast majority of scholars.

The date of Jesus' execution has been felt problematic. The problem has been debated at length.[43] The date which has commended itself to the greatest number of scholars is the Passover of 30 CE. If this date is accepted, Jesus would have been in his mid-thirties when he died. His manner of execution was the worst imaginable in the ancient world, being reserved for slaves and certain other categories of criminals.[44] It was death by asphyxiation, achieved over an excruciatingly long period of time. Uniquely in the case of this crucifixion victim, the history of subsequent Christianity insists that this painful death was simply the closing of one chapter, not the end of the story of Jesus himself. This post-mortem story of Jesus, which provides the link with the birth of Christianity, will be examined in Chapter 16.

THE MESSAGE OF JESUS

Had it not been for his teaching and of course his resurrection, Jesus would have been forgotten (or merely half-remembered) like most other Jewish figures of his time and outlook. As it is, Jesus of Nazareth remains one of the most revered figures from the whole of human history. Given the obvious lacunae in his history, we must examine his teaching to explain this astonishing reputation.

The Nature of his Preaching

The first thing to do is to ask what kind of teacher Jesus was. In many ways, it is easier to do this by eliminating possibilities than to propose an initial definition of Jesus as famous public speaker.

In the first place, Jesus was not (so far as we know) a literary figure. He left behind him no writings to parallel the works of the Jewish and Hellenistic philosophers, nor anything to match the scriptural exegeses of the rabbis or even the learning of the apocalypses. Jesus was not an author at all. He communicated in other media. The medium that Jesus preferred was oral. He loved a direct and striking image like the parable.[1]

Although Jesus was surrounded by a circle of twelve disciples, we should not confuse his movement with a 'school' in the rabbinic sense.[2] The rabbis collected pupils and taught the principles and practice of scriptural exegesis. Jesus' choice of *twelve* disciples shows that his movement had a symbolic element, whatever teaching was imparted. There is not much evidence that Jesus was a scriptural exegete in the technical sense, nor that he confined himself to scriptural texts as the basis of his preaching. His parables were essentially stories drawn from life. They made a point (generally an obvious point) on one or more levels of interpretation.

Jesus is thus best described as a preacher: someone with a message that he expounded in a variety of forms as occasion demanded. As a preacher, Jesus was an itinerant.[3] He travelled from village to village in Galilee, then in a final preaching campaign from Galilee to Jerusalem. His followers were also itinerants, sent out on their own on at least one occasion to spread the message that Jesus himself proclaimed.[4]

Jesus' distance from the scribes is a significant one.[5] The scribes, by and large, were held in popular esteem because of their historically determined status as expositors of the Torah. Although the Gospels record that Jesus was revered by the people, not least because of his miracles, they also state that he was opposed by the scribes (and latterly by the priests) on account of his message.[6] There is a definite irony in the fact that this influential religious teacher lived on the margins of society and proclaimed a message that in its time was by no means universally popular; especially not popular with the leading religious authorities. That irony is emphasized by the observation that, if Jesus wrote anything at all, not a word of it has managed to survive. The oral impact of his message was the critical thing.

The Kingdom of God

At the centre of Jesus' message stood his preaching of God's kingdom. The concept of a kingdom demands belief in a king; the king whom Jesus proclaimed was God.[7] Belief in God as Israel's king goes back at least to the period of the monarchy and probably behind it.[8] In the Hebrew Bible, God is the creator of everything that exists (Genesis 1). For a Jewish writer to speak of God as 'king' is no limited or local nationalistic concept. God is the king of the whole world, for he is its creator. In the post-exilic period, this belief came to be expressed in terms of emergent monotheism.[9] The God of Israel was declared unique in respect of all the diverse deities of the Ancient Near Eastern and mediterranean world. Ps. 47.3 gives formal expression to this view when it states that 'God is the king of all the earth.' The Jewish God – Yahweh, or 'the God who is' – was the only true divinity. In his light, all other heavenly beings were subordinates or even mere pretenders.

The Hebrew Bible contains more than one understanding of God's kingship.[10] One strand is inextricably linked to the cult. In the call–vision of the prophet Isaiah (eighth century BCE), the prophet exclaims that he has seen God the king (Isa. 6.5). In the Psalms God is said to be seated 'above the cherubim' (e.g. Ps. 99.1), as if this part of the temple (the ark of the covenant) is regarded as God's throne, or at least its visible and earthly counterpart. The Royal Psalms in particular attest the connection between God the heavenly king and the earthly monarch in his cultic capacity. It is said elsewhere that Solomon sits on God's own throne (2 Chron. 9.8); Josephus even calls the community in Jerusalem a 'theocracy' (*Apion* 2.164–6).

The wavering fortunes of the Jewish cult and people meant that the notion of God's kingship acquired a forward-looking aspect at times of uncertainty.[11] The return from exile announced by Deutero-Isaiah included the reminder that the Israelite God truly reigns (Isa. 52.7). There is relevant material also in Obadiah (21) and Zephaniah (3.15). The most striking material, however, comes in texts influenced by emergent apocalypticism.[12] The so-called Isaiah apocalypse (Isaiah 24–7) anticipates the future reign of God on Mount Zion (Isa. 24.23). Its author describes a situation which he thinks needs transformation through God's own appearance. Similarly, Zech. 14.9 expects that 'the LORD *will* become king over all the earth', as if this situation has yet to be fully realized. The Hebrew Bible apocalypse, Daniel, has an entire vision (chapter 7) describing the emergence of the Israelite kingdom after the destruction of chaotic powers at the divine decree. The dissonance between hope and reality in this apocalypse is breached by the decree of the heavenly court.[13]

This biblical background should be carefully considered when evaluating the concept of God's kingdom in the sayings of Jesus. It brings us to the heart of the problem as it has been posed in recent years.

Present, Future or Both at Once?

We saw in Chapter 11 that the Jesus tradition contains both present and future statements about God's kingdom. We shall briefly note the contents of each to understand the matter.

The present sayings are indisputably part of the Jesus tradition.[14] The most prominent is the statement of Lk. 17.21 that 'the kingdom of God is among you'.[15] While this is attested only in Luke among the canonical Gospels, it appears more than once (in different forms) in the *Gospel of Thomas* (3; 113). This makes it more difficult to dismiss the saying as a merely Lucan fancy. There has been a dispute about whether Luke understands this saying to signify an interior or an external reality;[16] but the crucial point is that Lk. 17.21 regards the kingdom as present already. This view is supported by several of the so-called 'parables of the kingdom'; most obviously perhaps by the Seed Growing Secretly (Mk 4.26-9), which makes sense only on the premise that the seed has been sown already. So, too, in the parable of the Sower (Mk 4.1-9), the sowing of the word is a present and relevant event, not a merely future possibility.[17]

In this connection, we shall consider Jesus' healing miracles and their interpretation in the Gospels.[18] The Gospels breathe the conviction that Jesus' activity cast out Satan. This is expressed in visionary terms by Lk. 10.18 (Satan's fall from heaven) and in narrative terms by Mk 3.22-7 and parallels (the Beelzebul controversy).[19] In Lk. 11.20 (= Mt. 12.28), in what appears to be an authentic saying, Jesus states that 'if it is by the finger of God that I cast out the demons, then the kingdom of God has come upon you'.[20] The Gospels insist that Jesus casts out the demons. The kingdom must surely be present for this to happen.

The saying beloved of Albert Schweitzer is relevant also.[21] In Mt. 11.12-13/Lk. 16.16 Jesus says that, since the days of John the Baptist, violent people take the kingdom of God by force.[22] Schweitzer held this saying programmatic for the mission of Jesus. Whether or not this is a viable exegesis, the kingdom of God must again be present if it is to be treated with violence in this way. The Beatitudes equally imply that the kingdom is sufficiently present to demand a response from Jesus' followers in the here and now.[23] If Mt. 12.41 is authentic, the statement made there that something greater than Jonah is present is as much a statement about the presence of the kingdom as it is about the status of Jesus himself.[24]

Future Also?

No-one who reads the Jesus material really needs convincing that Jesus taught God's kingdom as a present reality. Agreement has recently begun to recede, however, about whether Jesus also taught God's kingdom as a future and apocalyptic reality. Having already examined what others have thought about this matter, we turn now to the primary data.

The first point to note is that futurist eschatology is found in all the recorded strata of the sayings of Jesus.[25] This includes the putative Q and *Gos. Thom.* 51 where it is attributed to the disciples, although admittedly rebutted in the latter by Jesus himself.[26] This places Jesus in line with his forerunner John the Baptist, at least in terms of eschatological hope

The Beatitudes describe the kind of qualities appropriate to God's kingdom.[27] Significantly, they include the promise of future change. Mt. 5.3 states that the kingdom of heaven belongs (already) to the poor in spirit. The meek are reminded that they will inherit the earth (5.5). This must mean that they do not possess it already, so that a futurist element is intended. So also with the promise of change for those who hunger and mourn. Theissen and Merz note that the biblical picture (Psalm 72) is of God intervening on behalf of the poor and weak and that the 'spiritualization' of these virtues in Matthew ('poor in spirit'; 'hunger and thirst for righteousness') shows that the more concrete Lucan version is original. In both cases, the promise of change implies a future element. It is bound up with the perception of society as unequal, as Jesus radically criticized the way things were at present.

This future hope is sometimes expressed under the image of the messianic banquet.[28] Mt. 8.11 (= Lk. 13.28-9) expects that people will come from the ends of the earth to feast with the patriarchs. This is resonant of Hebrew Bible and post-biblical themes; not least that of the pilgrimage of the Gentiles to Zion (Isaiah 2; 43; Micah 4). Jesus here presents the banquet with its inclusion of the Gentiles as a future event. Paul by contrast taught that the Gentiles can be included in salvation immediately. In favour of the authenticity of this saying of Jesus, as Theissen notes,[29] is its dissonance from Paul and the fact that it has not been altered to suit the later conception. Mt. 8.11 belongs to that stock of sayings where Jesus speaks of the kingdom as a future entity.

Mk 14.25 and parallels, if authentic, constitute important evidence for the future element in Jesus' eschatology.[30] At the Last Supper Jesus tells his disciples he will not drink wine with them again 'until that day when I drink it new in the kingdom of God'. Whether or not this saying anticipates death and resurrection, which is a vexed question, on any reading of Mk 14.25 Jesus anticipates celebrating the kingdom's arrival as a future event.[31]

Mk 9.1 and parallels is a difficult saying. Here, Jesus presents the kingdom as a future entity but states that it will come in the lifetime of at least some of his disciples. The authenticity of this saying has again been questioned by some commentators.[32] Against the view that it was created by the early church is the fact that it is recorded in all three Synoptic Gospels, all of which were written after some of the leading Christians (notably James the brother of Jesus, Peter and Paul) had died. Its inclusion goes against the tendency to suppress what time was suggesting might no longer be true. The saying has an ambiguous timescale if the followers of Jesus were young men in the 30s, as they probably were. Mk 9.1 thus has a greater claim to authenticity than some have allowed. Even if this judgment is questioned, it is important to note that the futurist strand in Jesus' reported eschatology does not *depend* on this verse, but is supported by a variety of evidence from the Gospels.

Apocalyptic or Not?

We saw in Chapter 11 that this futurist strand has been evaluated differently in the history of scholarship. Weiss marked a sea-change in attitudes when he preferred eschatology to ethics in the discussion of Jesus and his preaching. Schweitzer offered a more comprehensive approach which examined the deeds as well as the words of Jesus. Dodd denied the prominence of the futurist strand, replacing it with his theory of 'realized eschatology'. More recently, Crossan has denied the futurist strand on different grounds. The history of research into Jesus' eschatology can hardly have been more diverse. As with all such pendulum swings, there is a plausible case for arguing that the truth lies somewhere in the middle.

The answer proposed in this book agrees with that of W.G. Kümmel, who showed most plausibly that Jesus preached a present *and* a future eschatology.[33] This is not as odd as it seems. Consistent logic is a feature of the modern Western mind but not necessarily of the mind of a first-century Galilean Jew. The issue turns on how we evaluate the two strands of eschatology and explain their relation to each other.

That Jesus taught a present eschatology cannot and should not be denied. We shall therefore ask whether it is appropriate to remove the futurist strand from the preaching of Jesus. Those who remove it do so for more than one reason. Some scholars feel that the so-called 'Son of Man' sayings (where Jesus appears to identify himself with a heavenly mediator) can hardly be authentic in their present form.[34] Others think that the futurist Son of Man sayings and other material were imposed on the Jesus tradition to accord with the preaching of the early church when it was realized after Easter that much of what Jesus had said had failed to occur as had been predicted.[35]

The removal of the futurist strand in some contemporary scholarship is bound up with suspicion towards apocalypticism.[36] Apocalypticism is mistrusted by people like Crossan and Borg because it is assumed to concentrate too narrowly on the 'end' of what currently is and to divert attention from the articulation of present demands and hopes.[37] Prophecies of the end have generally been associated with fringe groups within and beyond the Christian church, not least because of the demise of millenarianism in the patristic period through the redefinition of the eschatological hope (and the very odd nature of some groups today).[38]

Crossan and Borg divorce the preaching of Jesus from apocalyptic eschatology and marry it with their own vision of social transformation. It might not unfairly be said that this is a further example of Schweitzer's dictum that questors after Jesus tend to find their own image in the reconstructed portrait.[39] It is not difficult to see why the portrait of Jesus as a subversive sage should find acceptance on the North American scene, if not in Europe also.[40] *Of course* there are elements in the Jesus tradition which support such a view. The question is whether this is a fair assessment of the views, including apocalyptic eschatology, that the Gospels attribute to Jesus; and also whether it is necessary to remove Jesus from an apocalyptic environment once this subversiveness is acknowledged.

In Dialogue with Crossan and Borg

This approach to apocalypticism falters on its eschatological imbalance.[41] While the apocalypses have much to say about future judgment, that is not their only interest; and it is by no means true to say that the judgment the apocalypses expect is always of a cataclysmic variety.[42] The earliest apocalyptic literature – some parts of the composite *1 Enoch* – has relatively little to say about future cataclysm.[43] *1 Enoch* 22, for instance, locates the departed in appropriate chambers as they await their final reward or punishment. This implies a *post-mortem* judgment, not a sudden irruption. The essence of apocalypticism is in fact not so much the element of cosmic dissolution, even though that features in certain parts of the tradition, but the spatial distinction between heaven and earth which allows authoritative information to be disclosed in a way that creates hope.[44]

Probing further, the nature of the promised eschatology in apocalyptic literature varies widely across the tradition. Although 'apocalyptic eschatology' is rightly recognized as a generic classification in scholarship, there is no single or identifiable *expression* of apocalyptic eschatology that can be held generic. In the case of Jesus, assuming that his futurist eschatology is authentic, his preaching of God's kingdom signified something other than the bald prediction of cosmic dissolution and conflict. It involved the authoritative declaration, evidently made on the basis of heavenly revelation, that God's kingdom was in process of emerging and that it would be fully present at some future point. So far as we can tell, Jesus thought this would happen within the confines of the existing order and neither in an ethereal realm nor a cosmic void. His was not the hope for the end of the space-time universe but for its reordering and in that sense its perfecting.[45] Sayings about cataclysm and disaster are relatively infrequent in the Jesus tradition.[46] The apocalyptic aspect of his preaching concentrates more on the state of affairs that will result from God's intervention than on the manner of the intervention itself. Jesus is at one here with Paul who speaks in Rom. 8.21 about the groaning of creation to be set free from its bondage to decay.[47]

Burton Lee Mack argues that Christian tradition after Jesus, and especially the author of Mark's Gospel, introduced apocalyptic elements into the tradition which were not found in Jesus himself.[48] While the impact made by the resurrection should not be under-estimated (see Chapter 16), it does not seem convincing that the resurrection alone could have created the apocalyptic eschatology that we find first in Paul and then in the Gospels.[49] The vision Jesus is reported to have experienced at his baptism is a strong indication that apocalyptic elements shaped his preaching campaign; not to mention the other material noted in this Part of the book.[50] Given the long history of Jewish apocalypticism by the first century CE, the visionary tradition associated with Jesus throughout his ministry, his famed authority as a teacher and the present form of his sayings, there is a strong case for regarding the apocalyptic elements in the Gospels as authentic. My view is that it is easier to take this view than to see this strand as a merely later accretion.

This does not, either in theory or practice, deny that Jesus was a penetrating social critic. It simply draws attention to the means by which Jesus thought the ills of society would be redressed. Where Crossan thinks that the Jesus movement and its preaching contained innate transformative potential, the view of 'double eschatology' advocated in this book accepts that this was so but argues further that Jesus saw the kingdom's full realization as a future event that could and would be achieved by God alone; and that demands a supernatural intervention of some kind. To remove the apocalyptic elements from Jesus' preaching is in my view more likely to harm our interpretation than the undoubted difficulties of wrestling with the material in its present form.

My argument reaches its zenith in consideration of the archetypal Christian prayer, the Lord's Prayer. This is found in two different forms, in Matthew 6 and Luke 11. The majority of scholars believe that Matthew's text represents a later and expanded version of the original which is more precise about God's location ('in heaven') and is careful to include an ethical petition ('your will be done').[51] Notwithstanding, the

Lord's Prayer in both versions includes petitions for present *and future* benefits. The supply of bread and the forgiveness of sins are continuing daily needs. The coming of God's kingdom, which comes at the head of the list, is a present and future hope, as is the request to be spared 'trial' or judgment with which the prayer closes. If this prayer is in any sense authentic, it shows with clarity that Jesus thought in both present and future categories about God's kingly rule. It is not possible to remove the future element from his eschatology as Crossan and others have done. Such removal does violence to the texts, and inappropriately masks a more plausible conclusion.

A Preliminary Conclusion

The question of *how* Jesus thought the kingdom would be introduced can only be answered by considering some questions about Jesus' self-understanding and about the enigmatic figure known as the Son of Man. These will be addressed in the next chapter. Without tripping over myself to anticipate that material, I think it will be helpful to set out some broad lines of engagement.

We have seen that the Jesus tradition contains both present and future sayings about the coming of God's kingdom, and that neither can satisfactorily be removed without difficulties. The implication of this conclusion is that what will fully be completed in the future has already begun in the present, and that what is present already is directly related to that future state without realizing it completely.

It is evident that the linchpin in this is the figure of Jesus himself and his preaching. That is why we have to examine the view which Jesus took of himself and the view the first Christians took of him: the business known as 'Christology'. Christology is important because of Jesus' view of the role of himself and his disciples in the kingdom schema he constructed. *In some sense*, it is certain, the Jesus movement embodied the nascent kingdom and gave it shape and meaning. We can only discern the nature of that sense by considering Jesus' likely self-understanding and the way he viewed his movement as it grew around him. This is a large-scale task, even in a book which inevitably presents some of the information in summary form.

In consequence, the next chapter is the longest in the book. I make no apology for this because we must take time to do justice to complex material. We need to ask about how Jesus evidently understood himself and his movement. This includes further consideration of the extent to which apocalypticism undergirded the mission of Jesus.

That brings us to what has been identifed as one of the most difficult problems in New Testament scholarship: the meaning and orientation of the so-called 'Son of Man' sayings. In a number of passages Jesus speaks of a specific figure – '*the* Son of Man' – in a way which describes his present activity, his suffering or his heavenly state. It is clear that, as the Gospels stand, this figure is identified with Jesus himself. The question is whether this identification was actually made by Jesus or whether it was superimposed on the Jesus tradition after Easter by the earliest Christians.

This embodies the question of whether Jesus thought that God's kingdom would be introduced by a heavenly mediator or whether it would arise more naturally from within the historical process: the debate about the apocalyptic or the non-apocalyptic Jesus we have considered already. The debate is a difficult one because, as in other areas, some of the evidence is missing and some is disputed. It nevertheless impacts directly on the interpretation of the ministry of Jesus in a way which our consideration of his preaching has shown already.

WHO DID JESUS THINK THAT HE WAS?

I want to develop what has been said by asking whether Jesus thought about himself as the Messiah; and then what sense can be placed on the 'Son of Man' sayings I have mentioned.

Did Jesus Think that He Was the Messiah?

I start by recalling what we saw about the understanding of 'the Messiah' in first-century Judaism.[1]

The Hebrew Bible uses the term 'Messiah' for several different figures, of whom the Jewish monarch is the most prominent. 'Messiah' is never used in the Bible as the title for a future redeemer. Horbury contends that 'the word Messiah itself attests a special accepted notion at the end of the Old Testament period, in the second century BC and later'.[2] He argues strongly that messianism had a much greater coherence in post-biblical Judaism than is sometimes allowed. Although there was no single and precisely defined understanding of 'the Messiah' and his role in the first century CE (witness the ambiguity of the Qumran evidence on this point), the hope for the Messiah as such was firmly rooted in the Jewish mindset. This observation introduces our quest to discover whether Jesus thought about himself as the Messiah.[3]

Mark's Gospel is structured by the theme of the disciples' progressive recognition of Jesus as Messiah.[4] The narrator shares this truth with the readers at the beginning of the Gospel (1.1). The evil spirits know that Jesus is a supernatural being (not necessarily the Messiah), but Jesus forbids them to make his identity public (for example at 1.34). At Caesarea Philippi (Mk 8.29-33) Simon Peter declares Jesus the Messiah. This passage represents a watershed in Mark's Gospel.[5] As Mark tells his story, the disciples' recognition of Jesus as Messiah sets the stage for the journey to Jerusalem and the final scene in the drama. This is when Jesus becomes widely known in the holy city, is arrested, tried and crucified. At the crucial moment, on trial before the high priest, Mark's Jesus acknowledges that he is the Messiah (Mk 14.62).[6] The question we need to ask is how true is this story, with its unfolding revelation of messiahship, to the original events.

This question is a heavily nuanced one. In the Matthaean and Lucan versions of Mk 14.62, Jesus' admission to the high priest that he is the Messiah is either toned down or suppressed altogether (Mt. 26.64; Lk. 22.67).[7] This makes it more difficult than it would otherwise have been to conclude that Jesus thought about himself as the Messiah, or at least that he encouraged such a view in public. John's Gospel makes Jesus acknowledge his messiahship to the Samaritan woman at the well (Jn 4.26); but many scholars think that this and other episodes in John were created by the Fourth Evangelist. Moreover, while it may be true that Matthew and Luke perceptibly draw away from the 'revolutionary' element in the reasons for Jesus' condemnation,[8] the ancient sources make it difficult to decide whether Jesus spoke about himself as the Messiah from an early point in his ministry.

The question is – as more than once before – what degree of history lies behind Mark's story of Jesus.[9] It is inevitable that we enter the realm of conjecture, or at least of informed conjecture, when addressing this problem. We saw that the question was answered in different ways in twentieth-century research. Where Schweitzer and others had little difficulty in accepting that Jesus thought about himself as Messiah,[10] Ed Sanders (surprisingly) disallows the possibility that Jesus held this view.[11] The basis of Sanders' refusal is that there is little direct evidence that Jesus accepted or used this title. Sanders does, however, accept that Jesus may have advanced a higher self-claim, that of spokesman for God or even God's own viceroy.

A crucial factor to decide is what it might have meant for Jesus to call himself the Messiah. In the light of the information presented here, especially the research of William Horbury, we may be sure that 'the Messiah' was a recognizable title and concept in first-century Judaism. Although the sources vary considerably in their description of what the Messiah was expected to do, he was seen in general terms as the ideal king of the future (Horbury's 'eschatological ruler and Saviour'). The fact that the sources vary in their understanding suggests that, while there was a general expectation that the Messiah was coming, there was no precise blueprint which determined what he would do. The expectations seem to have changed according to time and circumstance, in a way that is easy to understand, but which does not actually help the process of interpreting Jesus to any fixed degree.

The evidence shows that anyone claiming to be the Messiah in the first century CE would have been conscious of claiming a kingly role; although there was a measure of flexibility in the way that role was understood. The militaristic approach suggested by the *Psalms of Solomon* was not the only option for a would-be Messiah. The apocalyptic literature encourages the view that to act in a decisive manner was the prerogative of God alone. That is probably why there is no reference to the Messiah in the book of Daniel; and why in *4 Ezra* 7 the Messiah is a human figure who dies in a natural way.[12] The fact that Jesus apparently rejected militaristic action cannot be taken as evidence that he did not think about himself as Messiah. It merely indicates that he did not conceive messiahship in that particular way.

Jesus and the Twelve

We can refine the question by considering some wider evidence from the Gospels. Jesus reportedly surrounded himself with twelve disciples.[13] Their names are given variously according to which list one consults.[14] Yet throughout the Gospels runs the conviction that there were twelve.[15] This figure is found in Paul as well (1 Cor. 15.5). This evidence is too substantial to permit the conclusion that it was a post-Easter accretion.

Twelve appears to have been a symbolic number. The reason why Jesus had twelve disciples is almost certainly linked to the biblical portrait of Israel as composed of twelve tribes.[16] This portrait is found in classical form in Genesis 49 (the so-called 'Blessing of Jacob'). Although there has been more than one explanation of the significance and dimensions of the tribes of Israel, the notion that Israel was made up of twelve 'tribes' remains constant in the Hebrew Bible and in subsequent literature.[17] No doubt the uncertainty caused by the division of the monarchy and the territorial encroachments of foreign powers sustained this traditional idea. It is found frequently in the post-biblical literature.[18]

In my view, there is no more convincing explanation of the twelve disciples than this link with the tribes of Israel. In surrounding himself with twelve disciples, it seems that Jesus was making a statement about himself and the nature of his movement. While this insight has been variously interpreted, I do not think that it can easily be denied. Affinity to the biblical concept of the twelve tribes is mentioned elsewhere in the Gospel tradition. At the end of Matthew 19 Peter asks Jesus about the benefits of belonging to his movement. Mt. 19.28 makes Jesus reply by looking forward to the eschatological climax: 'At the renewal of all things, when the Son of Man is seated on the throne of his glory, you who have followed me will also sit on twelve thrones, judging the twelve tribes of Israel.' (The Lucan equivalent is 22.30, 'You will sit on thrones judging the twelve tribes of Israel.')[19] Leaving aside the problematic 'Son of Man' saying in this reference, the crucial point in both versions is that the disciples are expected to exercise a judgmental or even a presidential role in respect of the tribes of Israel at the time of the eschatological climax. The implication is that they will come into their own when the kingdom arrives; and that they will then be significant figures in the Jewish nation. That the twelve knew and looked forward to this future role is suggested by the dispute about precedence which is recorded with some gusto in Mk 10.35–40 and parallels.[20]

We do not know precisely what Jesus thought would happen in the eschatological future.[21] Indeed, it is possible that Jesus himself had only a vague or limited understanding of this matter, especially if he thought that the critical action was God's own prerogative. There is, in my view, a comprehensible portrait of Jesus which sees him as a radical visionary who believed he was called to announce *that* change was coming while recognizing that the actual nature of the change (as suggested by the Hebrew Bible) could not be determined by human choice. The existence of twelve disciples, together with the evidence for their eschatological role, suggests somewhat strongly that Jesus thought about his own movement analogously with Israel; and that this is the matrix in which the dialectic between the present and the future in his eschatology should be interpreted.

Jesus in Jerusalem

Other features of the Jesus movement are consonant with this view. The death of Jesus was the result of a process that began with his journey to Jerusalem.[22] When Jesus entered Jerusalem for the last time, on what we now call 'Palm Sunday', it appears that his was a relatively unknown movement. For all Jesus' fame in Galilee (possibly over-stated by the Gospels?), his so-called 'cleansing of the temple' prompted the religious authorities to ask basic questions about him, as if they were initially uncertain who he was and what his circle was about. If Schweitzer is right, they had to bribe Judas to secure the crucial information that Jesus and his friends thought about him as the Messiah.[23]

It is in fact by no means certain that Jesus entered Jerusalem to general acclaim. In the next part of this chapter, I shall argue the case that the 'triumphal entry' was probably recognized by his own followers alone. Even Mark, who emphasizes the messiahship of Jesus in the second half of his Gospel, says only that the chief priests and scribes 'kept looking for a way to kill him' (Mk 11.18). He absolutely fails to mention their recognition of his messiahship before the trial. This looks like an authentic recollection, as if the messianic status of Jesus proved an uncertain or even an unknown issue up to the time of his arrest; and that fact-finding about a potentially awkward character was a pressing reason for the initial investigation of Jesus.

This uncertainty draws attention to a significant statement attributed to Jesus when in custody: 'Day after day I was with you in the temple teaching, and you did not arrest me' (Mk 14.49). This information is corroborated by Mark's earlier narrative (chapters 11 to 13) which records a series of encounters between Jesus and the authorities that were evidently intended as investigations of him. If Jesus was given so much leeway during this period, he must have had an opportunity to escape the horrors of arrest and crucifixion. If Mark 11–13 is in any way authentic, Jesus must have sensed some form of danger or hostility in Jerusalem. This raises the question of why he chose to remain there in the face of an increasingly hostile environment. The answer must be – and it is supported by the narrative structure of the Gospels – that *this* journey to Jerusalem was a decisive event in Jesus' mind. What happened in Jerusalem at that time, it appears, was connected with his own understanding of his mission and movement. This in turn reflects back on the question of whether Jesus thought about himself as the Messiah.

Nowadays, there is a growing tendency to follow Sanders' suggestion that Jesus anticipated the 'restoration' of Israel, hoping that God would act eschatologically to secure the fortunes of his chosen people.[24] I have no reason to question that assessment, but I want to relate it to the question we are considering of whether Jesus thought about himself as the Messiah. I suggest that Jesus' unswerving presence in Jerusalem and what he did there are strong indications that he did think about himself as the Messiah.[25] Added to this is the question of whether Christianity after Easter would really have superimposed messianic status on a non-messianic Jesus given that they thought of him as a heavenly being, not an earthly leader.

Caution is needed in interpretation, but the evidence does support the conclusion that Jesus thought about himself as the Messiah. Such a vew is strongly suggested by the Gospels. It is in fact surprising that Sanders can consider that Jesus thought about himself as the divine viceroy but not as the Messiah; a surprise, I believe, which is exacerbated by the flexibility surrounding the messianic understanding in first-century Judaism. The way was open for Jesus to define his own concept of messiahship. This is what his words and his deeds suggest that he did, on the balance of all reasonable probability.

Jesus and Apocalyptic Secrecy

Related to the question of who Jesus thought that he was is the question of how he understood the nature of the movement he founded. In my research, I have increasingly been drawn towards the theory of Albert Schweitzer that the device of apocalyptic secrecy does much to explain the nature of the Jesus movement, and especially its final days in Jerusalem.[26] In the next part of this chapter, I want to explore this approach to Jesus and the Gospels and to ask what light it sheds on the self-understanding of this would-be Messiah from Galilee.

We saw that apocalypticism flourished in Judaism from the third century BCE. The apocalyptic writers believed that they handled secret matters which had been disclosed through heavenly revelation. There are frequent instructions in the apocalypses to seal up or preserve their contents which suggest that these texts were intended for an inner circle of readers who shared the authors' position.[27] The apocalypses breathe an esoteric air. They use complex imagery and symbolism to establish a perspective whose precise contours and their interpretation are known only to members of the authors' circle.

This device of apocalyptic secrecy provides an interesting link with the reported preaching of Jesus. It has long been recognized that there is a 'messianic secret' in Mark whereby Jesus tells both the demons (1.34) and the disciples (8.30) not to make his identity known. It has sometimes been suggested that this is a literary device and was invented by Mark: that Mark superimposed secrecy on a less opaque tradition.[28] This theory is open to question. For one thing, there is considerable messianic proclamation in Mark. The opening verse tells the reader quite plainly that Jesus is the Christ. Peter correctly identifies Jesus as Messiah in Mark 8. The question of Jesus' messiahship becomes more urgent as Mark's Gospel unfolds, reaching its climax in Jesus' statement to the high priest in Mk 14.62. If Mark does include a messianic secret, he also controverts it by clear and unambiguous messianic identification. In my view, the theory that Mark created the messianic secret wrongly and unhelpfully obscures the possibility that this stemmed from Jesus himself.

In this chapter, developing what I said earlier, I want to argue that the device of *apocalyptic* secrecy does much to explain the present form of the Jesus tradition. There are several stages in the argument. First of all, the general probability that Jesus was influenced by apocalypticism. This brings with it the likelihood that the atmosphere of the apocalypses, where commands to secrecy are a central feature of the genre, influenced the mindset of Jesus and his disciples, so that we should positively expect some form of esotericism within the confines of an apocalyptic sect.

Secondly, the present form of Jesus' teaching, where it is clear (not least from the parables) that he made a distinction between public and private teaching, in a way which suggests that inner teaching actually formed the heart of the Jesus movement. This secret teaching appears to have had an eschatological dimension and to have concerned the identity of Jesus as the Messiah and the twelve as the tribal presidents-elect of the restored Israel, together with the belief that the Son of Man would shortly appear to effect a decisive transformation on God's behalf. These hopes are fully described in the Gospels, which also indicate that they were not perceived by those whom Jesus encountered outside his circle. Thus, when Jesus was itinerant in Galilee, he was revered first and foremost as the worker of miracles, not as an eschatological teacher. If the structure of Mark's Gospel is accurate historically, it may even be that Jesus' disciples took some time to understand the precise nature of his movement and the role which messianism occupied there. When Jesus entered Jerusalem for the last time, it is obvious that the priestly authorities knew very little about him and resorted to bribery to discover the inner secrets of his Jesus movement. All of this indicates that private teaching was a major feature of the Jesus movement, and that this was very successfully concealed until the last moment. The self-understanding of the Jesus circle was a matter for private discussion.

Related to this is the interpretation of what Jesus did during his final days in Jerusalem. The interpretation of the Triumphal Entry, the Cleansing of the Temple and the Last Supper has prompted much debate. In what follows, I want to argue that the key to understanding them is again provided by the device of apocalyptic secrecy so that, first and foremost, we are reading about events which Jesus and the disciples believed that they alone understood. In this sense, they are to be construed as symbolic acts, just as the apocalypses are replete with symbolism. The meaning of these symbols, of which one caused offence and two probably went unnoticed, lies in the eschatological consciousness of the Jesus movement and the significance of Jerusalem as the geographical and theological capital of Judaism, which Jesus entered as Messiah.

By journeying to Jerusalem, Jesus mounted what has been called a messianic challenge to the Jewish nation. By this, I mean that his journey was undergirded by messianic belief and the expectation that, once certain things had been done, the stage had finally been set for God to act eschatologically. An apocalyptic ambience explains the meaning of the acts in question. Thus, by entering Jerusalem on a donkey, Jesus deliberately entered Jerusalem as Messiah, surrounded by the twelve, in a self-understanding that could hardly have been perceived by anyone outside the movement since it occurred when large numbers of pilgrims were arriving. In Cleansing the Temple Jesus, like the Qumran sectaries, revealed his belief that the temple cult had become estranged from the divine purpose and needed to be reconstituted by God. What the temple authorities perceived as a public order offence, Jesus and his disciples intended either as a divine act, purifying the temple, or more likely a divine declaration that the temple would be purified by God. In company with other Jewish sectarians, it appears Jesus thought that the temple's purity was a crucial feature of the eschatological age. In Cleansing the Temple, Jesus acted to restore that purity in an act with clear eschatological implications.

This brings us to the Last Supper. The major interpretive question in the history of research has been whether or not this was a Passover meal. The answer depends in no small measure on which Gospel's chronology an interpreter chooses to follow. It is probably easier to suppose that it was a Passover meal, given the Supper's obvious importance to Jesus and his circle, than that it was an otherwise ordinary meal invested on that occasion with absolutely extraordinary significance. It is important to ask, however, not just whether this was a traditional though special meal, but whether it had a unique significance related to Jesus' last days in Jerusalem. While any interpretation of this matter remains conjectural, given the status of the Triumphal Entry and Cleansing as unique events which derived their meaning from the self-understanding of the Jesus movement, the likelihood is that something similar explains the Last Supper as well. In order to understand the Last Supper, therefore, we need to ask what Jesus and his disciples believed about themselves and consider our interpretation of the event in the light of that evidence. In what follows, I shall argue that the internal secret of Jesus' messiahship reached its zenith in the Last Supper, once the Messiah had entered Jerusalem and reclaimed the temple for God. The stage was now set for the most powerful messianic act of all. On my reading of the story, Jesus and his disciples celebrated the messianic banquet. This was nothing less than a celebration of the kingdom's arrival. It set the seal on Jesus' eschatological hopes, in a manner that we may now examine in more detail.

Secret Teaching

The Jesus tradition contains a clear and obvious distinction between public and private teaching; as for instance in Mark 4. Interpreters must ask why this should be recorded if Jesus did not give more detailed teaching to his disciples than to the general public? In Mk 4.11, moreover, Jesus presents the parables as teaching devices which concealed as well as revealed truth: 'To you has been given the secret of the kingdom of God, but for those outside, everything comes in parables.'[29] The implication of this statement is that the disciples were given *further* teaching than what is found in the parables.

This further teaching must surely have been something other than just the interpretation of the parables. By and large, the parables of Jesus are easy to understand. They deal with themes like the coming of the kingdom and the certainty of future judgment. This further teaching to the disciples, I suggest, was more detailed and precise than the parables disclose. I think it concerned the role of Jesus and his disciples in respect of the coming kingdom, especially Jesus' messianic status and their role when the kingdom came. I think that Peter's 'confession' in Mk 8.29 and the statement about the disciples in Mt. 19.28 are examples of this 'inner teaching'. It is likely that Jesus' 'Son of Man' sayings should be considered in this light as well (see below).

The Triumphal Entry

When Jesus entered Jerusalem for the last time, he did a number of things whose meaning is not fully explained. Into this category fall the Triumphal Entry, the Cleansing of the Temple and the Last Supper. Each of these, I suggest, has a meaning which originally only Jesus' inner circle knew. Although the Gospels would have us believe that the triumphal entry was a notable public event, the subsequent ignorance about Jesus on the part of the ruling authorities and the fact that he was not immediately arrested make it likely that those who acclaimed him on this occasion were probably his own followers alone.[30] In this case, the meaning of the triumphal entry should be deduced from its context within the Jesus movement and not from its presumed public importance.

The Gospels state that Jesus entered Jerusalem in triumph riding on a donkey. This story is found, with variations, in all four Gospels.[31] Matthew and Luke presuppose Mark's account; Matthew and John deliberately include the evidence of Zech. 9.9.[32] The Synoptic versions describe how Jesus sent two disciples who mysteriously found a colt which they brought to Jesus. Jesus then entered Jerusalem on the donkey as people strewed palm branches and garments in his path crying 'Hosanna! Blessed is the one who comes in the name of the Lord!' (11.9). John 12.12-19 lacks the sending of the disciples to find the donkey but includes the public acclamation of Jesus and the cry, 'Blessed is the one who comes in the name of the Lord – the king of Israel!'

The citation of Zech. 9.9 ('Lo, your king comes to you . . . humble and riding on a donkey') by Matthew and John explicitly makes this a messianic event, while the recollection of Mark and Luke that Jesus entered Jerusalem on a donkey arguably recalls that text as well (see esp. Mk 11.10, 'Blessed is the coming kingdom of our ancestor David!'). The requisitioning of the donkey by Jesus has been understood as a messianic act.[33] Derrett comments that 'the right to impress was a royal right . . . The ruler and his servants needed transport, and the people on the spot provided it.'[34] Derrett finds further support in the statement that the animal is said to be unridden (Mk 11.2). 'A true king would not choose an animal which had been ridden . . . Here was a moment for Jesus to show his royal dignity.'[35] Whatever the truth of Derrett's interpretation (and some scholars have questioned it), the textual evidence really does suggest that the four Gospels understand the triumphal entry as a messianic act.[36]

The story raises considerable problems of interpretation. The nature of historical verification make it impossible to *prove* that it happened in the way that is recorded, although it is difficult to see how and why it should have been invented were this not the case. It is easier to suppose that an event of this nature happened than to treat it as a subsequent and imaginary historical or theological explanation of the ministry of Jesus. What the Gospel writers have done is to describe this event with the eye of post-Easter faith where the universal acclaim of Jesus was a *desiderandum*. Once this is recognized, it becomes plausible to see the triumphal entry as a secret event whose meaning was known to Jesus and the disciples alone, and which in a very real sense illuminated, and probably also acted out, the significance of their movement in terms of its background in the idea of Israel, the Messiah and the twelve tribes with their titular presidents. The Hebrew Bible contains a number of stories about the prophets – notably Ezekiel – performing symbolic actions.[37] Such actions have almost the character of 'acted parables' whose symbolism resembles a divine message delivered dramatically at a critical point.

The triumphal entry was thus on my view a symbolic act in which Jesus entered Jerusalem as Messiah accompanied by the twelve as representatives of the restored Israel. This suggests a form of 'scene-setting' in which the conditions were beginning to be assembled that would yield the eschatological climax. The event can be seen as the 'acting out' by an apocalyptic group of an eschatological event whose meaning was denied to the public at large. Jesus and the disciples effected the advent of the Messiah to Jerusalem in a way that only they knew but whose significance they believed would soon be revealed when God intervened decisively from outside the historical process. The story cannot be understood apart from prophetic and apocalyptic convictions, notably the need for secrecy and the belief that the final event would be a matter of divine and not human activity.

This interpretation gives the triumphal entry a more important place in the Jesus story than some modern readings allow. Once the Messiah had entered the holy city, the conditions were ripe for the messianic age to appear. This makes that journey not the last desperate march on Jerusalem proposed by Albert Schweitzer but a journey towards the kingdom which was fired by prophetic and apocalyptic convictions. It is likely that, on arrival in Jerusalem, Jesus and the disciples expected something significant to happen. That is suggested also by the next event in the Holy Week calendar.

The Cleansing of the Temple

That next event is the 'cleansing of the temple'.[38] This event is reported in all four Gospels (Mk 11.15-19 and parallels; Jn 2.13-22). It is one of the most controversial of Jesus' deeds so far as modern scholarship is concerned. Interpretations have ranged from the suggestion that Jesus was merely purging the temple of dishonest or objectionable tradesmen to the view that he was symbolizing the replacement of the present temple by the eschatological temple through God's own intervention.

The story as narrated by Mk 11.15-19 is a relatively simple one. On entering Jerusalem Jesus goes to the temple and drives out the tradesmen, forbidding people to carry anything through the temple. He is made to utter the words, 'My house shall be called a house of prayer for all the nations . . . but you have made it a den of robbers.' The conclusion of the story in Mark (11.18) states that, as the result of this event, the chief priests and the scribes kept looking for a way to kill Jesus. Matthew adds some healing miracles performed by Jesus on this occasion (Mt. 21.14-16). Lk. 19.45-7 presents a shorter account which agrees with Mark that the religious authorities wanted to kill Jesus as the result of this event. John sets the incident at the beginning of the public ministry of Jesus (2.13-22), attributing to Jesus the words, 'Destroy this temple and in three days I will raise it up.'[39]

These last words are undoubtedly significant. They occur in different forms in the Synoptic tradition, and also in the *Gospel of Thomas*. Thus at the trial of Jesus, witnesses come forward who allege that Jesus said, 'I will destroy this temple that is made with hands, and in three days I will build another, not built with hands' (Mk 14.58); Matthew tones this down with his report, 'I am able to destroy the temple of God' (26.61), which removes the specific element of threatening. In Mark 13.2 – part of Jesus' major eschatological teaching – he is reported as having said, 'Do you see these great buildings? Not a stone will be left here upon another; all will be thrown down.' With this should be compared the saying of *Gos. Thom.* 71: 'I will destroy [this] house, and no one will be able to build it.'

Traditionally, interpretation of this event has started with the words attributed to Jesus on this occasion; notably the words, 'you have made it a den of robbers'. The latter phrase, it must be noted, is not mere descriptive commentary on the part of Jesus but a biblical citation. The source is Jer. 7.11. In that context, Jeremiah criticizes those who trust in the temple as a religious building but do things that are not consistent with the moral demands of belief in God. Similarly, the statement that the temple is a 'house of prayer for all the nations' (Mk 11.17) is a citation of Isa. 56.7 (LXX), so that all the words attributed to Jesus on this occasion have their roots in scripture.

This scriptural foundation mounts a serious challenge to those who would see the event as the act of a religious crusader concerned to rid the temple of petty dishonesty.[40] The only suggestion that the traders were acting dishonestly comes from the citation itself. As Sanders notes, a proper supply of sacrificial animals was in fact necessary to the efficiency of the temple (and with it to the priestly economy).[41] It is possible that some traders were dishonest; but dishonesty is not generally attributed to them in other literature, as we might expect had such an allegation been common knowledge.[42] Moreover, the statement that the chief priests wanted to kill Jesus does not make full sense on this theory; nor is it evident how this one act would actually have removed widespread dishonesty, had that been the intention.

It seems more likely that some kind of symbolism is involved. Jesus performs another of his symbolic acts, distancing himself from the temple and its administration, as did other sectarian Jews of his day. The Qumran community voiced their mistrust of the temple in the Dead Sea scrolls, regarding themselves as the perfect embodiment of the temple community.[43] There is no evidence in the Gospels, however, that Jesus intended to replace the temple with a religious community as such, still less with the community of his own followers. The early chapters of Acts show the Jerusalem community as not only faithful to temple observance, but even focused on it.[44] Jesus' was a different form of protest from that adopted by the Qumran community.

Every interpreter has to acknowledge that we are dealing with prob-abilities, hypotheses and conjectures when evaluating the 'cleansing of the temple'. The observation that Jesus' action cannot satisfactorily be referred to the dislike of a specific group within the temple, combined with the strong probability that symbolism is afoot, has led most to conclude that Jesus' criticism was directed against the temple institution as such and not just against those who bought and sold there; and that questions of purity or integrity are therefore involved in what he did. The statement that the priestly authorities wanted to kill Jesus is much easier to understand on these grounds. Moreover, there would then be grounds for holding together what Jesus *did* in the temple with what he is reported to have *said* about the temple, as John's Gospel does. The statement that Jesus threatened the temple's destruction (significantly toned down by Matthew and omitted by Luke, who attributes it to Stephen in Acts 7) is too difficult and widespread in the tradition to be regarded as a post-Easter accretion. This is strong evidence that Jesus did indeed hold a negative view of the present temple and that he regarded some kind of destruction or replacement as essential for the religious future of Israel.

If Jesus did threaten the temple's destruction, there is no evidence whatsoever in the 'cleansing' episode that he expected to destroy it *himself*; not even with the assistance of twelve disciples. The existing tradition (especially John 2.19f.) makes this clear. Nor is there con-vincing evidence in that tradition that Jesus and his movement har-boured revolutionary tendencies. The evidently symbolic nature of the 'cleansing' makes it clear that divine and not human action is involved. Jesus did and said something which referred the initiative to God, in keeping with his preaching of God's kingdom which we examined in Chapter 13. Jesus appears to be speaking of a future point when the present temple would be destroyed or replaced by God. The fact that the 'cleansing' occurred within a wider sequence of events – those of Holy Week – suggests an imminence to this belief; while Jesus' action, as distinct from his words, implies he may have thought God had delegated a part to himself in that destruction, whether that was as the divine spokesman who announced it or the Messiah whose advent had made it possible (and conceivably both of these).

I think that Sanders is correct in citing that Jewish evidence which speaks of the replacement of the present temple by God as relevant here.[45] Biblical examples include Isa. 60.3-7, which links the coming of the Gentiles to Israel's light with the glorification of 'my glorious house'; and Micah 4, where it is said that the 'mountain of the house of the Lord' will be made the highest mountain where many nations will come to learn the law. Tob. 14.5 says that 'the house of God will be rebuilt [in Jerusalem] with a glorious building for all generations for ever'. In *1 Enoch* the temple is apparently identified as the throne of God (25.3–5).

The author states that 'the Lord of the sheep brought a new house greater and loftier than the first, and set it in place of the first' (90.29; cf. 91.13). *Jub.* 1.15–17 predicts that national repentance will be accompanied by the construction of God's sanctuary in Israel. This expectation is found also in the *Psalms of Solomon* (17.32). It extended to the Qumran community to judge from 4QpPs 37 3.11: 'They shall possess the High Mountain of Israel [for ever], and shall enjoy [everlasting] delights in His Sanctuary' (cf. 11QTemple 29.8–10).

This complex of passages broadly agrees in its outlook with another group which predicts the reconstitution of the Israelite tribes in the eschatological age. Once again, the relevant material has been collected by Sanders.[46] He shows that a whole variety of passages articulates the hope that Israel will one day be its perfect self. These hopes have roots in the post-exilic prophets who responded to the disaster of 587 CE and the destruction of the Solomonic temple at that time.[47] Deutero-Isaiah strikingly anticipates the remaking of Israel according to biblical proportions. Isa. 49.5 hopes that Jacob will return to God and that Israel will be regathered. Isa. 56.1–8 (the prophecy significantly cited by Jesus during the 'cleansing of the temple') makes God promise to gather the outcasts of Israel. The author states that foreigners will offer sacrifice in the temple. This last theme is developed by Isaiah 60, which anticipates both the return of the exiles and the coming of the Gentiles to the light of the Jewish nation. In the apocryphal literature Baruch (4.37; 5.5) Ecclus (36.11) and 2 Macc. (1.27-8; 2.18) all anticipate the gathering of the tribes of Israel. The *Psalms of Solomon* contains more than one passage specifically anticipating the restoration of the tribes (chapters 11 and 17). According to the Qumran text 1QM 2 all the tribes will supply troops for the eschatological conflict. The hope for the regathering of the tribes continues in Jewish and Christian literature written after 70 CE (see *t.Sanh.* 13.10 and Rev. 21.12).

The notion that the temple needed replacement by God coheres with this wider articulated vision in Jewish literature for the perfecting of Israel. The triumphal entry and the cleansing of the temple are inextricably linked in the tradition. They belong together. If the Entry means that the Messiah and the tribal representatives had entered Jerusalem, and the Cleansing that the temple would soon be replaced by God, the second complex of passages illuminates the Jesus movement in the sense that it provides the background for the self-understanding of a group within the Jewish nation who thought that the biblical promises for the restoration or perfecting of Israel were about to be fulfilled. The arrival of the Messiah and the twelve symbolized the regathering of Israel; the Cleansing showed that the heart of Jewish religion was about to be revitalized.

There is evidence here of a programmatic consciousness which reinforces my suggestion that these last days in Jerusalem were crucially important for Jesus and disclose the distinctive nature of his movement. Jesus did not just *promise* that a transformed social order would emerge in the future. He said that this had *already begun* to emerge and that it was symbolized by the presence in Jerusalem of the very people who would be significant when God intervened to transform. Evidently, Jesus' strong desire to journey to Jerusalem was bound up with his belief that he and his disciples must be present in Jerusalem for the kingdom finally to come. Evidently, he would then be revealed as Messiah and the twelve would assume their eschatological role (Mt. 19.28; Lk. 22.30).

This reading of the evidence takes us back to Jeremiah. Jeremiah 7 is not just a criticism of those who trust in the temple while committing abominations, but it incorporates a prophecy of the temple's destruction. In Jer. 7.14 God promises to destroy the temple just as the sanctuary at Shiloh had been destroyed. Mark's narrator inserts the cursing of the fig tree by Jesus in between the triumphal entry and the cleansing of the temple (11.12-14). In cursing the barren tree, Jesus symbolically condemns the barrenness of Israel.[48] This further symbolic act casts further light on the Entry and the Cleansing by suggesting that Jesus is thinking of the Jewish nation as whole. Jesus apparently regarded the Cleansing as a necessary act which he thought would 'bring on' the kingdom in the imminent future.

Like the triumphal entry, the cleansing of the temple features as an act which initially had meaning for the inner circle alone. They saw the temple condemned in advance of its replacement by God. What appeared to outsiders as iconoclasm was in fact an eschatological sign performed by a prophet to those who knew its meaning.[49] In the symbolism of Holy Week, the tribes of Israel were now gathered in Jerusalem and the temple declared as about to be purified by God. This no doubt justified the raising of eschatological hope.

The Last Supper

Jesus' actions in the Last Supper had a similar symbolic meaning.[50] The major exegetical question that has preoccupied scholars concerning the Last Supper is whether or not it was a Passover meal.[51] This problem is compounded by a difference between the Synoptic and the Johannine chronology. The Synoptic Gospels unambiguously present the Last Supper as a Passover meal. In John, however, Jesus dies at the moment when the Passover lambs are slain so that the Last Supper is not a Passover meal as such (Jn 19.30-1). Joachim Jeremias argued strongly in favour of the Synoptic chronology.[52] Annie Jaubert tried to reconcile the two chronologies by pointing to the use of different calendars at the time, suggesting that Jesus had adopted an Essene calendar.[53] Theissen and Merz marginally prefer the Johannine chronology.[54] On the basis of this conflicting evidence, one cannot automatically *assume* that the Last

Supper was a Passover meal, as has been done in the past. This matter deserves a more nuanced consideration.

The Last Supper recalls the earlier meals of Jesus. These meals were a central feature of his movement, as they were in the Qumran community.[55] They appear to have been banquets rather than ordinary events.[56] Their distinctive feature is that anyone who followed Jesus – even the very worst kind of sinner – could attend.[57] In evaluating the Last Supper, we should note that it was far from a routine and typical meal, any more than the triumphal entry was haphazard or the cleansing of the temple an afternoon's excursion. The story as it is told in Mk 14.12-15 and parallels has an introduction in which two disciples are sent to follow a mysterious stranger; possibly the same person who had supplied the donkey for the triumphal entry (Mk 11.3-6). The disciples are shown the upper room. They make their preparations there. The scene is thereby set for Jesus' most powerful symbolic act.

The mysterious appearance of the stranger and the unexplained provision of the colt add to the secrecy surrounding the Jesus movement. This person was presumably a Jerusalem supporter whom Jesus had briefed in advance to act in this way. In a culture where women normally carried the water, the man stood out in the crowd and was instantly recognized by the disciples. Secrecy was effectively preserved, as befits an apocalyptic circle.

Whether or not the Last Supper was a Passover meal, the Gospels present it as something greater than the familiar annual ritual.[58] The meal clearly anticipates the death of Jesus in the scheme of events that is unfolding. The narrative presents Jesus' death as a sacrifice in which he peers into the eschatological future.[59] This is clear from his words, 'This is my blood of the covenant, which is poured out for many' (14.25).[60] If these words are authentic, Jesus apparently sees his death as a foreshadowing of the kingdom and even to that extent as facilitating the kingdom's appearance. Although the narrative raises substantial questions of authenticity – which are exacerbated by the differences between the Synoptic and the Pauline (1 Cor. 11.23-6) versions of the Last Supper – the eschatological significance of this meal seems assured. The Last Supper cannot therefore satisfactorily be evaluated without reference to the earlier preaching of Jesus with its concern for the kingdom of God.

The question of how those who participated at the Last Supper were encouraged by Jesus to understand its meaning can only be answered conjecturally, like so many questions about Jesus. I want to do this by asking what Jesus had already accomplished in his mission, with the preaching in Galilee and final journey to Jerusalem. Jesus had fully proclaimed the advent of God's kingdom, albeit with the distinction between public and private teaching noted here. He had entered Jerusalem; I think as Messiah, attended by the twelve as representatives of the reformed Israel. He had censured the temple as a prophetic sign indicating that its eschatological replacement was near. Now he celebrated a meal with only *some* of his followers present. Women and children were excluded. Those who sat down to the Last Supper were the Messiah and the twelve, who represented Israel.

Once again, the symbolism can hardly be ignored. In my book on Jesus, I suggested that one way of interpreting this event is to see it as the messianic banquet, coming as it does hard on the heels of the earlier symbolic acts.[61] Two different Jewish backgrounds set this interpretation in perspective. I want briefly to present the evidence and then to comment on its significance.

Several Jewish texts present the Messiah's revelation as sudden and mention his hidden origins. Jn 7.27, for instance, makes the Jews say that when the Messiah appears, no-one will know where he comes from. *j.Ber.* 5a states that the Messiah was mysteriously hidden after his birth in a storm. Targum Jonathan on Mic. 4.8 holds that the Messiah is already present, but concealed through the sins of his people. The notion that the Messiah's initial advent would be hidden, rather than sudden and dramatic, is thus not unknown in Jewish literature. In particular, we should note that the apocalyptic literature contains more than one passage describing the 'revelation' of the Messiah from either human or supernatural origins.

The notion of the messianic banquet was well known in Jewish and Christian apocalypticism, even though it cannot actually be said to be an indispensable element there. The background to it is both the connection between eating and drinking in the presence of the numinous which features in the Hebrew Bible (notably Exod. 24.1-11); and also the motif of the sacred banquet found in the prophets, notably in Isa. 25.6-8: 'On this mountain, the LORD of hosts will make for all peoples a feast of rich food, a feast of well-aged wines, of rich foods filled with marrow, of well-aged wines strained clear.' The messianic banquet features in apocalyptic texts such as *1 En.* 62.12–14: 'the righteous and elect ones . . . shall eat and rise with that Son of Man for ever and ever'. Significantly, it is referred to almost in commonplace terms even in rabbinic literature, as for instance in *Pirke Aboth* 3.20; 4.21 (cf. *Ex. R.* 25.8).

The most significant reference for our purposes is in the literature of the Qumran community. While the messianism of this Jewish sect is not entirely systematic, the text known as 1QSa describes the banquet that would attend the Messiah's arrival: 'Next the Messiah of Israel shall enter, and the heads of the thousands of Israel shall sit before him each according to his rank. . . . When they solemnly meet together at a table of communion or to drink the wine . . . The Messiah of Israel shall stretch out his hand to the bread' (1QSa 2.17–21). Communal meals were a regular feature of the Qumran community, as they were of the early Christians. This particular meal described in 1QSa seems to be something other than the communal meal that was celebrated regularly at

Qumran. It is a final meal, a messianic meal, celebrated once the Messiah(s) had arrived on the scene, with the intention of declaring that a new and eschatological phase had arrived in the community's existence (and that of Israel beyond it).

The familiarity of the messianic banquet in apocalyptic circles, combined with the strong evidence that Jesus and the disciples thought about him as Messiah and that their arrival in Jerusalem had brought matters to a head, suggests this may be a plausible interpretation of the Last Supper. I repeat the point that this is conjecture on my part and that nothing about Jesus' last days in Jerusalem can be made the subject of definitive interpretation, as scholar after scholar has acknowledged. My interpretation takes seriously the messianic self-consciousness of Jesus, the climactic nature of his last appearance in Jerusalem and the observation that his deeds on that occasion can be held to form a sequence once the hypothesis of apocalyptic secrecy is acknowledged as having something to contribute to interpretation.

On my view, at the Last Supper the Messiah takes his place among the tribes of Israel as represented by the twelve disciples who have already been identified as tribal presidents or figureheads (Mt. 19.28/Lk. 22.30). They celebrate the feast which inaugurates the eschatological age. The meaning of this symbolism (and indeed the feast itself) was known only by Jesus and the disciples. They believed that, in acting in this way, they had established the conditions which allowed God to act according to their apocalyptic paradigm. The scene was set for something much greater to occur, which Jesus and the disciples understood in terms of imminent divine intervention.

My argument is (as Schweitzer recognized) that we should pay careful attention to the deeds as well as to the words of Jesus. Jesus' actions in appointing twelve disciples and in journeying to Jerusalem *meant* something. These events in Jerusalem were 'messianic acts'. They were intended to signify and to effect the eschatological climax. That was their meaning. Acting on behalf of God, Jesus entered Jerusalem as Messiah, established himself there with the leaders of the eschatological Israel and celebrated the messianic banquet. The Last Supper forged the link between the promise and the fulfilment of eschatology. It constituted both a challenge to God to act and a declaration that God was about to act. In celebrating the messianic banquet, Jesus boldly opened the door to divine intervention. He crossed the Rubicon, demonstrating the 'all or nothing' of his trust in God. This was the final act of the Messiah who had prayed, 'Thy kingdom come!'

Immediately after the Supper, Jesus and his disciples go to the Mount of Olives (Mk 14.26). While this should not be pressed further than it deserves, there is a little evidence in Jewish tradition that the Mount of Olives was a place with eschatological associations.[62] If the Last Supper was undergirded by eschatological fervour, albeit with all the uncertainty surrounding the death of Jesus, there is nothing unusual about the fact that Jesus should go to a place associated with the divine glory and with resurrection. We have yet to consider the question of Jesus and the Son of Man. So far, however, we have found reasons for seeing the Last Supper as an event of momentous importance. In Jesus' mind, it was conceivably the final event that would 'bring on' the kingdom. We can only ponder what went through his mind as he left the upper room. The very least we can say is that his exit was fraught with possibilities.

The Role of Judas Iscariot

A further point to consider is the role of Judas Iscariot. Judas is the traditional villain of the Gospels.[63] Regarded as the 'betrayer' of Jesus, his name has become synonymous with multifarious forms of malice and deceit in all subsequent history.[64] On my reconstruction of events, it is possible that Judas suffered a failure of nerve rather than of loyalty. If Jesus expected God to act following the messianic banquet, a possible explanation of Judas' behaviour is that he began to doubt whether God would intervene in the manner Jesus had promised. Judas therefore took matters into his own hands. He went to the chief priests and told them what they wanted to know: that Jesus and his disciples thought about him as the Messiah. He did this to secure the public recognition of Jesus, acting with the same impetuosity that is sometimes predicated of Simon Peter. Judas acted against orders but with good intent. Judas' crime was to break the apocalyptic secrecy which Jesus had imposed and to force the climax by human means rather than through the divine intervention which Jesus had anticipated. In doing this, he created the conditions which led to the arrest of Jesus and his subsequent death (and resurrection).

Post-Easter Secrecy

Further evidence to support the theory that Jesus was concerned with apocalyptic secrecy comes from Christian circles after Easter. It concerns the protection of the so-called sacred formula (i.e. the words of eucharistic institution). Jeremias observes that the eucharistic narrative is absent from John's Gospel in such a way as to suggest that its author 'did not want to reveal the sacred formula to the general public'.[65] Jeremias inserts this Johannine silence into a wider pattern of secrecy in post-Easter Christianity which he thinks derived from Jesus himself. He notes the tendency of early Christianity to keep esoteric certain eschatological teachings, the deepest secrets of Christology and the secrets of the divine nature.

One does not have to agree with Jeremias' reconstruction of the extent of Jesus' secret teaching to recognize that the esotericism of post-Easter Christianity was in all probability related to the esotericism of

Jesus himself. It is certainly harder to account for the rise of Christian esotericism in the wake of an entirely non-apocalyptic Jesus than to argue for a continuity between the two on the hypothesis that the secrecy of the Jesus movement blossomed into the secrecy of the primitive church.

This is all by way of advocating the thesis that, with appropriate caution, apocalyptic secrecy undergirded the Jesus movement to the extent that it provided a way of thinking which set belief in Jesus' messiahship in the context of a definite eschatological scheme. Jesus evidently viewed himself as the Jewish Messiah and his movement as embodying the restoration of Israel through which God was acting and would finally intervene to reveal the Messiah and the new community once Jesus was present in Jerusalem. Until God intervened, Jesus chose to keep his messiahship and the nature of that community secret so that its revelation would be a divine task alone. The device of apocalyptic secrecy does much to explain the self-understanding of the Jesus movement; especially the events of Holy Week and the heightening of eschatological hope which prevailed at that time.

Did Jesus Expect to Die?

We shall briefly consider the question of whether Jesus expected to die. Although again ambiguity will remain the byword in this area, we should consider the evidence and see how it coheres with what has been said already.

The celebration of the messianic banquet by Jesus and his disciples did not mean that everything had by then been accomplished. The banquet signified that conditions were ripe for God to act. Jesus turned to God to act eschatologically in a symbolic meal which was effectively a dramatic form of prayer. This was not so much a last and desperate attempt to force God's hand, which is how Schweitzer interpreted Jesus' journey to Jerusalem, as an acted petition that God would act in the promised eschatological manner. This celebration of the Last Supper reveals an astonishing trust in God which rested on biblical foundations.

The question of whether Jesus expected to die has been variously posed and answered in the history of research – with no final agreement about how the evidence is to be interpreted.[66] One can see that Jesus might have expected some formal investigation with a predictable outcome were his messiahship to become public knowledge; but we cannot know when or in what form he thought that this would happen. Nothing in Mark's version of the Last Supper and its immediate aftermath *demands* the theory that Jesus expected to die, except the statement of 14.28 ('But after I am raised up, I will go before you to Galilee') whose specifics imply that it may have been introduced into the tradition at a subsequent point. The words of institution and the much-cited Mk

14.25 ('Truly I tell you, I will never again drink of the fruit of the vine until the day when I drink it new in the kingdom of God') are altogether more ambiguous. Mk 14.25 might mean that Jesus expected the kingdom to appear immediately and thus that he would celebrate the event which the banquet had inaugurated. It is only in the Christian retelling of the event that a definitive theology of martyrdom is added to cohere with the known fact that Jesus died and the belief that he had been revealed as a divine being in the resurrection. In this sense, me wonders how much Mk 14. 22–24 owes to post-Easter knowledge.

We should thus allow the ambiguity of Mark's Gospel to speak for itself once the likely provenance of Mk 14.28 is acknowledged. The evidence does not conclusively indicate that Jesus expected to die following the Last Supper.[67] Indeed, the element of apocalyptic secrecy draws away from that theory if Jesus celebrated the messianic banquet as a means of inaugurating the kingdom. To my mind, Jesus' standing as an apocalyptic figure suggests a mentality dominated by the belief that God would act and which delegated the significant action to him, rendering it unnecessary for Jesus to work out a plan for the future beyond the belief that God would intervene. I therefore regard it as an 'open question' whether Jesus either predicted his death or gave it a sacrificial interpretation in the way that Christian tradition records. What we can, however, conclude with some certainty is that Jesus expected God to act eschatologically in the aftermath of the Last Supper and that he regarded the final 'bringing-in' of the kingdom as a divine task for which the messianic party could make ready – as they did – but not themselves effect.

Jesus and the Son of Man

We now turn to what has been recognized as the most difficult question of all. This is the question of whether Jesus anticipated 'the Son of Man' as a heavenly mediator distinct from himself; and if he did, how he contemplated the distinctive roles of himself and that mediator in effecting the eschatological climax.

Here we enter territory that is among the most disputed of all New Testament issues.[68] In a number of passages, Jesus speaks of a figure called 'the Son of Man'. In some of these passages, it seems that 'the Son of Man' is a cipher for himself. This is particularly obvious in the so-called 'passion predictions' (Mk 8.31; 9.31; 10.33 and parallels) where Jesus speaks in the third person of the future suffering of this figure. In other passages, however, the Son of Man is apparently a heavenly figure and his connection with Jesus seems more remote. An obvious example is Jesus' promise to the high priest in Mk 14.62 and parallels, ' "you will see the Son of Man seated at the right hand of the Power", and "coming with the clouds of heaven." ' The 'Son of Man problem', as it has been called, lies in deciding whether Jesus himself used this form of words; if he did, whether he used them as a title; and if he did that, whether he used them as a title for himself. The only thing that can be said with certainty is that this problem does not permit of easy resolution.

We can narrow down the frame of reference for this discussion. Of the many occurrences of 'Son of Man' in the New Testament, all but three (Acts 7.56; Rev. 1.13; 14.14) are in the Gospels. In the Gospels, the phrase always occurs on the lips of Jesus, except for Jn 12.34 where the crowd ask about the Son of Man's identity. The title also occurs in *Gos. Thom.* 86. It is always introduced without comment and generally without explanation. Scholars often divide the 'Son of Man' sayings into three categories: those that concern the Son of Man's present activity, his future suffering and his heavenly activity. There are passages in the Gospels which illustrate all of these (see below).

Merely a Periphrasis?

The first question to resolve is what 'Son of Man' actually means. This is the question of whether or not it is used as a title in the Gospels. Vermes and Casey point to a proposed Aramaic background of these words and argue that they constitute a periphrasis on the part of the speaker for 'I' or 'me', so that they are not a title as such, either for the speaker or for anyone else.[69] The relevant evidence comes from rabbinic sources. Thus *j.Ber.* 3b reports R. Simeon ben Yohai (second century CE) as saying, 'If I had stood on Mount Sinai when the Torah was given to Israel, I would have asked the Merciful One to create two mouths for *bar nasha*, one for the study of the Torah and one for the provision of all his needs.' Here, *bar nasha* ('son of man') might mean humankind generally, an Israelite in particular or the speaker exclusively. Vermes (probably correctly) claims the third as the most plausible possibility. From the third century CE he cites the question of Rab Kahana to R. Johanan, 'If *bar nash* is despised by his mother, but honoured by another of his father's wives, where should he go?' Here again the speaker appears to be identifying himself in a circumlocutional way. Vermes argues from this evidence that in Galilean Aramaic 'son of man' was used as a circumlocutional reference to the self. It was used on occasions where death and humiliation were mentioned, to avoid dealing with difficult topics or when the avoidance of the first person was motivated by reserve and modesty.

On this view, the Christians converted what had been a periphrasis used by Jesus into a title for Jesus in the light of what was believed about the resurrection. Where Jesus had spoken of himself discreetly as 'son of man', the early Christians called him '*the* Son of Man' in a unique and titular sense.

This view links Jesus' sayings with the later rabbinic evidence but it poses more than one difficulty.[70] An obvious problem is that the Aramaic evidence cannot be proved to go back to the time of Jesus. We simply do not know that this periphrasis was common in first-century Galilee. On this interpretation, the earliest evidence for it comes from the Gospels themselves. We must then ask why the shift from periphrasis to title occurred and why, on that theory, the title does not feature more prominently in the New Testament when it is a central feature of the Synoptic Christology.

Moreover, the theory suits some of the 'Son of Man' sayings better than it suits others. Thus it provides a plausible background to Mk 2.10, where Jesus states that the Son of Man has authority on earth to forgive sins. Yet it makes much less sense of Mk 14.62 where Jesus promises the high priest a vision of the Son of Man in a context where it seems that the night-time vision in Dan. 7.13-14 is being recalled.

The periphrastic approach to the 'Son of Man' problem thus results in something of an *impasse*. On the one hand, we have a link with later Jewish evidence which it would be wrong to deny. On the other, this later evidence itself raises questions that are only incompletely satisfied by the Gospels. The shift from periphrasis to title is harder to explain than its advocates suggest. For this reason, we shall cast the net more widely to explain the 'Son of Man' sayings in the Gospels.

An Apocalyptic Background?

Scholars have also investigated the apocalyptic or visionary background of the Son of Man title. The use of a slightly different phrase in Dan. 7.13-14 ('one like a human being'), together with the use of 'Son of Man' as a title for a heavenly mediator in the *Similitudes of Enoch* (first century CE) and relevant material in *4 Ezra* (late first century CE), provides important comparative material, which is earlier than Vermes' rabbinic evidence, for the use of this phrase in the Gospels.[71] We shall examine each of these passages to assess the relevant material.

Daniel 7
Daniel 7 narrates the seer's vision of the heavenly court.[72] Chapter 7 marks the shift in the book from the court-tales which describe life in the Babylonian empire to the author's own visions of the heavenly world. Daniel 7 opens with a scene of chaos in which four beasts come up from the sea and exercise a terrible effect on those who witness them (Dan. 7.1-8).[73] The last beast has ten horns and grows another (Dan. 7.7-8). It is said of this last horn that 'there were eyes like human eyes in this horn, and a mouth speaking arrogantly' (Dan. 7.8).

Dan. 7.9 describes the seer's vision of the heavenly court through which this picture is set in perspective and overcome. 'As I watched, thrones were set in place, and an Ancient One took his throne.' This 'Ancient One' is God himself. The heavenly court sits in judgment and its ledgers are opened (Dan. 7.10). At this point Daniel reports that 'I saw one like a human being coming with the clouds of heaven. And he came to the Ancient One and was presented before him.' (Dan. 7.13) This subordinate figure is given 'dominion and glory and kingship, that all people, nations and languages should serve him' (Dan. 7.14). It is said that 'his dominion is an everlasting dominion that shall not pass away, and his kingship is one that shall never be destroyed' (Dan. 7.14 also).

This presentation of a subordinate at the heavenly court is not the end of Daniel's vision. Daniel asks an angel the meaning of what he has seen (Dan. 7.16). He is told that the four beasts symbolize four kingdoms (Dan. 7.23). The little horn on this view stands for Antiochus IV Epiphanes (Dan. 7.25). At the outbreak of his repression 'the court shall sit in judgment, and his dominion shall be taken away, to be consumed and totally destroyed' (Dan. 7.26). The result of this judgment is that, in the words of Dan. 7.27, 'the kingship and dominion and the greatness of the kingdoms under the whole heaven shall be given to the people of the holy ones of the Most High.'

This conclusion of the vision gives the revelation its meaning. The situation that Daniel describes is a thinly veiled pastiche of the Antiochian crisis, in the course of which the temple had been defiled in Jerusalem.[74] Daniel's vision of order proceeding from chaos is a promise that all will be well despite the persecution that had been launched against pious Jews at that time.[75] The presentation of 'one like a human being' at the heavenly court (Dan. 7.13-14) is connected with the acquisition of king-ship and dominion by those who are said to be 'the people of the holy ones of the Most High' in 7.27. These are the pious in Israel. They are promised a successful outcome despite what Antiochus and his sup-porters were doing in the Jewish capital. The social meaning of the vision is that the pious will prove victorious with heavenly support despite the superior forces which had been unleashed against them.

The identity of the subordinate figure in Daniel 7 has long puzzled commentators.[76] It used to be thought that he was merely a symbol in the prophet's dream, like the beasts who come out of the sea in Dan. 7.1-8.[77] An alternative suggestion of John J. Collins, however, has now firmly established itself in the scholarly mind.[78] This is that the 'one like a human being' is an angel analogous to or perhaps even identical with Michael who appears as Israel's heavenly patron in Daniel 10–12. On this view, Daniel 7 offers a visionary glimpse into the heavenly court and the author sees the moment when Israel's patron angel is proclaimed vic-torious there. In the apocalyptic logic of the vision, this means that nothing can stop the triumph of the faithful in Israel despite the factions opposing them. The mediator's heavenly installation anticipates the earthly triumph of the righteous.

This second interpretation has much to commend it. Daniel is domin-ated by the apocalyptic thought-world with its sharp division between earth and heaven which is also, albeit secondarily, the distinction between the present and the future. Angels play a prominent role in Daniel.[79] As early as Daniel 3, an angel occupies the fiery furnace with Daniel's friends. Angels mediate visions in Daniel 8, 9 and 10. Gabriel is mentioned by name in Dan. 8.16 and 9.21; Michael in 10.13 and 12.1. The reference in Dan. 7.13 to 'one like a human being' recalls the statement of Dan. 3.25 that 'four men unbound' were seen in the fiery furnace and that the fourth 'has the appearance of a god'; not to mention the description of Gabriel as 'having the appearance of a man' in Dan. 8.15. Although the figure of 7.13 is not identified by name, his connection with the heavenly court and his prominence there are evident in the text. It hardly stretches credulity to see this figure as an angel even if, as so often in apocalyptic visions, some of the details and imagery remain obscure and the figure in question is not identified. The most important thing is for the interpreter to ask about the social meaning which corresponds to the apocalyptic vision; and, given Daniel's situation, that is not in doubt.

The Similitudes of Enoch

The figure in Dan. 7.13-14 is described in the comparative: 'one like a human being', not '*the* Son of Man' of the Gospels. Nothing in the text of Daniel 7 indicates that he is the Messiah, although later exegesis understood him in that way.[80] Two passages from the first century CE, not themselves influenced by Christian theology, show how this passage was understood in the later apocalyptic tradition.[81]

The *Similitudes of Enoch* (*1 En.* 37–71), which form part of the composite *1 Enoch*, allude to Daniel 7 in more than one place.[82] In *1 En.* 46.1 it is said, 'And there I saw one who had a head of days, and his head (was) white like wool; and with him (there was) another, whose face had the appearance of a man . . .'. In *1 En.* 48.2 'that Son of Man was given a name in the presence of the Lord of the Spirits'. *1 En.* 62.7 adds that 'the Son of Man was concealed from the beginning, and the Most High One preserved him in the presence of his power; then he revealed him to the holy and the elect ones'; 62.9 continues that 'on that day, all the kings, the governors, the high officials, and those who rule the earth shall fall down before him on their faces, and worship and raise their hopes in that Son of Man'. This pleading is in vain, and results in their punishment by the mediator. Similar activities are predicated by the *Similitudes* to a mediator with a variety of other titles, notably 'Chosen One' and 'Anointed One'. Despite the variation, it seems that one and the same figure is described in this way so that the *Similitudes* present a coherent picture of judgment with symbolic variation in the title accorded the judge. *1 En.* 48.10; 52.4 identify this figure as the Messiah.

The *Similitudes* possibly close by identifying Enoch with the Son of Man ('You, son of man, who art born in righteousness'; *1 En.* 71.14).[83] This passage was the subject of an exegetical dispute in the last century. R.H. Charles emended the text to remove the identification of the Son of Man with Enoch.[84] More recently, John J. Collins has changed his mind on this matter. In his early work he argued that *1 En.* 71.14 was a secondary addition to the *Similitudes* which identified the mediator with Enoch, possibly as a Jewish rejoinder to Christian association of Jesus with the figure mentioned by Daniel.[85] In a 1992 article, however, Collins argues that 'son of man' in 71.14 is merely a nominative or vocative address to Enoch as a human being so that no such identification is intended.[86]

Whatever the resolution of this dispute, the *Similitudes of Enoch* show that 'Son of Man' was an established title for a heavenly mediator in at least some apocalyptic circles in first-century Judaism. The *Similitudes* offer a creative exegesis of Daniel in which fresh meaning is derived from that text. They articulate the world-view and self-understanding of a particular group – by no means necessarily a large one – in the late first century. This text expects that its mediator will discharge eschatological judgment. It seems that those who wrote the *Similitudes* found themselves uncomfortable with existing power structures and looked to eschatological intervention to redress this problem.[87]

The meaning of the 'Son of Man' title in the *Similitudes* deserves consideration.[88] It seems unlikely that this text was influenced by Christian theology. In view of what Collins now thinks, it is probably even questionable whether the *Similitudes* identify Enoch with the heavenly mediator in a way that provides a *close* parallel to Christian beliefs about Jesus. There certainly is nothing approaching Christian soteriology in the *Similitudes*. Instead, we find the hope that God will intervene on behalf of the righteous without any reference to human sacrifice or resurrection (let alone an earthly appearance of the Son of Man). The date of the *Similitudes* is a significant factor. The absence of any evidence that the author knew Christian theology is an argument in favour of a date in the early part of the first century CE. In this case it is possible, but by no means certain, that Jesus was using a title that was already current in at least one apocalyptic circle of Judaism. One possible – even plausible – way of reading the *Similitudes* is to conclude that its exegesis of Daniel 7 is original to that text and is not dependent on external influence. In this case, we should probably conclude that the Gospels and the *Similitudes* make independent use of the 'Son of Man' title in an apocalyptic ambience whose precise contours continue to elude us. It would appear impossible at this stage to unearth a full understanding of how Daniel 7 was interpreted in first-century Jewish apocalypticism.

4 Ezra

The other relevant text is *4 Ezra* 13, which comes from the late first century CE.[89] This passage describes how 'something like the figure of a man' comes up from the sea and flies with the clouds of heaven (*4 Ezra* 13.3). On this man's appearance 'an innumerable multitude' gather to make war against him (*4 Ezra* 13.5). The man carves himself a great mountain and consumes his opponents with breath from his mouth (*4 Ezra* 13.10–11). He is then joined by a peaceful multitude (*4 Ezra* 13.12–13). In the interpretation that follows, this man is described as 'he whom the Most High has been keeping for many ages, who will himself deliver his creation' (*4 Ezra* 13.26). Although this is not a specific messianic identification, both *4 Ezra* 7.28 and 12.32 expect the Messiah to be revealed at some future point. This makes it difficult not to read 13.26 in the light of these earlier passages. *4 Ezra* 13.35 identifies the mountain as Mount Zion, reinforcing the probable messianic allusion. Further reinforcement comes in 13.37 where the man in question is called 'my son', which is a title that the Hebrew Bible uses for the king.

Despite the reluctance of Helge Kvanvig to accept this conclusion,[90] it seems indisputable that *4 Ezra* 13 constitutes a further allusion to Daniel 7. Michael Stone has examined the prehistory of this chapter.[91] He thinks that *4 Ezra* 13 is an independent section, reinterpreted but not composed by the author of *4 Ezra* himself. Stone thinks that this source drew on Daniel 7, much as the author of *4 Ezra* himself used Daniel 7 in chapter 12 where the sea and the twelve kings are mentioned. Stone's conclusion is that 'the Son of Man' was not readily identifiable to his readers as a familiar concept, hence the author's reluctance to use that title, but that an allusion to Dan. 7.13 is certainly made in this text. This tends to confirm what we saw about the *Similitudes*, that there was no Son of Man *concept* as such in first-century Judaism; but there was indeed an exegetical interest in Daniel 7 which different circles explored in different ways.

Although the *Similitudes* and *4 Ezra* were not, so far as we know, connected, they share some common features with indications about the way in which Daniel 7 was understood in first-century Judaism. The figure mentioned by both texts is a specific individual who is identified as the Messiah. He is also understood as a heavenly being. This evidence shows something of the direction in which interpretation of Daniel 7 was travelling in the period of Christian origins. It provides us with ammunition with which to return to the 'Son of Man' problem in the Gospels.

The Son of Man in the Gospels

There is no doubt that the Gospels describe the Son of Man as a heavenly mediator and identify him with Jesus. The Gospels are also adamant that Jesus is the Messiah (see e.g. Mk 1.1). The question is whether this understanding of the phrase, including its messianic association, represents the authentic belief of Jesus himself. Allied to this are the questions of what, if any, of this Jewish apocalyptic material illustrates Jesus' usage of this phrase; and how the early church shaped the tradition of Jesus' sayings.

That Jesus used the phrase 'the Son of Man' is certain in view of its attestation in all four Gospels. The attempt to decide which of the two proposed Jewish backgrounds best suits the material is hampered by the different categories into which the Son of Man sayings fall. We saw that some sayings make good sense on the periphrastic hypothesis, but that others are less easy to explain on this theory. In Mk 14.62 a reference to Dan. 7.13-14 can hardly be denied. In Matthew's Gospel, particularly, the Son of Man is introduced as a heavenly mediator (see especially Mt. 13.41, 'The Son of Man will send his angels . . .'). This evidence complicates the periphrastic theory and poses an exegetical dilemma. Did Jesus use the phrase to describe his present activity, his future suffering and his heavenly glory; or were one or more of these categories set on his lips by the Christians after Easter?

It is certainly possible that Jesus used the phrase in the periphrastic sense. This is suggested by Mk 2.10, 28. In this case, we must conclude that the Gospels offer the earliest evidence for the circumlocutionary sense of 'Son of Man'. The only alternatives to this view would be to conclude, either that Jesus referred to himself as 'the Son of Man' in the titular sense, or that this titular usage was read back into Mk 2.10, 28 after Easter. These questions can only be resolved by considering whether those references which link Jesus with a heavenly mediator are also authentic to Jesus.

Two arguments have convinced me that they are. The first is essentially a negative argument. It seems implausible that, after Easter, the Christians should have seized on a periphrasis used by Jesus, converted it into a title and applied it to Jesus, only for that title then to disappear beyond the Synoptic tradition. I concede that such an occurrence is *possible*, particularly if Daniel 7 featured among the proof-texts that were culled by the Christians to support their views about Jesus; but I regard it as much more likely that the title derived in some form from Jesus himself and that it is preserved in the Gospel tradition for this reason. This is an argument based on relative probability.

More positively, Ed Sanders draws attention to convincing parallels between two Matthaean 'Son of Man' sayings and a passage in Paul's earliest letter:[92]

For this we declare to you by the word of the Lord, that we who are alive, who are left until the *coming of the Lord*, will by no means precede those who have died. For *the Lord* himself, with a cry of command, with the *archangel's* call and with the *sound of God's trumpet*, will *descend* from *heaven*, and the dead in Christ will rise first. Then we who are alive, who are left, will be *caught up* in the clouds together with them to meet the Lord in the air; (1 Thess. 4.15-17)

For *the Son of Man* is to come with his *angels* in the glory of his Father, and then he will repay everyone for what has been done. Truly I tell you, there are some standing here who *will not taste death* before they see the Son of Man coming in his kingdom. (Mt. 16.27-8)

Then the sign of the *Son of Man will appear* in heaven, and then all the tribes of the earth will mourn, and they will see '*the Son of Man coming* on the clouds of heaven' with power and great glory. And he will send out his *angels with a loud trumpet call*, and they will *gather* his elect from the four winds, from one end of heaven to the other. (Mt. 24.30-31)

Despite the differences between them, these passages all attest essentially the same saying. This asserts that a heavenly mediator will appear on earth with the sound of a trumpet. Paul adds to this saying his concern about the dead in Christ; Matthew modifies it to assert that only some will be alive at the eschatological climax. In this context Paul also replaces 'the Son of Man' with 'the Lord', which for him is a more familiar title.

This agreement discloses a saying which is older than the oldest New Testament document (1 Thessalonians) and whose source is the oral tradition deriving from Jesus. It is obvious that Paul's 'Lord' is a heavenly mediator. This is true also of Matthew's 'Son of Man'. Matthew 24 clearly alludes to Daniel 7, mentioning a named figure called '*the* Son of Man'. Since Paul preserves the essential content of the saying and modifies only the title – perhaps because he was writing for Gentile readers? – it seems fruitless to deny the possibility that Jesus did speak about 'the Son of Man' as a heavenly mediator, given its attestation across the entirety of the earliest Christian tradition that we can access.

Who is this Son of Man?

If my two arguments are accepted, there was more than one stage in the formation of our present 'Son of Man' sayings. Jesus apparently used 'son of man' in a periphrastic sense and also spoke of '*the* Son of Man' in a mediatorial sense similar to the *Similitudes of Enoch*. This does not in the first instance mean Jesus thought that Daniel's apocalyptic vision described *his own* activity. The evidence of these two Matthaean passages suggests a different understanding. There, 'the Son of Man' is by no means obviously identified with Jesus himself. Only in the Pauline version is this the case; and that is the result of a simple change of title. In the passages cited from Matthew – which can be paralleled throughout the Synoptic tradition – Jesus speaks of a mediator whom he distinguishes from himself. That mediator is presented as an apocalyptic figure who impinges onto the earthly scene by entry into it from the heavenly world.

Further evidence to support this view comes from Mk 8.38 and parallels. In this saying, Jesus formally distinguishes between himself and the Son of Man while noting a close affinity between their activity in terms of what will happen at the eschatological climax: 'Those who are ashamed of me and of my words in this adulterous and sinful generation, of them the Son of Man will also be ashamed when he comes in the glory of his Father with the holy angels.' This use of 'the Son of Man' is clearly titular and not a periphrasis. Moreover, the title appears to identify a figure other than Jesus himself; Jesus distinguishes between himself and the Son of Man in a way which differentiates their roles. The Son of Man is presented as the eschatological judge. Jesus makes the determining factor in how people will be judged by the Son of Man the issue of how they react to his own words now. The difference between the two figures is that Jesus is the Messiah who proclaims God's kingdom; the Son of Man is a heavenly mediator who will usher in that kingdom at God's behest.

Despite the separation of the two figures, it is clear that there is a moral or a collegial unity between them. This amounts to a very high Christology. Reaction to Jesus is made the criterion of impending judgment. The Son of Man (merely) acts on the information received. This implies that Jesus thought his own messianic authority ranked *above* that of the Son of Man, even though the Son of Man was a heavenly mediator. Jesus' claim to be united with God's eschatological action in a unique and specific way cannot be ignored here.

This seems to be the conclusion to the problem we have been considering in this chapter. Jesus evidently thought that, following the Last Supper, God would send the Son of Man as a heavenly mediator to introduce the kingdom on God's behalf. The preliminary task of Jesus as Messiah was to take up residence in the Jewish capital, surrounded by the twelve. There, they would be identified by the mediator when he appeared. The Triumphal Entry, the Cleansing of the Temple and the Last Supper all prepared for this eschatological climax by assembling the *dramatis personae* and by doing everything necessary to anticipate the Messiah's apocalyptic revelation.

The Messiah and the twelve not only symbolized but also embodied the restored Israel *in nuce*. What they did looked forward to the advent of the Son of Man, when the meaning of the events they performed secretly would become a matter of public revelation. The cleansing of the temple meant for Jesus that the replacement of the temple by God was imminent. The celebration of the Last Supper left nothing else to be done: its status as *the* banquet – the messianic banquet – meant for Jesus that the eschatological climax had arrived. This secrecy had a forward-looking aspect. It depended on the belief that the meaning of the Cleansing and the Supper would become clear when the apocalyptic intervention occurred. Its successful preservation (until Judas acted unilaterally) confirms the extent to which eschatology undergirded the hopes and expectations of the Jesus movement.

My Jesus thus apparently expected the appearance of the Son of Man at the end of the messianic banquet. Jesus thought that this mediator would effect the public revelation of himself as Messiah and the new

dimensions of Israel as represented by the twelve. Jesus would then preside as Messiah over the restored Israel, which would have the nature of a
theocracy where the divine will was obeyed. These events show an
irreversible trust in God – a Rubicon, as I called them – and I think also
represented a bold prayer that God would act in the expected manner. It
is in fact astonishing to ponder what was going through the mind of Jesus
at the Last Supper. The journey to the Mount of Olives (Mk 14.26)
rightly demands a response from each interpreter.[93]

On this view, the achievement of the Christian community after
Easter was to make the thoroughgoing identification of Jesus with the
Son of Man, which is reflected in the present form of the Gospels, in a
way that Jesus himself apparently did not do. The reason why this was
done will only become fully clear when we have considered the trial of
Jesus and studied the earliest Christian evidence for the resurrection.
Here, however, we must note that – at least to some extent – Jesus'
expectation of the immediate appearance of the Son of Man was frustrated by his arrest and subsequent execution. In the light of what
transpired eventually, the Christians reworked Jesus' belief about the
Son of Man into the identification of Jesus with the Son of Man combined with the hope that Jesus would return from heaven to preside
over God's kingdom Israel. The extent to which these hopes were con-
tinuous with what Jesus himself believed will be examined in Part III of
this book.

THE TRIAL OF JESUS

All of this represents an astonishing eschatological confidence. It is the confidence of someone who was so utterly convinced of his status as Messiah and by the promise of divine intervention that he neither stopped to work out a blueprint of what life would be like after the intervention nor imagined for one moment that God would fail to fulfil his promise. This is why I have revised my earlier view that Jesus expected to die in the course of this fulfilment. He may have been aware of official opprobium in the wake of the Cleansing of the Temple; but I believe that such fears were marginalized by the strength of his trust in God, which dominated his perspective to the extent that he never contemplated the possibility of failure up to and including the occasion of the Last Supper.

Perhaps this is why Judas has been cast as the traitor in Christian tradition.[1] The fact that Jesus was inevitably disappointed called for an explanation of what had gone wrong. This was done variously through emerging convictions about his resurrection and possibly by further thinking on the part of Jesus himself after his arrest. It was also done by making Judas the villain of the piece. Jesus was arrested following some kind of contact between Judas and the priestly authorities. I have suggested Judas probably told them the inner secrets of the Jesus movement. This alone would have warranted investigation and probably also the involvement of the Roman administration. We saw in Chapter 14 that Jesus' last days in Jerusalem were marked by increasing antagonism towards him by the priestly authorities on account of his behaviour in the temple. I drew attention to the statement of Mk 11.18 and parallels that 'when the chief priests and the scribes heard it, they kept looking for a way to kill him'. It seems that, following this incident, Jesus was a marked man when previously he had been barely distinguishable in Jerusalem. Mark's Gospel gathers pace from this moment onwards. Jesus now appears in a significant number of disputes with Jewish representatives (Mark 12). Mark 13 is the future-oriented passage often called the Synoptic Eschatological Discourse.[2] In Mark 14, before Mark narrates the Last Supper, he states again that before the Passover festival 'the chief priests and the scribes were looking for a way to arrest Jesus by stealth and kill him' (14.1). This statement forms the immediate prelude to the trial and death of Jesus which we shall consider in this chapter.

The Role of Judas Iscariot

I want to probe further the role of Judas Iscariot in the betrayal and arrest of Jesus.[3]

Jesus was arrested in the Garden of Gethsemane (Mk 14.32) when Judas accompanied the temple police to this location (Mk 14.43). There is a prevalent assumption among many people that what Judas 'betrayed' was the location of the secret place where Jesus used to go with his disciples. This hypothesis is intrinsically unlikely.[4] As history shows, every nation worth its salt has an intelligence service. One can hardly imagine that things were different in first-century Palestine, especially given the difficult political climate and the competing Jewish factions. The Romans had collaborators. The priestly authorities no doubt had spies. It would have been entirely easy and practicable for Jesus to be followed had the discovery of his secret place been the point at issue. Nor indeed is the Garden of Gethsemane particularly difficult to find.[5] It may even have been known that Jesus used to go there. Furthermore, for the priestly authorities to bribe one of Jesus' supporters was to run the risk of 'double bluffing'. That might have been considered dangerous given that Jesus was suspected of harbouring revolutionary tendencies.

The circumstances of Jesus' arrest point to a different explanation of the role of Judas Iscariot. This was suggested by Albert Schweitzer at the beginning of the last century and revived by Ed Sanders towards its end. We saw in Chapters 13 and 14 that the Jesus movement understood itself as an apocalyptic circle in which certain key beliefs were kept secret, to be disclosed when the kingdom finally came. Judas helped the priestly authorities out of a difficulty. They were outraged by Jesus' cleansing of the temple, but it is clear from the succeeding narrative that they were not really sure what Jesus was about. Various people ask Jesus nuanced questions in Mark 12, yet all that he does is to tease them with talk about the Messiah. He never provides a clear and unambiguous description of himself and his movement which would have given the authorities full understanding (and thus a reason to remove him). My strong view is that this concealment was deliberate and part of the inner logic of the Jesus movement.

I have suggested that Judas broke rank with Jesus over the issue of apocalyptic secrecy and, instead of waiting for God to act as Jesus had instructed, he went to the high priest in an abortive attempt to secure the public revelation of Jesus as Messiah.[6] This act was rash, but not inherently wicked. Judas may have been frustrated by the delay in the divine intervention or become convinced that God needed a human agent (other than Jesus and the Son of Man) to make the revelation. In any event, Judas told the chief priests what they wanted to know. They had previously mistrusted Jesus but not yet discovered enough to arrest him, despite informal consultations. Jesus at this stage was known to be the leader of a band of people, to have done something offensive in the temple and to have spoken about living as the people of God. Jesus' action in the temple was irritating but not inherently culpable, but there was always the fear that he might do something similar again. Additionally, there was the fear (a realistic one, I have suggested) that Jesus and his group held private teaching which none but his group knew.[7] Such secrecy was viewed as suspicious and probably as potentially seditious. Fears about secrecy themselves fuelled the suspicion that Jesus was up to no good; even that he might cause a disturbance during Passover which was a traditional time of confrontation between the Romans and the Jews.[8] It is not difficult to imagine the worry that this unknown but increasingly prominent figure would have caused the priestly authorities at that time of year.

The chief priests leaped at Judas' offer to tell them what Jesus was about, offering him money in exchange for information (Mk 14.11). My view is that Judas told the priests the inner secrets of the Jesus movement. This was that Jesus thought about himself as Messiah, the king of Israel. There is no reason to suppose that Judas told the priests anything about Jesus threatening to incite rebellion or about any proposed alliance with Jewish revolutionary groups, neither of which Jesus himself can convincingly be said to have contemplated. The decisive information was the formal identification of Jesus as the Messiah. This gave the priests grounds to arrest Jesus, *a fortiori* at Passover time, as a threat to public stability.

The authenticity of Judas' participation in the arrest of Jesus is probably open to doubt.[9] Jesus was in the Garden of Gethsemane, no doubt enveloped in eschatological fervour. He was arrested without a struggle and brought to Jerusalem. Despite official concern about the disciples of Jesus (Jn 18.19), they were not arrested because they were not felt to pose the same threat as Jesus himself. This probably focuses attention on the alleged messiahship of Jesus as the substantial reason for his arrest.

The Trial of Jesus of Nazareth

The trial of Jesus bristles with problems of both a source-critical and an historical nature.[10] Leaving aside the occasional references to the trial in Jewish tradition (not to mention Roman sources), we have no fewer than three different accounts of the matter in the Gospels (Mark–Matthew; Luke; and John).[11] These different accounts pose substantial problems of interpretation. Broadly speaking, these problems concern the questions of whether the 'trial' of Jesus was a trial in a formal sense, and if so what were the grounds for the death penalty. There are subsidiary questions such as the status of the trial before Herod which Luke records, and the precise nature of the exchanges between the Jewish and the Roman authorities which were needed to secure the death of Jesus.

We begin by examining the primary sources. I shall amass the evidence before considering its interpretation.

Mark and Matthew

Mark records hostility to Jesus at an early point in his ministry. Mark 3.6 states that, after Jesus had healed on the sabbath, 'the Pharisees went out and immediately conspired with the Herodians against him, how to destroy him'.

Mark's passion narrative begins in Mark 14 with the repeated decision of the 'chief priests and the scribes' to arrest Jesus and kill him.[12] This is followed by the story of Jesus at the home of Simon the leper when the woman pours ointment on his feet (14.3-9). In 14.10-11 Judas goes to the high priests with his offer of betrayal; 14.12-25 narrates the Last Supper; in 14.26-31 Jesus and the disciples go to the Mount of Olives and in 14.32 to Gethsemane where Jesus prays; and in 14.46 Jesus is arrested. At 14.51-2 is the tantalizingly brief story of the young man who escapes arrest, and who has sometimes been identified as the author of Mark's Gospel.[13]

In 14.53 Jesus is taken to the house of the high priest, Simon Peter following at a discreet distance. In 14.55 it is said that 'the chief priests and the whole council were looking for testimony against Jesus to put him to death; but they found none'. And 14.56 adds that 'many gave false testimony against him, and their testimony did not agree'. Jesus is accused of saying that he would destroy the temple and replace it with another temple not made with hands (14.58). In 14.61 the high priest asks Jesus if he is the Messiah, to which Jesus replies, 'I am; and "you will see the Son of Man seated at the right hand of the Power", and "coming with the clouds of heaven" ' (14.62).[14] In 14.64 Jesus is convicted of blasphemy and sentenced to death; 14.66-72 is the story of Peter's denial.

At the beginning of Mark 15 Jesus is brought before Pilate. Pilate asks Jesus if he is the king of the Jews, to which he replies, 'You say so' (15.2). At 15.6 the story of the yearly release of a prisoner is introduced, mentioning Pilate's desire to have Jesus released instead of Barabbas.[15] The crowd call for Barabbas to be released and for Jesus to be crucified. In 15.16-20 Jesus is mocked by the soldiers. In 15.21-4 Simon of Cyrene is made to carry the cross.[16] Jesus is crucified and dies; his body is placed in the tomb of Joseph of Arimathea in the remaining part of Mark 15.

Matthew generally follows the order of Mark, but inserts incidental details of his own.[17] At Mt. 26.1-29 the Gospel describes Jesus in the house of Simon the leper and the Last Supper. In 26.30 Jesus and the disciples go to the Mount of Olives; in 26.36 they proceed to Gethsemane, where Judas arrives in 26.47. Jesus is then taken to the home of Caiaphas the high priest (26.57).[18] Similar charges are put as in Mark, but Jesus answers the high priest's question of whether he is the Messiah with the more ambiguous, 'You have said so' (26.64). In 26.65-6 Jesus is sentenced to death for blasphemy; at 26.69-75 the story is told of Peter's denial.

At the beginning of Matthew 27 Jesus is brought before Pilate; 27.3-10 is an inserted story about the repentance of Judas; in 27.11-14 Pilate asks Jesus if he is the king of the Jews, and he receives the same reply as in Mark. In 27.15-26 Pilate fails in his attempt to persuade the Jews to accept Barabbas and reluctantly delivers Jesus for crucifixion, against the advice of his wife. The rest of Matthew 27 narrates the mocking, the execution and the burial of Jesus. We should note the strongly worded comment of 27.25 where the Jewish people say, 'His blood be on us and on our children!'

Luke

Luke 22 opens with the wish of the priests to kill Jesus (22.2) and the statement that Satan entered into Judas Iscariot (22.3).[19] The Last Supper occupies 22.7-38; then at 22.39 Jesus and the disciples go to the Mount of Olives.[20] In 22.47 Judas arrives with the temple police, and at 22.54 Jesus is brought to the house of the high priest. At 22.54-62 is the story of Peter's denial, and in 22.66-71 Jesus is examined by 'the assembly of the elders of the people'. They ask him specifically if he is the Messiah and the Son of God, and Jesus replies in very ambiguous terms: 'You say that I am' (22.70).

In Luke 23 Jesus is brought before Pilate, who gives Jesus a summary hearing (23.1-5), then sends him to Herod (23.6-12). In 23.13-16 Pilate tells the Jews that he finds Jesus innocent, but in 23.18-25 the Jews clamour for the death of Jesus. Pilate releases Barabbas to them and delivers Jesus for execution. In the rest of Luke 23 Jesus is crucified and buried.

John

John starts the hostile interest in Jesus mid-way through his Gospel.[21] In 11.45-53 many Jews are said to believe in Jesus but some complain to the Pharisees about him. The concern is raised in 11.48 that 'if we let him go on like this, everyone will believe in him, and the Romans will come and destroy both our holy place and our nation'. Caiaphas supplies the solution on this occasion when he declares that 'it is better for you to have one man die for the people than to have the whole nation destroyed'. This leads to the decision which is reported in 11.53 to put Jesus to death.

John 13 is the Johannine account of the Last Supper with its narrative of the foot-washing.[22] In chapter 17 Jesus pronounces his farewell speech (or prayer).[23] At the beginning of John 18 Jesus goes to the garden and is met by Judas with the soldiers. John differs from the Synoptics in not making Judas kiss Jesus. Jesus is taken initially to Annas, the father-in-law of Caiaphas the high priest; at 18.15-18, 25-7 is the story of Peter's denial. In 18.19 'the high priest questioned Jesus about his teaching and about his disciples'. This is evidently an informal hearing. In 18.24 Jesus is sent bound to Caiaphas himself. The hearing before Caiaphas is not reported. In 18.28 Jesus is taken to Pilate. Pilate initially tells the Jewish leaders to see to the matter themselves. A significant statement (which many scholars regard as historical) is made in 18.31 when 'the Jews' remind him that 'we are not permitted to put anyone to death'.

As the result of this encounter, Pilate investigates Jesus in 18.33-40 and decides that he is not guilty of any crime; not even of seditious claims to kingship. Pilate offers to release Barabbas. The narrative which follows astonishingly represents Jesus as in total control of the situation. Pilate appears here as weak and vacillating.[24] In 19.1-12 Pilate tries to persuade the Jews to let Jesus go, but he is countered by such cries as 'he ought to die because he has claimed to be the Son of God' (19.7); and 'everyone who claims to be a king sets himself against the emperor' (19.12). In 19.13-16 Pilate makes one last attempt to release Jesus but he is countered again by the Jews. Pilate therefore delivers Jesus to be crucified (19.16). The rest of John 19 describes the execution and burial of Jesus.

Sources Beyond the Gospels

We now turn to sources beyond the Gospels. These include Christian, Jewish and Roman material.[25]

The death of Jesus is mentioned briefly in two summary sections incorporated in the first- or second-century Christian apocalypse called the *Ascension of Isaiah*.[26] These summaries probably drew on a source which was held in common with the author of Matthew's Gospel. *Asc. Isa.* 3.13 mentions 'the persecution with which he would be persecuted, and the torments with which the children of Israel must torment him . . . and that before the sabbath he must be crucified on a tree, and be crucified with wicked men and that he would be buried in a grave'. *Asc. Isa.* 11.19–21 partially recalls the thought of 1 Cor. 2.6-8 when it states that 'after this the adversary envied him and roused the children of Israel, who did not know who he was, against him. And they handed him to the ruler, and crucified him, and he descended to the angel who (is) in Sheol. In Jerusalem, indeed, I saw how they crucified him on a tree.'

The *Gospel of Peter* was composed in Syria in the first half of the second century CE.[27] Discovered in an eighth-century manuscript in Egypt towards the end of the nineteenth century, this manuscript is incomplete and covers only the end of the trial, the death and the resurrection of Jesus. The fragment opens with Pilate and Herod together, Herod commanding that Jesus be marched off to the Jews. Jesus is mocked by the people and crucified between two criminals.

The second-century text known as the *Epistula Apostolorum* contains a brief reference (chapter 9) to the death of Jesus: 'He of whom we are witnesses we know as the one crucified in the days of Pontius Pilate and of the prince Archelaus, who was crucified between two thieves and was taken down from the wood of the cross together with them, and was buried in the place called qaranejo (i.e. the skull).'[28]

Several works are attributed to Pilate, all of them late and of dubious historical value. They were probably written by Christians for propaganda purposes. The most important is the *Acts of Pilate*.[29] This is the name given to an allegedly official record of the death of Jesus which is mentioned as early as Justin Martyr in the second century CE (*1 Apol.* 35, 48). It remains unlikely, however, that Justin had seen the document in question. The *Acts of Pilate* that we possess was not written before the fourth century CE. Sometimes combined with other writings and called the *Gospel of Nicodemus*,[30] it represents a development of tendencies that are found in the Fourth Gospel. The only trial mentioned is the trial before Pilate; the trial is thus a Roman one in which the Jews act as prosecutors. The charges are religious ones; the real issue is not the question of kingship as such but Jesus' blasphemous claim to divinity which is supported by other charges. Jesus is sentenced by Pilate in the garden where he was arrested. There is also a pseudonymous *Letter of Pilate* to the emperor Tiberius.[31]

The trial of Jesus is mentioned in Jewish tradition.[32] In the Babylonian Talmud, Jesus is remembered as someone who had led Israel astray: 'On the eve of Passover Yeshu was hanged. For forty days before the execution took place, a herald went forth and cried, "He is going forth to be stoned because he has practised sorcery and enticed Israel to apostasy. Any one who can say anything in his favour, let him come forward and plead on his behalf." But since nothing was brought forward in his favour he was hanged on the eve of the Passover' (*b.Sanh.* 43a). This view of Jesus comes to fuller expression in the medieval *Toledoth Yeshu*.[33] The fullest Aramaic version of this text exists in the Cambridge fragment from the Cairo Geniza collection. This text opens with a description of the trial and execution of five disciples of Jesus by R. Joshua b. Perachiach. This is followed by a discussion between the same rabbi and Pontius Pilate concerning the executions of Jesus and John the Baptist. Joshua suggests that both be brought before the emperor. Tiberius proposes a test-miracle of the virginal conception of his own daughter. This fails because of the prayers of the Jews: John and Jesus are handed over to the Jews for execution. Jesus, who attempted to escape, is crucified and stoned. He is buried in R. Judah's garden.

Finally, we shall consider Roman evidence for the trial of Jesus. Tacitus' *Annals* 15.44 states that the founder of the Christian sect, Jesus, was executed in the reign of Tiberius by the governor of Judaea, Pontius Pilate. (The Pilate literature cited above is clearly pseudonymous and cannot therefore appropriately be considered with the Roman sources.)

Was It a Trial and Who Were the Judges?

The value of these sources is clearly variable and demands careful consideration. It is undoubtedly problematic that the Gospels do not agree as to which processes resulted in the execution of Jesus. In the Marcan–Matthaean version, Jesus is tried before the high priest and assembly, sentenced to death, taken to Pilate, sentenced again and crucified. In Luke, Jesus is investigated before the assembly, not condemned at this stage, brought before Pilate, investigated by Herod Antipas, returned to Pilate and sentenced, apparently against Pilate's will. In John, Jesus is arrested, tried before the high priest but not sentenced, tried before Pilate and sentenced to death.

The Jewish evidence is different again. It cites sorcery as the reason for Jesus' death, indicating that his execution occurred as the result of a Jewish judicial process. It implies that Jesus had the chance to mount a defence but that no such convincing defence was offered. The Roman evidence supplies a more restricted reason for the death of Jesus. This is that Jesus was sentenced to death and executed by the Roman official, Pontius Pilate. The later Christian evidence adds little of substance to what we know of the trial of Jesus from these other sources.

The lack of uniformity in the Gospel tradition poses a serious historical problem. It raises doubt about whether Jesus was tried in the formal sense and if so in whose court and what the legal basis and outcome of that trial were.[34] This question is complicated by the fact that the Gospels, supported by the combined evidence of the Jewish and Roman tradition, mention two different 'trials': one before Jewish officials and the other before Pilate. This further raises the legal status of the Jewish trial given the documented need for the subsequent ratification of its verdict.

We start with the undisputed facts about the death of Jesus. This is that Jesus died on a Roman cross, having been sentenced to death by Pontius Pilate. It is hardly possible to deny that Jesus met his death by crucifixion rather than, say, by stoning. Crucifixion was a Roman method of punishment.[35] Although the Jews did exhibit the bodies of executed people on gibbets, this was done subsequently to death by stoning and was not a means of execution in itself.[36] Jesus died a Roman death – the very worst kind of death the Roman state could inflict. This of itself suggests substantial Roman involvement in the sentencing of Jesus, however much the Christian sources (notably Matthew) try to implicate the Jews and exonerate the Romans in this matter.[37]

For Jesus to have been executed demands the passing of a capital sentence. The sources (apart from the Talmud) indicate that Jesus was sentenced to death by Pilate, and there are no reasons to doubt this information. Theissen notes that, in other provinces, the Romans did not let capital sentences out of their hands.[38] Josephus states that the first prefect over Judaea, Coponius (6–9 CE) was given full powers including the right to pass capital sentences there (*War* 2.117). Furthermore, Jn 18.31 makes the Jews say that they have no legal right to carry out death sentences. This information is confirmed by the Mishnah, which states (*j.Sanh.* 1.18a; 7.24b) that the right to hold capital trials was withdrawn from the Jews forty years before the destruction of the temple (70 CE). If we take the figure of 'forty years' literally, this brings us to about the time of Jesus' death. It is possible, however, that it is a round figure and refers to a much earlier time, possibly to the imposition of direct Roman rule in 6 CE.

Jesus could have been executed as the result of two different procedures.[39] In the first place there was *coercitio*. This was essentially an expediency measure which allowed the governor to do anything that was necessary to maintain public order. A more considered approach was *cognitio*. This was a formal procedure in which charges were laid and a verdict given after interrogation. Opinions have varied on this matter but it seems more likely that Jesus was formally sentenced than summarily executed by the Romans. That is suggested particularly by the *titulus* on the cross (Mk 15.26 and parallels) which gives details of the offence for which he was executed. The designation 'king of the Jews' shows that Jesus was crucified as a pretender to kingship. This is suggested also by the Jewish accusation in Jn 19.12, 'Everyone who claims to be a king sets himself against the emperor.'

There are two possible charges on which Jesus could have been found guilty and executed. The first is *perduellio*: the charge of being a significant public enemy. The second is *crimen lasae maiestatis populi romani*. This was a more general charge which covered anything that brought the Roman nation and its representatives into disrepute. Both Tacitus (*Annals* 2.50; 3.38) and Suetonius (*Tiberius* 58) note that prosecutions on the second charge were increasing around the time that Jesus died. Many scholars think that Jesus was charged with this latter offence and summarily executed upon conviction.

This approach inevitably questions whether the Jewish 'trial' of Jesus was a real trial at all. Mark and Matthew say that Jesus was sentenced to death by the Jewish authorities. Luke and John, however, have no such record of indictment. The notion of a formal 'trial' of Jesus before the Sanhedrin goes against what is known about this Jewish body from the Mishnah.[40] There are at least five points where Mark's narrative comes into conflict with the Mishnaic regulations. First of all, the Mishnah legislates that capital trials must take place during daylight; but Jesus is investigated by night. Nor might they take place during the sabbath or on festivals; yet the Synoptics say that the trial of Jesus occurred on Passover night (and John on the Day of Rest). Thirdly, a death sentence could not be passed on the first day of a trial. Fourthly, the definition of 'blasphemy' in *m.Sanh.* 7.5 is speaking in the name of Yahweh, but in Mark Jesus never pronounces the divine name.[41] Finally, the Sanhedrin generally met in the temple whereas the so-called 'trial' of Jesus took place in the house of the high priest.

This problem has been addressed in several different ways by scholars. Joseph Blinzler takes the Marcan report at its face value, arguing that Jesus was condemned in accordance with Sadducean law, which was more stringent than Pharisaic law.[42] Strobel argues that Pharisaic law was set aside on this exceptional occasion because an 'extraordinary penal procedure' was invoked against Jesus.[43] Against this view it has been argued that the Sanhedrin trial is fictional, invented in order to exonerate the Romans.[44] Alternatively, it has been suggested that an informal hearing before the Sanhedrin was later written up as a formal trial and that several processes have been telescoped in the Marcan–Matthaean narrative to create a single and striking episode.[45]

The problem which stands irresistibly in the way of any attempt to portray the Jewish hearing as a formal trial is the reason supplied in Matthew and Mark for the condemnation of Jesus. This is the charge of blasphemy. It is difficult to see how Jesus could have been guilty of this charge when the Mishnaic evidence is considered. The Mishnah makes it clear that (at least by the time of its codification) blasphemy was defined as pronouncement of the divine name. Jn 19.7 makes the Jews state that Jesus must die 'because he has claimed to be the Son of God'; but even this statement is quite different from the Mishnaic definition of blasphemy. Mk 14.62 and parallels make Jesus promise the high priest a vision of the Son of Man seated at the right hand of God; but again, it is not certain that this involved pronouncement of the divine name. Added to the other difficulties we have discerned, it is highly problematic to assume that Jesus was formally tried and sentenced in a Jewish court. It has sometimes been suggested that Jn 18.31 supports the evidence of Mark and Matthew, indicating that Jesus was indeed tried and convicted but that the Jews lacked the power to carry out the capital sentence. Yet this theory is also unconvincing, particularly when we consider that Luke and John have no formal record of any Jewish condemnation of Jesus.

It is preferable to see the Jewish investigation as a 'fact-finding' mission based on the revelation made by Judas Iscariot that Jesus and the disciples harboured messianic convictions. The Jewish authorities were looking for a reason to hand Jesus over to the Romans and to rid themselves of someone whom they found troublesome. The information supplied by Judas proved decisive in this respect. In Mark's account, albeit toned down by the other Synoptists, Jesus admits to the high priest that he is the Messiah. A would-be Messiah who appeared at Passover with secret teachings definitely posed a threat to stability (cf. Jn 18.19, 'then the high priest questioned Jesus about his disciples and about his teaching'). The Jewish hearing found evidence to support the leaked belief that Jesus thought about himself as Messiah. Jesus was delivered to the Romans, tried, sentenced and executed on that charge. All of this happened in the immediate prelude to Passover, probably in the year 30 CE.

THE RESURRECTION OF JESUS

There have been occasional suggestions that Jesus of Nazareth did not really die on the cross but merely fainted and, in the coolness of the tomb, revived to make good an escape.[1] Such theories are entirely unconvincing. Jesus was severely flogged before he was crucified. Crucifixion itself inflicted horrific injuries resulting in the inability to breathe and consequent death through asphyxiation.[2] The only comparable injuries in contemporary terms are those sustained on the battlefield and in major road traffic accidents.[3] Roman soldiers were used to this method of execution. They knew when people were dead. Even in the most implausible case that Jesus was the only person in history to have survived this method of punishment, he could hardly have rolled the stone away unaided. The simplest explanation is the best one. Jesus of Nazareth was really dead when he was taken down from the cross. This much is acknowledged by the narrator's comment in Jn 19.34 that blood and water poured from the lanced side of Jesus. This suggests the first signs of bodily decomposition as the natural fluids were released.

The placing of the body of Jesus inside the tomb ought to have been the end of his story, but in fact it was not. In their different ways the Gospels and Paul indicate that Jesus enjoyed a new form of life beyond the grave: one which saw him acclaimed as a high heavenly being and through which his followers continued to claim that God's kingdom was at hand.[4] This chain of events, known collectively as the resurrection, was unprecedented so far as previous Judaism was concerned, although we saw in Chapter 10 that a whole variety of Jewish texts anticipated that it would happen at some future point.[5] The content of the earliest Christian preaching was thus the elevation of the crucified criminal Jesus to divine status through his transcendence of death; and the concomitant reflection which sought to explain the divine purpose in this strange manoeuvre.[6]

Paul's Understanding of the Resurrection of Jesus

The first step in our attempt to understand the resurrection of Jesus is to ask what the New Testament sources say about it.[7] We shall consider all the different nuances and only make a judgment when the entirety of the evidence has been considered. This will mean examining a variety of material and more than one New Testament way of describing the *post-mortem* history of Jesus.

The resurrection is everywhere presupposed in the New Testament, but it is described on a relatively small number of occasions. We can best approach the material chronologically, looking at the earliest texts first and moving from those to the later New Testament documents.

This means that we begin with the letters of Paul. We shall examine Paul in more detail in Part III; and here I am going to examine only those parts of Paul's letters which are relevant to the matter in hand. There are problems in reading Paul – sometimes quite difficult problems – but again I shall leave a formal statement of these problems until Part III of this book. We shall plunge straight into Paul, untroubled by some of the things that have troubled his commentators, and preface our study by an equally truncated look at the understanding of Jesus' resurrection which pertained in Christian circles before Paul.

Christianity before Paul

The twenty-year gap between the resurrection and the writing of 1 Thessalonians (Paul's first letter) in the early 50s is important analytically.[8] We can only hope to understand the nature of Paul's discussion of the resurrection in 1 Thessalonians and elsewhere by discerning something of its likely background. We saw that Jesus was a preacher of God's kingdom and that he thought God's kingdom would appear imminently. This sense of urgency is found with other New Testament figures. The justification for the Gentile mission in Paul seems to have been both the recognition that he had been called to this ministry by God (Gal. 2.7) and also the belief that the Gentiles played a crucial part in the biblical understanding of the eschatological age.[9] The carrying of the gospel to Rome, which resulted in the (presumed) death of both Peter and Paul, shows the desire that was felt in early Christian circles to evangelize the mediterranean world. The speed with which this was done reflected the belief that the time was short and that the good news must be preached to the Gentiles to ensure they were ready when the kingdom came.[10]

The earliest Christian preaching proclaimed the death and resurrection of Jesus and the new state of being which had emerged from those events. There are different ways of describing the resurrection in both Acts and Paul, but the emphasis in all New Testament literature is on the unexpected nature of the new event and on its consequences for eschatology.[11] The author of Acts is evidently faithful to Thucydides' canon of supplying authentic speeches to his characters when he makes Peter say in 3.19-21 that God would send Jesus the Messiah from heaven at the time of the 'universal restoration that God announced long ago through his holy prophets' (3.21).[12] This statement well preserves the sense of urgency that was implicit in all early Christian preaching. It makes the appearance of Jesus from heaven the event by which the universal restoration would be achieved.[13]

This last point marks a change from what Jesus himself had believed. Jesus anticipated the coming of God's kingdom. Whether or not Jesus expected to die remains an open question, but if he did, Mk14.28 substantially qualifies that belief with its expressed hope for resurrection. After the resurrection, it came to be believed that Jesus was a divine being in heaven. This led to the reinterpretation of his preaching to include the view that Jesus himself would return from heaven to introduce the kingdom: the role that Jesus had assigned to the Son of Man.[14] Jesus was thereafter identified with the Son of Man, as we saw in Chapter 14.

The result of this metamorphosis was the appearance of set formulae to describe the resurrection of Jesus.[15] The phrase 'God raised him from the dead' occurs so often in the Pauline literature that we can justifiably conclude it belonged to the Christian tradition before Paul. Also pre-Pauline are formulae such as 'Jesus died and rose again' (1 Thess. 4.14) and (in some form) the passion predictions found now in Mk 8.31; 9.31; 10.33 and parallels. This material testifies to the early Christians' pre-occupation with the resurrection of Jesus. It shows their willingness to codify such belief in set patterns of speech for the convenience of evangelism and their own internal understanding.

The Early Paul

Two passages in 1 Thessalonians are relevant for this study.[16] If 1 Thess. 1.9-10 is a summary of Paul's preaching to Gentile converts, as is widely conceded,[17] belief in the resurrection of Jesus is intimately linked to the fulfilment of eschatological hopes in Paul's earliest letter. Here it is said that God 'raised [Jesus] from the dead' and that Jesus 'rescues us from the wrath that is coming' (1.10). This future return is inconceivable without the past resurrection.

The question of the resurrection of believers is discussed in 1 Thessalonians 4.[18] Paul reassures those who were worried by the death of their friends that 'God will bring with [Jesus] those who have died' (4.14). The thought is that the archangel's trumpet will sound as Jesus descends from heaven, the dead will rise, and the living and the dead will ascend to the air to meet Jesus; either to escort him in triumph back to earth or to journey with him to heaven (probably the former).[19] The question has often been asked of why both parties speak as they do. The answer is probably that Paul had imparted insufficient teaching about the fate of the dead when he evangelized Thessalonica and that his converts had been left with the impression that one had to be alive to experience the 'rapture' (the ascent to meet Jesus) and the subsequent messianic kingdom.[20] Paul provides much-needed assurance that the dead will be raised, which in this context he connects with further embodied existence. He insists that the dead are not denied the eschato-logical benefits but kept safe by God precisely in order to enjoy them.

The Corinthian Correspondence

Paul offers further resurrectional teaching in 1 Corinthians 15.[21] This passage contains what is chronologically the earliest record of the resurrection appearances. The problem that Paul addresses is evidently the fact that some in Corinth had denied belief in the resurrection of the dead altogether. He responds by citing a formula which he explicitly states had derived from earlier Christianity (1 Cor. 15.3-4).[22] The precise extent of this citation is disputed, but that point only marginally concerns us here. The formula states that Christ, having died, was buried and rose again 'on the third day in accordance with the scriptures' (15.4). Paul (or his source) next describes a sequence of resurrection appearances, first to Peter and the Twelve (15.5); then to more than five hundred witnesses (15.6); next to James and all the apostles (15.7); and finally to Paul himself (15.8).[23] In this sequence, it seems that the resurrection appearances have a primarily evidential quality. They demonstrate the truth of the proposition that Jesus had been raised by explaining that the risen Jesus had appeared to an irrefutable number of witnesses.

This is not a complete description of the resurrection, still less a definition of it. One question that Paul annoyingly fails to address is the form of Jesus in his risen state.[24] The rest of the chapter, however, contains some clues to answer this question. In 1 Cor. 15.12-19 Paul deals with the objection that there is no such thing as resurrection by citing the resurrection of Jesus. In 15.20-8 he asserts that Christ *has* been raised, inserting this statement within a broader eschatological scenario. The crucial point of the chapter – at least for our purposes – is reached in 15.35. Here, Paul turns his attention to the nature of the resurrection existence (15.35–57). What he says at this point, although primarily about the future resurrection of believers, undoubtedly has implications for what Paul understood about the resurrection of Jesus himself. Some deductive reasoning exposes the probable connections.

The heart of the argument, however difficult the concept is to understand, is that the resurrection existence is embodied existence.[25] Paul argues that there will be a resurrection body just as there is a physical body which succumbs to death (15.44). The difference between the two bodies rests on the level of perishability. The present and physical body is a perishable body. The future and resurrection body will be an imperishable body. The meaning of the adjective 'spiritual' in 1 Cor. 15.45 is notoriously difficult; but it appears to signify the heavenly origin of the resurrection body and consequently its imperishable character.[26] That is the reason for Paul's contrast between Adam and Christ at this point in the chapter. Adam is an earthly man, Christ a heavenly being. Paul presents the two as archetypes of Christian existence when viewed in eschatological terms.[27] He states (15.49) that those who have borne the image of the man of dust will also bear the image of the man from heaven. This notion of future and permanent embodiment is the basic principle on which Paul's understanding of the resurrection rests.

This argument is developed further in 1 Cor. 15.50-7. Here Paul states that the perishable will be changed by the acquisition of the imperishable. That will be the final vanquishing of death (15.54). It is nothing less than the victory of God who provides an imperishable body to deal with the problem of human mortality. This leads Paul to his famous eulogy of the swallowing-up of death in the victory Jesus had accomplished.

The whole of 1 Corinthians thereby makes a link between the resurrection of Jesus and the resurrection of believers. We should say that what is true about the future nature of the believers' resurrection body is probably also true about the resurrection body that Jesus has acquired already. The link between Adam and Jesus in 15.42-9 is the key to this argument. It must mean that the risen Jesus, by analogy with Adam, was raised imperishable (15.42) and that he now enjoys what Paul calls a 'spiritual body' (15.44). This is a body appropriate to the heavenly world. That is why Paul can say in 15.49, 'Just as we have borne the image of the man of dust, we will also bear the image of the man of heaven.' The resurrectional life of Jesus, although clearly a heavenly life, is not for that reason a disembodied life. Jesus now has a different kind of body: a transformed and imperishable body, provided by God and destined to return to earth in Paul's understanding of things.

The Mature Paul

Paul develops this argument further in 2 Corinthians 5, but it is to Philippians 3 (Paul's last letter) that we turn to set the seal on this interpretation.[28] Phil. 3.20-1 shows that Paul continued to think about the return of Jesus from heaven to earth as the decisive moment for salvation.[29] He begins by stating that the Christians' citizenship is in heaven (3.20). This is not the view that Christians pass to heaven after death (although that view is found in some apocalyptic writings); but that Christians look to God as their heavenly king and derive their status from that presupposition.[30] From heaven, Paul continues, 'we are expecting a Saviour, the Lord Jesus Christ' (3.20). The return of Jesus means the climax of salvation so far as Paul is concerned. That is connected with impending transformation. Jesus 'will transform the body of our humiliation so that it may be conformed to the *body of his glory*' (3.21). The italicized phrase makes explicit the statement that Jesus' resurrectional existence is an embodied one, confirming that the risen Jesus has an imperishable body which serves as the model for the future transformation of believers.

Finally, and out of chronological sequence, we turn to what Paul says about his own conversion in Galatians. This is an allusive and less detailed account than the one found on three occasions in Acts.[31] Yet there are important parallels between Galatians and Paul's account of his vision of Jesus in 1 Cor. 15.8. In Gal. 1.15-16 Paul uses language reminiscent of the prophets to describe how God had chosen him for special ministry and how God had effected that calling in Paul. The crucial moment came, as Paul puts it, when God 'was pleased to reveal his Son to me'.[32] (The Greek says literally, 'in me', but most English versions translate it 'to me', as in the NRSV.) Paul appears to allude to a mystical vision similar to the resurrection appearances of 1 Corinthians 15. The language is allusive and difficult to interpret, but many scholars find it appropriate to read Galatians 1 in the light of 1 Corinthians 15. This link draws attention to Paul's status as a mystical theologian and to the significance of his apocalyptic vision of Jesus in the discerning of his own apostolate.[33]

The Resurrection Tradition in the Gospels

From Paul we turn to the Gospels. The Gospels were written later than Paul; Mark probably ten years after Philippians and John as much as thirty years later. We need to know when approaching this material that Matthew and Luke probably made independent use of Mark and that John may have known some if not all of the Synoptic Gospels, even though he presents his own distinctive understanding of the resurrection.

Mark's description of the resurrection leaves much to the reader's imagination. The original form of the Gospel probably ended in 16.8a. At some point, probably in the second century CE, a later hand or hands added the diffuse material which is now found in Mk 16.8b-20.[34] This material cannot safely be considered part of the original Gospel, but there has been more than one suggestion as to how it arose.

At the end of Mark 15 the body of Jesus is placed in the tomb. At 15.47 Mark specifically states that Mary Magdalene and another Mary saw where the body was laid. Since this was the day before the sabbath (Friday in modern terms), the women rested on the sabbath to avoid the impurity that would have been caused by contact with a corpse. Mary Magdalene and other women come to the tomb at the beginning of Mark 16 to anoint the body of Jesus in accordance with Jewish burial customs. They are worried about how they will gain entrance to the tomb (16.2). In the end, however, their worries prove groundless. The stone has already been rolled away when they get to the tomb (16.4). They enter the tomb and see a young man – clearly an angel – sitting on the right hand side (16.5). This angel tells them that Jesus 'has been raised', pointing to the place where his body had rested (16.6). This statement is accompanied by the command to tell the disciples that Jesus will meet them in Galilee (16.7). The original Mark ends on a highly effective note with the statement that 'they went out and fled from the tomb, for terror and amazement had seized them; and they said nothing to anyone, for they were afraid' (16.8).[35]

Mark's Gospel thereby ends with the empty tomb.[36] This marks a clear difference from Paul. The women who enter the tomb find, not the dead still less the risen Jesus, but an angel who tells them that Jesus has been raised. In the conventions of Jewish angelology, this message comes with the full authority of God of whom the angel is the messenger. This implies that Mark understands the resurrection as a divine act in which God's own power is disclosed.

The risen Jesus never appears to the disciples in the original version of Mark. This makes for an interesting contrast with Paul. Paul includes the resurrection appearances but not the empty tomb. Mark describes the empty tomb but has no resurrection appearances. We do not know why this is so.[37] One reason may be that the author of Mark is to some extent correcting the impression that Paul had inculcated. It is possible that concern about the missing tomb in Paul is not just a modern phenomenon. Since the tomb was known to have featured in the original tradition, Mark includes it to balance the description of the resurrection appearances which were already well known in the Pauline churches. There is, additionally, the promise that Jesus will meet the disciples in Galilee (16.7), even if this promise is never fulfilled in the original Mark. This statement shows that Mark is not ignorant of the resurrection appearances. He evidently chooses to omit them much as Paul had omitted the empty tomb.

The other Gospels augment Mark's picture, notably by describing the resurrection appearances. Thus Mt. 28.8-10 makes Jesus meet the women. He repeats the angelic command for the disciples to go to Galilee. Luke 24 includes the story of the journey to Emmaus and other appearances also. John 20 describes how Jesus meets Mary Magdalene in the garden. These resurrection appearances take us back to the approach of Paul, but significantly through the matrix of the empty tomb.

Mark's narrative closure is highly effective. The fear with which his Gospel ends is a striking commentary on the meaning of the resurrection. It denotes the reverential awe which attends the sudden discovery of the numinous. Mark's narrative genius is to capture this original moment and not to dissipate it through explanation.

Wrestling with the Sources

This diffuse material needs to be made the subject of careful interpretation.

The first question to ask is whether we can accept the Gospels' report that the tomb of Jesus was found empty on Easter morning.[38] There are two reasons for potentially doubting this report. In the first place, Paul does not mention the empty tomb. Secondly, there are a number of differences between the Gospels which raise the questions of literary dependence and historical objectivity. These need to be asked even by those who have no difficulty in accepting the basic reliability of the Gospels.

That Paul does not mention the empty tomb is not a convincing argument that he was ignorant of it. Paul's letters are occasional pieces, written from pastoral concern. Not even Romans is a systematic treatise as such. There are other things which Paul does not mention, such as a detailed itinerary of his own preaching campaign and a developed discussion of baptism. This does not mean that Paul did not know these other matters. It simply means that he did not judge them relevant to the topics discussed in his letters.

Paul's silence helps to clarify the status of the empty tomb in modern discussion of Jesus' resurrection. The empty tomb is an essentially ambiguous symbol.[39] This is shown by the body-stealing theory which is specifically rejected by two Matthaean passages (Mt. 27.61-6; 28.11-15). The ambiguity lies in the fact that the emptiness can be explained in more than one way. The empty tomb does not of itself *prove* that Jesus of Nazareth rose from the dead. It rather *contributes* to that theory when other evidence is considered. That is evidently why Paul describes the resurrection appearances and not the empty tomb in the early verses of 1 Corinthians 15. A Jesus who appears in an apocalyptic vision is a Jesus who has a heavenly existence and a contemporary relevance, and clearly also eschatological significance. He is a transformed Jesus whose life is now lived on the heavenly plane. The empty tomb supports such a view, but does not of itself create it in the absence of the resurrection appearances.

The ending of Mark supplies us with another possible reason for the suppression of the empty tomb tradition in Paul. Despite the angel's command, Mark presents the women as hesitant and fearful. They 'said nothing to anyone, for they were afraid' (16.8).[40] This implies, on the plain evidence of the text, that the women's report of the empty tomb was not the cause of resurrection faith. Mark does not say explicitly what *was* the cause of such faith. For this, we turn to Paul and the other Gospels where the resurrection appearances are described. Mark implies that the discovery of the tomb was initially a stumbling-block and not the joyful thing to which Mt. 28.8 alludes.[41]

We need not doubt the reliability of the statement that the tomb was found empty on Easter morning; but, in order to understand what the early Christians meant by their belief in resurrection, we shall augment it with the language of transformation and visionary appearance Paul uses in 1 Corinthians 15. In the next two Parts of this book we shall examine the effect that the conviction, 'Jesus is Lord' (Phil. 2.11), had on his previously disillusioned circle of followers. In bringing this study of Jesus to a close, we acknowledge the unexpected nature of this development and the enormous impact which the visions of the heavenly Jesus ('the resurrection appearances') exercised. They led, in words which Paul himself cites, to the reworking of Jewish theology and the conviction that 'for us there is one God . . . and one Lord, Jesus Christ' (1 Cor. 8.6). Belief that Jesus was the heavenly Lord swiftly became the centre of early Christian theology. The rest of this book will examine how this conviction became the very cradle of early Christianity.

PART III

PAUL AND CHRISTIAN BEGINNINGS

ON PAUL THE APOSTLE

After Jesus, the best-known figure in early Christianity was Paul the apostle.[1] Paul was the author of such key New Testament texts as Galatians and Romans, and moreover the author of the earliest New Testament text, which many people think was 1 Thessalonians but which some continue to think was Galatians. Paul's significance lies in the fact that he carried the good news about Jesus throughout the mediterranean world on his various preaching campaigns, transforming what was originally the proclamation of God's kingdom on Jewish soil into a religion which had the potential to change the world at large. Paul was not always appreciated in his own day, not even by fellow disciples of Jesus. In order to understand this man's religious and cultural significance, we shall look first at his own history and activity.

Saul of Tarsus

Paul nowhere tells us where he was born; but the author of Acts makes Paul say that he was born in Tarsus and brought up in Jerusalem at the feet of Gamaliel (Acts 22.3). This brief reference has become the focus of a scholarly dispute. In 1962, W.C. van Unnik argued that Paul may have been born in Tarsus but that he was taken to Jerusalem in early infancy and that his formative years were spent in the Jewish capital.[2] Van Unnik was followed in this assessment by Martin Hengel, who argued from Paul's knowledge of the Septuagint that 'Tarsus cannot be pushed completely into the background, even if it must take second place to Jerusalem in Paul's growth.'[3]

This reading of the evidence was challenged with typical acumen by Ernst Haenchen.[4] Haenchen observes that in Gal. 1.22 Paul tells the Galatian Christians he was 'unknown by sight to the churches in Judea'. This statement makes little sense if Paul had really been a long-established inhabitant of Jerusalem, particularly in view of what Paul himself says elsewhere in Galatians about being a zealous and well-known persecutor of the church. Moreover, Haenchen points to the symbolic role that Jerusalem occupies in the narrative of Acts, arguing that the author had an interest in inculcating the view of Paul the Jerusalemite. He notes that van Unnik implies the Hellenistic influence on Paul came only *after* his conversion, which seems unlikely; and that there is no evidence in Paul's letters that he knew Aramaic, the common language of Jerusalem.[5] Haenchen's conclusion is that Paul was not only born in Tarsus but that he was raised there as well. This rebuttal of van Unnik's hypothesis suggests we look to Tarsus to explain Paul's earliest interests and concerns.[6]

Tarsus was an important city in the ancient world, having been established in the second millennium BCE.[7] It is located in south-east Cilicia in Asia Minor, the modern Turkey. Its strategic location as a port meant that Hellenistic culture pervaded Tarsus from an early period. This cosmopolitan environment brought educational opportunities with it. Strabo said that 'the people at Tarsus have devoted themselves so eagerly, not only to philosophy, but also to the whole round of education in general, that they have surpassed Athens, Alexandria, or any other place that can be named where there have been schools and lectures or philosophers'.[8] It is known that ancient Tarsus housed both Cynic and Stoic philosophers. Their teachings would no doubt have been assimilated by Paul at a formative age.

Politically, Tarsus in the first century CE was the capital of Cilicia.[9] Cilicia had been annexed as a Roman province by Pompey in 67 BCE in his campaign against the mediterranean pirates. In 42 BCE Mark Antony was joined by Cleopatra in Tarsus. Antony made Tarsus a free city, which allowed it to set its own laws and mint its coinage. These privileges were reaffirmed by Augustus after the battle of Actium in 31 BCE. Tarsus when Paul was growing up was thus an esteemed city of the Roman empire, thoroughly pervaded by Hellenistic culture.

Tarsus was also an important centre of Judaism. Paul speaks of his respect for 'the traditions of the ancestors' (Gal. 1.14) in a way which shows that the Jewish presence in Tarsus was strongly established. It is clear from Paul's own writings that his Jewish education was profoundly influenced by Hellenism. He would have known the Hebrew Bible in the form of its Greek translation, the Septuagint.[10] We saw in Chapter 2 that this was a nuanced translation produced (in Alexandria) for a more cosmopolitan world where interaction with Gentiles was not only inevitable but in many cases found desirable. This is not to say that there were never tensions in Tarsus (as at Alexandria) between Jew and Gentile; but that Judaism as a minority religion had to find sensible ways of accommodating with the dominant culture which it could never effectively avoid. Such tension is found in a number of passages in Paul and is described vividly by Calvin Roetzel when writing on Romans: 'The tension between Paul's *kerygma* for the *oikoumene* (Rom. 10:18) and his affirmation of divine loyalty to Israel is so powerful that the letter almost throbs in our hands.'[11]

Recent studies of Paul have exposed the extent to which he was skilled in rhetoric and argument.[12] Paul clearly knew Stoic philosophy. This surfaces particularly in his concept of natural law in the early chapters of Romans.[13] A pressing question to address in the light of this information is that of Paul's social status. In Acts 22.28 Paul tells the Roman centurion that he is a Roman citizen. He thereby appeals successfully for his case to be heard in Rome. Although this statement is accepted as historical by prominent scholars such as Sherwin-White and

Hengel, there are strong arguments which bring it into doubt.[14] Two such arguments derive from Paul's status as a Jew of the eastern Mediterranean. The Romans rarely granted citizenship to such people; and when this was done it was normally the reward for distinguished service of some kind. If Paul was the kind of law-abiding Jew that his letters portray, he would have found it difficult (as would his parents) to participate in the civic cults which were a necessary requirement of Roman citizenship. Roetzel notes in addition that the myth of Roman citizenship clearly serves the narrative interests of Acts and that Paul's failure to mention such status in Romans is, to say the least, surprising.[15] These reservations raise at least a measure of doubt about whether Paul really was a Roman citizen.

If Paul was not a Roman citizen, the portrait of him as a well-placed and formally educated person becomes more difficult to believe than it would otherwise have been. In this light, we consider the tradition which surfaces in Acts 18.3 that Paul had learned the trade of a tent-maker. This evidence suggests that Paul is probably to be located in the artisan class. On the basis of these two observations, we should conclude that his learning was the result of exceptional industry and ability rather than the provision of opportunities that others of his generation had enjoyed. This of course makes it all the more exceptional that Paul (like Jesus himself) should have influenced the course of history in the way that he did.

The next question to consider is Paul's self-confessed status as a Pharisee (Phil. 3.4–6; cf. Acts 23.6).[16] In Chapter 8 we saw that Pharisaism was a lay movement concerned principally with matters of holiness based on study of the Torah. Josephus reports the Pharisees as teaching that future judgment awaits each human soul (*War* 2.162–3). The Pharisees strictly upheld the standards of priestly purity and saw themselves as next in line to the priests so far as holiness was concerned.

Potential Pharisaic influence is obvious in Paul's understanding of holiness and its boundaries. For Paul, as for most other Jews of his days including the Pharisees, God was the source of all holiness (Rom. 1.7; 1 Cor. 1.2). Paul's concept of the church is given by the Greek word *hagioi*, which in older English Bible translations is somewhat confusingly rendered as 'saints' and which is now more commonly translated as 'holy people'. These holy people to whom Paul refers are not exceptional members of the Christian community, but the Christian community in its entirety. Paul's understanding of 'holiness' is not that Christians are innately holy and called by God for that reason; but that they have been *made* holy by the holy God through the sacrificial achievement of Jesus. Christology, or more appropriately soteriology, is thereby linked to the concept of holiness because it is impossible for Paul to speak about humankind without speaking also of Jesus.

This holiness ideal undergirds Paul's concept of 'sanctification'. This understanding, simply put, is an ethical view in which Christians are called to be the holy people whom they are already. The new status of Christians as 'justified' demands new standards of behaviour in a radical understanding of the Torah which discloses the moral standards appropriate to those who share God's holiness.[17] Sanctification for Paul is a natural part of church life. It is at one and the same time the demonstration that Christians share God's holiness and the insistence that they must grow towards his holiness. This nexus of beliefs represents important contact with the Pharisaic movement.

I cannot explore Paul's connection with Pharisaism with the attention to detail that would be desirable and which others have done more fully. I simply note the opinion of many scholars that, although it is unlikely that Paul really studied at the feet of Gamaliel in Jerusalem, his writings show sufficient affinities with Pharisaism to make his connection with that movement plausible, if not likely. This is a further aspect of our emerging portrait of Paul's origins as a Jew in Tarsus which explains something of the concerns that surfaced in his later Christian ministry.

Paul's Conversion

In three places in Acts we read the story of Paul's 'conversion' (Acts 9.1-28; 22.1-21; and 26.4-23).[18] Acts 9 describes how Paul was journeying to Damascus when he saw a blinding light and heard a heavenly voice asking the reason for his persecution of the Christians. The owner of the voice then introduced himself: 'I am Jesus, whom you are persecuting' (Acts 9.5); Jesus instructed Paul to go to Damascus to await further instructions. The two later passages show some incidental variations on this theme, but without altering its basic thrust.

One of the problems raised by Acts is that we have no objective means of verifying its narrative reliability. Paul alludes to his 'conversion' in more than one passage, but without corroborating the specific details of the Damascus road story. In 1 Cor. 15.8-10 Paul mentions his vision of the heavenly Jesus within the sequence of resurrection appearances. Gal. 1.3-17 is more reserved in its description but speaks of a mystical encounter with Jesus. Occasional hints elsewhere support this general picture (1 Cor. 9.1; Phil. 3.4-11). We may thus have some confidence in supposing that a visionary or mystical encounter with Jesus was responsible for Paul's new and Christian position. The two questions that remain are whether this was a 'conversion' in the technical sense; and what this unusual experience contributed to the development of Paul's theology as such.

To speak of 'conversion' is to raise both sociological and psychological questions.[19] What constitutes 'conversion' has been variously discussed in modern sociology,[20] but there seems to be general agreement that it brings about a decisive and deliberate change in religious community, sometimes quite suddenly, and that it is often accompanied by the experience of inner conflict and hard decision. Acts would have us believe that Paul's experience on the Damascus road was a 'conversion' of this kind. Paul himself is more ambiguous, stating in Gal. 1.15 that God 'had set me apart before I was born'. For this reason Krister Stendahl has described Paul's espousal of Christianity as a 'call', not a 'conversion' as such.[21] There is some justification for this view. Despite the representative use of the pronoun 'I' in Romans 7, where Paul speaks corporately of the helpless state of humankind, there is not a great deal of evidence in Paul's writings that he was troubled by an inner turmoil of the kind that often attends a 'conversion'. Nor indeed did Paul repudiate his Jewish background when he became a Christian (see esp. Phil. 3.4-11). If conversion means the absolute and unprecedented change from one or no form of religion to another, then it is clear that Paul was not 'converted' in this sense.

Having said this, many historians of religion are prepared to allow that Paul was 'converted' in a broader or more general way on becoming a Christian.[22] The term is a valid one once we acknowledge that Paul moved from one sect of Judaism to another and that this involved a radical change of heart and the acquisition of a new self-understanding for him. The change in question was the shift from Pharisaism to Christianity. Alan Segal states the matter with precision: 'To read Paul properly . . . one must recognize that Paul was a Pharisaic Jew who converted to a new apocalyptic, Jewish sect and then lived in a Hellenistic gentile Christian community as a Jew among gentiles.'[23] Paul was used to living in a Hellenistic community – his time in Tarsus had prepared him for that – but he had not done so before as a Christian. This new Paul was gripped by his vision of Jesus and thereafter constructed his beliefs around the principle that God had acted eschatologically in Jesus. That was the basis of his change of heart. We are right in supposing that it amounted to a significant transformation of beliefs and expectations.

Segal continues with a fascinating discussion of what conversion meant in the context of early Christian communities. He observes that modern scholarship has generally moved away from the assumption of a universal explanation of conversion which holds good for all times and seasons and towards the view that individual communities set their own matrices which result in stereotypical narratives of conversion which are individual and particular to the community in question. This is conceivably why Luke has more than one account of Paul's conversion and why he presents incidental details of it in different ways in the two later passages in Acts.

Paul's conversion cannot be described without brief study of the nature of Jewish mysticism.[24] We saw in Part I that the essence of Jewish apocalypticism lay in its conviction that heavenly mysteries can be revealed for the benefit of people on earth. Although we do not know as much as we would like about the circumstances in which the apocalypses were written, the exceptional nature of the revelation to which they allude, together with the device of pseudepigraphy, shows that this mystical experience usually made a profound impression on the mind of the author. This is true even if some of the mystical experiences we find recorded in the apocalypses are fictitious creations based on the author's fertile imagination. These must be seen as attempts to *create* an impression on the reader and thus to authenticate the contents of the individual apocalypse. Apocalypticism, with its mystical component, offered heavenly disclosure and the possibility of new insight on the various situations that the different apocalypses addressed.[25]

Segal goes further, using Paul's narrative of his mystical encounter with Jesus as a 'missing link' in the story of Jewish apocalypticism.[26] He picks up Paul's language of 'transformation' from Rom. 12.2, arguing that it attests not just 'renewal' in the notional sense but a mystical union with Jesus which Paul thought would be shared by all Christian believers at the eschatological climax.[27] This view is found also in Phil. 3.10, 'I want to know Christ and the power of his resurrection and the sharing of his sufferings by becoming like him in his death.' On this passage, Segal comments that 'the language Paul uses is not merely that of analogy or imitation; it is that of transformation (*metamorphosis*) from one state of being to another, in which he has become the same substance as Christ through his death (*symmorphosis*) . . . This process of transformation will end in a glorious new body, spiritual rather than material, which corresponds with the body Christ has already revealed to him.'[28]

On this view, Paul's mystical encounter influenced the whole of his theology by revealing a new matrix in which to interpret the divine covenant with Israel. It is difficult to explain what this mystical conversion meant in practice beyond the observation that it brought to Paul a new form of life which had innate difficulties on account of its often misunderstood religious outlook.[29] The shift from persecutor to persecuted must have been a drastic one so far as Paul was concerned. It is probably fruitless to study Paul's letters for detailed psychological insights once it is recognized that the 'I' of Romans 7 is representative and not a description of Paul's own psychological state. Nevertheless, the futuristic element in Paul's thought is an important clue to his new state of mind. Although Paul regarded the decisive events of salvation as in the past, he also looked forward to the return of Jesus from heaven (1 Thess. 1.10) as the final event in the salvific process. He thought that this would be the time when both the mortal human body (1 Cor. 15.51; Phil. 3.21) and the creation itself (Rom. 8.21) would be transformed to accord with the heavenly originals. Paul's new psychology was thus one of a convert to an eschatological sect where the experience of living between the 'then' and the 'not yet' of salvation became the determinative factor.

It is problematic to achieve a precise explanation of the relationship between Paul's mystical experience and the subsequent development of his theology. The question of whether Paul's theology developed throughout his career has been exhaustively discussed and different answers given to it. We may conclude that Paul's eschatological understanding conceivably became more precise as he grew older, but that it did not alter in essentials once the so-called 'rapture' of 1 Thess. 4.17 is identified as a triumphal procession in which Christ is escorted back to earth.[30] In his last letter, Philippians, Paul continued to maintain that earth would be the realm of eschatological transformation and that the hope for the return of Jesus was a valid one (see Phil. 3.20-1). The same conclusion probably holds true for Paul's Christology and soteriology. Romans does not decisively contradict Galatians; but it represents a more detailed outworking of Paul's thought in which a degree of systematization is achieved. We do not of course know whether this represents a development in Paul's own understanding, or simply the committal to writing of ideas he had entertained for a while.

This observation means that we need not naively conclude that Paul's entire theological understanding was revealed to him in a single visionary moment.[31] Romans and Philippians show that Paul continued to think about things, not least because he was confronted by questions from the churches he had founded. Nonetheless, the intellectual impact of Paul's conversion needs to be considered in this assessment. Paul's visionary encounter with Jesus convinced him that Jesus was the Messiah and that what the Christians were saying about Jesus' resurrection was true, even though Paul had denied this information when persecuting the church as a Pharisee. Paul thereafter became a 'messianist', or follower of Jesus. From this will have flowed the fundamental principles of Paul's soteriology, doubtless under the influence of careful scriptural study.

The development of Paul's theology is a complex matter which cannot be addressed in a few paragraphs. We need to acknowledge that Paul probably developed his ideas but did not change them altogether; and also that he cannot be understood without recognizing the contribution made by mystical perception to his thought and activity. Albert Schweitzer made this point at the beginning of the last century.[32] In reading Paul's letters, we shall bear in mind the probable dialectic between his initial experience of calling and his subsequent reflection on his new position guided by the scriptures. This will become apparent not least in the study of Paul's eschatology in Chapter 21 of this book.

Paul's Missionary Journeys

Paul defines his ministry in Gal. 2.9 as a ministry to the Gentiles by divine calling and with the assent of the leading apostles. As the 'apostle to the Gentiles', Paul carried the good news about Jesus throughout the mediterranean world in the course of three missionary journeys. These journeys covered a considerable terrain and involved him in a variety of different experiences.

The date of Paul's conversion has been debated, but some scholars have placed it as early as 34 CE (October).[33] This would set it within a short span of the crucifixion of Jesus.[34] If Paul was converted that early, his claims to be a latecomer on the Christian scene (1 Cor. 15.8) should be assessed in relative terms. He must have been 'converted' not long after James the Just.[35] His career as a persecutor of the church (Gal. 1.13) would thus have been short and sharp rather than long and protracted.

After his conversion Paul says that he went to Arabia (Gal. 1.17), presumably to meditate on what had happened to him. He then returned to Damascus where he probably exercised a preaching campaign and studied the scriptures. After three years (perhaps by 'inclusive reckoning') Paul went down to Jerusalem for fifteen days (Gal. 1.18). This was probably the 'famine relief visit' described by Acts 11.27-30. Paul says that he met Cephas and James on this occasion (Gal. 1.18-19). We do not have a text of their conversations; but C.H. Dodd commented famously that 'presumably they didn't talk about the weather'.

The First Missionary Journey

Acts 13.1-3 reports that the Holy Spirit commissioned Barnabas and Saul for special ministry in the course of a revelation. As a result of this they set sail, with John Mark, from Seleucia to Cyprus. Following an initial preaching campaign in Salamis, they travelled westwards and came to Paphos (Acts 13.5). It was here that Paul met the magician bar-Jesus and subdued him to blindness, as a result of which the proconsul Sergius Paulus was converted.

From Cyprus, Paul and the others sailed to Perga in Pamphylia, on the southern shore of Asia Minor (Acts 13.13). At this point John Mark broke company with Paul and Barnabas and returned to Jerusalem (Acts 13.13). The remaining two proceeded to Pisidian Antioch in southern Galatia (Acts 13.14). Paul preached in the synagogue and was opposed by the Jews. According to Acts 13.46, Paul said that as a result of this rejection, 'It was necessary that the word of God should be spoken first to you. Since you reject it and judge yourselves to be unworthy of eternal life, we are turning now to the Gentiles.' This statement needs careful interpretation, for Acts later records Paul as preaching in the synagogues. Hereafter, Paul emerges as the leader of the party where Acts 13.2 had referred to 'Barnabas and Saul'. They were driven from the city by the Jews, men and women alike.

From Antioch they went to Iconium, Lystra and Derbe. Much the same sequence of events occurred in Iconium. Paul and Barnabas preached in the synagogues. Animosity was stirred up against them. The result was an attempt to stone Paul and Barnabas (Acts 14.5). At Lystra the people thought that Barnabas and Paul were gods, calling Barnabas Zeus and Paul Hermes and even attempting to sacrifice to them (Acts 14.12-13). The preaching there was successful until Jews came from Antioch and Iconium and turned the crowds against them. Arriving in Derbe, they 'made many disciples' (Acts 14.21). They then retraced their steps to Perga and returned to Antioch. All of this took place between 43 and 45 CE.

The Jerusalem Conference

Acts 15 describes a conference in Jerusalem at the end of the first missionary journey.[36] This conference was prompted by the increasing number of Gentile converts to Christianity. In Acts 15.1, which is supported by Paul's own words in Gal. 2.12, people from Jerusalem had begun to teach the Gentile converts in Antioch they must be circumcised and obey the Jewish Torah. The result was this conference at which the status of Gentile converts was debated.

The evidence of Acts 15 has been considered problematic when compared with its sister passage Galatians 2.[37] It has been debated whether Galatians 2 really describes the same event because Paul makes this his second visit to Jerusalem where Acts claims it as his third. Having said this, both Acts 15 and Galatians 2 refer to some kind of conference in Jerusalem. It would be strange if two such meetings occurred without formal evidence in Acts. There is no necessary reason why Galatians should include an historical log of all Paul's visits to Jerusalem. A second problem concerns the outcome of the conference. Paul says in Gal. 2.6 that the Jerusalem apostles 'contributed nothing to me'; but Acts 15.20 says Paul agreed that Gentiles should adopt four modest concessions to Jewish scruples ('to abstain only from things polluted by idols and from fornication and from whatever has been strangled and from blood').

The attempt of some to equate Galatians 2 with Acts 11 on the grounds of the number of journeys is not successful. If Galatians 2 corresponds to Acts 15, this raises the question of the formality of the decree issued on that occasion and the response that Paul made to it. There is some sense of conflict between Acts and Paul depending on the view that one takes of Acts 15.20. In 1 Corinthians 8, for instance, we find Paul arguing that it is permissible for Christians to eat meat sacrificed to idols. Some have seen the concessions of Acts 15.20 as a later and unhistorical accretion; others think that they were reached at a later time when Paul was not present; others again argue that Paul accepted the concessions as a working compromise with Jewish Christians; Floyd V. Filson thinks that 'Paul agreed to the "decree" not as a compromise but because it contained essentially the kind of arrangement which he had led Gentile Christians to accept from the beginning of the Gentile mission.'[38]

The overall outcome of the Conference is not in doubt, however. Paul and Barnabas were vindicated in their Gentile mission. The fury that provoked Galatians is probably to be explained in reaction to the Jerusalem Conference when Jewish Christians *continued* to tell the Galatian Christians that they must be circumcised and keep the Torah in defiance of the general agreement. The result of the Conference (which probably took place in 51 CE) was that Paul embarked on further missionary journeys.

The Second Missionary Journey

In Acts 15.36–41 Paul and Barnabas break company over the issue of John Mark. Barnabas takes Mark and returns to Cyprus. Paul takes Silas and goes to Syria and Cilicia.[39]

At first Paul revisited Derbe and Lystra where he arranged for Timothy to be circumcised and to join his party (Acts 16.3). Apocalyptic revelation dominates the itinerary as Acts tells the story of the second missionary journey. They went through Phrygia and Galatia, 'having been forbidden by the Holy Spirit to speak the word in Asia' (Acts 16.6). They then attempted to enter Bithynia 'but the Spirit of Jesus did not allow them' (Acts 16.7). Finally, Paul had a vision of a man from Macedonia and headed there, 'being convinced that God had called us to proclaim the good news to them' (Acts 16.10).

This decision brought the Pauline party (to which the author of Acts implicitly claims to belong) via Troas and Samothrace to Philippi.[40] Despite initial successes, Acts tells the curious story of how the conversion of a slave-girl with divinatory abilities provoked hostility and caused Paul and Silas to be dragged before the civic authorities, beaten and imprisoned. The Philippian jailer was converted when Paul and Silas refused to escape from prison when an earthquake destroyed the building (Acts 16.25-34). After identifying himself as a Roman citizen, Paul received an apology and was freed from prison (Acts 16.35-40).

In Acts 17 they proceed to Thessalonica where success is again followed by civic investigation, as a result of which they are packed off by the Thessalonian church to Beroea (Acts 17.10). Jewish hostility from Thessalonica pursued Paul there (Acts 17.13). Leaving Silas and Timothy behind, Paul went from Beroea to Athens where the second half of Acts 17 narrates his famous sermon on the Areopagus, in the course of which he told the Athenians, 'What . . . you worship as unknown, this I proclaim to you' (Acts 17.23).

From Athens Paul proceeded to Corinth (Acts 18). He stayed there with the fellow tent-makers Aquila and Priscilla (Acts 18.3). Acts speaks of further opposition, prompting Paul to say that from then on he would go to the Gentiles (18.6), but it is difficult to unravel actual history from the author's narrative interests at this point. Acts states also that public unrest among the Jews resulted from Paul's preaching in Corinth, leading to a hearing before the proconsul Gallio (Acts 18.12-17). From Corinth, Paul went to Ephesus and thence via Caesarea and Jerusalem to Antioch.

The Third Missionary Journey

The shift from the second to the third missionary journey is described somewhat clumsily in Acts with the words, 'After spending some time [in Antioch] he departed and went from place to place through the region of Galatia and Phrygia, strengthening all the disciples' (Acts 18.23).

The most substantial port of call on the third journey was Ephesus (Acts 19.1).[41] Acts 19.8 states that Paul spent at least three months there, initially using the synagogue but then withdrawing to the hall of Tyrannus. Acts 19.11-20 narrates some extraordinary miracles that Paul performed in Ephesus. These culminated in further civic unrest (Acts 19.23). In Acts 20 Paul set sail for Macedonia, proceeding from there to Greece. Acts 20.3 briefly mentions a plot laid against Paul by the Jews, as a result of which he returned through Macedonia. Acts 20.6 brings him to Troas, 20.13 to Assos, 20.14 to Mytilene and 20.15 to Miletus, where he spoke with the elders of the church at Ephesus. Acts 21 brings the third missionary journey to a close with Paul's return to Jerusalem, allegedly against more than one piece of advice.

Arrest and Imprisonment

The advice that Paul received not to go to Jerusalem proved to be sound. In Acts 21.27 Jews from Asia cause trouble for Paul. It was alleged that Paul had brought the Gentile Trophimus into the temple (Acts 21.29). This caused a riot (Acts 21.30). Paul is arrested but, claiming to be 'a citizen of an important city' (Acts 21.39), is given permission to speak. Paul narrates his own conversion (Acts 22). When the Jews angrily interrupt him, he pleads his Roman citizenship to save himself from a flogging (Acts 22.22-9).

There follows the story of how a plot against Paul's life was discovered by his nephew, who reported it to the tribune. Paul, now in prison, was provided with secure transport to Felix the governor at Caesarea. Formally accused by a man named Tertullus who had travelled from Jerusalem, Paul makes his defence before Felix in Acts 24. Felix listens to Paul and adjourns the hearing, evidently expecting to receive a bribe from Paul (Acts 24.26). After two years Felix was succeeded by Porcius Festus (Acts 24.27). At the preliminary hearing before Festus Paul appeals for his case to be heard in Rome (Acts 25.11).

Acts 26 records Paul's speech before Festus in the presence of King Agrippa and Bernice. Here again Paul narrates his conversion. Paul's speech leads Agrippa to comment to Festus that Paul could have been set free had he not appealed to the emperor (Acts 26.32).

The rest of Acts (chapters 27 and 28) is preoccupied with Paul's journey to Rome, including the famous shipwreck (Acts 27).[42] Acts closes on an ambiguous note with Paul under house arrest in Rome and 'proclaiming the kingdom of God and teaching about the Lord Jesus Christ with all boldness and without hindrance' (Acts 28.31). There has been no shortage of attempts to explain why Acts ends at this point and what happened to Paul beyond the close of the story.[43] It is most unlikely that Acts is incomplete, for 28.31 looks like a natural conclusion. We need to acknowledge that, for whatever reason, the author wanted to end his story here. It is vaguely possible that Luke planned a third volume which he never completed, but that is not really a satisfying solution to the problem.

Nor is it certain what happened to Paul. There are only two possibilities.[44] Towards the end of Romans Paul speaks of his desire to visit Spain and the West (Rom. 15.28). Some scholars hold that Paul was tried and released and made his journey beyond Rome. This theory is heavily obstructed by the objection that, had Paul been released or found innocent, the author of Acts would surely not have lost the opportunity to say so; and also to describe Paul's further career. Other scholars believe that Paul suffered martyrdom in Rome at some point in the early 60s. There is a little archaeological evidence to support this conclusion,[45] but we must acknowledge that Paul's end is shrouded in mystery. It is ironic that we should know so much about Paul in the period before he made, or expected to make, his most famous speech of all, but then lose sight of him before he addresses the emperor. There are more sinister possibilities, such as Paul having a post-Christian phase and reneging on what he had said; but there is no evidence for these theories at all, and they should clearly be dismissed for that reason.[46]

CHRISTIANITY BEFORE PAUL

Before we can turn to Paul's letters as such, we shall examine the nature of the Christianity that existed before Paul wrote.[1] This important issue turns in no small measure on the interpretation of sources like Acts and the value that we place on occasional sources of insight about earlier Christianity in the Pauline letters themselves.

The date of Paul's conversion is relevant to this discussion. If Paul was converted in 34 CE, and thus within a short span of the resurrection of Jesus, then we have a seventeen-year period between this event and the writing of 1 Thessalonians, his first letter, in 51 CE. This means that Paul himself was the witness of many of the events and developments we shall mention in this chapter. It would be wrong to pretend that he was not. On the other hand, the attempt to confine our discussion of Paul to the evidence of his acknowledged letters is a legitimate one. We cannot say what Paul *might* have thought about a particular situation without the evidence to support that assertion. We can only say what Paul himself said, and merely speculate about what other beliefs he may have held.

The evidence of Acts poses problems because of its relatively late date.[2] When Acts was written, no earlier than 90 CE, Paul had been off the scene for thirty years. That is as long a span as that between Paul's conversion and the end of his literary activity. We cannot be sure that Acts has got everything right, nor what sources its author used. There are places in Acts where the author seems to have introduced later ideas and to have followed his own literary design.[3] This does not necessarily vitiate the evidence; but it does call for caution in interpretation. We shall consider at every point the degree of certainty with which we say anything about the earliest Christianity. This relative certainty of course increases the more that we are able to use contemporary evidence.

The Impact of the Resurrection

The starting-point for this chapter is the recapitulation of the early Christian beliefs about the resurrection described in Chapter 16. We saw that, in the eighteen-month period between April 33 and Paul's conversion in October 34 CE, the risen Christ appeared in mystical visions to numerous people, including people who like James the Just and Paul had not originally been his disciples. The effect of these visions was to convince people that Jesus had transcended the experience of death to be revealed as the heavenly Lord. This resulted in the transformation of Jewish monotheism in a binitarian direction through belief in the divinity of Jesus.

One can hardly over-estimate the effect that these resurrection appearances had. They transformed the followers of Jesus from frightened people into the confident preachers of the good news about Jesus whom we meet in the early chapters of Acts. Christologically, they were responsible for the identification of Jesus with the Son of Man and the identification of Jesus as the heavenly Lord and Messiah.[4] As early as 1 Thessalonians 4 we find what appears to be the developed Pauline argument about the resurrection which is based on belief in the resurrection of Jesus and which is amplified in different ways in 1 Corinthians 15 and 2 Corinthians 5. The resurrection appearances seem to have been an historically limited phenomenon, ending (as Paul notes in 1 Cor. 15.8) with the appearance to Paul himself.[5] Yet they were enough to call Judaism's messianic sect into being and to determine its central beliefs. Christianity has subsequently acknowledged Jesus as Lord (Phil. 2.11) and presented this (in an appropriate trinitarian context) as the required feature of belief.[6]

The development of the doctrine of the Trinity itself requires brief comment.[7] Although the classical language of Christian trinitarianism derives from the fourth and fifth centuries and not from the New Testament period, it is important to recognize that these later developments were not creations *ex nihilo* but legitimate re-expressions of the beliefs that are found in the New Testament itself. 1 Thessalonians 1 already contains an implicit trinitarianism; Paul presents a more developed view in Romans 8. John's Gospel is a heavily nuanced trinitarian text. The development of trinitarian theology was a necessary manoeuvre in the wake of emerging beliefs about Jesus. The Hebrew Bible had long known that God's Spirit manifested itself on specific occasions (see below). The belief that Jesus was divine created the need for a synthesis in which the particular modes of divine action were explained by an overarching theory. The New Testament holds that God is the creator, Jesus his Son the redeemer and the Spirit the active presence of God and Jesus in the world. This understanding stemmed in essentials from the *beginning* of Christianity, and certainly before Paul. It was neither a patristic development nor even a development that can satisfactorily be assigned to the later New Testament period, whatever its subsequent outworking.

Acts and the History of Earliest Christianity

The essential problem with Acts is that, except in those places where we can compare it with Paul's letters, we have no means of verifying the information that it gives us about the very earliest Christianity.[8]

This problem has led to widely different estimates of the historical value of Acts. A conservative scholar such as Howard Marshall tries to maintain that the author was a careful and accurate historian who describes what actually happened.[9] Marshall is supported in this by Martin Hengel, who insists that Luke is no less trustworthy than other ancient historians.[10] This has not been the verdict of every commentator on the issue. Ernst Haenchen takes a more trenchant view.[11] He argues that the Paul of Acts is quite different from the Paul whom we meet in the acknowledged Pauline letters. For Haenchen, the Paul of Acts is quite unambiguously the Paul of a later age.

While it may be true that one's own perspective on Acts reflects the stance one adopts towards wider biblical and theological matters, the question of the historical reliability of Acts is posed acutely by its earliest chapters, where we have no parallel source to verify the information presented. All we can do is to examine this material and make an estimate of its likely probability. That can be done with greater or lesser confidence depending on the extent to which we acknowledge the possibility of legendary accretion in the story of the earliest Christianity.

Pentecost

One of the surprises of Acts' earliest chapters is their relative silence about the resurrection appearances and the substantial interest that the author takes in Pentecost.[12] Luke, if indeed he was the author,[13] has a tidy division between his two volumes in which the physical ascension of Jesus to heaven is made the decisive link, not the resurrection appearances themselves. Of course, it could be argued that the ascension *is* a resurrection appearance; but the fact that it is not described in the other Gospels demands our attention. The removal of Jesus prepares the way for the coming of the Holy Spirit, in what appears to be a scarcely concealed trinitarian perspective.

Pentecost has a clear theological agenda in its present position in Acts. This is quite apart from the question of its historicity, which again has been a disputed issue among the commentators. Even if we maintain that Acts preserves a reliable account of what happened on this occasion, it is difficult (if not impossible) to maintain that the author has preserved the exact words of Peter at Pentecost.[14] The most we can suggest is that he followed Thucydides' dictum that the author supplied what he genuinely thought the speaker would have said.[15] We must conclude that this is a very rough rule-of-thumb, particularly so far as Peter's reported use of scripture is concerned.

Fortunately, it is not necessary to resolve the question of the historicity of the Pentecost story to comment on its meaning. The purpose of this story is to describe the divine empowerment of the church. The Pentecost story supplies the key to the narrative in Acts. It makes the church a Spirit-filled community among whom the Spirit of God becomes the permanent gift of the eschatological age, where in the Hebrew Bible the Spirit had been manifested on specific occasions alone.[16]

Everything in Common

The end of Acts 2 presents what many take to be an idealistic view of the primitive church in Jerusalem. Acts 2.44 states that 'all who believed were together and had all things in common'. Acts 2.45 adds that 'they would sell their possessions and goods and distribute the proceeds to all, as any had need'.

The background to this passage has been explored in a fascinating series of papers by Brian J. Capper.[17] Capper draws attention to the parallel example of the community of goods among the Essene community. He suggests that the evidence of this, quite unrelated, Jewish sect is a good argument for taking Acts seriously at this point. He also thinks this is why Ananias and Sapphira are punished so severely in Acts 5.1-11; because they lied in the matter of property when becoming members of a covenant community. While there is no evidence that this communitarian practice extended beyond the primitive church in Jerusalem, it may well be an accurate recollection which suggests that Christianity had a sectarian organization from its very beginning. The question of the relationship between Christians and Essenes in Jerusalem is a fruitful one for further research which may do much to explain the ultimate origins of the Christian movement.[18]

Hebrews and Hellenists

The Ananias and Sapphira story is the first of several divisions that attended the birth of Christianity. It is followed in Acts 6 by the story of division between the Hellenists and the Hebrews which resulted in the appointment of 'deacons'. The ostensible cause of this dispute was the complaint that the widows of the Hellenists were being neglected in the daily distribution of food. The odd thing about the deacons, however, is that when appointed they do anything but wait on tables. The stories of Stephen in Acts 7 and Philip in Acts 8 show that the deacons were effectively early Christian missionaries and evangelists. We shall look closely at the division in Acts 6 to discern what is going on here.

There is widespread agreement that the 'Hebrews' and the 'Hellenists' were both Jews and that the names refer primarily to linguistic divisions.[19] The Hebrews spoke Aramaic and the Hellenists probably spoke Greek. This is very probably also the distinction between Palestinian and Diaspora Judaism. The dominant theory in respect of Acts 6 is typified by Martin Hengel's assessment that the dispute between the Hebrews and the Hellenists was seminally responsible for the first development of the Gentile mission even before Paul's missionary journeys.[20] The deacons whose names are given in Acts 6.5 are all Greek. Hengel thinks that they were the leaders of the Hellenist Christian congregation in

Jerusalem. On his view, they developed an idiosyncratic theology which was more critical of the temple and its cult than the Hebrew Christians. This theology is typified by Stephen's anti-temple speech in Acts 7. As a result, persecution broke out against the Hellenists in Jerusalem. Being driven from the city, the Hellenists took the Christian message with them, exemplified by Philip's travels in Acts 8. In Acts 11.19-20 they share the message with non-Jews in what Hengel regards as 'a mission to the Gentiles without the law.'

This view has met with criticism, not the least of which is that Acts 7 is much too slender to reconstruct a formal 'theology' of the Hellenists.[21] This is undoubtedly true, but there does seem to be a sense in which the division represents theological conflict as well as linguistic barriers. Acts 7 is difficult to ignore in this respect. Given this evidence, we are bound to conclude that Paul himself was not necessarily the originator of the mission to the Gentiles but that, as a Hellenist himself, he followed much more prominently in the paths which others had established. The importance of Acts 6 lies in its testimony to an early dispute between Hebrew and Greek Christians in which separate paths were followed almost from the very beginning of the religion.

The Gospel Before Paul

This conclusion leads us to consider the nature of the Christian message before Paul. At places in his letters Paul includes what appear to be earlier formulae, most notably as we have seen in the early verses of 1 Corinthians 15, where Paul states that 'I handed on to you as of first importance what I in turn had received: that Christ died for our sins in accordance with the scriptures, and that he was buried, and that he was raised on the third day in accordance with the scriptures' (1 Cor. 15.3-4).[22]

This passage places us in touch with the shared apostolic gospel of the very earliest Christianity. While it is clear from more than one passage that the words of Jesus were important in the construction of the Christian self-understanding (a point which has unfortunately been obscured in some work on this subject),[23] we should not ignore the theological consciousness that shines through 1 Cor. 15.3-4. This shows that it was not enough for the Christians simply to repeat the words of Jesus. They inserted them into a broader framework of interpretation. That framework is demonstrated by this passage, which we might call an early 'kerygmatic summary' of the events concerning Jesus.[24] This summary compares and contrasts the death and resurrection of Jesus and holds them of saving benefit; in this case, the 'for our sins' hints at the possibility of acceptance by God and thereby has an eschatological base which Paul himself would develop as his career progressed.

Other Pauline passages probably represent the beliefs of the common apostolic Christianity. One such is Rom. 1.3-4, where Paul speaks of 'the gospel concerning his Son who was descended from David according to the flesh and was declared to be Son of God with power according to the spirit of holiness by resurrection from the dead, Jesus Christ our Lord'. Although the meaning of the word translated here as 'declared' is debated, not least by those who think it attests an 'adoptionist Christology' by which Jesus was a human being whom God appointed Messiah at the resurrection, this passage certainly contrasts the two states of Jesus' life in kerygmatic terms and makes the resurrection the decisive moment in the Christians' perception of him as Saviour.[25] It is also likely that Paul's argument about baptism in Gal. 3.26-9 derived from earlier Christianity (although we shall see in Chapter 27 that it cannot necessarily be assumed that baptism was a universal feature of Christian praxis in the first century CE).

The ambiguity of this area lies in the lack of final certainty about whether these passages *definitely* represent pre-Pauline ideas, even though it seems likely that they do. Another problem is that, as has been noted in the case of Acts 7, we do not have sufficient evidence for pre-Pauline Christianity, still less a pre-Pauline Christian text, to make firm judgments about this period. We can but examine the Pauline material with caution and integrity, making judgments about relative plausibility. We are on firmer ground when we turn, as we now do, to the Pauline letters themselves.

THE WRITINGS OF PAUL

Paul is both the earliest and the most extensive New Testament writer. Study of Paul, however, is complicated by the recognition that there are letters in the New Testament which are attributed to Paul but which it is virtually certain that Paul himself did not write. A further complication is the possibility that some of Paul's genuine letters may have been interpolated at some later point by others, in the concern to bring him up to date as regards a new situation. All of this means that the task of reading Paul is not as straightforward as might be preferred. Readers must tread carefully and ask critical questions at every point.[1]

One cannot understand the New Testament without trying to understand Paul. Understanding Paul requires a critical reading of his texts. In this chapter we shall survey the Pauline corpus as it currently stands and try to discern parameters between the genuine and the pseudonymous letters. This is the first stage in responsible interpretation. At times, this will involve borderline decisions; but that is inevitable when studying Paul. It should be noted that some scholars believe *all* the Pauline letters are authentic, but that such people are very much in the minority.[2] The more common (and indeed plausible) view is to accept the hypothesis of pseudonymity in certain cases but to argue strongly for a genuine core of Pauline letters which gives us valuable material to work on.

The Acknowledged Letters

The acknowledged letters of Paul (in canonical order) are Romans, 1 Corinthians, 2 Corinthians, Galatians, Philippians, 1 Thessalonians and Philemon. The disputed letters (again in canonical order) are Ephesians, Colossians, 2 Thessalonians, 1 Timothy, 2 Timothy and Titus. The last three letters are generally placed together in a group and called 'the Pastoral letters' because of their concern with church order. This canonical order, let it be said, is not the correct chronological order of these letters. What constitutes the correct chronological order depends on the view that is taken of pseudonymous authorship. For this reason I shall examine all the Pauline letters, acknowledged and disputed alike, in the canonical and not what I take to be the chronological order. Only by doing this can we form a judgment about the chronological order. I shall examine the acknowledged letters first and follow this with a study of the disputed letters.

Romans

The first letter to be examined is Romans.[3] Romans is often regarded as Paul's most mature letter, but it was not in fact his last letter. That distinction rests (probably) with Philippians. Romans was evidently written in Corinth during Paul's three-month stay recorded by Rom. 15.25 and Acts 20.2-3. This has been dated to the years 55 or 56 CE. Paul is anxious to get his gospel accepted in the Roman capital so that he can use Rome as the base for his proposed visit to the west (Rom. 15.24, 28). Paul writes in Romans to a church that he does not know personally. He speaks to them with clarity and conviction about the basis of his gospel, urging them to a common mind that will enable his plans for mission.

Romans has sometimes been regarded as a manual of Christian doctrine (notably by Melanchthon) but this is an over-statement of its contents.[4] Romans does not *look* like a treatise in theology. It has the form of a letter, and in this it resembles the other letters of Paul. In terms of its theological outlook, Romans has essentially to do with Christology and soteriology, which in Paul's outlook include the related topic of anthropology.[5] There are important topics which are scarcely mentioned in Romans (e.g. eschatology) and others which are not mentioned at all (e.g. the eucharist and questions of church order). That notwithstanding, Romans has most appropriately been called by Ernst Käsemann 'the testament of Paul' in the sense that it gathers together distinctive Pauline themes and presents them in a more coherent way than Paul achieved in his other letters.[6] We should presume that this coherence was a matter of authorial intention, possibly because Paul was not reacting to a crisis and thus had the opportunity for more measured discourse in which certain key themes are elaborated with conviction.

Paul opens Romans by discussing the nature of the Christian gospel. He calls the gospel God's power to effect salvation for everyone who believes (1.18). This leads immediately to questions of judgment (chapter 1) and law (chapter 2). Chapter 1 states that humankind has rebelled against God, rightly incurring divine wrath which is expressed in its natural context of justice. Chapter 2 argues that Jews and Gentiles stand together before God, even though the Jewish people have been entrusted with the Torah.[7] In a famous phrase (unfortunately much misused today) Paul says that those Gentiles who obey the natural law are 'a law to themselves', even though they have no knowledge of the Torah (2.14). This understanding of 'natural law' is essentially a Stoic idea. It helps Paul to further his argument for the incorporation of the Gentiles in salvation. That is developed as the letter unfolds. Chapter 3 establishes the basic principle that all have sinned. Paul defines 'sin' in terms of falling short of the divine glory (3.23).[8] Here we have echoes of the Pharisaism I described in Chapters 8 and 17. Its effect is to remove the distinction between Jew and Gentile through appeal to a common anthropological basis. This anthropology rests on the principle of Christ-tology set forth by Rom. 3.25 that 'God put (Jesus) forward as a sacrifice of atonement by his blood, effective through faith.'

In Romans 4 Paul introduces the figure of Abraham.[9] Paul cites the covenant between God and Abraham and notes that Abraham received circumcision as the covenantal sign *after* his election by God.[10] For Paul, this means that Abraham's descendants are children of faith and that circumcision is a merely subordinate question when the question of true paternity is considered. This is the beginning of Paul's classic statement of his principle of 'justification by faith'.[11] The basis of this principle is found in the demonstration that Abraham believed God and that his faith (which means his trusting belief) 'was reckoned to him as right-eousness' (Rom. 4.3). We shall see in Chapter 20 that 'righteousness' is a covenantal term which denotes God's faithfulness to his revelation, involving faithfulness to himself. Romans 5 (followed by Romans 8) constitutes the theological heart of the letter. Here Paul states that Christians are justified by faith and have peace with God through the achievement of Jesus (5.1). There is an obvious theology of atonement in 5.9 ('we have been justified by his blood'), matching what Paul had said in 3.25.[12] The thought is that the sacrificial death of Christ as God's Son has reconciled humankind to God in a unique act of restoration. Rom. 5.20 significantly presents the law as a poultice designed to draw out latent transgression, giving it a positive place in the economy of salvation.

Romans 6 links soteriology to ethics through an argument based on baptism.[13] Given that Christians have been baptized, Paul argues, they have already been raised from death to life. This is an obviously 'mystical' idea in the sense for which I argued in Chapter 17.[14] Now they must live out the new life and bring divine standards of holiness to bear on their earthly situation.[15] This means resisting the demands of sin and becoming what Paul calls 'slaves of righteousness' (Rom. 6.18); this term, I think, is a good example of what Paul understands by the divinely willed imperative of grace.[16]

In Romans 7 Paul deals with the problem of human sinfulness in the light of the Torah. He argues that Christians have been discharged from the law because of the achievement of Jesus (Rom. 7.6). Paul states that the law has defined the nature of human transgression and made it possible for sin to be perceived as sin. As a result of this insight, there is a fatal tension in all human beings, including those who belong to Christ.[17] This tension is between knowing what is right and actually doing it. It is, as Paul concludes at the end of the chapter, the tension between mind and body (7.25); which, put another way, is an honest acknowledgment of the inability of mental effort to control human action. This passage represents the anthropological beginning of Paul's understanding of the work of the Holy Spirit; the Spirit for Paul indwells Christian believers and impels them to ethical action.[18]

Romans 8 is the most systematic chapter in this, Paul's most systematic letter. Romans 8 has the nature of a summary which brings together the striking ideas Paul has articulated so far: 8.1-7 summarizes the theological content of Romans, linking together Christology, soteriology and ethics; 8.9-17 introduces a partially new idea, that of the contribution made by the indwelling Spirit to the process of Christian living. Paul is convinced that the Spirit produces life, whatever happens to the mortal human body. This leads him to wax eschatological in 8.18-27. Paul states that the entire creation will enjoy the process of redemption that Christ's sacrificial death has inaugurated.[19] Although Paul does not deal here with the future transformation of the human body, he insists that the creation will be freed from its bondage to decay and enjoy the liberty of God's children. This is a way of saying that the entire universe as God's creation is also the sphere of God's redemption. For this reason, nothing can separate Christian believers from the love of God expressed in Christ (8.31-9).

There is a marked change in tone at the beginning of Romans 9.[20] Paul now turns to consider the fate of Israel in the scheme of salvation; and especially the problem that Israel rejected its Messiah when Jesus appeared. It is axiomatic for Paul (as no doubt for other Jews) that God is neither impotent nor wrong. The problem of Israel's standing turns on the question of divine election which Paul holds an intractable issue. He insists that God has grafted in the Gentiles 'to share the rich root of the olive tree' (11.17) – the olive a traditional image for the Jewish nation – and that 'all Israel will be saved' (11.26). As at the end of Romans 11, this leads to a paean of praise in which the depth of God's being is adored (11.33-6).

In Romans 12 Paul offers rules for behaviour in the Christian community, introducing his famous image of the body of Christ in a call for humble mutuality. This leads in 13.1-7 to a call for civil obedience (a passage which has sometimes been seen as a later insertion).[21] The rules for good behaviour persist until Romans 15. While 15.33 looks like the original conclusion to the letter, the bulk of Romans 16 has often been seen as a later insertion.

1 Corinthians

1 Corinthians answers questions put to him by the church Paul had founded in Corinth.[22] The letter was written in Ephesus (so 16.8) in 54 or 55 CE.

1 Corinthians opens by acknowledging tensions in the Corinthian community.[23] It seems that Paul's authority has been denigrated and that party factions relating to different Christian leaders have reared their head in Corinth. Paul responds by explaining the nature of the gospel which he says, in the face of his own alleged frailty, constitutes divine

power revealed in the guise of human weakness, including the apparent weakness of the cross (2.6–8).[24] The diffusing of tension by pointing to the corporate nature of Christian ministry occupies Paul in the first four chapters of 1 Corinthians. Chapter 5 deals with a notorious case of sexual immorality in which a man is living with his father's wife. Paul addresses this problem by advising the community to consign the man to Satan for the destruction of his flesh (a possible allusion to the book of Job) 'so that his spirit may be saved on the day of the Lord' (5.5). This difficult passage has been the subject of much discussion; but it shows the extent to which eschatological concerns motivated Paul.[25]

Chapter 6 criticizes the practice of litigation in the Corinthian church. Paul moves from there to further matters of sexual concern.[26] These occupy Paul until the end of chapter 7, where he turns to the question of meat sacrificed to idols. Although rather strange to our own world, this was a pressing question for Christians in antiquity since much of the meat that was eaten was butchered in sacrificial or liturgical rituals associated with pagan divinities.[27] The question was whether Christians as followers of the one true God were permitted to eat such meat. Paul says that this practice is admissible on the grounds that idols have no substantial existence, unless a Christian with a less robust conscience (what Paul calls a 'weak' person) is offended by the practice. This – very striking – argument cocks a snook at the pagan divinities and mocks their very existence in the spirit of Deutero-Isaiah.

In 1 Corinthians 9 Paul answers the charge that he is a sponger on hospitality by saying that he deserves to be supported by the Christian community but has in fact elected not to do so. 1 Corinthians 10 develops the theme of idolatry, reiterating the invitation to 'eat whatever is sold in the meat market without raising any question on the ground of conscience' (10.25); but also telling the readers to 'flee from the worship of idols' (10.14). This leads, in the controversial first half of 1 Corinthians 11, to a statement of the subordination of women to men and a warning about appropriate behaviour at the *agape*.[28]

Chapters 12 to 14 deal with the question of spiritual gifts and manifestations in the church.[29] Paul introduces the image of the body of Christ (as he did in Romans 12) to explain that no spiritual gift or person is somehow greater than another. The grounds for this assertion are that all Christians belong to the one body of Christ which is empowered in the world by one and the same Spirit. 1 Corinthians 13 is the famous celebration of the primacy of love over faith and hope.[30] 1 Corinthians 14 deals with the more esoteric gifts of prophecy and ecstasy, calling for sense and order in the practice of what cannot by nature be understood and which Paul says must therefore be used advisedly.

1 Corinthians 15 contains Paul's most detailed eschatological teaching.[31] Paul begins by citing the formula about the death, burial and

resurrection of Jesus. He details the resurrection appearances, including the mystical appearance to Paul himself (15.3-11). This leads to Paul's insistence on the actuality of Jesus' resurrection and his outworking of this event in theological terms. Mystical categories stand to the fore at this point.[32] Given that Paul presents the human body as liable to be transformed or superimposed by an imperishable body, we saw in Chapter 16 that it is a reasonable deduction this is what Paul thought had happened to the body of Jesus in the resurrection. The implied sense of 1 Corinthians 15 is that the continuity between the earthly Jesus and the heavenly Lord lies in the transformation of his human body through the acquisition of heavenly immortality. The heavenly body of Jesus is the paradigm of the believers' resurrection body. It is implied that full mystical communion with Christ will be achieved through the transformation of believers to resemble him at the eschatological climax. This is a theme that Paul develops in his last letter, Philippians (see below).

1 Corinthians 16 brings the letter to a close with instructions of various kinds.

2 Corinthians

2 Corinthians is more difficult to decipher than 1 Corinthians.[33] This is because the letter falls into three different blocks whose relationship to each other has caused much debate in the past.[34] These blocks are chapters 1–7, chapters 8–9 and chapters 10–13. It has also been observed that chapters 1–7 do not form an obvious unity and contain more than one awkward transition. In particular, 6.14–7.1 looks like an insertion for which a Qumran provenance has occasionally been suggested.[35]

This evidence has led many if not most scholars to conclude that 2 Corinthians as we have it is made up of more than one part. The crucial question is whether chapters 10–13 belong with the rest of the material. This contentious issue can hardly be considered in brief. Opinions have been voiced on both sides of the argument.[36] Certainly, the transition to Paul's self-defence in these chapters is unexpected, not least at this point in the letter. One wonders whether more than one Pauline letter has been combined in 2 Corinthians, with the proviso that there are no grounds for denying the bulk of the material to the authentic Paul. This view makes it difficult to date 2 Corinthians; but scholars often assume as a bench-mark that it was written in Macedonia and comes from the year 55 or 56 CE.

Paul begins by apologizing for the fact that he has not visited the Corinthians a second time. He refers to pain he has caused the community (2.2), which is otherwise unknown from 1 Corinthians and Acts. This delicate situation leads Paul to a celebration in chapters 2 and 3 of the apostolic ministry as one through which the divine glory is revealed. Chapter 4 describes the very evident clay of that human nature through which such glory is revealed (4.7). 2 Corinthians 5 contains further eschatological teaching in which Paul speaks again of the heavenly body that will be superimposed on the mortal human body at the resurrection. Chapter 6 contains the odd-looking passage I mentioned (6.14–7.1) which asks, 'What agreement does Christ have with Beliar?' (6.15). Chapter 7 further describes the tribulations Paul had suffered in his career as an apostle.[37]

Chapters 8–9 form a separate and self-contained section in 2 Corinthians.[38] Paul deals with the matter of the collection he was making for the church in Jerusalem, which had been hard hit by famine (cf. Acts 11.28-30).[39] There is a famous justification of this appeal in 2 Cor. 8.9 which refers to the self-emptying of Christ in what appears to be a clear allusion to his heavenly pre-existence ('You know the generous act of our Lord Jesus Christ, that though he was rich, yet for your sakes he became poor, so that by his poverty you might become rich'). It is certain that, in reading this passage, we hear the voice of the middle Paul.

Chapters 10 to 13 return to Paul's boasting just when we were beginning to think he had got beyond this stage.[40] The most obvious explanation of this section is that it represents the interpolation of previously written material; possibly the 'severe letter' of 2.3-4 which we know from 7.8 caused sorrow in the Corinthian church. Chapters 10 to 13 justify Paul's apostolic credentials. It is evident from 11.5 that (in the wake of the reference to party strife in 1 Corinthians) Paul had been denigrated by comparison with some of what he terms 'super-apostles'. He replies that he is not a fool, and especially not a fool when it comes to perceiving the hidden divine wisdom. This leads him in 2 Corinthians 12 to speak of a mystical vision he had received at some point after his conversion.[41] Paul says that he was caught up to paradise in the third heaven and 'heard things that are not to be told, that no mortal is to repeat' (12.4).[42] He adds that, because of these revelations, a thorn was given him in the flesh to prevent him from becoming too proud (12.7). Paul thereby boasts in his weakness – naming a divine origin for it – and defends his ministry before the Corinthians, as he feels obliged to do.

Galatians

Galatians, which is sometimes supposed to have been Paul's earliest letter and to have been written in 48 CE, stands with Romans at the very heart of the Pauline corpus.[43] Galatians was probably written at some point in 54 or 55 CE, in either Ephesus or Macedonia.

The letter is a harsh condemnation of those who taught Paul's Galatian converts what Paul in 1.6 ironically calls 'a different gospel'. This was a gospel based on Jewish principles in which circumcision and the demand to keep the Torah were imposed on Gentile converts. Paul deals with this problem by describing his own experience in Judaism and his espousal of

Christianity. He insists that his gospel – which advocated freedom from Jewish legislation – was no human innovation but had been received as the result of divine revelation (1.11-12). This leads Paul to describe a dispute between himself and Peter in Antioch when the latter allegedly adopted double standards in the matter of table-fellowship with Gentiles. On this occasion Paul said to Peter that 'If you, though a Jew, live like a Gentile and not like a Jew, how can you compel the Gentiles to live like Jews?' (2.14).[44]

The rest of Galatians contains theological argument which defends the inclusion of the Gentiles in salvation. In Galatians, Paul adopts a more polemical attitude towards Judaism than he does in the slightly later Romans. He states in 2.16 that 'a person is justified not by the works of the law but through faith in Jesus Christ'. In Galatians 3 he compares the law to a disciplinarian whose ministry was concluded with the coming of Christ.[45] In Galatians 4 Paul goes so far as to say that the two epochs of law and grace are signified by the two wives of Abraham, Hagar and Sarah.[46] He says of Hagar that she bore children for slavery (4.24), commanding (in a very striking phrase) 'Drive out the slave and her child; for the child of the slave will not share the inheritance with the child of the free woman' (4.30). This comes very close to a negative evaluation of the law, and indeed of Judaism itself, which it is possible that Paul felt to some extent obliged to correct in Romans.

Galatians 5 and 6 contain injunctions to live by the Spirit and not to gratify the desires of the flesh.[47] These link with the earlier chapters by relating the indwelling Spirit to the redemptive achievement of Jesus in a repudiation of the possible temptation to antinomianism (living as if there were no law) which Paul acknowledges in 6.2 with his reference to 'the law of Christ'. Being a Christian, he says, does not mean abandoning the law but following a different kind of law.

Philippians

Philippians is probably the last letter Paul wrote.[48] Like 2 Corinthians, but perhaps less obviously, it has been suggested that here we have more than one fragment of a Pauline letter.[49] It has sometimes been thought that Philippians originally concluded in 3.1 but that in 3.2 another section begins which looks like an interpolation and which runs until 4.3. This is not necessarily the case, for Philippians reads much more coherently than 2 Corinthians and Paul himself is liable to sudden changes in tone. Of the interpolation theory, no less an authority than Werner Georg Kümmel states that 'this whole line of argument is totally unconvincing'.[50]

The greater problem to solve in respect of Philippians is that of its provenance and date. No fewer than three places of origin have been suggested. Out of Caesarea, Ephesus and Rome, the Roman hypothesis is the most convincing.[51] This would place the letter in the early 60s before Paul's presumed martyrdom in Rome. The other suggested provenances demand earlier dates, so that on those theories Philippians would not be Paul's last letter.

Paul begins by explaining that what had happened to him through imprisonment had served to advance the cause of the gospel. Paul looks forward to his own demise, stating that he would prefer to 'depart and be with Christ' (1.23). This is the first time Paul has spoken of his death. Chapter 2 contains the so-called 'Christ Hymn' (2.6-11), the interpretation of which has been a major bone of contention.[52] The significant exegetical question is whether or not this part of the letter alludes to Christ's 'pre-existence' in the heavenly world, as I have suggested that 2 Cor. 8.9 does. Subsidiary questions are whether or not the passage was written by Paul or derived by him from a source. These questions aside, the passage describes the humility of Jesus which is exemplified by the manner of his death of the cross. It contrasts this humiliation with the exaltation of the resurrection in which Jesus is worshipped as a heavenly being subordinate to God. Although the content of the hymn is christological, indeed quite markedly so, the context in which it is used is ethical. Paul uses it to criticize back-biting in the Philippian community, which he claims is inimical to the gospel.

Philippians 3 contains further warnings against Judaizing (3.2-6), as if this continued to be a problem that Paul faced throughout his career. The second half of chapter 3 turns to matters eschatological. Following his expressed hope for the 'heavenly call' in 3.14, Paul reiterates the eschatological hope he had first expressed in 1 Thessalonians some ten years earlier.[53] This is the promise that Jesus will return from heaven. It has sometimes been suggested that Paul turned away from this expression of eschatology towards the end of his career but, if Philippians is Paul's last letter, that theory is difficult to sustain. If my date for Philippians is accepted, this so-called *parousia* hope dominated Paul's theological agenda from beginning to end.

Paul's eschatological hope is very much rooted in the present world. He states that 'our citizenship is in heaven, and it is from there that we are expecting a Saviour, the Lord Jesus Christ. He will transform the body of our humiliation so that it may be conformed to the body of his glory, by the power that also enables him to make all things subject to himself' (3.20-1). This passage picks up the hope for transformation from 1 and 2 Corinthians and states that it represents the climax of eschatology.[54] Paul retains the hope for Jesus' return and makes this central to his mature statement of what will happen in the eschatological future. The transformation of the human body will occur when Jesus returns to earth. This is the hope in which Christian life is currently lived. It would represent the completion of the Christian hope that Paul had first grasped in his mystical revelation of Jesus.[55]

Philippians 4 brings the letter to a close with some instructions and exhortations. This chapter includes some notable passages, not least the call for continual rejoicing in 4.4.

1 Thessalonians

1 Thessalonians, which comes near the end of the canonical sequence, is probably Paul's first letter.[56] Thessalonica was the capital of the Roman province of Macedonia. The church in Thessalonica was founded by Paul and Silvanus (Silas) in 49 CE. 1 Thessalonians was probably written in 50 CE. The letter is important, especially when we set it in the immediate context of Philippians, not least for understanding the early development of Paul's eschatological teaching.[57]

1 Thessalonians opens with Paul's praise of the faith of the Thessalonian community, together with an important formula which has often been regarded as a summary of Paul's (early?) preaching to Gentiles: 'You turned to God from idols, to serve a living and true God, and to wait for his Son from heaven, whom he raised from the dead – Jesus, who rescues us from the wrath that is coming' (1.9-10).[58] The 'wrath' mentioned here is the eschatological retribution which Romans and other Pauline texts say is impending over those who refuse to believe in Jesus. Paul states that Jesus will deliver those who wait for him from this 'wrath' so that they have nothing to fear from it.

In 1 Thessalonians 2, Paul reminds the community of his efforts among them and celebrates their faith, which he says imitated that of the Christian churches in Judaea. In chapter 3 Paul says that he had sent Timothy to Thessalonica to enquire after the church's faith. It seems that Timothy's report prompted the writing of the letter. The report was essentially a good one, but it raised some matters of moral and eschatological concern (chapter 4). Paul asks the community to abstain from fornication (4.3) and to maintain mutual love and support (5.9-12). Eschatological matters are addressed in the second half of chapter 4 and in the first half of chapter 5.

The problem at Thessalonica was the community's general concern that some of their number had died before the *parousia* of Jesus. There is more than one possible reading of this complaint. Plevnik plausibly argues that Paul had originally taught that one had to be alive to experience the 'rapture' mentioned in this passage and that the reality of death had created the fear that the dead would be deprived of eschatological benefits.[59] Paul replied by offering his assurance that this was not the case and (fortunately for subsequent Christianity) by restating his early eschatological understanding. This is based on the conviction that God will 'bring' with Jesus those who had died (4.14). The crucial event is the return of Jesus from heaven (4.15). The dead will rise when the *parousia* occurs (4.16). Curiously, and not found elsewhere in the Pauline writings, the living and the dead are expected to ascend to the clouds 'to meet the Lord in the air' (4.17) This strange reference has been interpreted in two different ways.[60] It is possible that it attests an early understanding of heavenly immortality for the faithful; but more likely that it uses the imagery of the triumphal procession in which the earthly saints greet the angels to escort the victorious Jesus back to earth.[61] That would bring 1 Thessalonians 4 into line with later Pauline eschatology and indicate that Paul, like Jesus, understood the kingdom of God as an earthly entity achieved by intervention from outside the historical process. Such an interpretation provides a natural explanation of the concluding words, 'and so we will be with the Lord for ever' (4.17).

1 Thessalonians 5 contains the earliest evidence we have that the delay in Jesus' return was felt to be a problem in the Christian communities. Although we have only one side of a conversation, and do not know for sure either what Paul had originally taught the Thessalonians or what they made of his teaching, the very fact that Paul reminds his readers that 'the day of the Lord will come like a thief in the night' (5.2) suggests at least some concern over the matter of the eschatological delay. This is particularly obvious in 5.6, where Paul exhorts, 'So, then, let us not fall asleep as others do, but let us keep awake and be sober.' Paul's early eschatological teaching thus occurs within a context where human death and the delayed *parousia* were thought to be problems.

The letter ends with a concluding call for peace and with Paul's blessing on the Thessalonian community.

Philemon

The last of the genuine Pauline letters is Philemon.[62] Philemon differs from the other genuine Paulines in that it is a personal letter, written to a prosperous Christian whom it is unlikely that Paul knew personally. Paul had met a runaway slave of his, Onesimus, and with due propriety decided to send Onesimus back to Philemon. Paul pleads for clemency, although significantly he does not call for the setting-aside of the institution of slavery itself or for the manumission of Onesimus. Philemon comes from the period 55–60 CE when Paul is in prison; but the brief nature of the letter makes it difficult to decide exactly when it was written.

The Disputed Letters

Now we turn to the disputed letters. This is a more contentious issue since scholars disagree about which texts should be placed in this category. I have decided to take a 'maximalist' view, grouping together all the disputed epistles, although I am less certain whether Colossians should be placed here than the other letters. As before, I shall introduce the letters in their canonical order. This is neither their chronological order nor the order of their probable authenticity.

We begin by briefly considering the problem of pseudepigraphy in the ancient Christian world.[63] We have seen that the question of whether the New Testament contains pseudonymous letters has been answered in different ways, but that the majority of critical scholarship accepts that it probably does. The background to this conclusion is the observation that a significant number of pre-Christian Jewish texts are pseudonymous, hence the generic classification 'Pseudepigrapha' which is often invoked to describe them.[64] The collected Enochic literature and the *Odes of Solomon* are well-known examples of this practice. Pseudepigraphy was a common feature of Christian writings of the second century CE and beyond, including such works as the *Acts of Paul* and the *Apocalypse of Peter*.[65]

The primary purpose of pseudepigraphy was not to deceive the readers but to gain authority for the views that are advanced in a particular work.[66] A substantial impetus towards the introduction of pseudepigraphy in Christian circles was the recognition that key figures such as Peter and Paul were dead and that authoritative advice was needed to deal with fresh problems. Paul's name (like that of other figures) was invoked to speak with his old familiar authority where advice was felt to be needed.

Ephesians

The first letter to be discussed in this category is Ephesians.[67] Ephesians cannot be reviewed without mentioning Colossians; the grounds for denying Pauline authenticity to Ephesians are stronger than in the case of Colossians.[68]

Ephesians claims to be by Paul (1.1). The letter was widely known in the second century CE.[69] Having said this, the letter looks conspicuously different from other Pauline texts. It lacks any realistic personal detail of the kind we encountered in the genuine Pauline letters. Kümmel comments that 'the author seems to lack any sort of relationship with the readers'.[70] Paul, however, spent three years in Ephesus. This makes the claim to Pauline authorship unconvincing.

Other arguments have been produced to support this denial.[71] The most important is the presence in Ephesians of certain terms which are not found in Paul but which occur in later New Testament writings and in the apostolic fathers. Examples include the Greek words *eusplanchnos* and *politeia*. In addition, Ephesians uses certain other words or phrases (notably, 'in the heavenly places') which mean approximately the same thing as genuine Pauline conceptions but which Paul himself characteristically expressed in different ways.

This idiosyncratic vocabulary comes to a head when Ephesians is compared with Colossians.[72] Mitton notes that about a third of the words used in Colossians are reproduced in Ephesians and that these verbal similarities are distributed relatively evenly in Ephesians.[73] Only brief parts of Ephesians have no verbal parallels in Colossians. One whole passage about Tychicus in Ephesians (6.21-2) agrees almost exactly with Col. 4.7 in such a way as to indicate that Ephesians is almost certainly dependent on Colossians.[74] That the dependency runs this way (rather than from Ephesians to Colossians) is indicated by the observation that Ephesians also shows dependence on the wider Pauline corpus (with the exception of 2 Thessalonians) in a way that Colossians does not. Another, and in fact crucial, factor is the observation that Ephesians holds the Tychicus passage in common with Colossians but that it *also* uses certain words held in common with Colossians in a very different sense. This makes the theory of simultaneous authorship by the same writer implausible if not impossible. Some scholars even think that Ephesians uses words and ideas in a way that Paul himself did not do and would not have done.[75]

This cumulative evidence is virtually decisive for identifying the pseudonymous nature of Ephesians. There is some evidence to support this view in the letter itself. The superscription 'in Ephesus' (1.1) is found in many but not all manuscripts, including the text of the letter read by the second-century heretic Marcion. Tertullian says that Marcion knew this letter with the superscription, 'to the Laodiceans'.[76] There is no specific reason why Paul should write to the Laodiceans as such. Several scholars think that Ephesians was originally written as a circular letter, either with a blank space left for the insertion of more than one destination or more likely with no specific destination at all. The view taken here is that it is a post-Pauline circular of this kind, which nevertheless represents a development if not a climax of Paul's ideas in a way that significantly values the persona and the influence of the apostle himself.

The date of Ephesians is clearly dependent on that of Colossians. This is a matter we have yet to resolve. Even if Colossians is thought to be genuinely Pauline, however, there is no reason to assume that Ephesians was written in its immediate aftermath. Conceptions such as the institutional nature of the church in Eph. 2.20 indicate that Ephesians is a product of the late first century CE at the very earliest. Somewhere in the 90s of the first century is the consensus opinion.

The contents of Ephesians resemble a pastoral and theological (if not a liturgical) homily. Chapter 1 has a 'timeless' quality which celebrates Christ's heavenly enthronement and relates this to the life of the church at large. Chapter 2 celebrates Christian redemption, commenting famously that God has broken down the 'dividing wall' of hostility between Jew and Gentile (2.14). In the light of Romans and Galatians, it would be astonishing to find Paul himself making this statement. At 2.20 the letter looks to the era of the apostles and prophets as already past, confirming that the letter comes from a time when a new order of authority pertained in the church. Chapter 3 contains fictitious information about Paul's imprisonment. Chapter 4 is an ethical appeal which requests that readers 'no longer live as the Gentiles live' (4.17). Chapter 5 contains rules for Christian households.[77] These persist into chapter 6, where the letter concludes with the Tychicus passage and a grace and peace formula.

Colossians

The case for pseudonymous authorship of Colossians is not perhaps as strong as with Ephesians, but it has certainly been made in the past.[78] In the early nineteenth century it was in fact believed (by Mayerhoff) that the letter was dependent on Ephesians, but this view is now generally abandoned even by those who accept that Colossians is pseudonymous.[79]

The disputed authenticity of Colossians makes for an interesting test-case in the history of Pauline interpretation. F.C. Baur thought that both Colossians and Ephesians were the products of a second-century Gnosticism.[80] This approach was countered by the so-called 'History of Religions' school, which suggested (notably through Martin Dibelius) that Colossians' cosmic interests might easily reflect the religious atmosphere of Paul's own lifetime.[81] There was a further shift in the 1950s under the influence of Rudolph Bultmann and his pupils, who studied Pauline theology from an essentially Lutheran background and found Colossians distant from the other letters when this perspective was adopted.[82] Whereas English commentators such as Houlden and Caird defended Pauline authorship, this opinion has gone by the board in the majority of contemporary research.[83] Colossians should be examined with care to weigh the balance for and against Pauline authorship.

The evidence comes from several quarters. The first of these is Christology. Colossians tends to give Christ a cosmic role in a way that marks a difference from other Pauline letters when its protology is considered. Col. 1.15 says of Jesus that 'he is the image of the invisible God, the firstborn of all creation; for in him all things in heaven and on earth were created, things visible and invisible . . .'[84] When we compare this with even an explicit statement of Christ's pre-existence in the genuine Paul such as 2 Cor. 8.9 cited above, the differences are clear to see. Colossians incorporates a much more mythological Christology which draws heavily on the Jewish Wisdom tradition.[85]

Similarly, there is a heavy emphasis on 'realized eschatology' in Colossians whereas Paul himself never abandoned the idea of the *parousia* as we saw from Philippians 3.[86] 'Realized eschatology' does not necessarily deny the possibility of a future consummation; but it concentrates on the provision of salvation in the here and now whether or not any future climax is intended. In its description of baptism, for instance, Col. 2.12

states that Christians have *already* been raised with Christ. This is different from Paul's more cautious statements in 1 Cor. 4.8-10; 13.8-13, and indeed from Paul's general sense that the resurrection is a yet-to-be-accomplished event.

The understanding of the church is also different in Colossians from that found in other Pauline letters. Though indeed Paul speaks more than once of the church as 'the body' of Christ (Romans 12; 1 Corinthians 12), in Colossians this metaphor is redeployed to present Christ as the 'head' of the body in what we might claim an uncharacteristically Pauline way (Col. 1.18).[87] This has the effect for ecclesiology of giving the church, like Christ, a cosmic dimension. Similarly, the rather affected statement of 1.24 that Paul completes 'what is lacking in Christ's afflictions for the sake of his body' goes beyond Paul's own understanding of the apostolic ministry, as does the apparent reference to the accomplishment of universal mission in Col. 1.23. Furthermore, the construction of a 'household code' of ethics in 3.18–4.1 has been thought to go beyond Paul's more rudimentary ethical pronouncements in a letter such as 1 Corinthians.[88]

Having said this, statistical analysis is divided in its attitude towards Colossians. A. Kenny concludes from his analysis that we have in the twelve Pauline letters 'the work of an unusually versatile author'.[89] Interestingly, while Neumann finds Colossians and Ephesians closer to the other Paulines than to the Pastorals or other New Testament texts,[90] Mealand sets the two apart from the other Paulines.[91] The jury is still out on this matter. At present, we can but note the significant difficulties surrounding Pauline authorship and concentrate on reading the text.

Colossians 1 presents Christ as the head of his body in a cosmic sense. There is a strong note of 'realized eschatology' in this chapter as the author explains that 'the mystery that has been hidden throughout the ages . . . has now been revealed to his saints' (1.26). Chapter 2 contains ethical teaching, including an interesting passage which requests, 'Do not let anyone disqualify you, insisting on self-abasement and worship of angels' (2.18).[92] This passage has been variously interpreted and the possibility that angelic mediators were worshipped at Colossae considered by the commentators. This culminates in the ethical appeal at the beginning of Colossians 3, 'So if you have been raised with Christ, seek the things that are above, where Christ is seated at the right hand of God' (3.1). Ethical exhortation continues in the 'household rules' already mentioned. Colossians 4 brings the letter to a close with further instructions and the Tychicus passage.

2 Thessalonians

Certain difficulties attend the suggestion that Paul wrote 2 Thessalonians as well as 1 Thessalonians.[93]

The most obvious difference is the letter's eschatological teaching; specifically, the apocalyptic strand to its eschatology.[94] This amounts to a shift between 2 Thessalonians 1 and 1 Thessalonians 4 concerning what will happen at the eschatological climax. Gone is the reference to the 'rapture'. In its place we find the statement that the Lord Jesus will be revealed from heaven with his angels 'to repay with affliction those who afflict you' (2 Thess. 1.6) and 'inflicting vengeance on those who do not know God and on those who do not obey the gospel of our Lord Jesus' (2 Thess. 1.8).

There is further eschatological dissimilarity in 2 Thessalonians 2.[95] Where previously Paul had spoken only of the *parousia*, now he mentions a specific figure called 'the lawless one', predicting that 'the Lord Jesus will destroy [him] with the breath of his mouth' (2 Thess. 2.8). 2 Thessalonians 2 prescribes a much broader eschatological scheme, mentioning both 'the workings of Satan' (2.9) and a 'powerful delusion' sent on the ungodly by God (2.11). 2 Thessalonians 3 contains essentially ethical teaching, including the command to keep away from idle believers (3.6).[96]

The question of authenticity turns on the issue of whether Paul could have offered the eschatological teaching that he did in 1 Thessalonians 4 and then followed this up with the rather different, or at least more explicit, teaching that we find in 2 Thessalonians. This is not impossible; but we must certainly say that 2 Thessalonians offers ideas which are not found elsewhere in the Pauline letters. The issue is difficult to decide with confidence; but many commentators think that 2 Thessalonians is a post-Pauline text. In the words of Raymond E. Brown, however, 'although the current tide of scholarship has turned against writing by Paul himself, biblical studies are not helped by being certain about the uncertain'.[97]

The Pastoral Letters

By contrast, we may be virtually certain that Paul did not write the Pastoral Letters, 1 Timothy, 2 Timothy and Titus.[98] These letters were perceived as a group and given this title in the eighteenth century.[99] They are called 'the Pastorals' because they offer teaching about the pastoral office in early Christian communities.

External attestation for the Pastorals is less strong than in the case of other Pauline letters, including Ephesians.[100] They are lacking, for instance, in Marcion's canon and in the early Chester Beatty papyrus. Although they were accepted as genuinely Pauline in the patristic church, doubts were expressed about this issue from the early nineteenth century onwards.[101] These doubts rest on a variety of arguments.

The first difficulty is the observation that the Pastorals cannot be fitted into any reconstruction of Paul's life that is made on the basis of Acts and the acknowledged Pauline letters. This difficulty is exacerbated by an argument based on language and style. The Pastorals lack many of the short words that Paul uses frequently. They include language, such as Hellenistic 'epiphany' language, which Paul himself does not use elsewhere. Added to this is a developed ecclesiology which cannot be matched in any of the acknowledged Pauline letters. Some of the difficulties are described by W.G. Kümmel: 'The Pastorals contain a string of statements which do correspond to the central ideas of Paul . . . But along with them appears Hellenistic terminology which is totally foreign to Paul . . . Still more striking than the divergent formulation of soteriological expressions is the description of Christian existence which one finds in the Pastorals.'[102]

It would appear virtually impossible in today's climate to defend genuine Pauline authorship of the Pastorals, although the attempt to do this has sometimes been made by conservative scholars.[103] This does not devalue the contents of these texts. As with Ephesians, it simply points to the continuing and growing influence of Paul which resulted in the desire to claim his authority for letters which addressed the problems of a later generation. The Pastorals probably come from the early second century CE. They have much in common with the understanding of church order that is found in the letters of Ignatius.[104]

1 Timothy contains primarily ecclesiological and ethical instruction.[105] 1 Tim. 2.12 contains the intractable statement, 'I permit no woman to teach or to have authority over a man; she is to keep silent', in the context of rules about order in worship. Chapter 3 deals with the question of the ministerial offices, offering instructions for bishops and deacons in the oversight of the Christian communities; chapter 4 extols the virtues of godliness; chapter 5 emphasizes the importance of care for older people, including respect for the elders of the church; chapter 6 is an ethical exhortation whose orientation (even in this early second-century text) is an eschatological one (6.14).

2 Timothy has an equally fictitious setting.[106] 2 Timothy 2 deals interestingly with eschatological concerns. In a context where the author promises future eschatological benefits (2.11-13), he criticizes the teaching of people 'who have swerved from the truth by claiming that the resurrection has already taken place' (2.18). This appears to be an early Gnosticizing view, although it is difficult at our distance to reconstruct the precise contours of the argument in question. 2 Timothy 3 relates the difficulties of the age to which the Pastorals were addressed by saying that 'in the last days distressing times will come' (3.1). There follows a catalogue of vices with some similarities to pagan ethical catalogues but with an implicit eschatological foundation.

Titus similarly contains ecclesiological and ethical instructions, including the statement that slaves must be submissive to their masters (2.9-10). This resembles Philemon in not criticizing the institution of slavery *per se*.

Reading the Pastorals, one is struck by their curious blend of eschatological hope and growing acceptance of the world order. There is no indication that the author has rejected the hope for the *parousia* of Jesus. Indeed, he emphasizes it in what might be regarded as more intense language than Paul himself used (for example, 'the manifestation of our Lord Jesus Christ', 1 Tim. 6.14). That notwithstanding, the detailed ethical prescription and awareness of typical situations shows a shift from first-century Christianity. This is characterized by the recognition that, although the last days may be nigh, these are of significant duration; the eschatological climax will occur at what the author quite ambiguously calls 'the right time' (1 Tim. 6.15).

And So . . .

This short reading shows that study of Paul cannot be divorced from literary-critical questions. We cannot assume that Paul wrote everything that is attributed to him, nor even that we necessarily have his letters in the precise form in which he composed them. We must examine the evidence with care and ask at every point whether we are dealing with a Pauline or a subsequent idea. This is in addition to the question of whether or not there is development in Paul's theology.

Having said this, there is no reason to be pessimistic about the study of Paul. We can read the central texts, beginning with Galatians and Romans, and discover Paul's distinctive concerns. As opposed to the theology of the Hellenists, we are fortunate in having considerable evidence of Paul's emerging understanding. This helps us chart the early course of Christian origins with relative clarity.

PAUL AND CHRISTIAN SALVATION

What follows is more of a whistlestop tour than a detailed guide to Paul's theology.[1] We begin with the questions of God and of Jesus, for it is there that Paul's theology itself begins. Indeed, it might reasonably be said that Paul's theology is an outworking of the conviction that God has acted eschatologically in Jesus. As I have hinted already, this was a belief that Paul shared with other Christians of the first century; but we only have *his* letters to make judgments about the unfolding nature of Christianity in the years following the resurrection. In examining the contours of Pauline theology, the question remains to some extent an open one of how far Paul differed from other Christians in the first century CE, and where the common ground was.

The Primacy of God

To speak about Jesus is for Paul simultaneously to speak about God.[2] Paul was not a Trinitarian writer in the credal sense but there are many indications in his writings that he thought in at least a rudimentary Trinitarian way.[3] By this, I mean that he saw the work of Jesus in the wider context of God's action and believed that this work was being continued in the church by the Holy Spirit. This rudimentary Trinitarianism is linked to belief in the resurrection and it represents a legitimate development of that belief.

Paul shared with other first-century Jews the belief in the primacy of the God of Israel.[4] Generally speaking, when Paul mentions his apostolate he refers it to the calling of God (as at 1 Cor. 1.1; Gal. 1.1). His mature letter Romans presents the concepts of divine election and wrath as the key to his entire theological understanding. The fact that there is little developed or formal 'theology' ('talk about God') in Paul should not lead us to the conclusion that belief in God was unimportant for him. The reverse is clearly the case. Paul does not often articulate a formal doctrine of God because he *assumes* it at every point in his letters. Paul held in common with contemporary Judaism belief in the oneness of the God who had created the physical universe and made Israel his special people. Paul would presumably have prayed the *Shema* on a daily basis. He also shared the Pharisaic belief that this God raises the dead (Rom. 4.17), together with the variety of messianic and eschatological hopes which appear in Christian form in his letters.

Paul's change of heart would certainly have been greater had he not held these Jewish beliefs before his conversion to Christianity. This is not to underestimate his change of mind, however. From the Jewish belief that God had chosen Israel as his special people, which in mainstream Judaism involved the rejection of Christian claims that Jesus was the Lord and Messiah (not to mention incipient trinitarianism), emerged the conviction that God was the Father of Jesus in a unique sense (for example, 2 Cor. 11.31). The most obvious source of this understanding, itself suggested by Rom. 1.3-4, is the Christology of pre-Pauline Christianity which Paul had learned in the days and months after his conversion.[5]

Paul's Christian understanding took the view that God had inaugurated the mission of Jesus. While we have yet to consider whether and to what extent Paul believed in Jesus' heavenly pre-existence, in general terms Paul presents God as the author of everything Jesus had accomplished. This is made obvious in Gal. 4.4-5, where Paul (possibly citing an earlier formula) states that 'when the fullness of time had come, God sent his Son, born of a woman, born under the law, so that we might receive adoption as children'.[6] Both the sending of the Son and the adoption of the Christians are presented as divine works which God the Father had inaugurated and Jesus effected. It follows that for Paul there would have been no Christian experience of salvation had God not acted eschatologically in Jesus. God, his being and his action are the basis of Pauline theology.

This is not said in ignorance of the theological distinction Paul makes in 1 Cor. 8.5-6.[7] Whether or not this formula derives from pre-Pauline Christianity, it formed the heart of the argument Paul used when addressing the question of meat sacrificed to idols. Paul recognizes the dominance of pagan polytheism but sets against it the Jewish conviction that 'there is no God but one' (8.4). Paul follows this up by offering a Christian account of the way all things began: 'For us there is one God, the Father, from whom are all things and for whom we exist, and one Lord, Jesus Christ, through whom are all things and through whom we exist' (8.6). This binitarian formula acknowledges God the Father as the creator of the physical universe and Jesus Christ as the agent or mediator through whom God had created the world. This distinction, which owes much to the Jewish wisdom tradition, unites Jesus and God within the same divine action but in a context where Jesus is manifestly subordinated to God as agent to cause. Such 'subordinationism' is a consistent feature of Pauline Christology (see e.g. 1 Cor. 15.28).[8] It is a way of preserving the divine initiative within the human action of Jesus and of providing a meaningful way to speak about God when Christology seems to dominate the scene in Paul. It follows that God can never be dismissed from the drama of Paul's theology even though at times he seems a silent actor. He is in fact not an actor at all but the director of the action. For that reason he is not often seen on stage.

Jesus of Nazareth

What did Paul make of the human Jesus of Nazareth, and how did he conceive of the relationship between the executed prophet from Nazareth and the heavenly Christ who had appeared in the mystical vision to call Paul to his apostolate (1 Cor. 15.8)?[9]

It is sometimes said that Paul takes no interest in Jesus of Nazareth, but this is a misrepresentation of the evidence.[10] Paul clearly knows that Jesus died and rose so that the historical fact of the crucifixion is important to him (1 Cor. 15.3; Gal. 3.13). The problem that has been felt in this area is that Paul only rarely refers to the life and words of Jesus.[11] He prefers to speak about what New Testament scholars like to call 'the Christ event'. This phrase denotes the saving achievement of Jesus when his death and resurrection are considered in eschatological terms. The presumed silence of Paul has theological implications. If Paul takes no interest in the human Jesus, that raises the question of whether the historical Jesus as opposed to the kerygmatic presentation of Jesus' death and *post-mortem* career is important for Christian theology.[12]

An initial response to this debate observes that Paul's letters are what Calvin J. Roetzel has called 'conversations in context'.[13] We have only one side of the dialogue, and have no idea of what conversations preceded the particular conversation to which we have access. Paul only occasionally gives glimpses of what he might have said to his churches (e.g. 1 Thess. 1.9-10). We are therefore *forced* to speculate about what Paul said, at least to a point, with the inevitable ambiguity I mentioned.

Although Paul does not provide any record of his lost conversations, we must surely presume that they included information about Jesus. Paul himself would have learned this information early in his Christian career; not least when he visited Jerusalem on the occasion described by Gal. 1.18.[14] We know that the Gospels drew extensively on oral tradition, whether or not we accept the 'Q' hypothesis.[15] Paul must have known these traditions about Jesus. He had met people who had known Jesus personally. It is impossible – and I use this word advisedly – that he knew nothing about Jesus' career in the period before the crucifixion.

This observation sets the agenda for our present discussion. The question is not whether Paul knew the traditions about Jesus, which he most certainly did, but why he did not make more of them in the letters that we have. In part, we have seen that this is circumstantial given that Paul's letters are neither systematic texts nor indeed Gospels as such. Yet Paul does on occasion allude to the teaching of Jesus. Such allusions are found in various forms in his acknowledged letters. Thus Paul knows about the Last Supper in 1 Corinthians 11 and he mentions Jesus' teaching about divorce in 1 Corinthians 7. He specifically refers to 'the Lord's' teaching about paying labourers (1 Cor. 9.14) and to a 'word from the Lord' about the *parousia* (1 Thess. 4.15). Several scholars also believe that Paul's use of the word *abba* in Gal. 4.6 and Rom. 8.17 is an echo of the Lord's Prayer.[16]

This represents a reasonable amount of information about the pre-Easter Jesus. Just as there are echoes of the Jesus tradition in Paul, so Paul also uses Jesus as an example when it comes to recommending certain patterns of behaviour to his readers.[17] This is most obvious in Phil. 2.6-11 where, despite the obviously 'high' view that is taken of Jesus' position in the heavenly world, Paul's real interest lies with the example of Jesus as the one who humbled himself and ultimately died on the cross. Such an argument is impossible without a real interest in the life of Jesus as such. It shows that Paul did indeed know about Jesus and that he made use of such knowledge in his letters.

The Event of Salvation

Nevertheless, it is specifically the death and resurrection of Jesus which claim Paul's greatest attention. This is because these events, on his view, gave the Christians access to the experience of salvation in which they stand.

The death of Jesus, as Paul notes more than once in his writings, caused an immediate evangelistic problem. Paul says in 1 Cor. 1.23, 'We proclaim Christ crucified, a stumbling block to Jews and foolishness to Gentiles.' In Gal. 3.13 Paul writes, in a predominantly Jewish context, 'Christ redeemed us from the curse of the law by becoming a curse for us – for it is written, "Cursed is everyone who hangs on a tree." '[18] The 'curse' is the censure in Deut. 21.23 of those who were publicly displayed on a gibbet having met their death by stoning. Paul extends this curse to cover crucifixion as a parallel means of execution. Paul believes that God's hidden wisdom evaded the understanding of 'the rulers of this world' when they crucified 'the Lord of glory' (1 Cor. 2.6). It was axiomatic for Romans and Greeks alike (not to mention Jews) that no-one who met their death in this way could be considered of much account. Paul's genius was to express the ironic contrast between this widespread prejudice and the gospel of the crucified Lord and Messiah which he presented as the only way to salvation.

In doing this, Paul moves dialectically from historical event to theological explanation. The actual history of Jesus was unchallenged, even by pagans. We saw in Chapter 15 that Jesus of Nazareth died because the Romans considered him a threat to stability. Paul, probably following the lead of earlier Christianity, insisted it was through his shameful death that Jesus' true status was revealed. This is why Paul views the death of Jesus through the lens of the resurrection. The resurrection as Paul understands it was God's demonstration that Jesus is Lord and Messiah, and in this sense his vindication of the man who had been faithful in death. In this, Paul moves beyond the narrative of the resurrection appearances to a theological scheme which treats the death and resurrection of Jesus as one coherent event. There could have been no resurrection without the death; the death without the resurrection would have meant the end of the claims of Jesus. Paul understands Jesus' death in the light of his resurrection. He identifies Jesus as the one through whom God had 'reconciled the world to himself' (2 Cor. 5.17).

If the evidence of 1 Cor. 15.3-4 is anything to go by, this theological interpretation pertained from the earliest days of Christianity. It is said there that 'Christ died for our sins in accordance with the scriptures.'[19] Paul's achievement was to develop this theological interpretation in dialogue with his churches in rhetorical contexts. Paul's evaluation of the link between Jesus' death and resurrection was responsible for the distinctive contours of his theology.

Adam and Christ

At the heart of Paul's theology lay the conviction that the death of Jesus had representative significance. Paul came to this view by setting Jesus in contrast with Adam, evidently on the grounds that Adam was the first created person and Jesus the first person whom God had raised from the dead.[20] The resurrection disclosed a status for Jesus which no human being had enjoyed before. This was the position as the divine Son which is described by Rom. 1.3-4 and the heavenly Lord of Phil. 2.9-11.

Paul makes much of this contrast between Jesus and Adam in his letters. 'Sharing Adam's nature' is a fundamental anthropological idea.[21] It surfaces prominently in the second half of 1 Corinthians 15 where Paul contrasts Adam and Jesus in terms of the permanence of the bodies they possess. Paul argues that the resurrection has revealed Jesus as the second Adam, as a consequence of which he has the imperishable body that he will bestow on believers when he returns to earth (cf. Phil. 3.20-1). Adam, by contrast, had a perishable body. Such a body is owned also by the rest of humankind on the grounds that they follow in Adam's footsteps. The present and perishable body contrasts with the future and imperishable body.

Sharing Adam's lot is the natural condition of humankind, achieved by virtue of birth. This is the realm that Paul describes variously under the metaphors of sin and death. There is a clear statement of this position in 1 Cor. 15.22, where Paul says starkly, 'all die in Adam'. The reality of human death provides the link between 1 Corinthians and Paul's description of the effects of sin in Rom. 6.23, 'the wages of sin is death'. Sin itself is shown to be sin by the law (Rom. 3.20); it is defined as '[falling] short of the glory of God' (Rom. 3.23). Characteristically, Paul expresses this view of humankind's stark position through the lens of what Jesus has achieved. This has the effect of making the Adam–Christ typology decisive for Paul's view of salvation. We can see this typological influence by citing the full text of two of the passages just cited. 1 Cor. 15.22 in its entirety reads: 'For as all die in Adam, so all will be made alive in Christ'; Rom. 6.23, 'For the wages of sin is death, but the free gift of God is eternal life in Christ Jesus our Lord.' To this we should add the statement of Rom. 5.12 that 'sin came into the world through one man, and death came through sin'.[22]

In these texts Paul holds Adam responsible for his sin but, in line with Jewish post-biblical literature,[23] he also holds that people are responsible for the sins that they commit. There is no sense in which the sins of the fathers are vented on the children; for Paul, the children are punished because they too are sinners and sin. Sin is the universal condition of humankind established by Adam and perpetuated with vigour by his descendants (so Rom. 5.12). Salvation in Christ liberates one from the effects of sin, which we have seen from both 1 Corinthians and Romans means also liberation from the effects of death. The link between Adam and Jesus thus has an eschatological dimension based on the conviction that salvation is a continuing process with present and future benefits.

Crucial here is the recognition that Philippians is Paul's last letter' and that in Philippians Paul continues to maintain that Jesus will return from heaven to 'transform the body of our humiliation so that it may be conformed to the body of his glory' (3.21). This means that, in the chronological span between 1 Thessalonians 4 and Philippians, Paul continued to think about eschatology in 'this-worldly' terms. He expected Jesus to return from heaven to earth and transform human bodies so that they acquired imperishable status. Paul did not abandon this idea towards the end of his writing career.

Paul thereby conceives of salvation in theologico-historical terms. The condition of humankind as needing salvation or rescue was established by Adam's transgression in the primaeval period. This condition was actualized and repeated in the sinful actions of every human being, despite God's provision of the law (Romans 2). The offer of redemption was made in the very recent past, through the death and resurrection of Jesus the Messiah. Paul envisaged the future in apocalyptic categories as the final entrance of one order into another and as the consequent transformation of present experience through the acquisition of immortality (Rom. 8.18-25). This was made possible by Paul's view that Jesus had provided the antidote for Adam's transgression and inaugurated a new order of humankind where sin and death were overcome.

The 'Adam–Christ' typology is sometimes glossed over by commentators, but it is in fact central to Paul's thought. At heart, it represents a theology of creation. Adam was the first created person, the representative of the original creation described in the early chapters of Genesis.[24] This creation formed the arena in which the historical Israel (and later Jesus the Messiah) emerged. Paul also speaks unambiguously in 2 Cor. 5.17 of the 'new creation' in Christ. 2 Cor. 5.16-21 is a crucial exposition of Paul's gospel: 'From now on, therefore, we regard no one from a human point of view; even though we once knew Christ from a human point of view, we know him no longer in that way' (2 Cor. 5.16). This is not a contrast between the humanity and the divinity of Christ but a contrast between the original human order represented by Adam and the new human order inaugurated by Jesus. The linchpin between the two orders is the resurrection of Jesus. This is when it was perceived that, by contrast with the old order, people could 'know [Christ] no longer in that way'. Christ is not of the original order because as the first resurrected person he represents the 'new creation' in which 'everything old has passed away; see, everything has become new!' He is the first member of a new class of human being of which Paul says in Phil. 3.20 that 'our citizenship is in heaven', implying that this is the imperishable order described in the second half of 1 Corinthians 15. That is why in Rom. 8.15 Paul calls Christians God's children by adoption. This means that they have been removed from the old Adamic order and adopted into the new Christian order with the family promise of imperishability as signified by the *post-mortem* career of Jesus. In 8.19-21 Paul hints that this emancipation will be extended to the whole of the created order.

This in turn shows how Paul understands the resurrection of Jesus. For Paul, the resurrection meant passage through human mortality to heavenly immortality. This would be extended to all humankind when Jesus returned to earth. That is the very heart of Paul's theology.

A Sacrificial Expiation

Now we shall look more carefully at the language that Paul uses to describe the Christian experience of salvation.

This brings us immediately to the language of sacrifice. We saw in Chapter 7 that sacrifice stood at the heart of all Jewish religion. It is hardly surprising that Paul should turn to such language to describe the achievement of Jesus, particularly when we consider that Christianity had its origins in the humiliating death of a youngish man.[25] Rom. 3.25 brings us straight to the issue as Paul understands it: 'God put [Jesus] forward as a sacrifice of atonement by his blood, effective through faith.'[26] This too is a theological interpretation of Jesus' death. His death is understood here as a sacrifice. The person making the sacrifice, astonishingly, is said to be God. The thought is that God had provided the sacrifice which reconciled humankind to himself and that the sacrificial victim in question was none other than God's own Son.

The Greek word used for 'sacrifice' in Rom. 3.25 is *hilasterion*. It is necessary to cite the Greek at this point because this word is often used in the Septuagint to describe the lid of the ark of the covenant, otherwise known as the 'mercy seat'. This was the place where, on the Day of Atonement, a blood-offering was made for the sins of Israel according to the regulation of Lev. 16.16-17. More than one question has been asked about the precise meaning of *hilasterion* in Rom. 3.25. An important issue – at least for English Bible translators – is whether the word should be translated 'propitiation' or merely 'expiation'. The difference between these two terms is that the former carries the sense of appeasing the wrath of an angry God whereas the latter does not. There are two arguments in favour of the translation 'expiation' in Rom. 3.25.[27] In the Hebrew Bible, God is never said to be the object of the verb 'atone'. The object is rather the sin which is presented as the cause of the blockage between humankind and God. Moreover, although Paul freely presents God as the author of the sacrifice in question, it probably strains credulity to suggest that God should find it necessary to find such an extreme remedy whereby his own wrath can be appeased. This is a moral as well as a theological argument.

Another question concerns the possible influence of Jewish martyrology on Rom. 3.25.[28] The word *hilasterion* is used in *4 Macc.* 17.21-2 to describe the sacrifice of the Maccabaean martyrs. While it is possible that this post-biblical understanding influenced at least some of what Paul says in Romans 3, it is more likely that Paul holds the cultic background in common with the author of *4 Maccabees* and that both authors make use of the same tradition in different ways. This conclusion is confirmed by the observation that God himself is said to provide the sacrifice in Rom. 3.25; it does not emerge from human heroism or the historical process. That emphasis on divine provision makes a cultic background likely even when we acknowledge the general importance of Jewish martyrology in the early Common Era.

Rom. 3.25 raises more questions than it solves due to its brief and formulaic nature. There is, for instance, no reference to 'sin' in this formula. To understand *how* Paul understood the death of Jesus as a sacrifice we need to examine other passages also. Further light is shed by Rom. 8.3, where Paul also includes a narrative of salvation: 'For God has done what the law, weakened by the flesh, could not do: by sending his own Son in the likeness of sinful flesh, and to deal with sin, he condemned sin in the flesh.' The difference between Rom. 8.3 and the formula of Rom. 3.25 is that sin is made the significant problem that the death of Jesus addresses. The foundation of this argument is the premise that the law was unable to deal with the problem of sin because all it had done was to expose the inability of humankind to keep the divine commandments. The law made sin sin by providing a definition of it (cf. Rom. 3.20-3). All Hebrew thought demanded a sacrifice as the remedy for transgressing God's will. The phrase translated 'and to deal with sin' in Rom. 8.3 is the Greek *peri hamartias*. This phrase is used in a number of places in the Septuagint to render the Hebrew phrase, 'as a sin offering'. It is likely that this sense is intended in Romans 8, Paul asserting that an offering has been made for human sin.[29] As in Rom.

3.25, the thought is that *God* has provided this sacrifice. Rom. 8.3 adds to the formula of Rom. 3.25 an explicit interest in the problem of sin in the statement that Jesus' sacrifice has dealt with sins, '[condemning] sin in the flesh'. The implication is that the death of Jesus had proved effective in this way precisely because it was a sacrifice.

At 1 Cor. 5.7 this unfolding idea is linked to the notion of the Passover sacrifice: 'Our paschal lamb, Christ, has been sacrificed.' Careful description of this passage is needed because the Passover lamb in Jewish ritual was not a sacrifice in the technical Jewish sense.[30] Nevertheless, the later chapters of Ezekiel (specifically 45.18-22) associate the festivals of Passover and Atonement in the statement that a young bull is provided 'for a sin-offering'. This supplies at least some precedent for associating the two different ideas. The origin of the idea that Jesus' death was a paschal sacrifice was probably the recollection that his death had occurred at Passover time combined with the desire to say, in the words of another formula Paul cites, that 'Christ died for our sins according to the scriptures' (1 Cor. 15.3), which suggests a sacrificial understanding. The formula in 1 Cor. 5.7 draws on the background in Ezekiel and earlier biblical literature and fuses together imagery which had coalesced in recent Christian experience to provide a striking new expression.

There is a further development of this idea in 2 Cor. 5.21.[31] Paul writes that 'for our sake he made him to be sin who knew no sin so that in him we might become the righteousness of God'. This 'making sin' of Jesus recalls the Day of Atonement. Paul thinks of the unblemished animal provided on that occasion and associates Jesus thereby with the 'scapegoat' of Lev. 16.21. This 'scapegoat' was sent into the wilderness and not slaughtered, but it is sufficiently closely linked with the sacrificial ritual to become the object of Christian development in this way.

These last two passages show a loose use of imagery in which ideas drawn from the Jewish sacrificial ritual were developed by the Christians to describe the death of Jesus. This was unquestionably a reworking of existing ideas. Strictly speaking, the sin offering dealt only with inadvertent sins. There was no prescribed atonement for deliberate, still less for unrepented sins. This was evidently not a barrier to Paul's sacrificial interpretation of the death of Jesus. Paul's thought moves from effect to theology. He reworks Jewish theology in the light of what he now recognized as the divinely ordained remedy for human sin.[32]

It is probable that, in constructing this imagery, Paul thought that Jesus took the place of the sacrificial animal and that the sin was transferred from the sinner to the victim along the lines suggested by Lev. 16.21 (where Aaron places his hand on the goat and thereby transfers human sin to it). Here is the origin of the New Testament understanding of the sinlessness of Jesus.[33] The levitical legislation required that the victim be 'without blemish'. The New Testament understanding is not that Jesus was unblemished in the physical sense, for we never find a description of the body of Jesus in the New Testament;[34] but that he was 'without sin' in the moral and more predominantly the anthropological sense by virtue of his divine origins. This is the ground of Jesus' status as the second Adam. It was in fact necessary for Christian theology to create belief in the heavenly origin of Jesus to underpin its swiftly constructed sacrificial understanding.[35] This required that Jesus be qualitatively different from other people while also sharing human nature to the fullest extent. This is the foundation of the patristic doctrine of the 'two natures' of Christ.

Appropriated by Faith

We now ask how this salvific process worked itself out in the lives of Christian believers. This leads us to Paul's distinctive view of 'justification by faith'.[36]

So far, our discussion has been relatively straightforward. Paul's 'Adam' terminology allowed him to see humankind in generic terms as having turned its back on God and needing to be reconciled to God for that reason. In Romans 1, Paul describes this condition almost as forgetfulness or ignorance of God ('for though they knew God, they did not honour him as God or give thanks to him', Rom. 1.21). The decisive act of reconciliation was accomplished by Jesus Christ. Jesus was the final sacrifice for sin whom God had provided. His unique status as human yet divine had established a new order of humanity based on the resurrection, offering the possibility of immortality for his followers at the eschatological climax.

We shall examine the nature of Paul's future hopes in Chapter 21. Here we note an eschatological tension which we shall see in Chapter 22 is related also to the topic of Pauline ethics. This tension is generally called 'the now and the not yet of salvation'.[37] Paul's claim is that Jesus' death and resurrection had established a new human order in which Adamic limitations were set aside. This new order had begun with the resurrection but it was not yet complete (as Paul notes especially in Romans 8–11). It would finally be completed when Jesus returned from heaven, the general resurrection occurred, the Gentiles were included in salvation and 'all Israel will be saved' (Rom. 11.26). Meanwhile, Paul is anxious to extend the parameters of his preaching so that as many people as possible can be included in Christ's new human order. This was the theological rationale of Paul's missionary journeys, and it undergirded the missionary zeal of the entire early Christian movement.

Paul insisted that what Jesus had achieved on the representative level should and could be appropriated on the individual level through the experience of becoming a Christian. Paul's Adam–Christ typology created the need for a perceptible shift from one state of being to another. This is what had happened in Paul's own conversion and what he continually preached on his journeys must happen to those who responded to his message. Paul speaks dramatically of this change of heart, using the categories of 'sin' and 'death' as well as 'transformation' to underscore the point. A good example of Paul's ability to mix metaphors in this regard is 1 Cor. 6.11: 'You were washed, you were sanctified, you were justified in the name of our Lord Jesus Christ and in the Spirit of our God.'

Paul's most characteristic (but not his only) language for this shift is his language of 'justification by faith'. This language must not be pressed further than it deserves, as is sometimes done by those who claim it as the absolute 'centre' of Pauline theology. It is one metaphor among others in Paul's Christian vocabulary of salvation. Nevertheless, this metaphor features heavily in Galatians and Romans. It is a legal metaphor drawn from the law-courts. Ever since the alleged 'rediscovery' of this principle by Martin Luther at the Reformation, the significance of 'justification by faith' has engendered fierce debates about the outlook of Pauline theology.[38] Luther's unfortunate denigration of Judaism as a legalistic religion produced a plethora of academic studies in which this misconception was perpetuated, despite the criticism of such occasional voices as George Foot Moore's in the 1920s.[39] It was due more than anyone else to E.P. Sanders in the last century that this Christian portrayal of Judaism was shown to be a caricature, as we saw in Part I of this book.[40] Judaism in general and Pharisaism in particular is not a legalistic religion based on salvation by works alone. Such a view has ramifications for the study of early Christianity, including Pauline theology. The approach that we adopt to ancient Judaism clearly affects our understanding of the principle of justification by faith.

Paul's starting-point for his language of 'justification by faith' is the concept of divine 'righteousness' that he expresses in Romans 1.16-17: 'For I am not ashamed of the gospel: it is the power of God for salvation to everyone who has faith, to the Jew first and also to the Greek. For in it *the righteousness of God is revealed* through faith for faith; as it is written, "The one who is righteous will live by faith." ' On the evidence of this passage, the righteous God acts righteously by making others righteous. 'Righteousness' for Paul is a property of God's own being. Unfortunately, there has been a lack of certainty in the history of research as to what this word group actually means.[41]

'Justice' in English has a detached and impartial, if not a disinterested quality. In Hebrew thought, 'righteousness' always has a relational sense which is not always adequately conveyed by English translation. In Gen. 38.26, for instance, Judah says of Tamar that 'she is more in the right than I' in a context where Tamar has spoken the truth; and in 1 Sam. 24.17 David is called 'more righteous' than Saul because he refused to slay the Israelite monarch. It is unlikely that Paul's 'justification' terminology ignores this Hebrew background despite the claims which have been made about its forensic character. The concept of 'righteousness' in Hebrew essentially denotes obligations and their proper fulfilment. This provides the correct background for Paul's concept of 'righteousness' in Romans.

God's 'righteousness' in Rom. 1.16-17 denotes God's fidelity to himself and, by extension, to his creation, although in practice Paul rarely discusses the question of *why* God chose to create the universe and its inhabitants. In revealing his righteousness, God shows that he acts righteously. This means that he continues to act relationally (and in accordance with the covenant he had made with Israel). The basis of Paul's gospel is that humankind had become estranged from God by virtue of Adam's transgression. The result of this alienation was the entrance of sin and death into the human condition. At the heart of Rom. 1.16-17 stands the affirmation that the alienated God refuses to act in an alienated way. He chooses to act relationally, to restore the broken relationship by revealing the gospel which pivots around the death and resurrection of Jesus and its overcoming of Adam's transgression and creation of a new order of humanity. This is an act of 'grace' (a favourite Pauline term) in the sense that God has done *more* than was required by the covenant obligations once the wilfulness of Adam's sin is perceived.[42]

This is not a surprising theology for those who know the Hebrew Bible.[43] The crucial issue is not so much the fact that God *is* righteous, which is a consistent biblical theme, but that, as is implied by the verb 'justified', he *makes his people* righteous. This means that he causes them to act in the same way as he does, so that they act relationally in respect of himself. That is expressed clearly by Rom. 3.26, 'It was to prove at the present time that he himself is righteous and that he justifies the one who has faith in Jesus.' God's righteousness is demonstrated in the fact that he makes his people righteous. The new status of the Christian believer is demonstrated by the collocation of the terms 'justified' and 'Jesus', between which the link term is 'faith'. God and humankind reach out to each other in the person of Jesus. God took the initiative; Jesus supplied the necessary sacrifice; humankind must now look back to that sacrifice and hold it effective for securing the much-needed reconciliation with God. That, very roughly, is what 'faith' means for Paul. 'Faith' is simultaneously the 'believing that' and the 'trusting in' Jesus' achievement, which in turn depends on the relational righteousness of God which had allowed humankind to act relationally in respect of himself and thereby of each other.

Paul expounds his understanding of 'justification by faith' in Galatians and Romans.[44] These two letters make use of the same proof-texts, Hab. 2.4 and Gen. 15.6 to explain the issue. Hab. 2.4 is cited in Gal. 3.11, 'the one who is righteous will live by faith'. Gen. 15.6, is cited in Gal. 3.6, 'Abraham "believed God, and it was reckoned to him as righteousness" '. It forms the exegetical subject of the whole of Romans 4. Hab. 2.4 led

Paul to argue that faith was an important principle: faith that Jesus was the reconciling sacrifice leading to trust in Jesus and his achievement. The Genesis passage problematized the relationship between Christianity and Judaism. Paul observes that Abraham trusted God and acquired his righteousness *before* he was circumcised. The implication of this is that the covenant principle existed before Genesis 17, hence Paul's interest in Adam (and not Abraham) as the primal human being. In Galatians, and more reservedly in Romans, Paul argues on this basis that one does not have to become a Jew to become a Christian, and thus that circumcision and law-observance are ancillary issues for the Christian dispensation. The crucial issue is that Jesus has inaugurated a new order of human existence and that everyone can enter it by believing in and trusting his sacrifice as the only effective reconciliation between humankind and God. This demonstrates and depends on God's own righteousness in providing the sacrifice through which the relationality had been restored.

Jesus, Human and Divine

I have said already that belief in the 'heavenly pre-existence' of Jesus was bound to enter Christian theology given its distinctive contours. The question is when this belief emerged and to what extent it influenced Paul's view of Jesus.[45]

We know that it had emerged by the time of the Johannine Prologue, which achieved its present form around the end of the first century CE, but which in separate form is probably somewhat older.[46] Jn 1.1-18 celebrates the activity of God's Word who assisted the Father in the work of creation and became incarnate as Jesus of Nazareth. Belief in Christ's 'pre-existence' is found also in Col. 1.15-20.[47] If we could prove that Colossians was written by Paul, we would have little doubt that Paul himself thought in these terms about Jesus. Yet we have seen that Colossians may be post-Pauline, so that this hypothesis remains problematic. This draws us to the acknowledged Pauline letters to discover whether Paul himself thought in this way.

It is a question of balancing evidence which, by itself, is often ambiguous and difficult to interpret. Everyone has their preferred starting-place from which to answer this question. Many if not most turn to Phil. 2.6-11, whose interpretation is itself a veritable bone of contention.[48] My own starting-place is 2 Cor. 8.9, where Paul includes what appears to be a formula describing Jesus and his compassion: 'You know the generous act of our Lord Jesus Christ, that though he was rich, yet for your sakes he became poor, so that by his poverty you might become rich.'[49] As with the alleged 'hymn' in Phil. 2.6-11, it is striking that this formula is used in an ethical and not primarily a christological context. The saying contrasts the two states of Jesus' existence and urges Paul's readers to react in a similar way. It is evident that this saying formed part of the christological understanding which derived from Paul's wider Christian background. It is somewhat difficult to conceive when Jesus might have been thought to be rich other than in an alleged heavenly pre-existence. The Gospels do not portray him as rich. They portray Jesus as despising riches and extolling the virtues of (relative) poverty. The growing narrative about Jesus' origins, which issued in the infancy narratives of Matthew and Luke, describes a humble birth and an ordinary home.[50] In short, there is nothing in the New Testament that supports the portrait of Jesus as a rich person in terms of his human circumstances. At 2 Cor. 8.9, Paul points by implication to the heavenly world, suggesting that Jesus was rich because of his association with God and that he assumed the poverty of the human condition to accomplish the task of salvation.

The debate that has surrounded Phil. 2.6-11 is whether this passage can be read in the same way. The answer to this question has generally centred on the meaning of the word 'form' in Phil. 2.6 ('though he was in the form of God . . .').[51] This word has been thought by many scholars to designate a heavenly pre-existence; but others have argued that it merely describes the human Jesus conceived as an antitype of Adam. If Phil. 2.6 is read in the light of the earlier 2 Cor. 8.9, there appears to be no difficulty in regarding the Philippians passage as describing a heavenly pre-existence for Jesus. In that case we might argue that the more explicit Christology of Philippians 2 reflects Paul's developing thought on this issue between the writing of 2 Corinthians and Philippians. The noun 'form' is certainly used for heavenly beings in other Jewish literature.[52] It is a pertinent point that, whenever Paul uses his Adam–Christ typology, Jesus is considered in the light of his resurrection state. This might imply that a heavenly existence for Jesus cannot be ruled out at this point in the 'Christ Hymn'. The exegetical debate concerning Phil. 2.6-11 will doubtless continue, but it must be conducted with an eye to the wider Pauline corpus. When 2 Cor. 8.9 is identified as a potential starting-point for that discussion, it becomes easier than it might otherwise have been to read Phil. 2.6-11 in 'pre-existence' categories.

Other Pauline passages support this view but remain ambiguous.[53] Gal. 4.4 and Rom. 8.3 both speak of the 'sending' of the Son yet fail to explain in precise detail what this mission signified. On the balance of probability, and with an eye to 2 Cor. 8.9, I accept that Paul did think in 'pre-existence' terms about Jesus. This was possibly inevitable given the prominence of sacrificial ideas in Pauline literature. These developed the view that God had provided a sacrifice which was anthropologically unique in terms of the victim's status, resulting in the creation of a new human order on the basis of the death and resurrection of Jesus. This was the basis of Paul's gospel with its eschatological and ethical dimensions.

PAUL AND THE FUTURE

I spoke in the last chapter of a tension in Pauline theology which I called 'the now and the not yet of salvation'. This is the indication, found throughout Paul's letters, that the decisive events of salvation have been inaugurated in the death and resurrection of Jesus but that there remains a period of waiting before the formal climax of eschatology with the return of Jesus from heaven.[1] It is impossible to understand Paul without recognizing this dialectic between the past, the present and the future in his evaluation of all Christian existence.[2] Paul calls on his readers continually to appropriate the benefits they had secured through faith in Jesus and to 'wait for his Son from heaven' (1 Thess. 1.10). This means that the Christian life as Paul understands it is located in the interim period between the two poles of eschatology in which the benefits of the past salvific intervention have been actualized but remain to be finalized with the acquisition of heavenly immortality.

We shall see in Chapter 22 that this tension formed the basis of Paul's ethics. Paul believed that the Holy Spirit resided in Christian believers to produce the pattern of behaviour that Paul deemed desirable. For the moment, however, we shall look beyond the past and even the present to establish what Paul regarded as the ultimate goal of eschatology. This can be done by reading through Paul's letters in chronological order and examining what he says about the future and its eschatological significance.

The Evidence of Paul's Letters

The theme of eschatology runs like a thread through Paul's letters from 1 Thessalonians to Philippians. Although we have noticed some of the relevant material already, it will be helpful to expound it more formally to present the evidence in a systematic way.

1 Thessalonians shows that eschatological concerns dominated Paul's earliest theology. Paul's formula of salvation in 1 Thess. 1.9-10 is often regarded as a summary of his preaching to Gentiles. This formula asserts that Gentiles 'turned to God from idols, to serve a living and true God' and that they 'wait for his Son from heaven, whom he raised from the dead'. This formula is significant for the fact that it refers the continuing history of Jesus to the experience of Christian believers. Jesus died, was raised and is now in heaven. Those who believe are 'waiting' for his return. They will see Jesus when he descends from heaven. The keynote of this summary is the firm assurance that the eschatological climax will happen despite the delay of which some had complained.

This passage confirms that the hope for Jesus' return formed the centre of Paul's early eschatology. This idea is developed in 1 Thessalonians 4; and 1 Thess. 4.13-18 counters the worried belief in the Thessalonian community that one had to be alive to enjoy the eschatological benefits. Paul makes the return of Jesus central to what he says, combining this belief with the long-standing Jewish idea of the resurrection of the dead. The thought is that Jesus will return from heaven, and uniquely in this passage that believers will ascend to meet him in the air. This last reference has been variously interpreted but it probably attests the ancient understanding of the triumphal procession in which the returning Jesus is escorted down by his community of followers to begin his reign on earth.[3] At this time – the eschatological climax – the dead will be raised. The messianic kingdom will consist of all who believe in the Lord Jesus. The dead will be given new life by means of resurrection. The messianic kingdom will thus be a community of the transformed and the resurrected.

Two questions arise when 1 Thessalonians 4 is compared with the later Pauline correspondence. The first is why Paul's readers were so concerned about the fate of the dead when resurrection is a dominant feature of all Pauline eschatology. Although we have only one side of the conversation, and have no precise knowledge about what Paul had taught the Thessalonians, the answer may be that he had veered away from a characteristically Jewish idea like resurrection when preaching to Gentiles, or that he had not stressed this because it was not immediately relevant to the situation in hand. This was perhaps because death had not yet become a problem in the Thessalonian community. Plevnik argues plausibly that the background to this passage is the belief among the Thessalonians that one had to be alive to experience the 'rapture' (or ascent to meet Jesus) and that death had created the fear that some might be deprived of this and other eschatological benefits.[4] This raises the related questions of the extent to which Paul developed his resurrectional teaching in the light of pastoral experience; and whether the 'rapture' is an early explanation which Paul subsequently suppressed or abandoned.

The second question is why there is no reference to the transformation of human bodies in this passage. Such a view is arguably implied by the concept of resurrection as such; but even so, the omission marks a significant difference from the Corinthian correspondence where the theme of transformation features strongly. It is an open question whether Paul omits the transformation in 1 Thessalonians because he had yet to develop this view or merely because he did not think it relevant to the matter in hand. The possibility that Paul's eschatological thinking developed on these two matters should not be neglected, and remains a matter for discussion.[5]

Paul's most explicit eschatological teaching is contained in 1 Corinthians 15. Paul had been asked to explain the resurrection by the

Christians in Corinth. This was presumably not idle speculation but the result of a pastoral difficulty; it seems from 1 Cor. 15.12 that some in Corinth had taught there was no such thing as resurrection from the dead. We do not know the background to this view but it may have owed something to Greek ideas about immortality which censured belief in (re-)embodied existence of the kind that Paul defends in this chapter.[6] Paul opposes such teaching by arguing that Christian faith has its origins, precisely, in the *resurrection* of Jesus as an accomplished event. If Jesus had not been raised from the dead, Paul argues, then the whole of Christianity was ill-founded (1 Cor. 15.15).

Arguing with such people led Paul to frame his first description of the resurrection life as embodied existence. He does this with vigour in 1 Cor. 15.35-57. Paul is hampered by the obvious truth that the body is subject to decay. This leads him to distinguish in 15.42 between the perishable nature of the natural human body and the imperishable nature of the resurrection body, imperishability being the distinguishing factor between the two. It leads to his classic definition – by no means easy to understand – in 15.44 that the human body 'is sown a physical body' but 'raised a spiritual body'. The adjective 'spiritual' in this context evidently refers both to the imperishable nature of the body in question and to its heavenly origin, as suggested by the Adam–Christ typology which Paul employs at this point in 1 Corinthians 15.[7] Whatever the resolution of this exegetical difficulty, the crucial point is that the resurrection body will not be subject to decay.

Paul asserts that this eschatological transformation will be enjoyed by the living as well as by the dead. He states quite specifically in 1 Cor. 15.51 that 'we will not all die, but we will all be changed'. This is connected with the notion of immortality; Paul asserts further that at 'the last trumpet . . . the dead will be raised imperishable, and we shall be changed' (15.52).[8] The result is that the living and the dead will be changed into the same imperishable state, so that effectively it does not matter whether one is dead or alive at the time that the eschatological climax occurs. Nothing is said about the duration of the resurrection state beyond the strong implication that it will be a permanent one by virtue of the imperishable nature of the body provided. This notion of immortality is the key to 1 Corinthians 15 and beyond it to Paul's understanding of the resurrection.

1 Corinthians 15 moves beyond 1 Thessalonians but without contradicting anything Paul said in that earlier letter. There is a further development of this view in 2 Corinthians 5 where Paul returns to the subject of the resurrection body and offers further assurance that an imperishable dwelling will be provided from heaven by God.[9] The source of this body – 'we have a building from God, not made with hands, eternal in the heavens', 5.1 – represents a more explicit development from what was implied by 1 Corinthians 15, that (in the conventions of apocalyptic

imagery) the future bodies of believers are already present in heaven and will be revealed in due eschatological course.[10]

Surprisingly perhaps, Galatians and Romans say rather little about the eschatological destiny of believers in terms of these bodily arguments; but both mention the salvation of Israel (see below) and Romans contains important eschatological teaching in chapter 8.[11] Rom. 8.18-25 widens the extent of the projected eschatological transformation. In this significant passage, what Paul has said already about the transformation of human beings is extended to cover the whole created order. Paul speaks of the present futility of creation (Rom. 8.20) and of the possibility 'that the creation itself will be set free from its bondage to decay and will obtain the freedom of the glory of the children of God' (Rom. 8.21). In the light of this passage, it seems evident that Paul's view of bodily transformation (which features prominently in the Corinthian correspondence) is but one aspect of his wider eschatological programme, according to which the whole creation will be transformed and given an imperishable quality. What Paul says here about 'decay' is no doubt related to his earlier link between death, sin and Adam, although Paul does not specifically relate the topic of creation's bondage to Adam's sin at this point in Romans. It seems that what Paul says about the 'new creation' in 2 Cor. 5.17 has a very realistic character in terms of the programme proposed.[12] This is that the new human order will exist in the new creation from which all trace of decay will be removed. That is no doubt why Paul says, at the end of Romans 8, that nothing in the entire creation can separate Christians from the love of God in Christ.

Paul's mature expression of eschatology is found in Philippians. We have seen that Philippians 3 includes the hope for the earthly return of Jesus which we found as early as 1 Thessalonians. Phil. 3.21 states specifically that the Saviour will come from heaven and 'will transform the body of our humiliation so that it may be conformed to the body of his glory'. This is the same hope for bodily transformation found in 1 and 2 Corinthians. The difference, if there is one, from the earlier letters is that in Phil. 1.23 Paul contemplates the possibility of his own death before the return of Jesus and thus that he will receive an imperishable body by resurrection rather than by transformation while still alive. This small change, however, hardly diminishes the force of the contact between Philippians and 1 Thessalonians, according to which the return of Jesus from heaven will set the seal on the eschatological age and result in the transformation of believers, not to mention the entire creation.

Israel in Paul's Thought

No study of Paul's eschatology would be complete without consideration of the place of Israel in Paul's thought.[13] Paul began life as a pious Jew and probably as a Pharisee. As a persecutor of the church, he enjoyed considerable notoriety. His credentials as a Jew are such that he feels able to boast about them in Phil. 3.4-6. It is certain that Israel continued to exercise an influence on Paul's thought even though he was convinced that he was called to carry the good news about Jesus to the Gentiles.

Paul's attitude towards Israel is most clearly displayed in Romans 9–11. In this passage, which is certainly neither an excursus nor an insertion into Romans, Paul wrestles with the question of how the Jewish people came to reject the Messiah. This embodies the question, which draws on the wider thought of Romans, of what status those who have faith enjoy in respect of the historic Israel (and vice versa).

Paul combines these approaches in the early verses of Romans 9. He says that 'not all of Abraham's children are his true descendants . . . but the children of promise are counted as descendants' (Rom. 9.7-8). This picks up a biblical analogy which Paul had employed earlier in Gal. 4.21-31 to assert that Abraham had two different kinds of children. In Romans 9, the distinction is between the birthright Israel and the eschatological Israel. This is very roughly also the distinction between Israel as a discrete social entity and the entire human race in which both Jews and Gentiles play a part. The problem as Paul sees it is outlined with clarity in Rom. 9.30-1: 'Gentiles, who did not strive for righteousness, have attained it, that is, righteousness through faith; but Israel, who did strive for the righteousness that is based on the law, did not succeed in fulfilling that law.' The true Israel as Paul understands that concept is based on righteousness through faith, which we saw in Chapter 20 is an enabled response towards God based on the initiative that God had taken in providing Jesus as the necessary sacrifice for sin. Paul believes that Israel will be *made* righteous by God. Through God's further initiative, this divine relationality had already transcended national boundaries and created a new understanding of Israel, in which the historic Israel was destined to play a full part.

In Romans 10 Paul offers further scriptural proof to support his assertion that Jesus has introduced a new era of righteousness by faith. The understanding of the new (or true) Israel and the fate of the old Israel are discussed in Romans 11. In Rom. 11.17 Paul explains the inclusion of the Gentiles through the analogy of the olive branch which is grafted onto the stem and derives its nourishment from that source. He proceeds to say in 11.25 even that 'a hardening has come upon part of Israel, until the full number of the Gentiles has come in'. The result of this process, in the words of Rom. 11.26, is that 'all Israel will be saved'.

The effect of this (rather laboured) scriptural argumentation is to present a definition of Israel which reflects Paul's understanding of faith. For Paul, the Christian view of Israel shows how the Jewish nation should truly be understood. The Jewish understanding is inadequate for Paul because it was conceived apart from Christ and without the recognition that the Messiah had come and that the eschatological age had begun. Readers of this book must decide for themselves whether Paul indulges in 'special pleading' in Romans 9–11. The effect of his argument, however this question is answered, is to present the true Israel as a messianic entity into which all who have faith in Jesus can be incorporated. Such an understanding is clearly related to Paul's view that Jesus has established a new human order which itself is part of the eschatological renewal of creation. The issue that determines member-ship of the people of God is thus not how one is born but where one stands in Christ.

To this synthesis is related the issue of where the law and the 'works of the law' cohere with the Christian dispensation.[14] The law is clearly defined in Rom. 3.20 as a standard which allows sin to be perceived as sin. This is true even for the Gentiles, who, although they lack the Jewish law, have the natural law which at times enables them to be a 'law unto themselves' in that much-misused phrase (Rom. 2.14). In both Galatians and Romans, Paul argues that the law had a temporary authority which was superseded with the coming of Christ. Paul expresses this contrast vividly in Gal. 4.30: ' "Drive out the slave and her child; for the child of the slave will not share the inheritance with the child of the free woman." '[15] This argument reaches its zenith in 2 Cor. 3.1-18, where Paul describes the Sinai covenant as 'the ministry of death' (3.7) and the 'ministry of condemnation' (3.9) as opposed to the 'ministry of justification' (3.9), which is what he holds that Christ has introduced.

The conclusion, which affects ethics, is not that the works of the law are inadequate to provide salvation but that they are irrelevant for that purpose. It is axiomatic for Paul that 'a person is justified not by the works of the law but through faith in Jesus Christ' (Gal. 2.16). The law with its temporary but nevertheless clear manifestation of the divine will had been set aside with the coming of Christ (Rom. 10.4). Paul says that those Jews who continue to read the law without knowledge of Christ have their understanding veiled (2 Cor. 3.15). This is not to say that Paul is an antinomian, advocating life without any kind of law. But it is to say that he teaches a radically different ethical understanding, which we shall examine in the next chapter.

Paul's Eschatology, in Summary

Two questions which emerge from this study of Paul's eschatology are those of its possible change and development and of its universal panorama.

The first of these questions is less easy to answer than the second. We simply do not have enough material on which to base a definite judg-ment. Nor do we have transcripts of Paul's everyday preaching that would enable a decision about whether or not Paul's various letters represent developmental markers in his unfolding thought. We can answer the question of change and development in Paul's eschatology (as in other aspects of his thought) only approximately. So far as the hope for the return of Jesus from heaven is concerned, we may have reasonable certainty that Paul adhered to this belief throughout his career once Philippians is acknowledged as his last letter. We may also conclude from the chronology of Philippians that Paul continued to maintain the hope for bodily transformation as the centre of his eschatological understanding. It is possible that this hope became more precise in the shift from 1 Corinthians to 2 Corinthians, as indeed it seems to do in the shift from 1 Thessalonians to 1 Corinthians.

It is not completely certain how we should interpret the silence of 1 Thessalonians about the eschatological transformation of the living. Another uncertainty is whether the 'rapture' of 1 Thess. 4.17 is an early aberration or simply an aspect of eschatology which Paul retained but did not mention in his later letters. If I am right in concluding that it denotes a triumphal procession in which Paul expects Jesus to be escorted back to earth, the point at any rate is a minor one. It does not describe the final destiny of believers but draws attention to the status of Jesus as the universal Lord and Messiah. Some scholars have concluded from this reference that the early Paul expected heavenly immortality for believers at the start of his career but afterwards abandoned this view in favour of belief in an earthly resurrection. This interpretation is extremely problematic when the Pauline letters are considered as a whole. The exegesis I have proposed of 1 Thess. 4.17 seems preferable in every respect. Paul would surely have mentioned a proposed 'heavenly immortality' elsewhere had this been a significant aspect of his thought. I retain an open mind as to whether or not Paul continued to believe in the proposed 'rapture', but note the absence of this aspect from the later letters as an important argument against the 'heavenly immortality' theory.

This panoramic view sets Paul's eschatology in its proper perspective. Earth is the sphere of redemption for Paul. It is there that the proposed resurrection will take place and there that believers will receive their bodies from heaven. Just as Paul thinks that the salvation offered in Christ is totalistic in its effects, he also thinks that it will be all-encompassing in its properties. It covers not only human beings but the entire created order in which they live. The renewal of human bodies is thus one aspect of creation's renewal, which Paul thinks will happen in the eschatological future when Jesus returns from heaven.[16] The strong implication of Rom. 8.18-25 is that this revelation of eschatological glory will be nothing less than the revelation of heaven on earth. This will be the time when, in the language of 1 Cor. 15.28, 'God will be all in all'. Perhaps it is true to say that the eschatology of Romans is by no means as distant from that of the book of Revelation as some commentators have thought. Apocalyptic categories are prominent in this aspect of Paul's thought.

PAULINE ETHICS

This brings us, finally, to the topic of Pauline ethics.[1] Having begun in the past, we journeyed with Paul to the future. Now we return to the present to discover how 'the now and the not yet' of salvation works itself out in everyday experience.

Christ-Mysticism in Paul

No student of the New Testament can safely ignore the work of Albert Schweitzer. Schweitzer asked, not just about the form of Paul's thought, but about the nature of Paul's religious experience. He set mysticism at the heart of that experience, arguing that Paul depicts the Christian life as a relationship between individuals and the church community with Jesus as the heavenly Lord and Messiah.[2] Schweitzer commented that 'we are always in the presence of mysticism when we find a human being looking upon the division between earthly and super-earthly, temporal and eternal, as transcended, and feeling himself, while still externally amid the earthly and the temporal, to belong to the super-earthly and eternal'.[3]

While we might want to question Schweitzer's use of the word 'eternal' on the grounds that it incorporates more Platonic overtones than does Paul himself, the focus of Schweitzer's argument is on the direct relationship with Jesus the heavenly Lord that forms the heart of Pauline (and, we should add, *all* early Christian) theology. I said in Chapter 20 that Paul's principle of 'justification by faith' was only one of the metaphors that he uses to describe the process of Christian salvation. The merely relative importance of the principle, implying criticism of the Lutheran interpretation of Paul, was clearly recognized by Schweitzer. He describes the doctrine of righteousness by faith as 'a subsidiary crater, which has formed within the rim of the main crater – the mystical doctrine of redemption through being-in-Christ'.[4]

It is fascinating, when observing the history of New Testament study in the twentieth century, to see how scholarship moves in a pendulum movement. Interest in mysticism as such, and with it much of the liberal optimism of the Victorian era, was swept away on the battlefields of the First World War.[5] The possibility that Paul had a mystical outlook was further assailed in the debate about Gnosticism and the suggestion that there was any such first-century entity.[6] Since the 1980s, however, and largely through the rediscovery of Jewish mysticism, it has become fashionable once again to interpret Paul in mystical categories. This is what we find in the work of Alan Segal and other scholars.[7]

The very existence of this pendulum makes us stop and ask what is being claimed when we present Paul as a mystic, and how that alleged mysticism relates to other aspects of his writing. In this chapter, we shall examine the practical interface between Paul and the world. Paul's theology is never an internal phenomenon leading only to private religious experience. It always tends outwards, as the indwelling Spirit prompts the believer to works of righteousness which demonstrate the benefits of salvation to a largely unredeemed world. The first point to recognize, then, is that, despite the traditional associations of mysticism,[8] mysticism is never an introverted quality for Paul. It may be an inner relationship, but that inner relationship leads to the going-out from the self and to the meeting of others in the body of Christ, enabling the presentation of a good Christian face in a pagan environment.

This debate about Paul leads me to make a methodological observation. This is that, as we have seen already, Paul is not a systematic theologian. It would therefore be wrong to approach his writings from the perspective of a fully systematic theology. We are unlikely ever to produce a theology of Paul in which everything is left tidy in the manner of a modern systematic text. Paul is not like that. We can but examine his different metaphors and comment on their likely place in his thought. This is what I shall do in this chapter. I shall move from Paul's understanding of being 'in Christ' to his view of the Spirit as the moral enabler and thence to his outworking of these theological convictions in his ethical regulations for the churches, such as we can discern them.

Being in Christ

We saw when discussing Paul's view of the resurrection that he understands the resurrection life as embodied existence of an immortal kind. The risen Jesus has a glorious heavenly body. A similar body will be imparted to believers when Jesus returns to earth and the resurrection occurs. Modern Western culture, except in its 'post-modern' phase, shies away from bodily matters, preferring to speak of the affairs of the mind and privileging the dimension of thought. This is a continuation of the Platonic view that the soul is immortal and the body doomed to decay.

Paul's view of the resurrection is always an embodied one. It follows from his eschatology that we need to take particular notice of passages where Paul speaks about the 'body of Christ', for the body is what links the present and the future existence: 'the now and the not yet of salvation'. It was a great merit of John Robinson that he drew attention to the 'realism' with which Paul expounds his view of the church as the body of Christ.[9] This idea is expounded in both Romans 12 and 1 Corinthians 12. We should examine both passages to see what lies at the heart of this argument.

Romans 12 introduces the language of sacrifice. Paul has said earlier that 'God put [Jesus] forward as a sacrifice of atonement by his blood, effective through faith' (Rom. 3.25). In Romans 12 he says that Christians must 'present your bodies as a living sacrifice, holy and acceptable to God, which is your spiritual worship' (Rom. 12.1). The link between these two passages, the one christological and the other ethical, is the notion that human bodies must be sacrificed. There is, of course, a difference between the two different kinds of sacrifice. Since Paul believes that the sacrifice of Jesus was the unique and final sacrifice, he does not encourage his readers towards a theology of voluntary martyrdom, still less of bodily mutilation. Romans 12 advocates the presentation of bodies to God as an act of worship of a kind disclosed by the ethical behaviour of those who make this offering. There are parallels in this with the self-understanding of the Qumran community, who thought that their assembly represented the true temple since the Jerusalem temple had become defiled; hence the call for strict standards of purity in the Qumran community.[10]

Paul's required sacrificial act represents a world–negating standard (12.2). It appears from the opening verses of Romans 12 that it is nothing less than the attempt to bring the standards of heaven to bear on the earthly situation. In other words, the true nature of the divine holiness is progressively revealed in the midst of the Christian communities and in the lives of its individual members. Romans was written after 1 Corinthians; what Paul says here looks back to the earlier problem of division which had occurred in the Corinthian community. In 1 Corinthians 12 Paul argues that, since all Christians are members of the body of Christ, they should not disparage the spiritual gifts of others but by contrast value what appear to be the weaker or more hidden members. The basic principle, articulated in 1 Cor. 12.27, is that 'you are the body of Christ and individually members of it'. We know this view is important for Paul for he repeats it in Rom. 12.5: 'so we, who are many, are one body in Christ, and individually we are members one of another'.

It is easy to see in general terms what Paul means by this assertion but more difficult to give a precise account of the nuances. There is an obvious use of metaphor: Paul does not pretend that the church is *actually* an inflated organism with corporeal properties. His readers did not think that he said this. In acknowledging the use of metaphor, however, we must bear in mind Robinson's point about the realistic nature of the image. There is a delicate interplay between the themes of presence and absence, which is also the apocalyptic dichotomy between heaven and earth. The body of Jesus is now a transformed heavenly body with which Jesus will return to earth to effect the resurrectional transformation of believers. Paul freely acknowledges that Jesus has a heavenly body. The bodiliness of the risen Jesus is in fact the significant point of his resurrection appearances.[11] In terms of the accessibility of Jesus, however, Paul is bound to conclude there is an obvious difficulty despite the embodiment. Jesus is no longer visible and accessible in the same way that he was before the crucifixion. He will one day be visible in bodily form. At the moment, though, he is represented on earth by the church which Paul holds up, without apparent qualification, as the body of Christ.

The Spirit of Jesus

This striking image raises the question of what makes the church the body of Christ. We cannot answer this question with reference to Paul's principle of justification by faith alone. That is a principle, not an ethical maxim or a physical entity. The essence of any body is that it is an animated, living entity. Paul significantly stops short of the view articulated in both Colossians and Ephesians that the logic of this image lies in the fact that Christ is the head of the body.[12] That is a much more direct perspective and as such a development of what Paul himself says in his acknowledged correspondence. We cannot understand Paul's view of the church as Christ's body without considering what he says about the Holy Spirit.[13]

The Holy Spirit in Paul's writings is the link between the heavenly Jesus and the church as Christ's body on earth. Paul makes this point in characteristically polarized terms in Rom. 8.9-10: 'But you are not in the flesh; you are in the Spirit, since the Spirit of God dwells in you. Anyone who does not have the Spirit of Christ does not belong to him. But if Christ is in you, though the body is dead because of sin, the Spirit is life because of righteousness.' This crucial passage explains the practical consequences of justification by faith. Bodiliness is again the underlying concept. Paul's readers, it goes without saying, are embodied human beings. In this theological assessment of human mortality, Paul relates the fact of human death to the entrance of sin into the world. The noteworthy element is the statement that the indwelling Spirit allows the death-laden human body to be a different kind of body. It becomes a body destined for transformation after the fashion of Christ's heavenly body. That point is made explicitly in Rom. 8.11: 'If the Spirit of him who raised Jesus from the dead dwells in you, he who raised Christ from the dead will give life to your mortal bodies also through his Spirit that dwells in you.'

The Spirit, Paul says, represents 'life'. 'Life' is an eschatological concept: the present possession of the Spirit guarantees the future transformation of believers with the final overcoming of death. The indwelling Spirit of God makes the church the body of Christ. The Spirit animates the church and qualifies it to be the body of Christ by bonding individual Christians together in one corporate entity. That is why Paul says in 1 Cor. 12.13, 'in the one Spirit we were all baptized into one body'. The Spirit makes a whole from all the different parts. This is the first half of what Paul understands by his concept of the body of Christ.

The second half of that concept involves consideration of the apocalyptic distinction between heaven and earth. Jesus is currently in heaven and in possession of his transformed resurrectional body. Christians remain on earth. Their status is determined by their possession of the Spirit as a gift from heaven and by the hope that the returning Jesus will transform their mortal bodies at some future point. Only apocalyptic categories adequately explain the assertion that the church *is* the body of Christ when this is taken at face value. This statement depends on the argument, not always fully considered by the commentators, that the body of Christ as represented by the spiritual corporation of Christians in the world is a copy or earthly representation of the true and heavenly body of Jesus in much the same way that Jewish apocalyptic writings speak about the present Jerusalem as a copy of the true and heavenly Jerusalem or the law as a copy of the heavenly original.[14] Of course, the church is not *literally* or physically a body. It is, however, perceived as a body when the true state of apocalyptic reality is recognized, according to which the earthly entity finds its meaning by association with its heavenly counterpart.

This combination of themes supplies the rationale of Pauline ethics. The Holy Spirit replaces the absent Jesus in what we note is an important trinitarian view.[15] The Spirit is primarily a bonding and animating entity who enables the Christians to be what they are called to be: one body in the world. This body is simultaneously the body of Christ in the realistic manner that it represents in the apocalyptic sense the heavenly body of Jesus. As in all Jewish apocalypticism, what is currently anticipated in this way will one day be realized with the return of Jesus from heaven. The church will then share the risen body of Jesus with all the appropriate distinctions, including personal distinctions, that Paul explains in Romans 12 and 1 Corinthians 12 and which are implied by the promised transformation of the individual believer.

The more that one reads Paul, the more one sees that bodiliness is the key to his theology. It undergirds the Adam–Christ typology, according to which the mortal body of Adam is contrasted with the heavenly and imperishable body of Jesus. Bodiliness explains the present position of Jesus and the current status of believers. The same animating Spirit who gave humankind the breath of life according to Gen. 2.7 is poured out afresh on believers to enable them to represent and ultimately to possess the risen body of Jesus. This in turn leads to right(eous) actions as the Spirit impels believers to live out the life of heaven on earth.

Cleanse Out the Old Leaven

So far, we have seen that Paul thinks the coming of Christ means the end of the law and that the indwelling Spirit of God has taken the place of law-keeping in the mindset of the Christian believer. Now we shall explain how this ethical theory works itself out in practice in the various parts of Paul's letters.

The first point is that Paul does not throw out the baby with the bathwater in his critique of the Jewish law.[16] Three times Paul mentions a Christian form of law in his writings: 'the law of faith' (Rom. 3.27), 'the law of the Spirit' (Rom. 8.2) and 'the law of Christ' (Gal. 6.2). It appears from this that Paul is not rejecting law as such, merely a historically limited expression of law which by virtue of its nature he thinks had to be redefined with the coming of Christ. There is an interesting ethical use of the term 'faith' in Rom. 14.23 where Paul says that 'whatever does not proceed from faith is sin'. Earlier, Paul had connected 'sin' with the law (notably in Rom. 3.20). Here, 'faith' is presented not so much as the antithesis of 'law' but as its continuation or natural replacement. It is now faith in Christ and not the Jewish law which shows sin to be sin. This combination of evidence indicates that we should look very carefully at the concepts of 'Spirit' and 'faith' in order to understand the true base of Pauline ethics.

When this is done, it appears that Paul has replaced one form of law with another, not abandoned the concept of law altogether. The external and objective force of the Jewish law has been replaced by the indwelling Spirit as the direct expression of God's will in the Christian communities. It follows that the reference to 'the law of the Spirit' (Rom. 8.2) is of immense importance in the particular context of Romans 8.[17] Rom. 8.2 states explicitly that 'the law of the Spirit of life in Christ Jesus has set you free from the law of sin and death'. Paul thinks that the Jewish law had produced knowledge of sin and legitimated death. The law of the Spirit had removed the effects of sin and made it possible for death to be overcome. Christians must therefore follow the prompting of the Spirit to remain within the hopeful boundaries of Christian eschatology.

The specific outworking of Pauline ethics takes account of the two different worlds to which the Christians belong.[18] That is to say, while recognizing that the present world order (indeed the whole creation) is destined to be transformed with the coming of Christ, Paul also acknowledges that the world order currently has a durable quality. He therefore advocates a healthy sense of realism while arguing that heavenly standards must be brought to bear upon each human situation. Nowhere is this more obvious than in his treatment of slavery. Paul is not a William Wilberforce who calls for the abolition of slavery as morally repugnant. The rationale of this – to us, disconcerting – silence is Paul's belief that all human standards, including social standards, will be radically changed with the coming of Christ and that, as in all apocalypticism, the decisive action must be divine and not human in origin. That is why Paul sends Onesimus back to Philemon and why he tells people not to change their servile status in 1 Cor. 7.21-4.[19]

This is not said in detriment to the probability that, in Paul's view, the standards of the age to come affect personal relationships within the Christian community. Paul certainly relativizes the relationship between Onesimus and Philemon when he says, 'Perhaps this is the reason he was separated from you for a while, so that you might have him back for ever, no longer as a slave but as more than a slave, a beloved brother' (Phlm. 15-16). Paul does not tell Philemon to manumit Onesimus. Equally, he says that Onesimus must treat Philemon in one sense as an equal because of their common faith in Christ.[20] The same is true of Paul's understanding of Christian worship which presupposes that the Christian body meets together as one regardless of their social status. This doubtless reflects something of the community of goods that we noticed in connection with the primitive Christian community in Jerusalem.

Paul's sexual ethics have a definite bodily basis.[21] The reason why in 1 Cor. 6.12-20 Paul criticizes prostitution is because it emerges from an incorrect understanding of the status of the Christian body as the temple of the Holy Spirit.[22] To unite oneself with a prostitute opens the door to a different kind of relationship in which the Spirit's presence is denied. So it is with the evidently incestuous relationship described by 1 Cor. 5.1-5. This provokes from Paul the demand that the immoral man must be removed from the Christian community. The remedy in this case is a drastic one, the deliverance of the man to Satan 'for the destruction of the flesh' (1 Cor. 5.5).[23] This demand apparently distinguishes between the external form of the body – 'the flesh' – and the notion of eschatological embodiment, the idea being that if this man's flesh is destroyed punitively his spirit will at least be saved, probably to be reconstituted in an imperishable body among the rest of the Christian community at the *parousia*.

The question of social relations with people outside the Christian communities was an important one for Paul as it was for other New Testament writers, notably the author of the book of Revelation.[24] In saying this, we should recognize the ideological basis which gave Christian people a social distinctiveness in the ancient world. In the early period the question of their status in respect of the Jews proved perplexing to outsiders. The Christians were known to have Jewish roots, but everywhere they were disowned by the Jews. Part of the problem lay in the manner of Jesus' death. He died the slave's death as a messianic pretender. This made the proclamation of the Christian gospel problematic to Jews and Gentiles alike. Jews persecuted the Christians for their preaching of Jesus as Messiah. Gentiles failed to see why so much was being made about a crucified man, especially since the Christians seemed to stir up trouble everywhere they went. This led to the Christians frequently being misunderstood and even being represented, in the words of Tacitus, as 'a class hated for their abominations'.[25]

This was the set of circumstances Paul's social teaching addressed. Paul works with the consciousness of being part of a missionary culture with a duty to bring the good news about Jesus to others.[26] His theology, not least its aspect of the indwelling Spirit of God, works with the understanding that Christian behaviour is a witness to the gospel in a largely secular world. That notwithstanding, Paul's doctrine of 'separateness' is by no means as rigorous as that which pertained, for instance, in the Qumran branch of the Essene community. This relative distance is evident particularly in Paul's discussion of the question of meat sacrificed to idols in 1 Corinthians 8.[27] Paul says effectively that, since idols have no real existence, it is permissible for Christians to buy meat which had been sacrificed to idols from the local meat-markets. This effectively kept open the boundaries with outsiders for Christians of all social classes: well-placed Christians, who would often have taken part in civic banquets; and poorer Christians, who would not have had regular access to quality meat. Paul adds the proviso that this meat could be eaten unless it offended the conscience of a 'weak believer'. That left open the possibility of conscientious objection on religious grounds; but did not of itself require it.

PART IV

THE BIRTH OF EARLY CHRISTIANITY

THE ESCHATOLOGICAL FRAMEWORK
OF CHRISTIANITY

We saw when discussing Jesus that he held an imminent eschatology in which the coming of the Son of Man was expected to introduce the eschatological climax. Despite the attempts that have been made to separate Jesus from apocalypticism, we found that this strand of belief best explains the received portrait of Jesus and sets him comprehensibly within his first-century environment. Paul also believed that the eschatological climax would be introduced by the appearance of a heavenly mediator; in this case, by Jesus himself, whose return from heaven dominates the first Pauline letter (see 1 Thess. 1.9-10; 4.16). On the evidence of Philippians, Paul did not abandon this hope for the return of Jesus throughout his career. Phil. 3.19-20 anticipates the return of Jesus from heaven as the moment when the bodies of believers will be transformed to resemble the glorious body of Jesus. If there is a difference between 1 Thessalonians and Philippians, it is that in the later letter Paul acknowledges that he himself may not be alive to see this event happen (Phil. 1.23).[1] In that case, we must conclude on the basis of numerous Pauline references that Paul thought he would be incorporated in the resurrectional transformation and not miss out on the eschatological benefits as his Thessalonian converts had feared that they might.

The preponderance of eschatology in the first two phases of the Christian movement – the preaching of Jesus and the mission of Paul – makes us ask what eschatology contributed to the development of first-century Christianity as a whole.[2] This is bound up with the question of whether eschatology developed significantly in the period that the New Testament documents; and of course beyond that period also. It is certainly not true that the hope for imminent supernatural intervention continued throughout the Christian movement. There was a major sea-change with Augustine in the fifth century CE, who interpreted the book of Revelation in allegorical categories and understood God's kingdom as occurring within the present order. This is in line with what major studies of millenarianism have shown, that the hope for immediate intervention is often only one stage in the wider articulation of a more general discontent that can issue in remarkably conservative form; suggesting that the articulation of protest as such is more basic than the precise form in which that protest is cast.[3]

We shall carefully consider the course that Christian eschatology took during and beyond the New Testament period. This survey will in part be historical and in part doctrinal. We need to explore how far the New Testament material actually coheres, asking additionally whether there is evidence for the significant reworking of eschatology in the second century and beyond it into the third. We shall also ask about the different strands of New Testament eschatology; particularly the relation between hopes for the resurrection of the body and the immortality of the soul. This will introduce the study of post-Pauline Christianity that constitutes Part IV of this book.

The Orientation of New Testament Eschatology

An obvious starting-place is 1 Thessalonians, given its early origin.[4] Although Paul insists that Jesus will return from heaven, in this earliest New Testament text we nevertheless find the consciousness that the delay in his return was felt to be a *problem* by at least one Christian group.[5] The problem in this case was not the fear that the eschatological hope might prove unfounded but the (mistaken) belief that death had deprived some of the community of their promised eschatological benefits. Paul insists this is not the case. He develops his resurrectional teaching to deal with that concern.

The problem of the death of Christian believers was not unique to the Thessalonian community. It is noteworthy that debate about the resurrection preoccupies Paul in his Corinthian correspondence. At Corinth, it had even been suggested that there was no such thing as resurrection from the dead (1 Cor. 15.12). There is more than one possible explanation of this view.[6] Among the Jewish parties, the Sadducees denied belief in the resurrection of the dead. If the background to this suggestion is pagan, it is possible that resurrection of the dead had been denied in favour of the immortality of the soul; or even that it had simply been denied altogether. Barrett thinks that a situation pertained in Corinth similar to that described by 2 Tim. 2.18 where some had claimed that the resurrection had occurred already in an incipient Gnostic view.[7] Whatever the background to this dispute, Paul insists that the resurrection of Jesus prefigures the resurrection of believers, and that Christians will be invested with a heavenly body similar to that of Jesus himself. This, with incidental variations, is what he says also in the later 2 Corinthians 5 and Philippians 3.

Nowhere in Paul do we find the abandonment of eschatological hope. What we do find is the refining of Paul's eschatology with reference to the problem of death. This process of refinement had begun even before the earliest New Testament text was written. It doubtless began as early as the first deaths of Christian people, which must have happened very early on. The developing New Testament message is that human death is no obstacle to membership of God's kingdom. Resurrectional belief, inherited from Judaism and refined by Paul, is presented as the answer to the problem of death on the eschatological basis of the resurrection of Jesus. Paul's answer, mirrored also in Revelation,[8] is that Jesus will return from heaven to preside over the messianic kingdom. This will involve the transformation of the entire existing order. Paul expresses this view classically in the second half of Romans 8.

On a methodological note, we need to distinguish two questions when considering this evidence. The first is the mode of the promised resurrection existence. Is it to be heavenly or earthly? The second is the means by which the resurrection will be effected. How far does a particular strand of Christian tradition really believe that Jesus will return from heaven in the promised manner? Although these two questions are related, they must not be confused. The abandonment of the hope for Jesus' return from heaven might be said to have contributed to the demise in the hope for bodily resurrection; but, formally, it must be distinguished from it. In this chapter we shall consider both questions and try to explain how they are held together in the first-century Christian imagination.

The Delayed *Parousia*

The continuing eschatological problem that first-century Christianity addressed was not the hope for resurrection as such, although that later became controversial in the dispute with Gnosticism,[9] but the growing recognition that things had not materialized with the speed that had at first been anticipated. Where Jesus and Paul had been confident of imminent supernatural intervention, later New Testament writers are by no means so confident that this will occur immediately. Thus the author of 2 Pet. 3.4 records the complaints of some: 'Where is the promise of his coming? For ever since our ancestors died, all things continue as they were from the beginning of the creation!'[10] This author answers such criticism with the pastoral reassurance, 'The Lord is not slow about his promise, as some think of slowness, but is patient with you, not wanting any to perish, but all to come to repentance' (2 Pet. 3.9) Whether or not this amounts to 'special pleading' is a matter which readers of this book must decide for themselves. The passage does, however, indicate that the need to offer pastoral advice about the delayed *parousia* was an important feature of post-Pauline Christianity.

It would be wrong to draw a sharp trajectory within the New Testament as to how the eschatological hope waxes and wanes there.[11] Much depends on the date of 2 Peter, which has been set anywhere between the late first century and the mid-second century CE.[12] It is more important to note that apocalyptic eschatology is a feature of many if not most of the New Testament texts.[13] Instead of drawing over-precise and inherently falsifiable lines of development, we need to look at the different ways the eschatological hope is expressed in the later New Testament documents, asking what such hopes meant for the people who held them.

The Millennial Hope

The hope of Jesus and Paul for an earthly kingdom of God is supported by this unknown author of 2 Pet. 3.10, who insists that 'the day of the Lord will come like a thief, and then the heavens will pass away with a loud noise, and the elements will be dissolved with fire, and the earth and everything that is done on it will be disclosed'. This hope for an earthly regime persisted for a considerable while in the thought of patristic Christianity.[14] Papias of Hierapolis preserves a saying of Jesus, from those who knew John the Elder, to the effect that corn and wine would produce in prodigious proportions in the eschatological age.[15] There are close parallels in this to *2 Bar.* 29.5. *Barnabas* uses the symbolism of the week to assert that God's Son would come to destroy the age of the lawless one, and that this sabbatarian period would be followed by the new creation.[16] Irenaeus asserts that the millennial age would be a paradisal period with miraculous portents.[17] Tertullian defended the millennial hope against Marcion, criticizing the latter's symbolic understanding of the messianic banquet as a merely *post-mortem* enjoyment of the delights of heaven.[18]

Tertullian's millenarian zeal increased during his Montanist phase.[19] Since Montanism was subsequently deemed heretical, the connection between Montanism and millenarianism somewhat tended to diminish the welcome status of the hope for God's earthly kingdom. This hope was weakened further through the reaction against Cerinthus, whom both Eusebius and Dionysius of Alexandria report as teaching that the resurrectional age was a time for desires and pleasures.[20] The fact that Cerinthus appealed to the book of Revelation to support his opinions tended to bring the latter's authority into disrepute. Gaius of Rome was the first to do this, interpreting the reference to the binding of Satan in Revelation 20 as the past achievement of Jesus on the basis of Mt. 19.29.[21] Hippolytus criticized this exegesis,[22] but millennialism was censured again by the Alexandrians Clement and Origen, who thought that those who subscribed to it were literalists and fools.[23]

Augustine changed his mind about millenarian eschatology towards the end of his career.[24] In his early period he understood the millennium as a universal sabbath with all its delights. Later, and under the influence of Tyconius,[25] Augustine rejected this interpretation, arguing in *The City of God* 20.7 that the millennium had already begun with baptism and penitence and that the figure of 1,000 years given by Rev. 20.4 denotes the *present* age of the church, which would last until the end of the world. For Augustine, the binding of Satan had taken place already and could not be regarded as a future event.

This abbreviated history shows the course that hopes for the earthly reign of Christ took throughout the first five centuries of the Christian era. Jesus and Paul proclaimed the hope for supernatural intervention and earthly transformation as the central feature of hope. The influence of the Montanists and Cerinthus did much to discredit such belief in Christian circles. Gaius of Rome, followed by Clement and Origen and then of course Augustine, advocated the exegesis of Revelation in symbolic and not literal terms. The result of this is that what Jesus and Paul had proclaimed as standard effectively became the prerogative of fringe groups in the church.[26] The millennial hope never completely passed from sight, for it was picked up again by such figures as Thomas Müntzer and flourishes in certain circles today.[27] The more standard Christian understanding, though, is that eschatology has to do with the provision of *post-mortem* hope. We noted the introduction of this view into dogmatic theology with Abraham Calov in Chapter 10.

Immortality as a Theme in New Testament Eschatology?

A possible alternative to this understanding of resurrection is belief in the immortality of the human soul.[28] In Greek philosophy, this view is associated particularly with Plato (*c.*428–348 BCE).[29] Plato thought that human beings were composed of two parts, the soul being radically distinct from the body and in that sense pre-existent and indissoluble. The soul was therefore an immortal entity, as opposed to the body, which was destined for dissolution.

The growing influence of Hellenistic culture on Judaism from the third century BCE onwards, not least in the Antiochian crisis in the second century BCE, meant that Greek ideas about immortality were assimilated by Jewish writers. Both the Wisdom of Solomon and *4 Maccabees* show traces of this influence in their eschatology.[30] In the reworking of the famous story about the mother and the seven brothers from 2 Maccabees 7, for instance, *4 Macc.* 13.17 and other passages expect them to be received into eternal life immediately after death.[31] The question we must ask is the extent to which such ideas influenced the eschatology of the New Testament literature.

We have seen that Paul contemplates a form of immortality but that this is a bodily immortality (the 'spiritual body' of 1 Cor. 15.44) which takes place in connection with the resurrection of the dead and which views earth as the place where human bodies will be transformed. Among possible exceptions to this view, we should consider the familiar Johannine phrase, 'eternal life'.[32] This *sounds* like the promise of immortality; but in fact John never uses the terms 'immortal' or 'immortality' in his writings, and we are bound to conclude that it marks a significant difference between the Fourth Gospel and Platonic philosophy. The word translated 'eternal' is the Greek *aionios*, which has if anything a cosmic and not a temporal reference. Seen in this light, the phrase 'eternal life' appears to mean 'the life of heaven', which brings us rather closer to Pauline (and indeed to standard) New Testament eschatology than at first sight might appear. The Johannine view is an apocalyptic one in which the life of heaven has already been made available on earth. This is why John's Jesus says of Lazarus without fear of contradiction that 'those who believe in me, even though they die, will live' (Jn 11.25; cf. Jn 6.40, 'This is indeed the will of my Father, that all who see the Son and believe in him may have eternal life; and I will raise them up on the last day'). This view of eternal life is parallel to John's view of Jesus that the Son of Man had descended from heaven to accomplish a unique and decisive revelation of God (Jn 3.13 and other references).

It is true that 2 Pet. 1.4 has an enigmatic reference to the possibility of Christians becoming 'participants of the divine nature'; but even this is not necessarily the promise of immortality in the Platonic sense. Given that 2 Peter is almost certainly pseudonymous, it is possible that this reference is based on the earlier (and probably authentic) 1 Pet. 5.1, where Peter calls himself 'one who shares in the glory to be revealed'. In any event, in a letter which also promises the intervention of apocalyptic eschatology (chapter 3), it would be wrong to conclude that 1.4 is a radical departure from the path of New Testament eschatology in the direction of a Hellenistic immortality. The notions of 'escaping the world's corruption' and 'sharing divine nature' which feature in 2 Pet. 1.4 are actually quite consonant with the Pauline understanding of future bodily transformation.

We should not rush to conclude, therefore, that ideas about 'immortality' undergird even the later New Testament literature. The New Testament is dominated by the hope for the resurrection of the body and the earthly kingdom of the Messiah. Such ideas persisted into the patristic period. They were only displaced in the third century CE and beyond. While the transformation must not be ignored in any study of Christian origins, it occurred somewhat after the period in which we are interested here.

About Part IV

This observation serves to introduce Part IV of this book. In this Part we shall survey the course of second-generation Christianity from approximately the death of Paul to round about the end of the first century CE, and beyond it with the rise of Gnosticism and other issues in the second century CE. This was a period when Christianity, after its first heady expansion, began to consolidate its beliefs and set itself on a firmer footing in a world which proved to be more durable than had at first been anticipated.

Having begun with eschatology, we move next to examine the post-Pauline writings of the New Testament (Chapter 24). This will be followed by a study of emerging trends in Christology (Chapter 25) and of the reasons for the breach between Christianity and Judaism (Chapter 26).

Chapters 27 to 29 examine the early Christian view of sacraments, ministry and ethics, in that order. Finally, Chapter 30 looks forward to the second century CE by considering the rise of Gnosticism and its significance for the status of Christianity as a developing world religion. Chapter 31 draws the book to a close; it is followed by an Appendix on the relationships of the four canonical Gospels as promised in Part II.

THE POST-PAULINE WRITINGS OF THE NEW TESTAMENT

As we did with the Pauline writings in Chapter 19, we shall now survey the post-Pauline writings of the New Testament in the canonical and not (what I take to be) the correct chronological order.[1] This will be followed by an explanation of how the New Testament canon achieved its present form.

Hebrews

The canonical approach means that we begin with Hebrews. Hebrews owes its position in the New Testament canon to the false assumption that Paul was its author.[2] The superscription 'to Hebrews' is found already in the earliest papyrus and is repeated in both Clement of Alexandria and Tertullian, confirming that when the early Christian letters were collected, this letter was thought to have been written primarily for Christians from a Jewish background.[3]

Hebrews fared differently in Eastern and Western Christianity. In the East, Origen thought that Hebrews was written by one of Paul's disciples. In Greek and Syrian Christianity, the letter was regarded as Pauline and canonical from the third century CE onwards. In the West, however, Hebrews was not regarded as Pauline until the fourth century CE. Hebrews is absent from the Muratorian canon, while both Irenaeus and Hippolytus dispute that Paul was its author.[4] It was only in the second half of the fourth century, when the final moves were being made towards universal agreement about the New Testament canon, that Hebrews was held to be a Pauline letter in the West. Its status was questioned again at the Reformation, Beza and Calvin declaring it non-Pauline but the Council of Trent insisting there were fourteen Pauline letters in the New Testament. The rejection of Pauline authorship has become increasingly common in the post-Enlightenment period, and is commonly found today.[5]

There are sound reasons for denying Pauline authorship to Hebrews. Its structure is conspicuously different from a typical Pauline letter, even from Romans. Where Paul generally has doctrine followed by exhortation, Hebrews mingles exhortation with its central teaching. Hebrews has its own distinctive vocabulary which owes more to a Hellenistic milieu than is found in Paul. These differences extend to matters of style, language and theology. While there are echoes of Paul, not least in the Christology of Hebrews, there are also significant differences which suggest the actual author may have been aware of Pauline theology but possessed the ability to think in his own distinctive way.[6] These differences are evident not least in the area of Christology. Where Paul speaks of Jesus' resurrection, in Hebrews we find references to his exaltation. Moreover, the key idea of Hebrews – that Jesus is the high priest as well as the sacrificial victim – is totally absent from Paul. Similarly, the contact between Hebrews and Alexandrian Judaism (especially Philonic exegesis) does not seem convincingly Pauline.

It is probably no longer possible to determine the actual author's identity with certainty, as Origen was the first to acknowledge.[7] Both Luke and Apollos have been canvassed, by Clement of Alexandria and Luther respectively. Hebrews is a product of the later first century CE. It may have been written in Egypt, although places as diverse as Rome, Ephesus and Antioch have been suggested by the commentators.

The theme of Hebrews is that those who have entered the Christian dispensation must not retreat into Judaism. The letter opens with a vivid demonstration of this point by asserting the superiority of Christ to all other beings, including the angels (chapter 1). There is an obviously 'incarnational' Christology in chapter 2 which emphasizes the full humanity of Jesus and insists that his unique sacrifice has destroyed the devil who holds the power of death (2.14).[8] Chapter 3 asserts Christ's superiority to Moses. Chapter 4 refers God's rest on the seventh day to the Christian period, conceived in sabbatarian terms.[9] This leads to the famous statement of 4.14 that Jesus is the 'great high priest who has passed through the heavens'.[10] This poses the author in chapters 5–7 with the difficult problem that Jesus came from the tribe of Judah when the law required that Jewish high priests should come from the tribe of Levi. He deals with this problem by asserting that Jesus came from a different priestly order altogether, that of Melchizedek, of whom the author says that he was 'without father, without mother, without genealogy, having neither beginning of days nor end of life, but resembling the Son of God, he remains a priest for ever' (Heb. 7.2).[11]

This establishment of the new priestly order allows for the possibility that Jesus' sacrifice had finally and uniquely rendered all subsequent liturgy irrelevant. This is the theme of chapters 8 to 10. The author argues that the first covenant was not faultless (8.7); and that the high priest, as a sinful member of a sinful people, had to offer sacrifice for his own sins as much as for the sins of his people (9.7). The author looks back to the tabernacle which the Israelites had erected in the wilderness to contrast it with Christ's final sacrifice on the grounds that the latter was offered in the *heavenly* sanctuary, which is the immediate presence of God. In one sense, the thought of Hebrews climaxes in 9.12 with the statement, '[Jesus] entered once for all into the Holy Place, not with the blood of goats and calves, but with his own blood, thus obtaining eternal redemption.'

In another sense, what is said here summarily is repeated in more detail in chapter 10. The author's premise is that 'it is impossible for the blood of bulls and goats to take away sins' (10.4). This leads to his assessment of the Jewish liturgy in 10.11: 'And every priest stands day after day at his service, offering again and again the same sacrifices that can never take away sins'; and of Christ's sacrifice in 10.14: 'by a single offering he has perfected for all time those who are sanctified'. A subtle distinction between Judaism and Christianity undergirds the whole letter, especially at this point. This is the further distinction between heaven and earth which is at the same time also the distinction between the reality and the copy. Scholars used to think this is the Platonic distinction between the form and the reality; but some interesting research has exposed the extent to which Hebrews depends on the thought-world of Jewish apocalypticism.[12] The distinction is thus between heaven and earth, bound up with the view that the mysteries of heaven can be revealed to privileged people on earth. The author thereby presents heaven as the dwelling-place of God and asserts that it contains the mysteries of the future (including the true Jerusalem of Hebrews 13).[13]

Hebrews' argument is that in dying Christ entered the heavenly sanctuary, which in chapter 2 it is implied that he vacated when incarnating himself as Jesus. Because of Christ's credentials as high priest, and because the heavenly sanctuary is the truly real sanctuary, his combined ministry as priest and victim proved efficacious for all time. The pastoral conclusion, expressed throughout the letter, is that Christians must not revert to Judaism, otherwise they will lose grasp of the significant religious breakthrough which Christ had achieved in recent days.[14]

An apocalyptic background explains the remaining portions of Hebrews. The key to understanding Hebrews 11 is the recognition that all the faithful people mentioned in this chapter set out to find a city which they never in fact discovered.[15] They are the 'great cloud of witnesses' mentioned by 12.1 who bear witness to what they never in fact saw. The author has in mind the heavenly Jerusalem where Jesus is, seated at the right hand of God. This theme is made specific in the second half of chapter 12, where 12.22 explains that Christians stand on the very threshold of this heavenly city: 'You have come to Mount Zion and to the city of the living God, the heavenly Jerusalem, and to innumerable angels in festal gathering . . . and to Jesus, the mediator of a new covenant, and to the sprinkled blood that speaks a better word than the blood of Abel' (12.22, 24).

Seen in this light, Hebrews constitutes a pastoral homily addressed to people who (for a reason we do not know precisely) were being tempted to espouse or to re-espouse Judaism. The letter warns them, in homiletic and theological terms, not to do this. It provides reasons to show that Jesus and Christianity had disclosed the full truth about God. The use of Jewish apocalyptic categories is very obvious in this letter.

James

James raises considerable problems of authenticity in view of its clear attribution to James (often called 'the Just'), the brother of Jesus.[16]

James was not recognized as authoritative very early by Christians.[17] It is missing from the Muratorian canon, and is not quoted by key figures from the second century such as Irenaeus and Hippolytus. The letter is, however, noted in a spurious letter attributed to Clement of Alexandria and by Origen. At the time of the Reformation it attracted the notorious censure of Luther, who called it 'a right strawy epistle' when compared with the other New Testament documents.[18] In the nineteenth century, critical suspicion was raised once again in the form of the question of whether someone like James, the Lord's brother, could actually have written a letter of this kind.

One recent assessment of James, that of Richard Bauckham,[19] begins by asking about the nature of the document in question. Bauckham calls it a 'paraenetic encyclical', for which a more familiar term might be 'circular letter'. The recipients of the letter are 'the twelve tribes in the Dispersion' (1.1). Bauckham refers these to the entirety of the dispersed Israel under the premise that 'Jewish Christians thought of themselves, not as a specific sort distinguished from other Jews but as the nucleus of the Messianic renewal of the people of Israel which was under way and would come to include all Israel.'[20] He accepts that the letter really does come from James the brother of Jesus. This view is vigorously disputed by other commentators (notably Raymond E. Brown).[21] We should note that, if James was indeed the author, the letter must have been written before 62 CE because James the Just was killed in that year (Acts 12.2); and that such an early date must be carefully compared with both the contents and the outlook of the letter to secure a responsible interpretation.

James does not make for easy reading because of its uncoordinated nature.[22] It includes chains of admonitions and sayings which are strung together sometimes in a more but generally in a less connected manner. The letter seems to be a collection of early Christian *halakah* and moral instruction, but the social context in which the letter was read and to which it was addressed is not immediately obvious.[23] The best way to approach this problem is to recognize the 'mixed' nature of early Christian churches, including the church at Antioch, and to recognize that the author is introducing ethics which have an obviously Jewish foundation, as if to deal with the problem of Hellenistic morals which might have become prevalent due to the suggestion of people such as Paul in Galatians that the Jewish law had effectively been set aside with the coming of Christ. This is not, of course, to suggest that Paul has said precisely this about ethics; but that some may have read or misquoted him in that way.

It is difficult to provide a guide to the contents of James without exhaustive detail, such is the encyclopaedic nature of the wisdom that is offered in this letter.[24] Among the striking features of James we note the statement that a person is *not* justified by faith alone (Jas. 2.24), the description of rich and poor in early Christian communities (2.1-7) and the remedy of prayer with anointing for the sick in 5.13-18. The first statement inevitably represents at least some distance from Pauline theology.[25]

1 Peter

Approximately the same problems assault the reader of 1 Peter as of James.[26] These are the problems of knowing whether to believe the claim to apostolic authorship, and in places also of deciphering the content. Once again, it is evident that we are dealing with paraenesis;[27] and noteworthy, perhaps, that similar teaching is attributed in 1 Peter to Peter as to James in James, in a way that looks rather different from Paul, the self-styled 'apostle to the Gentiles'.

The authorship of 1 Peter is less uncertain than that of James.[28] Indeed, Raymond E. Brown notes that 'of all the Catholic Epistles, 1 Peter has the best chance of being written by the figure to whom it is attributed'.[29] In potentially agreeing with this conclusion, we should be careful to distinguish 1 Peter from 2 Peter, which even a conservative commentator like Bauckham accepts is a pseudonymous letter.[30] Against the hypothesis that Peter wrote 1 Peter,[31] it has been argued that the letter is written in excellent Greek, which would have been beyond the ability of a Galilean fisherman; that 1 Peter evidently draws on the Pauline writings when it is suggested from other evidence that relations between Peter and Paul were less than cordial; that the references to the 'fiery ordeal' (4.12) and suffering suggest a sharp persecution which cannot be correlated with the known events of Peter's life, given that the Neronian persecution of 64 CE was relatively local and short-lived; that the church order of 5.1-4 seems impossibly advanced for a date in Peter's lifetime; that the use of the term 'Peter' is artificial, for Peter would have called himself 'Simon Peter'; and that other indications in the letter suggest a date perhaps not much later than the apostle's martyrdom, but nevertheless *after* that event.

The last argument is accepted as decisive by Brown.[32] He argues that a Christian letter addressed to Asia Minor would make more sense after the Roman destruction of the temple in 70 CE, as would the reference to Rome as 'Babylon' (5.13).[33] The best parallels to the church order of 1 Pet. 5.1-4 are in works written after 70 CE, so that a date in the last third of the first century CE (with a consequently pseudonymous authorship) is probably now the dominant view.

1 Peter 1 is a celebration of Christian existence which includes a clear Christology of 'pre-existence' in 1.20.[34] In 2.1-12, which is almost a

charter of the Christian religion, the Christians are called a 'holy priest-hood' who offer 'spiritual sacrifices' (2.5). This leads to some 'household rules' in 2.11–3.7, which is potentially an indicator between genuine and pseudonymous literature. The presence of such information in 1 Peter tends to confirm Brown's conclusion that 1 Peter comes from the period after Peter's death, and that the letter reflects conditions in the period between the destruction of the temple in 70 CE and the end of the first century CE.

1 Pet. 3.8–4.6 deals with the theme of suffering and of virtue under suffering, relating this to the suffering of Christ (3.18) and then to Christian eschatology; 3.19-22 is often held to support the doctrine of the 'descent to hell' in New Testament literature (cf. 4.6 in this context).[35] At 4.7 the letter states explicitly that 'the end of all things is near', which is significant if 1 Peter comes from nearer the end than the middle of the first century CE. The section from 4.12 to the end of the letter returns to the theme of suffering, either because this was a feature of the readers' experience or because the author thought that suffering might be unleashed on the Asian church at some future point.[36] This part of the letter is remarkable for its continuing witness to an apocalyptic eschatology in the words, 'when the chief shepherd appears, you will win the crown of glory that never fades away' (5.4). Clearly, apocalypticism did not pass from the scene with the deaths of the first Christians but inspired the later writings of the New Testament. The presence of eschatology within an apocalyptic ambience is a notable feature of 1 Peter, and serves as a litmus test of developing Christian thought.

2 Peter

2 Peter, as I said, is almost certainly peudonymous.[37] It is in fact the most obviously pseudonymous letter in the entire New Testament. This virtually unanimous agreement among commentators has not, however, been matched by a significant agreement about when the letter was written.

Arguments against genuine Petrine authorship are compelling. W.G. Kümmel goes so far as to italicize his conclusion, '*But this letter cannot have been written by Peter.*'[38] The clearest indication of pseudonymity is its unmistakable dependence on Jude;[39] 2 Pet. 2.1-18 and 3.1-3 show clear signs of similarity to Jude 4-13 and 16-18. The contact between these texts is not precise: each has allusions not found in the other (see Jude 11 and 2 Pet. 2.5, 7-8), while roughly the same kind of language is used to combat *different* kinds of false teaching in 2 Pet. 2.1-18 and Jude 4-13. The language is often close but not always identical; while 2 Peter uses a form of Greek whose style and vocabulary is quite different from Jude's.

There are three possible explanations of this evidence. Either both letters were written by the same person; or both used a common source; or else one of the two writers used the other document. This third explanation has three different forms: either Jude used 2 Peter, or the other way round, or one document was interpolated by the author of the other.

The theory of common authorship claimed a major supporter in John Robinson, but it seems an unlikely explanation of the evidence.[40] It ignores the substantial literary and stylistic differences between the two texts, whatever similarities there may be between them. This is especially true if the letters are regarded as contemporaries. The situation in that case would be analogous to that between Ephesians and Colossians, where we saw that the hypothesis of common authorship cannot convincingly be sustained because of the considerable differences between the letters. If 2 Peter was written by the same author as Jude, we would clearly have to assume that both were written within a relatively short time of each other; but this theory fails to explain the differences between the texts, especially the introduction of material about the *parousia* and judgment in 2 Peter which goes beyond the apocalyptic eschatology of Jude.

The case for a common source is stronger. Its most notable exponent was Bo Reicke, who thought that both authors used a common sermonic pattern.[41] Many commentators object that, given the extent of the overlap, this source must have been virtually identical with Jude so that it was more likely Jude himself; but Bauckham draws attention to the appeal in Jude 20-3 as the most important part of that letter, arguing that the author of Jude *might* have been citing a source in the earlier verses of his text. Even Bauckham, however, recognizes that this is a complicated hypothesis which leaves some ends untied.

For this reason, it is best to consider the theory of literary dependence. The work of Fornberg and Neyrey is important here.[42] Both scholars applied redaction-critical methods to the two letters and concluded that they use similar material to address *different* situations. These commentators, along with Cranfield, Kelly and Bauckham,[43] accept that 2 Peter used Jude and not the other way round. It is surely easier to suppose that this was so and that the author of 2 Peter expanded and edited Jude's biblical allusions for Gentile readers than to explain why Jude should have omitted large parts of 2 Peter, including the reference to a character as familiar as Noah (2 Pet. 2.5), but also introduced the more obscure references to Cain and Korah (Jude 11) which require detailed knowledge of Jewish post-biblical interpretation.

Bauckham mentions another argument for the priority of Jude over 2 Peter.[44] This is that Jude 4-18, with its catena of biblical allusions, has been very carefully composed while the structure of the corresponding passage 2 Peter 2.1–18 seems altogether looser. Those who wish to find support for the opposite position, that Jude used 2 Peter, must turn back to the commentaries of Spitta (1885) and Bigg (1901) to find it.[45] The alternative form of argument, that 2 Peter was interpolated by Jude, has failed to command wide assent.

Given this conclusion, it is important to emphasize that the author of 2 Peter was not merely a plagiarizer of Jude but made a creative use of it, not least by applying it to a different situation.[46] Just because 2 Peter is pseudonymous does not make its life-setting fictitious. Like Ephesians, 2 Peter is innovative and not simply imitative. And the fact that 2 Peter makes use of Jude does not mean that the situation addressed was any less specific; simply again that it was different.

The date of 2 Peter has troubled the commentators. It was set as late as 150 CE by Ernst Käsemann and as early as 80–90 by Richard Bauckham.[47] Käsemann's late date was based on the theory that 2 Peter exhibits a form of 'primitive Catholicism' which few if any scholars would accept today. Käsemann also thought the author's opponents were Gnostics, whereas more recent research (especially Neyrey's) regards them as Epicureans (see below). It is not impossible that 2 Peter was written in the first century CE, but we cannot be certain about this. Käsemann's late date for the letter was based on exegetical presuppositions which would not be accepted today. This lack of consensus in critical scholarship, however, is a pertinent reminder of the real difficulties which attend the interpretation of biblical material; and of the need for each interpreter to keep an open mind and exmaine the grounds on which his or her assumptions are made.

Epicureans denied the power of a provident deity.[48] They held that this world was made by randon atomic collision, not by the will of God. They denied the value of providence and prophecy, holding that there can be no serious telling of the future; and they criticized traditional theistic belief by the age-old argument (found also in the Hebrew Bible) that justice for the virtuous seems perpetually delayed.

When it is seen in the light of this philosophy, 2 Peter makes good sense. At 1.3 the letter presents God as the source of 'life and godliness';[49] 1.11 argues that 'entry into the eternal kingdom of our Lord and Saviour Jesus Christ will be richly provided for you'. Chapter 2 notes the appearance of 'false prophets' in the community. The author promises judgment on the basis of more than one biblical analogy. Presumably, the 'slander (of) the glorious ones' criticized by 2.11 denotes the false teachers' denial of heavenly powers. They are clearly promised judgment in 2.17.

Chapter 3 reasserts traditional Christian eschatological teaching. The background to this chapter is the complaint of some that the eschatological climax seemed impossibly delayed, and that such delay showed the failure of early Christian eschatological hopes *tout court*.[50] The author reminds his readers that the eschatological hope had been part of the Christian message from the beginning (2 Pet. 3.2); and that 'the Lord is not slow about his promise, as some think of slowness' (2 Pet. 3.9). The result is pastoral assurance, based on the words of Jesus himself, that 'the day of the Lord will come like a thief, and then the heavens will pass away with a loud noise' (2 Pet. 3.10). This allusion reasserts the traditional apocalyptic eschatology and presents it as still relevant to a situation near the end of the first century CE. In this, 2 Peter should be compared with 1 Peter if that letter is pseudonymous, and of course also with Revelation. The reassertion of the traditional hope leads to paraenesis in 3.11-13 which is essentially ethical in character.

The Johannine Letters

The Johannine letters (1, 2 and 3 John) should be considered together since they clearly come from the same circle, which is connected with that of the Fourth Gospel.[51]

The questions of how the Fourth Gospel achieved its present form and when John's letters were composed are clearly related to each other.[52] Both are difficult to answer. Most scholars posit more than one stage in the writing of the Gospel, even if it is difficult now to agree with Rudolph Bultmann's suggestion that the present form of the Gospel was the work of an ecclesiastical redactor and not just an author alone.[53] The acceptance of different stages in the Gospel is often combined with the conclusion that more than one person was responsible for the four texts that are connected with the figure of John. Some have distinguished as many as four significant figures in the Johannine school: the Beloved Disciple (the source of the tradition about Jesus); the evangelist who wrote the bulk of the Gospel; the presbyter who wrote the letters; and the redactor who gave the Fourth Gospel its present form.[54]

In evaluating these suggestions, most people would accept that Revelation is to be distinguished from the Fourth Gospel and the Johannine letters, even if there is a distant connection between Revelation and the acknowledged Johannine writings. It is difficult to be certain about the relationship between John and 1 John except to say that the two texts are closely related in vocabulary and style, and that 1 John exhibits some different concerns from the Gospel; notably, strong preoccupation with internal issues and the absence of any awareness that 'the Jews' constitute a problem for the community. The most likely interpretation of 1 John is that it represents a later stage of development when the differentiation between Johannine Christians and Jews had become so marked that Judaism was no longer seen as a threat, but where internal dangers had arisen in the form of a divided Christian community with doctrinal questions. Both 1 Jn 2.22-4 and 4.3 show that some form of docetism was the disputed issue, 2.22 asking directly, 'Who is the liar but the one who denies that Jesus is the Christ?' This, somewhat ambiguous, question seems to imply that the Johannine errorists had detracted from the human career of Jesus by refusing to accept that in him the Christ had come in the flesh.[55] In other words, they privileged the heavenly existence of Christ over and above his human manifestation. It is possible that the Johannine Prologue was introduced to deal with this problem given its insistence that 'the Word became *flesh* and lived among us' (1.14). For the author of 1 John, such false teaching removed the 'historical' element in the Christian faith by setting aside the human significance of Jesus, including of course the meaning of his death on the cross and tending away from the emerging doctrine of the incarnation.

This problem noticed by 1 John seems to have been a thing of the past; 1 Jn 4.1 states that 'many false prophets have gone out into the world'.[56] In the author's obviously 'world-negating' symbolism, this statement erects clear barriers between the Johannine community and other religious (and no doubt social) groups, censuring the opponents under the biblical heading of 'false prophets' in denigration of their activity. 1 John addresses the community following this, possibly protracted and no doubt painful experience of secession. There is little evidence that 1 John is a real letter as such. It is rather a polemical tract, designed to reassure members of the community and to explain to them why they adopt the stance that they do in respect of certain other kinds of people.

Such a view explains the somewhat rambling arrangement of material. Bultmann thought the author had a source which he utilized extensively, but again this view has failed to commend itself to subsequent commentators. Scholars nowadays posit a bipartite or even a tripartite division of the letter, depending on the extent to which it is thought that 1 John follows the twofold division of the Gospel.[57] It is also disputed to what extent the letter has a poetic structure. None of these uncertainties substantially hinders the attempt to read 1 John once its general repetitiousness is acknowledged. Chapter 1 is almost the religious charter of the Johannine community. The author views the readers as a redeemed community who continue to experience forgiveness by virtue of their relationship with God. Chapter 2 deals with pastoral, ethical and eschatological concerns. The author comments on the need to preserve loving, harmonious relations in the community and comments on the distance between those who accept this teaching and what the author, following the lead of the Fourth Gospel, calls 'the world' which is inimical to 'the Father' (2.15). This overarching distinction supplies the reason for the secession of the false teachers in 2.18-25. The author explains that 'by going out they made it plain that none of them belongs to us' (2.19).

The rest of the letter seems like commentary on this theme. 1 John 3 reiterates the call for mutual affection, combining this with the reminder to abstain from sin. 3.23 reiterates the demand to believe in Jesus, to which the love commandment is related. This combination of themes is repeated in chapter 4, 4.1-6 dealing with the question of right belief and 4.7-21 combining this with the exposition of right behaviour. Chapter 5 contains the passage, found mysterious by many commentators, which states that 'there are three that testify: the Spirit and the water and the blood, and these three agree' (1 Jn 5.7). The letter ends with a further call to avoid sin and to continue in the truth revealed by Jesus. Perhaps the clearest statement of dualism in 1 John is at 5.19: 'We know that we are God's children, and that the whole world lies under the power of the evil one.'

By contrast with 1 John, both 2 John and 3 John have the form of genuine letters, sent by a person who calls himself 'the elder' to 'the elect lady and her children' in the case of 2 John and to 'the beloved Gaius' in the case of 3 John.[58] There is much to be said for Raymond Brown's view that 2 John is addressed to an outlying church where the secessionist heresy has not yet penetrated but where the author thinks it is on the way.[59] That is why 2 Jn 10 instructs its readers not to welcome those who 'do not confess that Jesus Christ has come in the flesh' (2 Jn 7). The situation addressed by 3 John is more difficult to diagnose, for we read there neither of christological error nor of serious moral failure. It seems that one Diotrephes had refused hospitality to some travelling missionaries. The author asks the recipient Gaius to assume responsibility in the face of this failure, especially since a person called Demetrius is apparently travelling to conduct missionary work in the community. This is possibly a sign of expansion following the earlier difficulties.

Jude

On the view proposed in this chapter, Jude served as the source for 2 Peter.[60] Although other 'Judes' have occasionally been proposed, it seems obvious that the Jude presupposed here is the third brother of Jesus who is mentioned by Mk 6.3 (the fourth brother according to Mt. 13.55).[61] There is nothing in the text or style of Jude that definitely excludes authenticity; but several scholars have concluded that the author's familiarity with Jewish apocalyptic literature and his style of argumentation is a possible if not a probable indication of pseudonymity. More than this we cannot say. Clearly, if Jude is authentic it must be nearer to 50 than 100 CE. If pseudonymous, it need not have been written outside or at least much outside this span. We are dealing in all probability with a text of the first century CE whose purpose is to warn against false teaching in language that had become familiar from the Jewish apocalyptic tradition. Palestine is the most likely provenance for the letter.

Jude 4 sets the scene for the argument with its assertion that 'certain intruders have stolen in among you, people . . . who pervert the grace of our God into licentiousness and deny our only Master and Lord, Jesus Christ'. It is implied by Jude 7 that this had a sexual dimension. Jude 8 adds the tripartite criticism that 'these dreamers also defile the flesh, reject authority, and slander the glorious ones'. Jude 9-13 further criticizes their activity by setting them in the guise of notorious biblical sinners. Jude 14-15 is a promise of punishment for these wrongdoers, cast in language familiar from *1 En.* 1.9. Jude 17-22 reminds the readers that the appearance of such people had been foretold by the apostles, encouraging them to persevere in Christian faith until the time of the eschatological judgment.

Jude addresses a specific situation. The letter is important for understanding the course which Christianity took in the later first century CE, and for the use of Jewish apocalyptic traditions which continued to be made there.

Revelation

Lastly, we come to Revelation.[62] Originally included in the canon through its supposed authorship by John the Apostle,[63] Revelation has attracted many readers but repelled many others. Scholarly attitudes towards Revelation are changing. It is now, for instance, questioned whether there was a persecution of the Christians by Domitian towards the end of the first century CE. A book by Leonard L. Thompson asks whether it is appropriate to refer the New Testament Apocalypse to a 'crisis situation' at all.[64] Given the oddities of the work's form and contents, considerable uncertainty remains in trying to match Revelation to the known events of the first century CE.

Revelation is the only New Testament 'apocalypse'. In the Old Testament we have a similar work in the book of Daniel, and there are numerous apocalypses from either side of the beginning of the Common Era. The nature of this genre has been examined in scholarly literature. A research project, edited by J.J. Collins in 1979, proposed the following definition: an apocalypse is 'a genre of revelatory literature with a narrative framework, in which a revelation is mediated by an otherworldly being to a human recipient, disclosing a transcendent reality which is both temporal, insofar as it envisages eschatological salvation, and spatial, insofar as it involves another, supernatural world'.[65] Collins and his team support this definition from a review of all the Jewish, Christian, Gnostic, Classical and Persian apocalypses. It led them to construct a paradigm noting the different modes of revelation and the variety of subjects which feature in these texts. This subject-matter includes eschatology, especially eschatological upheaval and the question of punishment or salvation. It also includes topics such as cosmogony, angelology, historical review and theodicy.

The essence of the apocalypse is that it claims to reveal the secrets of heaven for the benefit of people on earth. The nature of the revealed material varies from text to text, but the conviction of presenting heavenly revelation is a constant theme of the apocalypses. Such revealed material is set within the context of an encounter with a supernatural mediator, and the manner of the revelation varies across the apocalypses. Some texts locate the seer on earth where he is greeted by an angel;

others describe an otherworldly journey in which the mediator acts as guide. Revelation interestingly does both.[66] The apocalypse generally gives its revelation a narrative framework. The seer reports what he hears and sees. No apocalypse outside Gnosticism contains an unbroken monologue by the heavenly mediator. The narrative draws attention to the revealed nature of the material by describing the exceptional circumstances under which it was received. Very often it describes the seer's helpless response to the revelation – in a trance, a dream or some other mode of reception; the statement that the seer is the passive recipient of revelation perpetuates the belief that his is no ordinary experience. The origin of this response lies deep in human psychology, as Rudolph Otto has shown.[67] There is also an important background in the Hebrew prophetic and wisdom traditions.

Revelation clearly belongs to the apocalypse genre. It has a narrative setting (chapter 1) and embodies the claim to revelation (see 1.10-11). Its subject-matter is the secrets of the heavenly world. These secrets permit an authoritative view of the readers' situation. Although Revelation clearly has the form of an apocalypse (especially in chapters 4–22), we should note that it has affinities with other genres too. Chapters 2 and 3 include a series of letters sent by the heavenly Christ to seven representative churches in Asia Minor. John thirdly calls his work 'prophecy' (1.3). 'Prophecy' was a familiar entity in early Christianity, formally distinct from apocalypticism and practised by a number of figures.[68] 'John' the author of Revelation was evidently a well-known Christian prophet. A particular feature of his prophetic consciousness is the use of Hebrew Bible passages which supply the raw material for the rebirth of imagery that takes place in his text.[69] Revelation offers no mere repetition of these biblical themes, but a brilliant meditation on them by which new meanings are skilfully presented.

Authorship and Date

The authorship of the New Testament Apocalypse is a major bone of contention.[70] The text says its author was 'John' (1.9), but John was a common name in early Christian circles. Justin Martyr says that the author of Revelation was 'John, one of the apostles of Christ' (*Dial.* 81.4). He appears to mean by this the author of the Fourth Gospel. Papias mentions a John the Elder who was a venerable Christian leader in Ephesus (see Eusebius, *Hist. Eccl.* 3.39).[71] In the third century the belief in the common authorship of Revelation and the Fourth Gospel began to be rejected, not least because of the support that Revelation offers for millenarianism which was beginning to be judged unsound at that time. Dionysius of Alexandria, who is reported by Eusebius in his *Hist. Eccl.* 7.25, is an early representative of the view that John the Evangelist was not the author of the Apocalypse. The majority of recent scholars agree with this assessment, even though it is often conceded that the author of the Apocalypse may have had a loose connection with the Johannine 'school' in Ephesus.

The reasons for denying common authorship of the Gospel and the Apocalypse are compelling, and they rest on matters of style and content. The language of the two texts is quite different, as is their eschatology. Although there are certain similarities between them, these are never so great as to *demand* a theory of common authorship; the differences militate against it. It is not difficult to see that the identification of common authorship brought a real benefit in the second century CE. It enabled mainstream Christians to claim apostolic authority for Revelation's eschatology, including its millenarianism (20.4), which was used against the Gnostic denial of belief in the bodily resurrection. However, modern criticism has identified too many differences for the hypothesis of common authorship to be retained convincingly.[72] We need to search further than John the Evangelist to find the author of the Apocalypse.

Some scholars think the Apocalypse is pseudonymous and that an unknown Christian prophet attributed his work to John the Apostle.[73] This theory is also unconvincing. The fact that the Apocalypse does not establish its author's identity as *this* John strongly suggests that the author himself did not make that connection. The situation is quite different, say, from the Pastorals and 2 Peter, which all make great efforts to present their authors as front-rank apostles. The theory of pseudonymous authorship in fact detracts from the prophetic impact of the Apocalypse. The work gains its force from the assertion that a contemporary prophet has been commissioned by Christ to write to the churches in this way. The importance of the revelation in that sense transcends the identity of the human mediator. The crucial thing about the Apocalypse is that it gives every sign of having been written in a living prophetic tradition. It is significant that the long-standing Jewish tradition of pseudonymity is abandoned for that reason, marking a clear delineator in this circle's Christian understanding of revelation.

The author's identity therefore remains obscure – frustratingly so – but we can surmise that he was a well-known prophet on the Asian Christian scene who had gone to Patmos for a purpose which also remains obscure.[74] Eusebius reports that John had been 'condemned' (i.e. banished) to Patmos 'because of his testimony to the word of God' (*Hist. Eccl.* 3.18.1). It is surprising how many scholars have treated this as an historically reliable statement. Eusebius reports a number of other events, such as the story of the grandsons of Jude being hauled before Domitian,[75] which makes one wonder whether he really had the ability to distinguish between history and legend in the discussion of first-century Christianity. The Apocalypse itself gives no indication that John had been banished to Patmos. We would expect the text to make it clear if he had been. Nor was Patmos the dark and depressing place it is sometimes made out to be.

There are no records that it was used as a prison settlement. The seer possibly went there as a form of retreat. Such seclusion may have resulted in the oracles of the Apocalypse. Alternatively, if John was a wandering prophet, as his awareness of responsibility for a number of churches suggests, he may have gone to Patmos in the normal exercise of his ministry. The reason for John's presence on Patmos should be held an open question and Eusebius' report treated with caution in the absence of corroborating evidence for the theory that John had been banished to Patmos.

There has been a scholarly debate as to whether Revelation should be dated in the reign of Domitian, in the last decade of the first century CE, or whether it was written earlier, just after the reign of Nero (69 CE). This problem can be approached by examining the available evidence. The earliest documented use of Revelation comes from the reign of Hadrian, probably between 125 and 135 CE, with Papias of Hierapolis. Andreas of Caesarea, who wrote in the sixth century, says that Papias knew the Apocalypse.[76] Both Justin Martyr (in c.150 CE) and Irenaeus (in c.180 CE) knew Revelation also.

This evidence shows that Revelation was in Christian use within a century of the resurrection of Jesus. The evidence of Papias places its origin almost certainly in the first century CE. A first-century origin is supported also by Irenaeus, who says that the Apocalypse was seen at the end of the reign of Domitian (d. 96 CE; *Adv. Haer.* 5.30.3). Eusebius adds to this the report that John was banished to Patmos *by Domitian* (*Hist. Eccl.* 3.18.1). This collective information has been responsible for the dominant theory that Revelation was written in the last decade of the first century, in the years preceding the death of Domitian.

This 'consensus theory' has been challenged by scholars who argue on internal grounds that Revelation was written in the 60s of the first century CE. This view is argued forcefully by John A.T. Robinson. Robinson bases his case on Rev. 17.9-11, which says that, of the seven horns (i.e. emperors), five have fallen, one is reigning and the last has yet to come.[77] Robinson thinks the first emperor is Augustus. He includes the so-called 'soldier emperors' (Galba, Otho and Vitellius) in his list. This leads him to suggest that the Apocalypse was written in the reign of Galba (68–9 CE) and before the accession of Otho (69 CE). Against this interpretation, however, it must be objected that the number 'seven' has a symbolic significance in the Apocalypse and that it is far from certain John offers an historically precise review in 17.9-11.[78] That information can be read in more than one way. If the list begins with Caligula, 17.9-11 yields a date in the reign of Domitian, on the grounds that Caligula was the first emperor to offend Jewish scruples, and the reigns of Galba, Otho and Vitellius are omitted as too short to be considered significant. The list would then consist of Caligula, Claudius, Nero, Vespasian and Titus. Domitian would be the reigning emperor. On this hypothesis, the author wrote before the accession of Nerva (96 CE), so that 17.9-11 can be made to support the consensus theory.[79]

The question is thus whether the internal evidence of the Apocalypse, which is quite ambiguous, should be allowed to outweigh the externally attested date for Revelation at the end of the first century CE. Despite the frequent references to martyrdom in the Apocalypse, there is little concrete evidence that martyrdom was a significant feature of the author's recent experience (see below on 2.13). We would expect more to be made of the Neronian persecution (64 CE) had the Apocalypse been written in close proximity to that event. Nor might John so readily have disclosed his own identity then. Given the uncertainty surrounding 17.9-11, it does not seem appropriate to set aside the external evidence, even when the question of Irenaeus' critical awareness is treated with some caution. The view adopted here is that Revelation was written in the last decade of the first century CE, at some point before the death of Domitian in 96 CE.

With this conclusion to hand, it is often suggested that Revelation was written during a Roman *persecution* of the Christians in the later years of Domitian's reign. But, again, scholars have assumed much too uncritically that there was such a persecution on the basis of the evidence of Eusebius.[80] Eusebius states that many people fell victim to Domitian's appalling cruelty and were executed, banished and fined in the later part of his reign (*Hist. Eccl.* 3.17–20). Yet the internal evidence of Revelation hardly supports the view that the Apocalypse was addressed to a situation dominated by martyrdom. The only martyr mentioned by name is the Antipas of Rev. 2.13. It is far from certain how this person died. The other references to martyrdom in Revelation are mainly symbolic. They must be judged in the wider context of the imagery that the Apocalypse constructs. The threat of widespread martyrdom is significantly unconfirmed by the letters to the seven churches which, if anything, indicate that the Apocalypse was addressed to a situation dominated by complacency and not by conflict.

Thompson's Theory

Leonard L. Thompson draws a very different conclusion about Revelation. He begins by asking why so many ancient sources adopt a pessimistic attitude towards Domitian.[81] Suetonius says for instance that from an early age Domitian 'exercised all the tyranny of his high position so lawlessly, that it was even then apparent what sort of a man he was going to be' (*Dom.* 1.3). Tacitus mentions his unbridled passions (*Hist.* 4.68); Pliny describes the imperial household as the place where 'that fearful monster built his defences with untold terrors, where lurking in his den he licked up the blood of his murdered relatives or emerged to plot the massacre and destruction of his most distinguished subjects' (*Pan.* 48.3).

Thompson argues that this harsh portrait of Domitian comes from writers who were concerned to eulogize the reign of Trajan. He draws attention to their promulgation of Trajan's reign as a 'new era' which had adopted a change in tone from its predecessor.[82] These writers consequently praised Trajan as a new-style libertarian. Pliny's *Panegyricus* is typical of this approach when it declaims that 'the sufferings of the past are over: let us then have done with the words which belong to them' (2.12).

The total silence about a Domitianic persecution in Christian sources before Eusebius is a significant thing. Thompson uses this silence to propose an alternative reading of the New Testament Apocalypse. He suggests that it was a response to social tension but not to martyrdom in the readers' environment.[83] Asia during the reign of Domitian was a relatively prosperous place to live.[84] The Jews of Asia were perhaps the most socially and culturally integrated of those outside Palestine (although in general they remained faithful to their religious traditions). The Asian Christians (as throughout the Empire) came from different economic backgrounds. Their leaders were relatively prosperous people with sufficient resources to let them travel, own large houses and act as patrons of the Christian congregations. These wealthier Christians took their full part in civic life. We know from the sources (especially Pliny, *Ep.* 10.96–7) that imperial officials did not go on the offensive to persecute Christians. Such trials as there were (at least by the second century) came from individual initiatives in which information was laid by private citizens. 'Atheism', by which was meant the refusal to honour the state pantheon, was the principal cause of offence in such investigations. This stemmed from the belief that the corporate well-being was threatened by unwise alienation of the gods.

The issue of how the church should relate to the world is crucial for Revelation. This had been a matter for Christian reflection from at least the Pauline letters onwards. John's perspective in the Apocalypse is more critical of Christians who were open to cultural assimilation than that of either Paul or the author of Acts.[85] John complains that more than one church had been tempted to eat food sacrificed to idols and to practise fornication (2.14, 20). This symbolism probably constitutes rhetoric against Christians who had assimilated the pagan ethos, and not warnings against sexual misbehaviour in the narrow sense. Thompson cites the research of Gerd Theissen to explain the likely background of this concern.[86] Theissen shows that people in late antiquity had the opportunity to eat meat in a cultic setting at both public occasions (festivals and funerals) and private (guild meetings and banquets). These occasions were representative of social connections. They indicated the status that an individual enjoyed in society. They almost invariably had religious connotations in the customary invocations that were offered to the gods. Theissen argues that this issue would have affected Christians of different status in different ways. Wealthier Christians with civic responsibility would have eaten meat sacrificed to idols more often than poorer Christians who had no such respectable connections. Wealthier Christians might even have found it necessary to host these occasions themselves. They would certainly have found it difficult to abstain from meat-eating if they wanted to retain their status.

Thompson's reading of the Apocalypse concludes that John was a rigorist who objected to Christians accommodating to this and other social demands of urban life in the late first century CE.[87] There is a variety of evidence in the Apocalypse to support this interpretation. John tells the churches at Pergamum and Thyatira to rid themselves of false teaching advocated by leaders who permitted the eating of meat sacrificed to idols (2.14-15, 20). Thompson compares these 'opponents' to the liberal wing of the Corinthian church, contrasting John's attitude with the partial support which Paul had offered for such behaviour in 1 Corinthians 8. John's criticism extends to the economic as well as the social order.[88] Buying and selling require the mark of the beast, he explains (13.16-17). This statement anticipates the extended description of the goods which can no longer be sold when Babylon falls (18.11-13). That catastrophe causes the merchants (18.15) and the shipmasters and seafarers (18.17) to regret the city's demise. The description of Babylon's fall is a symbolic rejection of Rome's attraction to those who had benefited from supplying her with goods. That probably included some of John's Asian readers, so that the criticism had a cutting edge.

Only the letters to Sardis and Laodicea fail to mention specific adversaries. Both are set in ironic terms: the Christians at Sardis are 'dead' (3.1) and the Laodiceans 'poor', among other things (3.17). Sardis and Laodicea were important centres of Judaism; yet Thompson notes that John does not mention opposition from Judaism there.[89] Jewish opposition, however, is mentioned in Smyrna and Philadelphia, where the Jewish presence was much less concentrated. From this information, Thompson infers a link between his readers' assimilation to their urban environment and the absence of conflict with Judaism, and the opposite situation where Jews persecuted Christians who maintained high social boundaries. The references to conflict in the letters depend on whether or not the churches were following John's teaching to keep themselves 'separate' from wider society, in a way that Paul had not required of his readers.

Thompson argues that this is why the Apocalypse was written. John *encourages* his readers to see themselves in conflict with society as part of his own distinctive vision of the world. The Apocalypse *creates* the notion of conflict through its choice of genre, where conflict and world-negation are prominent themes, and also through the language and imagery as the various visions unfold. Thompson thereby turns the long-established view of the Apocalypse as 'crisis literature' on its head. There is indeed a crisis in Revelation: but the crisis lies in the author's rhetoric and not in the actual situation addressed. The author wants his readers to *perceive* a crisis, and thus to take responsible action, when the lives of at least his wealthier readers may have been strikingly free from apprehension. By reworking apocalyptic traditions, John calls his churches to action and challenges the security of their existence. They needed decisive action to live as God's priestly people.

Reading Revelation

Revelation does not make for easy reading. It contains a series of visions which are only more or less related to each other. Nevertheless, the recognition that the work's thought reflects the dominance of eschatology in the Christian movement is an important one. The letter moves from celebration of Christ's sacrifice (chapters 4–5) to the theme of his return from heaven (chapter 19) and the establishment of his earthly kingdom (chapters 20–2).

Revelation juxtaposes the theme of the suffering righteous with that of their eschatological vindication. Following the vision of God and the Lamb (chapters 4–5), the Lamb opens seals which disclose a sequence of calamities (chapters 6–7). In chapter 7 the servants of God are sealed to prevent them from eschatological annihilation. The opening of the seventh seal in 8.1 provides the cue for seven angels to blow seven trumpets, the last of which is sounded in 11.15. These trumpets herald horrid calamities. Chapter 12 describes warfare in heaven in which the dragon is cast down to the earth. Chapter 13 describes the activity of the first beast, who has often been identified with the emperor Nero. Chapter 14 marks the transition to the *dénouement* of the Apocalypse with its vision of the Lamb and his elect on Mount Zion. This is a celebration of the redeemed community as those who survived the divine judgment unleashed against the earth.

Chapter 16 narrates 'the seven bowls of the wrath of God' (16.1), which result in yet further calamities. Chapter 17 describes the judgment of Babylon (Rome), mentioning a second beast in this context, and chapter 18 that city's downfall. Chapter 19 records the return of Jesus in pictorial language ('Then I saw heaven opened, and there was a white horse!', 19.1). Chapter 20 contains an odd scheme of eschatology in which Satan is bound for a thousand years but then allowed to exercise his tyranny on earth. In chapter 21 the present heaven and earth are replaced with new and perfect counterparts. Chapter 22 brings the Apocalypse to a close with a promise of the speedy return of Jesus (22.20).

The Development of the New Testament Canon

The last matter to consider is the development of the New Testament canon of scripture.[90] This topic can best be approached by revisiting what we saw about the emergence of the Hebrew canon in Part I.[91]

The earliest evidence that we have for the Hebrew canon comes from Josephus, who states that the Jews held twenty-two writings as authoritative (*Apion* 1.8).[92] At the Jamnian Academy which convened after the Fall of Jerusalem (70 CE), doubts were raised about a surprisingly small number of books. The Song of Solomon and Ecclesiastes were the principal texts to be questioned on this occasion. In the case of both, authorities were found who declared they 'rendered the hands unclean' (*m.Yad.* 3.5). Such suspicion as attached to them derived from their potentially unsuitable content; sexual content in the case of the Song of Solomon. This means that the Hebrew canon had achieved a virtually fixed form by the time that the New Testament canon was emerging.

There is always the danger of reductionism when writing on a complex topic. Nevertheless, we can chart without gross inexactitude the major steps by which the New Testament canon achieved its present form. The first point to make is that the development of the canon was an evolutionary phenomenon, not a design feature of the very earliest Christianity. Paul and the others did not set out to write 'scripture' as such. As we know from more than one New Testament reference, the Bible to which the early Christians appealed was 'the Law and the Prophets', no doubt also the Writings as well.[93] While the Christians interpreted the Hebrew Bible in the light of their beliefs about Jesus, the Bible nonetheless remained their principal source of authority.

As with the development of Christian theology, it was first the visionary perception and then the perceived authority of the heavenly Jesus which provided the impetus to authoritative utterance. In his first letter, 1 Thessalonians, we find Paul offering advice on the basis of a word of Jesus (1 Thess. 4.15). In a number of references in 1 Corinthians, Paul appeals to the words of Jesus to establish authoritative teaching (see e.g. 1 Cor. 9.9, 13, 14).[94] We find here the ultimate origins of the Gospel tradition in the belief that Jesus' words, before and after Easter, had divine authority.[95] Direct communication from Jesus in the form of prophetic utterances and revelations served to reinforce this view.[96]

Christian texts from around the end of the first century CE show a seachange in the perception of what passed for authority. The Hebrew Bible's authority is augmented by the words of Jesus in what appears to be a claim for parallel status (see e.g. *1 Clem.* 13.1f.; 2 Pet. 3.2). There is important evidence in Ignatius.[97] Ignatius designates the prophets *and* the gospel as witnesses to truth (*Smyrn.* 7.2); and on one occasion he places the deeds and words of Jesus *above* the 'holy documents' (*Phld.* 8). Ignatius certainly knew a collection of Paul's letters, and he may have known one or more of the Gospels. In the words of Bruce Metzger, however, 'there is no evidence that he regarded any of these Gospels or Epistles as "Scripture" '.[98] The primary authority for Ignatius was the apostolic preaching about Jesus, in whatever form this was transmitted.

The Pauline Corpus

The evidence of Ignatius shows that a collection of Pauline letters existed at least by the end of the first century CE.[99] Such a collection was available to the arch-heretic Marcion, who knew ten Pauline texts. The reason for this collection has been variously explained. It has been suggested (but also rebutted) that Paul passed out of fashion in the period between his death and the end of the century, and that Ephesians was written as a kind of introduction to explain what Paul was about and to rekindle interest in his writings.[100] There is, however, no formal evidence of this neglect. Much depends on questions of dating. All we can say is that a Pauline collection was made towards the end of the first century and that Ignatius and Marcion are witnesses of it. Perhaps the more convincing explanation is that Paul's normative significance was increasingly recognized when the breach between Christianity and Judaism was becoming complete.

The Gospels

The question of when the Gospels were collected and placed together in a canon (as opposed to when the individual Gospels were written) is less easy to answer.[101] If Ignatius knew Matthew and John (and conceivably Luke),[102] he gives no indication that this knowledge was derived from a formally recognized collection. It is only from around the *middle* of the second century CE that such a collection is acknowledged in Christian literature. Both the 'Unknown Gospel' and the Gospel of Peter seem to know all four Gospels.[103] Tatian's *Diatessaron*, or harmony of the four Gospels, which was written around this time, presupposes the authority of these four texts.[104] The evidence of the *Ascension of Isaiah*, however, which comes from the early second century CE, shows that the oral tradition continued to be used alongside the emerging Gospel tradition for a while.[105] The continuing use of oral and legendary material in this period is further attested by the various apocryphal Gospels, which form a topic of study in their own right.[106]

The Canon

The next question is when the collections of Gospels and epistles were put together and the entity that we call the 'New Testament' was born. The *Letter of Polycarp* and *2 Clement* are relevant here.[107] Polycarp, *Phil.* 6.3 refers to the commands of 'the Lord, the apostles and the prophets', as if the sayings of Jesus and the apostles are given equal authority with the Hebrew Bible. *2 Clem.* 14.2 names as authoritative in a doctrinal matter 'the books and the apostles', holding the two together. Earlier in the same letter, *2 Clem.* 2.4 follows a biblical citation with the words of Jesus, introduced with the formula 'and another writing says . . .'. Similarly, *Barn.* 4.14 introduces another saying of Jesus with the words, 'it is written'.

This evidence is probably indicative of a trend, rather than conclusive about a canon. The second half of the second century CE was the time when awareness of a canon as such makes its appearance in the Christian consciousness. Justin Martyr (*1 Apol.* 67.3) states that in the Christian worship service there were read 'the memoirs of the apostles and the writings of the prophets'.[108] Justin has earlier made it clear that by these 'memoirs' he means the Gospels (*1 Apol.* 66.3), much as he often cites Gospel passages with a similar formula of introduction. It is not certain that Justin knew John, and thus not certain that he knew a four-Gospel canon.[109] He does, however, cite Revelation in *1 Apol.* 28.1.

We have mentioned Marcion already.[110] Marcion was regarded as one of the arch-heretics of primitive Christianity. He rejected the view that the God of the Hebrew Bible was the God whom Jesus proclaimed. He rejected the Hebrew Bible as the product of an inferior deity. Marcion also believed that the twelve apostles had corrupted the teaching of Jesus by believing him to be the Messiah of that rejected deity. Marcion thought that Paul alone of the early Christians had understood the true nature of the gospel. He privileged ten letters of Paul (the exception being the Pastorals) and made them the basis of his theological programme. Among the Gospels, Marcion felt he could trust only the Gospel of Luke. He proceeded to expunge both Paul and Luke of what he regarded as 'interpolations', which he thought had been introduced by false and Judaizing apostles.

While there is no doubt that Marcion was the first to form a 'canon' of New Testament scripture, the broader and less nuanced canon which the mainstream church subsequently came to accept should not necessarily be seen as a direct reaction to Marcionism. Marcion doubtless accelerated a trend that was already in place, but he was not the first to identify certain Christian writings as authoritative on the basis of their connection with Jesus and the apostles.

Hard on the heels of Tatian, Irenaeus emphasized the authority of the four Gospels.[111] His *Adv. Haer.* 3.11.11 compares the existence of four Gospels to other more established 'fours', such as the four compass points and the four principal winds. This reflects the strong conviction that the four Gospels were recognized and distinguished from the other, apocryphal Gospels. Irenaeus was the first to recognize thirteen Pauline letters.

Tertullian was the first to acknowledge the existence of a formal New Testament alongside the Old Testament.[112] Although the contents of his canon were not significantly different from those of Irenaeus and other Christians, Tertullian introduced the two Latin words *instrumentum* and *testamentum* to describe the authoritative Christian writings.[113] These terms meant a 'written contract' and a 'will' respectively. In the context of his denuniciation of Marcion, Tertullian rebukes him for not accepting Acts; he defends each of the Pauline letters in turn. He quotes also from Hebrews, 1 John, 1 Peter and Revelation. In fact, he cites *all* the New Testament writings with the exception of 2 Peter, James, and 2 and 3 John. Tertullian originally viewed the *Shepherd of Hermas* as scripture but subsequently deemed it apocryphal.

Clement of Alexandria also knows 'the four Gospels which have been given over to us' (*Strom.* 3.93.1). He prepared expositions of 1 Peter, 1 John and Jude.[114] Clement regarded certain other writings as apostolic scripture, including the *Apocalypse of Peter, Hermas* and *Barnabas*.[115] This means that his canon was still rather 'open' when compared with what pertained subsequently. The so-called 'Muratorian Canon' identifies the recognized writings in the Roman church from around the same time. It mentions all the New Testament books with the exception of Hebrews, James, and 1 and 2 Peter.

It was only in the third and fourth centuries that our present understanding of the New Testament canon was agreed. Clement's successor as head of the catechetical school in Alexandria, Origen, drew up different classes of book according to the respect in which they were held by the worldwide church.[116] There were essentially three classes of text. The first class was those writings which were uncontested by the church generally. Into this category fell the four Gospels, the thirteen Paulines, 1 Peter, 1 John, Acts and Revelation. The second class was those writings which were held doubtful, including 2 Peter, 2 and 3 John, Hebrews, James and Jude. The third class was that of pseudonymous texts, including the *Gospel of the Egyptians*, the *Gospel of Thomas*, the *Gospel of Baileides*, and the *Gospel of Matthias*.

In the fourth century CE Eusebius similarly denoted three categories of scripture: homologoumena, antilegomena and completely senseless heretical concoctions.[117] The homologoumena were the four Gospels, Acts, the fourteen Pauline letters (including Hebrews), 1 Peter, 1 John and potentially Revelation. His antilegomena fell into two sub-categories: writings held in greater or lesser esteem by the majority of Christians. Those recognized by the majority were James, Jude, 2 Peter, and 2 and 3 John. The lesser-accepted group included the *Apocalypse of Peter, Hermas, Barnabas* and the *Didache*. However, Eusebius also says that the Greek church of his day knew seven Catholic letters (*Hist. Eccl.* 2.23.24f.). If his homologoumena and his first sub-category of antilegomena are grouped together, we have the entire New Testament as it was subsequently understood.

In the fourth and fifth centuries, the authority of only a very few books was contested. Interestingly, this happened on a regional basis. Revelation was held suspect in the East while Hebrews was treated with suspicion in the West. The question of the canonical books in the

Eastern church was settled by the letter of Athanasius in 367 CE which delimited the canon of the Old and New Testaments alike.[118] Athanasius designated the twenty-seven books of the New Testament as the only canonical ones. These were the four Gospels followed by the seven Catholic letters and the fourteen Pauline letters (Hebrews being included there again). In the West, it is possible that the Athanasian canon was adopted in 382 CE, but completely certain that it was adopted (or readopted) in 405 CE.[119] So ended the process which yielded our present form of the New Testament, after some three hundred years of sometimes acrimonious debate.

THE EMERGENCE OF BELIEFS ABOUT JESUS

The development but also the delay of the eschatological hope was the framework of the first-century Christian understanding. Another significant feature was the emergence and development of beliefs about Jesus.[1] Although the growing understanding of Jesus' achievement was clearly related to the delay in eschatology, it must be considered separately because the New Testament documents equally clearly provide evidence of an emerging doctrine *of* Jesus that paralleled beliefs about what Jesus would *do* at his return from heaven. Christology developed throughout the first century CE. Some quite sophisticated beliefs about Jesus emerged at an early stage of the Christian understanding. This happened even before 1 Thessalonians was written, to judge from such pre-Pauline passages as 1 Cor. 8.5-6 and Phil. 2.6-11.[2] Christology did not develop, as might be supposed, in a strict chronological sequence.[3] We shall investigate the development of beliefs about Jesus in order to understand the safe transition of Christianity from the first to the second generation and beyond.[4]

The Roots of Christology

The roots of Christology lie in one sense in the complex of Jewish hopes that existed before the period of Christian origins.[5] Christianity did not, however, just pick up existing Jewish messianic hopes and claim they had been fulfilled in the person of Jesus. There was no such precise Jewish 'blueprint' for action. We saw in Part I that it is more appropriate to speak of a variety of Jewish hopes for salvation. The Qumran community offers a perfect example of this in their expectation of two Messiahs and of a final conflict that would leave the Sons of Light victorious over the Sons of Darkness.[6] Christianity took up this complex of Jewish hopes and reworked them in a new and creative way which made allowance for and tried to explain the unexpected nature of the Easter event. This development produced some new forms of belief which were peculiar to the Christian religion itself.

The Preaching of Jesus

We look to the preaching of Jesus to discover the ultimate origin of Christology.[7] Jesus preached the dawn of God's kingdom. We saw that he probably thought about himself as Messiah and expected to preside over the transformed Israel with his twelve disciples when the Son of Man introduced the kingdom. It remains uncertain whether Jesus expected to die and thus to enter his messianic status through resurrection. In any event, Jesus almost certainly thought about himself as Messiah. He understood this to signify his own eschatological rule over Israel.

It is probably more important when researching the roots of Christology to decide what Jesus did *not* believe about himself than to decide what he actually did. Jesus did not, so far as we know, think about himself as God. Although this claim is attributed to him by the Jews in John's Gospel (Jn 5.18),[8] it is significantly unsupported by evidence from the Synoptic Gospels. It would have been unthinkable for a first-century Jew to call himself God. Jesus did not do this. He conceivably thought about God as his Father in a symbolic way, but the claim for 'paternal familiarity' once advocated by Joachim Jeremias and regarded as a firm conclusion of scholarship has more recently been criticized by James Barr, who questions the basis of the evidence Jeremias used to reach his conclusion.[9] Jesus' claim to divine sonship is more plausibly to be evaluated within the context of Jesus' redefinition of family ties in which the rejection of patriarchal values stands to the forefront of meaning.[10] In this sense, calling God 'Father' meant that 'Father' (i.e. patron) was not an applicable title for any human being (cf. Mt. 23.9). This had the effect of diverting attention from existing power structures to the theocracy that Jesus' preaching of the kingdom embodied.

We saw that Jesus probably used 'son of man' in more than one sense. The present form of the Gospels, where 'the Son of Man' is used as a title for Jesus, makes it difficult to discern what lies behind this phrase. It is probable that Jesus associated his own work with that of the cosmic mediator called the Son of Man and that after Easter the church conflated these two different figures. It is unlikely that Jesus said that *he* was the Son of Man, if by that he meant he was a heavenly being; still less that he was the *incarnation* of the Son of Man in the sense that John's Gospel speaks of Jesus as the incarnation of the divine Word (Jn 1.14, 18). Jesus more likely spoke about himself as 'son of man' in the self-referential sense and also about the Son of Man as a heavenly mediator distinct from himself. This combination of terms provided the resources for the church to speak of *Jesus* as the Son of Man after Easter.

Jesus, like most first-century Jews with the exception of the Sadducees, would have believed in the concept of resurrection.[11] There is evidence for this view in more than one passage from the Gospels,[12] and no sound reason for doubting that Jesus thought in this way. This is quite different, however, from the assertion that Jesus anticipated *his own* resurrection in the precise sense that the Christians proclaimed he had been raised after Easter. Just as Jesus did not think he was God, so he almost certainly did not anticipate the universal worship of himself which is described by Phil. 2.9-11 and implied by 1 Cor. 8.5-6. The most we can say is that Jesus held a view analogous to the martyrological tradition represented by 2 Maccabees 7 and other passages, according to which it was believed

that God would raise the righteous in recompense for their deaths. If
Mk 14.25 is an authentic saying, Jesus expected to appear as Messiah to
preside over the earthly kingdom of God. This is quite different, however, from the suggestion that Jesus thought he was a heavenly being who
would return to earth as Lord and Messiah, which is how the Christians
thought about him after Easter.

The Easter Experience

These observations show that the rise of Christology cannot be explained
from the preaching of Jesus alone. We should not under-estimate the
importance of the Easter experience in the development of beliefs about
Jesus. The transformation represented by Easter is demonstrated graphic-
ally by the apparent obvious change of heart and face among the followers of Jesus in Acts. At the conclusion of the Gospels, the disciples forsake
Jesus and flee (Mk 14.50). Only the women stand at the foot of his cross
(Mk 15.40). Following the Pentecost experience, in contrast to what had
pertained beforehand, the disciples emerge as bold and confident people
who are only too prepared to preach the resurrection of Jesus, despite the
personal risk to themselves.

This boldness is matched on the ideological level by new convictions
about Jesus.[13] We do not know for sure what the disciples felt in the
aftermath of his arrest and crucifixion. Presumably, they would have
felt animosity towards Judas Iscariot on the grounds that he had ruined
the plot.[14] There must also have been considerable soul-searching and
uncertainty about the relevance of the hope for God's kingdom and
even about the belief that Jesus was the Messiah. Jn 20.19 presents the
disciples as frightened on account of the Jews. In the light of the fact that
the disciples were not arrested with Jesus, however,[15] they are more likely
to have been disillusioned by the failure of Jesus' movement than frightened of reprisals from the Jews. What had happened to Jesus seemed like
the end of it all. What were they to do now their leader had been taken
from them?

We saw in Chapter 16 that it is difficult to reconstruct the precise
sequence of events connected with the resurrection of Jesus, as with
other aspects of the birth of Christianity. The first dramatic evidence of
change occurs in the so-called resurrection appearances which Paul
describes in 1 Corinthians 15. We need not doubt the historicity of the
empty tomb narrative, as some have done, but we must acknowledge that
the empty tomb by itself is an ambiguous symbol. The resurrection
appearances have the status of apocalyptic visions in which a heavenly
mediator appears to the disciples and communicates revelation to them.
In this case, the mediator is Jesus and the authoritative revelation is his
new and unprecedented heavenly status through which it came to be
believed that he shared the divine nature.

The first stem of Christology, pushing beyond its roots in the preaching of Jesus, was thus the recognition that the crucified Jesus was a divine being.[16] Once again, Acts supplies evidence of this development, bringing with it reconsideration of the concept of messiahship: 'This Jesus God raised up, and of that we are all witnesses. Being therefore exalted at the right hand of God . . . God has made him both Lord and Messiah, this Jesus whom you crucified' (Acts 2.32-3, 36). Leaving aside the question of whether Acts here introduces later christological ideas, which it arguably does,[17] Peter's Pentecost speech reveals the startling conviction which transformed the disciples of Jesus. This was the belief that Jesus was *Lord* and Messiah: a heavenly being analogous to God.

The Lordship of Jesus is a crucial concept for New Testament Christology.[18] 'Lord' (*ho kyrios*) in the Septuagint's title for God. It represents the strange formula known as the tetragrammaton in the Hebrew Bible. In calling Jesus 'Lord', the Christians associated Jesus with God. At the same time, they were generally reluctant, at least in the earlier New Testament documents, to call Jesus 'God', *ho theos* in the Greek.[19] The difference between the two titles 'Lord' and 'God' is summarized by the formula Paul incorporates in 1 Cor. 8.6. In a context which acknowledges pagan belief in a variety of gods, Paul states the grounds of Christian theology as the belief that 'for us there is one God, the Father, from whom are all things and for whom we exist, and one Lord, Jesus Christ, through whom are all things and through whom we exist'. This passage presents an effective binitarianism according to which the Lordship of Jesus augments and does not threaten belief in the one God. The two divine beings are related through the use of language derived from the Jewish wisdom tradition, according to which Jesus as Lord mediated the creation which was the original work of God the Father.[20] This embodies an implicit 'subordinationism' in which Jesus as Lord is not God the Father's *precise* co-equal but his divine associate.

The result of this understanding was that, like God himself, Jesus was accorded worship. This is the view Paul advocates in Phil. 2.9-11: 'Therefore God also highly exalted him and gave him the name that is above every name, so that at the name of Jesus every knee should bend, in heaven and on earth and under the earth, and every tongue should confess that Jesus Christ is Lord to the glory of God the Father.' In this context, the worship of Jesus is held to advance the glory of God; evidently under the belief that Jesus' eschatological manifestation had revealed the divine nature in a way that strongly implies (and many people think makes explicit) a Christology of heavenly pre-existence.[21]

As it Was in the Beginning

Early Christology had an eschatological basis, in an understanding which stemmed from Jesus himself. Jesus had preached God's imminent kingdom. After Easter, the Christians took up this belief and transformed it into their proclamation of Jesus' return from heaven. This was understood to be the event through which God's kingdom would finally be introduced. The belief that people were living in the last days motivated the Christians in their evangelism as they sought to spread the good news about Jesus throughout the mediterranean world, exemplified by the missionary journeys of Paul.

One of the subtle changes in first-century Christology was the attempt to link Jesus with the first as well as with the last things. We find the intellectual basis of this view in 1 Cor. 8.5-6 (cited above).[22] There, the pre-Pauline author (probably not long after the resurrection) explains the heavenly presence of Jesus by analogy with what pre-Christian Judaism had believed about the operation of divine wisdom. This led him to assert that the Lord was a heavenly being who had always been with God and who had assisted God in the work of creation. This implies that he had always existed, like God himself. This view is made more explicit in later Christology.

Development of this view is found in the hymn incorporated in Col. 1.15-20: 'He is the image of the invisible God, the firstborn of all creation; for in him all things in heaven and on earth were created, things visible and invisible . . . He himself is before all things, and in him all things hold together.' This hymn makes explicit what had been implicit in 1 Corinthians 8, that Jesus 'is before all things'. The author even insists that Jesus 'is the image of the invisible God'. This is as close as Paul comes to the assertion that Jesus is God; the difference between the two is preserved by the noun 'image', which implies that Christ's divine glory is reflected and not innate to his own being.[23]

The question arises of how the Christians understood the relationship between this heavenly Lord and the prophet Jesus from Nazareth. The classical answer to this question is provided by the Prologue to the Fourth Gospel, which uses the concept of incarnation. Incarnation means 'enfleshment'. John's Gospel describes the 'enfleshment' of the Word in the following way: 'And the Word became flesh and lived among us, and we have seen his glory, the glory as of a father's only son, full of grace and truth' (Jn 1.14).[24] This is the view, anticipated both in the Jewish angelophanic tradition and in classical mythology, that a heavenly being might appear on earth as a human being; quite properly, truly both. At the heart of this 'incarnational' Christology stands the conviction that Jesus was a human *and* a heavenly being. In the body of John's Gospel, we find the slightly different idea that the Son of Man (a heavenly mediator) had descended to earth from heaven where he was perceived as Jesus. This Son of Man was destined to return to heaven at the conclusion of the ministry of Jesus (see Jn 3.13; 6.62; 20.17).[25] This slight difference between the Prologue and the body of the Fourth Gospel should not be pressed further than it deserves. Such Christology allows

John's Jesus to accomplish a unique revelation which is first and foremost the revelation of himself as the one who discloses the things of God; and, in that context, a revelation of the God whom he himself knows personally and represents (see esp. Jn 3.11; 8.38).

It has long been disputed when this 'incarnational' understanding first entered the tradition of Christology.[26] Some would argue that John is the first incarnational writer, although they are prepared to concede that Wisdom categories enabled belief in the 'heavenly pre-existence' of Jesus at some point before the writing of the Fourth Gospel c.100 CE. Others point to the passage I cited from Philippians 2 to argue that this (conceivably pre-Pauline) author already describes the heavenly existence of Jesus as the first stage in a tripartite scheme of heavenly presence, earthly humility and heavenly acclamation. On this view, the scheme of Christology in Philippians 2 closely resembles a parabola in which Christ laid aside or concealed his heavenly dignity when appearing as Jesus.

This issue is difficult to decide absolutely, but several scholars do think that Philippians 2 represents this view and that belief in Christ's so-called 'heavenly pre-existence' emerged very early in the annals of Christology.[27] The issue turns on the interpretation of the Greek noun morphe in Phil. 2.6, which is generally translated 'form' ('who, though he was in the form of God, did not regard equality with God as something to be exploited'). Despite the attempts of some British scholars to argue that this term designates the earthly Jesus by comparison with his earthly counterpart Adam,[28] probably the greater body of scholars believes that the divine form is something that belongs to the heavenly world, much as in other references Paul speaks of the heavenly body of Jesus when comparing Jesus with Adam (notably in 1 Corinthians 15; 2 Corinthians 5). On this view of Philippians 2, Christ lays aside his divine prerogatives when appearing as Jesus, resuming them to universal acclamation following his shameful death on the cross through exaltation by the Father.

There is no intrinsic reason why an incarnational Christology should not have emerged at an early point in the Christian religion. An obviously uncertain factor is the date of the material in Philippians 2 and John 1. While a number of scholars assume a pre-Pauline origin for the material in Phil. 2.6-11, this view has been challenged by one commentator on the topic.[29] This might mean that the 'pre-existence' idea entered Christology not much earlier than Philippians, which was Paul's last letter.[30] It is also uncertain how much earlier than the Fourth Gospel John's Prologue actually is. Having said this, the evidence of earlier Pauline passages such as Gal. 4.4, Rom. 8.3 and 2 Cor. 8.9 shows that belief in Christ's heavenly existence before the ministry of Jesus was almost certainly an established feature of Pauline Christology.

In Part III, I claimed 2 Cor. 8.9 as perhaps the most obvious representative of this view: 'For you know the generous act of our Lord Jesus Christ, that though he was rich, yet for your sakes he became poor, so that by his poverty you might become rich.' It is difficult to make sense of this contrast between the riches and the poverty of Jesus, expressed in that order, except by recourse to a theory of heavenly pre-existence. Although the historical Jesus was not necessarily on the breadline, the Gospels indicate that he came from rural stock and challenged the values of the dominant society, including its differentials between rich and poor. Jesus could not possibly be described as 'rich' on the evidence of the Gospels. The most natural conclusion, reinforced by the statement about the sending of God's Son in Rom. 8.3, is that Jesus' riches belonged to the heavenly world and that, as in other Pauline apocalypticism, the glory of heaven had been revealed on earth in what amounts to the incarnation of God's Son.

On Earth as It Is in Heaven

Belief in the return of Jesus from heaven was sustained despite challenges throughout the New Testament period. It formed an important part of early Christology.

The major question to ask is whether this belief could have derived from Jesus himself. Given that it is unlikely that Jesus ever thought about himself as God, it is also unlikely that he identified himself with a divine being in the 'incarnational' sense. It is more likely that he identified his earthly activity with the heavenly activity of the Son of Man, while maintaining an appropriate distinction between the two figures (see Mk 8.38); but even this has been questioned by researchers. John's Gospel, if its evidence can be trusted, would appear to support this view.

There are more obvious indications in the Gospels that Jesus spoke in the language of the Jewish wisdom tradition, not least when describing the impact of his preaching in Israel. One such example is Mt. 11.28–30 ('Come to me, all you that are weary and are carrying heavy burdens, and I will give you rest.') where Jesus seems to imitate the language of *Ecclus* 51.[31] The implication is that Jesus may have seen himself as the earthly representative of wisdom, speaking in a well-established Jewish tradition. If Jesus did speak in this way, it is only one step from this to the assertion that Jesus be identified with *pre-existent* wisdom. So far as we can tell, this identification belonged to the period after Easter, when Jesus was also identified with the heavenly Son of Man.

If Jesus neither anticipated his heavenly exaltation nor presumed his heavenly pre-existence, it is unlikely that he predicted his own return from heaven. The most we can say is that Jesus conceivably predicted his resurrection, depending on the interpretation of Mk 14.25. The identification of Jesus with the Son of Man happened after Easter, not before. The doctrine of the return from heaven, which became the linchpin of Christian eschatology, emerged from the supernova represented by the resurrection.[32]

To speak of this development in Christology is to raise the question of why language about the 'Son of God' should have replaced that of 'Son of Man' in the Christian proclamation.[33] There are two probable answers to this question, one pragmatic and the other theological. The first is that 'Son of Man' simply proved unintelligible beyond an Aramaic environment because it implied a purely human figure to people who did not know the relevant background in Daniel 7. The second is that 'Son of Man' carried angelic overtones when the Christians believed that Jesus was a divine being who ranked above the angels (see Phil. 2.9-11; Hebrews 1).[34] To speak of Jesus as God's 'Son' picked up the language of the Jewish messianic tradition and allowed the possibility of a binitarian theology (with its implications for trinitarianism) which had been prepared for in the mystical aspect of the Hebrew royal tradition.[35]

THE BREACH BETWEEN CHRISTIANITY AND JUDAISM

Before the end of the first century CE, the Christians were recognized as a religious sect distinct from the Jews. Evidence for this distinction is found in Tacitus, who calls the Christians 'a class hated for their abominations' (*Annals* 15.44.3). Further evidence is found in the early second century in the exchange between Pliny and the emperor Trajan concerning the activities of the Christians in Bithynia.[1] The evidence of Acts, although it poses the problem of historical reliability, shows that the split between the Jews and the Christians took place very early, given that the Jews are presented as the principal enemies of Paul wherever he goes.

No doubt this split took place gradually and began with local opposition.[2] This later emerged as a full-scale distinction between Christians and Jews based on recognized theological distinctions. Jesus had anticipated the eschatological emergence of God's kingdom on Jewish soil. If he had also anticipated the inclusion of the Gentiles in that kingdom, which is by no means unlikely,[3] it was within this matrix and under the presupposition that the Gentiles would finally be subordinated to God. Paul also held the view that 'all Israel will be saved' (Rom. 11.26), even though in another passage he implies that the Christian concept of Israel is wider than the boundaries of the Jewish nation itself (see Gal. 6.16). There was thus no intention on the part of Jesus or the earliest Christians to separate themselves from Israel as such. The separation that occurred was the result of reaction against the Christians by people of Jewish descent. It was based increasingly on theological grounds, beginning with the scandal caused by the proclamation of the crucified Jesus as Lord and Messiah.

Reasons for the Breach

As early as 1 Corinthians, we find Paul claiming that the manner of Jesus' death posed a problem for Christian evangelism.[4] 'We proclaim Christ crucified', Paul wrote to his converts in Corinth, 'a stumbling block to Jews and foolishness to Gentiles' (1 Cor. 1.23). Gentiles baulked at the idea that a crucified person could be anyone significant, and there was greater insult to Jews in such preaching. The Jewish law held that 'cursed is everyone who hangs on a tree', as Paul reminds the Galatians in Gal. 3.13. Paul used this paradox to insist that 'Christ redeemed us from the curse of the law by becoming a curse for us' (also Gal. 3.13). By this rhetoric, the manner of Jesus' death was turned forcefully in the face of its critics and held to be a dramatic and saving intervention. For Jews, however, it remained a scandal because of the abiding significance of Deut. 21.23, which legislates that the person who hangs on a tree is accursed by God.[5]

Crucifixion was a humiliating death in the ancient world.[6] We have seen throughout this book that there would have been no Christian faith without the resurrection of Jesus, the essence of which was the sequence of resurrection appearances aided and explained by the discovery of the empty tomb. It was his resurrection from the dead which convinced the Christians that Jesus was divine and resulted in their change of heart of which I have spoken. Early Christian proclamation of the crucified Jesus as Messiah was made in the light of his resurrection, so that his life and death were seen in a different light when viewed from the perspective of Easter. This new perspective enabled and in fact impelled the apostolic preaching of the cross in a mainly hostile environment.

We cannot overestimate the importance of Paul in breaching the gulf between these two perceptions so far as the crucified Jesus was concerned. In 1 Corinthians, we find Paul arguing that God's wisdom overcame even the most intelligent human wisdom by revealing itself in an event which was universally perceived as folly.[7] Paul supplied the paradoxical logic which made it possible to explain the crucifixion to a largely sceptical world. This paradox was fuelled by the recognition that the full truth about Jesus had not been disclosed until after his death. Paul linked the divine purpose in Jesus' life to the revelation of his heavenly status after death, and interpreted the cross in that light. This led him to explain the Jewish and Gentile reaction to the proclamation of the crucified Messiah as within the divine plan, and as opposition that was destined to be overcome by the apocalyptic revelation represented by the apostolic preaching of the cross.[8]

The manner of Jesus' death was not the only christological problem experienced by the earliest Christianity. Given that Jesus was believed to be divine and entitled to worship, Jewish theology was of necessity remodelled in the light of the Christian proclamation. We have seen this already in 1 Cor. 8.5-6 where Jesus is associated with God as the Lord, distinguished from the Father by his mediation of creation of which the Father is held to be the cause and origin. This led to the form of belief, binitarianism, which has come to be popularly known as 'two powers in heaven'.[9] This kind of theology was prepared for by pre-Christian Judaism, not least its angelological strand, without being formally reached there.[10] The emergence of trinitarian theology was related to this development, and almost certainly occurred in parallel with it.[11] With the rise of Christian theology, the public scandal of the crucified Messiah was reinforced by theological distinctiveness. This combination of events formed a major reason for the breach between Christianity and Judaism which began almost immediately after the resurrection and was complete by the late first century CE.

A second reason was the attitude of at least some early Christians to the Jewish temple. Jesus, we have seen,[12] purified or reclaimed the temple for God in the event known as the 'cleansing of the temple'. Although the precise meaning of this event has been disputed by the commentators, it is presented in the Gospels as the reason why the Jewish authorities decided to kill Jesus. Certainly, Jesus was remembered as having done something that criticized the present functioning of the temple. In this, he is to be compared with the Qumran covenanters who believed that their community with its worship formed a true and perfect temple during the period that the Jerusalem temple was defiled.

Acts paints an ambivalent picture of early Christian attitudes towards the temple.[13] On the one hand, we have the idealized picture of the Christians in the temple which dominates the earliest chapters of the work. On the other, Stephen's speech in Acts 7 is consistently hostile towards the temple.[14] When I mentioned the problem posed by the Hebrews and Hellenists in Part III (pp. 174–5), I concluded that it is impossible to reconstruct a distinctively 'Hellenist' theology on the basis of the slender evidence that we have. Nevertheless, it is not impossible that the status of the temple should have posed a dispute among the followers of Jesus in the period after Easter. If the earliest chapters of Acts are correct, we can presume that those Christians who attended the temple assumed that Jesus had already satisfactorily purified the temple for God. Yet Christian hopes were dominated by belief in impending supernatural intervention, according to which Jesus would return from heaven to preside as Messiah over God's kingdom. More than one passage in the New Testament speaks of the true Jerusalem as present already in heaven, with the strong implication that it will be revealed in the eschatological age.[15] If this is so, one continues to wonder about the attitude of the earliest Christians towards the temple in Jerusalem.

One cannot be dogmatic about this issue in the absence of decisive evidence. It is possible, however, that at least some Christians held the view attributed to Stephen in Acts 7, which is far more negative towards Judaism and its religious institutions than the mature Paul, and which in fact calls to mind the Sarah–Hagar antitypology of Galatians 4 where the earlier Paul comes perilously close to presenting Christianity and Judaism in antithetical terms. If this is so, it provides another reason for the breach between Christianity and Judaism which follows a lead that Jesus had adopted. The question was whether the present temple was already purified or whether it must await replacement by God at the eschatological climax. This question conceivably divided different groups of Christians, and posed an acute problem in early Christian circles. It must be considered a second reason for the breach between Christianity and Judaism.

A third reason is the attitude to the Jewish law that pertained in early Christianity.[16] While Jesus in general upheld the Jewish law, he was critical of the interpretation of the law that pertained in some Jewish parties. He evidently prepared the way for a different view of the law in his authoritative pronouncements about it. There was no reason, *a priori* or otherwise, why Jesus should have set the Jewish law aside. So far as we can tell, he did not do this.

It was a different case with the followers of Jesus after Easter. We saw that in Galatians Paul comes close to declaring the Jewish law redundant, even if in Romans he qualifies that view by presenting the law as a poultice designed to draw out latent transgression. The point at issue was the question of what the death and resurrection of Jesus had achieved in terms of salvation. Given that it was believed that Jesus' death had been the final sacrifice which brought God's kingdom near, the status of the Jewish law as providing the effective standard of salvation was called into question. This is what we find in the early Paul, whose letters look back on what was no doubt a history of reflection on this problem.

Paul does not so much eradicate the Jewish law as present Jesus as its pre-ordained and necessary fulfilment. This view reaches its mature expression in Rom. 10.4 where Paul declares that 'Christ is the end of the law so that there may be righteousness for everyone who believes.' Paul's view is that Jesus brings what the law could not bring, namely righteousness in respect of God. This was made possible because Christians now shared the new human order inaugurated by Jesus which is distinguished from the old adamic order by its eschatological propensities. It means that the law had been replaced by a new means of salvation, namely the possibility of salvation in Christ. Paul speaks for this reason of 'the law of Christ' (Gal. 6.2), while continuing to allow the law a modified place in the scheme of salvation (Romans 2–4) and insisting that 'all Israel will be saved' (Rom. 11.26) at the eschatological climax.

To present Jesus – *a fortiori* the crucified Jesus – as the messianic fulfilment of the law was offensive to Jewish people. It implied that the law had much less status than that which the Jews accorded it, and it further discredited Christianity in the eyes of Jewish people. This explains the difficulties that the Christian preaching encountered from the very beginning. It supplies a third reason for the breach between Christianity and Judaism.

Evidence for the Breach: John and Matthew

The middle of the second century CE saw the writing of Justin Martyr's celebrated *Dialogue with Trypho*, in the course of which Justin attempts to prove on a systematic basis that Christianity is the proper fulfilment of Judaism.[17] Justin reminds the Jew Trypho no fewer than seven times in the *Dialogue* that 'you' (i.e. Jews) curse those who believe in Christ. In *Dial.* 16 and 96 it is said that this happens 'in your synagogues'.

A significant passage in *Dial.* 47 states that 'those in the synagogues anathematized and anathematize this Christ'.

This information has generally been interpreted with reference to the reformulation of the Eighteen Benedictions towards the end of the first century CE.[18] At some point after the formation of the Jamnian Academy following the events of 70 CE, the twelfth petition of the Eighteen Benedictions was reworked to curse 'heretics'. In some versions of this reworking, notably the Cairo Geniza version first published in 1898,[19] the reference to 'heretics' is specifically refined to include 'Christians'. This information is again often linked with information in the New Testament, notably Jn 9.22 but also Jn 12.42; 16.2, that the Christians were formally excluded from the synagogue at some point between 70 and 100 CE. This has led also to the conclusion that the reformulation of the Eighteen Benedictions at this time was a significant moment in the breach between Christianity and Judaism. In some modern work, however, this view has been called into question. Peter Schäfer, for instance, thinks that the Twelfth Benediction is directed as much against the Roman government as against the Christians.[20]

The argument is a complex one which cannot be simplified to one or two paragraphs. Suffice it to say, however, that William Horbury has examined the evidence with care and reached the conclusion that 'to describe the Twelfth Benediction as an anti-Roman as much as an anti-heretical prayer is to narrow its large biblical scope misleadingly, and to put second the purpose which from the Aramaic period onwards appeared primary'.[21] Horbury proceeds to examine the strength of the case that the prayer was directed against Christians. Although the wording of the Twelfth Benediction long continued to be variable, attention must be given to the Talmudic report (*b. Ber.* 28b–29a) that the change was 'ordered' by Samuel the Small at the request of Gamaliel II. Horbury argues in this connection that synagogues were places to which many non-Jews were attracted and that the cursing of the Christians in this context, where church and synagogue were vying for the same audience, makes good religious sense. The ambiguous New Testament picture of how Christians fared in the synagogues also makes sense within this context. At first, Christians were merely punished as members of the synagogue (Mk 13.9; Acts 22.19; 2 Cor. 11.24). Later, they withdrew from the synagogue or were expelled from there (Acts 13.50; 18.7). 'Such exclusion', Horbury notes, 'is the step reluctantly taken when punishment fails to correct.'[22]

In this light we may examine the evidence of John and Matthew, which in both cases comes from the latter part of the first century CE. The dispute reflected in John 9 is bound to be significant.[23] In the story of the man born blind, his parents refuse to comment on the source of his healing for fear of the Jews; 'for the Jews had already agreed that anyone who confessed Jesus to be the Messiah would be put out of the synagogue' (Jn 9.22). As with many stories in the Fourth Gospel, this particular story works on the dual level of a narrative about Jesus and the circumstances of the author's own day. It is difficult to escape the conclusion when reading John 9 that the author alludes to a definite policy of excommunication from the synagogue which in turn seems to have been based on a straightforward confessional test. It goes beyond the evidence to conclude that this was a *universal* policy enforced by Jews against Christians at that time. It may have been no more than a local innovation. Even so, we cannot ignore the sense of alienation the Johannine author feels, and which was no doubt in part responsible for the sharp lines of division which he draws between the Johannine community and the rest of humankind whom he categorizes as 'the world'.

This dispute is expressed elsewhere in the Fourth Gospel in a variety of images. It does much to explain the form of the Gospel's Christology, not least the clear depiction of Jesus as Messiah (Jn 1.45) and his precedence over Abraham (8.58) and Moses (6.32). It also explains why the Jewish scriptures are made to speak with a christological voice (5.46). In general, the situation presupposed by John is one in which Judaism and Christianity are recognized as separate entities and where attempts are being made to explain the religious superiority of Christianity to Judaism in the face of the religious assaults of the Jews.

The situation presupposed by Matthew's Gospel is somewhat different.[24] There is no evidence that the Christians were being excluded from the synagogues in the narrow and specific sense. Rather, the dispute waged by Matthaean Christianity is with the Pharisees as a particular sect in Judaism.[25] It seems that Matthew comes from a scribal circle, or possibly even a 'school', for whom interest in Jesus as an authoritative religious teacher was a dominant concern.[26] Matthew therefore depicts Jesus in the guise of Moses, especially when giving the Sermon on the Mount (Matthew 5–7). There is particular polemic against the Pharisees in Matthew 23, in the course of which they are called hypocrites and mere religious timeservers. Matthew 23, more than any other passage in the New Testament, has been responsible for the powerful portrait of the Pharisees which was so eloquently criticized by Ed Sanders in the last quarter of the twentieth century.[27]

Although we do not know precisely what kind of disputes were responsible for this form of polemic – and it is possible that such disputes themselves took place within the orbit of the synagogue – Matthew nevertheless presupposes a sufficiently strong differentiation between his own form of Christianity and the Pharisaic movement for the two to be recognized as standing on opposite sides of a debate. This again illustrates the breach between Christianity and Judaism in the last third of the first century CE, possibly just before the more developed situation described by the Fourth Gospel emerged. This was a critical time for the breach between the two religions. What began as a dispute about Jesus and God, encompassing the temple and law along the way, emerged as a powerful religious divide in which Christianity came to be recognized as an independent religion which stood over and against Judaism. This new position of Christianity as a nascent world religion is recognized in both Tacitus and Pliny, as I explained at the beginning of this chapter.

Justin Martyr's *Dialogue with Trypho*

We return briefly to Justin Martyr's *Dialogue with Trypho*.[28] We saw that this work comes from the period when the breach between Christianity and Judaism, on the scheme presented here, was already complete. Justin begins by describing his conversion to Christianity. On meeting Trypho, he tells how he once met an old man on the seashore. This man had spoken to him of the prophets, whom Justin in *Dialogue* 7 calls more ancient than the philosophers. Justin initially hears Trypho's criticisms of Christianity (*Dialogue* 7 again), but turns the tide away from conversation and indeed from philosophical discourse in the direction of biblical citation and exegesis. In this context, Justin says of recent Jewish history, notably the abortive Bar Kochbah revolt, that 'these things have happened to you properly and with justice, for you killed the just one, and before him his prophets; and now you reject and dishonour as far as you can those who hope in him and in Him who sent him, God the creator and maker of all things' (*Dialogue* 16).

This bold statement sets the tone for everything that follows in the *Dialogue*. The work is, in the words of Tessa Rajak, 'a defence of the Christian religion organized around an extended engagement with Judaism, an engagement which takes the dual and inevitable forms of appropriation and assault'.[29] As such, it sets out to 'prove' that Christianity has superseded Israel; as for instance in *Dial.* 11.4 where Justin states explicitly that 'we are the true Israel of the spirit and the race of Judah'. There is no room in Justin's economy for representatives of the old Israel.[30] Justin acknowledges that some Jews will be 'found in the portion of Christ' but he insists that others 'are like the sand on the seashore, which is barren and fruitless, copious and without number, bearing no fruit whatsoever, and only drinking the water of the sea . . . imbibing doctrines of bitterness and atheism, and spurning the word of God' (*Dialogue* 120). Justin thereby attacks what William Horbury has called 'the corporate Jewish rejection of Christianity',[31] including the curse of the heretics which is mentioned as early as *Dialogue* 38.

The intended audience of the *Dialogue* has been examined in recent research. Where Justin's two *Apologies* were clearly written for a pagan audience, nothing indicates this in the case of the *Dialogue*. Some commentators think that the work was targeted at pagans, but a wider body of opinion holds that the *Dialogue* was written to counter and convert Jews.[32] Rajak's essay, however, argues that the *Dialogue* was principally targeted at the Christians. She notes that a Christian audience of sorts must be posited for the attacks on various Jewish-Christian groups in *Dialogue* 35, and that Justin's struggle to define Christianity over against Judaism is of primary benefit to Christians themselves. Rajak thereby classifies the *Dialogue* as a contribution to *Christian* thought in the sense that it engages seriously with the prophetic texts and tries, through this and other means, to consolidate the experience of belonging to the Christian religion.

Jewish Christianity

The term 'Jewish Christianity', which was favoured by F.C. Baur in the nineteenth century,[33] has become a controversial one. It raises questions of content and orientation which have not been resolved to the satisfaction of every scholar who has studied the subject. The original Christians were all Jewish Christians in the sense that they were Jews who followed Jesus as Messiah. Having said that, they swiftly distinguished themselves from Judaism, as we have seen. The term 'Jewish Christianity' is now most commonly used to describe a number of sects in the second century CE which had an archaic constitution in the sense that they continued to define their Christianity through the matrix of Judaism at a time when mainstream Christianity had abandoned the Jewish matrix altogether. It is in this sense that the term will be used in this part of the book.

The evidence Acts offers for a split between Hebrews and Hellenists (primarily a linguistic split) seems to explain certain features of primitive Christianity, not least the origins of the Gentile mission which was taken up with vigour by Paul. The Jerusalem Council of Acts 15 vindicated the Gentile mission; but it also acknowledged (in a way that is supported by the earlier Galatians 2) the existence of a more conservative Christianity typified by James the Just in which considerably greater interest was taken in the religious norms and presuppositions of Judaism.[34] This caused difficulties on at least one occasion when Peter came to Antioch when Paul was present there (see Gal. 2.11-14).

James the Just was executed in 62 CE.[35] This event may have caused those of the Jewish-Christian position to rally their forces in the face of what was perceived as opposition from the Jews. Not much later, in 66 CE, we read in Eusebius (*Hist. Eccl.* 3.5.3) that the Christian community in Palestine fled to Pella in the Decapolis.[36] This report is an important one, for it is precisely in Transjordania and Syria that the church fathers of the second century locate the majority of the Jewish-Christian sects, whom they criticize with venom. While a connection between these two observations is a supposition and not a demonstrated fact, the supposition does seem a reasonable one. The abandonment of Palestine and the colonization of the Decapolis by Christians in the first century, and the presence there of Jewish–Christian sects in the second century, is probably not coincidental.

Justin briefly notices Jewish Christians (*Dialogue* 47–8), but he does not tell us where they lived. Harnack assumed they lived in Palestine or Syria; we should possibly conclude in favour of the latter.[37] We have to wait for sources *c*.180 CE, and specifically Irenaeus in his *Adversus Haereses*, to find such specific named groups as the Ebionites. It is difficult to know how many people belonged to such sects and what kind of influence they exercised; but as with many sects we may probably suppose not too many members and a very prominent ideology which kept such people separate from the mainstream church. The following were the principal lines of division.

The Ebionites were the best-known Jewish–Christian sect.[38] In *Adv. Haer.* 1.26.2 Irenaeus states that these people used only the Gospel of Matthew and repudiated Paul, practising circumcision and adopting a Jewish way of life. They allegedly had an adoptionist Christology according to which Christ descended upon Jesus at the moment of his baptism. Irenaeus adds in *Adv. Haer.* 3.21.1 that they denied the validity of the virgin birth. Tertullian (*de carne Christi* 14; *de praesc. haer.* 33.5) opines that their name derived from one Ebion; but it seems more likely that it is related to the Aramaic word for 'poor', hence Origen's pun on their poor understanding of the law (*De Princ.* 4.3.8; *c. Cels.* 2.1). Epiphanius (*Panarion* 30) specifically connects the origin of this sect with the flight of the Palestinian Christians to Pella; he holds the biblical translator Symmachus an Ebionite.

The Cerinthians were an Asian sect, the followers of one Cerinthus whom Irenaeus (*Adv. Haer.* 3.3.4) presents as the opponent of John at Ephesus.[39] Irenaeus states earlier (*Adv. Haer.* 1.26) that Cerinthus taught that the world was not the creation of the supreme God but of a power separated from the first principle. The Cerinthians, like the Ebionites, had a Christology of adoptionist type in which Christ descended upon Jesus at his baptism and departed before the crucifixion.

Epiphanius refers to a Christian sect called the Nazarenes (*Panarion* 29).[40] He associates them with the flight to Pella and states that, although they read the Old Testament and at least one Gospel, they also observed the law of Moses and Jewish customs. He observes further, almost certainly without foundation, that Ebion came from them (*Panarion* 30.2.1). Jerome (*Ep.* 112.13) gives his opinion that the Nazarenes were not Christians at all, but in other contexts he includes citations from their texts. Jerome adds that they held a mission to the Jews (*In Isa.* 31.6–9) and that they were involved in disputes with the Pharisees (*In Isa.* 8.14).

Various allegedly Jewish–Christian texts exist such as the *Pseudo-*

Clementine Recognitions and Homilies and the *Preaching of Peter*, but these lie beyond the period with which this book is concerned.[41] The Jewish-Christian Gospels, nonetheless, are a valuable source of information about Jesus traditions in the second century.[42] Two such texts are the *Gospel of the Ebionites* and the *Gospel of the Nazarenes*.

SYMBOLS OF THE KINGDOM

The next feature of early Christianity we shall examine is the means by which membership of that religion was controlled by symbols and rites of passage. We saw that at Qumran an introductory immersion admitted people into the community (similar in some respects to the practice of John the Baptist), and that the daily common meal was a central feature of community life among the Essenes.[1] There were distinctive rituals in early Christianity, with important differences from parallel Jewish rituals. In this chapter, we shall examine the significance of eucharist and baptism in the lives of early Christian communities.

No-one who studies this topic can ignore the work of Gerd Theissen in his book, *A Theory of Primitive Christian Religion* (1999).[2] Theissen includes an invaluable section in which he studies the nature and significance of early Christian ritual.[3] He argues that 'religions are sign systems which point to an ultimate reality'; and that 'rites are actions which become an end in themselves through the strict observance of rules'.[4] Within this context, Theissen presents baptism as the decisive rite of initiation and eucharist as a rite of integration by virtue of its constant repetition. Theissen notes other symbolic acts performed in Christian circles including the laying-on of hands and the ritual language of *glossolalia*.

The most significant feature of his research is the demonstration that in antiquity the co-ordination of life took place above all through sacrifices. This observation leads Theissen to argue that, in the case of early Christianity, a new ritual sign language arose from the prophetic and symbolic actions with which John the Baptist and Jesus delivered their eschatological message.[5] These symbolic actions became primitive Christian sacraments through their referral to the fate of Jesus, especially his death understood as a sacrifice. This new interpretation gave the Christian rituals the power to supersede the traditional Jewish sacrifices.

Baptism

The origins of Christian baptism are found in the reports of Matthew and Mark that Jesus was baptized by John the Baptist; and in the general Synoptic conviction that Jesus was originally an adherent of John the Baptist's movement. According to Jn 3.22, Jesus and his disciples baptized in the Judaean countryside.[6] It is not certain whether this is an authentic historical reference, or merely an attempt to claim Jesus as a baptizer on the part of the early church. There are no references to Jesus conducting baptisms in the Synoptic Gospels; John's statement is quickly qualified by the phrase, 'it was not Jesus who baptized but his disciples' (Jn 4.2). This addition shows that the Gospels were sensitive to the report that Jesus himself was a baptizer, as if they were anxious to put space between Jesus and John in the different ways disclosed by Matthew, Luke and the Fourth Gospel.

We saw when discussing John the Baptist that Josephus and the Gospels are divided about the motives for his rite. Josephus states that '[the Jews] must not employ it . . . as a consecration of the body implying that the soul was already thoroughly cleansed by right behaviour' (*Ant.* 18.17). The Gospels present John's baptism as a rite which resulted in 'the forgiveness of sins' (Matthew, however, omits this phrase), and thus as related to John's eschatological preaching. Jesus himself was baptized by John as Matthew's embarrassment (and Luke's omission) makes clear. The most recent studies of John the Baptist distinguish John from the Qumran community and make him the leader of a Jewish sectarian movement which had an ethical and eschatological basis, offering a once-for-all rite of initiation with a strong penitential dimension.[7]

The early Christian practice of baptism undoubtedly drew on the recollection that Jesus himself was baptized in this way, although something more than mere imitation was involved in the rite. There is evidence for the baptism of believers in a variety of New Testament sources.[8] While these are not inconsiderable in scope, the evidence has sometimes led to the question of whether baptism was practised as a *universal* rite in first-century Christianity. The author of Acts appears to take baptism for granted, associating it with Peter's Pentecost speech (Acts 2.38-41), Paul's conversion (Acts 9.18) and other lesser-known figures such as the Philippian jailer and his family (Acts 16.30-4). Four times the author of Acts cites what appears to be a baptismal formula, 'in(to) the name of the Lord Jesus' (Acts 2.38; 8.16; 10.48; and 19.5).

Paul himself mentions baptism in more than one place. This is generally done *en passant* rather than in the context of direct teaching. In 1 Cor. 1.12-17, in the context of a dispute about his apostolic credentials, Paul gives thanks that he had baptized only a few of the Corinthian community. In this context, he mentions the same formula as does Acts, baptism 'into the name' of Jesus (1 Cor. 1.13). In Rom 6.1-14 we find Paul arguing that baptism into Christ means baptism into his death, so that the introductory rite is linked to an ethical argument, not quite *ex opere operando* but certainly with an eye to the theological understanding of the inward transformation which Paul claims the Christians had experienced. In 1 Cor. 12.13, Paul acknowledges that the Spirit is at work in Christian baptism.

Elsewhere in the New Testament, 1 Pet. 3.21 mentions baptism. Indeed, the whole of that letter has often been thought to be a baptismal homily.[9] Heb. 10.19-25 probably contains an allusion to baptismal practice. Beyond the New Testament we may point to a passage such as *Did.* 7.1, 3 as evidence for a similar practice. In the *Didache*, baptism is followed by the eucharist.[10] This is doubtless because participation at the eucharist was forbidden to the unbaptized in primitive Christian circles.

This evidence has often led scholars to conclude that baptism was indeed universal in first-century Christianity, and that such universality pertained from the very beginning of the religion. That theory has been challenged in a significant but neglected article by Colin Hickling in 1990.[11] Hickling begins by noting the dissimilarity between second- and first-century sources in terms of the universal requirement for baptism. He cites Justin, *1 Apol.* 66 and *Did.* 9.5 as good and convincing evidence that baptism was universally practised in the second century CE. The latter passage dictates, 'Let no one eat or drink of this eucharistic thanksgiving but they that have been baptized into the name of the Lord' (the same point made above). This situation contrasts, however, with what we find in the New Testament literature. The clearest demand for universal baptism is found in the longer ending of Mark's Gospel ('the one who believes and is baptized will be saved; but the one who does not believe will be condemned', Mk 16.16); but this passage comes from the second century CE. Even here, Hickling argues that the omission of baptism from the second half of the passage 'suggests something a little short of the unambiguous confidence of Justin and the *Didache* that baptism was the necessary and indispensable qualification for admission – in their case – to the Eucharist'.[12]

Hickling holds the evidence of Mark 16 too late to modify his conclusion that the New Testament nowhere regards baptism in the same universal terms as Justin and the *Didache*. Although it is virtually certain that the Pauline churches practised baptism, he thinks that the same cannot necessarily be held true of other, more Jewish-Christian churches where 'the possibility that some adherents had not been baptized may well have been one that would arouse no sense of scandal'.[13] He mentions the brothers of Jesus and such people as Joseph of Arimathea as examples of people who broadly belonged to the Christian community but whose baptismal status is either unclear or even left improbable in the primary sources. He also raises the question, since we are not told that the disciples of Jesus were baptized, of who baptized them if indeed they were baptized. The same goes for the family of Jesus also.

Hickling thereby provides a necessary *caveat* to the prevalent assumption that everyone was baptized in first-century Christianity. His argument is not that such people necessarily were unbaptized; but that we cannot *assume* that every Christian in the first century was baptized. This marks a point of difference from second-century Christianity where that assumption can safely be made.

The question of what was meant by baptism 'into the name' of Jesus has been answered in more than one way.[14] Many scholars (such as

W. Heitmüller) argue that it means the baptized person was dedicated to Jesus as the heavenly Lord, in an extension of the mystical relationship to which I have alluded in Part III of this book.[15] Lars Hartman, however, thinks that the term is a referential one so that no mystical relationship is intended.[16] This formula was later expanded in a trinitarian direction as shown by Mt. 28.19; *Did.* 7.1; Justin, *1 Apol.* 61.3, 13 and other passages. *Did.* 7.4 and Justin *1 Apol.* 61.2 state that fasting was practised in connection with baptism. The *Apostolic Tradition* of Hippolytus (20.7) indicates that the candidates unrobed before baptism and dressed after-wards; but it is not certain that this practice goes back to the first century CE. That depends on the interpretation of the particular language used in Col. 3.5-17 and Eph. 4.22-3.

Eucharist

Baptism in Christian churches was a once-for-all event, similar in this sense to the rite dispensed by John the Baptist. The same cannot be said for early Christian eucharistic practice, which was a repeated ritual and which, as Theissen reminds us, finds its very meaning in that act of repetition.

The origins of the Christian eucharist take us back to the Last Supper, which we examined in Part II of this book.[17] The earliest Christian record of the Last Supper, which itself shows signs of later interpret-ation,[18] is 1 Cor. 11.23-6. Paul claims to pass on what he received 'from the Lord' (Jesus himself) that on the night when he was betrayed Jesus took bread, blessed and broke it with the words, 'This is my body that is for you. Do this in remembrance of me.' This was followed by the cup after supper, over which Jesus pronounced the words, 'This cup is the new covenant in my blood. Do this, as often as you drink this, in remembrance of me.'[19]

It lies beyond my purpose here to rehearse the arguments for and against the suggestion that the Last Supper was a Passover meal. I have already argued that, whether or not it enjoyed such a status, its signifi-cance for Jesus and his disciples was that it represented the messianic banquet and that as such it was related to their hopes for the coming of God's kingdom. Our purpose is to understand the role that the Lord's Supper fulfilled in the earliest Christian communities.

The practice of the Lord's Supper as *the* distinctive Christian rite, baptism apart, again undoubtedly reflects the fact that it was based on the Last Supper as an historical event in the life of Jesus. Although we do not know whether Jesus definitively anticipated his own death on that occasion, and if so whether he placed a sacrificial interpretation on it,[20] the repetition of the Lord's Supper as a ritual in early Christian churches certainly had a sacrificial outlook as we see from Paul. The Lord's Supper – a title that is evidently a familiar one in 1 Cor. 11.20 – is in this sense the liturgical outworking of Paul's conviction in Rom. 3.25 that God 'put [Jesus] forward as a sacrifice of atonement by his blood'. We may have little doubt that the account in 1 Corinthians 11 reflects the actual practice of the Pauline churches and that this practice was enjoined on them by Paul himself. By the early second century, 'eucharist' had become the technical name for this gathering (Ign., *Phld.* 4; *Smyrn.* 7.1, 8.1). It appears to have been celebrated on the Saturday evening during the first century but on Sunday morning in the second century CE.

Both the Last Supper and the Lord's Supper are related to the frequent meals Jesus shared with his disciples during his ministry. Meals were a familiar feature of wider Judaism, including as we have seen the Pharisaic movement.[21] The Gospels depict Jesus as eating meals with all kinds of people, including social outcasts (e.g. Mk 2.15-17). Interestingly, however, the Last Supper is the only meal that Jesus is recorded as having eaten with his disciples *alone* (apart from the problematic resurrection appearances).

The historical origins of the eucharist have become a matter of scholarly controversy. Cullmann argued that the origin lay in the disciples' experience of table-fellowship with the risen Jesus after Easter.[22] Hans Lietzmann distinguished two kinds of meal in early Christianity: the 'breaking of bread' and the Lord's Supper.[23] The first was a continuation of the table-fellowship that Jesus advocated when still alive. This made no reference to the death of Jesus and is reflected in the *Didache* (9–10), the shorter text of Lk. 22.19b-20 and elsewhere in Luke–Acts. Lietzmann linked this practice with the primitive Christian community in Jerusalem. Lietzmann's second type is exemplified by 1 Corinthians 11. It arose in response to the death of Jesus and was modelled particularly on the Last Supper.

Given that the text of Luke 22 is extremely problematic, the evaluation of Lietzmann's theory depends in no small measure on the interpretation of the *Didache*.[24] The *Didache* is a manual of church order which comes in all probability from the end of the first century CE. Since the final form of the *Didache* shows signs of editorial activity, it is probable that some of its contents are earlier.[25] This is true not least of the meal prayers which are found in *Didache* 9–10. These prayers have raised as many questions as they have solved. The liturgy has been interpreted both as an *agape*, or breaking of bread, and as a sacramental or eucharistic meal.[26] The problem is that Jesus is mentioned at this point but without any reference to his death or any use of sacrificial language. The interpretation of *Didache* 9–10 is often referred to the interpretation of *Didache* 14, where a sacramental outlook seems more assured. There, we find reference to the confession of sins: the word 'sacrifice' is used twice in what seems a clear allusion to the death of Jesus.

We may certainly read the *Didache* as a whole, even when it is acknowledged that it is the product of editorial activity. An important study of

Didache 9–10, by Johannes Betz,[27] concludes that the prayers in this section changed their form in the history of transmission from original eucharistic prayers to (mere) *agape* prayers in which the connection with the sacrificial death of Jesus was removed. This was conceivably because the *agape* as opposed to the Lord's Supper originally had no fixed form and one can see from 1 Cor. 11.21 how freely and unliturgically it could be conducted. The eucharistic formula was reworked in order to make the *agape* relate more neatly to the eucharist.

We may acknowledge that Lietzmann was correct in his suggestion that there was more than one form of table-fellowship in primitive Christianity, although whether he was correct to distinguish between 'Jerusalem' and 'Pauline' influence in this is more open to question. The *agape* was a meal in the true sense, reminiscent of the meals that Jesus shared with others. The eucharist was a recollection of the death of Jesus. It had specific reference to the Last Supper as 1 Corinthians 11 shows. The reference to abuse in 1 Cor. 11.21, supported by the contrast between *Didache* 9–10 and 14, shows that the eucharist was celebrated in the wider context of a meal, although we have no clear understanding about the different ways in which the two were combined. If the eucharist was celebrated weekly, as seems likely, there was nothing to stop the *agape* taking place more regularly.

The crucial element in the eucharistic liturgy of 1 Corinthians 11 is the repeated phrase, 'Do this in remembrance of me.' The Greek word used is *anamnesis*, which means something more substantial than recollection alone.[28] The *anamnesis* requested is not a nostalgic look-back to the death of Jesus but the making-present of that death so that its reality and meaning are brought to bear on the present situation of the Christians, not least in their community gathering. It is, if I can put it this way, an effective proclamation whereby the past is brought into the present and shown to be the decisive event by which the present is determined and enabled to be understood.

This brings us back to Theissen's point that sacrifice was the co-ordinating ritual of all ancient societies. In re-enacting the sacrifice of Jesus, the Christians reminded themselves that the uniquely efficacious sacrifice had already been offered on a once-for-all basis, and that what was necessary now was the constant representation of that sacrifice in the form of a ritual which reminded both God and the Christians of the basis of faith by which the Christian communities had been called into existence and continued to understand themselves.

As with all rituals, the eucharist had a forward-looking dimension as well as a recollective and representational sense. The crucial phrase in this respect is that of 1 Cor. 11.26, 'until he comes'. This phrase identifies the eucharist as a recollective rite with eschatological properties. That is to say, it made the reality of Jesus' death accessible to those who celebrated it; but it also affirmed their belief that Jesus would return from heaven to bring God's kingdom to completion. The origins of this forward-looking aspect are found in the outlook of Jesus himself, possibly his words at the Last Supper (although we have seen that the narratives raise considerable problems). If the Last Supper was the messianic banquet, it conceivably functioned as a prayer that God would act to bring in his kingdom. Early Christian eucharistic celebrations should be seen in a similar light. They made present Jesus' death as a reminder to themselves and as a prayer to God that he would effect the eschatological climax with the return of Jesus from heaven (cf. Acts 3.19–20). The interplay between recollection, community self-definition and the maintenance of eschatological hope is a powerful and effective one.

THE DEVELOPMENT OF THE
CHRISTIAN MINISTRY

The emerging Christian religion progressively developed a system of
authority, with recognized officials, which was the forerunner of professional ministry as we understand that term today.[1] Important questions
to ask of the sources include what form the earliest Christian ministry
took, and whether or not there were institutional offices from the very
beginning of the religion.

Ignatius of Antioch

We begin, to provide a fixed point, in the second century CE with Ignatius
of Antioch,[2] whose writings are generally recognized as constituting a
milestone in the development of Christian ministry. Ignatius was bishop
of Antioch in Syria, and he journeyed to Rome in or around the year
110 CE, where he was martyred as a Christian. His letters vividly illustrate
his impending martyrdom; they also contain evidence which sets the
topic of ministry in perspective, and allows us to reflect back on the
New Testament evidence from a perspective that seems more firmly
established.

Ignatius places great emphasis on the threefold order of deacons,
priests and bishops (see e.g. *Trall.* 3.1).[3] There are signs that this situation
was still somewhat fluid. Yet the crucial thing is that this threefold understanding is in place in Ignatius; the three offices are named together in
what appears to be a formulaic understanding. This marks a difference
from most of the New Testament, where we find no identical formulae
nor such a fixed understanding of ministry.

Within this context, Ignatius attaches great importance to episcopal
authority.[4] This seems to have been a feature of Ignatius' own belief,
which was not necessarily derived from the Christian world around him.
It was probably related to the circumstances that resulted in his own
martyrdom, including the probability that the Antiochene church was
divided over the doctrinal issue of docetism.[5] Many scholars think that,
when in *Eph.* 3.2 Ignatius states that monarchical bishops are found
everywhere in the church, he is indulging in probable hyperbole.

In many ways the Ignatian system, although itself a development of
the New Testament perspective, is somewhat crude when compared
with the later understanding.[6] There is no evidence in Ignatius of a
universal *theory* of the episcopate; merely the belief that the bishop over-
sees the local Christian congregation. The fact that, when writing to the
Romans, Ignatius appears to give the Roman bishop pre-eminence over

other bishops is probably due more to the recognition that Rome was the last port of call on his journey to martyrdom than to the incipient belief that the Roman bishop was universally pre-eminent. The bishop for Ignatius was essentially a local figure who, in the presence of disputes, formed the visible icon of unity in the church.[7]

Nor was Ignatius' theory of the episcopate reinforced by the idea of episcopal succession as it would be in the later understanding.[8] Ignatius mentions the apostles as figures from the past, not as people with contemporary significance in connection with his own understanding of the ministry. The likelihood is, as Schoedel observes,[9] that Ignatius conceives the bishops as deriving their authority from God independently of each other. One should therefore beware of reading more into Ignatius' view of the Christian ministry than is actually present in his texts.

A potential problem when reading Ignatius derives from the language that he uses to describe the Christian ministry with reference to God's own being.[10] *Magn.* 6.1 supplies crucial evidence: 'I exhort you: be eager to do all things in godly concord, with the bishop set over you in the place of God, and the presbyters in the place of the council of the apostles, and the deacons, most sweet to me, entrusted with the service of Jesus Christ, who before the ages was with the Father and appeared at the end.' Elsewhere, Ignatius speaks almost as if divine and episcopal authority are interchangeable. This is most obvious in *Eph.* 6.1: 'One must regard the bishop as the Lord himself.' It is an open question what this language means. Ignatius is perfectly capable of speaking in metaphorical as well as literal terms. This seems to be the case here, rather than any implied view of the bishop as divine.

The Ministry of Jesus

What relevance do Ignatius and his ecclesiology have to the world of first-century Christianity? To answer this question, we return to the case of Jesus.

Jesus was the leader of a Jewish sectarian movement with eschatological hopes.[11] He taught that God's kingdom – Israel's messianic age – would be introduced by the Son of Man and that, following this intervention, Jesus would rule as Messiah over Israel. The question of whether Jesus intended to found a church has been much discussed in the past.[12] In part, the answer depends on what is meant by the term 'church'. If by 'church' is meant the modern ecclesiastical entity with its hierarchy and committees, the answer is almost certainly not. Jesus probably at most anticipated the gathering of the Gentiles within Israel and not the gradual separation of the church from Judaism which happened towards the end of the first century CE. Given the uncertainty that surrounds Jesus' own view of his personal resurrection, he may have expected his followers to represent his cause after his death. In terms of his understanding of ministry, Jesus' notions of 'servanthood' (e.g. Mk 10.45) have sometimes been taken out of context, but they generally stand within the view that Jesus took of the transformation of society around him. Jesus taught his followers a new understanding of 'family' in which mutual support was the crucial factor and not patriarchal ties. This provided a gadfly's challenge to the norms of first-century Palestine, which embodied a culture of inequality and indebtedness.[13]

Jesus' understanding of 'ministry' must therefore be seen in the context of his eschatological understanding and his vision of the impending kingdom. Jesus certainly appointed disciples, including the twelve to whom he attributed the representative function suggested by their number and which we have seen was to reveal its meaning and significance when the kingdom came (see esp. Mt. 19.28; Lk. 22.30). Jesus probably also appointed others in an ancillary capacity. He may have sent them out as independent preachers as the Gospels imply. If so, this was the forerunner of the missionary campaigns of Paul and to a lesser extent of the deacons Peter and Philip.

Between Jesus and Paul

The question of what happened between Jesus and Paul is hampered by the relative lack of evidence.[14] I have mentioned as problematic the twenty-year gap between the resurrection and the writing of 1 Thessalonians. This is particularly difficult if (as seems likely) the early chapters of Acts, although they claim to describe the earliest history of the church, are not free from later interpretation, and indeed were among the later New Testament documents to be written. This uncertainty means that we need to tread carefully in this area.

Jesus' death inevitably led to demoralization among his disciples. Having been convinced that the messianic age was impending, they must have felt let down and demotivated when he died as a common criminal. They were not expecting the apocalyptic visions which created the belief in his resurrection. These came as a complete surprise.[15] They made Jesus' followers reconsider what they had previously believed, and reaffirm the eschatological orientation of their movement in a way which worshipped Jesus as the heavenly Lord and derived its impetus from that conviction.

How Jesus regarded his own family must be treated as an open issue. Jesus preached a new understanding of family ties in which patriarchal norms and assumptions were swept aside. It is possible that this approach explains the often ambivalent attitude of Jesus towards his family which is recorded in the Gospels. Thus when Jesus says, 'Who are my mother and my brothers?' (Mk 3.33 and parallels), he may be posing a rhetorical question and not personally rejecting his family as such. This notwithstanding, it is evident that Jesus' immediate family are not mentioned as his key followers by the Gospels; and that Mk 3.21 mentions the attempt by Jesus' family to restrain him on the grounds that people thought he was mad. We can only speculate on this matter; but it is possible that, within the context of his redefinition of family ties, Jesus saw his own disciples as his 'family' and that his choice of Peter, James and John for special activities implies that he thought them his natural successors on this new-found family basis.

It is therefore a little surprising to discover that the real leader of the church in Jerusalem was not Simon Peter but James, surnamed the Just, the brother of Jesus.[16] We find at 1 Cor. 15.7 a partial explanation of this fact when it describes an apocalyptic vision of Jesus to James in the context of the resurrection appearances. As in all Jewish society, family ties proved to be important when it came to redefining the Jesus movement after Easter. James the Just took the place of Jesus while the twelve evidently retained their status (thus 1 Cor. 15.5). There is a little evidence that James was succeeded by another relative, Symeon, so that the family of Jesus occupied a central role in the administration of early Christianity.[17]

Ministers in the New Testament Period

On another count, 1 Corinthians 15 is informative; 1 Cor. 15.5 mentions the resurrection appearance of Jesus to Cephas and the twelve; 1 Cor. 15.7 adds to this the statement that 'then he appeared to James, then to all the apostles'. This implies that there was a difference between 'the twelve' and 'the apostles' in post-Easter Christianity.[18]

Apostles

Paul (albeit by implication) spells out the basis of the apostolate in 1 Corinthians 15.[19] It was not simply the case that norms of authority which pertained before Easter were carried over and reaffirmed after Easter. Paul states that the basis of the apostolic calling, in which the twelve were clearly involved as a particular group, was their vision of the risen Jesus by which they became conscious of a special calling. While not all witnesses of the resurrection appearances were apostles, all the apostles were witnesses of the resurrection appearances. The twelve were all apostles on the evidence of this passage (although they are not named, and we cannot therefore make a precise judgment about their identity). The circle of the apostles was wider than the twelve, however.[20] It included Paul and presumably James the Just and an unspecified number of others (1 Cor. 15.7).

The apostles were not static functionaries but active missionaries. They carried the good news of Jesus beyond Palestine in the manner that Peter and Paul exemplify. They represented Jesus and preached the onset of God's kingdom, in this sense as ambassadors of a king. Although Paul is the only apostle whose career is substantially documented, this should not lead to the conclusion that he was the only apostle, still less the only effective apostle. Acts tells a very selective picture of emerging Christianity, but it is clear from this that other apostles discharged an effective ministry. The ancient tradition that Paul *and* Peter died as martyrs in Rome warns us not to be narrow-minded on this issue.

The probable fluidity of the term 'apostle' in the earliest Christianity is signified by the fact that Paul is willing to call James an apostle when we know from Gal. 2.12 that Paul found difficulties with the position James adopted, and when he was clearly not one of the twelve (as Paul himself was not). The meaning of the term 'apostle' should be deduced from its internal sense and its relation to the Jewish agency concept as a 'sent one' in the sense of an agent's possession of his master's full authority.[21]

There is a technical background to this in Jewish law, as a number of studies have demonstrated. In Greek literature the term *apostolos* means an envoy in a general sense (e.g. Plato, *Ep.* 7.346a). There is a similar term in Jewish literature (e.g. Ezra 7.14; Dan. 5.24). If it is true that early Christian language picked up an existing technical term, it is also true that the meaning which that term acquired in the new religion drew in no small measure on the influence of Jesus himself. Jesus' ministry was undergirded by the conviction that he had been called by God to proclaim the impending kingdom. Jesus' choice of others is related to this sense of calling, in a way that is exemplified by Jn 17.18, 'As you have sent me into the world, so I have sent them into the world.' Although the precise nature of the Jewish background of the 'apostleship' concept continues to be discussed, it is certain that a redefined form of that concept lies at the heart of this term.

We should note that the New Testament itself contains one passage in which the activity of 'the apostles' is seen as a thing of the past. The deutero-Pauline author of Eph. 2.20 states that the church is 'built upon the foundation of the apostles and prophets', as if their activity was recognized as already historical rather than contemporary at that time. The author of Ephesians clearly regards Paul as an apostle (so Eph. 1.1), and thus does not restrict 'apostle' to 'the twelve' in the Lucan sense. He does, however, acknowledge that all the apostles belonged to an earlier generation. This implies a change in eschatological (and ecclesiological) understanding in which the metaphor of the building or body had replaced the specifically Jewish hope for the reconstitution of Israel on biblical lines (see esp. Eph. 2.15 in this context). This is an important step towards Ignatius, where the church is recognized as an organism with an identifiable system of ministry in its local constitutions.

The Twelve

The question of how many apostles there were in primitive Christianity is different from that of the role of the twelve in the period after Easter.[22] If my reading of the evidence is correct, the role of the twelve was determined not so much by Jesus' personal commission (although it involved that) as by their future and eschatological role when the kingdom came. The twelve were representatives of Israel who, the Last Supper implies, were to continue, and in fact more definitely to assume, that role after the death of Jesus.

In view of what I have said, it is surprising that we hear little of more than a few named apostles in either Acts or Paul. When Acts refers to 'the apostles', as it does not infrequently, we know from Luke that the author means the twelve, as he explains in Lk. 6.13. It is possible that, as before Easter, 'the twelve' remained a representative concept so that the names were perhaps irrelevant; but the silence is nevertheless awkward, and it draws attention both to the existence of an 'inner circle' within the twelve and also to other ministerial titles in the New Testament literature (see below). There is no reason to doubt the continuity before and after Easter of the concept of 'the twelve' or to question the eschatological significance of this concept. The fact that the New Testament literature was all written on the 'unrealized' side of eschatology probably explains why we do not hear more about 'the twelve' as named and active leaders. Luke's refinement of the term 'apostle' to become the equivalent of 'the twelve' is probably related to the desire to preserve this link with the past at a time when the Christian eschatological hope was under review.

Within the twelve, both Peter singly, and Peter, James and John corporately, are given special status. The historicity of this evidence has been exhaustively sifted. It is generally agreed that the extended form of Peter's commission in Mt. 16.18-19 is unhistorical, but there is evidence also in Mk 16.7; Lk. 22.31-2 and Jn 21.15-18 (a later tradition) that Peter was singled out with special favour by Jesus. Given the nature of Jesus' preaching and the attitude of his family towards him that we noticed, it is possible that Jesus saw Peter as his natural successor, especially if he contemplated his own death in the later stages of his preaching campaign. Those passages which name Peter, James and John as the recipients of special favour (notably the transfiguration narrative) are also conceivably historical, but it is more difficult to see what meaning can be placed on this choice of individuals within the twelve.

Prophets

Besides the apostles, we now consider the role of the prophets in early Christianity.[23] Prophecy is a familiar conception from the Hebrew Bible, and the second section of the tripartite division in the Bible is called 'the Prophets'. Hebrew prophecy began in the eighth century BCE and continued until long after the exile, when it was gradually superseded by the phenomenon of apocalypticism. The Hebrew prophets claimed to have received the divine word directly and to speak out to particular human situations on that basis. They were followed in this by their Christian counterparts, albeit with certain differences from their Jewish predecessors.

At the heart of the Christian conception of prophecy stood the conviction that the Holy Spirit was powerfully active in the church in the aftermath of Jesus' resurrection. Jesus himself is regarded as a prophet in the New Testament, in the sense that he spoke the divine word with an authoritative immediacy that marked him out from others, not least as we have seen during his last few days in Jerusalem. The original impetus of the Spirit after Easter is described by Acts 2, which may preserve an authentic historical reminiscence when it says, 'All of them were filled with the Holy Spirit and began to speak in other languages, as the Spirit gave them ability' (Acts 2.4). We know from the Pauline correspondence (and especially from 1 Corinthians 12–14) that charismatic speech and praxis were a distinctive feature of the early Christian communities. Prophecy is mentioned as a potentially universal gift by 1 Cor. 14.5. It is defined in that context as '[speaking] to other people for their upbuilding and encouragement and consolation'; no doubt under the conviction of direct divine inspiration. The fact that Paul specifically claimed 'visions and revelations of the Lord' (2 Cor. 12.1) shows the charismatic basis of much if not most early Christianity.

Paul's statement that he wanted all to prophesy (1 Cor. 14.5) must not be pressed further than it deserves, however. It may simply be rhetorical hyperbole. While all gifts of the Spirit were potentially available to all Christians, there is also evidence to indicate that in practice there was a differentiation of gifts in the Corinthian community. Prophecy in early Christianity was in the main the prerogative of recognized practitioners, such as the Agabus who is mentioned by name in Acts 11.27-30; 21.1-14. While the divine hand in their ministry was accepted, it did not obviate the perceived need to test what was said by the prophets. Paul specifically told the Corinthian church: 'Let two or three prophets speak, and let the others weigh what is said' (1 Cor. 14.29). This coheres with the series of warnings about prophetic authenticity which is found in the Letters to the Seven Churches in Revelation 2, and with the Johannine command to 'test the spirits' (1 Jn 4.1).

Revelation 2 is an important passage for the study of early Christian prophecy. John the Divine complains against the Thyatiran church, 'But I have this against you: you tolerate that woman Jezebel, who calls herself a prophet and is teaching and beguiling my servants to practise fornication and to eat food sacrificed to idols' (Rev. 2.20). The author, who clearly regards himself as a prophet and in that sense as a true prophet, complains about another person who also regards herself as a prophet but whom he regards as a false prophet. The phenomenon of false prophecy is further illustrated by 2 Jn 7, where it is said of some – apparently former members of the community – that 'many deceivers have gone out into the world, those who do not confess that Jesus Christ has come in the flesh'.[24] It is clear that the possibility of immediate divine communication brought with it the problem of authentication. It is likely that the demise of prophecy in the church, which is mentioned as an issue by Eph. 2.20, was related to this issue and that the appearance of more formalized ministerial orders was an attempt to deal with the question of authority by locating it in recognized offices rather than in a particular individual's inspiration.

The question of prophetic authority is posed acutely by the *Didache*.[25] The *Didache* knows a situation where there is awareness of the possibility of unforgivable sin, which is defined as challenging a prophet when he spoke in the Spirit (*Did.* 11.7); but also the notion that certain prophetic statements did not necessarily have to be tolerated. Source-critical analysis has divided *Didache* 11–13 into two constituent parts. Significantly, such analysis holds the section 11.4–12 together, as if this apparent collocation of antitheses represents the earliest strata of the *Didache* to which we can gain access. In the *Ascension of Isaiah*, which was written not much later than the *Didache*, we read of a group of prophets who find themselves out of sorts in an increasingly institutional church, as if the dispute between institutional and charismatic authority was an acute one at the time when these texts were written.[26] It is possible (but not certain) that the *Ascension of Isaiah* comes from a group of wandering charismatics, as if itineracy became a marked feature of the prophetic ministry at a time when it was recognized that there were no longer prophets in every Christian community.

Deacons

In the early chapters of Acts (chapters 6–8), we read of the ministry of seven men who are sometimes called 'deacons'. This identification must be handled with considerable care. The noun 'deacon' is not used to describe them, although the verb and the related noun *diakonia* occur. Of this passage, C.K. Barrett concludes that 'even though the Seven are appointed to do what would later be thought of as work appropriate for deacons it is impossible that anyone should set out to give an account of the origin of the diaconate without calling its first holders deacons'.[27] Although Luke may have modelled the appointment of the Seven on his contemporary perception of appointment to ecclesiastical offices, their choice is clearly related to welfare concerns as this part of Acts amply evidences. In this case, the difference is between Hellenists and Hebrews.

'Hebrews' were apparently Aramaic-speaking Christians and 'Hellenists' were Greek-speaking Christians.[28] The Seven were appointed as over-seers of the Greek-speaking church in Jerusalem, in which capacity they appear as both welfare officers and evangelists.

The later use of the term 'deacon' is related to its implied meaning, that of 'servant'.[29] A whole passage in the Pastoral Epistles (1 Tim. 3.8-13) prescribes rules for their behaviour, including the behaviour of women deacons. The fact that the same epistle forbids women to teach or to have authority over men (1 Tim. 2.12) is an indicator of the subordinate role of deacons in the communities addressed at that time. Deacons are associated both with bishops (Phil. 1.1) and with presbyters (Polycarp, *Ep.* 5.2) in early Christian literature, and we can assess their role by examining the post-biblical sources. We read of deacons distributing the eucharist in the Sunday assembly (Justin, *1 Apol.* 67); assisting with baptisms and at the agape (Hippolytus, *Trad. Ap.* 21.26); and taking messages between churches (Ignatius, *Phld.* 10). We know from Jerome (*Ep.* 146) that deacons sometimes got ideas above their station and thought themselves superior to the presbyters.

Presbyters

The next category of minister we shall consider is that of presbyters.[30] The term was apparently derived from Judaism, where the noun *zaken* ('elder') denoted a member of the community council who interpreted the law and settled disputes among Jewish people. In the New Testament period, there were seventy members of the so-called Great Sanhedrin in Jerusalem who were known as 'elders'. The early Christians translated the Semitic term into Greek, producing the noun *presbuteros*. We see from both Acts (11.30; 15.6) and the Pastorals (1 Tim. 5.17) that they discharged the analogous functions of overseeing communities and resolving disputes.

The earliest discernible form of the presbyterate was a plurality in which a number of presbyters exercised authority in a Christian congre-gation. The letters of Ignatius, which speak of a single bishop, describe the presbyters in the plural as standing with the bishop in the place of the apostles (Ignatius, *Polyc.* 6; *Smyrn.* 8). Bishops themselves were called 'presbyters' (Clement, *Strom.* 3.12.90) even when their primacy was acknowledged. So far as the two different offices were distinguished, the bishop tended to be a teacher while the presbyters exercised discipline and issued judgments.

The presence of a single presbyter as the head of a Christian congrega-tion arose from the expansion of Christianity in the patristic period.[31] This led naturally to the establishment of the monarchical episcopate first designated by Ignatius. The theology on which this was based also derived from Ignatius, as we have seen. The terms 'priest' and 'priesthood' were not used for either presbyters or bishops until after the second century CE.

Bishops

The senior figure in the triad of bishops, priests and deacons was the bishop.[32] In the earliest literature bishops are introduced in the plural, different in this respect from Ignatius' monarchical episcopate. The most important evidence comes from the opening of Paul's letter to the Philippians: 'To the saints in Christ Jesus who are in Philippi, with the bishops and deacons' (Phil. 1.1). This reference, which is not free from textual problems,[33] has been found difficult by the commentators because of the plurality of the noun *episkopoi*, the association of bishops with deacons and the absence of any reference to presbyters. The most obvious reconciliation of this difficulty is to accept that Paul did indeed write as recorded and that his letter reflects an early stage of church organization which was superseded historically by that recorded in the Pastoral Epistles and then again in Ignatius. In Philippians, the 'bishops' are effectively presbyters; the evolution of the monarchical episcopate was the work of a later generation.

This notwithstanding, the monarchical episcopate, which evidently began as an Ignatian invention, was almost everywhere in place by the middle of the second century CE. Justin Martyr speaks in this sense of the 'president' of the assembly (*1 Apol.* 67). Around 170 Dionysius (according to Eusebius, *Hist. Eccl.* 4.23) wrote to a number of churches mentioning a bishop in each of them. The terms 'bishop' and 'presbyter' are used interchangeably by Irenaeus and Clement, but only because all bishops were presbyters as we have seen already. (Not all presbyters were bishops, however.) Irenaeus has an important passage outlining his view of apostolic succession (*Adv. Haer.* 3.3.1–3) which, given that the church in Jerusalem seems to have had a designated leader from the very beginning, did much to reinforce the Ignatian model as the norm for the church.

Long beyond the New Testament period, the theory of the episcopate was powerfully articulated by Cyprian (*c.*200–58 CE).[34] Cyprian presented the episcopate as the corporate possession of the entire church in which each individual bishop was permitted to share (*Unit. Eccl.* 5). Cyprian also developed the use of 'priestly' language as applied to the bishop, especially in connection with eucharistic presidency (*Unit. Eccl.* 17). The Council of Nicaea (325 CE) acknowledged that some bishops (e.g. Rome, Alexandria) had a wider jurisdiction than their local area alone. The Council of Chalcedon (451 CE) stated that such bishops were five in number, from the sees of Rome, Constantinople, Antioch, Alexandria and Caesarea.

The Body of Christ

The church is described under a number of images in the New Testament, none of them more prominent than that of the body of Christ.[35] This is a major theme of Pauline theology, set out as such in the two key passages 1 Corinthians 12 and Romans 12. The image of the body provides an important link with the ministry of Jesus, who in the period that the New Testament documents was coming to be seen as the 'incarnation' (embodiment) of the divine Son who had revealed the things which he had seen in the heavenly world.[36] The prominence of the bodily image was conceivably suggested by the mystery surrounding the resurrection of Jesus, whereby the discovery of the empty tomb created the need for an explanation of what had happened to the body of Jesus. The answer that the church provided to this conundrum was that Jesus' earthly body had been *transformed* into his heavenly body along the lines suggested by 1 Corinthians 15; and that the present company of believers formed the earthly representation of Christ's body, in an ecclesiology conceived along apocalyptic lines.

This interpretation returns us briefly to the narrative of the Last Supper, and especially to the words of institution which are reported to have been used on that occasion.[37] If Jesus conceived the Last Supper as the messianic banquet, can it truly be said that he pronounced the words of institution with their present, sacramental significance? One should beware of thinking in modern, Western categories when addressing this question. The Aramaic word *gupa* ('body') can also stand for the personal pronoun, 'I'. If Jesus contemplated his own death, he may also have said that he would always be with his disciples, presumably until the act of resurrection anticipated by Mk 14.25. The tension between my portrait of the Jesus who expected God to act swiftly and the Jesus who expected to die and be resurrected is deeply rooted in the sources; it has been explained by scholars in several different ways. We should note that Mk 14.25 places no time-scale on the projected resurrection, and that Jesus may have contemplated his own resurrection at the advent of the Son of Man, which he held an imminent phenomenon. We cannot be precisely certain about events, hopes and fears which the sources themselves leave quite uncertain.

John Robinson was certainly right to comment on the realistic sense in which the image of Christ's body is used in the New Testament literature.[38] The term has a dynamic and not a static sense as it is employed there. It denotes not so much 'an individual person in and of himself/herself, but . . . someone's being, living and acting in relationship with others'.[39] This dynamic sense explains the dispute about spiritual gifts which is found in 1 Corinthians 12 and the corporate notion of the spiritual sacrifice in Romans 12. The sources of the body image have been much discussed. There is a conviction among many scholars that it stemmed from Jewish ideology.[40] In the ancient Jewish view, a patriarch represented the whole of his present and future tribe. The experience of having belonged to a messianic movement with tribal convictions possibly prompted the Christians to introduce this terminology in the aftermath of the Last Supper with its words of institution and following the apocalyptic experience of the resurrection, which was based on visions of the heavenly body of Jesus. In this case, the image of Christ's body was intended to perpetuate the ideals of Jesus in the world and to make them present until the time of his return from heaven.

The body image allowed Christian believers to believe that they represented Christ. It also permitted them to make hierarchical distinctions analogous to the tribal system. The church order of the Pastoral Epistles and the threefold order of Ignatius was not an innovation as such but a legitimate development from the understanding of ministry shared by Jesus and the first disciples. This is particularly true if, as seems likely, there was a hierarchy within the twelve and certain members were ranked by Jesus more highly than were others. The essential point of the Pauline correspondence (1 Corinthians 12–14) is that the body remained a connected organism in spite of internal distinctions. The future of the church lay in the anticipated eschatological transformation of each individual body through the acquisition of the heavenly body, when the Lord Jesus would finally render the church like himself through the presentation of that kind of immortality (Phil. 3.21).

EARLY CHRISTIAN ETHICS

In order to discuss the developing ethical perspective of early Christianity, we need to know something about the social position of the Christians in the ancient mediterranean world.[1] Christianity began with the preaching of Jesus firmly on Palestinian soil, and probably with the belief that imminent eschatology had rendered widespread evangelism impossible and maybe even irrelevant. The presence of the Hellenists (Greek-speaking Jews) in Jerusalem from an early stage, however, shows that the original Aramaic formulation of Christianity was almost bound to be widened as time wore on.[2] Paul's apocalyptic conviction that he was the apostle to the Gentiles did much to broaden this framework. His missionary journeys carried the Christian message to Rome, where legend has it that he and Peter died as martyrs in service of the Christian gospel.[3] The delayed *parousia* conspicuously set the problem of who could be admitted into God's kingdom on something broader than ethnic lines.

Christianity first emerged on the fringes of Judaism, which by the first century CE was a well known if in general a somewhat difficult religious grouping in the popular mindset.[4] The book of Acts is undoubtedly correct when it describes the first and most hostile opposition to the Christians as stemming from the Jews. The Jews hated the Christians for their messianic convictions, especially the proclamation that the crucified Jesus was the Messiah. The Christians responded by accusing the Jews of hardness of heart and of defying God's will which had been revealed, first in scripture then supremely in Jesus. Suetonius says of the relations between Jews and Christians in Rome in the middle of the first century that 'since the Jews constantly made disturbances at the instigation of Chrestus, [the emperor] expelled them from Rome' (*Claudius* 25.4). One plausible interpretation of this statement is that conflict between Jews and Christians was a significant feature of first-century city life, which in this instance prompted a response from the authorities.

Certainly, by the time of the Neronian persecution in 64 CE, we find it said that Nero seized on the Christians as an unpopular group to deflect criticism that he himself had started the fire of Rome: 'To get rid of this report, Nero fastened the guilt on a class hated for their abominations, called Christians by the populace. Christus, from whom the name had its origin, suffered the extreme penalty at the hands of one of our procurators, Pontius Pilate, and a deadly superstition, thus checked for the moment, again broke out not only in Judaea, the first source of the evil, but also in the City, where all things hideous and shameful from every part of the world meet and become popular' (Tacitus, *Annals* 15.44). Though indeed Nero was misinformed in certain respects, not least in mentioning nefarious practices committed by the Christians, this passage shows the way in which a deviant religious group could easily become stigmatized in late antiquity, and thus find itself faced with a difficult problem of credibility. This problem of credibility stemmed in the first instance from the manner of the death of Jesus (1 Cor. 1.23).

The Research of Wayne Meeks

This approach to the moral world of the first Christians has been followed with brilliance by Wayne Meeks in his book of that name.[5] Meeks demonstrates the centrality of the *polis* (city) in the Graeco-Roman world, then approaches Christianity through an analysis of the dominant traditions of Greece, Rome and Israel which had determined the nature of the world into which Christianity was born. This leads him (in chapter 4) to examine the nature of the earliest Christian communities. He depicts Christianity as a messianic sect of Judaism which identified itself in the world at large through the distinctive rite of baptism, and which made initiates part of a special community.

Meeks next explores the morals of an apocalyptic sect.[6] He challenges Schweitzer's identification of an 'interim ethic', preferring to speak of 'the promise that the world was soon to be transformed or replaced by a better world, in which righteousness would prevail'.[7] Given that apocalyptic sects fall into more than one distinctive pattern (witness the differences between the Essenes and the early Christians) Meeks concludes that the *form* of a particular sect inevitably affects its internal perception of ethical issues, not least because of the gulf between the elect and all others which is a feature of sectarian ideology.

The most significant shift in the outlook of nascent Christianity lay in the development of an urban Christian culture where originally the religion had sprung from rural roots. While some Christians maintained the tradition of itineracy, the greater majority of Christians lived in the towns where Christian churches emerged in the penumbra of Jewish assemblies. Although the early chapters of Acts document Christian devotion to the temple, Acts (followed by Paul) records that the Christians met in private houses beyond Jerusalem. The earliest Christian building unearthed by archaeologists, in Dura Europos, was remodelled for exclusive Christian use only in the third century CE. The householder often acted as the church's patron, implying that he or she had a modicum of wealth and enjoyed relative importance in the city's social circles.

The rise of urban Christianity and the emergence of the community-with-patron posed new social problems for Christian people. Where Jesus told his disciples not to worry where their next meal was coming from (Mt. 6.25), the dispute recorded in 1 Corinthians 8–10 concerns the all too accessible supply of meat in the local market.[8] Some of the

more complicated sexual problems discussed by Paul seem never to have
troubled the Jesus movement, so far as we know. What was to be done,
for instance, with a man who committed incest with his stepmother
(1 Cor. 5.1)? And what of those who slept with temple prostitutes
(1 Cor. 6.15)? Such problems arose from the more complicated world of
the city, and they formed one of the major motives for Paul's letters.[9]

Meeks has a fascinating section in which he discusses the difference
between a cult and a school.[10] Ancient religious cults contained little
direct ethical teaching. The Christians, however, taught appropriate
norms of behaviour from the very beginning. This is no doubt because
Christianity arose in a Jewish context, where ethics is a familiar feature of
most genres of literature. Paul's letters contain as much ethical as eschatological material, if not more. This included (but was not restricted by) the
desire to preserve the teaching of Jesus and to apply it to new situations.
Among the motives that led to the writing of the Gospels, the desire to
preserve such teaching was an important factor. The late first century
witnessed the production of the *Didache*, while Hippolytus in the third
century produced *The Apostolic Tradition* because he thought that the
church was deviating from a certain ethical standard. In this context,
Hippolytus mentions a process of initiation in which a three-year
'catechumenate' was proposed for would-be Christians.

Alongside these regulatory writings arose a didactic tradition of
Christian literature. It has commonly been noted by supporters of the
'Q' hypothesis that one of the features of that alleged source was a
tradition of scholarly or scribal wisdom.[11] The Gospels present Jesus as a
teacher of wisdom as well as a prophet, as some North American scholars
have been quick to observe. The later New Testament literature (especially Hebrews and 1 Peter) is conspicuously acquainted with Greek
rhetorical conventions. By the third century the so-called Alexandrian
school under Clement and Origen had laid down the foundation of a
distinctively Christian philosophy. All of this had implications for the
emerging Christian understanding of ethics. Meeks concludes that

the emergence of Christian scholarship was an important means by which the counter-
cultural sect of the crucified Messiah's followers would eventually assimilate to the new
society that would take shape in late antiquity. From the beginning, it seems, there were
some leaders in the sect who were able, consciously or unconsciously, to connect the
Christian movement's moral and religious reflection with the Great Traditions, both
Jewish and Gentile.[12]

This was the origin of serious Christian moral reflection.

Christian Ethics and the Delayed *Parousia*

A crucial question to consider is whether the rise of a distinctively
Christian ethic, alongside a system of doctrine, was a response to the

delayed *parousia*, or failure of Jesus to return from heaven in the promised manner. This issue fuelled a famous controversy in twentieth-century research. In 1941 Martin Werner's *Die Entstehung des christlichen Dogmas* explored the subject and touched, in what was perceived as a dangerous manner, on the topic of angel or angelomorphic Christology. It produced a somewhat hasty response from Wilhelm Michaelis, *Zur Engelchristologie im Urchristentum: Abbau der Konstruktion Martin Werners* (1942), who argued that Werner's approach was fundamentally misplaced. The subject was further examined by David Aune in 1975, who concluded that the delayed *parousia* was by no means necessarily a decisive factor in the reinterpretation of Christianity which took place in the second and third generations.[13]

We shall approach this problem by returning (for the last time) to the person of Jesus. We saw that Jesus, although he believed that the Son of Man would introduce God's kingdom in the very near future, nevertheless also believed that he and his disciples embodied the kingdom in the here and now, and that he had to do certain key things in Jerusalem which would hasten the kingdom's arrival. After Easter, the Christians continued to live in hope of the kingdom, and they also worshipped Jesus as the heavenly Lord. This meant that they understood their present existence in spatial as well as temporal categories in a way that is exemplified by Phil. 3.20 ('But our citizenship is in heaven, and it is from there that we are expecting a Saviour, the Lord Jesus Christ. He will transform the body of our humiliation so that it may be conformed to the body of his glory'). I have argued in this book that this is an essentially apocalyptic view.

Although eschatology stood at the heart of Jesus' preaching, his was by no means a non-ethical message.[14] There is an *implied* ethic in the hope that God would soon introduce his kingdom by supernatural means. This led to the explicit ethical teaching of the Gospels, which centres around the radical nature of life in the present and the demand to live by the truth of impending change in a way which dynamically affected all present relationships and commitments. Eschatological urgency did not displace ethical realism in the preaching of Jesus. The saying about divorce in Mt. 5.32, which acknowledges valid grounds, holds true even if no eschatological climax occurs. The tradition of the sayings of Jesus is in fact a diverse one in which ethics features alongside eschatology and where there is obvious ethical overlap (with important differences) between Jesus and contemporary Judaism.

The same is true of Paul's ethical teaching.[15] Paul's view (Gal. 5.22) was that the indwelling Spirit prompted the believer to good works, so that ethical orientation and action stood at the heart of his view of Christian faith. Ethics in this sense demonstrated the realism of the Christian eschatological hope. Given Paul's central image of the church as the body of Christ, the relation between temporal and spatial categories in eschatology is relevant for this question. Paul's ethics were not simply a temporal pledge of eschatological hope. They had a prominent spatial dimension, in the sense that Christians were *already* citizens of heaven (Phil. 3.20). This complemented the temporal aspect of eschatology by demonstrating that the life of heaven had already been introduced on earth, with its potential to transform the world at large.

It is thus not correct to say that the delayed *parousia* was *alone* responsible for the development of Christian ethics, any more than it will do to claim that doctrine was a secondary product of Christian reflection. Ethics formed part of the Christian eschatological hope from the very beginning. It complemented the temporal aspect of eschatology by drawing attention to the mystical relationship between the heavenly Christ and the church on earth. Nor indeed did eschatology vanish with the work of Augustine in the fifth century CE. It was simply reinterpreted to allow for the fact that the earthly kingdom had so far failed to materialize by drawing attention to the reality of *post-mortem* judgment in the spirit of Jewish apocalyptic literature. This eschatological shift emphasized the moral significance of the entirety of human life and developed the need for sustained and coherent moral teaching.

A Moral Centre?

With these comments to hand, we ask whether it is possible to discern a centre of early Christian morality, or merely a series of related themes.[16]

So far as Jesus is concerned, the moral centre of his message was the kind of life demanded by the kingdom of God and the nature of the people who belonged to the kingdom. Like many visionaries, Jesus was more concerned to articulate the *promise that* God's kingdom was in process of becoming than to offer a *precise blueprint* of what the kingdom would be like. We nowhere find a sustained description of God's kingdom in Jesus' reported teaching; merely a sequence of images that contrast the nature of the kingdom with the general state of reality. Jesus conceived the distinction between the kingdom and everyday reality in apocalyptic terms; by which I mean that he accorded it both a temporal and a spatial dimension. He taught that the kingdom was already present among his disciples, but accepted that its public revelation was a matter for the future. The rationale of this view was the belief that the apocalyptic mystery of the kingdom had been revealed to the elect in advance of its more general disclosure.

This means that we need to examine Jesus' circle and the messianic convictions which sustained them, to discover the heart of Jesus' ethical convictions. In the future, Jesus believed, God would send the Son of Man to introduce the kingdom over which he himself would then preside as Messiah. This would be the time of judgment which the Hebrew

Bible had predicted. Given that God's kingdom was already present among the elect, Jesus envisaged at least some continuity between the present and the future. That is why he spoke about the kingdom and the judgment as 'this-worldly' entities, brought from heaven to earth through the apocalyptic Son of Man. The future would fully disclose the divinely willed order of things. It would *not* mark the end of all things in the sense of cataclysmic cosmic destruction. The centre of Jesus' morality thus combined the twin aspects of apocalypticism and made the judgment and the revelation of his messiahship the crucially determinative factor. This appears to be the meaning of the (evidently authentic) distinction between Jesus and the Son of Man in Mk 8.38 ('Those who are ashamed of me and my words in this adulterous and sinful generation, of them will the Son of Man also be ashamed when he comes in the glory of his Father with the holy angels').

There is the threat of judgment here, to be sure, but the dominant motif is that of revelation. Although there are passages especially in Matthew which speak of retribution (e.g. Mt. 13.41–2), we should not ignore the traditional nature of such language or miss its relative absence from the Gospel of Mark. Many of Matthew's judgment sayings occur in the context of parables which are, precisely, stories about God and the future and not literal representations of reality. The crucial point of the parable of the wheat and the tares (Mt. 13.24-43) is that God's kingdom means righteous dealing and not ethical misbehaviour. It would be wrong to place the destructive aspect at the centre of Jesus' message in isolation from the themes of apocalyptic disclosure and divinely ordered change. Jesus was not a prophet of doom and hellfire but an ethically motivated preacher of apocalyptic revelation. It is attractive to suppose that Jesus did indeed speak about 'the renewal of all things', as he is reported to have done in Mt. 19.28. This new order is precisely what motivated an apocalyptic visionary, as we see both from Jewish literature (for example *The Similitudes of Enoch*) and the eschatology of Paul (Rom. 8.18-24).

Paul

The centre of Paul's ethical perspective is also provided by eschatology. The passage just cited from Romans is central to his thought, along with Paul's mature expression of eschatology in Phil. 3.20-1. In development of his individualized resurrectional teaching in 1 Corinthians 15 and 2 Corinthians 5, Paul depicts the entire universe as the sphere of God's redemptive action. This is set firmly within an apocalyptic orbit in the words, 'For the creation waits with eager longing for the revealing of the children of God' (Rom. 8.19). This amounts to a new and Christian reinterpretation of the Genesis story of the creation: 'For the creation was subjected to futility, not of its own will, but by the will of the one who subjected it, in hope that the creation itself will be set free from its bondage to decay and will obtain the freedom of the glory of the children of God' (Rom. 8.20-1).

The meaning of the noun translated here as 'futility' has been much discussed by the commentators.[17] Whether it means 'decay' or simply 'frustration', its fruit is the bondage to decay which is mentioned as a problem by 8.21 and which Paul thinks will be overcome in the final apocalyptic revelation: 'The creation itself will be set free from its bondage to decay and will obtain the freedom of the glory of the children of God.' The effect of the passage is to contrast the present status of creation with its yet-to-be-experienced, and in that sense unprecedented, liberty. Paul looks back to the story of Adam's transgression and the curse on the serpent (Genesis 3) to set the Christian understanding within a total eschatological scheme in which the end is destined to represent the perfection of God's revealed will.

The significant thing about this passage is that the present imperfection is seen as divinely mandated in the light of the apocalyptic revelation accomplished in Jesus. The end result of the frustration or decay was the inability of the creation to reflect the divine glory which Paul had earlier mentioned as a problem for human beings (Rom. 3.21). As with the description of human incapacity in Romans 7, it is made further evident here that *nothing* in creation – both human and non-human – can please God without God's own assistance. This ethical problem receives an apocalyptic remedy. The present and frustrating tendency to decay will be removed at the coming *apocalypsis*, when the children of God will be revealed in the manner described by Rom. 8.21. This will presumably involve the appearance of the heavenly mediator, whom Paul in all his writings identifies as Jesus himself (1 Thess. 4.16; Phil. 3.20-1). That will be the time of revelation when those who already know themselves to be God's children will be publicly revealed in the final marriage of spatial with temporal categories. This will be the moment when the entire creation 'will obtain the freedom of the glory of the children of God' (Rom. 8.21). That in one sense, we might say, is the fulfilment of what Jesus had believed about the future coming of the kingdom.

This magnificent ethical vision is unique in Paul and certainly poetic in form. It expresses, almost as the crown of Paul's theology, the mutual relationship between ethics and eschatology which we noticed also in the preaching of Jesus. In the light of Jesus' revelation, Paul acknowledges problems in the created order which he assigns to God's initiative (in what must certainly be regarded as a bold theological argument). Those who become God's children are enabled to see things from this perspective, and to overcome their moral failings through the indwelling Holy Spirit who entered believers when they turned to Christ. If there is a difference between the ethics of Paul and of Jesus, it is that in Paul the Spirit marks the bond between ethics and eschatology by prompting the

believer to good works as the outworking of what Jesus had achieved.
The Spirit is in this sense the 'first fruit' which guarantees the full revelation, with its hope for change: 'We ourselves, who have the first fruits of
the Spirit, groan inwardly while we wait for adoption, the redemption
of our bodies' (Rom. 8.23).

We saw in Part III that Paul continued this hope for bodily transformation throughout his career, expressing the belief very powerfully in his
last letter, Philippians (3.20-1). Paul's doctrine of the Spirit as ethical
impetus receives its most substantial exposition in 2 Corinthians 3. Here,
the Old Testament legislation is held a fading glory when compared with
the Christian revelation which is maintained in the world by the Holy
Spirit. This coheres with the thought of Romans 8 in the sense that the
entire created order, including pre-Christian Israel, is held to be
imperfect in the light of the Christian revelation with its hope for perfection and change; and in that sense destined for perfection at some future
point.

The centre of New Testament ethics, then, lies in the relationship
between ethics and eschatology, with the difference between Jesus
and Paul noted in the latter's doctrine of the Holy Spirit. We shall
now enquire about the course of ethical development in the period
between the death of Paul and the rise of Gnosticism in the second
century CE.

In the Second and Third Generations

The earliest New Testament documents were occasional pieces, written
to deal with problems in the Pauline churches as and when they arose.
The Gospels are more studied texts, drawing on an established oral tradition and preserving the teaching of Jesus at a time when it was recognized that contact with the original eyewitnesses was being lost through
death. The history of Christianity in and beyond the second generation
shows an increasing interest in drawing up moral rules and norms, not
necessarily as a direct response to eschatological lacklustre but certainly
because it was realized that Christianity was defining its own place in the
world, and needed moral self-consciousness in order to be true
both to the new situation and to the original foundation.

The interesting thing about this period is the way in which more than
one literary genre was used to convey moral teaching; often in didactic
or prescriptive form.[18] While it is impossible to survey all the Christian
texts of the second and third generations, it will be helpful to survey five
representative texts or authors where moral teaching is heavily fore-
grounded. This will provide at least a survey of the issues I have raised
here. The texts in question are the Pastoral Epistles, James, the *Didache*,
the *Ascension of Isaiah* and the letters of Ignatius.

The Pastoral Epistles

The Pastoral Epistles (1 Timothy, 2 Timothy, Titus) claim to have been written by Paul, but in reality they are the work of a deutero-Pauline imitator from the early second century CE.[19] The atmosphere is quite different from that of the genuine Paulines. The letters come from a situation where it is known there are competing varieties of teaching (1 Tim. 2.1-7). Of particular interest is the way in which the Spirit is conceived in more directly trinitarian terms, vindicating the risen Jesus (1 Tim. 3.16) and predicting the rise of doctrinal disputes (1 Tim. 4.1). The inevitable result of this is that the Spirit is less obviously linked with the lives of individual Christians (although that link is never formally denied) but associated with the emerging office-holders, so that the Spirit seems a more ecclesiastical entity in the Pastorals than in Paul.[20] Thus (in obvious contrast to 1 Corinthians 12–14) 1 Tim. 4.14 associates the gift of prophecy with the rite of ordination, as if the only genuine spiritual utterance were produced by those who held authority in the church, and not by unauthorized or suddenly inspired practitioners.

This institutionalized view has an ethical corollary. The awareness of the church as an institution leads the author to show awareness of other institutions and also of the realistic balance of power in the world at large. This is evident not least in 1 Tim. 2.1-12 where the author urges that 'supplications, prayers, intercessions, and thanksgivings be made for all men, for kings and all who are in high positions, that we may lead a quiet and peaceable life, godly and respectful in every way'. Somehow, this seems different from the missionary fervour of the earliest Christian texts. It bespeaks the wish to settle down and get on with the wider world, where old age was becoming a more realistic prospect than imminent intervention.[21] The Pastorals show a different kind of piety from the acknowledged Pauline writings. Words such as *eusebeia* and *semnotes* show a contact with Hellenistic ethics, and represent what Schrage calls 'extensive agreement with the ideals of bourgeois Hellenistic morality'.[22] This issues in the distinctive *via media* of the Pastorals' ethical position which advocates neither total abstinence nor gross indulgence but a sensible balance which keeps all things in proportion.

Office-holders in the church are thereby presented as bastions of Hellenistic morality.[23] The precepts for bishops and deacons in 1 Timothy are broadly the same, advising them to be good citizens and to manage their households well. Of the bishop it is said that he 'must be above reproach, married only once, temperate, sensible, respectable, hospitable, an apt teacher, not a drunkard, nor violent but gentle, not quarrelsome, and not a lover of money' (1 Tim. 3.2-3). Hans von Campenhausen famously commented on this situation that 'the Christian ministry thus becomes another ordinary profession'.[24] These are not exclusively

Christian qualities, but qualities which show the suitability of the church to the wider world in this crucial period of self-definition.

The shift both doctrinally and ecclesiastically from earlier Christianity is remarkable. Not only do we find the substantial absence of any direct references to eschatology or apocalypticism; we also discover a situation in which Hymenaeus and Philetus had been able to teach that the resurrection had occurred already (2 Tim. 2.18). The description of Jesus' death in 1 Tim. 6.13 says only that he 'made the good confession' before Pontius Pilate. Although the author does not deny the truth of future judgment (see Tit. 2.13), it can hardly be said that he bases his ethical system on it. The very nature of the Pastorals is an indication of the way in which the Christian life is now conceived. People are told the rules they should obey and how they should behave in the various aspects of their lives. This prescriptive morality is not the same as we find in Paul; it represents what Schrage calls '[the moralization of] the Christian message'.[25] It is in fact quite incredible that some scholars can maintain the Pastorals were written by Paul given this sense of distance from the earliest Christianity.

James

We saw that scholars have questioned the authenticity of James.[26] The point at issue is both whether James was written by *the* James, the brother of Jesus and leader of the church in Jerusalem; and also whether or not James as such is a 'real' letter. James certainly has the formal opening that is characteristic of the ancient letter. If it is a letter, however, it is certainly an official and not a personal one. It is probably best described in Richard Bauckham's words as a 'paraenetic encyclical' in which teaching of a moral nature is offered to the recipients.[27] The style and contents of the letter probably indicate that it is pseudonymous and claims James' authority for later opinions. This was evidently done to inculcate a particular moral perspective.

The identity of those described by Jas. 1.1 as 'the twelve tribes in the Dispersion' has been variously given, but in fact James does not make any further identification of its readers, and it may be that the reference has mainly symbolic value. As with the Pastorals, there is a considerable distance from Paul. This is evident not only in the bald statement of 2.24 that 'a man is justified by works and not by faith alone'; but also in the actual nature of the writing which, even more than the Pastorals, is filled with ethical concerns which demonstrate this very point.

The ethical approach James adopts is a polarized one. James voices early (and no doubt programmatic) criticism of the double-minded man who is neither one thing nor the other (1.2-8). What James requires is a radical commitment which in his view involves ethical rigorism. This is particularly obvious in 4.1-12, where the author states that 'friendship with the world is enmity with God' (4.4); and that 'there is one lawgiver and judge, he who is able to save and to destroy' (4.12). Interestingly, this rigorism has an apocalyptic dimension in the distinction between earthly and heavenly wisdom in 3.13-18, and especially in the vignette of the judge standing at the door (5.9). Although James is not dominated by eschatology, its ethics are given a Christian dimension in the words of 2.1 that the letter concerns 'the faith of our Lord Jesus Christ, the Lord of glory'. The profound influence of Jewish literature (of a variety of genres) combines to secure the moral effect of this encyclical, allowing it to offer a Christian version of a broader Jewish morality.

This contact with Judaism poses the question of why James was written. It has the form of a moral anthology in which teaching is threaded together, not always with clear division between the various sections. Where Martin Dibelius commented in 1921 on the letter's essentially incoherent order,[28] subsequent commentators have tried to rescue the author from the charge of being a merely vacillating dilettante. Bauckham divides James into three unequal parts in which Prescript (1.1) is followed by Introduction (1.2-27) and then by Exposition (chapters 2–5). Within the Exposition, Bauckham discerns twelve sections of unequal length, corresponding to the twelve tribes of Israel who are mentioned by 1.1 (in a numerological symbolism adopted in a different way also by the author of the New Testament Apocalypse). These twelve sections deal with various questions including faith and works (2.14-22), denunciation of merchants (4.13-17) and reclaiming those who err (5.19-20).

The very form of James, with its Christian indication and primarily ethical content, tells us much about the purpose of the work. It is a treatise of ethics or practical wisdom designed to show what constituted appropriate living in the social world of emergent Christianity. Perhaps the author was suspicious of Pauline liberalism and substituted his own opinions for it. At the centre of his text stands the demand to make the connection between faith and living ('works'). While the background and genre of James has sometimes been compared with the preaching of Jesus, there is of course a significant difference in genre between James and the Gospels, although less so with the *Gospel of Thomas*. For a work to have been issued in this particular genre implies the need for sustained moral teaching, possibly because the author disliked the attempt of the Paulinists to drive a wedge between Judaism and Christianity; but certainly because ethical instruction was perceived as a need at the time.[29]

Within this sustained teaching, we find a particular concern about riches and practical ethics. The fact that Bauckham's third section deals with favouritism towards the rich implies this was, or was coming to be, a problem in the different churches addressed.[30] At least we may conclude that the communities addressed contained the kind of better-off people who might have been cultivated in this way. This leads to the teaching about faith and works, and thence in chapter 3 to some easily overlooked teaching about the human tongue. This implies there was backbiting in the churches, which led no doubt to the disputes mentioned by 4.1. The result is the call to be humble, not proud, and to live an honourable Christian life.

The contact with Jewish literature which Bauckham has examined does much to explain the form of James' aphorisms, and even to some extent of the book itself; but it does not necessarily provide a full explanation of why the book was written. If James is pseudonymous, the clue to this is likely to lie in the obvious anti-Paulinism of 2.24 combined with the evident Jewish and probably Palestinian setting of much of the material. Where the Pastorals represent a stage beyond Pauline Christianity, James represents an attempt to preserve the original nature of the Christian faith by legislating in a thoroughly Jewish way for the internal workings of the Christian communities.[31] The concern with the law and the interest in 'works' show the author's concern to retain affinities with Judaism, while presenting a distinctively Christian face to the world. This was no doubt as much an ethical as a religious concern.

As with the Pastorals, therefore, we have an important exercise in self-definition which has obvious moral consequences. Where the Pastorals urged church leaders to be good Graeco-Roman citizens, James warns its readers not to lose touch with their Jewish heritage. We might suppose that the author of James would not have had full sympathy for the position adopted by the Pastorals. The difference between the two sets of texts shows the different ways in which Christianity achieved moral definition in the period following its first expansion. This is evident also from the *Didache* and the *Ascension of Isaiah*.

The Didache

Niederwimmer divides the *Didache* into four constituent parts: a baptismal catechism, the Treatise on the Two Ways (1.1–6.3); a liturgy (7.1–10.7); a church order (11.1–15.4); and an eschatological conclusion (16.1-8).[32] A glance at these four parts reveals the moral significance of the material in question.

The first is founded on a dualism, similar to the dualism we discerned in James, but more explicitly formulated in the reference to Two Ways (1.1). This contrasts the behaviour God approves, including the Ten Commandments,[33] with the kind of behaviour that leads to death (chapter 5). There is obvious contact with Jewish ethics in the rejection of murder, adultery, deceit and sorcery. This part of the *Didache* has the form of a moral anthology which attempts to explain the basis of Christian ethics in relatively systematic form. There is obvious influence by the New Testament literature as well as by Jewish principles so that we may speak of a broadly based moral outlook with definite Jewish sympathies. The social setting of this material is, like James, the need to achieve a more systematic statement of Christian ethics in the later first century when a more comprehensive understanding was needed as Christianity developed its place in the world.

The social setting of the liturgy is similar, with an expressed desire to distinguish the church from Judaism in the requirement for fasting (8.1). This section outlines such distinctively Christian practices as baptism in the name of the Father, the Son and the Holy Spirit, the Lord's Prayer and the eucharist. One can see that this material would have proved useful to new entrants into the Christian faith, telling them what essentially was to be believed and practised in their new religion.

The church order (11.1–15.4) is of great interest for discerning the character of Christianity in this transitional period. It contains rules for unmasking false prophets. The situation presupposed is apparently one where not every church has a prophet (13.4), and where the prophetic ministry is sustained by itinerant practitioners.[34] There is still contact with 1 Corinthians 12–14, in the sense that the prophetic ministry is valid and current; and not yet the position adopted by the *Ascension of Isaiah* (as we shall see) that the prophets are dying out and being repressed by the church leaders (*Asc. Isa.* 3.21–31). The *Didache* marks a transitional stage between these two positions. It knows a situation where some prophets were not above sponging on hospitality (11.6), but where their authority was still supremely valued (11.4). This is a situation where itinerant prophets apparently functioned in tandem with the bishops and deacons (15.1), who were settled, local figures. The difference from 1 Corinthians 12–14 lies in the statement that not every church now has a prophet; hence what is said about intineracy in the text.

This transitional nature of the *Didache*, standing effectively between the first and the second centuries CE, is demonstrated by its ecclesiastical conclusion. There is particular contact with the apocalyptic eschatology of Matthew, or possibly with a source held in common with Matthew given the likely origin of both texts around the same time.[35] At 16.1 the statement is repeated that 'you do not know the hour when our Lord is coming' (cf. Mt. 24.42; Lk. 12.35). There is reference to a 'deceiver' who would appear in the likeness of God's Son (16.4). The *Didache* ends with the familiar apocalyptic saying, deriving from Zech. 14.5 and possibly also from Daniel 7, that 'the Lord will come and all his saints with him. Then the world will see the Lord coming on the clouds of the sky.'[36]

The text thus runs from a baptismal catechism to an eschatological statement in a form which is quite significant for the development of later systematic theology. It sets the presentation of Christian beliefs within a confessional formula still dominated by apocalypticism, and with a moral framework which attempts to make the connection between belief and living in a way that echoes the teaching of the early New Testament but which also shows the hardening moral resoluteness of James. The result is a greater coherence than Paul had achieved, and indeed a broader moral vision than James itself. The *Didache* allows us to 'take a level' on Christianity at the end of the first century CE. It shows the emerging religion still dominated by the eschatological hope; but, most importantly, explaining itself in a concise way to converts and providing them with an instructional manual that taught the basis of Christian ethics. This is not yet a fully systematic theology or ethical treatise; but it represents a first step in that direction. The *Didache* is a crucial text for understanding the end of the New Testament period and the transition to patristic Christianity; not least so far as the presentation of ethics is concerned.[37]

The Ascension of Isaiah

Our fourth text is the *Ascension of Isaiah*.[38] This Christian apocalypse was probably written in the early second century CE, around the same time as the Pastorals and the letters of Ignatius. This text has received increased attention in recent years because of the nature of its apocalypticism and the light that it sheds on the development of Christian ministry and prophecy in the period after the *Didache*. The text comes from a prophetic circle who lament the fact that prophecy is progressively dying out in the church (3.21–31). In this, the author goes beyond the position witnessed by the *Didache*. He is the complete opposite of the author of the Pastorals, for whom the Spirit was associated mainly with the exercise of ecclesiastical authority. The author of the *Ascension* says of the institutional leaders that 'many will love office, although lacking wisdom' (3.24). He thinks that (at least in his terms) 'the Holy Spirit will withdraw from many' (3.26) and that 'among the shepherds and the elders there will be great hatred towards one another' (3.29). Setting the *Ascension* alongside the Pastorals shows two different sides of the picture. It is clear there was a considerable dispute about the nature of authority in early second-century Christianity, as for different reasons later in that century as well. The Pastorals show the understanding of the side that triumphed in the development of the monarchical episcopate. The *Ascension* is consequently much to be valued for the light that it sheds on the side which vanished: the early Christian charismatic prophets who subsequently passed from the scene.

In form, the *Ascension of Isaiah* is an apocalypse, a conspicuously Jewish genre of literature which speaks in this case with a Christian voice. No doubt this genre was deliberately adopted to show continuity with the mystical and apocalyptic tradition as opposed to the bourgeois Hellenistic *mores* that we meet in the Pastorals. The ethical position of the *Ascension* is determined by its dualism. Those who agree with the author are compared with king Hezekiah, while it is implied that his opponents are disciples of the wicked king Manasseh. It is said that

Manasseh was a demonically inspired king who permitted serious forms of lawlessness to flourish in Jerusalem (*Asc. Isa.* 2.5). The ethical view is one that people's behaviour is determined by their spiritual or super-natural allegiance, so that human behaviour is linked inexorably to the activity of cosmic powers. This echoes, but goes beyond, what was said in the deutero-Paulines.[39] This ethical determinism should be interpreted through the recognition that the author writes for a beleaguered group in the church who dealt with their sense of isolation by positing a grand cosmic contest which explained to them why the majority of people behaved in what they reassured themselves was a wicked and an immoral fashion.

The ethical conviction of the *Ascension of Isaiah* is that the church has suffered serious decline in recent days, and that this was due to the poor example set by its shepherds and elders (3.21–31).[40] The result is a call to return to foundations, exemplified in the statement of 3.21 that 'after-wards, at his return, his disciples will abandon the teaching of the twelve apostles, and their faith, and their love, and their purity'. The fact that the actual consequences of this decline are not spelled out in detail, except in codified form in the narrative that describes the behaviour of Manasseh, almost certainly means that the text was written for a close-knit group of readers who already knew what the problem was.

This means that the *Ascension of Isaiah* is not so much a manual of ethics as a call to persevere with a particular Christian position which for the author had definite ethical corollaries. At a complete distance from the Pastorals, it shows how one particular group tried to deal with the problems of change and self-definition at the crucial period of the early second century CE. They reintroduced the determinism of the Jewish apocalyptic tradition and that with a call to preserve prophetic standards of morality, linked to the suggestion that those who did this were the oral and spiritual heirs of the original Christians. It is intriguing to observe how near contemporaries the *Ascension of Isaiah* and the Pastorals probably were.

Ignatius of Antioch

These remarks bring us to Ignatius of Antioch. We have seen that Ignatius journeyed from Antioch to Rome, where he was martyred around 110 CE. Ignatius wrote a series of letters to the churches through which he would pass. These letters are informative of a variety of topics, ethics included. They represent a milestone between the New Testament literature and the Gnostic controversies of the second century.

With Ignatius, we find a considerable emphasis on the monarchical episcopate. We have seen that this was probably an Ignatian innovation, fuelled by fears about docetism and no doubt by his own desire to exercise a controlling influence in view of his impending death. The result, mirrored to a lesser degree and vigorously challenged by the *Ascension of Isaiah*, was the focusing of authority in a particular *person*: an institutional figure whom Ignatius claimed was worthy of respect because of the position he occupied.[41] This view is undergirded by a theological and christological appeal: 'But since love forbids me to keep silent about you, I hasten to urge you to harmonize your actions with God's mind. For Jesus Christ – that life from which we can't be torn – is the Father's mind, as the bishops too, appointed the world over, reflect the mind of Jesus Christ' (*Eph.* 3.2).

Although we have noted the probably hyperbolic character of Ignatius' comparison between God and the bishop, there is undeniably a shift in this from first-century Christianity. Where for Paul Jesus is the primary focus of authority, for Ignatius it is the bishop on the grounds that the bishop stands in the place of Jesus and thereby represents the Father to the people.[42] The bishop for Ignatius is the guardian of right teaching and ethics. There is a delicate interplay of the themes of imitating Jesus and imitating the bishop; not least, perhaps, because of the superficial similarities between the passion of Jesus and the death of Ignatius. Thus the ideal bishop is a modest, unassuming figure (*Eph.* 6.1). The bishop's mildness must be reflected in the mildness of Christian believers, which in turn is a reflection of the mildness of Jesus Christ: 'Return their violence with mildness and do not be intent on getting your own back. By our patience let us show we are their brothers, intent on imitating the Lord, seeing which of us can be the more wronged, robbed, and despised' (*Eph.* 10.3).

The subtle nature of this ethical shift must not be under-estimated. From the original emphasis on the teaching of Jesus made effective by the indwelling Spirit, we have moved to an institutional view of succession in which the bishop stands in the place of Jesus Christ and where his behaviour and teaching supplies the illustrative norm for the Christian community. Such 'routinization of charisma' was no doubt necessary for a religion that originated in strong supernatural experiences; but it paved the way for the subsequent history of Christian ethical teaching in which the clergy (especially bishops) were seen as figures of moral authority.[43] By virtue of their office, clergy were able to command great respect and to issue moral guidance of the kind that we still find in the Christian denominations today. That it was only really in the twentieth century that the role of lay people as teachers of faith and morals was publicly recognized shows the enormous influence which the principle deriving from Ignatius exercised.

The study of ethical traditions in the late first and early second century is an intriguing one. The Pastorals and Ignatius show the emerging authority of institutional figures, vigorously challenged by the *Ascension of Isaiah*. The *Didache* (along with parts of Matthew) is probably the earliest Christian manual of ethics, written specifically to educate people in their faith and encourage right norms of living. These divergent streams were all fuelled by first-century Christianity. In their different ways, they contributed to the formation of the patristic period by building on the original apocalyptic bedrock of Christianity and meeting the need for ethical elaboration.

THE RISE OF GNOSTICISM

The natural terminus of this book comes in the middle of the second century CE with the rise of the syncretistic religious movement known as Gnosticism.[1] Gnosticism is the name given to a variety of quasi-philosophical systems, of greater and lesser sophistication, which were opposed by the church fathers Irenaeus and Tertullian at that time. The term 'Gnosticism' is a comparatively modern invention, first appearing in the eighteenth century and not in ancient times. It almost always carries a pejorative sense when used today. While based on the Greek noun *gnosis*, which means 'knowledge', the use of 'Gnosticism' as a polemical term serves to set this syncretism in a particular light; and by no means, as it happens, a favourable one. This reflects the view taken of Gnosticism by the church fathers themselves, which perceived the Gnostic nexus of ideas as a dangerous heresy which had to be rejected to preserve the integrity of the emerging Christian faith.

This polemical, and indeed blanket, use of the term in modern scholarship immediately causes a problem, because there was no single, identifiable form of belief known as 'Gnosticism' in the world of late antiquity. We would do well to speak rather of a nexus of ideas, by no means always homogeneous, which reflected a particular world-view, projecting a cosmic myth of salvation and involving a particular understanding of human existence. What united the different varieties of 'Gnosticism' was a radical dualism, according to which the present world was held the work of an inferior deity, or demiurge, and where salvation was essentially a process of illumination in which people were told how this world had come to be and how they could be released from the depressing effects of its decay and their mortality, being repatriated with the true and heavenly world from which they had originally come.

Of all the New Testament literature, John's Gospel comes closest to this perspective with its distinction between 'above' and 'below' and its portrait of Jesus as the descending-ascending redeemer (Jn 3.13; 6.62).[2] Two aspects of John, however, serve to distinguish the Gospel from Gnosticism and thereby illustrate the dangers which Gnosticism posed to the early church. John's Gospel starts by declaring that 'the Word became flesh' (Jn 1.14) and by insisting that the human Jesus really died on the cross (Jn 19.34). John also indicates that Jesus imparted all his necessary teaching before death, devoting little space to post-resurrectional teaching which became the main revelatory mode of many if not most Gnostic texts.

In the framework of Gnostic soteriology, the psychology of Jesus was reworked to distinguish between the human prophet and the heavenly mediator, some Gnostic texts insisting that Christ left Jesus before the crucifixion and mocked those who thought they had killed him. The appearance of the risen Saviour in Gnosticism also led to the denial of the validity of certain sacred texts, Jewish and Christian alike. The tendency to decry acknowledged writings, to devalue the human significance of Jesus and to place great store by revisionist teaching revealed only after his death were the three principal reasons that the church became suspicious of Gnosticism. The erection of barriers between Christians and Gnostics marks the conclusion of this study because of its importance as a milestone between early and patristic Christianity. Such a procedure helped to set Christianity decisively on its path as an independent religion in which, even at that time, the awareness of having had a *tradition* featured prominently.

The Nag Hammadi Library

Until about the middle of the last century, our knowledge of Gnosticism was confined to polemical reports in the church fathers, and a sparse body of other material. In 1945, however, an Egyptian farmer unearthed a clay jar containing 46 different texts on papyrus codices which were copied in the fourth century CE.[3] These codices contained texts which, previously unknown at the time, have now become quite familiar. These include *The Apocryphon of John, The Treatise on the Resurrection* and *The Dialogue of the Saviour.*

The majority of the codices are of single quire. They represent the work of perhaps as many as fourteen different scribal hands. Birger A. Pearson helpfully divides the material into its constituent literary genres.[4] These include apocalypses, revelation dialogues, revelation discourses and what he calls 'rewritten Bible'. There are also Gospels, Acts and Epistles, together with wisdom books, homilies, prayers, hymns and anthologies. It is clear that the corpus contains the work, not just of more than one scribe, but also of a variety of different communities. Not all the works are actually 'Gnostic' in their outlook; and those texts which are Gnostic evince a variety of Gnostic perspectives. What holds the corpus together is a generally common interest in asceticism. This indicates a monastic provenance for the cache. Wisse thinks that the books were secretly buried by Christian monks in an established burial-ground because their contents had come under suspicion with the passage of time; and, in that case, we should add, it was because mainstream Christianity ultimately triumphed over the Gnostic movement.[5]

The value of the discovery at Nag Hammadi was that it put study of Gnosticism (long recognized as a milestone in early church history) on a properly scientific basis by offering actual evidence to work on. The material thus bears on the study of early Christianity, but also of late Judaism, and not least on its apocalyptic strand. We can now proceed to discover more about Gnosticism by considering in some detail one of its central writings.

The *Apocryphon of John*

The *Apocryphon of John* is an interesting text because it offers a coherent and comprehensive account of the redeemer myth which stands at the heart of Gnosticism.[6] While we should probably beware of using language such as 'typical' or 'central', in view of what has just been said, the text nevertheless does illustrate the substance of what it means to call a particular world-view 'Gnostic' in orientation. In this, it makes for excellent illustrative material.

The text is preserved in four Coptic manuscripts from Codices II, III and IV of the Nag Hammadi collection. There are differences between the four manuscripts such as to yield the conclusion that it exists in two separate versions, one of which is longer than the other. The particular Coptic dialect used is Sahidic. The ascription to John, son of Zebedee and disciple of Jesus, is clearly pseudonymous. The work was certainly in existence at the end of the third century CE when the codices were copied. How much earlier than this it was written is difficult to say. Certain similarities have been noticed between the *Apocryphon* and the Gnostic teachings of a man called Barbelo, who is cited without favour by Irenaeus (*Adv. Haer.* 1.29). This might date it as early as the second century CE. If the original text was written then, the resulting modifications represented by the different recensions might have taken place over a considerable time. A recent study of the text has examined the differences between the versions with reference to the established principle of *diaskeue*, a revision involving modification in details.

In form, the *Apocryphon* is an apocalypse, containing a revelation purportedly given by the risen Christ to the son of Zebedee. As with the Jewish and Christian apocalypses, the text has a narrative framework which serves as the setting for other material. That other material consists of a revelation discourse and a commentary on Genesis 1–6. The commentary has itself been the subject of editorial work, resulting in a certain amount of internal confusion, while it is evident also that a number of sources have been used to yield the present form of the work. Despite these difficulties, which are relatively superficial, the structure of the text is plain to see.

Birger A. Pearson's work is crucial for understanding the religious outlook and orientation of the *Apocryphon of John*.[7] His view is that the present form of the material represents a secondary Christianization of what was previously non-Christian material. When the narrative framework and the dialogue features between Christ and John are removed, we have essentially non-Christian material which contains some rather obvious Christian glosses. Pearson argues further that its various sections are based on the Bible and Jewish traditions of biblical interpretation, and Jewish apocryphal writings. This is an important insight for considering the origins and orientation of Gnosticism. If indeed a major Gnostic work can be shown to have Jewish rather than Christian origins, but to exist now in obviously Christian form, this must mean that the study of Gnosticism is considerably wider than the hypothesis that it is a Christian deviation alone.

The adjective 'synthetic' shows the basic point at issue here. Gnosticism must be evaluated both on the evidence for its diverse origins, considered across the totality of the extant literature, and also with reference to the social outlook of its mythology. Given that the mythology is essentially revisionist, and criticizes the opinions of Jews and Christians alike, we must conclude that the Gnostics were concerned to carve out their own identity by distinguishing themselves from all other religious groups. The fact that the mythology is essentially Jewish shows the religious ambience from which Gnosticism, as indeed Christianity, emerged. The fact that the author of the *Apocryphon of John* feels the need to revise Christian teaching as well as the Hebrew Bible is a measure of the foothold that Christianity had come to hold, in distinction from its Jewish parent, by the time the *Apocryphon* achieved its present form.

The narrative framework is provided by an appearance of the heavenly Jesus to John, who had become disconsolate due to criticism from a Pharisee named Arimanius. John asks the rhetorical question: 'How [then was] the saviour [chosen], and why was he sent [into the world] by [his Father, and who is his] Father who [sent him, and of what sort] is [that] aeon [to which we shall go]?' (II. 1. 21). This is a typically Gnostic *angst*. It links the myth of the Saviour's descent into the world with a theology in which God is called Father, and the notion of an 'aeon', by which the author means the heavenly world considered against the background of a variety of different emanations. These emanations form the mythical substratum of the work, providing the logic into which the myth of the saviour's descent is set.

In response to John's questioning, lo and behold (and in language derived from the apocalyptic tradition) the Saviour appears to provide authoritative answers. The Saviour has the ability to change his form at will; a phenomenon possibly derived from the Jewish angelological tradition. The Saviour is clearly identified with the heavenly Jesus; but he is not the same kind of Jesus familiar from the Gospels and other New Testament literature. His speech is quite different: 'I [am the Father], I am the Mother, I am the Son' (II. 1. 2). We should remember how much it went against the grain in antiquity for any Jew to conceive of God in female, let alone hermaphrodite terms. The Saviour continues by exegeting the state of heavenly reality, in terms which clearly owe something to the Platonic doctrine of divine transcendence presented in Jewish guise: 'The Monad [is a] monarchy with nothing above it. It is [he who] exists as [God] and Father of everything, [the invisible one] who is above [everything, who is] imperishability, existing [as] pure light which no [eye] can behold' (II. 1. 2).

The supreme God, then, is unknowable: except by revelation to the Gnostic initiate on the basis of the revelation disclosed in the *Apocryphon of John*. The main feature of the aeonic system, which conceives of the heavenly world in a pluriform way, is that there are a number of emanations, or derivations of being, from the supreme God. Chief among these are the *Ennoia* ('Thought') of God and her derivative, *Autogenes* ('Self-begotten'). From the latter derive four luminaries, known as Armozel, Oriel, Daveithai and Eleleth. There are also heavenly prototypes of Adam and Seth. The last of the aeons is *Sophia*, meaning 'Wisdom'.

Cosmic and mythological problems emerge when *Sophia* acts spontaneously to bring an emanation out of herself, despite her comparatively lowly status within the aeonic system. This is described in II. 9ff.: 'She wanted to bring forth a likeness out of herself without the consent of the Spirit – he had not approved – and without her consort and without his consideration.' The result of this disobedience is that something less than perfect emerged: 'And because of the invincible power which was in her, her thought did not remain idle and a thing came out of her which was imperfect and different from her appearance, because she had created it without her consort. And it was dissimilar to the likeness of its mother, for it has another form' (II. 1. 10).

This emanation is introduced as 'an archon' whose name is Yaltabaoth. He, too, continued the process of emanation, so that we have a second series of aeons, all of them imperfect when compared with the higher order because of their rebellious origin. Cain and Abel are mentioned in this context. There follows a typically Gnostic contrast and a theological description of this debased existence: 'And when the light had mixed with the darkness, it caused the darkness to shine. And when the darkness had mixed with the light, it darkened the light and it became neither light nor dark, but it became weak.' Yaltabaoth is made to say of himself: 'I am God and there is no other God beside me', in evident parody of Deutero-Isaiah (II. 1. 11). Following his emergence, *Sophia* evidently repents and casts out the Demiurge; failing, however, to destroy him or the aeonic system which he then created.

The rest of the *Apocryphon* constitutes exegetical development of a kind of Genesis 1–6. The birth of Seth is described in some detail, because his 'seed' constitutes the race of Gnostic initiates. Seth is therefore the Gnostic prototype.[8] He is the descendant of Adam, the first created man. It is made clear that human beings in their natural state have no idea about the emanations which had resulted in their particular condition in the world:

Likewise the mother also sent down her spirit which is in her likeness and a copy of those who are in the pleroma, for she will prepare a dwelling place for the aeons which will come down. And he made them drink waters of forgetfulness, from the chief archon, in order that they might not know from where they came. (II. 1. 25)

The result of this is that a distinction is made between different kinds of human being. Only *certain* people understand the truth of things:

Great things have arisen in your mind, for it is difficult to explain them to others except to those who are from the immovable race. Those on whom the Spirit of life will descend and (with whom) he will be with the power, they will be saved and become perfect and be worthy of the greatnesses and be purified in that place from all wickedness and the involvements in evil . . . They are not affected by anything except the state of being in the flesh alone, which they bear while looking expectantly for the time when they will be met by the receivers. (II. 1. 25–26, abridged)

There follows a theodicy in which it is explained that these people will be saved, while others will be imprisoned and subjected to eternal punishment.

The central means of redemption is a myth of the Saviour's descent in which he went down to Hades three times in order to illuminate the souls in prison, which is interpreted as the prison of the body:

Still for a third time I went – I am the light which exists in the light, I am the remembrance of the Pronoia – that I might enter into the middle of the darkness and the inside of Hades. And I filled my face with the light of the completion of their aeon. And I entered into the middle of their prison, which is the prison of the body. And I said, 'He who hears, let him get up from the deep sleep.' And he wept and shed tears. Bitter tears he wiped from himself and he said, 'Who is it that calls my name, and from where has this hope come to me, while I am in the chains of the prison?' And I said, 'I am the Pronoia of the pure light; I am the thinking of the virginal Spirit, he who raised you to the honored place. Arise and remember that it is you who hearkened, and follow your root, which is I, the merciful one, and guard yourself against the angels of poverty and the demons of chaos and all those who ensnare you, and beware of the deep sleep and the enclosure of the inside of Hades.' (II. 1. 31)

The *Apocryphon of John* is thus an apocalyptic text which fuses together a variety of cosmological speculations with an interest in personal salvation and the disclosure of the means by which this can be attained. The present human condition is presented in terms of a profound and indeed by now unwitting alienation from divine origins as a result of rebellion in the aeons before the creation of the world and humankind. Salvation consists in the first place of illumination, or knowledge gained by revelation, of this true state of being. One can only be saved by knowing what one is. This is not possible, on the author's view, to the unaided human intellect since the decisive events happened before the intellect itself emerged. Only the Saviour's revelation, and its perpetuation in Gnostic circles, can bring people to a knowledge of the proper state of being, and to the necessary asceticism which enabled the return to aeonic perfection.

There are clear and obvious features of this mythology which show why Gnostic teaching was perceived as a threat by the Christians. In the first place, the text is not distinctively Christian but essentially Jewish with inserted Christian overtones. This meant that its religious character was open to question through the fact of syncretism. Secondly, there is the tendency to denigrate the biblical basis on which mainstream Christianity was founded. This occurs in two different ways in the *Apocryphon of John*: first of all, in the reworking of the early chapters of Genesis to imply that the world and its inhabitants are children of a lesser God; secondly, in the explicit denial that what the Hebrew Bible said was true. More than once the Saviour says: 'It is not the way Moses wrote (and) you heard' (II. 1. 23). This calls into question the value of the Hebrew Bible; and indeed explicitly contradicts the approach to Moses which is found in Matthew and the mature Paul. Furthermore, there is the implied consideration that Jesus when on earth had left considerable gaps in his disclosure of divine truth. This is implied by the rebuke of Arimanius, and countered by the revelation which sets the record straight so far as the author's understanding of salvation is concerned.

The extent to which this mythology is consistent, let alone easy to understand, does not concern us here. The crucial point is that the Gnostic narrative looks, and is, recognizably different from what mainstream Christians were saying about the understanding of salvation and the role of Jesus, scripture and human receptivity within it. This difference in outlook caused grave concern in the second century. It made people consider what they really believed about things; and led them to identify those reliable writings where the truth about Jesus and Christianity could be confidently found. Nowhere perhaps is this more true than in the Gnostic portrayal of Jesus.

Gnostic Views of Jesus

The Jesus whom we encounter in the Gospels is an apocalyptic figure who journeyed to Jerusalem in the expectation that he would do certain distinctive things before God's kingdom came. His death on the cross was an all too real event, while his resurrection (and resurrection sayings) are described with relative brevity. The Gospels seem to place equal weight on Jesus' words and actions, even if in most cases the latter have to be interpreted with reference to the former. In the second century, with key figures such as Ignatius, Irenaeus and Justin Martyr, we find the emerging conviction that certain authoritative texts present an accurate Christology which cannot be set aside by any revision or new discovery. By virtue of using both of these, the Gnostic portrait of Jesus was a thorn in the flesh for the mainstream church, and served in the long run as a significant delineating factor.

Just as *The Apocryphon of John* set aside the traditions of Moses, several Gnostic texts offer a revised version of the teaching and significance of Jesus. The evidence in this respect has been helpfully collected by Gerard P. Luttikhuizen.[9]

The *Letter of Peter to Philip* describes how Jesus appeared to the disciples on the Mount of Olives and imparted teaching to them.[10] This text has two noteworthy features which match information already deduced from *The Apocryphon of John*. First, the author makes Jesus an essentially Gnostic teacher who dispenses revelation by virtue of his status as a heavenly being. Secondly, he insists that this Gnosticized teaching is entirely consistent with what Jesus said before Easter. Reading the text in brief shows the issues involved here.

The Gnostic element in Jesus' teaching is introduced by what is hardly an innocuous question from the apostles: 'Lord, we would like to know the deficiency of the Aeons and their Pleroma' (VIII. 134. 21). Jesus then makes a significant statement: 'It is you yourselves who are witnesses that I spoke all these things to you. But because of your unbelief I shall speak again' (VIII. 135. 6–8). The strong implication is that Jesus is going to repeat what he had said already, and that what he says in this respect is, indeed, merely repetition, not fresh teaching. The need to do this is referred to the disciples' unbelief, which has now been set aside in their willingness to hear things again.

It follows that the nature of the teaching provides a clear indication of the nature of the Christology this text exudes. There is no mere repetition of the Gospel narrative, but a Gnosticizing portrait whereby Jesus radically qualifies what was said in the Gospels. The literary device in this case is a blatant one. Repetition does not mean simple rehearsing of the Gospels' portrait, but the disclosure of an entirely new portrait, the justification for this being that the disciples did not believe what they had been told before. The question of whom this argument might convince is an open, if not an opaque one. It is transparently literary in character, allowing the author to introduce a radically different kind of Jesus whom the church fathers would have had no difficulty in dissociating from orthodox Christology.

The message imparted by this Jesus is similar in many respects to that found in the *Apocryphon of John*. There is a cosmogonic myth, involving disobedience and deficiency, resulting in ignorance of the supreme God by the inhabitants of earth. The text also includes a doctrine of the descending redeemer: 'And I came down to their dead product. But they did not recognize me; they were thinking of me that I was a mortal man' (VIII. 136. 20–1). Salvation is presented in terms of the stripping-away of mortality in order to become 'illuminators in the midst of dead men.' (VIII. 137.7). This is reminiscent of, but also rather different from, Paul's understanding of the resurrection in 2 Corinthians 5, where he expected the heavenly body to be superimposed over the present, mortal body. In the Gnostic text, by contrast with the doctrine of the resurrection in the New Testament, the mortal body must be stripped away in order to yield a form of illumination. Like the other words of Jesus in *The Letter of Peter to Philip*, this is conceptually quite different from anything found in the New Testament.

The *Apocalypse of Peter* offers a distinctive view of the passion of Jesus which again is at variance from what first-century Christianity had believed. Just as the *Apocryphon of John* rewrote the teaching of Moses, the *Apocalypse of Peter* startlingly reinterprets the meaning of the cross. The Saviour tells Peter, 'He whom you saw on the tree, glad and laughing, this is the living Jesus. But this one into whose hands and feet they drive the nails is his fleshly part, which is the substitute being put to shame, the one who came into being in his likeness.' (VII. 81. 15–25). This part of the work makes a distinction between the human (and therefore mortal) Jesus and the immortal Saviour. This is simultaneously the distinction between the heavenly world and the earthly, for the Saviour is the agent of the supreme God, while Jesus in this text is made 'the son' of the cosmic powers. This means that those who crucified Jesus may have despised a human body, but that their actions had no effect on the Saviour; and, therefore, in terms of the overall drama, very little effect on actual reality at all. As if to make this point, the Saviour appears above the cross (VII. 82), while Jesus laughs at the blindness of those who crucified him as the Saviour's substitute.

This approach to Jesus can be paralleled in Gnostic works that lie outside the Nag Hammadi corpus, and also in the reports of the church fathers.[11] The implications of this Christology for the development of Christology in the second century are clear. We find here, not just the suggestion that Jesus meant something other than what he is recorded as having said in the Gospels, but the plain declaration that his death on the cross did not involve suffering for a divine being. The view of the *Apocalypse of Peter* requires deception or discernment, depending on the perspective of the interpreter. Where Paul had retained the preaching of the cross while noting its difficulties (1 Cor. 1.23), the Gnostic text deals with the difficulties by reworking the preaching of the cross. For mainstream Christians who looked to the death of Jesus as an eschatological sacrifice, this was clearly a step too far because it denied the saving significance of the passion. Devaluing the cross meant devaluing baptism and the New Testament doctrine of the resurrection, and thus the entire basis on which first-century Christianity had been based.

The reason that Gnosticism posed such a threat in the second century has thus been made clear. In reworking what were coming to be regarded as cherished traditions, it called attention to the value of those traditions and the need to preserve them in a form which had continuing meaning but which still remained faithful to the original understanding. In ending my study with Gnosticism, I have reached a point which might be regarded as a terminus. The church fathers perceived, perfectly correctly, that to accept the premises of Gnosticism would be both to sever any effective links with first-century Christianity, and to open up a revelatory stream where almost anything might be held true by virtue of the claim to revelation. In this case, and for the first time, the words of the heavenly Jesus were tested with reference to the words of the earthly Jesus, and the suggestion that the former could take precedence over the latter was decisively rejected. Christianity thereby closed the door to timeless truth, insisting that what had been believed in the past could be believed today, on the basis of writings which by now had come to be valued as fully authoritative.

SUMMARY AND CONCLUSION

At the end of the book, it is time to look back and take stock of what has been accomplished here. We have covered quite a lot of ground in a single volume and, for that reason, necessarily at some speed. Historically, we have moved from the search for ancient Israel through the ministry of Jesus, the activity of Paul to the rise of second- and then third-generation Christianity. Intellectually, we have surveyed the nature of pre-Christian Judaism, and then examined the unique religious insight of Jesus, together with the impact made by his resurrection.

Certain fundamental convictions have emerged from this quite wide-ranging enquiry. The first of these is that the story of early Christianity cannot be told monolithically. This is obvious in the disputes between the Hebrews and the Hellenists recorded in Acts, but also in the outlook of a work like James with its implied criticism of those who misread Paul. Early Christianity was not a homogeneous entity but a growing and developing organism which produced some sophisticated ideas at an early date. What we read in the New Testament is essentially the story of a religion that is in process of becoming. The emergence of beliefs about Jesus, combined with the need to form a more coherent ethical under-standing, brought the Christian faith to the kind of position represented by the Johannine literature at the end of the first century, where the portrait of the heavenly Jesus had already yielded an incarnational Christology, and where the need to maintain correct forms of belief had been identified in tandem with the love commandment. We need to take account of the entire range of Christian life and thought, making due allowance for change and development while remembering that this did not happen according to a strict chronological sequence. Only by con-sidering the totality of the evidence, sensibly and responsibly, can we gain an adequate understanding of how Christianity emerged.

A second conviction concerns the phenomenon of apocalypticism. I showed how apocalypticism arose in Israel in the third century BCE with the writings of the Enochic scribes. The ministry of Jesus was certainly fuelled by apocalypticism, as can be seen once it is recognized that the Son of Man in the Gospels is a heavenly mediator whom Jesus expected would usher in the kingdom. The distinctive feature of my research into Jesus has been the demonstration that his movement had the nature of an apocalyptic circle and that, in deference to that tradition, certain things were said or done there in advance of their more general disclosure. I have identified the triumphal entry, the cleansing of the temple and Last Supper as events which had a crucial meaning for the Jesus circle, functioning as acted symbols with eschatological significance in the sense that they created the conditions which enabled the imminent coming of the kingdom.

Related to this is a third conviction, that the Jesus tradition is not as clear-cut as we would like it to be, and that consequently final certainty on the vital question of the self-understanding of Jesus is likely to elude us. We do not know for sure whether he expected to die, or about the extent to which he himself held fixed ideas about the nature of the kingdom following the Son of Man's intervention. We can, by all means, ponder and prioritize the possibilities. But this is not the same thing as reaching certain conclusions; and the difference between what we would like to say and what we can reliably say must be maintained at all costs. Humility is the byword in this area. We can but remember the warning of Albert Schweitzer that those who quest after the historical Jesus tend to reconstruct him in their own image and likeness.

This brings us, fourthly, to the conviction, both that the resurrection was a pivotal event in early Christianity, and that we need to hold in mind certain parameters concerning its likely and most obvious inter-pretation. I have ventured to suggest that Jesus did not think about him-self as God, and that he hardly anticipated the worship of himself as divine which emerged in close proximity to his death. In evaluating the evidence for the resurrection, we need to distinguish between the visions of the risen Jesus (which are mentioned in the earliest accounts, by Paul) and the empty tomb which is a feature of the Gospel tradition. I have insisted that the latter can and must derive its meaning from the former. The empty tomb is an ambiguous symbol which gains its meaning from the apocalyptic declaration that Jesus is a heavenly being. The narrative outworking of this view is the story of the ascension which bridges the stories of Luke and Acts. What the early Christians meant when they said that Jesus had been raised is that the theological conceptions of Judaism had been redefined by the revelation that the crucified visionary from Nazareth shared the divine glory and was entitled to worship. What had not been recognized previously transformed the followers of Jesus when they perceived the nature of the apocalyptic intervention which emerged from the death of Jesus.

Fifthly, there is a conviction about Paul. Reading Paul is not always an easy experience, both because of the occasional nature of his letters but also because Paul himself did not represent the totality of the Christianity that existed in the first century CE. Paul has been viewed in various ways in the history of scholarship. Some scholars think that Paul passed out of fashion in the later first century, but the silence from him after the writing of Philippians can be explained in more than one way. If Paul *did* die a martyr in Rome, his early demise clearly left a gap which no-one could fill in quite the same way. If James is to be believed, some of what Paul said caused a problem when it came to carrying on the process of self-definition in the later part of the first century. Paul did not always make for easy reading; particularly if Galatians is privileged over the other correspondence.

The most obvious conclusion is that there was an anxious gap after Paul which Gentile Christianity did not quite fill completely, and which in one sense was responsible for the doctrinal disputes that we find in the Johannine literature and in Ignatius. The problem with Paul is that he established a path towards separateness but did not live sufficiently long to fill in the necessary details. This would take centuries to accomplish; Augustine in that sense marks the next significant milestone in the development of Christian thought. Paul, however, took the first decisive steps in separating Christianity from Judaism when he said that the law was not *necessary* as a means of salvation in Christ, even though it contained much that was useful. In reading Paul, we are taking steps along a way that becomes rather less certain for a time when Paul stops speaking.

This brings us, finally, to the question of how boundaries were defined. Jesus worked with an imminent eschatology, which was reworked after his death through the emergence of beliefs about the resurrection. Paul took up the preaching of Jesus and presented the religion of Jesus as one that had a separate place in antiquity different from Judaism and paganism but not in fact inimical to either. It was inevitable that the first disputes which rocked the Christian faith, local disputatiousness apart, were disputes about Jesus and disputes about authority. *In what sense* could it be held that the prophet from Nazareth was divine? And which writings from Christian circles could be trusted, and why should that be so? In both cases, reassurance came from excluding those whom the emerging mainstream church decided really had crossed unacceptable boundaries and were saying something other than what ought to be believed. This took the form of saying, either that the human Jesus was not divine or that the divine Saviour was not ordinarily human; or of rejecting texts which long use and respectability indicated had acquired a certain authority for Christian people. Marcion and the Gnostics were critical influences here. By denying the authority of certain books, and by insisting that the human career of Jesus was not the plain and full truth of the matter, they forced people like Irenaeus to explain which books could be trusted and to uphold the connection between the human Jesus and the heavenly Christ which is found in the canonical Gospels.

Establishing boundaries and excluding unwelcome opinions is a sign that a history has taken place. What the earliest history of Christianity teaches subsequent Christianity is that the interpretation of canonical literature and the meaning of Christology are not things that were achieved once and for all in the second century CE. The process of biblical interpretation and the task of Christology continue afresh in every generation, almost by necessity in view of the way the canon was formed and Christian doctrine created. The discovery both of the

Qumran scrolls and of the Nag Hammadi library in the last century is an indication of the need for fresh thinking; while the way that disputes about Christology continued with venomous fury in the wake of *Honest to God* and *The Myth of God Incarnate* shows the pain which probing the uncertainties of first-century Christianity continues to cause.[1]

I learned much from editing John Sturdy's book on the date of the early Christian literature.[2] Sturdy is a good example of what I mean because he self-consciously swims against the tide and challenges fellow scholars to come up with good reasons for holding the opinions that they do. In researching the history of Christian origins, we need constantly to ask ourselves what we know and how we believe that we know it. I very much hope that this book has managed to ask at least some critical questions and to identify the religious distinctiveness of Jesus and his successors as something quite unusual in the world of late antiquity.

APPENDIX

The Gospels as sources for Jesus

I said in Chapter 11 that, in his review of my book on Jesus,[1] Anthony Harvey rightly criticized me for failing to include a discussion of the relationship between the four Gospels as a means of penetrating back to the authentic Jesus of history.[2] In acknowledging that he was right to do this, I look back to my own experience of being an undergraduate and then a research student at Cambridge. During the time I was there, the Tripos was changed from a paper on the Synoptic Gospels (which I sat as an undergraduate) to a paper on Jesus (which I taught to undergraduates). I remember the sense of relief as a graduate supervisor of not having to begin with a problem which, so far as I understood it then, everyone knew perfectly well was insoluble. That is why I decided to press on with my section on Jesus in this book (Part II), and to leave till later an indication of the reliability of the sources and the problems of the inter-relationship between them. Nevertheless, these *are* significant issues. In what follows, I would like to give an indication of the main lines of argument, and to show that it really is difficult, if not impossible, to reach absolute agreement about the greater majority of them.

I have considered the nature of the Gospel genre already. This Appendix is therefore an introduction to 'The Synoptic Problem', and then the relationship of the Fourth Gospel (John) to the other three.[3]

What Is the Synoptic Problem?

We begin by considering what it is about the first three Gospels that allows them to be called 'Synoptic', and then by asking why the existence of three such texts should be thought to constitute a problem.

The reason the first three Gospels are called 'Synoptic' is not because they incorporate eyewitness testimony, although in places they rather obviously do, but because they can be set alongside each other in a large number of places and comparisons can be made of the way in which a particular story is told in Matthew, Mark and Luke. A number of synopses are available, both in English and in Greek.[4] It is obvious that the first three Gospels, as well as having quite a similar 'storyline', generally follow the same narrative/plot sequence in which Jesus ministers in Galilee and journeys finally to Jerusalem to death and resurrection. Mark begins his story with the ministry of John the Baptist. Matthew and Luke describe the birth of Jesus; but otherwise these generally follow Mark's sequence of events, augmenting and adapting it in places, but leaving the reader in no doubt that we are dealing with the same basic story.

John is conspicuously different. Not only does he read the story of Jesus back to the event of creation itself (1.1-14); he also adopts a different narrative structure which is determined by the three Passover visits that Jesus made to Jerusalem, from which is derived the traditional understanding that Jesus' ministry lasted three years. John also includes some obvious symbolism based around the number 'seven', as if symbolic and theological purposes played a considerable role in shaping the Fourth Gospel.

In addressing the question, 'Are the first three Gospels very similar?', we are bound to come up with the answer 'yes and no'. Yes, there are many similarities, both of structure and content. But yes, also, there are many differences, more of content than structure, including some significant 'minor agreements' between Matthew and Luke against Mark.[5] The reason this constitutes a 'Synoptic *problem*' is because it raises the question of which of the texts came first. The most common answer is that Mark was the first Gospel to be written. A variant hypothesis, however, argues for Matthew, while the status and origin of Luke in respect of the others has become a contested matter in research.

The Synoptic problem, briefly put, is the difficulty of knowing which Gospel was written first, and in what order and with what sources the subsequent Gospels were written. In addressing the first of these issues, it is evident that there is an amount of material found in Matthew and Luke, and further material in each of these Gospels individually, which is not found in Mark. Some scholars have argued that Matthew and Luke also used an oral or sayings source known as Q, from the German *Quelle*, which means 'source'. Other scholars (including myself) vigorously deny that Q is a necessary or even a convincing hypothesis. We may review the so-called Synoptic Problem in the following way.

The Priority of Mark

The majority of scholars who have worked on the Synoptic problem think that Mark was the first Gospel to be written. The exception is the group of scholars who accept the 'Griesbach hypothesis': the belief that Matthew wrote first, Luke used Matthew, and Mark then used both Matthew and Luke.[6] The majority hypothesis needs careful statement for we cannot necessarily assume that our version of Mark is its original form.[7] Mark was certainly expanded by the addition of material at the end of chapter 16, and it may have existed in a now-lost but abbreviated version which stands behind the present text (the so-called *Ur-Markus*, or Proto-Mark, theory). To argue for Marcan priority is thus not to argue that Mark reached its *present* form before the other Gospels were written;

but that what we now know as Mark represents the earliest written Gospel.

The grounds for accepting Marcan priority have been stated in an article by Geoffrey Styler which, to the best of my knowledge, has never successfully been repudiated.[8] Styler observes a number of passages where individual points of style and detail suggest that Matthew and Luke were written with a knowledge of Mark. So far as Matthew is concerned, Styler notes his description of the death of John the Baptist (Mt. 14.3-12 = Mk 6.17-29). There are features in Matthew's story which he thinks betray knowledge of Mark's. The words 'and the King was sorry' are integral to Mark but alien to Matthew, who has already said that Herod *wanted* to kill John. Matthew also forgets that the story is told as a 'flashback', and builds a smooth transition to the next pericope at its conclusion (14.12-13).

Another example is Pilate's offer to release a prisoner in Mt. 27.15-18 (= Mk 15.6-10). Mark's sequence is clear and intelligible, but Matthew blurs it badly. He removes Mark's logic by *first* making Pilate offer a choice between Jesus and Barabbas (27.17); and *then* stating that 'he knew it was from envy that they had delivered him up' (27.18). Matthew's confusion suggests that he knew Mark and inexpertly retained his flow of thought. The six examples which Styler produces have a certain cumulative force. They explain some features of Matthew which are otherwise difficult to account for.

It might be objected, as I shall show in a moment, that there are places in the Synoptic Gospels where the similarity between all three Gospels is best explained on the hypothesis that *Matthew* and not Mark is the middle in the sequence. I do not think this invalidates the case for Marcan priority once we recognize that Mark itself possibly passed through more than one version. It is probably true to say that in places Matthew does represent the most original form of text (and indeed this could be said in places also of Luke). It is, however, easier to support Marcan priority over Matthew than the other way round (and very difficult to support absolute Lucan priority over either). Marcan priority over Matthew is thus a hard-and-fast rule but not an absolute rule. It claims more supporters than detractors today.

Styler also argues for Marcan priority over Luke. This is easier to sustain because Luke follows Mark's order more closely than does Matthew. Styler identifies several passages where it is easy to believe that Luke's version is 'secondary', and hard to believe otherwise.[9] The best example is the sermon in the Nazareth synagogue, Lk. 4.16-30. Here Luke retains themes that are prominent in Mk 4.1-6, but works many of them in artificially and presents what appears to be a 'secondary' version of the story. In the story of Jairus' daughter (Lk. 8.51, cf. Mk 5.37, 40), Luke blunders in allowing the mother to enter the house – for she has been there all the time – and appears to stumble in suggesting that the inner group who witness the miracle scoff at Jesus. This statement, however, is comprehensible when Mark's version is read, for there Jesus allows only three disciples to accompany him and the people scoff when Jesus says that the child is merely asleep. In compressing Mark's account, Luke becomes guilty of carelessness and unwittingly discloses his source. Luke is clearly secondary at this point to a Gospel which has a fuller narrative.

Belief in Marcan priority has often been combined with belief in Q.[10] Q has never been found, evidently because it was never committed to writing, but several scholars offer confident (in some cases, rather *too* confident) reconstructions of it.[11] This fusion of sources yields what has come to be called the 'two-source' hypothesis, according to which Matthew and Luke used Mark and Q independently of each other, and their own private material too. The advantage of the Q hypothesis, it might unfairly be said, is that a putative source can never be examined and so can be held to contain anything a Gospel critic would like it to contain (as long as it is a saying). That Luke used Mark and Q and worked independently of Matthew has been the dominant theory in the past century. Only more recently has a scholarly consensus begun to emerge that this is not correct.

Boo to Q

There are greater objections to the 'two-source' theory than its protagonists are prepared to concede. These have been cogently stated by Sanders and Davies.[12] The theory's fatal flaw is the strong evidence that Matthew and Luke were not written independently of each other but that one of them used the other. The 'triple tradition' – incidents which occur in all three Synoptists – throw up about a thousand agreements between Matthew and Luke against Mark. These are far too many to be simply coincidental. They suggest – indeed, confirm – that Matthew and Luke did *not* use Mark independently of each other. This calls into question the existence of Q, because it cannot then be shown that the material in either of Matthew or Luke is derived from independent reading of Mark backed up by oral tradition.

We must also consider those places where Mark and Q overlap (e.g. in the Temptation story). This overlap, noted by B.H. Streeter in 1911, raises the possibility that Mark himself knew Q.[13] That would mean the end of the 'two-source' hypothesis because Mark could not then be held to have been uncontaminated by Q.

If Q is regarded as an invalid hypothesis, this must mean that either Matthew or Luke used the other. Sanders and Davies observe that, in places in the triple tradition, Matthew and not Mark (but never Luke) is the most plausible middle in the sequence.[14] This indicates that, of all three Synoptic Gospels, Luke is the most likely to be dependent on the others. The hypothesis that Luke used Matthew which they form from this information requires careful statement. To prove it, we must look for something more precise than just Luke's knowledge of Matthaean passages or even of Matthaean themes. These would indicate only that Luke knew Matthew's sources, which brings us back to the beginning of the Synoptic problem. We must find evidence that Luke knew Matthew's *style and editorial activity* to place his knowledge of Matthew beyond doubt. According to Sanders and Davies, such evidence is indeed forthcoming from the text of Luke.[15]

I reproduce here their argument, which seems to me quite plausible. In the story of the 'many from East and West', Lk. 13.28 preserves the phrase from Mt. 8.12 that there will be 'weeping and gnashing of teeth' among those who deserve eschatological punishment. It is easier to suppose that Luke copied Matthew in this than that both independently copied Q, because Matthew often uses the phrase but Luke never does again (and Mark never does at all). In the commission of the twelve (Lk. 9.1-6 = Mk 6.6b-13 = Mt. 9.35; 10.1, 7-11, 14), there are several agreements between Matthew and Luke. One of them is very striking. In 9.5 Luke says the disciples, if rejected, must shake off the dust from their feet when they leave 'that town'. This phrase agrees verbatim with Mt. 10.14, but the context is strikingly different: Lk. 9.4 says 'whatever *house* you enter' and nothing about towns. Mt. 10.11 has the words 'whatever town or village you enter' which make the succeeding phrase relevant. Lk. 9.4 is based apparently on Mk 6.10 ('when you enter a house . . .') and not on Matthew. The best explanation is that Luke has used both Matthew and Mark. The alternative – that Luke's reading is coincidental – is not at all convincing.

Thirdly, in the story of John the Baptist (Mk 1.2-3 and parallels), Mark's statement about John ('Behold I send . . .') is from Mal. 3.1 or Exod. 23.20, but not a precise citation of either. Matthew and Luke lack the 'Behold I send' (but agree in placing it elsewhere; see Mt. 10.11 = Lk. 7.27); and have their own version of the scriptural citation which in both cases ends with the words *emprosthen sou*, 'before you'. *Emprosthen* is a favourite word of Matthew's, and here Luke agrees with Matthew against Mark, Exodus and Malachi. This makes the suggestion that Luke used Matthew an irresistible one, for otherwise Luke would coincidentally have produced a citation which Matthew also records. That would stretch credulity to breaking point.

The Griesbach Hypothesis

Sanders and Davies also include a discussion of the Griesbach hypothesis (the view that Mark is a redaction of Matthew and Luke).[16] They see it as 'mechanically feasible', but ask why Mark should have written a Gospel that contains so many omissions of consequence which are balanced by merely trivial insertions. The lack of a convincing reason for the writing of Mark is the Achilles heel of the Griesbach hypothesis. This argument represents a substantial objection to the theory that Mark is the third Gospel in the chronological sequence. And the observation that Mark is more often the middle term than Matthew tends to support the theory of Marcan priority, with the proviso noted here again that there may have been more than one edition of Mark.

I conclude therefore that Mark was the first Gospel to be written, that Matthew came second and used Mark and his own special material, and that Luke came third in the canonical sequence. Luke's sources were (or included) Mark and Matthew; I am far from convinced that it is necessary to posit the hypothetical Q; but I emphasize that we do not know for sure that our version of Luke is the original one. Such uncertainty continues to make all study of Gospel relations a troublesome area.

The Synoptics: When and Where?

All of this raises the questions of when and where the Synoptic Gospels were written.

The first Gospel to be written, on the dominant hypothesis, was Mark (or a version of Mark).[17] The major question to address is whether Mark was written before the Roman destruction of Jerusalem in 70 CE. It is interesting to observe how scholarship moves in a pendulum cycle. Before 1975, there was a perceptible tendency to set the Gospel around the year 70 CE.[18] In 1975, in his *Redating the New Testament*, John Robinson argued for an earlier date. This book proved quite influential, with conservative scholars fascinated by the opinions of a radical. The difficulties of Robinson's approach to the New Testament in general are exposed in John Sturdy's posthumously published book where some of the flaws in his arguments are exposed, together with a massive compendium of nineteenth-century German New Testament scholarship.[19]

Thirty years on, most scholars posit a date between 65 and 75 CE, the influential commentary of Hooker arguing that Mark 13 reflects the trauma of those who had witnessed the temple's destruction. Clement of Alexandria (according to Eusebius, *Hist. Eccl.* 2.15.1f.), supported by the anti-Marcionite Prologue and some evidence in Irenaeus (*Adv. Haer.* 3.1.1ff.), states that Mark was written in Rome.[20] This conclusion, however, is based on the link between Mark and Peter; and, despite the evidence of *Asc. Isa.* 4.3, Peter's presence in Rome has been questioned in at least some recent scholarship.[21] It is probably safe to say that Mark was written somewhere in the Roman empire; but rather less safe to narrow this down to a particular locality.

One of the most interesting aspects of Marcan studies in the present decade has been the growth of narrative approaches to the Gospel. I have listed some examples in the notes. If Mark is the earliest Gospel, as it almost certainly is, its author is to be credited with having devised the Gospel genre, despite drawing on earlier precedents. His narrative has a stark simplicity; and, even if truncated, a really brilliant ending with an unresolved caesura (16.8). We should neither under-estimate Mark's narrative genius nor ignore the sources which he used.

Matthew and Luke

On my view, Matthew used Mark and must therefore have been written later than Mark.[22] If Mark was written c.70 CE, a date for Matthew c.80 CE will not be too wide of the mark. Matthew has a strong Jewish influence,[23] and was probably written in Syria.

It is difficult to characterize a Gospel in a single paragraph. A recent study of Matthew's reworking of Mark, however, examines the critical features of this revision, which is a manifest feature of the text.[24] There are two major ways in which this is done. First of all, Matthew reorganizes Mark's narrative of Jesus into 'poly-structures', based around symbolic use of the numerals two, three, five, seven and twelve. Matthew then embeds Old Testament scripture within the reconstructed narrative. The result is a more obviously nuanced and 'Jewish' portrait of Jesus as Messiah, ending with his post-resurrectional depiction as the heavenly Lord (Mt. 28.18) in a way that is absent from Mark. Matthew's Jewishness is thus a literary phenomenon as well as an indication of the work's outlook and probable provenance.

If Luke used Mark *and* Matthew, as seems likely, a date c.90 CE is in order. Luke's Gospel was written outside Palestine, but it is difficult to say precisely where. The dominant hypothesis that the author of Luke also wrote the Acts of the Apostles receives vigorous criticism from John Sturdy, but continues to be maintained by the majority of scholars.[25]

Luke is in many ways the most charming of the Gospels.[26] What emerges is a text whose author writes after the model of Mark and with a knowledge of Matthew, but who at points adapts his sources and even tries to correct what he regarded as unhelpful tendencies in the earlier literature (Matthew especially). Luke emphasizes the present reality of Christian salvation, and tries to make the link between faith and ethics which we have seen was an important feature of second-generation Christianity. If indeed the author also wrote the Acts of the Apostles, Luke significantly modifies the status of the Gospel genre by adding a second volume to it.

John's Gospel

This brings us to John's Gospel.[27] John was described as a 'spiritual' Gospel by Clement of Alexandria.[28] This reflects John's interest in the heavenly world, and his insistence that the Son of Man descended from heaven to be identified with the earthly Jesus (3.13). Such a view represents a stage of belief where Jesus had been fully identified with the heavenly Christ. John is a product of the end of the first century CE, seventy years after the resurrection and forty years after Paul's last letter. It thus looks back on two if not three generations of Christian experience. It is impossible to accept that the process of change and development has not done something to shape John's theological outlook.

The date of John is an important question because on it rests the argument of his probable knowledge of the Synoptists.[29] There is a little evidence that Ignatius knew John, although this argument has been disputed by some scholars. The discovery of the papyrus P52, which comes from the early second century CE, dates John to the first century, while John is known also to the author of the fragment of the 'Unknown Gospel' which is a close contemporary of P52. How much earlier than 100 CE is difficult, if not impossible, to say. The general tenor of the Gospel suggests that it comes from the last decade of the first century and not earlier than that. While there is a little early evidence that the Gospel was written in Ephesus, it seems more likely that John was written in Syria, not least because of the connection in thought with the *Odes of Solomon*.[30]

This makes it likely that some if not all of the Synoptic Gospels were known to the author, who is often thought to have had a particular knowledge of Luke. The crucial point to make is that, if John did know Mark, he has made a completely different use of Mark than either Matthew or Luke. Where Matthew, and especially Luke, generally follow Mark's narrative order, John produces a different order of events in which Jesus' three journeys to Jerusalem are made the overarching structure. This makes the issue of which sources John used difficult to resolve with certainty.

John thus provides a Gospel, but a different kind of Gospel from the Synoptic Gospels. At places, it seems obvious that he reflects a later view: notably, perhaps, in matters of Christology. In other places, however, John preserves what appears to be authentic historical recollection, particularly when he appears to be using a source. The most obvious example of this is Jn 18.31, where the Jews tell Pilate they no longer have the legal right to carry out capital sentences.

This last piece of evidence serves as a sobering reminder of our nature of Gospel tradition. Just because a text is later than others does not mean that it is necessarily less reliable; merely that there is a greater distance between event and reporting, which draws attention to the need to ask questions about sources, and to evaluate the evidence of the Gospels across the board, not monolithically. This, of course, is what is true in a different context also about the development of Christology. The identification of Jesus with the heavenly Christ before his ministry emerged at an early date, to judge from the evidence of Phil. 2.6-11. In commending the study of the Gospels to my reader, therefore, I call for both care and open-mindedness in interpretation, together with a healthy pessimism about the possibility of solving the question of Gospel inter-relationships with absolute satisfaction.

NOTES

Chapter 1

1. See also Christopher Rowland, *Christian Origins* (London, [2]2002); George W.E. Nickelsburg, *Ancient Judaism and Christian Origins: Diversity, Continuity, and Transformation* (Minneapolis, 2003); Ron Cameron and Merill P. Miller (eds), *Redescribing Christian Origins* (Atlanta, 2004); and Robert A. Horsley (ed.), *Christian Origins*, vol. i (PHC, 1; Minneapolis, 2005). Earlier studies include Elizabeth Schüssler Fiorenza, *In Memory of Her: A Feminist Theological Reconstruction of Christian Origins* (London, 1983); Howard Clark Kee, *Christian Origins in Sociological Perspective* (London, 1980); Floyd V. Filson, *A New Testament History* (London, 1965); F.F. Bruce, *New Testament History* (London, 1969); and Henry Chadwick, *The Early Church* (reprinted Harmondsworth, 1990).
2. *Paulus und Jesus: Eine Untersuchung zur Präzisierung der Frage dem Ursprung der Christologie* (Tübingen, 1967). By the same author see also *God as the Mystery of the World: On the Foundation of the Theology of the Crucified One in the Dispute between Atheism and Theism* (ET Grand Rapids, 1983).
3. See E.P. Sanders *et al.* (eds), *Jewish and Christian Self-Definition* (3 vols.; London, 1980–2).
4. See Lewis Ayres and Gareth Jones, *Christian Origins: Theology, Rhetoric and Community* (London, 1998).
5. Hence the titles of two books on the subject: Alan F. Segal, *The Other Judaisms of Late Antiquity* (BJS, 127; Atlanta, 1987); and J. Neusner, W. Scott Green and E.S. Frerichs (eds), *Judaisms and Their Messiahs at the Turn of the Christian Era* (Cambridge, 1987). The use of the plural 'Judaisms' in these books is striking.

Chapter 2

1. See O. Eissfeldt, *The Old Testament: An Introduction* (ET Oxford, 1965); N.K. Gottwald, *The Hebrew Bible: A Socio-literary Introduction* (Philadelphia, 1985); J. Alberto Soggin, *Introduction to the Old Testament: From its Origins to the Closing of the Alexandrian Canon* (ET London, 1989); and Barry L. Bandstra, *Reading the Old Testament: An Introduction to the Hebrew Bible* (Belmont, 1995).
2. On the historical reasons for this reorganization see F.F. Bruce, *The Canon of Scripture* (Downers Grove, 1988), pp. 68–114; and the various essays in Lee Martin Macdonald and James A. Sanders, *The Canon Debate: On the Origins and Formation of the Bible* (Peabody, 2002). A readable guide is John W. Rogerson, *An Introduction to the Bible* (London, 1999).
3. See e.g. Raymond B. Dillard and Tremper Longman III, *An Introduction to the Old Testament* (Leicester, 1995), p. 47: 'In the final analysis, it is possible to affirm the substantial Mosaic authorship of the Pentateuch in line with the occasional internal evidence and the strong external testimony, while allowing for earlier sources as well as later glosses and elaboration.'

4. Celebrated studies of Moses include H. Gressmann, *Moses und seine Zeit* (Göttingen, 1913); S. Freud, *Moses and Monotheism* (ET London, 1939); M. Buber, *Moses: The Revelation and the Covenant* (London, 1940); and E. Auerbach, *Moses* (ET Detroit, 1975).
5. E.g. by J. van Seters, *Encyclopaedia of Religion*, vol. x, p. 116.
6. For a controversial view of the Torah's origin, see James W. Watts (ed.), *Persia and Torah: The Theory of an Imperial Authorization of the Pentateuch* (SBLSS, 17; Atlanta, 2001).
7. See Emil Schürer, revised and edited by Geza Vermes, Fergus Millar and Matthew Black, *The History of the Jewish People in the Age of Jesus Christ*, vol. ii (Edinburgh, 1979), p. 315. On the Priestly Code, see Baruch J. Schwartz, trans. Pamela Barmesh, *Holiness Legislation: Studies in the Priestly Code* (ET Jerusalem, 1999).
8. *Jub.* 3.10; 4.5 and indeed *passim*. See Martha Himmelfarb, 'Torah, testimony and heavenly tablets: the claim to authority of the Book of Jubilees', in B. Wright (ed.), *A Multiform Heritage: Studies on Early Judaism and Christianity in Honor of Robert A. Kraft* (SPHS, 24; Atlanta, 1999), pp. 19–29.
9. See R. Rendtorff and R.A. Kugler (eds), *The Book of Leviticus: Composition and Reception* (Leiden, 2003).
10. On Deuteronomy see Gary N. Knoppers and J. Gordon McConville, *Reconsidering Israel and Judah: Recent Studies on the Deuteronomistic History* (SBTS, 8; Winona Lake, 2000).
11. See the histories of research provided by E.J. Young, *An Introduction to the Old Testament* (London, 1949), pp. 109–53; and Antony F. Campbell and Mark A. O'Brien, *Sources of the Pentateuch* (Minneapolis, 1993), pp. 1–20; *idem, Rethinking the Pentateuch: Prolegomena to the Theology of Ancient Israel* (Louisville, 2005).
12. Johann Gottfried Eichhorn, *Einleitung in das Alte Testament* (Leipzig, 1780–3).
13. Karl David Ilgen, *Die Urkunden des jerusalemischen Tempelarchivs in ihrer Urgestalt* (Halle, 1798).
14. Wilhelm Martin Lebrecht de Wette, *Beiträge zur Einleitung in das Alte Testament* (Halle, 1806–7). On this man see John W. Rogerson, *W M L de Wette: Founder of Modern Biblical Criticism: An Intellectual Biography* (Sheffield, 1992).
15. Hermann Hupfeld, *Die Quellen der Genesis und die Art ihrer Zusammensetzung* (Berlin, 1853).
16. Karl Heinrich Graf, *Die geschichtlichen Bücher des Alten Testaments. Zwei historisch-kritischen Untersuchungen* (Leipzig, 1866).
17. Abraham Kuenen, *De Godsdienst van Israel* (1869–70).
18. See e.g. Duane A. Garrett, *Rethinking Genesis: The Sources and Authorship of the First Book of the Pentateuch* (Grand Rapids, 1991); and R.N. Whybray, *Introduction to the Pentateuch* (Grand Rapids, 1995).
19. The classic studies are Gerhard von Rad, *The Message of the Prophets* (ET London, 1968); and J. Lindblom, *Prophecy in Ancient Israel* (Oxford, 1962). See also Joseph Blenkinsopp, *A History of Prophecy in Israel from the Settlement in the Land to the Hellenistic Period* (London, 1984). An interesting comparative study is M. Nissinen (ed.), *Prophecy in its Ancient Near Eastern Context: Mesopotamian, Biblical, and Ancient Perspectives* (SBLSS, 13; Atlanta, 2000).

20. See D.N. Premnath, *Eighth Century Prophets: A Social Analysis* (St Louis, 2003).

21. Lindblom, however, makes much of the phenomenon of prophetic ecstasy; see his *Prophecy*, ch. 3. On the latter see Frederick H. Cryer, *Divination in Ancient Israel and its Near Eastern Environment: A Socio-historical Investigation* (JSOTSup, 142; Sheffield, 1994).

22. See Schürer, *History of the Jewish People*, vol. ii, pp. 316–21; Thomas Henshaw, *The Writings: The Third Division of the Old Testament Canon* (London, 1963); and S.Z. Leiman, *The Canonization of Hebrew Scriptures: The Talmudic and Midrashic Evidence* (New Haven, 1991).

23. See Julio C. Trebolle Barrera, 'The origins of a tripartite Old Testament canon', in Macdonald and Sanders (eds), *Canon Debate*, pp. 128–45. In the same volume see also Jack N. Lightstone, 'The Rabbis' Bible: The canon of the Hebrew Bible and the Early Rabbinic Guild', pp. 163–85. All references to Josephus in this book are cited according to The Loeb Classical Library division of material.

24. See Jack P. Lewis, 'Jamnia revisited', in Macdonald and Sanders (eds), *Canon Debate*, pp. 142–62.

25. A. Samely, *Rabbinic Interpretation of Scripture in the Mishnah* (Oxford, 2002).

26. The critical edition is *Septuaginta, Vetus Testamentum Graecum* (Göttingen, 1931–); use also A. Rahlfs, *Septuaginta, id est Vetus Testamentum Graece iuxta LXX interpretes* (Stuttgart, 1935). See S. Jellicoe, *The Septuagint and Modern Study* (Oxford, 1968); E. Tov, *The Text-Critical Use of the Septuagint in Biblical Research* (JBS, 3; Jerusalem, 1981); and George J. Brooke and Barnabas Lindars, *Septuagint, Scrolls and Cognate Writings* (Atlanta, 1992). An important study is Michael A. Knibb (ed.), *The Septuagint and Messianism* (Leuven, 2006).

27. See Jellicoe, *Septuagint*, pp. 29–58; and Schürer, revised and edited by Eliza Vermes. *History of the Jewish People*, vol. iii.1 (Edinburgh, 1985), pp. 677–87.

28. See M. Hengel, *The Septuagint as Christian Scripture* (ET Edinburgh, 2002); and R. Timothy McLay, *The Use of the Septuagint in New Testament Research* (Grand Rapids and Cambridge, 2003). All references to Philo are cited according to The Loeb Classical Library division of material.

29. For an introduction see E.J. Goodspeed, *The Story of the Apocrypha* (Chicago, 1939); B.M. Metzger, *An Introduction to the Apocrypha* (New York, 1957); G.W.E. Nickelsburg, *Jewish Literature between the Bible and the Mishnah* (Philadelphia, 1981); H.F.D. Sparks (ed.), *The Apocryphal Old Testament* (Oxford, 1984); B.M. Metzger (ed.), *The Oxford Annotated Apocrypha: Expanded Edition* (New York, 1991); Schürer, *History of the Jewish People*, vol. iii, (Edinburgh, 1985, 1987), pp. 177–341, 470–808; M.E. Stone (ed.), *Jewish Writings of the Second Temple Period* (CRINT, 2.2; Assen and Philadelphia, 1984); Daniel J. Harrington, *Invitation to the Apocrypha* (Grand Rapids, 1999); David A. De Silva, *Introducing the Apocrypha: Message, Context, and Significance* (Grand Rapids, 2002); and O. Kaiser, *The Old Testament Apocrypha: An Introduction* (Peabody, 2004).

30. See J.J. Collins, *Daniel, First Maccabees, Second Maccabees* (Wilmingon, 1981); R. Doran, *Temple Propaganda: The Purpose of 2 Maccabees* (CBQMS, 12; Washington DC, 1981); and John R. Bartlett, *First Maccabees* (GAP; Sheffield, 1998).

31. I shall discuss the Antiochian crisis in Chapter 3.
32. See Michael E. Stone, *Fourth Ezra* (Hermeneia; Minneapolis and London, 1992); Bruce W. Longenecker, *2 Esdras* (GAP; Sheffield, 1995); and *idem*, 'Looking at 4 Ezra: a consideration of its social setting and function', *JSJ* 28 (1997), pp. 271–93.
33. Josephus is most conveniently accessible with English translation in the Loeb Classical Library series. See also Shaye J.D. Cohen, *Josephus in Galilee and Rome: His Vita and Development as a Historian* (Leiden, 1979); Tessa Rajak, *Josephus: The Historian and His Society* (Philadelphia, 1983); Steve Mason, *Josephus and the New Testament* (Peabody, 1992); Steve Mason (ed.), *Understanding Josephus: Seven Perspectives* (Sheffield, 1998); Joseph Sievers and Gaia Lembi (eds), *Josephus and Jewish History in Flavian Rome and Beyond* (JSJSup, 104; Leiden, 2005); Shaye D. Cohen and Joshua J. Schwartz (eds), *Studies in Josephus and the Varieties of Ancient Judaism* (AGJU, 67; Leiden, 2007); and Zuleika Rodgers (ed.), *Making History: Josephus and Historical Method* (JSJSup, 110; Leiden, 2007).
34. This aspect of Josephus is surveyed by Steve Mason, *Flavius Josephus on the Pharisees: A Composition-Critical Study* (Leiden, 1991).
35. See F. Parente and J. Sievers (eds), *Josephus and the History of the Graeco-Roman Period: Essays in Memory of Morton Smith* (SPB, 41; Leiden, 1994); and Eric D. Huntsman, 'The reliability of Josephus: can he be trusted?', in J.F. Hall and J. Welch (eds), *Masada and the World of the New Testament* (Provo, 1997), pp. 392–402.
36. See James E. Bawley, 'Josephus's use of Greek sources for biblical history', in John C. Reeves and John Kampen (eds), *Pursuing the Text: Studies in Honor of Ben Zion Wacholder on the Occasion of his 70th Birthday* (JSOTSup, 184; Sheffield, 1994), pp. 202–15.
37. See Philip A. Stadter (ed.), *The Speeches in Thucydides: A Collection of Original Studies with a Bibliography* (Chapel Hill, 1973).
38. Like Josephus, Philo is available with English translation in the Loeb Classical Library series. See E.R. Goodenough, *An Introduction to Philo Judaeus* (Oxford, 1940); H.A. Wolfson, *Philo: Foundations of Religious Philosophy in Judaism, Christianity, and Islam* (Cambridge MA, 1947); S. Sandmel, *Philo of Alexandria: An Introduction* (New York, 1979); W. Haase (ed.), *Aufstieg und Niedergang der römischen Welt*, 2.21.1 (Berlin and New York, 1984); M. Niehoff, *Philo on Jewish Identity and Culture* (TSAJ, 86, Tübingen, 2001); Roland Deines and Karl-Wilhelm Niebuhr (eds); *Philo und das Neue Testament: wechselseitzige Wahrnehmungen* (WUNT, 172; Tübingen, 2004); and Kenneth Schenlk, *A Brief Guide to Philo* (Louisville, 2005).
39. See P. Borgen, 'Philo of Alexandria', in Stone (ed.), *Jewish Writings*, pp. 233–82; *idem*, *Philo of Alexandria: An Exegete for His Time* (Leiden, 1997); and *idem*, 'Philo of Alexandria as exegete', in Alan J. Hauser and Duane F. Watson (eds), *A History of Biblical Interpretation*, vol. i: *The Ancient Period* (Grand Rapids and Cambridge, 2003), pp. 114–43.
40. See Carsten Colpe, 'Von der Logoslehre des Philon zu der des Clemens von Alexandrien', in A. Ritter (ed.), *Kerygma und Logos* (Göttingen, 1979), pp. 89–107.
41. See Ellen Birnbaum, 'The place of Judaism in Philo's thought: Israel, Jews,

and proselytes', in E. Lovering (ed.), *Society of Biblical Literature: 1993 Seminar Papers* (Atlanta, 1993), pp. 54–69.

42. See James H. Charlesworth (ed.), *The Old Testament Pseudepigrapha* (2 vols.; New York and London, 1983–5); A.-M. Denis, *Introduction aux pseudépigraphes grecs d'Ancien Testament* (SVTP, 1; Leiden, 1970); Nickelsburg, *Jewish Literature*; D.S. Russell, *The Pseudepigrapha* (Philadelphia, 1987); Lester L. Grabbe and Robert D. Haak (eds), *Knowing the End from the Beginning: The Prophetic, the Apocalyptic, and their Relationships* (JSPSup, 46; London, 2003); and James R. Davila, *The Provenance of the Pseudepigrapha: Jewish, Christian, or Other?* (Leiden, 2005).

43. See Paul D. Hanson, *The Dawn of Apocalyptic* (Philadelphia, 1975); Christopher Rowland, *The Open Heaven* (London, 1982); David Hellholm (ed.), *Apocalypticism in the Mediterranean World and the Near East* (Tübingen, 1983); John J. Collins and James H. Charlesworth (eds), *Mysteries and Revelations: Apocalyptic Studies since the Uppsala Colloquium* (JSPSup, 9; Sheffield, 1991); John J. Collins, *The Apocalyptic Imagination* (Grand Rapids, ²1998); and Jonathan Knight, *Apocalypticism in Early Christianity and its Jewish Environment* (forthcoming).

44. *IDBSup* (1976), p. 30.

45. *ABD*, vol. i, p. 283.

46. The classic study is Hanson, *Dawn of Apocalyptic*. See also the remarks of J.J. Collins, 'Apocalyptic eschatology as the transcendence of death', *CBQ* 36 (1974), pp. 21–43.

47. *IDBSup* (1976), p. 30.

48. 'Apocalypse: morphology of a genre', *Semeia* 14 (1979), p. 22.

49. 'Christian writers on Judaism', *HTR* 14 (1921), pp. 197–254; and 'Intermediaries in Jewish theology', *HTR* 15 (1922), pp. 41–79.

50. *Open Heaven*. See also Christopher Rowland and John Barton (eds), *Apocalyptic in History and Tradition* (JSPSup, 43; London, 2002); and Stephen L. Cook, *The Apocalyptic Literature* (Nashville, 2003).

51. On this aspect of apocalypticism see I. Gruenwald, *Apocalyptic and Merkabah Mysticism* (AGJU, 14; Leiden, 1980); and G. Scholem, *Major Trends in Jewish Mysticism* (London, 1955).

52. See John J. Collins, 'Testaments', in Stone (ed.), *Jewish Writings*, pp. 325–56.

53. The scrolls are most easily accessible in the translation by Geza Vermes, *The Complete Dead Sea Scrolls in English* (London, 1998). For a readable introduction to the Qumran community see James Vanderkam, *The Dead Sea Scrolls Today* (Grand Rapids, 1994); and also Hartmut Stegemann, *The Library of Qumran: On the Essenes, Qumran, John the Baptist, and Jesus* (Grand Rapids, 1998). See also Laurence Schiffman, *Reclaiming the Dead Sea Scrolls: The History of Judaism, the Background of Christianity and the Lost Library of Qumran* (Philadelphia, 1994); Geza Vermes, *The Dead Sea Scrolls: Qumran in Perspective* (London, ³1994); Robert A. Kugler and Eileen M. Schuller (eds), *The Dead Sea Scrolls at Fifty: Proceedings of the 1997 Society of Biblical Literature Qumran Meetings* (Atlanta, 1999); James R. Davila (ed.), *The Dead Sea Scrolls as Background to PostBiblical Judaism and Early Christianity: Papers from an International Conference at St. Andrews in 2001* (Leiden, 2001); and Y. Hirschfeld, *Qumran in Context* (Peabody, 2004).

54. See Schürer, *History of the Jewish People*, vol. iii.1, pp. 380–469.

55. See George J. Brooke, *Exegesis at Qumran: 4QFlorilegium in its Jewish Context* (JSOTSup, 29; Sheffield, 1985); Frederick H. Cryer and Thomas L. Thompson (eds), *Qumran between the Old and the New Testaments* (JSOT-Sup, 290; Sheffield, 1998); Moshe J. Bernstein, 'The contribution of the Qumran discoveries to the history of early biblical interpretation', in H. Najman and Judith H. Newman (eds), *Idea of Biblical Interpretation: Essays in Honour of James L. Kugel* (Leiden, 2004), pp. 215–38; Jonathan G. Campbell, William J. Lyons and Lloyd K. Pietersen (eds), *New Directions in Qumran Studies: Proceedings of the Bristol Colloquium on the Dead Sea Scrolls, 8–10 September 2003* (LSTS, 52; London, 2005); Katharina Galor, Jean-Baptiste Humbert and Jürgen Zangenberg (eds), *Qumran, the Site of the Dead Sea Scrolls: Archaeological Interpretation and Debates: Proceedings of a Conference held at Brown University, November 17–19, 2002* (STDJ, 57; Leiden, 2006); and J.J. Collins and Craig A. Evans (eds), *Christian Beginnings and the Dead Sea Scrolls* (Grand Rapids, 2006). Two further contributions are Eileen M. Schuller, *The Dead Sea Scrolls: What Have We Learned?* (London, 2006); and Judith Anne Brown, *John Marco Allegro: The Maverick of the Dead Sea Scrolls* (Grand Rapids, 2005).

56. See the two essays by Joseph A. Fitzmyer, 'The Dead Sea scrolls and Christian origins: general methodological considerations', and 'The Dead Sea scrolls and early Christianity', in his *The Dead Sea Scrolls and Christian Origins* (2 vols.; Grand Rapids and Cambridge, 2000); and cf. Stegemann, *Library*, pp. 256–7: 'With the Essenes Jesus shared a high estimation of the Torah and the Prophets. But he took a totally different stance towards these writings than the Essenes did at the time. Especially in the interpretation of the Torah, he followed paths that neither the Essenes nor any other Jews before him had done.'

57. On the background to this see Simon Schwarzfuchs, *A Concise History of the Rabbinate* (Oxford and Cambridge, 1993); Martin S. Jaffee, *Torah in the Mouth: Writing and Oral Tradition in Palestinian Judaism, 200 BCE–400 CE* (Oxford, 2001); M. Fishbane, *Biblical Myth and Rabbinic Mythmaking* (Oxford, 2003); Jacob Neusner, *Rabbinic Literature: An Essential Guide* (Nashville, 2005); Carol Bakhos (ed.), *Current Trends in the Study of Midrash* (JSJSup, 106; Leiden, 2006); *idem* (ed.), *Ancient Judaism in its Hellenistic Context* (JSJSup, 95; Leiden, 2005).

58. The Mishnah is translated by H. Danby, *The Mishnah* (Oxford, 1933). See also J. Neusner, *The Modern Study of the Mishnah* (Leiden, 1963); *idem*, *Judaism: The Evidence of the Mishnah* (Chicago and London, 1981); and H.L. Strack and G. Stemberger, translated and revised by Markus Bockmuehl, *Introduction to the Talmud and Midrash* (Minneapolis, 1992).

59. See his detailed outworking of this theory in the two books *Jewish Law from Jesus to the Mishnah: Five Studies* (London and Philadelphia, 1990); and *Judaism: Practice and Belief 63 BCE–66 CE* (London and Philadelphia, 1992).

60. See Alexander Samely, *Rabbinic Interpretation of Scripture in the Mishnah* (Oxford, 2002).

61. See Abraham Goldberg, 'The Tosefta: companion to the Mishnah', in Shemuel Safrai (ed.), *The Literature of the Sages* (Assen and Philadelphia, 1987), pt. I, pp. 283–302; Jack Yaakov Elman, *Authority and Tradition: Toseftan Baraitot in Talmudic Babylonia* (New York, 1994); Harry Fox and

Tirzah Meachen (eds), *Introducing Tosefta: Textual, Intratextual and Intertextual Studies* (New York, 1999); and Jacob Neusner (trans.) *The Tosefta, Translated from the Hebrew, with an Introduction* (Peabody, 2002).

62. Translation of *The Babylonian Talmud* by I. Epstein (London, 1947); French translation by M. Schwab of *Le Talmud de Jérusalem* (Paris, 1960). Critical study of this material includes Jacob Neusner, *The Formation of the Babylonian Talmud* (Leiden, 1970); Abraham Goldberg, 'The Babylonian Talmud' in Safrai (ed.), *Literature*, pt. I, pp. 325–45; D. Goodblatt, 'The Babylonian Talmud' in Jacob Neusner (ed.), *The Study of Ancient Judaism* (New York, 1981), vol. ii, pp. 120–38; Strack and Stemberger, rev. Bockmuehl, *Introduction*; Jeffrey L. Rubenstein, *The Culture of the Babylonian Talmud* (Baltimore, 2003); and *idem* (ed.), *Creation and Composition: The Contribution of the Bavli Redactors (Stammain) to the Aggada* (TSAJ, 114; Tübingen, 2005).

63. See P.S. Alexander, 'Jewish Aramaic translations of Hebrew scriptures', in M.J. Mulder (ed.), *Mikra: Text, Translation, Reading and Interpretation of the Hebrew Bible in Ancient Judaism and Early Christianity* (CRINT, 2.1; Assen and Philadelphia, 1988), pp. 217–53; Derek Robert George Beattie and M.J. McNamara (eds), *The Aramaic Bible: Targums in Their Historical Context* (JSOTSup, 166; Sheffield, 1994); and Paul V.M. Flesher (ed.), *Targum and Scripture: Studies in Aramaic Translations and Interpretation in Memory of Ernest G. Clarke* (Leiden, 2002).

64. This is translated from the Coptic and introduced in James M. Robinson (ed.), *The Nag Hammadi Library in English* (Leiden, [3]1988). The literature was discovered in Upper Egypt in 1945. On it, see Karen L. King, *What is Gnosticism?* (Cambridge MA, 2003).

65. See Birger A. Pearson, 'The problem of "Jewish Gnostic" literature', in C. Hedrick and R. Hodgson (eds), *Nag Hammadi, Gnosticism, and Early Christianity* (Peabody, 1986), pp. 15–35; and Attilio Mastrocinque, *From Jewish Magic to Gnosticism* (Tübingen, 2005).

66. See Gershom Scholem, *Jewish Gnosticism, Merkabah Mysticism and Talmudic Tradition* (New York, 1965); and Ithamar Gruenwald, *From Apocalypticism to Gnosticism: Studies in Apocalypticism, Merkavah Mysticism and Gnosticism* (BEATAJ, 14; Frankfurt, 1988).

Chapter 3

1. There are many standard treatments of this issue. See M. Noth, *The History of Israel* (ET London, [2]1961); John Bright, *A History of Israel* (London, [3]1981); J.M. Miller and J.H. Hayes, *A History of Ancient Israel and Judah* (London, 1986); J. Alberto Soggin, *An Introduction to the History of Israel and Judah* (ET London, [2]1993); H. Jagersma, *A History of Israel from Alexander the Great to Bar Kochba* (London, 1994); and Walter C. Kaiser, *A History of Israel: From the Bronze Age through the Jewish Wars* (Nashville, 1998). On the subject of Israelite historiography see Philip R. Davies, *In Search of Ancient Israel* (JSOTSup, 148; Sheffield, 1992); Mark Zvi Brettler, *The Creation of History in Ancient Israel* (London, 1995); and Keith W. Whitelam, *The Invention of Ancient Israel: The Silencing of Palestinian History* (London, 1996). See also

Robert D. Miller, *Chieftains of the Highland Clans: A History of Israel in the 12th and 11th Centuries BC* (Grand Rapids, 2005).

2. On whom see James Barr, 'Why the world was created in 4004 BC; Archbishop Ussher and biblical chronology', *BJRL* 67 (1984–5), pp. 575–608; and also Saul Leeman, 'Was Bishop Ussher's chronology influenced by a midrash?', *JBQ* 31 (2003), pp. 195–6.

3. There is an excellent study of this topic by Karl Robert Gnuse, *No Other Gods: Emergent Monotheism in Israel* (JSOTSup, 241; Sheffield, 1997), ch. 1.

4. See Robert D. Miller, 'Identifying earliest Israel', *BASOR* 333 (2004), pp. 55–68.

5. Neil Asher Silberman, 'Who were the Israelites?', *Archaeology* 45.2 (1992), pp. 22–30. Compare Albert Schweitzer's view of historical Jesus research. See Chapter 11, note 4.

6. *Kleine Schriften zur Geschichte des Volkes Israels* (Munich, 1953), vol. i, pp. 126–92.

7. Noth, *History*, pp. 53–84; Soggin, *Joshua* (ET Philadelphia, 1972), p. 4 and elsewhere; Aharoni, 'Nothing early and nothing late: re-writing Israel's conquest', *BA* 39 (1976), pp. 55–76.

8. Albright, *The Biblical Period from Abraham to Ezra* (New York, 1963), pp. 24–34; Bright, in the second edition of his *History* (Philadelphia, 1972), pp. 127–30; and Yadin, 'Is the biblical conquest of Canaan historically reliable?', *BAR* 8.2 (1982), pp. 16–23.

9. Mendenhall, *The Tenth Generation; the Origins of the Biblical Tradition* (Baltimore, 1973); Gottwald, *The Tribes of Yahweh: A Sociology of the Religion of Liberated Israel 1250–1050 BCE* (Maryknoll, 1979).

10. See N.P. Lemche, *Early Israel: Anthropological and Historical Studies on the Israelite Society before the Monarchy* (VTSup, 37; Leiden, 1985), pp. 66–76; and I. Finkelstein, *The Archaeology of the Israelite Settlement* (Jerusalem, 1988), p. 304.

11. Silbermann, 'Who were the Israelites?'; and M. Chaney, 'Ancient Palestinian Peasant Movements and the Formation of Premonarchic Israel', in D. Freedman and D. Graf (eds), *Palestine in Transition: The Emergence of Ancient Israel* (SWBA, 2; Sheffield, 1983), pp. 39–90.

12. See G. Ramsey, *The Quest for the Historical Israel* (Atlanta, 1981), pp. 69–73.

13. See e.g. Noth, *History*, pp. 262–82; Gottwald, *Tribes*, pp. 192–203; and Roland de Vaux, 'On the right and wrong uses of archaeology', in J. Sanders (ed.), *Near Eastern Archaeology in the Twentieth Century: Essays in Honor of Nelson Glueck* (New York, 1970), pp. 64–80.

14. G. Ahlström, *Who were the Israelites?* (Winona Lake, 1986), pp. 1–118.

15. Ramsey, *Quest*, pp. 93–8; and Keith Whitelam, *The Emergence of Early Israel in Historical Perspective* (SWBA, 5; Sheffield, 1987), pp. 49–80.

16. This is described by Gnuse, *No Other Gods*, pp. 32–61.

17. Callaway, 'A new perspective on the hill country settlement of Canaan in Iron Age I', in J.N. Tubb (ed.), *Palestine in the Bronze and Iron Ages: Papers in Honour of Olga Tufnell* (London, 1985), pp. 31–49; Fritz, 'Conquest or settlement? The Early Iron Age in Palestine', *BA* 50 (1987), pp. 84–100; Finkelstein, *The Archaeology of the Israelite Settlement* (Jerusalem, 1988).

18. 'Village subsistence at Ai and Raddana in Iron Age I', in H. Thompson

(ed.), *The Answers Lie Below: Essays in Honor of Lawrence Edmund Toombs* (Lanham, 1984), pp. 51–66.

19. See his further article, 'The Israelite "Conquest" in light of recent excavations at Khirbet el-Mishnah', *BASOR* 241 (1981), pp. 61–73; and Mordechai Haiman, 'Negev', in Suzanne Richard (ed.), *Near Eastern Archaeology: A Reader* (Winona Lake, 2003).

20. See also Ram Gophna and Dan Grazil, 'The southern frontier of Canaan during the early Bronze Age III. Some neglected evidence', in Aren M. Maeir and Pierre de Miroschedji (eds), *'I Will Speak the Riddles of Ancient Times'*, vols. i and ii: *Archaeological and Historical Studies in Honor of Amihai Mazar on the Occasion of his Sixtieth Birthday* (Winona Lake, 2006), pp. 33–38.

21. On which see Mark S. Smith, *The Origins of Biblical Monotheism: Israel's Polytheistic Background and the Ugaritic Texts* (Oxford, 2001); and Nathan Macdonald, *Deuteronomy and the Meaning of Monotheism* (FAT, 12; Tübingen, 2003).

22. See A. Alt, 'The formation of the Israelite state in Palestine', in his *Essays in Old Testament History and Religion* (Oxford, 1966), pp. 171–237; and R.B. Coote and K.W. Whitelam, 'The emergence of Israel: social transformation and state formation following the decline in Late Bronze Age trade', *Semeia* 37 (1986), pp. 107–47.

23. See Andrew G. Vaughn and Ann E. Killebrew (eds), *Jerusalem in Bible and Archaeology* (Atlanta, 2003); John Day (ed.), *In Search of Pre-exilic Israel: Proceedings of the Oxford Old Testament Seminar* (London, 2004); Simcha Shalom Brooks, *Saul and the Monarchy: A New Look* (SOTSMS; Aldershot, 2005); and Carl S. Ehrlich and Marsha White (eds), *Saul in Story and Tradition* (FAT, 47; Tübingen, 2006).

24. On this period see Sigfried H. Horn, 'The divided monarchy: the kingdoms of Judah and Israel', in H. Shanks (ed.), *Ancient Israel: A Short History from Abraham to the Roman destruction of the Temple* (Washington DC, 1989), pp. 109–49; and Wayne A. Brindle, 'The causes of the division of Israel's kingdom', *Bibliotheca Sacra* 141 (1984), pp. 223–33.

25. Notably in John 4. See also Alan D. Crown, Reinhard Plummer and Abraham Tal (eds), *A Companion to Samaritan Studies* (Tübingen, 1993).

26. For a review of the issues see Eric Eynikel, *The Reform of King Josiah and the Composition of the Deuteronomistic History* (OS, 33; Leiden, 1996); and Lowell K. Handy, 'Josiah in a new light: Assyriology touches the reforming king', in W. Holloway Steven (ed.), *Orientalism, Assyriology and the Bible* (Sheffield, 2006), pp. 415–35.

27. See Peter Ackroyd, *Exile and Restoration: A Study of Hebrew Thought of the Sixth Century BC* (London, 1968). For a commentary on Jeremiah, Walter Brueggemann, *A Commentary on Jeremiah: Exile and Homecoming* (Grand Rapids, 1998); and for revisionist thinking on the subject from more than one direction, Lester Grabbe (ed.), *Leading Captivity Captive: 'The Exile' as History and Ideology* (JSOTSup, 278; Sheffield, 1998). From a different perspective, Shaye J.D. Cohen and Ernest S. Frerichs (eds), *Diasporas in Antiquity* (Atlanta, 1993); and Beake Ego, 'Interpreting the Exile: the experience of the destruction of the temple and the desecration of the land as reflected within the nonpentateuchal biblical Abraham tradition', in

Armin Lange, Kristin de Troyer, Katie M. Goetz and Susan Bond (eds), *Reading the Present in the Qumran Library* (Atlanta, 2005), pp. 165–79.

28. On Diaspora Judaism see further John M.G. Barclay, *Jews in the Mediterranean Diaspora: From Alexander to Trajan (323 BCE–117 CE)* (Edinburgh, 1996).

29. *History*, p. 363.

30. See Rainer Albertz and Bob Becking (eds), *Yahwism after the Exile: Perspectives on Israelite Religion in the Persian Era* (Assen, 2003).

31. See James A. Sanders, 'The Exile and canon formation', in J. Scott (ed.), *Exile: Old Testament, Jewish, and Christian Conceptions* (Leiden, 1997), pp. 37–61; Joseph Blenkinsopp, *Treasures Old and New: Essays in the Theology of the Pentateuch* (Grand Rapids, 2004); and Mark A. O'Brien, *Rethinking the Pentateuch: Prolegomena to the Theology of Ancient Israel* (Louisville, 2005).

32. On the history of this period see Lester L. Grabbe, *Judaism from Cyrus to Hadrian* (London, 1992), vol. i, ch. 4; and the same author's *Judaic Religion in the Second Temple Period: Belief and Practice from the Exile to Yavneh* (London, 2000).

33. On whom see U. Wilcken, *Alexander the Great* (ET New York and London, 1967); W.W. Tarn, *Alexander the Great* (Cambridge, 1948); and A.B. Bosworth, *Conquest and Empire: The Reign of Alexander the Great* (Cambridge, 1988).

34. *Judaism and Hellenism* (ET London, 1974), vol. i, pp. 39–47.

35. *Judaism and Hellenism*, vol. i, p. 47.

36. See Emil Schürer, revised and edited by Geza Vermes and Fergus Millar, *The History of the Jewish People in the Age of Jesus Christ*, vol. i (Edinburgh, 1973), pp. 137–73; and Paul Niskanen, 'Daniel's portrait of Antiochus IV: echoes of a Persian king', *CBQ* 66 (2004), pp. 378–86.

37. The religious tensions of the period are described by the book of Daniel as well as by the two books of the Maccabees. Among the secondary literature see E. Bickerman, *The God of the Maccabees* (ET Leiden, 1979); and V. Tcherikover, *Hellenistic Civilization and the Jews* (ET Philadelphia, 1966).

38. See 1 Macc. 1.41–51; 2 Macc. 6.1–2; and Dan. 11.31.

39. On this key text see John J. Collins, *Daniel: A Commentary on the Book of Daniel* (Philadelphia, 1993); and the same author's 'New light on the book of Daniel from the Dead Sea scrolls', in Florentino García Martínez and Edward Noort (eds), *Perspectives in the Study of the Old Testament and Early Judaism: A Symposium in Honour of Adam S. van der Woude on the Occasion of his 70th birthday* (VTSup, 73; Leiden, 1998), pp. 180–96.

40. See Jan W. van Henten, *The Maccabean Martyrs as Saviours of the Jewish People: A Study of 2 and 4 Maccabees* (JSJSup, 57; Leiden, 1997).

41. In addition to the *History* by Schürer, for this period see E. Mary Smallwood, *The Jews under Roman Rule* (Leiden, 1981).

42. See M. Stern, 'The reign of Herod and the Herodian dynasty', in S. Safrai and M. Stern (eds), *The Jewish People in the First Century* (CRINT, 1; Assen, 1974), ch. 5; *idem*, 'Social and political realignments in Herodian Judaea', in L.I. Levine (ed.,), *The Jerusalem Cathedra* (Jerusalem, 1982), vol. ii, pp. 40–62; and Peter Richardson, *Herod, King of the Jews and Friend of the Romans* (Columbia, 1999).

43. On the latter see Duane W. Roller, *The Building Program of Herod the Great* (Berkeley, 1998).
44. See David M. Jacobson, 'Herod's Roman temple', *BAR* 28 (2002), pp. 18–27, 60.
45. See Brian Lalor, 'The Temple Mount of Herod the Great at Jerusalem: recent excavations and literary sources', in John R. Bartlett (ed.), *Archaeology and Biblical Interpretation* (London, 1997), pp. 95–116.
46. See H.W. Hoehner, *Herod Antipas* (SNTSMS, 17; Cambridge, 1980).
47. The history of the Revolt is told by Schürer, *History of the Jewish People*, vol. i, pp. 484–513; and by Smallwood, *Jews*, pp. 293–330. See also Martin Goodman, *The Ruling Class of Judea: The Origins of the Jewish Revolt against Rome AD 66–70* (Cambridge, 1989); and Andrea M. Berlin and J. Andrew Overman (eds), *The First Jewish Revolt: Archaeology, History, and Ideology* (London, 2002).
48. See Schürer, *History of the Jewish People*, vol. i, pp. 514–57; and Smallwood, *Jews*, pp. 428–66. For a perspective on the aftermath of the Second Revolt, Martin Goodman, *State and Society in Roman Galilee AD 132–212* (Totowa, 1983).
49. Eusebius preserves a tradition that the Christians of Judaea fled to Pella in the Decapolis before the city fell; *Hist. Eccl.* 3.5.3.
50. See the article 'Zealots' by David Rhoads, in *ABD*, vol. vi, pp. 1043–54.
51. Smallwood, *Jews*, pp. 284–92.
52. Smallwood, *Jews*, p. 293.
53. See Yigael Yadin, *Masada: Herod's Fortress and the Zealots' Last Stand* (New York, 2000).

Chapter 4

1. E.P. Sanders, *Judaism: Practice and Belief 63BCE–66CE* (London, 1992); A.R.C. Leaney, *The Jewish and Christian World 200 BC to AD 200* (CCW-JCW, 7; Cambridge, 1984); J. Neusner, *Judaism in the Beginning of Christianity* (Philadelphia and London, 1984); John K. Riches, *The World of Jesus: First Century Judaism in Crisis* (Cambridge, 1990); Herschel Shanks (ed.), *Christianity and Rabbinic Judaism: A Parallel History of the Origins and Early Development* (Washington DC, 1992); J. Neusner (ed.), *Judaism in Late Antiquity*, pt. ii: *Historical Synthesis* (HOA, 17; Leiden, 1995); Lester L. Grabbe, *An Introduction to First-Century Judaism: Jewish Religion and History in the Second Temple Period* (Edinburgh, 1996); idem, *A History of Jews and Judaism in the Second Temple Period*, vol. i (LSTS, 47; London, 2004); and Karl P. Donfried and Peter Richardson (eds), *Judaism and Christianity in First Century Rome* (Grand Rapids, 1998).
2. See P. Athanassiadi and M. Frede (eds), *Pagan Monotheism in Late Antiquity* (Oxford, 1999); Mark S. Smith, *The Origins of Biblical Monotheism: Israel's Polytheistic Background and the Ugaritic Texts* (Oxford, 2001); Bob Becking, *Only One God? Monotheism in Ancient Israel and the Veneration of the Goddess Asherah* (London, 2001); and Nathan Macdonald, *Deuteronomy and the Meaning of 'Monotheism'* (FAT, 1; Tübingen, 2003).
3. See Richard Bauckham, *God Crucified: Monotheism and Christology in the New Testament* (Grand Rapids, 1998); and Carey C. Newman, James R.

Davila and Gladys S. Lewis, *The Jewish Roots of Christological Monotheism* (Leiden, 1999).

4. See Baruch A. Levine, 'Assyrian ideology and Israelite monotheism', *Iraq* 67 (2005), pp. 411–27.

5. *No Other Gods: Emergent Monotheism in Israel* (JSOTSup, 241; Sheffield, 1997). See also Fritz Stolz, 'Der Monotheismus Israels im Kontext der altorientalischen Religionsgeschichte – Tendenzen neuren Forschung', in Walter Dietrich and M.A. Klopfenstein (eds), *Ein Gott allein? YHWH-Verehrung und biblischer Monotheismus im Kontext der israeliticshen und altorientalischen Religionsgeschichte* (OBO, 139: Fribourg and Göttingen, 1994); and Diana Edelman (ed.), *The Triumph of Elohim: From Yahwisms to Judaisms* (CBET, 13; Kampen, 1995).

6. See Mark S. Smith, 'The divine family at Ugarit and Israelite monotheism', in Stephen L. Cook, Corrine L. Patton and James W. Watts (eds), *The Whirlwind: Essays on Job, Hermeneutics and Theology in Memory of Jane Morse* (London, 2001); Manfred Krebernik and Jürgen von Oorschot (eds), *Polytheismus und Monotheismus in den Religionen des Vorderen Orients* (AOAT, 298; Münster, 2002); and G. del Olmo Lete, *Canaanite Religion according to the Liturgical Texts of Ugarit* (Winona Lake, 2004).

7. On which see A.S. Kapelrud, *Baal in the Ras Shamra Texts* (Copenhagen, 1952); *idem, The Ras Shamra Discoveries and the Old Testament* (Oxford, 1965); J. Gray, *The Legacy of Canaan* (VTSup, 5; Leiden, [2]1965); H. Ringgren, *Religions of the Ancient Near East* (London, 1973); A. Caquot and R. Sznycer, *Ugaritic Religion* (Leiden, 1980); and J. Day, *God's Conflict with the Dragon and the Sea: Echoes of a Canaanite Myth in the Old Testament* (Cambridge, 1985).

8. For an exploration of this material, which has met with a certain degree of criticism from other scholars, see Margaret Barker, *The Older Testament* (London, 1987).

9. 'The geography of monotheism', in H.T. Frank and W. Reed (eds), *Translating and Understanding the Old Testament: Essays in Honor of Herbert Gordon May* (Nashville, 1970), pp. 253–78.

10. 'Geography of monotheism', pp. 272–73.

11. See Baruch Halpern, ' "Brisker pipes than poetry": the development of Israelite monotheism', in Jacob Neusner, Baruch A. Levine and Ernest S. Frerichs (eds), *Judaic Perspectives on Ancient Israel* (Philadelphia, 1987), pp. 77–115; Michael S. Horton, *Covenant and Eschatology: The Divine Drama* (Louisville KY, 2002); Stanley E. Porter and Jacqueline C.R. de Roo (eds), *The Concept of Covenant in the Second Temple Period* (JSJSup, 71; Leiden, 2003); A.D. Hayses and R.B. Salters (eds), *Covenant as Context: Essays in Honour of E.W. Nicholson* (Oxford, 2003); and John van Seters, *A Law Book for the Diaspora: Revision in the Study of the Covenant Code* (Oxford, 2003).

12. 'Geography of monotheism'.

13. See G. Mendenhall, 'Covenant forms in Israelite tradition', *BA* 17 (1954), pp. 50–76; K. Baltzer, *Das Bundesformular* (WMANT, 4; Neukirchen-Vluyn, 1964); W. Beyerlin, *Origins and History of the Oldest Sinai Traditions* (Oxford, 1965); and J. Levenson, *Sinai and Zion* (New York, 1985).

14. These were described by V. Korosec, *Hethitische Staatsverträge* (Leipzig, 1931). For a review of how this theory has fared see Rolf Rendtorff, *The*

Covenant Formula: An Exegetical and Theological Investigation (Edinburgh, 1998).

15. See G. Mendenhall, 'The suzerainty treaty structure: thirty years later', in Edwin B. Firmage, Bernard Weiss and John W. Welch (eds), *Religion and Law: Biblical-Judaic and Islamic Perspectives* (Winona Lake, 1990), pp. 85–100; and Frank H. Polak, 'The covenant at Mount Sinai in the light of texts from Mari', in Chaim Cohen, Avi Hurvitz and Shalom M. Paul (eds), *Sefer Moshe: The Moshe Weinfeld Jubilee Volume* (Winona Lake, 2004).

16. On the significance of the Ebla archives see Giovanni Pettinato, *The Archives of Ebla* (New York, 1981); and Cyrus H. Gordon and Gary A. Rendsburg (eds), *Eblaitica: Essays on the Ebla Archives and Eblaite Language*, vol. iii (Winona Lake, 1990).

17. *Die Ursprünge des israelitischen Rechts* (Leipzig, 1934). This theory was developed also by J.J. Stamm and M.E. Andrew, *The Ten Commandments in Recent Research* (SBT, 2; London, 1967).

18. R.E. Clements, *Abraham and David* (SBT, 2.5; London, 1967).

19. 'The nature and purpose of the Abrahamic tradition', in P.D. Miller, P.D. Hanson and S.D. McBride (eds), *Ancient Israelite Religion: Essays in Honor of Frank Moore Cross* (Philadelphia, 1987), pp. 337–56.

20. On this prayer see R.W.L. Moberly, 'Towards an interpretation of the Shema' in C. Seitz and K, Greene-McCreight, *Theological exegesis: Essays in Honor of Brevard S. Childs* (Grand Rapids, 1999), pp. 124–44.

21. Sanders, *Judaism*, as at note 1 above. See also the same author's *Paul and Palestinian Judaism* (London, 1977).

22. *Judaism*, ch. 5.

23. See the article 'Hammath', in *EncycJud*, vol. vii, cols 1242–4.

24. See Michael Knibb, 'Eschatology and messianism in the Dead Sea scrolls', in Peter W. Flint and James C. Vanderkam, *The Dead Sea Scrolls After Fifty Years* (Leiden, 1999), vol. ii. pp. 379–402.

25. *Judaism*, ch. 7.

26. *Judaism*, pp. 257–60.

27. For reviews of this term see Morna D. Hooker, 'Paul and "covenantal nomism"', in M.D. Hooker and S. Wilson (eds), *Paul and Paulinism* (London, 1982); James D.G. Dunn, 'The new perspective on Paul', *BJRL* 65/2 (1983), pp. 95–122; Timo Eskola, 'Paul, predestination and "covenantal nomism": re-assessing Paul and Palestinian Judaism', *JSJ* 28 (1997), pp. 390–412; A. Andrew Das, *Paul, the Law, and the Covenant: Beyond Covenantal Nomism to the Newer Perspective* (Peabody, 2001); Donald A. Carson, Peter T. O'Brien and Mark A. Seifrid (eds), *Justification and Variegated Nomism*, vol. ii: *The Paradoxes of Paul* (WUNT, 181; Tübingen, 2004); and Simon J. Gathercole, 'Early Judaism and covenantal nomism: a review article', *EQ* 76 (2004), pp. 153–62.

28. Sanders writes in the wake of George Foot Moore, 'Christian writers on Judaism', *HTR* 14 (1921), pp. 197–254.

Chapter 5

1. See the bibliography in Chapter 2, n. 1. An important contribution is Peter W. Flint, Emanuel Tov and James C. Vanderkam (eds), *Studies in the Hebrew*

Bible, Qumran and the Septuagint Presented to Eugene Ulrich (VTSup, 101; Leuven, 2006).

2. For a review of this issue see the collection of essays edited by A. van der Kooij and K. van der Toorn, *Canonization and Decanonization* (Leiden, 1998).

3. See also Andrew E. Steinmann, *The Oracles of God: The Old Testament Canon* (St Louis, 1999); and Stephen B. Chapman, *The Law and the Prophets: A Study in Old Testament Canon Formation* (Tübingen, 2000).

4. See especially Emil Schürer, revised and edited by Geza Vermes, Fergus Millar and Matthew Black, *The History of the Jewish People in the Age of Jesus Christ*, vol. ii (Edinburgh, 1979), pp. 314–80.

5. On the early moves that led to this development see James A. Sanders, 'The Exile and canon formation', in J. Scott (ed.), *Exile: Old Testament, Jewish, and Christian Conceptions* (Leiden, 1997), pp. 37–61.

6. See Steve Mason, 'Josephus and the twenty-two book canon', in Lee Martin Macdonald and James A. Sanders, *The Canon Debate: On the Origins and Formation of the Bible* (Peabody, 2002), pp. 110–27.

7. For the cultural background to this association see John G. Gammie and Leo G. Perdue (eds), *The Sage in Ancient Israel and the Ancient Near East* (Winona Lake, 1990); and K. Watanabe (ed.), *Priests and Officials in the Ancient Near East* (Heidelberg, 1999).

8. See Schürer, *History of the Jewish People*, vol. ii, pp. 314–55; Anthony J. Saldarini, *Pharisees, Scribes and Sadducees* (Edinburgh, 1989); Sanders, *Judaism*, chs. 11 and 12; E.C. Ulrich and J.W. Wright (eds), *Priests, People and Scribes: Essays on the Formation and Heritage of Second Temple Judaism in Honour of Joseph Blenkinsopp* (JSOTSup, 149; Sheffield, 1992); and Philip R. Davies, *Scribes and Schools: The Canonization of the Hebrew Scriptures* (Louisville and London, 1998). An important contribution is Craig A. Evans (ed.), *Of Scribes and Sages: Early Jewish Interpretation and Transmission of Scripture*, vol. i: *Ancient Versions and Tradition*; vol. ii: *Later Versions and Tradition* (London, 2004).

9. See Philip R. Davies, *Scribes and Schools*; *idem*, 'The scribal school of Daniel', in John J. Collins and Peter W. Flint (eds), *The Book of Daniel: Composition and Reception*, vol. ii (Leiden, 2001), pp. 247–65; and Christiane Schams, *Jewish Scribes in the Second Temple Period* (Sheffield, 1998).

10. See James C. Vanderkam, *Enoch: A Man for All Generations* (Columbia, 1995); and George W.E. Nickelsburg, ' "Enoch" as scientist, sage, and prophet: content, function, and authorship in 1 Enoch', *SBL Seminar Papers 1999*, pp. 203–30.

11. On this point see Joachim Jeremias, *Jerusalem in the Time of Jesus* (ET London, 1969), pp. 233–45. Jeremias also draws attention to the function of the scribes as the guardians of the mystical tradition in Judaism.

12. The best recent study is Michael Fishbane, *Biblical Interpretation in Ancient Israel* (Oxford, 1985). See also Peter Richardson and Stephen Westerholm, *Law in Religious Communities in the Roman Period: The Debate over Torah and Nomos in Post-biblical Judaism and Early Christianity* (Waterloo, 1991); and Markus Bockmuehl, *Jewish Law in Gentile Churches: Halakah and the Beginning of Christian Public Ethics* (Edinburgh, 2000).

13. See Schürer, *History of the Jewish People*, vol. ii, pp. 314–80.

14. For a summary of Jewish haggadah see Louis Ginzberg, *Legends of the Jews* (Baltimore and London, reissued, 1998).
15. On which see H.G.M. Williamson, *1 and 2 Chronicles* (NCB; London, 1982).
16. See Philip S. Alexander, 'Retelling the Bible', in D.A. Carson and H.G.M. Williamson (eds), *It is Written: Scripture Citing Scripture* (Cambridge, 1988), pp. 99–121; and G.W.E. Nickelsburg, 'Patriarchs who worry about their wives: a haggadic tendency in the Genesis Apocryphon', in Michael E. Stone and Esther Glickler Chazon (eds), *Biblical Perspectives: Early Use and Interpretation of the Bible in Light of the Dead Sea Scrolls* (Leiden, 1998), pp. 137–58.
17. But see Matthew Magenstein, 'A new clue to the original length of the Genesis Apocryphon', *JJS* 47 (1996), pp. 345–7.

Chapter 6

1. See Emil Schürer, revised and edited by Geza Vermes, Fergus Millar and Matthew Black, *The History of the Jewish People in the Age of Jesus Christ*, vol. ii (Edinburgh, 1979), pp. 423–54; L.I. Levine (ed.), *Ancient Synagogues Revealed* (Jerusalem, 1981); L.I. Levine, *The Synagogue in Late Antiquity* (Philadelphia, 1987); *idem*, 'The nature and origin of the Palestinian synagogue reconsidered', *JBL* 115 (1996), pp. 425–48; *idem*, 'The development of synagogue liturgy in late antiquity', in E. Meyers (ed.), *Galilee through the Centuries: Confluence of Cultures* (Winona Lake, 1999), pp. 123–44; *idem*, *The Ancient Synagogue: The First Thousand Years* (New Haven, 2000); S. Fine (ed.), *Jews, Christians, and Polytheists in the Ancient Synagogue* (New York, 1999); Anders Runesson, *The Origins of the Synagogue: A Socio-historical Study* (Stockholm, 2001); and Birger Olsson and Magnus Zetterholm (eds), *The Ancient Synagogue from its Origins until 200 CE: Papers Presented at an International Conference at Lund University* (Stockholm, 2003).
2. On the origins of this development see N. Drazin, *History of Jewish Education from 515 BCE to 220 CE* (Baltimore, 1940); and R. de Vaux, *Ancient Israel: Its Life and Institutions* (ET London, 1961), pp. 48–50.
3. On this see Howard Clark Kee, 'Defining the first-century CE synagogue: problems and progress', *NTS* 41 (1995), pp. 481–500; and Matthew J. Martin, 'Interpreting the Theodotus inscription: some reflections on a first century Jerusalem synagogue inscription and E.P. Sanders' "common Judaism" ', *ANETS* 39 (2002), pp. 160–81.
4. On the latter see Y. Yadin, 'The synagogue at Masada', in Levine (ed.), *Ancient Synagogues*, pp. 19–23; and E. Jan Wilson, 'The Masada synagogue and its relationship to Jewish worship during the Second Temple period', in J.F. Hall and J.W. Welch (eds), *Masada and the World of the New Testament* (Provo, 1997), pp. 269–76.
5. E.g. Acts 18.7.
6. See Schürer, *History of the Jewish People*, vol. ii, pp. 454–63; and William Horbury, 'The benediction of the minim and early Jewish–Christian controversy', *JTS* 33 (1982), pp. 19–61. I discuss this problem in Chapter 26.
7. See Levine, 'The development of synagogue liturgy in late antiquity'.
8. See Schürer, *History of the Jewish People*, vol. ii, pp. 423–54.

Chapter 7

1. See M. Stern, 'The reign of Herod and the Herodian dynasty', in S. Safrai and M. Stern (eds), *The Jewish People in the First Century* (CRINT, I.2; Assen, 1974), pp. 216–307; and the standard histories cited in this book.
2. See Duane P. Roller, *The Building Program of Herod the Great* (Berkeley, 1998); and Patrick Joseph, 'Herod's theatre in Jerusalem: a new proposal', *IEJ* 52 (2002), pp. 231–9.
3. See Carol Meyers, 'Herodian Temple', in *ABD*, vol. vi, pp. 364–5; K. and L. Ritmyer, 'Reconstructing Herod's Temple Mount in Jerusalem', *BAR* 15/6 (1989), pp. 23ff.; and David M. Jacobson, 'Herod's Roman temple', *BAR* 28 (2002), pp. 18–27.
4. See Andrew Teasdale, 'Herod the Great's building programme', *BYUS* 36/3 (1996–7), pp. 84–98; and Brian Lalor, 'The Temple Mount of Herod the Great at Jerusalem: recent excavations and literary sources', in J. Bartlett (ed.), *Archaeology and Biblical Interpretation* (London, 1997), pp. 95–116.
5. These taxes are generally recognized as having contributed to the burden imposed on the Galilean peasants who responded to the preaching of Jesus. This theme is explored by Richard A. Horsley, *Jesus and the Spiral of Violence* (Minneapolis, 1993 [1987]), pp. 13–14.
6. See E.P. Sanders, *Judaism: Practice and Belief 63BCE–66CE* (London and Philadelphia, 1992), ch. 5.
7. See Sanders, *Judaism*, pp. 47–76. Several scholars, however, think that some form of the temple sacrifice continued between 70 and 135 CE.
8. Noted by Sanders, *Judaism*, pp. 47–76.
9. *Judaism*, p. 49.
10. Thus Sanders, *Judaism*, pp. 69, 87.
11. Sanders, *Judaism*, pp. 78–9.
12. *Judaism*, p. 130.
13. See Shimon Finkelman, *Pesach: Passover: Its Observance, Laws, and Significance* (Brooklyn, 1994); and Theodor Herzl Gaster, *Passover: Its History and Traditions* (Westport, 1984).
14. See Sanders, *Judaism*, p. 134.
15. See Lawrence A. Hoffmann, 'The Passover meal in Jewish tradition', in P. Bradshaw and Lawrence A. Hoffmann (eds), *Passover and Easter: Origin and History to Modern Times* (Notre Dame, 1999), pp. 8–26.

Chapter 8

1. Very relevant to our topic are L.I. Levine (ed.), *The Galilee in Late Antiquity* (New York and Jerusalem, 1992); Richard A. Horsley, *Archaeology, History, and Society in Galilee: The Social Context of Jesus and the Rabbis* (Valley Forge, 1996); and Eric M. Meyers (ed.), *Galilee through the Centuries: Confluence of Cultures* (Winona Lake, 1999).
2. See James S. McLaren, 'Josephus' summary statements regarding the Essenes, Pharisees and Sadducees', *ABR* 48 (2000), pp. 31–46. There is valuable material in William Horbury, W.D. Davies and John Sturdy (eds), *The Cambridge History of Judaism*, vol. iii (Cambridge, 1999); see the essays by J. Schaper, 'The Pharisees', pp. 402–27, 1123–9; by G. Stemberger, 'The

Sadducees: their history and doctrine', pp. 428–43, 1129–31; and O. Betz, 'The Essenes', pp. 444–70, 1131–5.

3. What I say about the Pharisees here is based on the research of E.P. Sanders in his *Judaism: Practice and Belief 63BCE–66CE* (London, 1992), p. 444. For review and criticism of this see Martin Hengel, 'E.P. Sanders' "common Judaism", Jesus and the Pharisees', *JTS* 46 (1995), pp. 1–70. On the Pharisees see also Steve Mason, *Flavius Josephus on the Pharisees: A Composition-Critical Study* (Leiden, 1991); Gunther Stemberger, *Jewish Contemporaries of Jesus: Pharisees, Sadducees, Essenes* (Minneapolis, 1995); and Joseph Sievers, 'Who were the Pharisees?', in J.H. Charlesworth (ed.), *Hillel and Jesus: Comparative Studies of Two Major Religious Leaders* (Minneapolis, 1997), pp. 137–55. See also J. Patrick Mullen, *Dining with Pharisees* (Collegeville, 2004).

4. *Judaism*, p. 389.

5. See further James C. Vanderkam, 'Those who look for smooth things: Pharisees and oral law', in Paul M. Shalom, Robert A. Kraft, Laurence H. Schiffmann and Weston W. Fields (eds), *Emanuel: Studies in Hebrew Bible, Septuagint and Dead Sea Scrolls in Honor of Emanuel Tov* (VTSup, 94; Leiden, 2003), pp. 465–77; and Martin Goodman, 'A note on Josephus, the Pharisees and ancestral tradition', *JJS* 50 (99), pp. 17–20.

6. Not the least of which is Matthew 23.

7. A point made effectively by Sanders, *Judaism*, p. 389.

8. *Judaism*, pp. 438–40. See also Shaye J.D. Cohen, 'Were the Pharisees and Rabbis the leaders of communal prayer and Torah study in antiquity? The evidence of the New Testament, Josephus and the early church fathers', in Howard Clark Kee and Lynn H. Cottick (eds), *Evolution of the Synagogue* (Harrisburg PA, 1999), pp. 89–105.

9. Besides the literature cited see G. Baumbach, 'Der sadduzaische Konservatismus', in J. Maier and J. Schreiner (eds), *Literatur und Religion des Frühjudentums* (Würzburg, 1973), pp. 201–3; *idem*, 'The Sadducees in Josephus', in L. Feldman and G. Hata (eds), *Josephus, the Bible, and History* (Leiden, 1989), pp. 173–97; Cecilia Wassén, 'Sadducees and halakah', in P. Richardson and S. Westerholm (eds), *Law in Religious Communities in the Roman Period* (Waterloo, 1991), pp. 127–46; Daniel R. Schwarz, 'Law and truth: on Qumran-Sadducean and rabbinic views of law', in D. Dimant and U. Rappaport (eds), *The Dead Sea Scrolls: Forty Years of Research* (Leiden, 1992), pp. 229–40; Hans Burgmann, '11QT: the Sadducean Torah', in G. Brooke (ed.), *Temple Scroll Studies* (JSPSup, 7; Sheffield, 1989), pp. 257–67; David Daube, 'On Acts 23: Sadducees and angels', *JBL* 109 (1990), pp. 493–97; Benedict T. Viviano, 'Sadducees, angels, and resurrection (Acts 23.8–9)', *JBL* 111 (1992), pp. 496–8; Steve Mason, 'Chief priests, Sadducees, Pharisees, and Sanhedrin in Acts', in R. Bauckham (ed.), *The Book of Acts in its Palestinian Setting* (Grand Rapids, 1995); and finally Martin Goodman, 'Sadducees and Essenes after 70 CE', in Stanley E. Porter, Paul Joyce and David Orton (eds), *Crossing the Boundaries: Essays in Biblical Interpretation in Honour of Michael D. Goulder* (BIS, 8; Leiden, 1999), pp. 347–56.

10. See Mason, 'Chief priests, Sadducees, Pharisees, and Sanhedrin in Acts'.

11. See Sanders, *Judaism*, p. 328.

12. See Geza Vermes and Martin Goodman (eds), *The Essenes according to the Classical Sources* (Sheffield, 1989); André Paul, 'Flavius Josèphe et les

Esséniens', in Dimant and Rappaport (eds), *Dead Sea Scrolls* pp. 274–93; Martin Goodman, 'A note on the Qumran sectarians, the Essenes and Josephus', *JJS* 46 (1995), pp. 161–6; and Curtis Hutt, 'Qumran and the ancient sources', in Donald W. Parry and Eugene Ulrich (eds), *Provo International Conference on the Dead Sea Scrolls* (STDJ, 30; Leiden, 1999), pp. 274–93. Useful also is James R. Davila (ed.), *The Dead Sea Scrolls as Background to Postbiblical Judaism and Early Christianity: Papers from an International Conference at St. Andrews in 2001* (Leiden, 2003).

13. On this point see James C. Vanderkam, *The Dead Sea Scrolls Today* (Grand Rapids, 1994), pp. 71–98; and Lena Cansdale, *Qumran and the Essenes: A Re-evaluation of the Evidence* (TSAJ, 60; Tübingen, 1997).

14. See Philip R. Davies, *Behind the Essenes: History and Ideology in the Dead Sea Scrolls* (BJS, 94; Atlanta, 1987); *idem*, 'The prehistory of the Essenes', in Dimant and Rappaport (eds), *Dead Sea Scrolls*, pp. 116–25.

15. See Philip R. Davies, 'The birthplace of the Essenes: where is "Damascus"?', *RQ* 14 (1990), pp. 503–19; and Charlotte Hempel, 'Community origins in the Damascus Document in the light of recent scholarship', in Parry and Ulrich (eds), *Provo International Conference*, pp. 316–29.

16. See Michael O. Wise, 'Dating the Teacher of Righteousness and the floruit of his movement', *JBL* 122 (2003), pp. 53–87.

17. On the Jerusalem branch see Bargil Pixner, 'Jerusalem's Essene gateway: where the community lived in Jesus' time', *BAR* 23 (1997), pp. 22–31, 64, 66; Bonnie Rochman, 'The missing link? Rare tombs could provide evidence of Jerusalem Essenes', *BAR* 23 (1997), pp. 20–1; and John J. Collins, 'Forms of community in the Dead Sea scrolls', in Shalom, Kraft, Schiffmann and Fields (eds), *Emanuel*, pp. 97–111.

18. See Berndt Schaller, '4000 Essener – 6000 Pharisäer; zum Hintergrund und Wert antiker Zahlenangaben', in Bernd Kollmann, Wolfgang Reinhold and Annette Steudel (eds), *Antikes Judentum and frühes Christentum: Festschrift für Hartmut Stegemann zum 65 Geburtstag* (Berlin, 1999), pp. 172–82.

19. See Brian J. Capper, 'The Palestinian cultural context of the earliest Christian community of goods', in R.J. Bauckham (ed.), *The Book of Acts in its Palestinian Setting* (Grand Rapids, 1995), pp. 323–56; and Justin Taylor, 'The community of goods among the first Christians and among the Essenes', in David Goodblatt, Avital E. Pinnick and Daniel R. Schwartz (eds), *Historical Perspectives: From the Hasmoneans to Bar Kochba in Light of the Dead Sea Scrolls* (Leiden, 2001), pp. 147–61.

20. See Émile Puech, 'Les Esséniens et le temple de Jérusalem', in J. Petit (ed.), *Où demeures-tu? (Jn 1, 38): La maison depuis le monde biblique* (Montreal, 1994); and Deborah Dimant, 'Men as angels: the self-image of the Qumran community', in A. Berlin (ed.), *Religion and Politics in the Ancient Near East* (Bethesda, 1996), pp. 93–103.

21. See Vanderkam, *Dead Sea Scrolls*, pp. 175–6. There is valuable material also in M. Becker and W. Fenske, *Das Ende der Tage und die Gegenwart des Heils: Begegnunung mit dem Neuen Testament und seiner Umwelt: festschrift für Heinz-Wolfgang Kuhn zum 65 Geburtstag* (AGJU, 44; Leiden, 1999).

22. See further Brian J. Capper, 'With the oldest monks ... light from Essene history on the career of the Beloved Disciple?', *JTS* 49 (1998), pp. 1–55.

23. See the excellent article by David Rhoads, 'Zealots', in *ABD*, vol. vi, pp. 1043–54.
24. On this subject see Tessa Rajak, *Josephus: The Historian and His Society* (Philadelphia, 1984); and R. Horsley, 'Josephus and the Bandits', *JJS* 10 (1979), pp. 37–63. There is an interesting study of *The Roman–Jewish War 66–70 AD: Its Origins and Consequences* by M. Aberbach (London, 1966).
25. S.G.F. Brandon, *Jesus and the Zealots* (Manchester, 1967); and Martin Hengel, *The Zealots* (ET Edinburgh, 1989).
26. Besides his *ABD* article, see *Israel in Revolution: 6–74 CE* (Philadelphia, 1976).
27. Sanders, *Judaism*.

Chapter 9

1. The classic study of this issue is Martin Hengel, *Judaism and Hellenism* (ET 2 vols.; London, 1974).
2. See T.C. Mitchell, 'The Babylonian Exile and the Restoration of the Jews in Palestine (*c*.586 BC–500 BC)', in John Boardman *et al.* (eds), *The Cambridge Ancient History*, vol. iii, pt. ii (Cambridge, ²1991), pp. 410–60; and James M. Scott, 'Exile and self-understanding of Diaspora Jews in the Greco-Roman period', in James M. Scott (ed.), *Exile: Old Testament, Jewish and Christian Conceptions* (Leiden, 1997).
3. A classic study of this intermingling is Hengel's *Judaism and Hellenism*. See also Leonard V. Rutgen, 'The hidden heritage of diaspora Judaism', *JBL* 119 (2000), pp. 124–5. There is valuable material in William Horbury, W.D. Davies and John Sturdy (eds), *The Cambridge History of Judaism*, vol. iii (Cambridge, 1999); see the essay by E.M. Smallwood, 'The diaspora in the Roman period before CE 70', pp. 168–91, 1099–1104.
4. *Jews in the Mediterranean Diaspora: From Alexander to Trajan (323 BCE–117 CE)* (Edinburgh, 1996).
5. See L.L. Thompson, *The Book of Revelation: Apocalypse and Empire* (New York and London, 1990); and Jonathan Knight, *Revelation* (Sheffield, 1999; ²2008).
6. Barclay, *Jews*, p. 184.
7. Barclay, *Jews*, pt. iii.
8. Barclay, *Jews*, pp. 418–24.
9. Barclay, *Jews*, p. 420.
10. Barclay, *Jews*, pp. 19–34.
11. Barclay, *Jews*, pp. 424–8. See also Emil Schürer, rev. Geza Vermes, Fergus Millar and Matthew Black, *The History of the Jewish People in the Age of Jesus Christ (175 BC–AD 135)*, vol. ii (Edinburgh, 1979), pp. 314–80.

Chapter 10

1. See the essay by Marcus J. Borg, 'Jesus and eschatology: current reflections', in *Jesus in Contemporary Scholarship* (Valley Forge, 1994), pp. 69–96. Borg attributes this recognition to Gerhard Sauter, 'The concept and task of theology: theological and philosophical reflections', *SJT* 41 (1988), pp. 499–515. See also the article 'Eschatology (early Jewish)' by George

W.E. Nickelsburg, in *ABD*, vol. ii, pp. 579–94; and Nickelsburg's earlier study, *Resurrection, Immortality, and Eternal Life in Intertestamental Judaism* (HTS, 26; Cambridge MA, 1972).

2. See the different treatments of this theme by John Hick, *Death and Eternal Life* (London, 1976); Eberhard Jüngel, *Death: The Riddle and the Mystery* (ET Edinburgh, 1975); and J. Moltmann, *The Coming of God: Christian Eschatology* (ET Minneapolis, 1996).

3. See N. Tromp, *Primitive Conceptions of Death and the Nether World in the Old Testament* (BibOr, 21; Rome, 1969); K. Spronk, *Beatific Afterlife in Ancient Israel and the Ancient Near East* (AOAT, 219; Neukirchen-Vluyn, 1986); Theodore J. Lewis, 'Dead, abode of the', in *ABD*, vol. ii, pp. 101–5; John Jarick, 'Questioning Sheol', in Stanley E. Porter, Michael A. Hayes and David Tombs (eds), *Resurrection* (JSNTSup, 186; Sheffield, 1999), pp. 22–32; and Philip S. Johnston, *Shades of Sheol: Death and Afterlife in the Old Testament* (Downers Grove IL, 2002).

4. The Jewish messianic hope is examined by William Horbury, *Jewish Messianism and the Cult of Christ* (London, 1998), pp. 5–63. He has a bibliography and discussion of earlier writings on this subject. See also Horbury's *Messianism among Jews and Christians: Twelve Biblical and Historical Studies* (London, 2003). Significant other books include H. Gressmann, *Der Messias* (Göttingen, 1929); J. Klausner, *The Messianic Idea in Israel* (ET London, 1956); H. Ringgren, *The Messiah in the Old Testament* (SBT, 18; London, 1956); S. Mowinckel, *He that Cometh: The Messiah Concept in the Old Testament and Later Judaism* (ET Oxford, 1956); G. Scholem, *The Messianic Idea in Judaism, and other Essays on Jewish Spirituality* (ET London, 1971); J. Neusner, *Messiah in Context* (Philadelphia, 1984); J. Neusner, W.S. Green and E.S. Frerichs (eds), *Judaisms and Their Messiahs at the Turn of the Christian Era* (Cambridge, 1987); J.H. Charlesworth (ed.), *The Messiah: Developments in Earliest Judaism and Christianity* (Minneapolis, 1992); I. Baldermann (ed.), *Der Messias* (JBTh, 8; Neukirchen-Vluyn, 1993); J.J. Collins, *The Scepter and the Star* (New York, 1995); K.E. Pomykala, *The Davidic Dynasty Tradition in Early Judaism, Its History and Significance for Messianism* (Atlanta, 1995); and Michael A. Knibb (ed.), *The Septuagint and Messianism* (Leuven, 2006). There is important material also in John J. Collins and Craig A. Evans (eds), *Christian Beginnings and the Dead Sea Scrolls* (Grand Rapids, 2006); and Magnus Letterholm (ed.); *The Messiah in Early Judaism and Christianity* (Minneapolis: Fortress Press, 2007).

5. In his article, 'Eschatology', in *ABD*, vol. ii, pp. 575–9. See also Donald E. Gowan, *Eschatology in the Old Testament* (Edinburgh, [2]2000).

6. The significant book here is Paul D. Hanson, *The Dawn of Apocalyptic* (Philadelphia, 1975). More recently, see John J. Collins, 'From prophecy to apocalypticism: the expectation of the end', in John J. Collins (ed.), *The Encyclopedia of Apocalypticism*, vol. i: *The Origins of Apocalypticism in Judaism and Christianity* (New York, 1998), pp. 129–61; F. Dailey, 'Non-linear time in apocalyptic texts: the spiral model', in *SBL Seminar Papers* 38 (1999), pp. 231–45; Albert I. Baumgarten, *Apocalyptic Time* (SHR, 86; Leiden, 2000); and Paul L. Redditt, 'The rhetoric of Jewish apocalyptic eschatology', *PRS* 28 (2001), pp. 361–71.

7. H.H. Rowley, *The Relevance of Apocalyptic* (London, 1944), p. 38.

8. Besides the literature already cited, see E. Schürer, revised by Geza Vermes, Fergus Millar and Matthew Black, *The History of the Jewish People in the Age of Jesus Christ (175 BC–AD 135)*, vol. ii (London, 1979), pp. 488–554; and Carl E. Braaten and Robert W. Jenson (eds), *The Last Things: Biblical and Theological Perspectives on Eschatology* (Grand Rapids, 2002).

9. There is an important study of this issue by John J. Collins, *The Apocalyptic Imagination* (Grand Rapids, ²1998). My own *Apocalypticism in Early Christianity and its Jewish Environment* is forthcoming. A fascinating exploration of the Enochic material is offered by Gabriele Boccaccini (ed.), *Enoch and Qumran Origins: New Light on a Forgotten Connection* (Grand Rapids and Cambridge, 2005).

10. See Paul D. Hanson, 'Rebellion in heaven, Azazel, and euhemeristic heroes in 1 Enoch 6–11', *JBL* 96 (1977), pp. 195–233; George W.E. Nickelsburg, 'Apocalyptic and myth in 1 Enoch 6–11', *JBL* 96 (1977), pp. 383–405; and Devorah Dimant, '1 Enoch 6–11: a methodological perspective', in Paul J. Achtmeier (ed.), *Seminar Papers SBL* (1978), pp. 323–39.

11. See Patrick A. Tiller, *A Commentary on the Animal Apocalypse* (Atlanta, 1993); and James C. Vanderkam, 'Open and closed eyes in the Animal Apocalypse (1 Enoch 85–90)', in H. Najman and Judith H. Newman (eds), *The Idea of Biblical Interpretation: Essays in Honor of James L. Kugel* (JSJSup, 83; Leiden, 2004).

12. See John J. Collins, 'The kingdom of God in the Apocrypha and Pseudepigrapha', in W. Willis (ed.), *The Kingdom of God in Twentieth-Century Interpretation* (Peabody, 1987), pp. 81–95.

13. See John J. Collins, *Daniel: A Commentary on the Book of Daniel* (Minneapolis, 1993).

14. For discussion of Daniel 7, including the question of its influence on Jesus and the early Christians, see Chapter 14.

15. See A.S. van der Woude, 'Prophetic prediction, political prognostication, and firm belief: reflections on Daniel 11:40–12:3', in C. Evans (ed.), *The Quest for Context and Meaning: Studies in Biblical Intertextuality in Honor of James A. Sanders* (Leiden, 1997), pp. 63–73.

16. See my discussion of the *Similitudes* in Chapter 14. On the issues raised by its messianism, and its relation to early Christian belief, see Timo Eskola, *Messiah and the Throne: Jewish Merkabah Mysticism and Early Christian Exaltation Discourse* (WUNT, 142; Tübingen, 2001); Darrell D. Hannah, 'The throne of his glory: the divine throne and heavenly mediators in Revelation and the Similitudes of Enoch', *ZNW* 94 (2003), pp. 68–96; and Andrei A. Orlov, *The Enoch-Metatron Tradition* (TSAJ, 107; Tübingen, 2005). Important studies are George W.E. Nickelsburg and James C. Vanderkam, *1 Enoch: A New Translation based on the Hermeneia Commentary* (Minneapolis, 2004); and Boccaocini (ed.), *Enoch and Qumran Origins*.

17. See Tom W. Willet, *Eschatology in the Theodicies of 2 Baruch and 4 Ezra* (JSPSup, 4; Sheffield, 1989); and Bruce W. Longenecker, *Eschatology and the Covenant: A Comparison of 4 Ezra and Romans* (JSNTSup, 57; Sheffield, 1991).

18. See Frank Zimmerman, 'The language, the date, and the portrayal of the Messiah in 4 Ezra', *Hebrew Studies* 26 (1985), pp. 203–18; and Michael E. Stone, 'The question of the Messiah in 4 Ezra', in Jacob Neusner and others (eds), *Judaisms and Their Messiahs*, pp. 209–24.

19. See Rivka Nir, *The Destruction of Jerusalem and the Idea of Redemption in the Syriac Apocalypse of Baruch* (SBLEJL, 20; Atlanta, 2003).

20. See Schürer, *History of the Jewish People*, vol. ii, Appendix B; John J. Collins, 'The expectation of the end in the Dead Sea scrolls', in Craig A. Evans and Peter W. Flint (eds), *Eschatology, Messianism, and the Dead Sea Scrolls* (Grand Rapids, 1997), pp. 74–90; B. Nitzan, 'Eschatological motives in Qumran literature: the messianic concept', in H.G. Reventlow (ed.), *Eschatology in the Bible and in Jewish and Christian Tradition* (JSOT-Sup, 243; Sheffield, 1997); and Michael A. Knibb, 'Eschatology and messianism in the Dead Sea scrolls', in Peter W. Flint and James C. Vanderkam (eds), *The Dead Sea Scrolls after Fifty Years* (2 vols.; Leiden, 1999), pp. 379–402. There are several important essays in the volume edited by Eva Ben David, Weston W. Fields, Laurence H. Schiffmann, Shalom M. Paul and Robert A. Kraft, *Emanuel: Studies in Hebrew Bible, Septuagint and Dead Sea Scrolls in Honor of Emanuel Tov* (Leiden and Boston, 2003). See especially Hermann Lichtenberger, 'Qumran-messianism', pp. 323–33; and Geza Vermes, 'Eschatological world view in the Dead Sea scrolls and the New Testament', pp. 479–94. Important also is James H. Charlesworth, Hermann Lichtenberger and Gerbern S. Oegema (eds), *Qumran-Messianism: Studies on the Messianic Expectation in the Dead Sea Scrolls* (Tübingen, 2002).

21. On the dimensions of a 'sect', see Bryan Wilson, *Religious Sects: A Sociological Study* (London, 1970).

22. On the general self-understanding of the Qumran community, see James C. Vanderkam, *The Dead Sea Scrolls Today* (Grand Rapids, 1994). Other literature is mentioned in Chapter 8.

23. See Florentino Garcia Martinez, 'Two messianic figures in the Qumran texts', in Donald W. Parry and Eugene Ulrich (eds), *The Provo International Conference on the Dead Sea Scrolls: Technological Innovations, New Texts, and Reformulated Issues* (STDJ, 30; Leiden, 1999), pp. 14–40; and John J. Collins, 'The nature of messianism in the light of the Dead Sea scrolls', in Timothy Lim (ed.), *The Dead Sea Scrolls in their Historical Context* (Edinburgh, 2000), pp. 199–217.

24. See the bibliography at n. 4 above. One can hardly over-estimate the importance of Horbury's study, *Jewish Messianism*.

25. See Collins, *Daniel*, pp. 354–7.

26. See F. Hesse in *TDNT*, vol. ix, pp. 496–509; de Jonge in *ABD*, vol. iv, pp. 777–88; and Horbury, *Jewish Messianism*, p. 7.

27. *Jewish Messianism*, p. 5.

28. *Jewish Messianism*, pp. 36–63.

29. On this subject see John Day (ed.), *King and Messiah in Israel and the Ancient Near East: Proceedings of the Oxford Old Testament Seminar* (JSOTSup, 270; Sheffield, 1998); especially the essay by John Barton on pp. 365–79 of that volume, 'The messiah in Old Testament theology'.

30. See Day (ed.), *King and Messiah*.

31. A. R. Johnson, *Sacral Kingship in Ancient Israel* (Cardiff, [2]1967).

32. See Stan Rummel (ed.), *The Ras Shamra Parallels: The Texts from Ugarit and the Hebrew Bible* (Rome, 1981); and also Adrian Curtis, *Ugarit (Ras Shamra)* (CBW, 4; Grand Rapids, 1985).

33. Horbury, *Jewish Messianism*, p. 7.
34. *Jewish Messianism*, pp. 7–13.
35. Besides Horbury, see J. Klausner, 'The messianic idea in the apocryphal literature', in M. Avi-Yonah (ed.), *Society and Religion in the Second Temple Period* (Jerusalem, 1977), pp. 153–86.
36. See Andrew Chester, 'The Sibyl and the temple', in W. Horbury (ed.), *Templum Amicitiae* (JSNTSup, 48; Sheffield, 1991), pp. 37–69.
37. See Kenneth Atkinson, 'On the Herodian origin of militant Davidic messianism at Qumran: new light from Psalms of Solomon 17', *JBL* 118 (1999), pp. 435–60.
38. Richard A. Horsley, 'Messianic figures and movements in first-century Palestine', in Charlesworth (ed.), *The Messiah*, pp. 276–95.
39. William Horbury, 'The messianic associations of "The Son of Man" ', *JTS* 36 (1985), pp. 34–55; Klaus Koch, 'Messias und Menschensohn: die zweitufige Messianologie der jüngeren Apokalyptik', in Baldermann (ed.), *Der Messias*, pp. 73–102; James C. Vanderkam, 'Righteous One, Messiah, Chosen One, and Son of Man in 1 Enoch 37–71', in Charlesworth (ed.), *The Messiah*, 169–91.
40. Standard treatments of this issue include R. Martin-Achard, *From Death to Life: A Study of the Development of the Doctrine of the Resurrection in the Old Testament* (ET Edinburgh, 1960); G. Stemberger, *Der Leib der Auferstehung: Studien zur Anthropologie und Eschatologie des palästinischen Judentums im neutestamentlichen Zeitalter (ca. 170 v. Chr.–100 n. Chr.)* (AnBib, 56; Rome, 1972); George W.E. Nickelsburg, *Resurrection, Immortality, and Eternal Life in Intertestamental Judaism* (HTS, 26; Cambridge MA, 1972); C. Barth, *Die Errettung vom Tode in den individuellen Klage- und Dankliedern des Alten Testaments* (Zolliken, 1974); H.C.C. Cavallin, *Life after Death* (CB 7/1; Lund, 1974); E. Schürer, revised by G. Vermes, F. Millar and M. Black, *The History of the Jewish People in the Age of Jesus Christ (175 BC–AD 135)*, vol. ii (Edinburgh, 1979), pp. 539–44; and the articles by Robert Martin-Achard, 'Resurrection – Old Testament', in *ABD*, vol. v, pp. 680–4; George W.E. Nickelsburg, 'Resurrection – early Judaism and Christianity', in *ABD*, vol. v, pp. 684–91; Jacob Neusner and Alan J. Avery-Peck (eds), *Judaism in Late Antiquity*, pt. iv: *Death, Life after Death, Resurrection and the World to Come in the Judaism of Antiquity* (Leiden, 2000); Friedrich Avemarie and Hermann Lichtenberger (eds), *Auferstehung = Resurrection: The First Durham–Tübingen Research Symposium: Resurrection, Transfiguration and Exaltation in the Old Testament, Ancient Judaism and Early Christianity* (WUNT, 135; Tübingen, 2001); Claudia Setzer, *Resurrection of the Body in Judaism and Early Christianity: Doctrine, Community and Self-definition* (Boston, 2004); and James H. Charlesworth, *Resurrection: The Origin and Future of a Biblical Doctrine* (London, 2006).
41. See the bibliography, n. 40 above.
42. For a review of this issue see John Day, 'The dependence of Isaiah 26:13–27:11 on Hosea 13:4–14:10 and its relevance to some theories of the redaction of the "Isaiah apocalypse" ', in Craig Broyles and Craig A. Evans (eds), *Writing and Reading the Scroll of Isaiah: Studies of an Interpretive Tradition*, vol. i (VTSup, 70/1; Leiden, 1997).
43. See Collins, *Daniel*, pp. 394–8; and Ulrich Kellerman, 'Das Danielbuch und

die Märtyrtheologie der Auferstehung', in J. Henten (ed.), *Die Entstehung der jüdischen Märtyrologie* (Leiden, 1989), pp. 51–75.

44. See Nickelsburg, in *ABD*, vol. v, p. 685; and Collins, *Daniel*, p. 396 n.235. M.-T. Wacker, (*Weltordnung und Gericht: Studien zu 1 Henoch 22* (FB, 45; Würzburg, 1982), pp. 107–8) discerns two stages in the text at this point.

45. See the discussion of this material by Collins, *Apocalyptic Imagination*, pp. 43–84.

46. Gene L. Davenport, *Eschatology of the Book of Jubilees* (SPB, 20; Leiden, 1971). On *Jubilees* more generally, M. Albani, J. Frey and A. Lange (eds), *Studies in the Book of Jubilees* (Tübingen, 1997).

47. Nickelsburg, *Resurrection*.

48. See R.J. Taylor, 'The eschatological meaning of life and death in the book of Wisdom', *ETL* 42 (1966), pp. 72–137; John J. Collins, 'Cosmos and salvation: Jewish wisdom and apocalyptic in the Hellenistic age', *HR* 17 (177), pp. 121–42; Otto Kaiser, 'Die ersten und die Letzten Dinge', *NZSThR* 36 (1994), pp. 75–91; and Marco Nobile, 'La thématique eschatologique dans le livre de la Sagesse en relation avec l'apocalyptique', in N. Calduch-Benages and J. Vermeylen (eds), *Treasures of Wisdom: Studies in Ben Sira and the Book of Wisdom* (Louvain, 1999), pp. 303–12.

49. See F. Gerald Downing, 'The resurrection of the dead: Jesus and Philo', *JSNT* 15 (1982), 42–50; and Jan W. van Henten, *The Maccabean Martyrs as Saviours of the Jewish People: A Study of 2 and 4 Maccabees* (JSJSup, 57; Leiden, 1997).

50. There are obvious parallels with subsequent Christian ritual actvity. See Barnabas Lindars, 'Joseph and Asenath and the Eucharist', in Barry P. Thompson (ed.), *Scripture: Meaning and Method: Essays Presented to Anthony Tyrrell Hanson for his Seventieth Birthday* (Hull, 1987), pp. 181–98.

51. See Fausto Parente, 'Flavius Josephus' account of the anti-Roman riots preceding the 66–70 war, and its relevance for reconstruction of Jewish eschatology during the first century AD', *JANES* 16–17 (1984–5), pp. 183–205; and Joseph Sievers, 'Josephus and the afterlife', in Steve Mason (ed.), *Understanding Josephus: Seven Perspectives* (JSPSup, 32; Sheffield, 1998), pp. 20–34.

52. See Anitra Bingham Kolenkow, 'The fall of the temple and the coming of the end: the spectrum and process of apocalyptic argument in 2 Baruch and other authors', in Kent Harold Richards (ed.), *SBL Seminar Papers* 21 (1982), pp. 243–50; Bernhard Lang, 'No sex in heaven: the logic of procreation, death, and eternal life in the Judaeo-Christian tradition', in A. Caquot, S. Légasse and M. Tardieu, *Mélanges bibliques et orientaux en l'honneur de M. Matthias Delcor* (AOAT, 25; Neukirchen-Vluyn, 1985), pp. 237–57; Willet, *Eschatology*; and Longenecker, *Eschatology and the Covenant*.

53. Nickelsburg, *Resurrection*.

54. Oscar Cullmann, 'Immortality of the soul or resurrection of the dead', in Krister Stendahl (ed.), *Immortality and Resurrection* (New York, 1965), pp. 9–35.

Chapter 11

1. See G.N. Stanton, *The Gospels and Jesus* (Oxford, 1989); *idem, Jesus and Gospel* (Cambridge, 2004); Richard A. Burridge, *Four Gospels, One Jesus? A Symbolic Reading of the Gospels* (Grand Rapids, 1994; 2005); Richard Bauckham (ed.), *The Gospels for All Christians: Rethinking the Gospel*

Audiences (Grand Rapids, 1998); Richard A. Burridge and Graham Gould, *Jesus Now and Then* (London, 2004); Stanley E. Porter (ed.), *Reading the Gospels Today* (Grand Rapids, 2004); and Dale C. Allison, *Resurrecting Jesus: Earliest Christian Tradition and its Interpreters* (London and New York, 2005). Among the recent books on Jesus, see Dale C. Allison, *Jesus of Nazareth: Millenarian Prophet* (Minneapolis, 1998); Markus Bockmuehl (ed.), *The Cambridge Companion to Jesus* (Cambridge, 2001); Leander E. Keck, *Who is Jesus? History in Perfect Tense* (Edinburgh, 2001); Jonathan Knight, *Jesus: An Historical and Theological Investigation* (London, 2004); Sean Freyne, *Jesus a Jewish Galilean: A New Reading of the Jesus Story* (London, 2004); James D.G. Dunn and Scot McKnight (eds), *The Historical Jesus in Recent Research* (SBTS, 10; Winona Lake, 2005); James D.G. Dunn, *A New Perspective on Jesus: What the Quest for the Historical Jesus Missed* (Grand Rapids, 2005); James H. Charlesworth (ed.), *Jesus and Archaeology* (Grand Rapids, 2006); and Craig A. Evans, *Fabricating Jesus: How Modern Scholars Distort the Gospels* (Nottingham, 2007).

2. On the genre of the Gospels see R.A. Burridge, *What are the Gospels? A Comparison with Graeco-Roman Biography* (SNTSMS, 70; Cambridge, 1992, 2004); and Jonathan Knight, *Luke's Gospel* (NTR London, 1998), pp. 21–69. There is a valuable introduction to the study of this literature by E.P. Sanders and Margaret Davies, *Studying the Synoptic Gospels* (London, 1989). Written from a conservative viewpoint I note Craig Blomberg's *The Historical Reliability of the Gospels* (Leicester, 1987).

3. On whom see James M. Robinson, 'The legacy of Albert Schweitzer's Quest of the Historical Jesus', in Marvin Meyer and Kurt Bergel (eds), *Reverence for Life: The Ethics of Albert Schweitzer for the Twenty-First Century* (Syracuse, 2002), pp. 246–55.

4. *The Quest of the Historical Jesus* (ET London, 1910), p. 4: 'But it was not only each epoch that found its reflection in Jesus; each individual created Him in accordance with his own character. There is no historical task which so reveals a man's true self as the writing of a Life of Jesus.'

5. As for instance the discovery of the Dead Sea scrolls in 1947.

6. On the relations between the two see H. Koester 'Apocryphal and canonical Gospels', *HTR* 73 (1980), pp 105–30; *idem, Ancient Christian Gospels: Their History and Development* (London, 1990); and James H. Charlesworth and Craig A. Evans, 'Jesus in the agrapha and apocryphal Gospels', in Bruce Chilton and Craig A. Evans (eds), *Studying the Historical Jesus* (Leiden, 1994), pp. 479–533.

7. The view of Morna D. Hooker, *A Commentary on the Gospel According to St Mark* (London, 1991).

8. This date for the finished form of John is given by Martin Hengel, *The Johannine Question* (ET London, 1989).

9. For advocacy of the 'Q' hypothesis see Christopher M. Tuckett, *Q and the History of Early Christianity: Studies on Q* (Edinburgh, 1996). For a characteristically robust rebuttal of the theory, Michael D. Goulder, *Luke* (JSNTSup, 20; 2 vols.; Sheffield, 1989). On the work of the latter, see Mark S. Goodacre, *Goulder and the Gospels* (JSNTSup, 133; Sheffield, 1996).

10. *What are the Gospels?*

11. *The Gospels and Jesus*, p. 19. See also D.L. Barr and J.L. Wentling, 'The

conventions of classical biography and the genre of Luke–Acts', in C.H.
Talbert (ed.), *Luke–Acts: New Perspectives from the Society of Biblical Literature
Seminar* (New York, 1984), pp. 63–88.

12. Broadly related to this topic see F. Kermode, *The Genesis of Secrecy: On
the Interpretation of Narrative* (Cambridge, 1979); Rudolph Schnackenburg,
Jesus in the Gospels: A Biblical Christology (ET Louisville, 1995); and Stanley
E. Porter, Michael A. Hayes and David Tombs (eds), *Images of Christ:
Ancient and Modern* (RILP, 2; Sheffield, 1997).

13. See Chapter 15.

14. On this aspect see Mk 3.21-35. His family thought Jesus mad; he in turn
ignored them.

15. *Theology* 108 (2005), pp. 442–3.

16. *Reden über die Religion* (Göttingen, 1899); *Der christliche Glaube* (Berlin,
new edn, 1960). On this man see Stephen W. Sykes, *Friedrich Schleiermacher*
(London, 1971).

17. *Das Wesen des Christentums* (Leipzig, 1900); ET *What is Christianity?*
(London, 1901).

18. *Christianity and the Social Crisis* (New York, 1907).

19. Weiss, *Jesus' Proclamation of the Kingdom of God*, translated and edited by
Richard H. Hiers and D. Larrimore Holland (Philadelphia, 1971), p. 133.

20. *Die christliche Lehre von der Rechtfertigung und Versöhnung* (Bonn, [4]1895), vol.iii,
p. 271; translation from Richard H. Hiers and D. Larrimore Holland's edition of *Jesus' Proclamation*, pp. 7–8.

21. *Jesus' Proclamation*, p. 9.

22. *Jesus' Proclamation*, pp. 84–92.

23. *Jesus' Proclamation*, pp. 87–8.

24. *Jesus' Proclamation*, pp. 105–14.

25. See Robert Morgan, 'From Reimarus to Sanders: the kingdom of God,
Jesus, and the Judaisms of his day', in R. Barbour (ed.), *The Kingdom of God
and Human Society* (Edinburgh, 1993), pp. 80–139.

26. Works in English about Albert Schweitzer include H. Clark, *The Philosophy
of Albert Schweitzer* (London, 1964); and J.C. O'Neill, *The Bible's Authority*
(Edinburgh, 1991), pp. 248–65. In French, see Pierre Lassus, *Albert Schweitzer*
(Paris, 1995); and Laurent Gagnebin, *Albert Schweitzer* (Paris, 1999).

27. Albert Schweitzer, *The Mystery of the Kingdom of God* (ET London, 1914),
p. 253.

28. *Mystery*, p. 254.

29. *Mystery*, p. 136.

30. *Mystery*, p. 94.

31. *Mystery*, p. 261.

32. *Mystery*, p. 266.

33. *Mystery*, p. 267.

34. '*Then Judas betrayed to them the secret*. Now he was condemned', *Mystery*,
p. 271. Italics original.

35. *Mystery*, p. 253.

36. *The Parables of the Kingdom* (London, 1935). See also his *The Founder of
Christianity* (reprinted London, 1986). An interesting article is John Tudno
Williams, 'The contribution of Protestant nonconformists to biblical schol-
arship in the twentieth century', in Alan P.F. Sells and Anthony R. Cross

(eds), *Protestant Nonconformity in the Twentieth Century* (Carlisle, 2003), pp. 1–32.

37. *Promise and Fulfilment* (ET SBT, 23; London, 1957) [1956].

38. *Jesus and Judaism*, pp. 1–58.

39. *Jesus and Judaism*, p. 11.

40. *Jesus and Judaism*, p. 75.

41. *Jesus and Judaism*, pp. 77–90.

42. *Jesus and Judaism*, pp. 91–119.

43. *Jesus and Judaism*, pp. 98–106.

44. *Jesus and Judaism*, pp. 123–56.

45. *Jesus and Judaism*, pp. 106–13.

46. Notably Crossan's *The Historical Jesus: The Life of a Mediterranean Jewish Peasant* (San Francisco, 1991). See also *In Parables: The Challenge of the Historical Jesus* (New York, 1973). By Marcus J. Borg see especially *Jesus, a New Vision: Spirit, Culture, and the Life of Discipleship* (San Francisco, 1991); *Jesus in Contemporary Scholarship* (Valley Forge, 1994); and Marcus J. Borg and N.T. Wright, *The Meaning of Jesus: Two Visions* (London, 1999).

47. On Cynicism see D.R. Dudley, *A History of Cynicism from Diogenes to the 6th Century AD* (London, 1937); Harold W. Attridge, *First-Century Cynicism in the Epistles of Heraclitus: Introduction, Greek Text and Translation* (HTS, 29; Missoula, 1976); Abraham J. Malherbe, *The Cynic Epistles* (SBLSBS, 12; Atlanta, 1977); and L. Schotroff and W. Stegemann, *Jesus von Nazareth: Hoffnung der Armen* (Stuttgart, 1978).

48. Bryan R. Wilson, *Sects and Society: A Sociological Study of Three Religious Groups in Britain* (London, 1961); *Religious Sects: A Sociological Study* (London, 1970); *Magic and the Millennium: A Sociological Study of Religious Movements of Protest Among Tribal and Third-World Peoples* (New York, 1973).

49. *Historical Jesus.*

50. *Historical Jesus*, pp. 287–91.

51. *Historical Jesus*, pp. 291–2.

52. *Historical Jesus*, pp. 421–2.

53. *JEH* 45 (1994), pp. 115–16.

54. *JTS* 45 (1994), pp. 209–10.

55. *Jesus and the Victory of God* (London, 1996), pp. 210–14. See further Robert B. Stewart (ed.), *The Resurrection of Jesus: John Dominic Crossan and N.T. Wright in Dialogue* (London, 2006).

56. *Jesus the Jew* (London, 1973); *Jesus and the World of Judaism* (London, 1983); *The Religion of Jesus the Jew* (London, 1993); *The Changing Faces of Jesus* (London, 2000); and *Jesus in His Jewish Context* (London, 2003).

57. *Jesus the Jew*, pp. 58–82.

58. See also W.S. Green, 'Palestinian holy men: charismatic leadership and rabbinic tradition', in *ANRW* II.19.2, pp. 614–47; and J. Neusner, 'The sage, miracle, and magic', in *Why no Gospels in Talmudic Judaism?* (BJS, 135; Atlanta, 1988), pp, 13–30.

59. See also Vermes, 'Hanina ben Dosa', in *Post-biblical Jewish Studies* (SJLA, 8; Leiden, 1975), pp. 178–214.

60. *Jesus the Jew*, p. 79.

61. *Religion*, pp. 46–75.

62. Gerd Theissen and Annette Merz, *The Historical Jesus: A Comprehensive Guide* (ET London, 1998), p. 308.
63. Especially in his two books, *Jesus and the Spiral of Violence* (Minneapolis, 1993); and *Sociology and the Jesus Movement* (New York, 1994). See also his *Galilee: History, Politics, People* (Valley Forge, 1995); the later *Jesus and Empire: The Kingdom of God and the New World Disorder* (Minneapolis, 2003) and Richard A. Horsley and Neil A. Silberman, *The Message and the Kingdom: How Jesus and Paul Ignited a Revolution and Transformed the Ancient World* (Minneapolis, 2002).
64. See especially pt. iii of *Jesus and the Spiral of Violence.*
65. *Jesus and the Spiral of Violence*, pp. 231–42.
66. *Sociology*, p. 125.
67. *Sociology*, ch. 7.
68. In demonstration of this point, see Dunn's *A New Perspective on Jesus*, which I cited at note 1 above.

Chapter 12

1. Among attempts to do this, see Gerd Theissen, *Jesus als historische Gestalt: Beiträge zur Jesusforschung* (FRLANT, 202; Göttingen, 2003); Sean Freyne, *Jesus, a Jewish Galilean: A New Reading of the Jesus Story* (London, 2004); and Charles W. Hedrick, *Many Things in Parables: Jesus and His Modern Critics* (Louisville, 2004).
2. The Greek text is accessible in C. Tischendorf, *Evangelia Apocrypha* (2nd edn, 1876). There are English translations in J.K. Elliott, *The Apocryphal New Testament* (Oxford, 1993), pp. 48–67; H.R. Smid, *Protevangelium Jacobi: A Commentary* (ANT, 1; Assen, 1965); by O. Cullmann in E. Hennecke, rev. W. Schneemelcher, *New Testament Apocrypha*, vol. i: *Gospels and Related Writings* (ET Cambridge, 1991), pp. 421–39. See also E. Cothenet, 'Le Protévangile de Jacques: origine, genre et signification d'un premier midrash chrétien sur la nativité de Marie', *ANRW* II.25.6, pp. 4252–69; John L. Allen, 'The Protevangelium of James as an historia: the insufficiency of the Infancy Gospel category', in Eugene H. Lovering (ed.), *Society of Biblical Literature: 1991 Seminar Papers* (Atlanta, 1991), pp. 508–17; Ronald F. Hock, *The Infancy Gospels of James and Thomas* (Santa Rosa, 1995); James P. Sweeney, 'Modern and ancient controversies on the virgin birth of Jesus', *BS* 160 (2003), pp. 142–58; and Timothy J. Horner, 'Jewish aspects of the Protevangelium of James', *JECS* 12 (2004).
3. See P. Benoît, 'L'emplacement de Bethlehem au temps de Jésus', *Dossiers de l'Archéologie* 10 (1975), pp. 58–63.
4. See Jaroslav Pelikan, *Mary: Images of the Mother of Jesus in Jewish and Christian Perspective* (Minneapolis, 2005).
5. Pertinent literature includes R.E. Brown, *The Birth of the Messiah* (London, new edition 1993); George J. Brooke (ed.), *The Birth of Jesus: Biblical and Theological Reflections* (Edinburgh, 2000); and Edwin D. Freed, *The Stories of Jesus' Birth: A Critical Introduction* (Sheffield, 2001).
6. See Brown, *Birth*, Appendix VII, pp. 547–56; A.N. Sherwin-White, *Roman Society and Roman Law in the New Testament* (Oxford, 1963), pp. 162–71; and

John M. Rist, 'Luke 2.2: making sense of the date of Jesus' birth', *JTS* 56 (2005), pp. 489–91.

7. Thus R. Syme, 'The Titulus Tiburtinus', in *Vestigia: Akten des VI Internationalen Kongresses für Griechische und Lateinische Epigraphik, 1972* (BAG, 17; Munich, 1972).

8. This evidence comes from second- and third-century sources and is noted by Markus Bockmuehl, *This Jesus: Martyr, Lord, Messiah* (Edinburgh, 1994), pp. 28–9. Bockmuehl argues that Joseph's family owned property in Bethlehem.

9. On these features see Richard Horsley, *The Liberation of Christmas: The Infancy Narratives in Social Context* (New York, 1989). A birth at Bethlehem is denied by at least some prominent scholars. See for instance Gerd Theissen and Annette Merz, *The Historical Jesus: A Comprehensive Guide* (ET London, 1998), pp. 164–6. They argue in favour of Nazareth. I acknowledge my use of this book in this chapter.

10. See George Ogg, 'Hippolytus and the introduction of the Christian era', *VC* 16 (1962), pp. 2–18; and G. Fedalto, *Quando festiggiare il 2000? Problemi di chronologia cristiana*, (Rome, 1998).

11. The story of the twelve-year-old Jesus in the temple; Lk. 2.41-51. This again raises considerable questions of historicity.

12. On John the Baptist see Robert L. Webb, *John the Baptizer and Prophet: A Socio-Historical Study* (JSNTSup, 62; Sheffield, 1991); J.P. Meier, *A Marginal Jew*, vol. ii (New York and London, 1994), pp. 19–233; Joan E. Taylor, *The Immerser: John the Baptist within Second Temple Judaism* (Grand Rapids, 1997); Theissen and Merz, *Historical Jesus*, pp. 196–207; and Catherine M. Murphy, *John the Baptist: Prophet of Purity for a New Age* (Collegeville, 2003). Older studies include C.H. Scobie, *John the Baptist* (London, 1964); and Walter Wink, *John the Baptist in the Gospel Tradition* (SNTSMS, 7; London, 1968).

13. See Webb, *John the Baptizer*, pp. 39–41.

14. Origen states in this passage that Josephus did not believe in Jesus as Christ. The writings of Josephus, however, contain the so-called *Testimonium Flavianum* (*Ant.* 18.63–4) in which this opinion about Jesus is advanced. The *Testimonium Flavianum* throws up notorious problems of interpretation; many would say of reconstruction. On the issues raised here see Theissen and Merz, *Historical Jesus*, pp. 64–74.

15. But see Bruce D. Chilton, 'Recovering Jesus' *Mamzerut*', in James H. Charlesworth (ed.), *Jesus and Archaeology* (Grand Rapids, 2006), pp. 84–110.

16. The *Gospel of the Ebionites* is a Jewish–Christian apocryphal Gospel mentioned by both Irenaeus and Eusebius. ETs in Elliott (ed.), *Apocryphal New Testament*, pp. 14–16; and Hennecke, rev. Schneemelcher, *New Testament Apocrypha*, vol. i: *Gospels and Related Writings*, pp. 166–71. See also William L. Petersen, 'Gospel of the Ebionites', in *ABD*, vol. ii, pp. 261–2.

17. See the arguments for this view set out by Raymond E. Brown, 'The Dead Sea scrolls and the New Testament', in James H. Charlesworth (ed.), *John and Qumran* (London, 1972), pp. 4–5.

18. *John the Baptizer*, pp. 209–13.

19. See Taylor, *The Immerser*. She concludes (p. 48) that John should not be associated with the Essenes. A similar conclusion is advocated by Hartmut

Stegemann, *The Library of Qumran: On the Essenes, Qumran, John the Baptist, and Jesus* (ET Grand Rapids, 1998), pp. 212–27. Stegemann concludes in a pithy paragraph: 'John the Baptist was neither an Essene nor a spiritual pupil of the Essenes. Were he ever to have made the effort to walk over to Qumran, as a non-Essene he would have been denied entry, and at best provided with enough food and drink for the long walk back.'

20. See Craig A. Evans, 'Jesus, John and the Dead Sea scrolls: assessing typologies of restoration', in John J. Collins and Craig A. Evans (eds), *Christian Beginnings and the Dead Sea Scrolls* (Grand Rapids, 2006), pp. 45–62.

21. On this topic see F. Lentzen-Deis, *Die Taufe Jesu nach den Synoptikern* (FTS, 4; Frankfurt, 1970); Meier, *Marginal Jew*, vol. ii, pp. 100–30; Theissen and Merz, *Historical Jesus*, pp. 207–13; J. Ernst, 'Johannes der Taufer und Jesus von Nazareth in historischer Sicht', *NTS* 43 (1997), pp. 161–83; R. Alastair Campbell, 'Jesus and his baptism', *Tyndale Bulletin* 47 (1996), pp. 191–214; Craig A. Evans, 'The baptism of John in typological context', in Stanley E. Porter and Anthony R. Cross (eds), *The Dimensions of Baptism: Biblical and Theological Studies* (JSNTSup, 234, London, 2002), pp. 45–71; and Morna D. Hooker, 'John's baptism: a prophetic sign', in Graham N. Stanton, Bruce W. Longenecker and Stephen C. Barton (eds), *The Holy Spirit and Christian Origins: Essays in Honor of J.D.G. Dunn* (Grand Rapids, 2004), pp. 22–40.

22. Luke seems to represent a link between Matthew and John in this respect when he mentions Jesus' baptism only *after* the story of John's imprisonment, creating doubt as to who baptized Jesus (Lk. 3.18-22).

23. See Graham Neville, 'Sinlessness and uncertainty in Jesus', *ExpT* 166 (2005), pp. 361–5.

24. The classic study of this issue is N.P. Williams, *The Ideas of the Fall and Original Sin* (London, 1927).

25. Cf. Ezek. 1.1; Rev. 4.1; and see Christopher Rowland, *The Open Heaven* (London, 1982), pp. 358–68.

26. It recalls Ps. 2.7 and Isa. 42.1.

27. 'Jesus' baptismal vision', *NTS* 41 (1995), pp. 512–21.

28. On this point see Theissen and Merz, *Historical Jesus*, p. 554.

29. This point has been explored, with distinctive emphasis, by Maurice Casey, *From Jewish Prophet to Gentile God: The Origin and Development of New Testament Christology* (Cambridge, 1991).

30. On Capernaum see V. Tzaferis, *Excavations at Capernaum* (Winona Lake, 1991); John C.H. Laughlin, 'Capernaum from Jesus' time and after', *BAR* 19 (1993), pp. 54–61, 90; and Henry Innes MacAdam, 'Domus domini: where Jesus lived; Capernaum and Bethany in the Gospels', *TR* 25 (2004), pp. 47–70.

31. See Theissen and Merz, *Historical Jesus*, 291–7; Gerd Theissen, *The Miracle Stories of the Early Christian Tradition* (ET Philadelphia, 1983); Graham H. Twelftree, *Jesus the Miracle Worker: A Historical and Theological Study* (Downers Grove IL, 1999); Wendy Cotter, *Miracles in Greco-Roman Antiquity: A Sourcebook for the Study of New Testament Miracle Stories* (London, 1999); Eric Eve, *The Jewish Context of Jesus' Miracles* (JSNTSup, 231; Sheffield, 2002); and Esther Eshel, 'Jesus the exorcist in light of epigraphic sources', in Charlesworth (ed.), *Jesus and Archaeology*, pp. 178–85.

32. See E. Bowie, in *ANRW* II.16.2 (1978), pp. 1652ff.; and G. Anderson, *Sage, Saint and Sophist* (London, 1994), *passim*.
33. *Marginal Jew*, vol. ii, pt. iii.
34. M. Dibelius, *From Tradition to Gospel* (1919; ET London, 1934); G. Schille, *Die urchristliche Wundertradition. Ein Beitrag zur Frage nach dem irdischen Jesus* (AT 1, 29; Stuttgart, 1967).
35. Theissen, *Miracle Stories*, p. 94.
36. *Miracle Stories*, pp. 94–5.
37. *Miracle Stories*, p. 99.
38. *Miracle Stories*, p. 103.
39. *Miracle Stories*, p. 106.
40. See my comments in *Jesus: An Historical and Theological Investigation* (London, 2004), pp. 156–8.
41. See R. Steven Notley, Marc Turnage and Brian Becker (eds), *Jesus' Last Week: Jerusalem Studies in the Synoptic Gospels*, vol. i (Leiden, 2006) and Marcus J. Borg and John Dominic Crossan, *The Last Week: A Day-by-day Account of Jesus' Final Week in Jerusalem* (San Francisco, 2006).
42. See my outworking of this thesis in *Jesus*, chs. 5 and 7; and in the later chapters of this Part of this book.
43. See Theissen and Merz, *Historical Jesus*, pp. 157–61.
44. See Martin Hengel, *Crucifixion* (ET London, 1977); and Gerard S. Sloyan, *The Crucifixion of Jesus: History, Myth, Faith* (Minneapolis, 1995).

Chapter 13

1. There is a forest of literature on the parables of Jesus. Classic studies include C.H. Dodd, *The Parables of the Kingdom* (London, 1935); and J. Jeremias, *The Parables of Jesus* (ET New York, 1963). More recent studies include Charles W. Hedrick, *Parables as Poetic Fictions: The Creative Voice of Jesus* (Peabody, 1994); William R. Herzog, *Parables as Subversive Speech: Jesus as Pedagogue of the Oppressed* (Louisville, 1994); Ivor H. Jones, *The Matthean Parables: A Literary and Historical Commentary* (NovTSup, 80; Leiden, 1995); Ruth Etchells, *A Reading of the Parables of Jesus* (London, 1998); V.G. Shillington, *Jesus and his Parables: Interpreting the Parables of Jesus Today* (Edinburgh, 1997); and Luise Schotroff, trans. Linda M. Maloney, *The Parables of Jesus* (Minneapolis, 2006).
2. Though see Bruce D. Chilton, *Rabbi Jesus: An Intimate Biography* (New York, 2000); and Beatrice Bruteau (ed.), *Jesus Through Jewish Eyes: Rabbis and Scholars Engage an Ancient Brother in New Conversation* (Maryknoll NY, 2001).
3. See Richard A. Horsley, *Sociology and the Jesus Movement* (New York, 1989), esp. pp. 43–50. Horsley criticizes Gerd Theissen's attempt to portray the Jesus movement as consisting primarily of wandering charismatics (Theissen, *The Sociology of Early Palestinian Christianity*; ET London, 1978).
4. See Mk 6.7–13 and parallels.
5. See William E. Arnal, *Jesus and the Village Scribes: Galilean Conflicts and the Setting of Q* (Minneapolis, 2001).
6. See Chapter 15 for evaluation of this.
7. Of all the available literature, Gerd Theissen and Annette Merz, *The Historical*

Jesus: A Comprehensive Guide (ET London, 1998), pp. 240–80, is perhaps the clearest and most accessible study of this issue. Other important studies include Bruce J. Malina, *The Social Gospel of Jesus: The Kingdom of God in Mediterranean Perspective* (Minneapolis, 2000); and Richard A. Horsley, *Jesus and Empire: The Kingdom of God and the New World Disorder* (Minneapolis, 2003).

8. See my study of this theme in Part 1.
9. I mentioned the work of Robert Karl Gnuse, *No Other Gods: Emergent Monotheism in Israel* (JSOTSup, 241; Sheffield, 1997).
10. See Keith W. Whitelam, 'King and kingship', in *ABD*, vol. iv, pp. 40–8. Among the older literature, S. Mowinckel, *The Psalms in Israel's Worship* (2 vols.; ET Oxford, 1962).
11. See Paul S. Hanson, *The Dawn of Apocalyptic* (Philadelphia, 1975), esp. ch. 3.
12. See Hanson, *Dawn*, ch. 4.
13. On this aspect of Daniel see John J. Collins, *The Apocalyptic Vision of the Book of Daniel* (Missoula MT, 1977), ch. 6.
14. This conclusion is accepted by all scholars, as I observed in Chapter 11.
15. See W.G. Kümmel, *Promise and Fulfilment* (ET SBT, 23; London, 1957) [1956], pp. 32–6, 103–5; G.R. Beasley-Murray, *Jesus and the Kingdom of God* (Grand Rapids and Exeter, 1986), pp. 313–21; D.R. Catchpole, 'The Law and the Prophets in Q', in G.F. Hawthorne and O. Betz (eds), *Tradition and Interpretation in the New Testament* (Tübingen and Grand Rapids, 1987), pp. 95–109; J.M. Robinson, 'The study of the historical Jesus after Nag Hammadi', *Semeia* 44 (1988), pp. 45–55; and J. Ramsey Michaels, 'Almsgiving and the kingdom within: Tertullian on Luke 17:21', *CBQ* 60 (1998), pp. 475–83.
16. See Theissen and Merz, *Historical Jesus*, p. 260.
17. See Hedrick, *Parables*, pp. 7–35.
18. See Chapter 12; and Theissen and Merz, *Historical Jesus*, ch. 10.
19. See Simon J. Gathercole, 'Jesus' Eschatological Vision of the Fall of Satan Reconsidered', *ZNW* 94 (2003), p. 143–63.
20. On this verse see Martin Hengel, 'Der Finger und die Herrschaft Gottes in Lk 11,20', in René Kieffer and Jan Bergman (eds), *Le Main de Dieu/Die Hand Gottes* (WUNT, 94; Tübingen, 1997), pp. 87–106; Pieter W. van der Horst, ' "The finger of God": miscellaneous notes on Luke 11:20 and its *Umwelt*', in William L. Petersen, Johan S. Vos and Henk J. de Jonge (eds), *Sayings of Jesus: Canonical and Non-Canonical. Essays in Honour of Tjitze Baarda* (Leiden, 1997), pp. 89–103; and R.W. Wall, 'The finger of God: Deuteronomy 9:10 and Luke 11:20', *NTS* 33 (1987), pp. 144–50.
21. *The Kingdom of God and Primitive Christianity* (ET London, 1968), pp. 123–5.
22. See also Gerd Theissen, 'Jünger als Gewalttäter (Mt 11,12f.; Lk 16,16). Der Stürmerspruch als Selbststigmatisierung einer Minorität', in David Hellholm, Halvor Moxnes and Turid Karlsen Seim (eds), *Mighty Minorities? Minorities in Early Christianity – Positions and Strategies* (Oslo, 1995), pp. 183–200; and Chris Mearns, 'Realized eschatology in Q: a consideration of the sayings in Luke 7:22, 11:20 and 16:16', *SJT* 40 (1987), pp. 189–200.
23. See Mark Allan Powell, 'Matthew's Beatitudes: reversals and rewards of the kingdom', *CBQ* 58 (1996), pp. 460–79.
24. See Theissen and Merz, *Historical Jesus*, p. 266.

NOTES TO CHAPTER 13

25. A point made helpfully by Theissen and Merz, *Historical Jesus*, p. 252.
26. See Helmut Koester, 'The sayings of Q and their image of Jesus', in Petersen, Vos and de Jonge (eds), *Sayings of Jesus*, pp. 137–54. His conclusion (p. 154) is that 'the Jesus of the earliest formation of the Sayings Gospel Q proclaims the arrival of God's kingdom as a challenge to the disciples, who are asked to realize that their own existence belongs to a new eschatological moment. This may not be a direct and unbroken mirror of the preaching of the historical Jesus; but it certainly excludes any recourse to a Jesus who was but a social reformer or a philosopher in the tradition of the Cynic preacher.' On this saying from *Gos. Thom.* see Stephen J. Patterson, *The Gospel of Thomas and Jesus* (Sonoma, 1993), pp. 208–13.
27. See Theissen and Merz, *Historical Jesus*, pp. 252–4. On the Beatitudes see also Simon Tugwell, *The Beatitudes: Soundings in Christian Tradition* (Springfield, 1980); Dennis Hamm, *The Beatitudes in Context: What Luke and Matthew Meant* (Wilmington, 1990); Powell, 'Matthew's Beatitudes'; and Michel Gourgues, 'Sur l'articulation des béatitudes matthéennes (Mt 5:3–12): Une proposition', *NTS* 44 (1998), pp. 340–56.
28. On which see Chapter 15.
29. Theissen and Merz, *Historical Jesus*, p. 255.
30. Cf. Martin Hengel, *The Atonement* (ET London, 1981), p. 72: 'We are probably to understand Mark 14.25, the reference to the coming meal in the kingdom of God, as meaning that Jesus wanted to prepare the way for the coming of the kingdom of God through his sacrificial death in the face of the apparent supremacy of evil and sin in God's own people and all mankind.' A more recent study of this passage is Marinus de Jonge, 'Mark 14:25 among Jesus' words about the kingdom of God', in Petersen and others (eds), *Sayings of Jesus*, pp. 123–35; see also Jack T. Sanders, 'The criterion of coherence and the randomness of charisma: poring through some aporias in the Jesus tradition (Mk. 11.7-19; Lk. 7.24-5; Mk 3.21, 4.10-11, 12.13-17, 14.25, 15:2-5; Lk. 16.1-9, 18.1-8 as read by J.D. Crossan, J. Jeremias, N. Perrin, E.P. Sanders, G. Vermes)', *NTS* 44 (1998), pp. 1–25.
31. I note, however, that de Jonge, in 'Mark 14:25', considers the attestation uncertain. An influential supporter of the authenticity of Mk 14.25 is J.P. Meier, *A Marginal Jew*, vol. ii (New York and London, 1994), p. 308.
32. See Theissen and Merz, *Historical Jesus*, p. 255. Meier also concludes that Mk 9.1 derives from the early church (*Marginal Jew*, vol. ii, pp. 341–4). For a different view see David Wenham and A.D.A. Moses, ' "There are some standing here . . ." Did they become the "reputed pillars" of the Jerusalem church?', *NovT* 36 (1994), pp. 146–63.
33. *Promise and Fulfilment*. His argument is accepted as convincing by Theissen and Merz, in *Historical Jesus*.
34. See my review of this issue in Chapter 15.
35. See Meier, *Marginal Jew*, vol. ii, pp. 341–4.
36. This point is made by N.T. Wright, *Jesus and the Victory of God* (London, 1996), pp. 210–14. See also Robert J. Miller, *The Apocalyptic Jesus: A Debate* (Santa Rosa, 2001).
37. Marcus Borg, in his two books *Jesus: A New Vision* (San Francisco, 1991); and *Jesus in Contemporary Scholarship* (Valley Forge, 1994).
38. See Chapter 23.

39. It is significant in this respect that Borg should call himself an 'unbelieving son of the church'; *Jesus: A New Vision*, Preface.
40. Notably, with the much-hyped interest in post-modernism.
41. See Wright, *Jesus and the Victory of God*, pp. 210–14.
42. The first point is made with conviction by Christopher Rowland, *The Open Heaven* (London, 1982). On the second, see the 'Systematic presentation' of eschatology in E. Schürer, revised by Geza Vermes, Fergus Millar and Matthew Black, *The History of the Jewish People in the Age of Jesus Christ (175 BC–AD 135)*, vol. ii (London, 1979), pp. 514–47.
43. See Chapter 10.
44. These two axes of the apocalyptic matrix were appropriately brought out in John J. Collins (ed.), *Apocalypse: Morphology of a Genre* (*Semeia* 14, 1979).
45. See further Chapter 14.
46. They feature particularly in the non-Marcan material. See David Sim, *Apocalyptic Eschatology in the Gospel of Matthew* (SNTSMS, 88; Cambridge, 1996).
47. See Ben Witherington, *Jesus, Paul and the End of the World: A Comparative Study in New Testament Eschatology* (Exeter, 1992).
48. *A Myth of Innocence: Mark and Christian Origins* (Minneapolis, 1988).
49. For Paul's early eschatology see 1 Thess. 1.9-10; 4.13-18; and 1 Corinthians 15. See also Chapters 21 and 23.
50. See Chapter 12.
51. So Theissen and Merz, *Historical Jesus*, pp. 261–5. Among recent studies see also Douglas E. Oakman, 'The Lord's Prayer in social perspective', in Bruce Chilton and Craig A. Evans (eds), *Authenticating the Words of Jesus* (Leiden, 1999), pp. 137–86; and Vernon K. Robbins, 'Divine dialogue and the Lord's Prayer: sociorhetorical interpretation of sacred texts', *Dialogue* 28 (1995), pp. 117–46.

Chapter 14

1. See Chapter 10. To the literature mentioned there, add Sean Freyne, 'A Galilean Messiah?', *ST* 55 (2001), pp. 198–210; Richard S. Hess and M. Daniel Carroll (eds), *Israel's Messiah in the Bible and the Dead Sea Scrolls* (Grand Rapids, 2003); and John J. Collins, 'A Messiah before Jesus?' in John J. Collins and Craig A. Evans (eds), *Christian Origins and the Dead Sea Scrolls* (Grand Rapids, 2006), pp. 15–35.
2. *Jewish Messianism and the Cult of Christ* (London, 1998), p. 7.
3. See Aquila H. Lee, *From Messiah to Pre-existent Son: Jesus' Self-consciousness and Early Christian Exegesis of Messianic Psalms* (WUNT, 192; Tübingen, 2005).
4. For different (and in places conflicting) approaches to Mark as a narrative see Burton Lee Mack, *A Myth of Innocence: Mark and Christian Origins* (Philadelphia, 1991); Robert W. Funk with Mahlon H. Smith, *The Gospel of Mark: Red Letter Edition* (Sonoma, 1991); John Painter, *Mark's Gospel: Worlds in Conflict* (London, 1997); and Mark Allan Powell, 'Towards a narrative-critical understanding of Mark', in J.D. Kingsbury (ed.), *Gospel Interpretation: Narrative-Critical and Social Scientific Approaches* (Harrisburg, 1997),

pp. 65–70. Valuable also is Suzanne Watts Henderson, *Christology and Discipleship in the Gospel of Mark* (SNTSMS, 135; Cambridge, 2006).

5. The classic demonstration of this point in English-speaking commentaries is in Dennis Nineham, *The Gospel of Saint Mark* (originally published Harmondsworth, 1963).

6. At least in Mark's version of this event.

7. See Lidija Novakovic, *Messiah, the Healer of the Sick: A Study of Jesus as the Son of David in the Gospel of Matthew* (WUNT, 170; Tübingen, 2003); and Brandon Byrne, 'Jesus as Messiah in the Gospel of Luke: discerning a pattern of correction', *CBQ* 65 (2003), pp. 80–95.

8. See the review of the evidence in the essays collected in E. Bammel and C.F.D. Moule (eds), *Jesus and the Politics of His Day* (Cambridge, 1984); and Chapter 15 below.

9. For a review of this issue see Martin Hengel, 'Jesus, the Messiah of Israel: the debate about the "Messianic Mission" of Jesus', in Bruce D. Chilton and Craig A. Evans (eds), *Authenticating the Activities of Jesus* (Leiden, 1999), pp. 323–49.

10. See Chapter 11.

11. *Jesus and Judaism* (London, 1985); *idem, The Historical Figure of Jesus* (London, 1993), pp. 240–3.

12. See Michael E. Stone, 'The question of the Messiah in 4 Ezra', in J. Neusner, W. Green and E. Frerichs (eds), *Judaisms and Their Messiahs at the Turn of the Christian Era* (Cambridge, 1987), pp. 209–24.

13. That Jesus did this is acknowledged as 'almost indisputable' by Ed Sanders, *Jesus and Judaism*, p. 11. See further Eckhard J. Schnabel, *Early Christian Mission*, vol. i: *Jesus and the Twelve* (Downers Grove and Leicester, 2004).

14. See Martin Hengel, *The Johannine Question* (London, 1989), p. 18.

15. For further discussion of this issue see John P. Meier, 'The circle of the twelve: did it exist during Jesus' ministry?', *JBL* 116 (1997), pp. 635–72.

16. See especially Sanders, *Jesus and Judaism*, pp. 91–106.

17. See N.K. Gottwald, *The Tribes of Yahweh* (Maryknoll NY, 1979); A.H.D. Mayes, 'Amphictyony', in *ABD*, vol. i, pp. 212–16.

18. The evidence is set out by Sanders, *Jesus and Judaism*, pp. 95–8.

19. See further David C. Sim, 'The meaning of *palingenesia* in Matthew 19.28', *JSNT* 50 (1993), pp. 3–12; and I. Howard Marshall, 'The hope of a new age: the kingdom of God in the New Testament', *Themelios* 11 (1985), pp. 5–15.

20. See Sanders, *Jesus and Judaism*, pp. 98–106.

21. On this subject see Dale C. Allison, 'The eschatology of Jesus', in J.J. Collins (ed.), *The Encyclopedia of Apocalypticism*, vol. i: *The Origins of Apocalypticism in Judaism and Christianity* (New York, 1998), pp. 267–302.

22. See Marcus J. Borg and John Dominic Crossan, *The Last Week: A Day-by-day Account of Jesus' Final Week in Jerusalem* (San Francisco, 2006); and R. Steven Notley, Marc Turnage and Brian Becker (eds), *Jesus' Last Week: Jerusalem Studies in the Synoptic Gospels* (Leiden, 2006).

23. *The Mystery of the Kingdom of God* (London, 1914), p. 271.

24. Sanders, *Jesus and Judaism*.

25. See further Chapter 15.

26. See my *Jesus: An Historical and Theological Investigation* (London, 2004), pp. 138–45.

27. See e.g. Dan. 12.4. The esotericism of the apocalypses is examined by
    D.S. Russell, *The Method and Message of Jewish Apocalyptic, 200 BC–100 AD*
    (London, 1964), pp. 107–18.
28. Notably by Burton Lee Mack.
29. Dated but still valuable is Schuyler Brown's article, 'Secret of the kingdom
    of God, Mark 4:11', *JBL* 92 (1973), pp. 60–74. I mention also the study
    of Joachim Jeremias, translated by Norman Perrin from the German 3rd
    edition, *The Eucharistic Words of Jesus* (ET London, 1964), pp. 125–37.
30. For interpretations of this story see David R. Catchpole, 'The "triumphal
    entry" ', in Bammel and Moule (eds), *Jesus and the Politics of His Day*,
    pp. 319–34; N.T. Wright, *Jesus and the Victory of God* (London, 1996),
    pp. 490–3; Sanders, *Jesus and Judaism*, pp. 306–8; M.D. Hooker, *A Commen-
    tary on the Gospel according to St. Mark* (London, 1991), pp. 255–60; and Brent
    Kinman, *Jesus' Entry into Jerusalem* (Leiden, 1995).
31. Mk 11.1-10; Mt. 21.1-9; Lk. 19.29-40; Jn 12.12-19.
32. Sanders (*Jesus and Judaism*, p. 306) considers the possibility that Jesus staged
    the triumphal entry to fulfil Zech. 9.9.
33. See J. Duncan M. Derrett, 'Law in the New Testament: the Palm Sunday
    colt', in *Studies in the New Testament*, vol. ii: *Midrash in Action and as a Literary
    Device* (Leiden, 1978), pp. 165–83.
34. 'Law in the New Testament', p. 168.
35. 'Law in the New Testament', pp. 172–3.
36. See Wright, *Jesus and the Victory of God*, p. 491.
37. See Morna D. Hooker, *Signs of a Prophet: Prophetic Actions of Jesus* (London,
    1997), pp. 2–6.
38. See Hans Dieter Betz, 'Jesus and the purity of the temple (Mark 11:15–18): a
    comparative religion approach', *JBL* 116/3 (1997), pp. 455–72. He sees Jesus
    objecting to the commercialization of the temple. For a different under-
    standing see Sanders, *Jesus and Judaism*, pp. 61–76, 77–90; idem, *Historical
    Figure*, pp. 42, 254–7.
39. On the Johannine version of the story see Larry J. Kreitzer, 'The temple
    incident of John 2.13-25: a preview of what is to come', in Christopher
    Rowland and Crispin Fletcher-Louis (eds), *Understanding, Studying and
    Reading: New Testament Essays in Honour of John Ashton* (JSNTSup, 153;
    Sheffield, 1998), pp. 93–101.
40. A variant on this theme is the suggestion of Hans Dieter Betz ('Jesus and
    the purity of the temple') that Jesus was irritated by the fact that the
    merchants and bankers had moved inside the sacred precinct to conduct
    their business. It is, however, difficult to explain the immediate decision of
    the religious authorities to *kill* Jesus on this hypothesis. This decision
    implies that Jesus was perceived as threatening the temple, not extending the
    limits of its holiness. Other interpretations of this event include Crossan's,
    who thinks Jesus criticized the temple's non-egalitarian system (*The Histori-
    cal Jesus: The Life of a Mediterranean Jewish Peasant* (San Francisco, 1991),
    pp. 127–33); and Neusner's, who thinks that Jesus was establishing a
    new religious system – 'Money-changers in the temple: the Mishnah's
    explanation', *NTS* 35 (1989), pp. 287–90.
41. *Jesus and Judaism*, ch. 8.
42. See Sanders, *Historical Figure*, p. 255.

43. See Sanders, *Jesus and Judaism*, pp. 65–6; and C.A. Evans, 'Opposition to the temple: Jesus and the Dead Sea scrolls', in James H. Charlesworth (ed.), *Jesus and the Dead Sea Scrolls* (New York, 1992), pp. 235–53. The latter has a list of pertinent literature.

44. See Daniel K. Falk, 'Jewish prayer literature and the Jerusalem church in Acts', in Richard Bauckham (ed.), *The Book of Acts in its First Century Setting*, vol. iv: *The Book of Acts in its Palestinian Setting* (Grand Rapids and Carlisle, 1995), pp. 267–301.

45. *Jesus and Judaism*, pp. 61–76.

46. Sanders, *Jesus and Judaism*.

47. Sanders, *Jesus and Judaism*, pp. 77–90.

48. See William R. Telford, *The Barren Temple and the Withered Tree* (JSNTSup, 1; Sheffield, 1980).

49. See the interesting exploration of this theme by Morna Hooker, *Signs*.

50. A most interesting, and I believe important, article is David Wenham, 'How Jesus understood the Last Supper: a parable in action', *Churchman* 105 (1991), pp. 246–60; reprinted in *Themelios* 20 (1995), pp. 11–16. See also Jonathan Klawans, 'Interpreting the Last Supper: sacrifice, spiritualization and anti-sacrifice', *NTS* 48 (2002), pp. 1–17; and Robin L. Routledge, 'Passover and Last Supper', *Tyndale Bulletin* 53 (2002), pp. 203–21.

51. Jeremias, *Eucharistic Words*, pp. 41–84 accepts it as a Passover meal. For a different view see Hooker, *Mark*, p. 333.

52. *Eucharistic Words*, pp. 15–88.

53. *La Date de la Cène* (Paris, 1957).

54. Gerd Theissen and Annette Merz, *The Historical Jesus: A Comprehensive Guide* (ET London, 1998), p. 159.

55. See James D.G. Dunn, 'Jesus, table-fellowship, and Qumran', in James H. Charlesworth (ed.), *Jesus and the Dead Sea Scrolls* (New York, 1992), pp. 254–72. Dunn concludes that 'Jesus was probably aware of the strictness of the Qumran ideal and, on at least one occasion, deliberately spoke out against it' (p. 268).

56. See Marcus Borg, *Jesus a New Vision: Spirit, Culture, and the Life of Discipleship* (New York, 1987), pp. 131–3.

57. Mt. 8.11 provides interesting evidence for this view. Jesus tells those who criticized the healing of the centurion's servant, 'Many will come from east and west and will eat with Abraham and Isaac and Jacob in the kingdom of heaven.'

58. Only in 1 Cor. 5.7 in the New Testament do we find a reference to Christ as the 'paschal lamb'. This suggests that paschal categories were not dominant in early Christian interpretation of the passion of Jesus.

59. For a review of this issue see Peter M. Head, 'The self-offering and death of Christ as a sacrifice in the Gospels and the Acts of the Apostles', in Roger T. Beckwith and Martin T. Selman (eds), *Sacrifice in the Bible* (Carlisle, 1995), pp. 111–29.

60. There is a difficult textual problem in the Lucan account of the Last Supper. Some manuscripts omit Lk. 22.19b-20. An important study of the form of the institution narratives is H. Merklein, 'Erwägungen zur Uberlieferungs-geschichte des neutestamentlichen Abendmahlstraditionen', *BZ* 21 (1977), pp. 235–44.

61. Jonathan Knight, *Jesus: An Historical and Theological Investigation* (London, 2004). See J. Priest, 'A note on the messianic banquet', in J.H. Charlesworth (ed.), *The Messiah: Developments in Earliest Judaism and Christianity* (Minneapolis, 1992), pp. 222–38; Dennis E. Smith, 'The messianic banquet reconsidered', in B. Pearson (ed.), *The Future of Early Christianity: Essays in Honour of Helmut Koester* (Minneapolis, 1991); and Laurence Schiffmann, 'Communal meals at Qumran', *RQ* 10 (1979), pp. 45–56.

62. In Ezek. 11.23 (by implication) the Mount of Olives was the place from which the divine glory departed, while Ezek. 43.2-5 explains that the glory returned and entered the eschatological temple. *Lam. Rab.* Proem 25 opines that the glory tarried three and a half years on Olivet, while *m. Ketub.* 111a states that those Jews who died abroad would be resurrected on the Mount of Olives (see Warren J. Heard, 'Mount of Olives', in *ABD*, vol. v, pp. 13–15).

63. See H. Klauck, 'Judas der "Verräter"? Eine exegetische und wirkungsgeschichtliche Studie', in *ANRW* II.26.1, pp. 717–40; William Klassen, *Judas: Betrayer or Friend of Jesus?* (Minneapolis, 1996); *idem*, 'The authenticity of Judas' participation in the arrest of Jesus', in Chilton and Evans (eds), *Authenticating the Activities of Jesus*, pp. 389–410; and William Klassen, 'Judas and Jesus: a message on a drinking vessel of the Second Temple period', in J.H. Charlesworth (ed.), *Jesus and Archaeology* (Grand Rapids, 2006), pp. 503–20.

64. On this point, see the characteristically nuanced work of Hyam Maccoby, *Judas Iscariot and the Myth of Jewish Evil* (New York, 1992).

65. *Eucharistic Words*, p. 125.

66. See, for instance, Wright, *Jesus and the Victory of God*, ch. 12, who considers the evidence and summarizes earlier scholarship. Wright's conclusion (p. 609) is that 'Jesus, then, went to Jerusalem not just to preach, but to die. Schweitzer was right: Jesus believed that the messianic woes were about to burst upon Israel, and that he has to take them upon himself, solo.'

67. My view has become more cautious than I expressed in my *Jesus*, pp. 176–7. I concluded there (p. 177) that 'the possibility that Jesus spoke of his own death in sacrificial terms and even that he predicted his own resurrection remains a reasonable one'. I still think that a resurrectional reference *can* be found in Mk 14.25 *if* the reference to the body and blood are interpreted as references to the death. But I have become more open to the possibility that these are purely symbolic and that Jesus remained convinced God would intervene immediately after the Last Supper. My own uncertainty mirrors the perplexity of almost everyone who has tried to make sense of this problem. This is perhaps the uncertainty of Jesus himself as he remained focused on imminent divine action.

68. The subject has provoked a plethora of scholarly literature. Among the more important contributions, see H.E. Tödt, *The Son of Man in the Synoptic Tradition* (ET London, 1965); Morna D. Hooker, *The Son of Man in Mark* (London, 1967); F.W. Borsch, *The Son of Man in Myth and History* (London, 1967); *idem, The Christian and Gnostic Son of Man* (SBT, 14; London, 1970); R. Leivestad, 'Exit the apocalyptic Son of Man', *NTS* 18 (1971–2), pp. 243–63; C. Colpe, '*ho huios tou anthropou*', in *TDNT*, vol. viii, pp. 400–77; A.J.B. Higgins, *The Son of Man in the Teaching of Jesus* (SNTSMS, 39; Cambridge, 1980); B. Lindars, *Jesus, Son of Man: A Fresh*

Examination of the Son of Man Sayings in the Gospels in the Light of Recent Research (Grand Rapids, 1983); C.C. Caragounis, *The Son of Man: Vision and Interpretation* (WUNT, 38; Tübingen, 1986); J.J. Collins, 'The Son of Man in first century Judaism', *NTS* 38 (1992), pp. 448–66; G.W.E. Nickelsburg, 'Son of Man', in *ABD*, vol. vi, pp. 137–50; Adela Yarbro Collins, 'The Influence of Daniel 7 on the New Testament', in John J. Collins, *Daniel: A Commentary on the Book of Daniel* (Hermencia: Minneapolis, 1993), pp. 90–123; Bruce Chilton, '(The) Son of (the) Man, and Jesus', in Bruce D. Chilton and Craig A. Evans (eds), *Authenticating the Words of Jesus* (Leiden, 1999), pp. 259–87; Delbert Burkett, *The Son of Man Debate: A History and Evaluation* (SNTSMS, 107; Cambridge, 1999); Walter Wink, *The Human Being: Jesus and the Enigma of the Son of Man* (Minneapolis, 2002); Robert M. Price, *The Incredible Shrinking Son of Man: How Reliable is the Gospel Tradition?* (Amherst NY, 2003); and Karl A. Kuhn, 'The "one like a Son of Man" becomes the "son of God" ', *CBQ* 69 (2007), pp. 22–42.

69. G. Vermes, *Jesus the Jew* (London, 1973), pp. 160–91; *idem, Jesus and the World of Judaism* (London, 1983), pp. 89–99; Maurice Casey, *The Son of Man: The Interpretation and Influence of Daniel 7* (London, 1979); *idem, From Jewish Prophet to Gentile God: The Origins and Development of New Testament Christology* (Cambridge and Louisville KY, 1991), pp. 46–54; 'The use of the term [*bar nasha*] in the Aramaic Translation of the Hebrew Bible', *JSNT* 54 (1994), pp. 87–118.

70. On the problems see Theissen and Merz, *Historical Jesus*, pp. 541–53.

71. See especially Collins, 'The Son of Man in First Century Judaism'.

72. See Collins, *Daniel*, pp. 274–326; Arthur J. Ferch, *The Son of Man in Daniel 7* (Andrew University Seminary Doctoral Dissertation Series, 6; Berrien Springs MI, 1979): *idem,* 'Daniel 7 and Ugarit: a reconsideration', *JBL* 99 (1980), pp. 75–86; and Christopher M. Tuckett, 'The Son of Man of Daniel 7: inclusive aspects of early Christology', in Kieran J. O'Mahony (ed.), *Christian Origins* (JSNTSup, 241; London, 2003).

73. See John A. Emerton, 'The origin of the Son of Man imagery', *JTS* 9 (1958), pp. 225–42.

74. On which see Chapter 3.

75. On the notion of the 'chaotic' in ancient Judaism, see Norman Cohn, *Cosmos, Chaos and the World to Come: The Ancient Roots of Apocalyptic Faith* (New Haven, 1983).

76. This in one sense is the crux of the 'Son of Man' problem.

77. For this interpretation see C.F.D. Moule, *The Origin of Christology* (Cambridge, 1977), pp. 11ff.; and Leivestad, 'Exit the apocalyptic Son of Man'.

78. Collins, *Apocalyptic Vision*, pp. 112–13; *idem, Daniel*, pp. 304–10.

79. On the importance of angels in Judaism, see Robert Hayward, 'Heaven and earth in parallel: the key role of angels in ancient Judaism', in D. Brown and A. Loades (eds), *Christ the Sacramental Word: Incarnation, Sacrament and Poetry* (London, 1996), pp. 57–74.

80. A messianic interpretation of Daniel 7 is found in the Gospels, *4 Ezra* 13 and the *Similitudes of Enoch*. See Collins, 'The Son of Man in first century Judaism'.

81. See Thomas B. Slater, 'One like a Son of Man in first century CE Judaism', *NTS* 41 (1995), pp. 183–98.

82. On this aspect of the *Similitudes* see J. Theisohn, *Der auserwählte Richter. Untersuchungen zum traditionsgeschichtlichen Ort der Menschensohngestalt der Bilderreden des Aethiopischen Henoch* (SUNT, 12; Göttingen, 1975); and Collins, 'The Son of Man in first century Judaism'.

83. See Daniel C. Olson, 'Enoch and the Son of Man in the Epilogue of the Parables', *JSP* 18 (1998), pp. 27–38; and James C. Vanderkam, 'Righteous One, Messiah, Chosen One, and Son of Man in 1 Enoch 37–71', in J. Charlesworth (ed.), *The Messiah: Developments in Earliest Judaism and Christianity* (Minneapolis, 1992), pp. 169–91. On the figure of Enoch in Jewish post-biblical understanding, James C. Vanderkam, *Enoch and the Growth of an Apocalyptic Tradition* (CBQMS, 66; Washington DC, 1984); *idem*, '1 Enoch, Enochic motifs, and Enoch in early Christian literature', in James C. Vanderkam and William Adler (eds), *The Jewish Apocalyptic Heritage in Early Christianity* (CRINT, 3/4; Assen and Minneapolis, 1996), pp. 33–101; and Margaret Barker, *The Lost Prophet: The Book of Enoch and Its Influence on Christianity* (London, 1988).

84. *The Apocrypha and Pseudepigrapha of the Old Testament* (2 vols.; London, 1913), vol. ii, p. 237.

85. 'The heavenly representative: the 'Son of Man' in the *Similitudes of Enoch*', in George W.E. Nickelsburg and John J. Collins (eds), *Ideal Figures in Ancient Judaism* (Chico, 1980), pp. 111–33.

86. 'The Son of Man in first century Judaism'.

87. See George W.E. Nickelsburg, ' "Enoch" as scientist, sage, and prophet: content, function, and authorship in 1 Enoch', in E. Lovering (ed.), *Society of Biblical Literature: 1999 Seminar Papers* (Atlanta, 1999), pp. 203–30.

88. See Gillian Bampfylde, 'The *Similitudes of Enoch*: historical allusions', *JSJ* 15 (1984), pp. 9–31.

89. There is a commentary on this passage by Michael E. Stone, *Fourth Ezra* (Minneapolis, 1990), pp. 381–7.

90. *Roots of Apocalyptic* (WMANT, 61; Neukirchen-Vluyn, 1988), pp. 517–20.

91. Michael E. Stone 'The concept of the Messiah in IV Ezra', in Jacob Neusner (ed.) *Religions in Antiquity: Essays in Memory of E.R. Goodenough* (SHR, 14; Leiden, 1968), pp. 305–6; *idem, Features of the Eschatology of 4 Ezra* (HSS, 35; Atlanta, 1989), pp. 123–5; *idem*, 'The question of the Messiah in 4 Ezra'.

92. *Historical Figure*, pp. 180–2.

93. This point is pure speculation but it continues to fascinate me because the Mount of Olives had eschatological associations in post-biblical Judaism. We have here the same problem of dating external evidence that we noticed in connection with the Son of Man problem. The possibility, however, that Jesus went to the mountain with high eschatological hopes does not *depend* on this evidence. It merely augments what I have suggested from elsewhere.

Chapter 15

1. Though see William Klassen, 'Judas and Jesus: a message on a drinking vessel of the Second Temple period', in J.H. Charlesworth (ed.), *Jesus and Archaeology* (Grand Rapids, 2006), pp. 507–20; and below.

2. Besides the literature already cited on Mark 13, see G.R. Beasley-Murray, *Jesus and the Future: An Examination of the Criticism of the Eschatological Discourse, Mark 13, with Special Reference to the Little Apocalypse Theory* (London, 1954); *idem, A Commentary on Mark 13* (New York, 1957); and *idem*, 'Second thoughts on the composition of Mk. 13', *NTS* 29 (1983), pp. 414–20. For a different view see Robert W. Funk and Roy W. Hoover, *The Five Gospels: The Search for the Authentic Words of Jesus* (New York, 1993), p. 107.

3. For previous research in this area see Albert Schweitzer, *The Kingdom of God and Primitive Christianity* (ET London, 1968), p. 111; E.P. Sanders, *Jesus and Judaism* (London, 1985), pp. 99–101, 309; and William Klassen, *Judas: Betrayer or Friend of Jesus?* (London, 1996).

4. Thus Schweitzer, *Kingdom of God*, p. 111: 'The betrayal cannot have consisted in giving away the most convenient location for Jesus' arrest. That he went each evening to Bethany could easily have been found out from spies. At the arrest Judas was needed only to enable the soldiers to recognize clearly in the dark the man they were to seize. What concerned the high priest and the elders of the people first and foremost was to find something that would enable them to proceed against him and put him out of the way. Judas gave it to them.'

5. Four rival locations claim to be the site of Gethsemane. See Donald A.D. Thorsen, 'Gethsemane', in *ABD*, vol. ii, pp. 997–8.

6. See Chapter 14.

7. I mention again the work of J. Jeremias, *The Eucharistic Words of Jesus*, translated by Norman Perrin from the 3rd German edition (ET London, 1964), pp. 125–37.

8. On the volatility of the Passover season see Richard A. Horsley, *Jesus and the Spiral of Violence* (Minneapolis, 1993), pp. 33–43.

9. Though note William Klassen, 'The authenticity of Judas' participation in the arrest of Jesus', in Bruce D. Chilton and Craig A. Evans (eds), *Authenticating the Activities of Jesus* (Leiden, 1999), pp. 389–410.

10. See J. Blinzler, *The Trial of Jesus* (Cork, 1959); S.G.F. Brandon, *The Trial of Jesus of Nazareth* (London, 1968); E. Bammel (ed.), *The Trial of Jesus* (SBT, 13; London, 1970); D. Catchpole, *The Trial of Jesus* (Leiden, 1971); E. Bammel and C.F.D. Moule (eds), *Jesus and the Politics of His Day* (Cambridge, 1984); R.E. Brown, *The Death of the Messiah* (2 vols.; New York and London, 1993); and Gerd Theissen and Annette Merz, *The Historical Jesus: A Comprehensive Guide* (ET London, 1998), pp. 440–73. I acknowledge my use of the last-mentioned work. See also Brad M. Young, 'A fresh examination of the cross, Jesus and the Jewish people', in R. Steven Notley, Marc Turnage and Brian Becker (eds); *Jesus' Last Week: Jerusalem Studies in the Synoptic Gospels* (Leiden, 2006), pp. 191–209; and John W. Welch, 'Miracles, maleficium, and maiestas in the trial of Jesus', in Charlesworth (ed.), *Jesus and Archaeology*, pp. 349–83.

11. See Brandon, *Trial*, pp. 81–139; and the two volumes of Brown, *Death*.

12. See Werner H. Kelber (ed.), *The Passion in Mark: Studies on Mark 14–16* (Philadelphia, 1976); and Morna D. Hooker, *The Gospel According to St. Mark* (London, 1991), pp. 350–71.

13. See Michael J. Haran, 'The naked young man: a historian's hypothesis on Mark 14, 51–52', *Biblica* 79/4 (1998), pp. 521–30.

14. See Brown, *Death*, vol. i, pp. 462–83.
15. Some scholars think the Barabbas episode is fictitious; see e.g. S.J. Davies, 'Who is called Bar Abbas?', *NTS* 27 (1980), pp. 260–2. Yet R.L. Merrit finds widespread evidence of prisoner releases at festivals; 'Jesus Barabbas and the Paschal pardon', *JBL* 104 (1985), pp. 57–68.
16. In connection with this person see the interesting article of J.P. Kane, 'Ossuary inscriptions of Jerusalem', *JSS* 23 (1978), pp. 268–82.
17. On which see Donald Senior, 'Revisiting Matthew's special material in the passion narrative: a dialogue with Raymond Brown', *ETL* 70 (1994), pp. 417–24.
18. See Craig A. Evans, 'Excavating Caiaphas, Pilate and Simon of Cyrene: assessing the literary and archaeological evidence', in Charlesworth (ed.), *Jesus and Archaeology*, pp. 323–40.
19. See Marion L. Soards, *The Passion According to Luke: The Special Material of Luke 22* (JSNTSup, 14; Sheffield, 1987); and Jerome Neyrey, *The Passion According to Luke: A Redaction Study of Luke's Soteriology* (New York, 1985).
20. See Joel B. Green, 'Jesus and the Mount of Olives (Luke 22:34–46): tradition and theology', *JSNT* 26 (1986), pp. 29–46.
21. On John's perspective see Andrew T. Lincoln, 'Trials, plots and the narrative of the Fourth Gospel', *JSNT* 56 (1994), pp. 3–30.
22. See Richard J. Bauckham, 'Did Jesus wash his disciples' feet?', in Chilton and Evans (eds), *Authenticating the Activities of Jesus*, pp. 411–29.
23. See E. Käsemann, *The Testament of Jesus: A Study of the Gospel of John in the Light of Chapter 17* (ET London, 1968).
24. On the portrait of this person see Helen K. Bond, *Pontius Pilate in History and Interpretation* (SNTSMS, 100; Cambridge, 1998).
25. See Theissen and Merz, *Historical Jesus*, pp. 469–73.
26. See Richard J. Bauckham, 'The Ascension of Isaiah: genre, unity and date', in his *The Fate of the Dead* (NovTSup, 93; Leiden, 1998), pp. 363–90; and my own *Disciples of the Beloved One: Studies in the Christology, Social Setting and Theological Context of the Ascension of Isaiah* (JSPSSup, 18; Sheffield, 1996), pp. 44–8. Text available in P. Bettiolo *et al.*, *Ascensio Isaiae: Textus* (CCSA, 7; Turnhout, 1995); Italian commentary in E. Norelli, *Ascensio Isaiae: Commentarius* (CCSA, 8; Turnhout, 1995).
27. ET in J.K. Elliott (ed.), *The Apocryphal New Testament* (Oxford, 1993), pp. 150–8; and E. Hennecke, rev. W. Schneemelcher, *New Testament Apocrypha*, vol. i (ET London, 1991), pp. 216–27.
28. Text and introduction by C. Detlef and G. Müller in Hennecke, rev. Schneemelcher, *New Testament Apocrypha*, vol. i, pp. 249–84. See also C. Schmidt, *Gespräche Jesu mit seinen Jüngern nach der Auferstehung* (TU, 43; Berlin, 1919); M. Hornschüh, *Studien zur Epistula Apostolorum* (PTS, 5; Berlin, 1965); and Charles E. Hill, 'The *Epistula Apostolorum*: an Asian tract from the time of Polycarp', *JECS* 7 (1999), pp. 1–53.
29. See G.W.H. Lampe, 'The trial of Jesus in the Acta Pilati', in Bammel and Moule (eds), *Jesus and the Politics of His Day*, pp. 173–82; Theissen and Merz, *Historical Jesus*, pp. 578–9; and Marek Starowieyski, 'Eléments apologétiques dans les Apocryphes', in B. Pouderon and J. Doré (eds), *Les apologistes chrétiens et la culture grecque* (TH, 105; Paris, 1998).
30. See Zbigniew Izydorczyk (ed.), *The Medieval Gospel of Nicodemus: Texts,*

Intertexts, and Contexts in Western Europe (MRTS, 158; Binghampton NY, 1997).

31. Translation in Theissen and Merz, *Historical Jesus*, pp. 472–3; and Hennecke, rev. Schneemelcher, *New Testament Apocrypha*, vol. i, p. 527.

32. See Theissen and Merz, *Historical Jesus*, pp. 74–6, 463; and J. Maier, *Jesus von Nazareth in der talmudischen Überlieferung* (EdF, 82; Darmstadt, 1978), pp. 210–35.

33. See William Horbury, 'The trial of Jesus in Jewish tradition', in Bammel (ed.), *Trial of Jesus*, pp. 103–21; and Hillel I. Newman, 'The death of Jesus in the Toledot Yeshu literature', *JTS* 50 (1999), pp. 59–79.

34. See the literature cited at n. 10 above.

35. See Martin Hengel, *Crucifixion* (ET London, 1977); and Gerard S. Sloyan, *The Crucifixion of Jesus: History, Myth, Faith* (Minneapolis, 1995).

36. This observation explains Paul's argument in Gal. 3.13.

37. See Mt. 27.25; and Theissen and Merz, *Historical Jesus*, pp. 449–51.

38. Theissen and Merz, *Historical Jesus*, p. 455

39. See Theissen and Merz, *Historical Jesus*, pp. 457–8.

40. The evidence is helpfully set out by Theissen and Merz, *Historical Jesus*, pp. 460–5. See also Laurna L. Berg, 'The illegalities of Jesus' religious and civil trials', *BS* 161 (2004), pp. 330–42,

41. The Talmud restricts capital punishment to blasphemy of the divine name. See Leonard W. Levy, *Blasphemy: Verbal Offense against the Sacred, from Moses to Salman Rushdie* (New York, 1993); Craig A. Evans, 'In what sense blasphemy? Jesus before Caiaphas in Mark 14.61-64', in Eugene H. Lovering (ed.), *SBL 1991 Seminar Papers*, pp. 215–34; Darrell L. Bock, 'Key Jewish texts on blasphemy and exaltation and the Jewish examination of Jesus (Mk 14.53-65)', in Eugene H. Lovering (ed.), *SBL 1997 Seminar Papers*, pp. 115–60; and Adela Yarbro Collins, 'The charge of blasphemy in Mark 14.64', *JSNT* 26 (2004), pp. 379–401.

42. *Trial*, pp. 134ff.

43. A. Strobel, *Die Stunde der Wahrheit* (WUNT, 21; Tübingen, 1980), pp. 46–61.

44. H. Lietzmann, 'Bemerkungen zum Prozess Jesu I + II', *Kleine Schriften II* (TU, 68; Berlin, 1958), pp. 264–8, 269–76.

45. The view of J. Gnilka, *Das Evangelium nach Markus* (EKK II/2; Zurich and Neukirchen-Vluyn, 1979), pp. 284–8.

Chapter 16

1. This theory was first advocated by H.E.G. Paulus (1761–1851), *Kommentar über die drey ersten Evangelien III* ([1]1802), pp. 797–806; *idem, Das Leben Jesu als Grundlage einer reinen Geschichte des Urchristentums* (Heidelberg, 1828), pp. 277–305. Other so-called 'explanations' of the resurrection of Jesus include the suggestions of H.S. Reimarus (1694–1768), based on Mt. 28.11–15, that the disciples stole the body of Jesus; and of H.J. Holtzmann that Joseph of Arimathea secretly reburied the body of Jesus ('Das leere Grab und die gegenwärtigen Verhandlungen über die Auferstehung Jesu', *ThR* 9 (1906), pp. 79–86, 119–32).

2. See Martin Hengel, *Crucifixion* (ET London, 1977), pp. 22–32.

3. See W. Reid Litchfield, 'The search for the physical cause of Jesus Christ's death', *BYUS* 37/4 (1997), pp. 93–109.
4. See Acts 1.3; Gal. 5.21; 1 Thess. 2.12; and many other references. Three studies of this issue are Richard Bauckham, *God Crucified: Monotheism and Christology in the New Testament* (Carlisle, 1998; Grand Rapids, 1999); Carey C. Newman, James R. Davila and Gladys S. Lewis (eds), *The Jewish Roots of Christological Monotheism* (JSJSup, 63; Leiden, 1999); and Larry W. Hurtado, *How on earth did Jesus become a God?* (Grand Rapids, 2005).
5. On the Jewish resurrectional hope see R. Martin-Achard, *From Death to Life: A Study of the Development of the Doctrine of the Resurrection in the Old Testament* (ET Edinburgh, 1960); G.W.E. Nickelsburg, *Resurrection, Immortality, and Eternal Life in Intertestamental Judaism* (HTS, 26; Cambridge MA, 1972); H.C.C. Cavallin, *Life after Death. Paul's Argument for the Resurrection of the Dead in 1 Cor. 15*, pt. i: *An Enquiry into the Jewish Background* (CB, 7/1; Lund, 1974); E. Schürer, rev. G. Vermes *et al.*, *The History of the Jewish People in the Age of Jesus Christ*, vol. ii (Edinburgh, 1979), pp. 539–44; and J.H. Charlesworth (ed.), *Resurrection: The Origin and Future of a Biblical Doctrine* (London and New York, 2006).
6. Cf. Martin Hengel, writing on Phil. 2.6-8: 'The discrepancy between the shameful death of a Jewish state criminal and the confession that depicts this executed man as a pre-existent divine figure who becomes man and humbles himself to a slave's death is, as far as I can see, without analogy in the ancient world'; *The Son of God* (ET London, 1976), p. 1.
7. See W. Marxsen, *The Resurrection of Jesus of Nazareth* (ET London, 1970); C.F. Evans, *Resurrection and the New Testament* (SBT, 12; London, 1970); P. Perkins, *Resurrection* (London, 1984); P. Carnley, *The Structure of Resurrection Belief* (Oxford, 1987); S. Davis, D. Kendall and G. O'Collins (eds), *The Resurrection: An Interdisciplinary Symposium on the Resurrection of Jesus* (Oxford, 1997); P. Avis (ed.), *The Resurrection of Jesus Christ* (London, 1993); G. Lüdemann, *The Resurrection of Jesus: History, Experience, Theology* (ET London, 1994); S. Barton and G.N. Stanton (eds), *Resurrection: Essays in Honour of Leslie Houlden* (London, 1994); Richard N. Longenecker (ed.), *Life in the Face of Death: The Resurrection Message of the New Testament* (Grand Rapids, 1998); A.J.M. Wedderburn, *Beyond Resurrection* (London, 1999); Richard G. Swinburne, *The Resurrection of God Incarnate* (Oxford, 2003); N.T. Wright, *Christian Origins and the Question of God*, vol. iii: *The Resurrection of the Son of God* (Minneapolis, 2003); Robert B. Stewart (ed.), *The Resurrection of Jesus: John Dominic Crossan and N.T. Wright in Dialogue* (London, 2006); and Émile Puech, 'Jesus and resurrection faith in the light of Jewish texts', in J.H. Charlesworth (ed.), *Jesus and Archaeology* (Grand Rapids, 2006), pp. 639–59.
8. This was studied classically by C.H. Dodd, *The Apostolic Preaching and its Developments* (London, 1936).
9. See C.K. Barrett, 'The Gentile mission as an eschatological phenomenon', in W. Gloer (ed.), *Eschatology and the New Testament: Essays in Honour of George R. Beasley-Murray* (Peabody, 1988); and Terence L. Donaldson, 'Israelite, convert, apostle to the Gentiles: the origins of Paul's Gentile mission', in R. Longenecker (ed.), *The Road from Damascus* (Grand Rapids, 1997), pp. 62–84.

10. The inclusion of the Gentiles was an important theme in contemporary Jewish eschatology. See the discussion of this theme by E.P. Sanders, *Jesus and Judaism* (London, 1985), pp. 212–21.

11. For a review of this topic see Thomas E. Schmidt (ed.), *To Tell the Mystery: Essays on New Testament Eschatology* (JSNTSup, 100; Sheffield, 1994).

12. John Robinson asked whether this was 'The most primitive Christology of all?', *JTS* 7 (1956), pp. 177–89.

13. See A.L. Moore, *The Parousia in the New Testament* (NovTSup, 13; Leiden, 1966); Barnabas Lindars, 'The sound of the trumpet: Paul and eschatology', *BJRL* 67 (1985), pp. 766–82; and Joseph Plevnik, *Paul and the Parousia: An Exegetical and Theological Investigation* (Peabody, 1997).

14. Chronologically, the earliest statement of the *parousia* hope in the New Testament is in 1 Thess. 1.9-10.

15. See Martin Hengel, *Studies in Early Christology* (Edinburgh, 1995), pp. 359–89.

16. For important background issues to this letter, see Raymond F. Collins (ed.), *The Thessalonian Correspondence* (Louvain, 1990).

17. See U. Wilckens, *Die Missionsreden der Apostelgeschichte. Form- und traditions-geschichtliche Untersuchungen* (WMANT, 5; Neukirchen-Vluyn, 1974), pp. 80–6.

18. See J. Plevnik, 'The parousia as implication of Christ's resurrection: an exegesis of 1 Thes. 4:13-18', in J. Plevnik (ed.), *Word and Spirit: Essays in Honor of David Michael Stanley* (Willowdale, Ontario, 1975), pp. 199–277; and Robert A. Jewett, *The Thessalonian Correspondence: Pauline Rhetoric and Millenarian Piety* (Philadelphia, 1986), pp. 94–100.

19. The latter view is supported by Plevnik, *Paul and the Parousia*, p. 88: 'The living faithful in 1 Thess. 4:17 are similarly taken on a cloud into heaven.' I shall find reasons for questioning this exegesis in Part III.

20. See further Plevnik, 'The taking up of the faithful and the resurrection of the dead in 1 Thessalonians 4.13-18', *CBQ* 46 (1984), pp. 274–83.

21. See Murray J. Harris, 'Resurrection and Immortality in the Pauline Corpus', in Richard L. Longenecker (ed.), *Life in the Face of Death: The Resurrection Message of the New Testament* (Grand Rapids, 1998), pp. 147–70; *idem*, *Raised Immortal* (London, 1983), pp. 114–33; C.M. Tuckett, 'The Corinthians who say "There is no resurrection of the dead" (1 Cor 15, 12)', in R. Bieringer (ed.), *The Corinthian Correspondence* (Louvain, 1996), pp. 247–303; M. de Boer, 'Paul's use of a resurrection tradition in 1 Cor 15, 20-28', in Bieringer (ed.), *Corinthian Correspondence*, pp. 639–51; Plevnik, *Paul and Parousia*, ch. 5; and Edith M. Humphrey, 'Which way is up? Revival, resurrection, assumption, and ascension in the rhetoric of Paul and John the seer', *ARC* 33 (2005), pp. 328–39.

22. See Hans Conzelmann, *1 Corinthians* (ET Philadelphia, 1975), pp. 251–4.

23. For a discussion of Paul's vision of Jesus see Lüdemann, *Resurrection*, pp. 49–70.

24. See my discussion of this matter below; and also David A. Ackerman, *'Lo, I Tell You a Mystery': Cross, Resurrection, and Paraenesis in the Rhetoric of First Corinthians* (PTMS, 52; Eugene Or, 2006).

25. Thus Harris, *Raised Immortal*, pp. 114–32.

26. See Harris, 'Resurrection', in Longenecker (ed.), *Life*, p. 153; Schweizer in

TDNT, vol. vi, pp. 420–2; and Alan F. Segal, 'Paul's "soma pneumatikon" and the worship of Jesus', in Newman *et al.* (eds), *Jewish Roots*, pp. 258–76.

27. I shall have more to say on this subject when reviewing Paul in Part III of this book.

28. On which see Plevnik, *Paul and Parousia*, pp. 170–93.

29. This suggestion is reviewed by Richard N. Longenecker, 'Is there development in Paul's resurrection thought?', in Longenecker (ed.), *Life*, pp. 171–202.

30. See Darrell J. Doughty, 'Citizens of heaven: Philippians 3.20-21', *NTS* 41 (1995), pp. 102–22. On the dialogue between notions of resurrection and heavenly immortality in Jewish antiquity, see George W.E. Nickelsburg, *Resurrection, Immortality, and Eternal Life in Intertestamental Judaism* (HTS, 26; Harvard, 1967).

31. For a variety of perspectives on how Paul's so-called 'conversion' shaped his future preaching, see Longenecker (ed.), *Road from Damascus*.

32. With this passage cf. Paul's brief statement in 1 Cor. 9.1, 'Have I not seen Jesus our Lord?'

33. See further Part III; and Albert Schweitzer, *The Mysticism of Paul the Apostle* (ET London, 1931); and Alan F. Segal, *Paul the Convert: The Apostolate and Apostasy of Saul the Pharisee* (New Haven, 1990).

34. See Morna D. Hooker, *The Gospel According to St Mark* (London, 1991), pp. 387–94; and John Fenton, 'The ending of Mark', in Barton and Stanton (eds), *Resurrection*, pp. 1–7.

35. Unsurprisingly, this verse has appealed to feminist exegetes. See Marie Sabin, 'The ending of Mark is the beginning of wisdom', *Cross Currents* 48 (1998), pp. 149–68; and Judith Lieu, 'The women's resurrection testimony', in Barton and Stanton (eds), *Resurrection*, pp. 34–44.

36. See Robert M. Price and Jeffrey Jay Lowder (eds), *The Empty Tomb: Jesus beyond the Grave* (New York, 2005); and Susan Miller, 'The empty tomb', *ExpT* 117 (2006), pp. 246–8.

37. On the relation between the two strands, see Barnabas Lindars, 'The resurrection and the empty tomb', in Avis (ed.), *Resurrection*, pp. 116–35.

38. For a sensible review of this debate, see Stephen T. Davis, *Risen Indeed* (Grand Rapids, 1993), pp. 62–84.

39. For a philosopher's perspective on this issue, see Richard Swinburne, 'Evidence for the resurrection', in Davis *et al.* (eds), *Resurrection*, pp. 191–212.

40. See further Mary Cotes, 'Women, silence and fear (Mark 16:8)', in G. Brooke (ed.), *Women in the Biblical Tradition* (Lewiston NY, 1992), pp. 150–66.

41. One must therefore consider the possibility of development especially between Matthew and Mark when evaluating the early Christian narratives of the resurrection.

Chapter 17

1. There are any number of studies of Paul. Among the important contributions see E.P. Sanders, *Paul and Palestinian Judaism* (London, 1977); *idem*, *Paul* (Oxford, 1991); C.K. Barrett, *Paul: An Introduction to his thought* (London and New York, 1994); James D.G. Dunn, *The Theology of Paul the Apostle*

(Edinburgh and Grand Rapids, 1998); Calvin Roetzel, *Paul: The Man and the Myth* (Minneapolis and Edinburgh, 1999); David Horrell, *An Introduction to the Study of Paul* (London and New York, 2000, 2006); Seyoon Kim, *Paul and the New Perspective: Second Thoughts on the Origin of Paul's Gospel* (Grand Rapids, 2002); James D.G. Dunn, *The Cambridge Companion to Paul* (Cambridge, 2003); Jerome Murphy O'Connor, *Paul: His Story* (Oxford, 2004); John Dominic Crossan and Jonathan L. Reed, *In Search of Paul: How Jesus' Apostle Opposed Rome's Empire with God's Kingdom: A New Vision of Paul's Words and World* (London, 2005); Edwin D. Freed, *The Apostle Paul and His Letters* (London, 2005); N.T. Wright, *Paul: Fresh Perspectives* (London, 2005); James D.G. Dunn (ed.), *The New Perspective on Paul: Collected Essays* (WUNT, 185; Tübingen, 2005); and Stanley E. Porter (ed.), *Paul and His Theology* (PS, 3; Leiden, 2006). Further studies will be mentioned throughout this Part of the book.

2. W.C. van Unnik, *Tarsus or Jerusalem? The City of Paul's Youth* (ET London, 1962). For a review of this debate see Roetzel, *Paul*, pp. 8–24.

3. *The Pre-Christian Paul* (ET London and Philadelphia, 1991), p. 39.

4. *Acts of the Apostles: A Commentary* (ET Philadelphia, 1971).

5. See also J. Paul Sampley (ed.), *Paul in the Greco-Roman World: A Handbook* (Harrisburg, 2003).

6. For an interesting study of the geography of Paul's world, see Richard Wallace and Wynne Williams, *The Three Worlds of Paul of Tarsus* (London, 1998). An earlier study of the same theme is S.E. Johnson, *Paul the Apostle and His Cities* (Wilmington, 1987).

7. See W. Ward Gasque, 'Tarsus', in *ABD*, vol. vi, pp. 333–4; and Roetzel, *Paul*, pp. 12–19. Among the older studies, Hans Böhlig, *Die Geisteskultur von Tarsos im augustischen Zeitalter mit Berücksichtigung der paulinischen Schriften* (Göttingen, 1913), pp. 8–178; A.H.M. Jones, *The Cities of the Eastern Roman Provinces* (Oxford, 1937), pp. 192–216; and W.M. Ramsay, *The Cities of St Paul: Their Influence on His Life and Thought* (Grand Rapids, 1907), pp. 95–244.

8. *Geography* 13.5.13.

9. On the religious life of the region, see Terence Bruce Mitford, 'The cults of Roman rough Cilicia', in *ANRW* II.18.3, pp. 2131–60. On its religious importance, Mark Wilson, 'Cilicia: the first Christian churches in Anatolia', Tyndale Bulletin 54 (2003), pp. 15–30.

10. See Roetzel, *Paul*, pp. 16–19; James Barr, 'Paul and the LXX: a note on some recent work', *JTS* 45 (1994), pp. 593–601; Margaret E. Thrall, 'Paul of Tarsus: a Hellenistic Jew', in Robert E. Pope (ed.), *Honouring the Past and Shaping the Future* (Leominster, 2003), pp. 97–111; and Martin Hengel, *The Septuagint as Christian Scripture: Its Prehistory and the Problem of its Canon* (Edinburgh, 2002).

11. Roetzel, *Paul*, p. 18.

12. The groundbreaking work is that of G.A. Kennedy, *New Testament Interpretation through Rhetorical Criticism* (Chapel Hill, 1984). See also Robert A. Jewett, *The Thessalonian Correspondence: Pauline Rhetoric and Millenarian Piety* (Philadelphia, 1986); Stanley E. Porter, 'Paul of Tarsus and his letters', in Stanley E. Porter (ed.), *Handbook of Classical Rhetoric in the Hellenistic Period, 330 BC–AD 400* (Leiden, 1997), pp. 533–85; and Thomas H. Tobin, *Paul's Rhetoric in its Contexts: The Argument of Romans* (Peabody, 2004).

13. See Stanley K. Stowers, *A Rereading of Romans: Justice, Jews, and the Gentiles* (New Haven, 1994); and Runar M. Thorsteinnson, 'Paul and Roman Stoicism: Romans 12 and contemporary stoic ethics', *JSNT* 29 (2006), pp. 139–61.

14. A.N. Sherwin-White, *Roman Society and Roman Law in the New Testament* (Oxford, 1963), esp. pp. 181–5 where he argues that Paul's claim to dual citizenship in Tarsus and Rome would have been impossible since this policy had been reversed before Paul's time; Martin Hengel, *The Pre-Christian Paul* (London and Philadelphia, 1991), pp. 11–12. A more recent supporter of this hypothesis is Peter van Minnen, 'Paul the Roman citizen', *JSNT* 56 (1994), pp. 43–52. A considerable number of scholars, however, doubt the probability of this conclusion. One such critic is E.R. Goodenough, 'The perspective of Acts', in Leander E. Keck and J.L. Martyn (eds), *Studies in Luke–Acts* (New York, 1966), p. 55. The arguments are summarized by Roetzel, *Paul*, pp. 20–2.

15. Roetzel, *Paul*, p. 21.

16. On this topic see Leander E. Keck, 'The quest for Paul's Pharisaism: some reflections', in Douglas A. Knight and Peter J. Paris (eds), *Justice and the Holy: Essays in Honor of Walter Harrelson* (Atlanta, 1989), pp. 163–75; Alan F. Segal, *Paul the Convert: The Apostolate and Apostasy of Saul the Pharisee* (New Haven, 1990); Brad H. Young, *Paul, the Jewish Theologian: A Pharisee among Christians, Jews, and Gentiles* (Peabody, 1997); and Roetzel, *Paul*, pp. 24–38.

17. See Chapter 20 for a discussion of these key terms in Paul.

18. See Segal, *Paul*, pp. 117–83; Richard N. Longenecker (ed.), *The Road from Damascus: The Impact of Paul's Conversion on His Life, Thought and Ministry* (Grand Rapids, 1997); Willy Rordorf, 'Paul's conversion in the canonical Acts and in the Acts of Paul', *Semeia* 80 (1997), pp. 137–44 (with replies by J.V. Hills, pp. 145–58; and V.K. Robbins, pp. 291–303); E. Krentz, 'Conversion in early Christianity', in Adela Yarbro Collins (ed.), *Ancient and Modern Perspectives on the Bible and Culture: Essays in Honor of Hans Dieter Betz* (SPHS, 22; Atlanta, 1998); Roetzel, *Paul*, pp. 43–6; and Stephen J. Chester, *Conversion at Corinth: Perspectives on Conversion in Paul's Theology and the Corinthian Church* (London, 2003).

19. On the psychological aspect, see Segal, *Paul*, pp. 285–300. The cultural background is studied by Zeba A. Crook, *Reconceptualizing Conversion: Patronage, Loyalty, and Conversion in the Religions of the Ancient Near East* (BZNW, 136; Berlin, 2004).

20. See the summary in Segal, *Paul*, pp. 72–114. The classic study is that of Arthur Darby Nock, *Conversion* (Oxford, 1933).

21. 'The apostle Paul and the introspective conscience of the west', *HTR* 56 (1963), pp. 199–215.

22. See for instance Segal, *Paul*. The term 'the conversion of Paul' is a familiar one in Christian religious discourse. The matter is discussed by Peter T. O'Brien, 'Was Paul converted?', in Donald A. Carson, Peter T. O'Brien amd Mark A. Seifrid (eds), *Justification and Variegated Nomism*, vol. ii: *The Paradoxes of Paul* (Tübingen, 2004), pp. 361–91.

23. Segal, *Paul*, pp. 6–7.

24. This is done by Segal, *Paul*, pp. 38–58. Other pertinent literature includes Gerschom G. Scholem, *Major Trends in Jewish Mysticism* (New York, 1955);

Ira D. Chernus, *Mysticism in Rabbinic Judaism: Studies in the History of Midrash* (SJ, 11; Berlin, 1982); Peter Schäfer, *Hekhalot-Studien* (TSAJ, 19; Tübingen, 1988); and David Halperin, *The Merkabah in Rabbinic Literature* (AOS, 62; New Haven, 1980); *idem*, *The Faces of the Chariot: Early Jewish Responses to Ezekiel's Vision* (TSAJ, 16; Tübingen, 1988).

25. See Michael Mach, 'From apocalypticism to early Jewish mysticism', in John J. Collins (ed.), *The Encyclopedia of Apocalypticism*, vol. i (London, 2000), pp. 229–64.

26. Segal, *Paul*, p. 22. See also Ulrich Luz, trans. Martin Kitchen, 'Paul as mystic', in Graham N. Stanton, Bruce W. Longenecker and Stephen C. Barton (eds), *The Holy Spirit and Christian Origins: Essays in Honor of J.D.G. Dunn* (Grand Rapids, 2004), pp. 131–43.

27. I offer my own development of this theme in Chapter 21.

28. Segal, *Paul*, pp. 22–3.

29. See the different perspectives offered in Longenecker (ed.), *Road from Damascus*.

30. On this subject see Richard N. Longenecker, 'Is there development in Paul's resurrection thought?', in Richard N. Longenecker (ed.), *Life in the Face of Death: The Resurrection Message of the New Testament* (Grand Rapids, 1998), pp. 171–202.

31. Such a view tends to mar the study of Seyoon Kim, *The Origin of Paul's Gospel* (WUNT, 4; Tübingen, 1981).

32. *The Mysticism of Paul the Apostle* (ET London, 1931). See Ulrich Luz, 'Paul as mystic'.

33. The matter is examined by Robert Jewett, *Dating Paul's Life* (London, 1979), pp. 29–30. He accepts a date for Paul's conversion in 34 CE if the crucifixion of Jesus occurred in 33 CE. Other studies of this part of Paul's career include Martin Hengel and Anna Maria Schwemer, *Paul between Antioch and Damascus* (London, 1997); and Rainer Riesner, *Paul's Early Period: Chronology, Mission Strategy, Theology* (Grand Rapids, 1998). See also Jerome Murphy-O'Connor, *Paul: A Critical Life* (Oxford, 1996).

34. *A fortiori* if a date for the crucifixion in 33 CE is preferred, which is technically possible. See Ingo Broer, 'Neues zur Pauluschronologie', *BZ* 50 (2006), pp. 99–104.

35. James the Just was the brother of Jesus mentioned by the Gospels. After Easter he became the leader of the primitive Christian community in Jerusalem. On this figure see Richard Bauckham, 'James and the Jerusalem church', in R. Bauckham (ed.), *The Book of Acts in its Palestinian Setting* (Grand Rapids and Carlisle, 1995), pp. 415–80; John Painter, *Just James: The Brother of Jesus in History and Tradition* (Columbia, 1997); and Bruce D. Chilton and Craig A. Evans (eds), *James the Just and Christian Origins* (NovTSup, 98; Leiden, 1999).

36. See Hans Dieter Betz, *Galatians* (Hermeneia; Philadelphia, 1979), pp. 81–3; William O. Walker, 'Acts and the Pauline corpus revisited: Peter's speech at the Jerusalem conference', in Richard P. Thompson and Thomas E. Phillips (eds), *Literary Studies in Luke–Acts: Essays in Honor of Joseph B. Tyson* (Macon, 1998), pp. 77–86; David Trobisch, 'The Council of Jerusalem in Acts 15 and Paul's Letter to the Galatians', in C. Seitz (ed.), *Theological Exegesis: Essays in Honor of Brevard S. Childs* (Grand Rapids, 1999), pp. 331–8; and, more

generally, the volumes of essays edited by Bruce Chilton and Craig Evans (eds), *The Missions of James, Peter, and Paul: Tensions in Early Christianity* (NovTSup, 115; Leiden, 2005).

37. See the remarks of Jewett, *Dating Paul's Life*, ch. 4; and Roetzel, *Paul*, pp. 178–83.

38. Floyd V. Filson, *A New Testament History* (London, 1965) p. 220.

39. See Robert Jewett, 'Mapping the route of Paul's "Second Missionary Journey" from Dorylaeum to Troas', *Tyndale Bulletin* 48 (1997), pp. 1–22.

40. The possibility that the author of Acts was a travelling companion of Paul has been much discussed in research. See the comments of Stanley E. Porter, 'The "we" passages in Acts', in David W.J. Gill and Conrad H. Gempf (eds), *The Book of Acts in its Greco-Roman Setting*, vol. ii (Grand Rapids and Carlisle, 1994), pp. 545–74. He has a bibliography of earlier research.

41. See Scott Shauf, *Theology as History, History as Theology; Paul in Ephesus in Acts 19* (BZNW; 133, Berlin, 2005).

42. On which see J.M. Gilchrist, 'The historicity of Paul's shipwreck', *JSNT* 61 (1996), pp. 29–51.

43. See the review of C.K. Barrett, 'The end of Acts', in H. Cancik (ed.), *Geschichte–Tradition–Reflexion: Festschrift für Martin Hengel zum 70 Geburtstag*, vol. iii (Tübingen, 1996), pp. 545–55.

44. See Roetzel, *Paul*, pp. 170–6. The *Acts of Paul* (second century CE) describes Paul's glorious career as a martyr. See the translation of this text in J.K. Elliott (ed.), *The Apocryphal New Testament* (Oxford, 1993), pp. 350–89; and Dennis R. MacDonald, 'Apocryphal and canonical narratives about Paul', in W.S. Babcock (ed.), *Paul and the Legacies of Paul* (Dallas, 1990), pp. 55–70.

45. See Henry Chadwick, 'St. Peter and St. Paul in Rome: the problem of the *Memoria Apostolorum ad Catacumbas*', in *History and Thought in the Early Church* (London, 1982), pp. 313–18.

46. A tongue-in-cheek article: N. Clayton Croy, ' "To die is gain" (Philippians 1.19-26); does Paul contemplate suicide?', *JBL* 122 (2003), pp. 517–31.

Chapter 18

1. On this subject see, among other contributions, Martin Hengel, *Between Jesus and Paul* (London, 1983); and particularly, Ron Cameron and Merrill P. Miller (eds), *Redescribing Christian Origins* (SBLSS, 28; Atlanta, 2004).

2. See C.K. Barrett, 'The Historicity of Acts', *JTS* 50 (1999), pp. 515–34.

3. On this topic see William S. Kurz, *Reading Luke–Acts: Dynamics of Biblical Narrative* (Louisville, 1993); Ben Witherington, *The Acts of the Apostles: A Socio-Rhetorical Commentary* (Grand Rapids, 1998); Clare K. Rothschild, *Luke–Acts and the Rhetoric of History* (WUNT, 175; Tübingen, 2004); and Charles H. Talbert, *Reading Acts: A Literary and Theological Commentary on the Acts of the Apostles* (revised edition; Macon, 2005).

4. See further Chapters 16 and 25.

5. See Friedrich Avemarie and Hermann Lichtenberger (eds), *Auferstehung= Resurrection: The Fourth Durham–Tübingen Research Symposium: Resurrection, Transfiguration and Exaltation in Old Testament, Ancient Judaism and Early Christianity* (WUNT, 135; Tübingen, 2001); and N.T. Wright, *The Resurrection of the Son of God* (London, 2003).

6. See Larry W. Hurtado, *How on Earth Did Jesus Become a God? Historical Questions about Earliest Devotion to Jesus* (Grand Rapids and Cambridge, 2005); and Christopher R. Matthews, 'From Messiahs to Christ: the pre-Pauline Christ cult in scholarship', in Cameron and Miller (eds), *Redescribing Christian Origins*, pp. 349–63

7. See G.C. Stead, 'The origins of the doctrine of the Trinity', *Theology* 77 (1971), pp. 582–8; A.W. Wainwright, *The Trinity in the New Testament* (London, 1962); K. Rahner, *The Trinity* (ET London, 1970); D. Brown, *The Divine Trinity* (London, 1985); and T.F. Torrance, *The Trinitarian Faith: The Evangelical Theology of the Ancient Catholic Church* (Edinburgh, 1988).

8. See Joel B. Green and Michael C. McKeever, *Luke–Acts and New Testament Historiography* (Grand Rapids, 1994).

9. I.H. Marshall, *The Acts of the Apostles* (Leicester, 1980).

10. *Acts and the History of the Earliest Christianity* (London, 1979).

11. *The Acts of the Apostles* (ET Oxford, 1971). For an investigation of this topic, see Stanley E. Porter, *The Paul of Acts: Essays in Literary Criticism, Rhetoric, and Theology* (WUNT, 115; Tübingen, 1999).

12. On Pentecost see James D.G. Dunn, *Jesus and the Spirit* (Grand Rapids, 1997), ch. 6; and I.H. Marshall, 'Significance of Pentecost', *SJT* 30 (1977), pp. 347–69.

13. On this subject see Mikeal C. Parsons and Richard I. Pervo, *Rethinking the Unity of Luke and Acts* (Minneapolis, 1993).

14. See further David P. Moessner, 'Two Lords "at the right hand"? The Psalms and an intertextual reading of Peter's Pentecost speech (Acts 2.14-36)', in Richard P. Thompson and Thomas E. Phillips (eds), *Literary Studies in Luke–Acts: Essays in Honor of Joseph B. Tyson* (Macon, 1998), pp. 215–32.

15. On this topic see Joel B. Green and Michael C. McKeever, *Luke–Acts and New Testament Historiography* (Grand Rapids, 1994), pt. ii; and the collection of essays edited by Robert L. Gallagher and Paul Hertig, *Mission in Acts: Ancient Narratives in Contemporary Context* (Maryknoll, 2004).

16. On the New Testament understanding of the Spirit, see James D.G. Dunn, *The Christ and the Spirit: Collected essays*, vol. ii: *Pneumatology* (Edinburgh, 1998).

17. 'The Interpretation of Acts 5:4', *JSNT* 19 (1983), pp. 117–31; 'In der Hand der Ananias: Erwägungen zu 1QS 6:20 und der urchristlichen Gütergemeinschaft', *RQ* 12 (1986), pp. 223–36; 'The Palestinian cultural context of earliest Christian community of goods', in R.J. Bauckham (ed.), *The Book of Acts in its Palestinian Setting* (Grand Rapids, 1995), pp. 323–56; and 'Essene community houses and Jesus' early community', in James H. Charlesworth (ed.), *Jesus and Archaeology* (Grand Rapids, 2006), pp. 472–502.

18. See further Capper, 'With the oldest monks . . . light from Essene history on the career of the Beloved Disciple?', *JTS* 49 (1998), pp. 1–55; and Richard J. Bauckham, 'The early Jerusalem church, Qumran, and the Essenes', in James R. Davila (ed.), *The Dead Sea Scrolls as Background to Postbiblical Judaism and Early Christianity* (Leiden, 2003), pp. 63–89.

19. See Paul Hertig, 'Dynamics in Hellenism and the immigrant congregation: Acts 6:8–8:2', in Gallagher and Hertig (eds), *Mission in Acts*, pp. 73–86.

20. Hengel thinks the Hellenists originally shared the Christian gospel with non-Jews; *Between Jesus and Paul* (London, 1983), pp. 1–29.

21. Craig Hill, *Hellenists and Hebrews: Reappraising Division within the Earliest Church* (Minneapolis, 1992). See also F. Scott Spencer, 'Neglected widows in Acts 6.17', *CBQ* 56 (1994), pp. 715–33; *idem*, *The Portrait of Philip in Acts: A Study of Roles and Relations* (JSNTSup, 67; Sheffield, 1992).

22. The classic study of this material is Klaus Wengst, *Christologische Formeln und Lieder des Urchristentums* (SNT, 7; Gutersloh, 1972).

23. See David Wenham, *Paul and the Historical Jesus* (Cambridge, 1998); *idem, Paul: Follower of Jesus or Founder of Christianity?* (Grand Rapids and Cambridge, 1995); and Seyoon Kim, 'The Jesus tradition in 1 Thess. 4:13–5:11', *NTS* 48 (2002), pp. 225–42.

24. The significance of these summaries was noted by C.H. Dodd, *The Apostolic Preaching and its Developments* (London, 1936).

25. On the meaning of this term in first-century Christianity see Francis Watson, 'Is John's Christology adoptionist?' in Larry J. Hurst and N.T. Wright (eds), *The Glory of Christ in the New Testament: Studies in Christology in Memory of G.B. Caird* (Oxford, 1987), pp. 113–24.

Chapter 19

1. Good introductions include Calvin J. Roetzel, *The Letters of Paul: Conversations in Context* (Louisville, ³1991); and James D.G. Dunn, 'The Pauline letters', in J. Barton (ed.), *The Cambridge Companion to Biblical Interpretation* (Cambridge, 1998), pp. 276–89. More detailed studies include the relevant parts of W.G. Kümmel, *Introduction to the New Testament* (revised ET; London, 1975); and Raymond E. Brown, *An Introduction to the New Testament* (ABRL; New York, 1997). There are valuable introductions to all the New Testament letters in the Sheffield New Testament Guides series. The Cambridge series on the theology of the different Pauline letters is valuable also.

2. One such is Donald Guthrie in his *New Testament Introduction* (Leicester, 1990).

3. Important commentaries and studies include C.E.B. Cranfield, *A Critical and Exegetical Commentary on the Epistle to the Romans* (Edinburgh, 1975); James D.G. Dunn, *Romans 1–8, Romans 9–16* (WBC, 38a, 38b; Dallas, 1988); Joseph A. Fitzmyer, *Romans: A New Translation with Introduction and Commentary* (AB, 33; New York, 1993); and Peter Stuhlmacher, *Paul's Letter to the Romans: A Commentary* (ET Louisville, 1994). See also Philip F. Esler, *Conflict and Identity in Romans: The Social Setting of Paul's Letter* (Minneapolis, 2003); Klaus Haacker, *The Theology of Paul's Letter to the Romans* (Cambridge, 2003); Ben Witherington, *Paul's Letter to the Romans: A Socio-rhetorical Commentary* (Grand Rapids, 2004); Thomas H. Tobin, *Paul's Rhetoric in its Contexts: The Argument of Romans* (Peabody, 2004); Mark Reasoner, *Romans in Full Circle: A History of Interpretation* (Louisville, 2005); and Robert Jewett, assisted by Ray D. Kotansky, edited by Eldon Jay Epp, *Romans: A Commentary* (Hermeneia; Minneapolis, 2006).

4. Philipp Melanchthon, *Commentary on Romans* (reissued St Louis, 1992).

5. On this topic, see Hans Dieter Betz, 'The concept of the "inner human

being" in the anthropology of Paul', *NTS* 46 (2000), pp. 315–41; Sang-Wen Son, *Corporate Elements in Pauline Anthropology: A Study of Selected Terms, Idioms, and Concepts in the Light of Paul's Usage and Background* (AnBib, 148; Rome, 2001).

6. Käsemann, *Commentary on Romans* (ET Grand Rapids, 1980).
7. The topic of Paul and the law is discussed by numerous scholars. Among the most important, see E.P. Sanders, *Paul, the Law and the Jewish People* (Philadelphia, 1983); Heikki Räisänen, *Paul and the Law* (WUNT, 29; Tübingen, ²1987); and James D.G. Dunn (ed.), *Paul and the Mosaic Law* (WUNT, 89; Tübingen, 1996). See also A. Andrew Das, *Paul and the Jews* (Peabody, 2004); Femi Adeyemi, *The New Covenant Torah in Jeremiah and the Law of Christ in Paul* (SBL, 94; New York, 2006); and Martin G. Abegg, 'Paul and James on law in light of the Dead Sea scrolls', in James H. Charlesworth (ed.), *Christian Beginnings and the Dead Sea Scrolls* (Grand Rapids, 2006), pp. 63–74.
8. There is an interesting discussion of the background to this conception in Serge Ruger, 'The seat of sin in early Jewish and Christian sources', in J. Assmann and G.A.G. Stroumsa (eds), *Transformations of the Inner Self in Ancient Religions* (SHR, 83; Leiden, 1999), pp. 367–91.
9. See George W.E. Nickelsburg, 'Abraham the convert: a Jewish tradition and its use by the apostle Paul', in M.E. Stone and T.A. Bergren (eds), *Biblical Figures Outside the Bible* (Harrisburg, 1998), pp. 151–75; and Nancy Calvert Koysis, *Paul, Monotheism and the People of God: The Significance of Abraham Traditions for Early Judaism and Christianity* (JSNTSup, 273; London, 2004).
10. On circumcision see John J. Collins, 'A symbol of otherness: circumcision and salvation in the first century', in Jacob Neusner and Ernest S. Frerichs (eds), *'To See Ourselves as Others See Us': Christians, Jews, 'Others' in Late Antiquity* (Chico, 1985), pp. 163–86; and John M.G. Barclay, 'Paul and Philo on circumcision: Romans 2.25-9 in social and cultural context', *NTS* 44 (1998), pp. 536–56.
11. On which see M. Seifrid, *Justification by Faith: The Origin and Development of a Central Pauline Theme* (Leiden, 1992); J. Ziesler, *The Meaning of Righteousness in Paul* (Cambridge, 1972); Simon J. Gathercole, 'The doctrine of justification in Paul and beyond: some proposals', in Bruce L. McCormack (ed.), *Justification in Perspective: Historical Developments and Contemporary Challenges* (Grand Rapids, 2006), pp. 219–41; and David E. Aune, 'Recent readings of Paul relating to justification by faith', in David E. Aune (ed.), *Rereading Paul Together: Protestant and Catholic Perspectives on Justification* (Grand Rapids, 2006), pp. 188–245; together with further literature mentioned later in this chapter. There has been a substantial debate about whether the principle of 'righteousness by faith' constitutes the *centre* of Paul's theology. The belief that it does stems from Martin Luther (1483–1546). A prominent critic of this view is Albert Schweitzer, who called it a merely 'subsidiary crater' in the landscape of Pauline mysticism; see his *The Mysticism of Paul the Apostle* (London, 1931).
12. This aspect of Paul's thought has been studied by Daniel P. Bailey, 'Jesus as the Mercy Seat: the semantics and theology of Paul's use of *hilasterion* in Romans 3.25' (Unpublished PhD thesis, University of Cambridge, 1999).
13. See Chapter 22 on the subject of Pauline ethics.

14. The matter is explored post-Schweitzer by Alan F. Segal, *Paul the Convert: The Apostolate and Apostasy of Saul the Pharisee* (New Haven, 1990). See also Ulrich Luz, trans. Martin Kitchen, 'Paul as mystic', in Graham N. Stanton, Bruce W. Longenecker and Stephen C. Barton (eds), *The Holy Spirit and Christian Origins* (Grand Rapids, 2004), pp. 131–43; and Ithamar Gruenwald, 'Ritualizing death in James and Paul in the light of Jewish apocalypticism', in Bruce D. Chilton and Craig E. Evans (eds), *The Missions of James, Peter and Paul: Tensions in Early Christianity* (Leiden, 2005), pp. 467–86.

15. See further C.E.B. Cranfield, 'Paul's teaching on sanctification', *Reformed Review* 48 (1995), pp. 217–29.

16. See D.B. Martin, *Slavery as Salvation: The Metaphor of Slavery in Pauline Christianity* (New Haven, 1990).

17. The background is explored by H. Hömmel, 'Das 7. Kapitel des Römerbriefs im Licht antiker Überlieferung', *ThViat* 8 (1961–2), pp. 90–116. See also Gerd Theissen, *Psychological Aspects of Pauline Theology* (Edinburgh, 1987), esp. pp. 212–19.

18. Again, see Chapter 22 for an exploration of this matter. An important study is A.J.M. Wedderburn, 'Pauline pneumatology and Pauline theology', in Stanton *et al.* (eds), *The Holy Spirit and Christian Origins*, pp. 144–56. A number of other studies in this *Festschrift* are relevant also.

19. Henry Alan Hahne, *The Corruption and Redemption of Creation: Nature in Romans 8.19–22 and Jewish Apocalyptic Literature* (LNTS, 36; London, 2006).

20. See H. Räisänen, 'Römer 9–11: Analyse eines geistigen Ringens', in *ANRW* II.25.4 (1987), cols 2891–2939; O. Hofius, 'Das Evangelium und Israel: Erwägungen zu Römer 9–11', in *Paulusstudien* (Tübingen, 1989), pp. 175–202; and R.H. Bell, *Provoked to Jealousy: The Origin and Purpose of the Jealousy Motif in Romans 9–11* (WUNT, 63; Tübingen, 1994); *idem, The Irrevocable Call of God: An Inquiry into Paul's Theology of Israel* (WUNT, 184; Tübingen, 2005); and Kari Kuula, *The Law, the Covenant and God's Plan*, vol. ii: *Paul's Treatment of the Law and Israel in Romans* (PFES, 85; Helsinki, 2003).

21. For this view see E. Käsemann, 'Principles of the interpretation of Romans 13', in *New Testament Questions of Today* (ET London, 1969), pp. 196–216; E. Bammel, 'Romans 13', in E. Bammel and C.F.D. Moule (eds), *Jesus and the Politics of His Day* (Cambridge, 1984), pp. 365–83. The opposite case is argued by V. Riekkinen, *Römer 13: Aufzeichnung und Weiterführung der exegetischen Diskussion* (Helsinki, 1980), esp. chs. 1 and 2

22. Important commentaries include H. Conzelmann, *1 Corinthians* (Hermeneia; ET Philadelphia, 1975); and C.K. Barrett, *A Commentary on The First Epistle to the Corinthians* (London, 1992). See also James D.G. Dunn, *1 Corinthians* (NTG; Sheffield, 1995); R. Bieringer (ed.), *The Corinthian Correspondence* (BETL, 125; Louvain, 1996); Anthony C. Thiselton, *The First Epistle to the Corinthians: A Commentary on the Greek Text* (NIGTC; Grand Rapids and Carlisle, 2000); David E. Garland, *1 Corinthians* (Grand Rapids, 2003); Trevor J. Burke and J.K. Elliott (eds), *Paul and the Corinthians: Studies on a Community in Conflict* (NovTSup, 109; Leiden, 2003); Judith L. Kovacs, *1 Corinthians Interpreted by Early Christian Commentators* (ET Grand Rapids, 2005); John Paul Heil, *The Rhetorical Role of Scripture in 1 Corinthians* (SBL, 15; Atlanta, 2005); Craig S. Keener, *1–2 Corinthians* (NCBC; Cambridge,

2005); and Anthony C. Thiselton, *First Corinthians: A Shorter Exegetical and Pastoral Commentary* (Grand Rapids, 2006).

23. See David Horrell, *The Social Ethos of the Corinthian Correspondence: Interests and Ideology from First Corinthians to First Clement* (Edinburgh, 1996). It used to be thought that the problem Paul faced in Corinth was a form of incipient Gnosticism. This hypothesis was stated classically by W. Schmithals, *Gnosticism in Corinth* (ET Nashville, 1971). For criticism of this view, however, see Dunn, *1 Corinthians*, pp. 34–41 and the literature cited there.

24. See P. Marshall, *Enmity in Corinth: Social Conventions in Paul's Relations with the Corinthians* (WUNT, 23; Tübingen, 1987); and M.M. Mitchell, *Paul and the Rhetoric of Reconciliation: An Exegetical Investigation of the Language and Composition of 1 Corinthians* (HUT, 28; Tübingen, 1991).

25. An interesting perspective is offered on this by J.H. Neyrey, 'Perceiving the human body: body language in 1 Corinthians', in *Paul in Other Words: A Cultural Reading of his Letters* (Louisville, 1990), pp. 102–46.

26. See Alistair Scott May, *'The Body for the Lord': Sex and Identity in 1 Corinthians 5–7* (JSNTSup, 278; London, 2004).

27. See W.L. Willis, *Idol Meat in Corinth: The Pauline Argument in 1 Corinthians 8 and 10* (SBLDS, 68; Chico, 1985); and John Fotopolos, *Food Offered to Idols in Roman Corinth: A Socio-rhetorical Reconsideration of 1 Corinthians 8:1–11:1* (WUNT, 151; Tübingen, 2003)

28. See M.D. Hooker, 'Authority on her head: an examination of 1 Corinthians 11.10', in *From Adam to Christ: Essays on Paul* (Cambridge, 1990), pp. 113–20. From a different perspective, E. Schüssler Fiorenza, *In Memory of Her: A Feminist Theological Reconstruction of Christian Origins* (London, 1983).

29. See W.A. Grudem, *The Gift of Prophecy in 1 Corinthians* (Lanham, 1982); R.P. Martin, *The Spirit and the Congregation: Studies in 1 Corinthians 12–15* (Grand Rapids, 1984); and D.A. Carson, *Showing the Spirit: A Theological Exposition of 1 Corinthians 12–14* (Grand Rapids, 1987).

30. See Carl R. Holladay, '1 Corinthians 13: Paul as apostolic paradigm', in David L. Balch, Everett Ferguson and Wayne A. Meeks (eds), *Greeks, Romans, and Christians: Essays in Honor of Abraham J. Malherbe* (Minneapolis, 1990), pp. 80–98; and J. Smit, 'The genre of 1 Corinthians 13 in the light of classical rhetoric', *NovT* 33 (1991), pp. 193–216.

31. See M.C. de Boer, *The Defeat of Death: Apocalyptic Eschatology in 1 Corinthians 15 and Romans 5* (JSNTSup, 22; Sheffield, 1988); and Chapter 21 below.

32. Thus also Segal, *Paul the Convert*, p. 65.

33. Major commentaries include C.K. Barrett, *A Commentary on the Second Epistle to the Corinthians* (London, 1973); R.P. Martin, *2 Corinthians* (WBC; Waco, 1986); Ernest Best, *Second Corinthians* (Westminster, 1987); V.P. Furnish, *2 Corinthians* (AB, 32a; New York, 1984); M.E. Thrall, *A Critical and Exegelical Commentary on The Second Epistle to the Corinthians* (ICC; 2 vols.; Edinburgh, 1994, 2000); Frank J. Matera, *2 Corinthians: A Commentary* (NTL; Louisville, 2003); Frederick J. Long, *Ancient Rhetoric and Paul's Apology: The Compositional Unity of 2 Corinthians* (SNTSMS, 131; Cambridge, 2004); and Murray J. Harris, *The Second Epistle to the Corinthians: A Commentary on the Greek Text* (Grand Rapids, 2005).

34. For a summary of the difficulties and how they have been resolved in the past, see Larry Kreitzer, *2 Corinthians* (NTG; Sheffield, 1996), ch. 2. There

is important material also in R. Bieringer and J. Lambrecht, *Studies on 2 Corinthians* (BETL, 112; Louvain, 1994).

35. Major studies of this section include J. Gnilka, '2 Cor. 6.14–7.1 in the light of the Qumran texts and the Testaments of the Twelve Patriarchs', in J. Murphy-O'Connor (ed.), *Paul and Qumran: Studies in New Testament Exegesis* (London, 1968), pp. 48–68; J.A. Fitzmyer, 'Qumran and the interpolated paragraph in 2 Cor. 6.14–7.1', in *Essays on the Semitic Background of the New Testament* (London, 1971), pp. 205–17; and H.D. Betz, '2 Cor. 6.14–7.1: an anti-Pauline fragment?', *JBL* 92 (1973), pp. 88–108. See also W.J. Webb, *Returning Home: New Covenant and Second Exodus as the Context for 2 Corinthians 6.14–7.1* (JSNTSup, 85; Sheffield, 1993).

36. See further L.L. Welborn, 'The identification of 2 Corinthians 10–13 with the "Letter of Tears" ', *NovT* 37 (1995), pp. 138–53.

37. On the rationale of this part of the letter, see L.L. Belleville, 'A letter of apologetic self-commendation: 2 Cor. 1.8–7.16', *NovT* 31 (1989), pp. 142–63.

38. See H.D. Betz, *2 Corinthians 8–9* (Hermeneia; Philadelphia, 1985).

39. On this aspect see K.F. Nickle, *The Collection: A Study in Paul's Strategy* (SBT, 48; London, 1966); Kreitzer, *2 Corinthians*, ch. 6; J. Murphy-O'Connor, *The Theology of the Second Letter to the Corinthians* (NTT; Cambridge, 1991), pp. 75–95; A.J.M. Wedderburn, 'Paul's collection: chronology and history', *NTS* 48 (2002), pp. 95–110; and David J. Downs, 'Paul's collection and the Book of Acts revisited', *NTS* 52 (2006), pp. 50–70.

40. Cf. Simon J. Gathercole, *Where is Boasting? Early Jewish Soteriology and Paul's Response in Romans 1–5* (Grand Rapids, 2002).

41. This enigmatic passage has stimulated a great deal of interest. Beside the work of Segal already mentioned, see J.W. Bowker, ' "Merkabah" visions and the visions of Paul', *JJS* 16 (1971), pp. 157–73; A.T. Lincoln, ' "Paul the visionary": the setting and significance of the rapture to paradise in II Corinthians XII. 1–10', *NTS* 25 (1979), pp. 204–20; P. Schäfer, 'New Testament and Hekalot literature: the journey into heaven in Paul and Merkavah mysticism', *JJS* 35 (1984), pp. 19–35; C.R.A. Morray-Jones, 'Paradise revisited (2 Cor. 12:1–12): the Jewish mystical background of Paul's apostolate', *HTR* 86 (1993), pp. 177–217, 265–92; M.E. Thrall, 'Paul's journey to paradise: some exegetical issues in 2 Cor 12, 2–4', in Bieringer (ed.), *Corinthian Correspondence*, pp. 347–63; and M.D. Goulder, 'Vision and knowledge in Paul', *JSNT* 56 (1994), pp. 53–71.

42. See Paula R. Gooder, *Only the Third Heaven? 2 Corinthians 12.1-10 and Heavenly Ascent* (LNTS, 313; London, 2006).

43. Commentaries include H.D. Betz, *Galatians* (Hermeneia; Philadelphia, 1983); R.N. Longenecker, *Galatians* (WBC, 41; Dallas, 1990); J.D.G. Dunn, *The Epistle to the Galatians* (Peabody, 1993); and J.L. Martyn, *Galatians* (AB, 33a; London, 1997). See also Susan Elliott, *Cutting Too Close for Comfort: Paul's Letter to the Galatians in its Anatolian Cultic Context* (JSNTSup, 248; London, 2003); D. François Tolmie, *Persuading the Galatians: A Text-Centered Rhetorical Analysis of a Pauline Letter* (WUNT, 190; Tübingen, 2005); and Justin Kee Hardin, *Galatians and the Imperial Cult? A Critical Analysis of the First-Century Social Context of Paul's Letter* (Cambridge, 2006).

44. On this episode see the discussion of Martyn, *Galatians*, pp. 228–45.

45. R.B. Hays, *The Faith of Jesus Christ: An Investigation of the Narrative Substructure of Galatians 3.1–4.11* (SBLDS, 56; Chico, 1983).

46. See G.W. Hansen, *Abraham in Galatians: Epistolary and Rhetorical Contexts* (JSNTSup, 29; Sheffield, 1989); Nancy Calvert Koyzis, *Paul, Monotheism and the People of God: The Significance of Abraham Traditions for Early Judaism and Christianity* (JSNTSup, 273; London, 2004); and James R. Harrison, *Paul's Language of Grace in its Graeco-Roman Context* (WUNT, 172; Tübingen, 2003).

47. See further D.J. Lull, *The Spirit in Galatia* (SBLDS, 49; Chico, 1980).

48. Commentaries include G.F. Hawthorne, *Philippians* (WBC; Waco, 1987); P.T. O'Brien, *The Epistle to the Philippians: A Commentary on the Greek Text* (NIGTC; Grand Rapids, 1991); G. Fee, *Paul's Letter to the Philippians* (Grand Rapids, 1995); Markus Bockmuehl, *A Commentary on the Epistle to the Philippians* (London, 1997); Bonnie B. Thurston and Judith M. Ryan, *Philippians and Philemon* (SPS; Collegeville, 2005); and Stephen E. Fowl, *Philippians* (THNTC; Grand Rapids, 2005). See also Peter Oakes, *Philippians: From People to Letter* (SNTSMS, 110; Cambridge, 2001); and James Patrick Ware, *The Mission of the Church in Paul's Letter to the Philippians in the Context of Ancient Judaism* (NovTSup, 120; Leiden, 2005).

49. For a review of this theory see Brown, *Introduction*, pp. 496–500.

50. *Introduction*, p. 333.

51. This is accepted by Bockmuehl, *Philippians*, pp. 30–2.

52. An important study is Markus Bockmuehl, ' "The form of God" (Phil 2:6): variations on a theme of Jewish mysticism', *JTS* 48 (1997), pp. 1–23. The best-known study is the republished *Carmen Christi* by R.P. Martin (Grand Rapids, 1983). See also Adela Yarbro Collins, 'Psalms, Philippians 2:6-11 and the origin of Christology', *Biblical Interpretation* 11 (2003), pp. 361–71.

53. See Chapter 21.

54. See Peter Doble, 'Vile bodies or transformed persons? Philippians 3:21 in context', *JSNT* 86 (2002), pp. 3–27.

55. See the articles by Luz and Gruenwald mentioned at note 14 above.

56. Commentaries include E. Best, *A Commentary on the First and Second Epistles to the Thessalonians* (London, 1972); F.F. Bruce, *1 and 2 Thessalonians* (WBC; Waco, 1982); Charles A. Wanamaker, *The Epistles to the Thessalonians: A Commentary on the Greek Text* (NIGTC; Grand Rapids, 1990); Earl J. Richard, *First and Second Thessalonians* (SPS; Collegeville, 1995); David J. Williams, *1 and 2 Thessalonians* (NIBC, 12; Peabody, 1995); and Ben P. Witherington, *1 and 2 Thessalonians: A Socio-rhetorical Commentary* (Grand Rapids, 2006). An important study is R. Jewett, *The Thessalonian Correspondence: Pauline Rhetoric and Millenarian Piety* (Philadelphia, 1986); and see also Colin R. Nicholl, *From Hope to Despair in Thessalonica: Situating 1 and 2 Thessalonians* (SNTSMS, 126; Cambridge, 2004); and Angus Paddison, *Theological Hermeneutics and 1 Thessalonians* (SNTSMS, 133; Cambridge, 2005).

57. See C.F. Mearns, 'Early eschatological development in Paul: the evidence of I and II Thessalonians', *NTS* 20 (1980–1), pp. 136–57.

58. See Karl P. Donfried, '1 Thessalonians, Acts and the early Paul', in Raymond F. Collins (ed.), *The Thessalonian Correspondence* (Louvain, 1990), pp. 3–26; and Morna D. Hooker, '1 Thessalonians 1:9-10: a nutshell – but what kind

of nut?', in H. Cancik, H. Lichtenberger and P. Schäfer (eds), *Geschichte–Tradition–Reflexion: Festschriften für Martin Hengel zum 70 Geburtstag*, vol. iii (Tübingen, 1996), pp. 435–48.

59. J. Plevnik, 'The taking up of the faithful and the resurrection of the dead in 1 Thessalonians 4:13-18', *CBQ* 46 (1984), pp. 274–83; *idem, Paul and the Parousia* (Peabody, 1997), ch. 3; and '1 Thessalonians 4:17: the bringing in of the Lord or the bringing in of the faithful?', *Biblica* 80 (1999), pp. 537–46.

60. See Michael R. Cosby, 'Hellenistic formal reception and Paul's use of *apantesis* in 1 Thessalonians 4:17', *BBR* 4 (1994), pp. 15–33; and Robert H. Gundry, 'A brief note on "Hellenistic formal reception and Paul's use of *apantesis* in 1 Thessalonians 4:17" ', *BBR* 6 (1996), pp. 39–41.

61. The alternatives are explored by Plevnik in the literature cited. He opts for the first interpretation. See also Seth Turner, 'The interim, earthly messianic kingdom in Paul', *JSNT* 25 (2003), pp. 323–42.

62. See Hans Hübner, *An Philemon. An die Kolosser. an die Epheser* (HNT, 12; Tübingen, 1997); James Tunstead Burtchaell, *Philemon's Problem: A Theology of Grace* (Grand Rapids, 1998); and Marianne Meye Thompson, *Colossians and Philemon* (THNTC; Grand Rapids, 2005).

63. See N. Brox, *Falsche Verfasserangaben: Zur Erklärung der frühchristlichen Pseudepigraphie* (SBS, 79; Stuttgart, 1975); N. Brox (ed.), *Pseudepigraphie in der Heidnischen und Jüdisch-Christlichen Antike* (WF, 484; Darmstadt, 1977); D.O. Meade, *Pseudonymity and Canon* (WUNT, 39; Tübingen, 1986); and Kent D. Clarke, 'The problem of pseudonymity in biblical literature and its implications for canon formation', in Lee Martin Macdonald (ed.), *The Canon Debate: On the Origins and Formation of the Bible* (Peabody, 2002). A conservative evaluation is E. Randolph Richards, *Paul and First-Century Letter Writing: Secretaries, Composition and Collection* (Downers Grove, 2004).

64. On this material see J.H. Charlesworth (ed.), *The Old Testament Pseudepigrapha* (2 vols.; London, 1983, 1985).

65. See J.H. Charlesworth and J.R. Mueller, *The New Testament Apocrypha and Pseudepigrapha* (ATLABS, 17; Metuchen, 1987).

66. See B.M. Metzger, 'Literary forgeries and canonical pseudepigrapha', *JBL* 91 (1972), pp. 3–14; and Terry L. Wilder, 'New Testament pseudonymity and deception' (unpublished PhD thesis, University of Aberdeen, 1999).

67. Commentaries include C.L. Mitton, *Ephesians* (Grand Rapids, 1976); M. Barth, *Ephesians* (AB, 34; 2 vols.; New York, 1974); A.T. Lincoln, *Ephesians* (WBC, 92; Waco, 1990); R. Schnackenburg, *The Epistle to the Ephesians* (LET; Edinburgh, 1991); Pheme Perkins, *Ephesians* (ANTC; Nashville, 1997); E. Best, *A Critical and Exegetical Commentary on Ephesians* (ICC; Edinburgh, 1998); and Harold W. Hoehner, *Ephesians: An Exegetical Commentary* (Grand Rapids, 2002). See also Martin Kitchen, *Ephesians* (London, 1994); E. Best, *Essays on Ephesians* (Edinburgh, 1997); George H. van Kooten, *Cosmic Christology in Paul and the Pauline School: Colossians and Ephesians in the Context of Graeco-Roman Cosmology, with a New Synopsis of the Greek Texts* (WUNT, 171; Tübingen, 2003); and N. Yee Tet-Lim, *Jews, Gentiles and Ethnic Reconciliation: Paul's Identity and Ephesians* (SNTSMS, 130; Cambridge, 2005). An important study is Paul Trebilco, *The Early Christians in Ephesus from Paul to Ignatius* (WUNT, 166; Tübingen, 2004).

68. Critical literature here includes J.A. Robinson, *St. Paul's Epistle to the Ephesians* (London, 1904); C.L. Mitton, *The Epistle to the Ephesians* (Oxford, 1951); E.J. Goodspeed, *The Meaning of Ephesians* (Chicago, 1933); and *idem*, *The Key to Ephesians* (Chicago, 1956).

69. See Kümmel, *Introduction*, pp. 357–63.

70. *Introduction*, p. 352.

71. See the works by Goodspeed and Mitton mentioned at note 68. A more recent work is A. van Roon, *The Authenticity of Ephesians* (NovTSup, 39; Leiden, 1974).

72. See E. Best, 'Who wrote whom? The relationship of Ephesians and Colossians', *NTS* 43 (1997), pp. 72–96.

73. In Mitton, *Ephesians* and *Epistle to the Ephesians*.

74. See Mitton, *Epistle to the Ephesians*, pp. 28, 59, 75, 249.

75. E.g. Kümmel, *Introduction*, p. 361.

76. *Adv. Marc.* V.11.17.

77. See James D.G. Dunn, 'The household rules in the New Testament', in S. Barton (ed.), *The Family in Theological Perspective* (Edinburgh, 1996), pp. 43–63.

78. Commentaries include E. Lohse, *Colossians and Philemon* (Hermeneia; ET Philadelphia, 1971); Peter T. O'Brien, *Colossians, Philemon* (WBC, 44; Waco, 1984); Petr Pokorny, *Colossians: A Commentary* (ET Peabody, 1991); James D.G. Dunn, *The Epistles to the Colossians and Philemon: A Commentary on the Greek Text* (Grand Rapids and Carlisle, 1996); and R. McL. Wilson, *A Critical and Exegetical Commentary on Colossians and Philemon* (ICC; London, 2005) A useful study is Outi Leppä, *The Making of Colossians: A Study on the Formation and Purpose of a Deutero-Pauline Letter* (PFES, 86; Helsinki and Göttingen, 2003).

79. Ernst Theodor Mayerhoff, *Der Brief an die Colosser, mit vornehmlicher Berücksichtigung der drei Pastoralbriefe kritisch geprüft* (Berlin, 1838).

80. *The Church History of the First Three Centuries* (ET London and Edinburgh, 1878), p. 127. On the phenomenon of Gnosticism, see Chapter 30 below.

81. *An die Kolosser, Epheser, on an Philemon* (HNT, 12; Tübingen, 1927). See also E. Percy, *Die Probleme der Kolosser- und Epheserbriefe* (Lund, 1946) and George H. van Kooten, *Cosmic Christology in Paul and the Pauline School: Colossians and Ephesians in the Context of Graeco-Roman Cosmology, with a New Synopsis of the Greek Texts* (WUNT, 171; Tübingen, 2003),

82. Bultmann, *Theology of the New Testament*, vol. ii (ET New York, 1955).

83. J.L. Houlden, *Paul's Letters from Prison* (Harmondsworth, 1970); G.B. Caird, *Paul's Letters from Prison* (London, 1976). On the latter view see M. Kiley, *Colossians as Pseudepigraphy* (BS, 4; Sheffield, 1986).

84. See Christopher Rowland, 'Apocalyptic visions and the exaltation of Christ in the letter to the Colossians', *JSNT* 19 (1983), pp. 73–83; Jarl E. Fossum, 'Colossians 1.15a–18a in the light of Jewish mysticism and Gnosticism', *NTS* 35 (1989), pp. 183–201; and Walter Wink, 'The hymn of the cosmic Christ', in Robert T. Fortna and Beverley Roberts Gaventa (eds), *The Conversation Continues: Studies in Paul and John in Honor of J. Louis Martyn* (Nashville, 1990), pp. 235–45.

85. See G.E. Cannon, *The Use of Traditional Materials in Colossians* (Macon, 1983). On the proposed Jewish background to the Colossian syncretism,

F.O. Francis and W.A. Meeks, *Conflict at Colossae: A Problem in the Interpretation of Early Christianity* (SBS, 4; Missoula, 1973); M.D. Hooker, 'Were there false teachers in Colossae?', in B. Lindars and S.S. Smalley (eds), *Christ and the Spirit in the New Testament* (Cambridge, 1973), pp. 315–31; J.D.G. Dunn, 'The Colossian philosophy: a confident Jewish apologia', *Biblica* 76 (1995), pp. 153–81; and C.E. Arnold, *The Colossian Syncretism* (WUNT, 77; Tübingen, 1995).

86. On this topic see David E. Aune, *The Cultic Setting of Realized Eschatology in Early Christianity* (NovTSup, 28; Leiden, 1972); Clayton Sullivan, *Rethinking Realized Eschatology* (Macon, 1988); and Todd D. Still, 'Eschatology in Colossians: how realized is it?', *NTS* 50 (2004), pp. 125–38

87. See James D.G. Dunn, 'The "body" in Colossians', in Thomas E. Schmidt and Moisis Silva (eds), *To Tell the Mystery: Essays on New Testament Eschatology in Honor of Robert H. Gundry* (JSNTSup, 100; Sheffield, 1994), pp. 163–81; C. Arnold, 'Jesus Christ: "head" of the church (Colossians and Ephesians)', in Joel B. Green and Max Turner (eds), *Jesus of Nazareth: Lord and Christ: Essays on the Historical Jesus and New Testament Christology* (Grand Rapids and Carlisle, 1994), pp. 346–66.

88. See Andrew T. Lincoln, 'The household code and Wisdom mode of Colossians', *JSNT* 74 (1999), pp. 93–112.

89. *A Stylometric Study of the New Testament* (Oxford, 1986).

90. K.J. Neumann, *The Authenticity of the Pauline Epistles in the Light of Stylostatistical Analysis* (Atlanta, 1990).

91. D.G. Mealand, 'The extent of the Pauline corpus: a multivariate approach', *JSNT* 59 (1995), pp. 61–92.

92. On this passage, see the literature on Colossian syncretism cited at note 86 above.

93. Beside the commentaries on 1 and 2 Thessalonians already mentioned, see Gerhard A. Krodel, *The Deutero-Pauline Letters: Ephesians, Colossians, 2 Thessalonians* (PC; Minneapolis, 1993); and G.S. Holland, *The Tradition that You Received from Us: 2 Thessalonians in the Pauline Tradition* (HUT, 24; Tübingen, 1988). There are several useful articles in Collins (ed.), *Thessalonian Correspondence.*

94. See Helmut Koester, 'From Paul's eschatology to the Apostolic Schemata of 2 Thessalonians', in Collins (ed.), *Thessalonian Correspondence*, pp. 441–58.

95. See Koester, 'Paul's eschatology'.

96. See R. Russell, 'The idle in 2 Thess. 3:6-12: an eschatological or social problem?', *NTS* 34 (1988), pp. 105–19.

97. Brown, *Introduction*, p. 596.

98. Commentaries and studies include M. Dibelius and H. Conzelmann, *The Pastoral Epistles* (ET Philadelphia, 1972); G. Fee, *1 and 2 Timothy, Titus* (NIBC; Peabody, 1988); M. Davies, *The Pastoral Epistles: 1 and 2 Timothy and Titus* (EC; London, 1996); Jerome D. Quinn, *The Letter to Titus: A New Translation with Notes and Commentary* (AB, 35; New York, 1990); *idem, The First and Second letters to Timothy: A New Translation with Notes and Commentary* (EdCC; Grand Rapids, 2000); Raymond F. Collins, *I and II Timothy and Titus* (NTL; Louisville, 2002); and Ray van Neste, *Cohesion and Structure in the Pastoral Epistles* (JSNTSup, 280; London, 2004). See

I. Howard Marshall, 'Some recent commentaries on the Pastoral Epistles', *ExpT* 117 (2006), pp. 140–3.

99. The title was first used for Titus by D.N. Bardot in 1703; and for all three letters by P. Anton, *Exegetische Abhandlungen der Past. Pauli* (1753–5).

100. See Kümmel, *Introduction*, pp. 370–1.

101. See Kümmel, *Introduction*, pp. 370–84.

102. Kümmel, *Introduction*, pp. 382–3. See further L.R. Donelson, *Pseudepigraphy and Ethical Argument in the Pastoral Epistles* (HUT, 22; Tübingen, 1986).

103. Such as Guthrie in the work mentioned at note 2 above.

104. On whom see Chapter 28.

105. See Craig A. Smith, *Timothy's Task, Paul's Prospect: A New Reading of 2 Timothy* (NTM, 12; Sheffield, 2006).

106. See note 18 above.

Chapter 20

1. There are plenty of detailed guides for readers to follow if their appetite is whetted by this topic. See e.g. H.J. Schoeps, *Paul: The Theology of the Apostle in the Light of Jewish Religious History* (London and Philadelphia, 1961); D.E.H. Whiteley, *The Theology of St. Paul* (Oxford, 1964); E.P. Sanders, *Paul and Palestinian Judaism* (London, 1977); J. Fitzmyer, *Paul and His Theology: A Brief Sketch* (Englewood Cliffs, ²1989); J. Ziesler, *Pauline Christianity* (Oxford and New York, ²1990); James D.G. Dunn, *The Theology of Paul the Apostle* (Edinburgh and Grand Rapids, 1998); and J. Louis Martyn, *Theological Issues in the Letters of Paul* (Nashville and Edinburgh, 1997).

2. See F. Hahn, 'The confession of the one God in the New Testament', *HBT* 2 (1980), pp. 69–84; H. Moxnes, *Theology in Conflict: Studies in Paul's Understanding of God in Romans* (Leiden, 1980); and Larry. J. Kreitzer, *Jesus and God in Paul's Eschatology* (JSNTSup, 19; Sheffield, 1987). The theological climate of early Christianity is assessed by Richard Bauckham, *God Crucified: Monotheism and Christology* (Grand Rapids and Carlisle, 1998); Carey C. Newman, James R. Davila and Gladys S. Lewis (eds), *The Jewish Roots of Christological Monotheism* (JSJSup, 63; Leiden, 1999); Max Turner, ' "Trinitarian" pneumatology and Pauline Theology', *ATJ* 57–8 (2002–3), pp. 167–86; Larry W. Hurtado, *How on Earth Did Jesus Become a God?* (Grand Rapids, 2005); and Nancy Calvert Koyzis, *Paul, Monotheism, and the People of God: The Significance of Abraham Traditions for Judaism and Christianity* (JSNTSup, 73; London, 2004).

3. See Gordon Fee, 'Paul and the Trinity: the experience of Christ and the Spirit for Paul's understanding of God', in Stephen T. Davis, Daniel Kendall and Gerald O'Collins (eds), *The Trinity* (Oxford and New York, 1999).

4. The background to this is explored by Robert K. Gnuse, *No Other Gods: Emergent Monotheism in Israel* (JSOTSup, 241; Sheffield, 1997).

5. This point is carefully argued by Alan F. Segal in his *Paul the Convert: The Apostolate and Apostasy of Saul the Pharisee* (New Haven and London, 1990).

6. See below; and Dunn, *Theology*, pp. 224–5.

7. On the theology proposed here see the above literature; and Kreitzer, *Jesus and God*.
8. See W. Marcus, *Der Subordiatianismus* (Munich, 1963); and Craig S. Keener, 'Is subordination within the Trinity really heresy?', *Trinity Journal* 20/1 (1999), pp. 39–51.
9. See Jerome Murphy O'Connor, 'The origins of Paul's Christology: from Thessalonians to Galatians', in Kieran J. Mahoney (ed.), *Christian Origins: Worship, Belief, and Society: The Miltown Institute and Irish Association Millennium Conference* (London, 2003).
10. This has been a perennial problem in Pauline and other New Testament theology. For the view that Paul took no interest in the historical Jesus, see Rudolph Bultmann, 'The significance of the historical Jesus for the theology of Paul', in *Faith and Understanding: Collected Essays* (London and New York, 1969), pp. 220–46. This view is now no longer held by New Testament scholars. On the subject see E. Jüngel, *Paulus und Jesus. Eine Untersuchung zur Präzisierung der Frage nach dem Ursprung der Christologie* (Tübingen, ³1967); V.P. Furnish, *Jesus According to Paul* (Cambridge, 1993); J.D.G. Dunn, 'Jesus tradition in Paul', in B. Chilton and C.A. Evans (eds), *Studying the Historical Jesus: Evaluation of the State of Current Research* (Leiden, 1994), pp. 155–78; and David Wenham, *Paul: Follower of Jesus or Founder of Christianity?* (Grand Rapids, 1995).
11. See Michael B. Thompson, *Clothed with Christ: The Example and Teaching of Jesus in Romans 12.1–15.13* (JSNTSup, 59; Sheffield, 1991).
12. See Stephen W. Sykes, 'The theology of the humanity of Christ', in Stephen W. Sykes and John Paul Clayton, *Christ, Faith and History: Cambridge Studies in Christology* (Cambridge, 1972); and John P. Galvin, 'From the humanity of Christ to the Jesus of history: a paradigm shift in Catholic Christianity', *TS* 55 (1994), pp. 252–73.
13. *The Letters of Paul: Conversations in Context* (Louisville, ³1998).
14. See the comment by C.H. Dodd I mentioned in Chapter 17 (p. 166).
15. For 'Q' see Christopher M. Tuckett, *Q and the History of Early Christianity: Studies on Q* (Edinburgh, 1996). Against, Michael D. Goulder, *Luke* (JSNTSup, 20; 2 vols; Sheffield, 1989).
16. See Dunn, *Theology*, pp. 183–206; and Wenham, *Paul*.
17. See Morna D. Hooker, 'Interchange in Christ and ethics', *JSNT* 25 (1985), pp. 3–17.
18. See R.G. Hamerton-Kelly, 'Sacred violence and the curse of the law (Galatians 3:13): the death of Christ as a sacrificial travesty', *NTS* 36 (1990), pp. 98–118; and Gerd Theissen, *Psychological Aspects of Pauline Theology* (Edinburgh, 1987), pp. 228ff.
19. The question of *which* scriptures are meant here has been answered in different ways. Probably, the Hebrew Bible in its entirety is designated. The succeeding reference, 'that he was raised on the third day in accordance with the scriptures', evidently has a narrower focus and calls to mind passages such as Hos. 6.1-2 and Jon. 1.17.
20. On the background to Paul's 'Adam' terminology see J. Jervell, *Imago Dei: Gen. 1.26f. im Spätjudentum, in der Gnosis und in den paulinischen Briefen* (FRLANT, 76; Göttingen, 1960); C.K. Barrett, *From First Adam to Last: A Study in Pauline Theology* (London and New York, 1962); R. Scroggs, *The*

Last Adam: A Study in Pauline Anthropology (Philadelphia, 1966); and J.R. Levison, *Portraits of Adam in Early Judaism From Sirach to 2 Baruch* (JSPSup, 1; Sheffield, 1988).

21. See further Robert H. Gundry, *Soma in Biblical Theology: With Emphasis on Pauline Anthropology* (SNTSMS, 29; reprinted Cambridge, 2005); and A.J.M. Wedderburn, 'Adam in Paul's letter to the Romans', in E.A. Livingstone (ed.), *Studia Biblica 1978*, vol. iii (JSNTSup, 3; Sheffield, 1980), pp. 413–30.

22. On the interpretation of this verse see A.J.M. Wedderburn, 'The theological structure of Romans 5.12', *NTS* 19 (1972), pp. 339–54; and J.L. Houlden, 'Fall and salvation: a case of difficulty', *ExpT* 109/8 (1998), pp. 234–7.

23. The closest parallel is *2 Bar.* 54.19: 'Adam is . . . not the cause, except only for himself, but each of us has become our own Adam.' There is a clear summary of the relevant material in Dunn, *Theology*, pp. 84–90.

24. See further Paul S. Minear, *Christians and the New Creation: Genesis Motifs in the New Testament* (Louisville, 1994).

25. Among a substantial bibliography on this topic, see G. Barth, *Der Tod Jesu Christi im Verständnis des Neuen Testaments* (Neukirchen-Vluyn, 1992); M. Barth, *Was Christ's Death a Sacrifice?* (Edinburgh, 1961); J.T. Carroll and J.B. Green, *The Death of Jesus in Early Christianity* (Peabody, 1995); C.B. Cousar, *A Theology of the Cross: The Death of Jesus in the Pauline Letters* (Minneapolis, 1990); J.D.G. Dunn, 'Paul's understanding of the death of Jesus as sacrifice', in Stephen W. Sykes (ed.), *Sacrifice and Redemption: Durham Essays in Theology* (Cambridge and New York, 1991), pp. 35–56; R.G. Hamerton-Kelly, *Sacred Violence: Paul's Hermeneutic of the Cross* (Minneapolis, 1992); M. Hengel, *The Atonement: The Origins of the Doctrine of Atonement in the New Testament* (London and Philadelphia, 1981); J.D. Levenson, *The Death and Resurrection of the Beloved Son* (New Haven, 1993); F.M. Young, *Sacrifice and the Death of Christ* (London and Philadelphia, 1975); and Richard H. Bell, 'Sacrifice and Christology in Paul', *JTS* 53 (2002), pp. 1–27.

26. See Daniel P. Bailey, 'Jesus as the Mercy Seat: the semantics and theology of Paul's use of *hilasterion* in Romans 3.25' (unpublished PhD thesis, University of Cambridge, 1999). There is valuable material also in W. Kraus, *Der Tod Jesu als Heiligtumsweihe. Eine Untersuchung zum Umfeld der Sühnevorstellung in Römer 3.25.26a* (WMANT, 66; Neukirchen-Vluyn, 1991).

27. Noted by Dunn, *Theology*, pp. 213–18.

28. See D. Seeley, *The Noble Death: Graeco-Roman Martyrology and Paul's Concept of Salvation* (JSNTSup, 28; Sheffield, 1990).

29. For the evident difference from the Hebrew sacrificial ritual which dealt only with inadvertent sins, see Dunn, *Theology*, pp. 218–19.

30. Again, see Dunn, *Theology*, pp. 216–18.

31. Richard K. Moore, '2 Cor. 5,21: the interpretive key to Paul's use of *dikaiosune theou*?', in R. Bieringer (ed.), *The Corinthian Correspondence* (BETL, 125; Louvain, 1996), pp. 707–15.

32. Interestingly, the (non-)sacrifice of Isaac in Genesis 22 features comparatively rarely in New Testament thought; see Alan Segal, 'He who did not spare his own son: Jesus, Paul, and the Akedah', in P. Richardson and J. Hurd (eds), *From Jesus to Paul* (Waterloo, 1984), pp. 169–84; and J.D. Levenson,

The Death and Resurrection of the Beloved Son: The Transformation of Child Sacrifice in Judaism and Christianity (New Haven, 1993).

33. On this topic see Trevor A. Hart, 'Sinlessness and moral responsibility: a problem in Christology', *SJT* 48 (1995), pp. 37–54.

34. For different views of this problem see David J.A. Clines, 'Ecce vir, or gendering the Son of Man', in J. Cheryl Exum and Stephen D. Moore, *Biblical Studies/Cultural Studies: The Third Sheffield Colloquium* (JSOTSup, 266; Sheffield, 1998), pp. 352–75; and Graham Ward, 'Bodies: the displaced body of Jesus Christ', in J. Milbank, C. Pickstock and G. Ward (eds), *Radical Orthodoxy: A New Theology* (London, 1999), pp. 163–81.

35. See further below.

36. Again, there is a daunting bibliography. Among the major studies see P. Stuhlmacher, *Gerechtigkeit Gottes bei Paulus* (Göttingen, 1965); E. Käsemann, ' "The righteousness of God" in Paul', in *New Testament Questions of Today* (ET London, 1969), pp. 60–101; J.A. Ziesler, *The Meaning of Righteousness in Paul: A Linguistic and Theological Inquiry* (SNTSMS, 20; Cambridge, 1972); J. Reumann, *Righteousness in the New Testament: justification in the United States Lutheran-Roman Catholic dialogue* (Philadelphia and New York, 1982); M.A. Seifrid, *Justification by Faith: The Origin and Development of a Central Pauline Theme* (NovTSup, 68; Leiden, 1992); E. Lohse, *Paulus: Eine Biographie* (Munich, 1996), pp. 199–214; Donald A. Carson, Peter T. O'Brien and Mark A. Seifrid (eds), *Justification and Variegated Nomism*, vols. i and ii (WUNT, 140, 181; Tübingen, 2001, 2004); Joseph A. Burgess and Marc Kolden (eds), *By Faith Alone: Essays on Justification in Honor of Gerhard O. Forde* (Grand Rapids, 2004); David E. Aune (ed.), *Rereading Paul Together; Protestant and Catholic Perspectives on Justification* (Grand Rapids, 2006); and Bruce L. McCormack (ed.), *Justification in Perspective: Historical Developments and Contemporary Challenges* (Grand Rapids, 2006).

37. The classic study is O. Cullmann, *Christ and Time: The Primitive Christian Conception of Time and History* (rev. ET London and Philadelphia, 1962).

38. See Alister E. McGrath, *Iustitia Dei: A History of the Christian Doctrine of Justification* (Cambridge, [3]2005).

39. 'Christian writers on Judaism', *HTR* 14 (1921), pp. 197–254.

40. Sanders in the literature cited in Chapter 4, notes 1, 21.

41. See the summary in Dunn, *Theology*, pp. 334–89.

42. See I. Howard Marshall, 'Salvation, grace and works in the Pauline corpus', *NTS* 42 (1996), pp. 339–58.

43. For a different telling of this story, see Stephen W. Sykes, *The Story of Atonement* (London, 1997).

44. See Douglas A. Campbell, *The Rhetoric of Righteousness in Romans 3:21-26* (JSNTSup, 65; Sheffield, 1992).

45. See Martin Hengel, 'Präexistenz bei Paulus?', in C. Landmesser, H. J. Eckstein and H. Lichtenberger (eds), *Jesus Christus als die Mitte der Schrift: Studien zur Hermeneutik des Evangeliums* (Berlin, 1997), pp. 479–518; and J.D.G. Dunn, 'Christ, Adam and preexistence', in R.P. Martin and Brian J. Dodd (eds), *Where Christology Began: Essays on Philippians 2* (Louisville, 1998), pp. 74–83. For the later documents, Simon J. Gathercole, *The Pre-Existent Son: Recovering the Christologies of Matthew, Mark, and Luke* (Grand Rapids, 2006).

46. See O. Cullmann, 'The theological content of the prologue to John in its present form', in Robert T. Fortna and Beverley Roberts Gaventa (eds), *The Conversation Continues: Studies in Paul and John in Honor of J. Louis Martyn* (Nashville, 1990), pp. 295–8.
47. See Walter Wink, 'The hymn of the cosmic Christ', in Fortna and Gaventa (eds), *The Conversation Continues*, pp. 235–45.
48. See R.P. Martin, *Carmen Christi* (Grand Rapids, 1983); and Markus Bockmuehl, ' "The Form of God" (Phil 2:6): variations on a theme of Jewish mysticism', *JTS* 48 (1997), pp. 1–23.
49. See Brendan Byrne, 'Christ's pre-existence in Pauline soteriology', *TS* 58 (1997), pp. 308–30.
50. On this material see Edwin D. Freed, *The Stories of Jesus' Birth* (BS, 72; Sheffield, 2001).
51. See the examination of Bockmuehl, 'The Form of God'.
52. A point noted by Bockmuehl.
53. See the discussion of Dunn, *Theology*, pp. 266–93.

Chapter 21

1. The return of Jesus from heaven is often called by its Greek name, *parousia*. Two important studies are Joseph Plevnik, *Paul and the Parousia: An Exegetical and Theological Investigation* (Peabody, 1997); and Osvaldo D. Vena, *The Parousia and its Rereadings: The Development of the Eschatological Consciousness in the Writings of the New Testament* (SBL, 27; New York, 2001). See also I. Howard Marshall, 'The parousia in the New Testament and today', in M. Wilkins and T. Paige (eds), *Worship, Theology, and Ministry in the Early Church: Essays in Honor of Ralph P. Martin* (JSNTSup, 87; Sheffield, 1992), pp. 194–211; and the earlier work by Arthur L. Moore, *The Parousia in the New Testament* (NovTSup, 13; Leiden, 1966).
2. See further I. Howard Marshall, 'A new understanding of the present and the future: Paul and eschatology', in Richard N. Longenecker (ed.), *The Road from Damascus: The Impact of Paul's Conversion on his Life, Thought, and Ministry* (Grand Rapids, 1997), pp. 33–54; M. de Boer, 'Paul and apocalyptic eschatology', in J.J. Collins (ed.), *The Encyclopedia of Apocalypticism*, vol. i (New York, 1998), pp. 345–93; *idem, The Defeat of Death: Apocalyptic Eschatology in 1 Corinthians 15 and Romans 5* (JSNTSup, 22; Sheffield, 1988); and James H. Charlesworth (ed.), *Resurrection: The Origin and Future of a Biblical Doctrine* (FSCS; New York, 2006).
3. I disagree in this with Plevnik, *Paul and the Parousia*, p. 97, who thinks that Paul originally taught a doctrine of assumption to heaven.
4. J. Plevnik, 'The taking up of the faithful and the resurrection of the dead in 1 Thessalonians 4:13-18', *CBQ* 46 (1984), pp. 274–83; *idem, Paul and the Parousia*, ch. 3; *idem* 'The destination of the apostle and of the faithful: Second Corinthians 4:13b-14 and First Thessalonians 4:14', *CBQ* 62 (2000), pp. 83–95.
5. See Richard N. Longenecker, 'Is there development in Paul's resurrection thought?', in Richard N. Longenecker (ed.), *Life in the Face of Death: The Resurrection Message of the New Testament* (Grand Rapids and Cambridge, 1998), pp. 171–202.

6. The different possibilities are discussed by C.K. Barrett, *The First Epistle to the Corinthians* (London, [2]1992), pp. 347–8.

7. On the meaning, see Alan F. Segal, 'Paul's *"soma pneumatikon"* and the worship of Jesus', in Carey C. Newman, James R. Davila and Gladys S. Lewis (eds), *The Jewish Roots of Christological Monotheism* (JSJSup, 63; Leiden, 1999), pp. 258–76.

8. On the significance of the trumpet, see M. Bockmuehl, ' "The trumpet shall sound": shofar symbolism and its reception in early Christianity', in William Horbury (ed.), *Templum Amicitiae: Essays on the Second Temple Presented to Ernst Bammel* (JSNTSup, 48; Sheffield, 1991), pp. 199–225.

9. See Murray J. Harris, *Raised Immortal* (London, 1983), ch. 4.

10. See Calvin J. Roetzel, 'Paul as organic intellectual: the shaper of apocalyptic myths', in Julian V. Hills, Richard B. Gardner and Robert Jewett (eds), *Common Life in the Early Church: Essays Honoring Graydon F. Snyder* (Harrisburg, 1988), pp. 221–43; and Robert W. Scholla, 'Into the image of God: Pauline eschatology and the transformation of believers', *Gregorianum* 78 (1997), pp. 33–54.

11. See Barnabas Lindars, 'The sound of the trumpet: Paul and eschatology', *BJRL* 67 (1985), pp. 766–82; J. Ramsey Michaels, 'The redemption of our body: the riddle of Romans 8:19–22', in S. Soderlund and N.T. Wright (eds), *Romans and the People of God: Essays in Honor of Gordon D. Fee on the Occasion of his 65th Birthday* (Grand Rapids, 1999), pp. 92–114; and also Eberhard Jüngel, 'Predigt über Rom. 8,18ff.', in Peter Neuner and Harald Wagner (eds), *In Verantwortung für den Glauben: Beiträge zur Fundamentaltheologie und Ökumenik* (Freiburg, 1992), pp. 391–8.

12. I am reminded here of the emphasis expounded by John Robinson in his important work, *The Body: A Study in Pauline Theology* (SBT, 5; London, 1952).

13. See W.D. Davies, 'Paul and the people of Israel', in his *Jewish and Pauline Studies* (Philadelphia, 1984), pp. 123–52; J. Munck, *Christ and Israel: An Interpretation of Romans 9–11* (Philadelphia, 1967); N.T. Wright, *The New Testament and the People of God* (London, 1992); Sigurd Grindheim, *The Crux of Election: Paul's Critique of the Jewish Confidence in the Election of Israel* (WUNT, 202; Tübingen, 2005); Richard H. Bell, *The Irrevocable Call of God: An Inquiry into Paul's Theology of Israel* (WUNT, 184; Tübingen, 2005); and the literature cited in the notes to Chapter 20, especially notes 1 and 20.

14. See James D.G. Dunn (ed.), *Paul and the Mosaic Law* (WUNT, 89; Tübingen, 1996), especially the contributions of Stephen Westerholm and Heikki Räisänen; and J.C. O'Neill, 'Did you receive the Spirit by the works of the law? (Gal. 3:2): the works of the law in Judaism and the Pauline corpus', *ABR* 46 (1998), pp. 70–84.

15. See G.W.E. Nickelsburg, 'Abraham the convert: a Jewish tradition and its use by the apostle Paul', in Michael E. Stone and Theodore A. Bergren (eds), *Biblical Figures Outside the Bible* (Harrisburg, 1998), pp. 151–75.

16. For different developments of this idea, see Sally McFague, *The Body of God: An Ecological Theology* (Minneapolis and London, 1993); and Jonathan Clatworthy, *Good God: Green Theology and the Value of Creation* (Charlbury, 1997).

Chapter 22

1. Among recent literature see David G. Horrell, *Solidarity and Difference: A Contemporary Reading of Paul's Ethics* (London, 2005); and J.G. van der Wette and F.S. Malan (eds), *Identity, Ethics and Ethos in the New Testament* (BZNW, 141; Berlin, 2006).
2. *The Mysticism of St. Paul* (ET London, 1931). See also his *Paul and His Interpreters: A Critical History* (ET London and New York, 1912).
3. *Mysticism*, p. 1.
4. *Mysticism*, p. 225.
5. Witness the emergence of Barthianism subsequent to this conflict.
6. See for instance Birger A. Pearson, 'The problem of "Jewish Gnostic" literature', in C. Hedrick and R. Hodgson (eds), *Nag Hammadi, Gnosticism, and Early Christianity* (Peabody, 1986).
7. Alan F. Segal, *Paul the Convert: The Apostolate and Apostasy of Saul the Pharisee* (New Haven and London, 1990); *idem*, 'Paul and the beginnings of Jewish mysticism', in J.J. Collins and M. Fishbane (eds), *Death, Ecstasy, and Other Worldly Journeys* (Albany, 1995), pp. 95–122.
8. There is a good collection of essays on this topic, edited by Richard Woods, *Understanding Mysticism* (New York, 1980). For an example of this kind of mysticism see Rowan Williams, *Teresa of Avila* (London, 1991).
9. *The Body: A Study in Pauline Theology* (SBT, 5; London, 1952).
10. See Chapter 8.
11. See Robert Morgan, 'Flesh is precious: the significance of Luke 24:36-43', in S. Barton and G.N. Stanton (eds), *Resurrection: Essays in Honour of Leslie Houlden* (London, 1994), pp. 8–20.
12. For this view see James D.G. Dunn, 'The "body" in Colossians', in Thomas E. Schmidt and Moisis Silva, *To Tell the Mystery: Essays on New Testament Eschatology in Honor of Robert H. Gundry* (JSNTSup, 100; Sheffield, 1994), pp. 163–81; C. Arnold, 'Jesus Christ: "head" of the church (Colossians and Ephesians)', in Joel B. Green and Max Turner (eds), *Jesus of Nazareth: Lord and Christ: Essays on the Historical Jesus and New Testament Christology* (Grand Rapids and Carlisle, 1994), pp. 346–66.
13. See M. Welker, *God the Spirit* (ET; Minneapolis, 1994); Gordon D. Fee, *God's Empowering Presence: The Holy Spirit in the Letters of Paul* (Peabody, 1994); *idem, Paul, the Spirit, and the People of God* (Peabody, 1996); James D.G. Dunn, *The Christ and the Spirit: Collected Essays of James D.G. Dunn* (Edinburgh, 1998); Graham N. Stanton, Bruce W. Longenecker and Stephen C. Barton (eds), *The Holy Spirit and Christian Origins: Essays in Honor of James D.G. Dunn* (Grand Rapids, 2004); and Finny Philip, *The Origins of Pauline Pneumatology: The Eschatological Bestowal of the Spirit upon Gentiles in Judaism and in the Early Development of Paul's Theology* (WUNT, 194; Tübingen, 2005). An older study is C.F.D. Moule, *The Holy Spirit* (London, 1978).
14. It would be helpful to read both *Jubilees* and *2 Baruch* to gain an understanding of this point.
15. See Gordon D. Fee, 'Paul and the Trinity: the experience of Christ and the Spirit for Paul's understanding of God', in Stephen T. Davis, Daniel Kendall and Gerald O'Collins (eds), *The Trinity: An Interdisciplinary Symposium* (New York, 1999), pp. 49–72.

16. See the interesting article of Klaus Haacker, 'Der "Antinomismus" des Paulus im Kontext antiker Gesetzestheorie', in H. Cancik (ed.), *Geschichte–Tradition–Reflexion: Festschriften für Martin Hengel zum 70 Geburtstag*, vol. iii: *Frühes Christentum* (Tübingen, 1996), pp. 387–404.

17. See James D.G. Dunn, ' "The law of faith", "the law of the Spirit" and "the law of Christ" ', in Eugene H. Lovering and Jerry L. Sumney (eds), *Theology and Ethics in Paul and His Interpreters: Essays in Honor of Victor Paul Furnish* (Nashville, 1996), pp. 62–82.

18. On early Christian ethics see Wayne A. Meeks, *The Moral World of the First Christians* (Philadelphia, 1986); idem, *The Origins of Christian Morality: The First Two Centuries* (New Haven and London, 1993); Markus Bockmuehl, *Jewish Law in Gentile Churches: Halakah and the Beginning of Christian Public Ethics* (Edinburgh, 2000); and Edwin D. Freed, *The Morality of Paul's Converts* (London, 2005).

19. See John M.G. Barclay, 'Paul, Philemon and the dilemma of Christian slave-ownership', *NTS* 37 (1991), pp. 161–86; and J. Albert Harrill, 'Paul and slavery: the problem of 1 Corinthians 7:21', *Biblical Research* 39 (1994), pp. 5–28.

20. On the handling of social distinctions in the context of early Christian worship, see R. Banks, *Paul's Idea of Community: The Early House Churches in their Historical Setting* (Peabody, [2]1994).

21. See L.W. Countryman, *Dirt, Greed and Sex: Sexual Ethics in the New Testament and Their Implications for Today* (Philadelphia, 1988); and B.S. Rosner, *Paul, Scripture and Ethics: A Study of 1 Corinthians 5–7* (Leiden, 1994).

22. See B. Byrne, 'Sinning against one's own body: Paul's understanding of the sexual relationship in 1 Corinthians 6.18', *CBQ* 45 (1983), pp. 608–16.

23. See V. George Shillington, 'Atonement texture in 1 Corinthians 5.5', *JSNT* 71 (1998), pp. 29–50.

24. On the latter see Leonard L. Thompson, *The Book of Revelation: Apocalypse and Empire* (New York and London, 1990); and Jonathan Knight, *Revelation* (Sheffield, 1999; [2]2008).

25. *Annals* 15.44

26. See Michael Barram, *Mission and Moral Reflection in Paul* (SBL, 75; New York, 2006),

27. See Wendell L. Willis, *Idol Meat in Corinth: The Pauline Argument in 1 Corinthians 8 and 10* (SBLDS, 68; Chico, 1985); P.W. Gooch, *Dangerous Food: 1 Corinthians 8–10 in its Context* (Waterloo, 1993); J.J. Meggitt, 'Meat consumption and social conflict in Corinth', *JTS* (1994), pp. 137–41; and A.T. Cheung, *Idol Food in Corinth: Jewish Background and Pauline Legacy* (JSNTSup, 176; Sheffield, 1999).

Chapter 23

1. Though I reject the suicide hypothesis; see N. Clayton Croy, ' "To die is gain" (Philippians 1.19-26): does Paul contemplate suicide?', *JBL* 122 (2003), pp. 517–31.

2. See Heikki Räisänen, 'Last things first: "Eschatology" as the first chapter in an overall account of early Christian ideas', *Temenos* 39–40 (2003–4), pp. 9–49.

3. Thus the classic study of Kenelm Burridge, *New Heaven, New Earth* (Oxford, 1969) detects three stages in the history of a millenarian movement. Other important studies include Norman Cohn, *The Pursuit of the Millennium: Revolutionary Millenarians and Mystical Anarchists in the Middle Ages* (London, 1970); Peter Worsley, *The Trumpet Shall Sound: A Study of 'Cargo' Cults in Melanesia* (London, 1970); Sylvia E. Thrupp (ed.), *Millennial Dreams in Action: Studies in Revolutionary Religious Movements* (New York, 1962); Bryan R. Wilson, *Magic and the Millennium: Movements of Protest among Tribal and Third-World Peoples* (London, 1973); and Thomas Robbins and Susan J. Palmer (eds), *Millennium, Messiahs, and Mayhem: Contemporary Apocalyptic Movements* (New York, 1997). Early Christian millennialism is examined by Stanley E. Porter, 'Was early Christianity a millenarian movement?', in Stanley E. Porter, Michael A. Hayes and David Tombs (eds), *Faith in the Millennium* (RILP, 7; Sheffield, 2001), pp. 243–59. In the same volume see Andrew Bradstock, 'Reading the signs of the times: millenarian and apocalyptic movements now and then', pp. 289–309; and also Fiona Bowie with Christopher Deacy (eds), *The Coming Deliverer: Millennial Themes in World Religions* (Cardiff, 1997).

4. See Robert Jewett, *The Thessalonian Correspondence: Pauline Rhetoric and Millenarian Piety* (Philadelphia, 1986).

5. This theme is explored by Joseph Plevnik, *Paul and the Parousia: An Exegetical and Theological Investigation* (Peabody, 1997), pp. 65–98.

6. See my discussion of this view, with bibliography, in Chapter 21.

7. C.K. Barrett, *The First Epistle to the Corinthians* (London, ²1992), pp. 347–8.

8. On which see A.Y. Collins, 'The book of Revelation', in John J. Collins (ed.), *The Encyclopedia of Apocalypticism*, vol. i: *The Origins of Apocalypticism* (New York, 1998), pp. 384–414; and my own *Revelation* (Sheffield, 1999; ²2008). Crucial evidence derives from Revelation 19.

9. On which see Chapter 30 below.

10. See Charles H. Talbert, '2 Peter and the delay of the parousia', *VC* 20 (1966), pp. 137–45; David E. Aune, 'The significance of the delay of the parousia for early Christianity', in Gerald F. Hawthorne (ed.), *Current Issues in Biblical and Patristic Interpretation: Studies in Honor of Merrill C. Tenney Presented by his Former Students* (Grand Rapids, 1975); Richard J. Bauckham, 'The delay of the parousia', *Tyndale Bulletin* 31 (1980), pp. 3–36; and Osvaldo D. Vena, *The Parousia and its Rereadings: The Development of the Eschatological Consciousness in the Writings of the New Testament* (SBL, 27; New York, 2001).

11. But see the collected studies of W.D. Davies and D. Daube (eds), *The Background of the New Testament and its Eschatology* (Cambridge, 1956); Thomas E. Schmidt and Moisis Silva, *To Tell the Mystery: Essays on New Testament Eschatology in Honor of Robert H. Gundry* (JSNTSup, 100; Sheffield, 1994); and Edward Adams, 'What is the promise of his coming? The complaint of the scoffers in 2 Peter 3.4', *NTS* 51 (2005), pp. 106–22.

12. See Chapter 24.

13. Including of course the developing Gospel tradition; see David C. Sim, *Apocalyptic Eschatology in the Gospel of Matthew* (SNTSMS, 88; Cambridge, 1996).

14. The classic study remains that of H. Bietenhard, 'The millennial hope in

the early church', *SJT* 6 (1953), pp. 12–30. See also Richard B. Hays, ' "Why do you stand looking up toward heaven?" New Testament eschatology at the turn of the millennium', *Modern Theology* 16 (2000), pp. 115–35; and Brian E. Daley, *The Hope of the Early Church: A Handbook of Patristic Eschatology* (Cambridge, 1991; Peabody MA, 2003).

15. Papias was bishop of Hierapolis in Asia Minor whom Irenaeus states was a disciple of one 'John' and a companion of Polycarp. His fragments, which stem from a substantial work know as 'Expositions of the oracles of the Lord', are collected and published by U.H.J. Körtner, *Papias von Hierapolis: Ein Beiträg zur Geschichte des frühen Christentums* (FRLANT, 133; Göttingen, 1983). See Charles E. Hill, 'What Papias said about John (and Luke): a new "Papian" fragment', *JTS* 49 (1998), pp. 582–629; *idem*, 'Papias of Hierapolis', *ExpT* 117 (2006), pp. 309–15; and esp. E. Norelli, *Papias of Hierapolis. Esposizione degli oracoli del Signore. I frammenti* (LCPM, 36; Milan, 2005).

16. *Barnabas* is a Jewish Christian text from the first or second century CE, probably written in Alexandria. See J. Carleton-Paget, *The Epistle of Barnabas: Outlook and Background* (WUNT, 64; Tübingen, 1994); and Everett Ferguson, 'Was Barnabas a Chiliast? An example of Hellenistic number symbolism in Barnabas and Clement of Alexandria', in David L. Balch, Everett Ferguson and Wayne A. Meeks (eds), *Greeks, Romans and Christians: Essays in Honor of Abraham J. Malherbe* (Minneapolis, 1990), pp. 157–67.

17. Irenaeus was bishop of Lyons in the second century CE. His work *Adversus Haereses* was a detailed attack on Gnosticism. Among the secondary literature see J. Lawson, *The Biblical Theology of Irenaeus* (London, 1948); and D. Minns, *Irenaeus* (London, 1994). With specific reference to this topic, A. Orbe, 'San Ireneo y el régimen del milenio', *Studia Missionalia* 32 (1983), pp. 345–72; Terrance Tiessen, 'Irenaeus on salvation and the millennium', *Didaskalia* 3 (1991), pp. 2–50; and D. Jeffrey Bingham, 'Hope in Irenaeus of Lyons', *ETL* 76 (2000), pp. 265–82.

18. Marcion was a notorious heretic of the second century CE. He rejected the Hebrew Bible, claiming that its God was not the loving God whom Jesus proclaimed. The standard study is E.C. Blackman, *Marcion and His Influence* (London, 1948). See also Peter M. Head, 'The foreign God and the sudden Christ: theology and Christology in Marcion's Gospel redaction', *Tyndale Bulletin* 44 (1993), pp. 307–21; Heikki Räisänen, 'Marcion and the origins of Christian anti-Judaism', *Temenos* 33 (1997), pp. 121–35; Gerhard May and Katharina Greschat (eds), *Marcion and his Impact on Church History* (TU, 150; Berlin, 2002); and John Barton, 'Marcion revisited', in Lee M. Macdonald and James A. Sanders (eds), *The Canon Debate* (Peabody, 2002), pp. 341–54. Tertullian was a North African who espoused Montanism towards the end of his life. Among the secondary literature see T.D. Barnes, *Tertullian: A Historical and Literary Study* (reprinted Oxford, 1985).

19. Montanism was a prophetic and apocalyptic movement which flourished in the second half of the second century CE. Sources for it are found in P. Labriolle, *Les sources de l'histoire du montanisme* (Paris, 1913); R.E. Heine, *The Montanist Oracles and Testimonies* (Macon, 1989); and William Tabbernee, *Montanist Inscriptions and Testimonia: Epigraphic Sources Illustrating the History of Montanism* (Macon, 1997); *idem*, 'Portals of the Montanist New Jerusalem: the discovery of Pepouza and Tymion', *JECS* 11 (2003), pp. 87–93. See

also Charles E. Hill, 'The marriage of Montanism and millenarianism', in Elizabeth A. Livingstone (ed.), *Studia Patristica*, vol. xxvi (Louvain, 1993), pp. 140–6; Christine Trevett, *Montanism: Gender, Authority and the New Prophecy* (Cambridge, 1996); Peter Lampe, 'Die montanistischen Tymion und Pepouza im Lichte der neuen tymionschrift', *ZAC* 8 (2004), pp. 498–512.

20. Cerinthus was a Gnostic heretic of the early second century whom Eusebius and Irenaeus report as an opponent of John in Ephesus. See G. Bardy, 'Cérinthe', *RB* 30 (1921), pp. 344–73; A.F.J. Klijn and G.S. Reininck, *Patristic Evidence for Jewish-Christian Sects* (NovTSup, 36; Leiden, 1973), pp. 3–19; and Charles E. Hill, 'Cerinthus, gnostic or chiliast? A new solution to an old problem', *JECS* 8 (2000), pp. 135–72.

21. See Bietenhard, 'Millennial hope', p. 18.

22. Hippolytus was bishop of Rome in the early third century CE.

23. Clement and especially Origen were significant figures who inherited Philo's allegorical method of exegesis and developed it for Christian purposes. On these figures see C. Bigg, *The Christian Platonists of Alexandria* (London, 1913); J. Daniélou, *Origen* (ET London, 1948); E.F. Osborn, *The Philosophy of Clement of Alexandria* (Texts and Studies, 3; London, 1957); R.P.C. Hanson, *Allegory and Event: A Study of the Sources and Significance of Origen's Interpretation of Scripture* (London, 1959); H. Chadwick, *Early Christian Thought and the Classical Tradition: Studies in Justin, Clement, and Origen* (Oxford, 1966); Karl-Heinz Uthemann, 'Protogie und Eschatologie: zur Rezeption des Origenes im 4 Jahrhundert vor dem Ausbruch der ersten origenistischen Kontroverse', in Wolfgang A. Bienert and Uwe Kühneweg (eds), *Origeniana Septima: origenes in den Auseinandersetzungen des 4 Jahrhunderts* (BETL, 137; Leuven, 1999), pp. 399–458; Henryk Pietras, 'I Principi II, di Origene e il millenarismo', in Lorenzo Perrone, P. Bernardino and D. Marchini (eds), *Origeniana Octava: Origen and the Alexandrian Tradition* (Leuven, 2003), pp. 707–14; and in the same volume, Yves-Marie Duval, 'Vers le commentaire sur Sophonie d'Origène l'annonce de la disparition finale du monde et le retour dans la Jérusalem céleste', pp. 525–39. See also John R. Sachs, 'Apocatastasis in patristic theology', *TS* 54 (1993), pp. 617–40; and Dieter Zeller, 'Philons spiritualisierunde Eschatologie und ihre Nachwirkung bei den Kirchenvätern', in E. Goodman-Thau (ed.), *Vom Jenseits: Jüdische Denken in der europäischen Geistesgeschichte* (Berlin, 1997), pp. 19–35.

24. See Ingo U. Dalferth, 'Zeit der Zeichen: Vom Anfang der Zeichen und dem Ende der Zeiten', in W. Härle, M. Marquard and W. Nethöfel, *Unsere Welt – Gottes Schöpfung: Eberhard Wölfel zum 65 Geburtstag* (MTS, 32; Marburg, 1992), pp. 161–79; Pamela Bright, 'Augustine and the thousand year reign of the saints', in Joseph T. Lienhard, Earl C. Muller and Roland J. Teske (eds), *Augustine: Presbyter Factus Sum* (CA, 2; New York, 1993), pp. 447–53; Avihu Zakai and Anya Mali, 'Time, history and eschatology: ecclesiastical history from Eusebius to Augustine', *JRH* 17 (1993), pp. 393–417; Bruce W. Speck, 'Augustine's tale of two cities: teleology/eschatology in the City of God', *Journal of Interdisciplinary Studies* 8 (1996), pp. 104–30; Paul B. Harvey, 'Approaching the Apocalypse: Augustine, Tyconius, and John's Revelation', in Mark Vessey, Karla Pollman and Allan P. Fitzgerald (eds), *History,*

Apocalypse, and the Secular Imagination: New Essays on Augustine's City of God (Bowling Green OH, 1999), pp. 133–51; Richard A. Norris, 'Augustine and the close of the ancient period of interpretation', in Alan J. Hauser and Duane F. Watson (eds), *A History of Biblical Interpretation*, vol. i: *The Ancient Period* (Grand Rapids, 2003), pp. 380–408; C. Everett Berry, 'Highlighting the link between the millenium and replacement thought: Augustinian nonchiliasm as a test case', *Creswell Theological Review* 3 (2005), pp. 71–91.

25. Tyconius was a Donatist theologian who drew up seven rules for the interpretation of scripture in the fourth century CE. See Charles Kannengiesser, 'Tyconius of Carthage, the earliest Latin theoretician of biblical hermeneutics: the current debate', in Mario Maritano (ed.), *Historiam perscrutari: Miscellanea di studi offerti al Prof. Ottorino Pasquato* (BSR, 180; Rome, 2002), pp. 297–311.

26. See the literature mentioned in n. 3 above.

27. See Cohn, *Pursuit*; R. Schwarz, *Die apokalyptische Theologie Thomas Müntzers und der Taboriten* (BHT, 5; Tübingen, 1977); Christopher Rowland, *Radical Christianity* (Oxford, 1988); and T. Scott, *Thomas Müntzer, Theology and Revolution in the German Reformation* (Basingstoke, 1989).

28. See Murray J. Harris, 'Resurrection and immortality in the Pauline corpus', in Richard N. Longenecker (ed.), *Life in the Face of Death: The Resurrection Message of the New Testament* (Grand Rapids, 1998), pp. 147–70. Also Claudia Setzer, *Resurrection of the Body in Early Judaism and Early Christianity* (Leiden, 2004).

29. See Rudolph Rehn, 'Tod und unsterblichkeit in der platonischen Philosophie', in G. Binder and B. Effe (eds), *Tod und Jenseits im Altertum* (BAC, 6; Trier, 1991), pp. 103–21.

30. This is noted by G.W.E. Nickelsburg, *Resurrection, Immortality, and Eternal Life in Intertestamental Judaism* (HTS, 26; Cambridge MA, 1972).

31. See Jan W. van Henten, *The Maccabean Martyrs as Saviours of the Jewish People: A Study of 2 and 4 Maccabees* (JSJSup, 57; Leiden, 1997).

32. See Marianne Meye Thompson, 'Eternal life in the Gospel of John', *Ex Auditu* 5 (1989), pp. 35–55; John Painter, 'Inclined to God: the quest for eternal life – Bultmannian hermeneutics and the theology of the Fourth Gospel', in R. Alan Culpepper and C. Clifton Black (eds), *Exploring the Gospel of John: In Honor of D. Moody Smith* (Louisville, 1996), pp. 346–68; and *idem*, 'John and the quest for eternal life', in R. Alan Culpepper (ed.), *Critical Readings of John 6* (BIS, 22; Leiden, 1997), pp. 61–74.

Chapter 24

1. Once again, I mention the Sheffield New Testament Guides series and the Cambridge New Testament Theology series as both important, but without necessarily listing every relevant volume here. A radical treatment of the topic with substantial bibliography is J.V.M. Sturdy edited by Jonathan Knight, *Redrawing the Boundaries: The Date of Early Christian Literature* (London, 2007).

2. This view is found as early as the Beatty Papyrus II (P46), which places Hebrews in canonical order immediately after Romans. In both Alexandria

and Rome in the fourth and fifth centuries, Hebrews was counted with the Pauline letters, which were held to be fourteen in number. The desire to claim Pauline authorship was no doubt bound up with the wish to emphasize the authority of Hebrews. It is still possible to find advocates of Pauline authorship. One such is David Alan Black in the journal *Faith and Mission* 16 (1999), pp. 32–51, 78–86; but the view is almost universally rejected. Commentaries on Hebrews include R.McL. Wilson, *Hebrews* (NCB; London, 1987); Harold W. Attridge, *The Epistle to the Hebrews* (Hermeneia; Philadelphia, 1989); W.L. Lane, *Hebrews 1–8, 9–13* (WBC, 47a, b; Dallas, 1991); P. Ellingworth, *The Epistle to the Hebrews: A Commentary on the Greek Text* (Grand Rapids and Carlisle, 1993); and Craig R. Koester, *Hebrews: A New Translation with Introduction and Commentary* (AB; New York, 2001). See also Gabriella Gelardini (ed.), *Hebrews: Contemporary Methods, New Insights* (BIS, 75; Leiden, 2005); and Andrew T. Lincoln, *Hebrews: A Guide* (London, 2006).

3. Again, this view is increasingly questioned in research. The view that Hebrews was sent to Rome (and thus to Gentiles) is considered by Raymond E. Brown, *An Introduction to the New Testament* (New York, 1997), pp. 697–701. Interesting is Clark M. Williamson, 'Anti-Judaism in Hebrews?', *Interpretation* 57 (2003), pp. 266–79.

4. The Muratorian canon is the oldest list of New Testament writings we possess. It was discovered by L.A. Muratori in an eighth-century manuscript but dates from the second century CE. The beginning and the end are missing; it mentions all the New Testament books with the exception of Hebrews, James, and 1 and 2 Peter. See Geoffrey M. Hahneman, *The Muratorian Fragment and the Development of the Canon* (Oxford, 1992); *idem*, 'The Muratorian fragment and the origins of the New Testament canon', in Lee M. Macdonald and James A. Sanders (eds), *The Canon Debate* (Peabody, 2002), pp. 405–15.

5. See the list of scholars reproduced by W.G. Kümmel, *Introduction to the New Testament* (ET London, 1973), pp. 401–3; and D. Georgi, 'Hebrews and the heritage of Paul', in Gelardini (ed.), *Hebrews*, pp. 239–44.

6. The distinctive ideas of Hebrews are surveyed by Barnabas Lindars, *The Theology of the Letter to the Hebrews* (Cambridge, 1991). See also Simon J. Kistemaker, *Exposition of the Epistle to the Hebrews* (Grand Rapids, 1984).

7. Reported by Eusebius, *Hist. Eccl.* 7.25.11ff. Origen thought that Hebrews was written by a disciple of Paul's who wanted to communicate the master's ideas in his own way.

8. See L.D. Hurst, 'The Christology of Hebrews 1 and 2', in L.D. Hurst and N.T. Wright (eds), *The Glory of Christ in the New Testament: Studies in Christology in Memory of G.B. Caird* (Oxford, 1987), pp. 151–64; H. Anderson, 'The Jewish roots of the Christology in Hebrews', in J. Charlesworth (ed.), *The Messiah: Developments in Earliest Judaism and Christianity* (Minneapolis, 1992), pp. 512–35; Ekkehard W. Stegemann and Wolfgang Stegemann, 'Does the cultic language in Hebrews represent sacrificial metaphors? Reflections on some basic problems', in Gelardini (ed.), *Hebrews*, pp. 13–27; and Christian Eberhart, 'Characteristics of sacrificial metaphors in Hebrews', in the same volume, pp. 37–64.

9. On this theme see E. Käsemann, *The Wandering People of God* (ET Minneapolis, 1984); and Otfried Hofius, *Katapausis. Die Vorstellung von endzeitlichen Ruheort im Hebräerbrief* (WUNT, 11; Tübingen, 1970).

10. See Paul Desalaers and Dorothea Sattler, 'Jesus hat "die Himmel durchschritten" (Hebräerbrief 4,14)', in Samuel Vollenweider and Dorothea Sattler (eds), *Die Himmel* (Neukirchen-Vluyn, 2006), pp. 293–302.

11. See further Fred L. Horton, *The Melchizedek Tradition: A Critical Examination of the Sources to the Fifth Century* AD, and in the Epistle to the Hebrews (SNTSMS, 30; Cambridge, 1976). More recent studies include Birger A. Pearson, 'Melchizedek in early Judaism, Christianity, and Gnosticism', in Michael E. Stone and Theodore A. Bergren (eds), *Biblical Figures Outside the Bible* (Harrisburg, 1998), pp. 176–202; Anders Aschim, 'Melchizedek and Jesus: 11QMelchizedek and the Epistle to the Hebrews', in Carey C. Newman, James R. Davila and Gladys S. Lewis (eds), *The Jewish Roots of Christological Monotheism* (JSJSup, 63; Leiden, 1999), pp. 129–47; and Deborah W. Rooke, 'Jesus as royal priest: reflections on the interpretation of the Melchizedek tradition in Hebrews 7', *Biblica* 81 (2000), pp. 81–94.

12. See C.K. Barrett, 'The eschatology of the epistle to the Hebrews', in W.D. Davies and D. Daube (eds), *The Background of the New Testament and its Eschatology* (Cambridge, 1956), pp. 363–93; Otfried Hofius, *Der Vorhang vor dem Thron Gottes* (WUNT, 14; Tübingen, 1972); L.D. Hurst, *The Epistle to the Hebrews: Its Background of Thought* (SNTSMS, 65; Cambridge, 1990); and M.E. Isaacs, *Sacred Space: An Approach to the Theology of the Epistle to the Hebrews* (JSNTSup, 73; Sheffield, 1992). The Jewish apocalyptic background of Hebrews is well brought out in the commentaries of Wilson and Attridge.

13. See Floyd V. Filson, *Yesterday* (SBT, 4; London, 1967); and George W. Macrae, 'Heavenly temple and eschatology in the letter to the Hebrews', *Semeia* 12 (1978), pp. 179–99.

14. See D. Peterson, *Hebrews and Perfection* (SNTSMS, 47; Cambridge, 1982); and D.A. deSilva, *Despising Shame: Honor Discourse and Community Maintenance in the Epistle to the Hebrews* (SBLDS, 152; Atlanta, 1995).

15. See Michael R. Cosby, *The Rhetorical Composition and Function of Hebrews 11 In Light of Example Lists in Antiquity* (Macon, 1988); and Pamela M. Eisenbaum, *The Jewish Heroes of Christian History: Hebrews 11 in Literary Context* (SBLDS, 156; Atlanta, 1997).

16. On this person see Bruce D. Chilton and Craig A. Evans, *James the Just and Christian Origins* (NovTSup, 98; Leiden, 1999); Bruce Chilton and Jacob Neusner (eds), *The Brother of Jesus: James the Just and his Mission* (Louisville, 2001); and Bruce D. Chilton and Craig A. Evans (eds), *The Missions of James, Peter, and Paul: Tensions in Early Christianity* (Leiden, 2005). Commentaries on James include M. Dibelius, *A Commentary on the Epistle of James* (rev. ET; Hermeneia; Philadelphia, 1976); S. Laws, *A Commentary on the Epistle of James* (London, 1980); L.T. Johnson, *The Letter of James: A New Translation with Introduction and Commentary* (AB, 37a; New York, 1995); and William F. Brosend, *The Letters of James and Jude* (NCBC; Cambridge, 2004). See also A. Chester and R.P. Martin, *The Theology of the Letters of James, Peter, and Jude* (Cambridge, 1994).

17. See Kümmel, *Introduction*, pp. 405–7.

18. Luther, *Preface to the Epistles of James and Jude* (1522).
19. *James* (London, 1999).
20. *James*, p. 16.
21. Brown, *An Introduction to the New Testament* (New York, 1997), pp. 741–3.
22. See Mark Edward Taylor, *A Text-Linguistic Investigation into the Discourse Structure of James* (LNTS, 311; Louisville, 2006).
23. See Markus Bockmuehl, *Jewish Law in Gentile Churches* (Edinburgh, 2000), ch. 4.
24. Important studies of the contents include Todd C. Penner, *The Epistle of James and Eschatology: Re-reading an Ancient Christian Letter* (JSNTSup, 121; Sheffield, 1996); and W.H. Wachob, *The Voice of Jesus in the Social Rhetoric of James* (SNTSMS, 106; Cambridge, 2000).
25. For a consideration of this issue see Bauckham, *James*, pp. 120–40.
26. Commentaries include E.G. Selwyn, *The First Epistle of Peter* (London, ²1947); Leonhard Goppelt, *A Commentary on 1 Peter* (ET Grand Rapids, 1993); P.J. Achtemeier, *1 Peter: A Commentary on 1 Peter* (Hermeneia; Minneapolis, 1996); and Karen H. Jobes, *1 Peter* (BECNT; Grand Rapids, 2005). See also J.H. Elliott, *The Elect and the Holy: An Exegetical Examination of 1 Peter* (NovTSup, 12; Leiden, 1966); *idem*, *A Home for the Homeless: A Sociological Exegesis of 1 Peter* (new edn; Minneapolis, 1990); *idem*, 'Disgraced yet graced: the gospel according to 1 Peter in the key of honor and shame', *BTB* 25 (1995), pp. 166–78; Torrey Seland, *Strangers in the Light: Philonic Perspectives on Christian Identity in 1 Peter* (BIS, 76; Leiden, 2005); and J. de Waal Dryden, *Theology and Ethics in 1 Peter: Paraenetic Strategies for Christian Character Formation* (WUNT, 209; Tübingen, 2006).
27. See L. Thurén, *Argument and Theology in First Peter: The Origins of Christian Paraenesis* (JSNTSup, 114; Sheffield, 1995).
28. On the figure of Peter in early Christianity, see K. Heussi, *Die römische Petrustradition in kritischer Sicht* (Tübingen, 1955); R.E. Brown, Karl P. Donfried and John Reumann (eds), *Peter in the New Testament: A Collaborative Assessment by Protestant and Roman Catholic Scholars* (Minneapolis, 1973); T.V. Smith, *Petrine Controversies in Early Christianity: Attitudes towards Peter in Christian Writings of the First Two Centuries* (WUNT, 15; Tübingen, 1985); Carsten P. Thiede, *Simon Peter: From Galilee to Rome* (Exeter, 1986) [to be used with caution]; P. Perkins, *Peter: Apostle for the Whole Church* (Columbia, 1994); William Thomas Kessler, *Peter as the First Witness of the Risen Lord: An Historical and Theological Investigation* (TGT, 37; Rome, 1998); and F. Lapham, *Peter: The Myth, the Man and the Writings: A Study of the Early Petrine Text and Tradition* (JSNTSup, 239; Sheffield, 2003).
29. Brown, *Introduction*, p. 718.
30. See below.
31. See the presentation and consideration of these arguments in Kümmel, *Introduction*, pp. 421–4; and Brown, *Introduction*, pp. 718–22.
32. Brown, *Introduction*, pp. 718–19.
33. See further Carsten Peter Thiede, 'Babylon, der andere Ort: Anmerkungen zu 1 Petr 5:13 und Apg 12:17', in Carsten Peter Thiede (ed.), *Das Petrusbild in der neueren Forschung* (Wuppertal, 1987), pp. 221–9.
34. On this form of Christology see Chapter 25.
35. Important discussions of this passage include Bo Reicke, *The Disobedient*

Spirits and Christian Baptism (ASNU, 13; Copenhagen, 1946); William J. Dalton, *Christ's Proclamation to the Spirits* (Rome, [2]1989); and Achtemeier, *1 Peter*, pp. 239–74.

36. See the interesting article by Paul J. Achtemeier, 'Suffering servant and suffering Christ in 1 Peter', in A. Malherbe and W. Meeks (eds), *The Future of Christology: Essays in Honor of Leander E. Keck* (Minneapolis, 1993), pp. 176–88.

37. Commentaries include J.N.D. Kelly, *A Commentary on the Epistles of Peter and of Jude* (London, 1969); R.J. Bauckham, *Jude, 2 Peter* (WBC, 50; Dallas, 1990); and J.H. Neyrey, *2 Peter, Jude: A New Translation with Introduction and Commentary* (AB, 37a; New York, 1993). See also my own *2 Peter and Jude* (Sheffield, 1995); Robert W. Wall, 'The Canonical Function of 2 Peter', *Biblical Interpretation* 9 (2001), pp. 64–81 and Peter H. Davids, *The Letters of 2 Peter and Jude* (PNTC; Grand Rapids, 2006).

38. Kümmel, *Introduction*, p. 430.

39. This is noticed by Bauckham, *Jude, 2 Peter*, pp. 138–51.

40. *Redating the New Testament* (London, 1976), pp. 193–4. Robinson is heavily criticized in his approach by Sturdy in the book mentioned in n. 1.

41. *The Epistles of James, Peter and Jude* (AB, 32; New York, 1964).

42. T. Fornberg, *An Early Church in a Pluralistic Society: A Study of Peter* (Lund, 1977); Neyrey, *2 Peter, Jude*.

43. C.E.B. Cranfield, *1 and 2 Peter and Jude: Introduction and Commentary* (London, 1960); J.N.D. Kelly, *A Commentary on the Epistles of Peter and of Jude* (New York, 1969); Bauckham, *Jude, 2 Peter*.

44. *Jude, 2 Peter*, p. 142.

45. F. Spitta, *Die zweite Brief des Petrus und der Brief des Judas* (Halle, 1885); C. Bigg, *A Critical and Exegetical Commentary on the Epistles of St. Peter and St. Jude* (ICC; Edinburgh, 1901).

46. See D. Watson, *Invention, Arrangement and Style: Rhetorical Criticism of Jude and 2 Peter* (SBLDS, 104; Atlanta, 1988).

47. Käsemann, 'An apologia for primitive Christian eschatology', in *Essays on New Testament Themes* (SBT, 41; ET London, 1964), pp. 169–91; Bauckham, *Jude, 2 Peter*.

48. On the Epicureans, see J.M. Rist, *Epicurus: An Introduction* (Cambridge, 1972); P. Mitsis, *Epicurus' Ethical Theory* (Ithaca, 1988); and J. Annas, *Hellenistic Philosophy of Mind* (Berkeley and London, 1992). Since Neyrey wrote, there have been other attempts to trace the influence of Epicureanism on the New Testament. See for instance Paul A. Holloway, 'Notes and observations *bona cognitare*: an Epicurean consolation in Phil. 4.8-9', *HTR* 91 (1998), pp. 84–96; and Abraham J. Malherbe, 'Anti-Epicurean rhetoric in 1 Thessalonians', in S. Maser and E. Schlarb, *Text und Geschichte: Facetten theologischen Arbeitens aus dem Freundes und Schülerkreis: Dieter Lührmann zum 60 Geburtstag* (MTS, 50; Marburg, 1999), pp. 136–42. There is valuable material also in Dorothea Frede and André Lahy (eds), *Traditions of Theology: Studies in Hellenistic Theology, Its Background and Aftermath* (Leiden, 2002).

49. See J. Daryl Charles, *Virtue amidst Vice: The Catalog of Virtues in 2 Peter 1* (JSNTSup, 150; Sheffield, 1997).

50. See Edward Adams, 'Where is the promise of his coming? The complaint of the scoffers in 2 Peter 3.4', *NTS* 51 (2005), pp. 106–22.

51. Commentaries include R. Bultmann, *The Johannine Epistles* (Philadelphia, 1973); R.E. Brown, *Epistles of John* (AB, 30; New York, 1982); S.S. Smalley, *1, 2 and 3 John* (WBC, 51; Waco, 1984); G. Strecker, *The Johannine Letters: A Commentary on 1, 2 and 3 John* (Hermeneia; Minneapolis, 1996); John Painter, *1, 2 and 3 John* (SPS; Collegeville, 2002); and Martin M. Culy, *1, 2, 3 John: A Handbook on the Greek Text* (Waco, 2004). See also Terry Griffith, *Keep Yourselves from Idols: A New Look at 1 John* (JSNTSup, 233; Sheffield, 2002).

52. See Martin Hengel, *The Johannine Question* (ET London, 1989); and the commentaries mentioned here.

53. Rudolph Bultmann, *The Gospel of John* (ET London, 1971).

54. Thus Brown, *Introduction*, p. 389.

55. This is a form of the heresy known generically as docetism. See Strecker, *Johannine Letters*, pp. 69–76; *idem*, 'Chiliasmus und Doketismus in der Johanneischer Schule', *Kerygma und Dogma* 38 (1992), pp. 30–46; Nathalie Depraz, 'Phénoménologie et docétisme: l'apparaître charnel', in Nathalie Depraz and Jean-François Marquet (eds), *La gnose, une question philosophique* (Paris, 2000), pp. 87–105; and Guy G. Stroumsa, 'Christ's laughter: docetic origins reconsidered', *JECS* 12 (2004), pp. 267–88.

56. See R.W.L. Moberley, ' "Test the spirits": God, love and critical discernment in First John 4', in Graham N. Stanton, Bruce W. Longenecker and Stephen C. Barton (eds), *The Holy Spirit and Christian Origins: Essays in Honor of James D.G. Dunn* (Grand Rapids, 2004), pp. 296–307.

57. See Brown, *Introduction*, p. 392.

58. See Judith Lieu, *The Second and Third Epistles of John* (Edinburgh, 1996); but note that her approach is criticized by Hengel, *Johannine Question*, pp. 29–30.

59. Brown, *Introduction*, p. 395.

60. See note 37 above on 2 Peter for commentaries on Jude.

61. On the family of Jesus, see R.J. Bauckham, *Jude and the Relatives of Jesus in the Early Church* (Edinburgh, 1990).

62. Commentaries include Austin Farrer, *The Revelation of St. John the Divine: Commentary on the English Text* (Oxford, 1964); M. Eugene Boring, *Revelation* (Louisville, 1989); J.P.M. Sweet, *Revelation* (reissued London, 1990); Christopher Rowland, *Revelation* (London, 1993); David E. Aune, *Revelation 1–5, 6–16* (WBC, 52a, b; Dallas, 1997–8); Jonathan Knight, *Revelation* (Sheffield, 1999; ²2008); Bruce J. Malina, *Social-Science Commentary on the Book of Revelation* (Minneapolis, 2000); Simon J. Kistemaker, *Revelation* (NTC; Grand Rapids, 2001); Judith Kovacs and Christopher Rowland, *Revelation* (BBC; Oxford, 2004); Joseph L. Trafton, *Reading Revelation: A Literary and Theological Commentary* (Macon, 2005); and Stephen J. Smalley, *The Revelation to John: A Commentary on the Greek Text of the Apocalypse* (London, 2005). See also R.J. Bauckham, *The Climax of Prophecy: Studies on the Book of Revelation* (Edinburgh, 1993); *idem*, *The Theology of the Book of Revelation* (Cambridge, 1993); and Steven J. Friesen, *Imperial Cults and the Apocalypse of John: Reading Revelation in the Ruins* (Oxford, 2001).

63. On which see Kümmel, *Introduction*, pp. 469–72.

64. *The Book of Revelation: Apocalypse and Empire* (New York and Oxford, 1990).

65. 'Apocalypse: morphology of a genre', *Semeia* 14 (1979), p. 9. Collins reviews this definition in his later article, 'Genre, ideology and social movements in Jewish apocalypticism', in J.J. Collins and J.H. Charlesworth (eds), *Mysteries and Revelations: Apocalyptic Studies since the Uppsala Colloquium* (JSPSup, 9; Sheffield, 1991), pp. 11–32. The revelatory element in the apocalypses is explored also by C.C. Rowland, *The Open Heaven* (London, 1982), pp. 70–2.

66. See 1.12-16; 4.1; 10.1. In the first of these references the mediator is Christ and not an angel.

67. *The Idea of the Holy: An Inquiry into the Non-Rational Factor in the Idea of the Divine and Its Relation to the Rational* (reprinted ET; Oxford, 1981).

68. See the studies of it by D.E. Aune, *Prophecy in Early Christianity and the Ancient Mediterranean World* (Grand Rapids, 1983); and D. Hill, *New Testament Prophecy* (London, 1979).

69. This aspect of Revelation is brilliantly explored by A.M. Farrer in his *A Rebirth of Images* (Westminster, 1949).

70. See Kümmel, *Introduction*, pp. 456–74.

71. On this man see Hengel, *Johannine Question, passim*.

72. The evidence is set out by Kümmel, *Introduction*, pp. 330–1.

73. See A.Y. Collins, *Crisis and Catharsis: The Power of the Apocalypse* (Westminster, 1984), p. 27, for an explanation of this view.

74. The author's status as a Christian prophet is explored by Collins, *Crisis and Catharsis*, pp. 37–46. Another valuable study is E. Schüssler Fiorenza, *The Book of Revelation: Justice and Judgment* (Philadelphia, 1985) pp. 133–56.

75. This story derives from Hegesippus and is reported by Eusebius in his *Hist. Eccl.* 3.19.1–20.8. On this report see Bauckham, *Jude and the Relatives of Jesus*, pp. 94–106.

76. See Collins, *Crisis and Catharsis*, p. 25. There is an important discussion of Papias in Hengel, *Johannine Question*, pp. 16–23.

77. *Redating*, pp. 221–53.

78. See Felise Tavo, 'The structure of the Apocalypse: re-examining a perennial problem', *NovT* 47 (2005), pp. 47–68.

79. See Sweet, *Revelation*, pp. 21–7.

80. This cautionary remark is made by Thompson, *Book of Revelation*, pp. 15–17.

81. *Book of Revelation*, pp. 95–115.

82. *Book of Revelation*, pp. 111–15.

83. *Book of Revelation*, pp. 116–32.

84. *Book of Revelation*, pp. 133–45.

85. Cf. Thompson, *Book of Revelation*, p. 174: 'Christian leaders who espouse participation in the life of the empire as harmless and as irrelevant to Christian existence are made homologous to evil, mythic forces such as Babylon, the Great Whore. The peace and prosperity of Roman society is, from his point of view, not to be entered into by faithful Christians.'

86. *Book of Revelation*, p. 122; citing G. Theissen, *The Social Setting of Pauline Christianity: Essays on Corinth* (Edinburgh, 1982), pp. 132–6. See also David L. Barr (ed.), *The Reality of The Apocalypse: Rhetoric and Politics in the Book of Revelation* (SBLSS, 39; Atlanta, 2006).

87. Thompson, *Book of Revelation*, pp. 123, 174.

88. *Book of Revelation*, p. 175.

89. *Book of Revelation*, pp. 124–5.
90. See Kümmel, *Introduction*, pp. 475–503; B. Metzger, *The Canon of the New Testament: Its Origin, Development, and Significance* (Oxford, 1987); Linda L. Belleville, 'The canon of the New Testament', in David S. Dockers, Kenneth A. Mathews and Robert B. Sloan (eds), *Foundations for Biblical Interpretation: A Complete Library of Tools and Resources* (Nashville, 1994), pp. 374–95; Arthur G. Patzia, *The Making of the New Testament: Origin, Collection, Text and Canon* (Downers Grove and Leicester, 1995); Macdonald and Sanders (eds), *Canon Debate*; John Barton and Michael Wolter (eds), *Unity of Scripture and Diversity of the Canon* (Oxford, 2003); Christine Helmer and Christof Landmesser, *One Scripture or Many? Canon from Biblical, Theological and Philosophical Perspectives* (Oxford, 2004); Tomas Bokedal, *The Scriptures and the Lord: Formation and Significance of the Christian Biblical Canon: A Study in Text, Ritual, and Interpretation* (Lund, 2005); and Gabriella Aragione, Eric Junod and Enrico Norelli (eds), *Le canon du Nouveau testament: Regards nouveaux sur l'histoire de sa formation* (Geneva, 2005).
91. See especially M. Saebo (ed.), *Hebrew Bible/Old Testament: The History of its Interpretation*, vol. i: *From the Beginnings to the Middle Ages (until 1300)*, pt. i: *Antiquity* (Göttingen, 1996).
92. See Chapter 5.
93. E.g. Mt. 11.13; Lk. 16.16.
94. See David Wenham, *Paul: Follower of Jesus or Founder of Christianity?* (Grand Rapids and Cambridge, 1995).
95. See Jens Schröter, 'Jesus and the canon: the early Jesus traditions in the context of the origins of the New Testament canon', in Richard A. Horsley, Jonathan A. Draper and John Miles Foley (eds), *Performing the Gospel: Orality, Memory, and Mark* (Minneapolis, 2006), pp. 104–22, 222–8.
96. Note especially the reference to the 'Spirit of Jesus' in Phil. 1.19.
97. See Charles E. Hill, 'Ignatius and the apostolate: the witness of Ignatius to the emergence of Christian scripture', in Maurice F. Wiles, Edward Yarnold and P.M. Parvis (eds), *Studia Patristica*, vol. xxxvi (Louvain, 2001), pp. 226–48.
98. Metzger, *Canon*, p. 49.
99. See Andreas Lindemann, 'Der Apostel Paulus im 2 Jahrhundert', in J. Sevrin (ed.), *The New Testament in Early Christianity* (Louvain, 1989), pp. 39–67; *idem*, 'Paul in the writings of the apostolic fathers', in W. Babcock (ed.), *Paul and the Legacies of Paul* (Dallas, 1990), pp. 25–45; and Stanley E. Porter (ed.), *The Pauline Canon* (PS, 1; Leiden, 2004).
100. This is Goodspeed's hypothesis; *The Key to Ephelians* (Chicago, 1956).
101. See F.F. Bruce, 'Some thoughts on the beginning of the New Testament canon', *BJRL* 65 (1983), pp. 37–60; William L. Petersen, *Gospel Traditions in the Second Century: Origins, Recensions, Text, and Transmission* (CJA, 3; Notre Dame, 1989); Helmut Koester, 'Written Gospel or oral tradition?', *JBL* 113 (1994), pp. 293–7; Harry Y. Gamble, *Books and Readers in the Early Church: A History of Early Christian Texts* (New Haven and London, 1995); Loveday Alexander, 'Ancient book production and the circulation of the Gospels', in Richard Bauckham (ed.), *The Gospels for all Christians:*

Rethinking the Gospel Audiences (Grand Rapids and Cambridge, 1998), pp. 71–105.

102. Early use of Matthew is examined by E. Massaux, *L'Influence de l'Évangile de Saint Matthieu sur la littérature chrétienne avant Saint Irénée* (BETL, 175: reprinted Louvain, 1986); ET of this, *The Influence of the Gospel of Saint Matthew on Christian Literature Before Saint Irenaeus* (3 vols.; Macon, 1990–3); W.-D. Köhler, *Die Rezeption des Matthäusevangeliums in der Zeit vor Irenäus* (WUNT, 24; Tübingen, 1987); and William R. Farmer, 'The Gospel of Matthew in the second century', *Second Century* 9 (1992), pp. 193–275. Use of Luke is studied by Arthur J. Bellinzoni, 'The Gospel of Luke in the second century CE', in Richard P. Thompson and Thomas E. Phillips (eds), *Literary Studies in Luke–Acts: Essays in Honor of Joseph B. Tyson* (Macon, 1998), pp. 59–76; and of John, by Hengel, *Johannine Question*, ch. 1.

103. See David Wright, 'Apocryphal Gospels: the "Unknown Gospel" (Pap Egerton 2) and the Gospel of Peter', in D. Wenham (ed.), *The Jesus Tradition Outside the Gospels* (GP, 5; Sheffield, 1984), pp. 207–32; John Dominic Crossan, 'The cross that spoke: the earliest narrative of the passion and resurrection', *Forum* 3 (1987), pp. 3–22; Raymond E. Brown, 'The Gospel of Peter and canonical Gospel priority', *NTS* 33 (1987), pp. 321–42; and Alan Kirk, 'Examining priorities: another look at the Gospel of Peter's relationship to the New Testament Gospels', *NTS* 40 (1994), pp. 572–95.

104. See Bruce M. Metzger, *The Early Versions of the New Testament* (Oxford, 1977), pp. 10–36; William L. Petersen, *Tatian's Diatesseron: Its Creation, Dissemination, Significance, and History in Scholarship* (VCSup, 25; Leiden, 1994); *idem*, 'From Justin to Pepys: the history of the harmonized Gospel tradition', in E. Livingstone (ed.), *Studia Patristica*, vol. xxx (Louvain, 1997), pp. 71–96; and Emily J. Hunt, *Christianity in the Second Century: The Case of Tatian* (London, 2003).

105. See Jonathan Knight, *Disciples of the Beloved One: Studies in the Christology, Social Setting and Theological Context of the Ascension of Isaiah* (JSPSup, 18; Sheffield, 1996), ch. 4; and Richard J. Bauckham, *The Fate of the Dead: Studies on the Jewish and Christian Apocalypses* (London, 1998), pp. 363–90.

106. See Stephen Gero, 'Apocryphal Gospels: a survey of textual and literary problems', in W. Haase (ed.), *ANRW* II.25.5, pp. 3969–96; Frans Neirynck, 'The apocryphal Gospels and the Gospel of Mark', in Sevrin (ed.), *The New Testament in Early Christianity*, pp. 123–75; and James H. Charlesworth and Craig A. Evans, 'Jesus in the agrapha and apocryphal gospels', in Bruce D. Chilton and Craig A. Evans (eds), *Studying the Historical Jesus: Evaluation of the State of Current Research* (Leiden, 1994), pp. 479–533.

107. See Kümmel, *Introduction*, pp. 483–4.

108. See Craig D. Allert, *Revelation, Truth, Canon and Interpretation: Studies in Justin Martyr's Dialogue with Trypho* (VCSup, 64; Leiden, 2002).

109. See Graham N. Stanton, 'The fourfold Gospel', *NTS* 43 (1997), pp. 317–46; *idem*, 'Jesus traditions and Gospels in Justin Martyr and Irenaeus', in J.-M. Auwers and H.J. de Jonge (eds), *The Biblical Canons* (BETL, 163; Leuven, 2003), pp. 353–70.

110. Besides the literature cited, see Gilles Quispel, 'Marcion and the text of

the New Testament', *VC* 52 (1998), pp. 349–60; Wolfgang Schenk, 'Die Jesus-rezeption des Markion als theologisches Problem', in Rudolph Hoppe and Ulrich Busse (eds), *Vom Jesus zum Christus: christologische Studien: Festgabe für Paul Hoffmann zum 65 Geburtstag* (BZNW, 93; Berlin, 1998), pp. 507–28; and John Barton, 'Marcion revisited', in Macdonald and Sanders (eds), *Canon Debate*, pp. 341–54.

111. See Pierre Nautin, 'Irénée et la canonicité des épîtres pauliniennes', *RHR* 182 (1972), pp. 113–30; T.C. Skeat, 'Irenaeus and the four-Gospel canon', *NovT* 34 (1992), pp. 194–9; and Yves Marie Blanchard, *Aux sources du canon, le témoignage d'Irénée* (CF, 175; Paris, 1993).
112. See John F. Jansen, 'Tertullian and the New Testament', *Second Century* 2 (1982), pp. 191–207; Cecil M. Robeck, 'Canon, regulae fidei, and continuing revelation in the early church', in J. Bradley and R. Muller (eds), *Church, Word and Spirit: Historical and Theological Essays in Honor of Geoffrey W. Bromiley* (Grand Rapids, 1987), pp. 65–91; and Enrico Norelli, 'La tradizione ecclesiastica negli antichi prologhi latini alle Epistole Paoline', in W. Rordorf, P. Grech and M. Tabet (eds), *La tradizione: forme e modi: XVIII Incontro di studiosi dell'antichità cristiana, Roma 7–9 maggio 1989* (Rome, 1990), pp. 301–24.
113. *Apol.* 18.1, 19.1; *De praesc. haer.* 38; *Adv. Marc.* 4.1 and *Adv. Prax.* 20.
114. See Helmut Merkel, 'Clemens Alexandrinus über die Reihenfolge der Evangelien', *ETL* 60 (1984), pp. 382–5; James A. Brooks, 'Clement of Alexandria as a witness to the development of the New Testament canon', *Second Century* 9 (1992), pp. 41–55; and A. le Boulluec, 'De l'usage de titres "néotestementaires" chez Clément d'Alexandre', in M. Tardieu (ed.), *La formation des canons scripturaires* (Paris, 1993), pp. 191–202.
115. See Annewies van der Hoek, 'Clement and Origen as sources on "non-canonical" scriptural traditions during the late second and earlier third centuries', in G. Dorival (ed.), *Origeniana sexta: Origène et la Bible* (Louvain, 1995), pp. 93–113.
116. *Tomoi in Johannem*, 20.10.66. See Everett R. Kalin, 'Re-examining New Testament canon history: pt I, The canon of Origen', *Currents in Theology and Mission* 17 (1990), pp. 274–82
117. See Gregory Allen Robbins, 'Eusebius' Lexicon of "canonicity" ', in E. Livingstone (ed.), *Studia Patristica*, 25 (Louvain, 1993), pp. 134–41; and Armin Daniel Brown, 'Der neutestamentliche Kanon bei Eusebius (*Hist. Eccl.* III, 25, 1–7) im Kontext seiner literaturgeschichtlichen Arbeit', *ETL* 73 (1997), pp. 307–48.
118. See David Brakke, 'Canon formation and social conflict in fourth-century Egypt: Athanasius of Alexandria's thirty-ninth festal letter', *HTR* 87 (1994), pp. 395–419.
119. See M. Moreton, 'Rethinking the origin of the Roman canon', in E. Livingstone (ed.), *Studia Patristica*, vol. xxvi (Louvain, 1993), pp. 63–6.

Chapter 25

1. See Oscar Cullmann, *The Christology of the New Testament* (ET London, ²1963); R.H. Fuller, *The Foundations of New Testament Christology* (London, 1965); A. Grillmeier, *Christ in Christian Tradition*, vol. i: *From the Apostolic*

Age to Chalcedon (ET London, 1975); Petr Pokorny, *The Genesis of Christology: Foundations for a Theology of the New Testament* (ET Edinburgh, 1987); L.D. Hurst and N.T. Wright, *The Glory of Christ in the New Testament: Studies in Christology in Memory of George Bradford Caird* (Oxford, 1987); Arland J. Hultgren, *Christ and His Benefits: Christology and Redemption in the New Testament* (Philadelphia, 1987); I. Howard Marshall, *The Origins of New Testament Christology* (Leicester, 1990); Maurice Casey, *From Jewish Prophet to Gentile God: The Origins and Development of New Testament Christology* (Louisville and Cambridge, 1991); Martinus C. de Boer, *From Jesus to John: Essays on Jesus and New Testament Christology in Honor of Marinus de Jonge* (JSNTSup, 84; Sheffield, 1993); Abraham J. Malherbe and Wayne A. Meeks, *The Future of Christology: Essays in Honour of Leander E. Keck* (Minneapolis, 1993); Raymond E. Brown, *An Introduction to New Testament Christology* (Mahwah, NJ, 1994); Joel B. Green and Max Turner (eds), *Jesus of Nazareth, Lord and Christ: Essays on the Historical Jesus and New Testament Christology* (Grand Rapids, 1994); James D.G. Dunn, *Christology in the Making: A New Testament Inquiry into the Origins of the Doctrine of the Incarnation* (reissued, Grand Rapids, 1996); Richard Bauckham, *God Crucified: Monotheism and Christology in the New Testament (Grand Rapids, 1999); Frank J. Matera, New Testament Christology* (Louisville, 1999); Christopher M. Tuckett, *Christology and the New Testament: Jesus and his Earliest Followers* (Edinburgh, 2001); George H. van Kooten, *Cosmic Christology in Christ and the Pauline School: Colossians and Ephesians in the Context of Graeco-Roman Cosmology, with a New Synopsis of the Greek Texts* (WUNT, 171; Tübingen, 2003); Jiri Mrazek and Jan Roskovec (eds), *Testimony and Interpretation: Early Christology and its Judeo-Hellenistic Milieu. Studies in Honor of Petr Pokorny* (JSNTSup, 272; London, 2004); and Richard N. Longenecker (ed.), *Contours of Christology in the New Testament* (Grand Rapids, 2005).

2. See Christopher R. Matthews, 'From Messiah to Christ: the pre-Pauline Christ cult in scholarship', in Ron Cameron and Merill P. Miller (eds), *Redescribing Christian Origins* (Atlanta, 2004), pp. 349–63.

3. Cf. Martin Hengel, *The Son of God* (ET London, 1976), p. 2: 'The "apotheosis of the crucified Jesus" must already have taken place in the forties, and one is tempted to say *that more happened in this period of less than two decades than in the whole of the next seven centuries, up to the time when the doctrine of the early church was completed*' (italics original).

4. In this context see Frank J. Matera, 'Christ in the theologies of Paul and John: a study in the diverse unity of New Testament theology', *TS* 67 (2006), pp. 237–56.

5. See Jarl Fossum, *The Image of the Invisible God: Essays on the Influence of Jewish Mysticism on Early Christology* (NTOA, 30; Göttingen, 1995); John M.G. Barclay and John P.M. Sweet (eds), *Early Christian Thought in its Jewish Context* (Cambridge, 1996); Bauckham, *God Crucified*; and Carey C. Newman, James R. Davila and Gladys S. Lewis (eds), *The Jewish Roots of Christological Monotheism* (JSJSup, 63; Leiden, 1999).

6. See Chapter 10.

7. See Chapters 13 and 14.

8. See Wayne A. Meeks, 'Equal to God (Jn 5:18)', in R. Fortna and B. Gaventa

(eds), *The Conversation Continues: Studies in Paul and John in honor of J. Louis Martyn* (Nashville, 1990), pp. 309–21.

9. Jeremias, *New Testament Theology*, vol. i (ET London, 1967), p. 67; James Barr, ' "Abba" isn't "daddy" ', *JTS* 39 (1988), pp. 28–47; *idem*, 'Abba, father, and the familiarity of Jesus' speech', *Theology* 91 (1988), pp. 173–9.

10. On which see Richard A. Horsley, *Jesus and the Spiral of Violence* (Minneapolis, 1993), pp. 231–45.

11. See Chapter 10.

12. See Mk 12.18–27 and parallels; and the various material in John 11.

13. See Chapter 16.

14. Though see Anthony Cane, *The Place of Judas Iscariot in Christology* (Aldershot, 2005).

15. (And this despite the seemingly historical evidence of Jn 18.19, 'Then the high priest questioned Jesus about his disciples and about his teaching.').

16. See Larry W. Hurtado, *One God, One Lord: Early Christian Devotion and Ancient Jewish Monotheism* (London, 1988); *idem*, *Lord Jesus Christ: Devotion to Jesus in Earliest Christianity* (Grand Rapids, 2003); *idem*, *How on Earth Did Jesus Become a God? Questions about Earliest Devotions to Jesus* (Grand Rapids, 2005).

17. For a review of the evidence see Christopher M. Tuckett, 'The Christology of Luke–Acts', in J. Verheyden (ed.), *The Unity of Luke–Acts* (BETL, 142; Louvain, 1999), pp. 133–64.

18. Among the studies of this title, see Martin Hengel, 'Christological titles in early Christianity', in *Studies in Early Christology* (Edinburgh, 1995), pp. 359–89; and Otfried Hofius, ' "Einer ist Gott – Einer ist Herr": Erwägungen zu Struktur und Aussage des Bekenntnisses 1 Kor 8, 6', in Martin Evang, Helmut Merklein and Michael Wolter (eds), *Eschatologie und Schöpfung: Festschrift für Erich Grässer zum siebzigsten Geburtstag* (BZNW, 89; Berlin, 1997), pp. 95–108.

19. On the uses of the *ho theos* title for Jesus in the New Testament, see Murray J. Harris, *Jesus as God: The New Testament Use of Theos in Reference to Jesus* (Grand Rapids, 1992)

20. See further Hurtado, *One God, One Lord*.

21. See Adela Yarbro Collins, 'Psalms, Philippians 2.6-11 and the origins of Christology', *Biblical Interpretation* 11 (2003), pp. 361–72; and Jerome Murphy-O'Connor, 'The origins of Paul's Christology: from Thessalonians to Galatians', in Kieran J. Mahony (ed.), *Christian Origins: Worship, Belief and Society* (JSNTSup, 241; London, 2003), pp. 113–42

22. See Hofius, ' "Einer ist Gott" '; and the research of Hurtado, *One God, One Lord*.

23. See Walter Wink, 'The image of the cosmic Christ', in Fortna and Gaventa (eds), *The Conversation Continues*, pp. 235–45; Jarl E. Fossum, '1 Corinthians 1:15-18a in the light of Jewish mysticism and Gnosticism', *NTS* 35 (1989), pp. 183–201; *idem*, 'The image of the the invisible God: Col. 1, 15a-18, Jewish mysticism and Gnosticism', in *The Image of the Invisible God, pp. 13–39. See also Robert W. Scholla, 'Into the image of God: Pauline eschatology and the transformation of believers', Gregorianum* 78 (1997), pp. 33–54.

24. See Manfred Görg, 'Fleischwerdung der Logos: Auslegungs- und religionsgeschichte Anmerkungen zu Joh 1, 14a', in R. Hoppe and U. Busse

(eds), *Von Jesus zum Christus: christologische Studien: Festgabe für Paul Hoffmann zum 65 Geburtstag* (BZNW, 93; Berlin, 1998), pp. 467–82.

25. On the problems raised by this Johannine strand, see J.-A. Bühner, *Der Gesandte und sein Weg im vierten Evangelium* (WUNT, 2; Tübingen, 1977); and Francis J. Moloney, *The Johannine Son of Man* (BSR, 14; Rome, ²1978).

26. See the history of research summarized in Dunn, *Christology in the Making*; and Ralph P. Martin and Brian J. Dodd, *Where Christology Began: Essays on Philippians 2* (Louisville, 1998).

27. See for instance Markus Bockmuehl, ' "The form of God" (Phil. 2:6): variations on a theme of Jewish mysticism', *JTS* 48 (1997), pp. 1–23. On the Gospels, Simon J. Gathercole, *The Pre-existent Son: Recovering the Christologies of Matthew, Mark and Luke* (Grand Rapids, 2006).

28. Notably Dunn in his *Christology in the Making*. See also Morna D. Hooker, 'Philippians 2.6-11', in *From Adam to Christ: Essays on Paul* (Cambridge, 1990), pp. 88–100; and Stephen J. Hultzen, 'The origin of Paul's doctrine of the two Adams in 1 Corinthians 15.45-49', *JSNT* 25 (2003), pp. 343–70.

29. By Bockmuehl, ' "The form of God" '.

30. See further Martin Hengel, 'Präexistenz bei Paulus', in Christof Landmesser, Hans Joachim Eckstein and Hermann Lichtenberger (eds), *Jesus Christus als die Mitte der Schrift: Studien zur Hermeneutik des Evangeliums* (BZNW, 86; Berlin, 1997), pp. 479–518.

31. On this topic see Celia Deutsch, 'Wisdom in Matthew: transformation of a symbol', *NovT* 32 (1990), pp. 13–47; and Russell Pregeant, 'The wisdom passages in Matthew's story', in D. Lull (ed.), *SBL 1990 Seminar Papers* (Atlanta, 1990), pp. 469–93.

32. On which, see Anthony J. Godzieba, Lieven Boere and Michele Saracino, 'Resurrection–interruption–transformation: incarnation as hermeneutical strategy: a symposium', *TS* 67 (2006), pp. 777–815.

33. See Hengel, 'Christological titles in early Christianity'; and *idem*, *The Son of God*.

34. See further Chapter 26.

35. See the exploration of these themes by Jey J. Kanagaraj, 'Jesus the king, merkabah mysticism, and the Gospel of John', *Tyndale Bulletin* 47 (1996), pp. 349–66; and William Horbury, *Jewish Messianism and the Cult of Christ* (London, 1998), pp. 78–86.

Chapter 26

1. Pliny, *Ep.* 10.96–7.

2. On the breach in general, see E. P. Sanders *et al.* (eds), *Jewish and Christian Self-Definition* (3 vols.; London, 1980–82); James D.G. Dunn, *The Partings of the Ways Between Christianity and Judaism and their Significance for the Character of Christianity* (London, 1991); and James D.G. Dunn (ed.), *Jews and Christians: The Parting of the Ways, AD 70–135* (WUNT, 66; Tübingen, 1992).

3. See Chapter 13 for discussion of this point.

4. The best study of this theme is still that of Martin Hengel, *The Son of God* (ET London, 1976).

5. See Martin Hengel, *Crucifixion* (ET London, 1977), pp. 84–5; and R.G. Hamerton-Kelly, 'Sacred violence and the curse of the Law (Galatians 3:13): the death of Christ as a sacrificial travesty', *NTS* 36 (1990), pp. 98–118.

6. A theme explored by Hengel, *Crucifixion*.

7. See Richard B. Hays, 'Wisdom according to Paul', in Stephen Barton (ed.), *Where Shall Wisdom Be Found? Wisdom in the Bible, the Church and the Contemporary World* (Edinburgh, 1999), pp. 111–23.

8. Note 1 Cor. 2.7 in this context, 'We speak God's wisdom, secret and hidden, which God decreed before the ages for our glory.'

9. The title was coined by Alan F. Segal, *Two Powers in Heaven: Early Rabbinic Reports about Christianity and Gnosticism* (SJLA, 25; Leiden, 1977). See also Larry W. Hurtado, *One God, One Lord: Early Christian Devotion and Ancient Jewish Monotheism* (London, 1988), and his later writings mentioned in the last chapter (n. 16); Carey C. Newman, James R. Davila and Gladys S. Lewis (eds), *The Jewish Roots of Christological Monotheism* (JSJSup, 63; Leiden, 1999); Richard Bauckham, *God Crucified: Monotheism and Christology in the New Testament* (Grand Rapids, 1999); and Loren T. Stuckenbruck and Wendy E.S. North (eds), *Early Jewish and Christian Monotheism* (JSNTSup, 263; London, 2004). An interesting comparative text is Polymnia Athanassiadi and Michael Frede (eds), *Pagan Monotheism in Late Antiquity* (Oxford, 1999).

10. A judicious study of this issue is Peter Carrell, *Jesus and the Angels: Angelology and the Christology of the Apocalypse of John* (SNTSMS, 95; Cambridge, 1997).

11. See the various contributors to Stephen T. Davis, Daniel Kendall and Gerald O'Collins (eds), *The Trinity: An Interdisciplinary Symposium on the Trinity* (Oxford and New York, 1999).

12. Chapter 12.

13. See Nicholas H. Taylor, 'Luke–Acts and the temple', in J. Verheyden (ed.), *The Unity of Luke–Acts* (Louvain, 1999), pp. 709–21.

14. See Edvin Larsson, 'Temple-criticism and the Jewish heritage: some reflexions on Acts 6–7', *NTS* 39 (1993), pp. 379–95; and Michael Bachmann, 'Die Stephanusepisode (Apg 6,1–8,3): ihre Bedeutung für die lukanische Sicht des jerusalemischen Tempels und des Judentums', in Verheyden (ed.), *Unity*, pp. 545–62.

15. See e.g. Gal. 4.26; Heb. 12.22.

16. Besides the various works of Ed Sanders cited already in this book, see Markus Bockmuehl, *Jewish Law in Gentile Churches: Halakah and the Beginning of Christian Public Ethics* (Edinburgh, 2000).

17. See below on this text.

18. On this Jewish prayer see Emil Schürer, revised by Geza Vermes and others, *The History of the Jewish People in the Age of Jesus Christ (175 BC–AD 135)*, vol. ii (Edinburgh, 1979), pp. 454–63; and David Instone-Brewer, 'Eighteen Benedictions and the Minim before 70 CE', *JTS* 54 (2003), pp. 25–44.

19. See Y. Luger, 'Versions of the Amidah in the Cairo Genizah: a new perspective', in David Assaf (ed.), *Proceedings of the Eleventh World Congress of Jewish Studies, Div C, Thought and Literature*, vol. i: *Rabbinic and Talmudic Literature*, pp. 79–86.

20. 'Die sogenannte Synode von Jabne', *Judaica* 31 (1975); reprinted in his

Studien zur Geschichte und Theologie des rabbinischen Judentums (Leiden, 1978), pp. 45–55.

21. 'The Benediction of the *Minim* and early Jewish–Christian controversy', *JTS* 33 (1982), pp. 19–61; here p. 47.

22. 'The Benediction of the *Minim*', p. 51.

23. See Wayne O. McCready, 'Johannine self-understanding and the synagogue episode of John 9', in D. Hawkin (ed.), *Self-Definition and Self-Discovery in Early Christianity: A Study in Changing Horizons* (SBEC, 26; Lewiston, 1990), pp. 147–66; Christopher J. Probst, *Anti-Judaism and the Fourth Gospel* (Louisville, 2001); and Raimo Hakola, *Identity Matters: John, the Jews, and Jewishness* (NovTSup, 118; Leiden, 2005).

24. See J. Andrew Overman, *Matthew's Gospel and Formative Judaism: The Social World of the Matthean Community* (Minneapolis, 1990); David C. Sim, *The Gospel of Matthew and Christian Judaism: The History and Setting of the Matthean Community* (Edinburgh, 1998); and Anthony O. Ewherido, *Matthew's Gospel and Judaism in the Late First Century CE: The Evidence from Matthew's Chapter on Parables* (SBL, 91; New York, 2006).

25. See Meg Davies, 'Stereotyping the other: the "Pharisees" in the Gospel according to Matthew', in J. Cheryl Exum and Stephen D. Moore (eds), *Biblical Studies/Cultural Studies: The Third Sheffield Colloquium* (Sheffield, 1998), pp. 415–32; and Wolfgang Reinhold, 'Das Matthäus-evangelium, die Pharisäer und die Tora', *BZ* 50 (2006), pp. 51–73.

26. The classic statement of this view is that of Krister Stendahl, *The School of Saint Matthew and Its Use of the Old Testament* (ASNU, 20; Copenhagen, 1954). See also Petri Luomanen, 'The "sociology of sectarianism" in Matthew modeling the genesis of early Jewish and Christian communities', in Ismo Dunderberg, Christopher M. Tuckett and Kari Syreeni (eds), *Fair Play – Diversity and Conflicts in Early Christianity: Essays in Honor of Heikki Räisänen* (Leiden, 2002), pp. 107–30.

27. See Chapter 8.

28. See E.R. Goodenough, *The Theology of Justin Martyr* (Jena, 1923); Henry Chadwick, 'Justin Martyr's defence of Christianity', *BJRL* 47 (1965), pp. 275–97; L.W. Barnard, *Justin Martyr: His Life and Thought* (Cambridge, 1967); E.F. Osborn, *Justin Martyr* (BHT, 47; Tübingen, 1973); O. Skarsaune, *The Proof from Prophecy: A Study in Justin Martyr's Proof-Text Tradition: Text-Type, Provenance, Theological Profile* (NovTSup, 56; Leiden, 1987); Timothy J. Horner, *Listening to Trypho: Justin Martyr's Dialogue Reconsidered* (Leuven, 2001); Craig D. Allert, *Revelation, Truth, Canon, and Interpretation: Studies in Justin Martyr's Dialogue with Trypho* (Leiden, 2002); and the very important Justin Martyr, *Dialogue avec Tryphon: édition critique*, edited by Philippe Bobichon (2 vols; Fribourg, 2003).

29. 'Talking at Trypho: Christian apologetic as anti-Judaism in Justin's Dialogue with Trypho the Jew', in Mark Edwards, Martin Goodman, Simon R.F. Price and Christopher Rowland (eds), *Apologetics in the Roman Empire: Pagans, Jews and Christians* (Oxford, 1999), pp. 59–80; citation p. 71.

30. See David Rokéah, *Justin Martyr and the Jews* (Leiden, 2002).

31. Horbury, 'The Benediction of the *Minim*'.

32. See the review of scholarship in Rajak, 'Talking at Trypho', pp. 75–80.

33. See his classic essay, 'Die Christuspartei in der korinthischen Gemeinde,

der Gegensatz des petrinischen und paulinischen Christenthums in der alten Kirche, der Apostel Petrus in Rom', *TZTh* (1831), pp. 61–206; and G. Lüdemann, *Opposition to Paul in Jewish Christianity* (ET Minneapolis, 1989), p. 321. More recent studies include G. Hoennicke, *Das Judenchristentum im ersten und zweiten Jahrhundert* (Berlin, 1908), pp. 1–19; A.F.J. Klijn, 'The study of Jewish Christianity', *NTS* 20 (1974), pp. 419–31; A.F.J. Klijn and G.S. Reininck, *Patristic Evidence for Jewish-Christian Sects* (NovTSup, 36; Leiden, 1973); and James Carleton-Paget, 'Jewish Christianity', in William Horbury, W.D. Davies and John Sturdy (eds), *The Cambridge History of Judaism*, vol. iii: *The Early Roman Period* (Cambridge, 1999), pp. 731–75; and Peter J. Tomson and Doris Lambers-Petry (eds), *The Image of the Judaeo-Christians in Ancient Jewish and Christian Literature* (WUNT, 158; Tübingen, 2003); Judith Frishman, Willemien Otten and Gerard Rouwhorst (eds), *Religious Identity and the Problem of Historical Foundation: The Foundational Character of Authoritative Sources in the History of Christianity and Judaism* (JCPS, 8; Leiden, 2004).

34. See Bruce Chilton and Craig Evans (eds), *The Missions of James, Peter and Paul: Tensions in Early Christianity* (NovTSup, 115; Leiden, 2005).

35. See Bruce Chilton and Craig Evans (eds), *James the Just and Christian Origins* (NovTSup, 98; Leiden, 1999); and Bruce Chilton and Jacob Neusner (eds), *The Brother of Jesus: James the Just and His Mission* (Louisville, 2001).

36. See the discussion of this passage by Craig R. Koester, 'The origin and significance of the Flight to Pella tradition', *CBQ* 51 (1989), pp. 97–105; J. Verheyden, 'The flight of the Christians to Pella', *ETL* 66 (1990), pp. 369f.; Carleton-Paget, 'Jewish Christianity', pp. 746–9; and P.H.R. van Houwelingen, 'Fleeing forward: the departure of Christians from Jerusalem to Pella', *WTJ* 65 (2003), pp. 181–200.

37. *Judentum und Judenchristentum in Justins Dialog mit Trypho* (Leipzig, 1913), p. 90.

38. See Klijn and Reininck, *Patristic Evidence*, pp. 19–43; Glenn Alan Koch, 'A critical investigation of Epiphanius' Knowledge of the Ebionites' (Unpublished PhD dissertation, University of Pennsylvania, 1976); James R. Edwards, 'The Gospel of the Ebionites and the Gospel of Luke', *NTS* 48 (2002), pp. 568–86; Josef Verheyden, 'Epiphanius on the Ebionites', in Tomson and Lambers-Petry (eds), *Image*, pp. 182–208; and Michael D. Goulder, 'Hebrews and the Ebionites', *NTS* 49 (2003), pp. 393–406.

39. See Klijn and Reininck, *Patristic Evidence*, pp. 3–19.

40. See Klijn and Reininck, *Patristic Evidence*, pp. 44–52; R. Pritz, *Nazarene Jewish Christianity* (Jerusalem and Leiden, 1988); and W. Kinzig, ' "Non-Separation": closeness and cooperation between Jews and Christians in the fourth century', *VC* 41 (1991), pp. 27–53.

41. See Carleton-Paget, 'Jewish Christianity', pp. 761–4.

42. See Carleton-Paget, 'Jewish Christianity', pp. 764–6; P. Vielhauer and G. Strecker, 'Jewish-Christian Gospels', in E. Hennecke, rev. W. Schneemelcher, *New Testament Apocrypha* (rev. ET Cambridge, 1991), pp. 134–78; A.F.J. Klijn, *Jewish-Christian Gospel Tradition* (Leiden, 1992); Andrew Gregory, 'Prior or posterior? The Gospel of the Ebionites and the

Gospel of Luke', *NTS* 51 (2005), pp. 344–60; *idem*, 'Hindrance or help: does the modern category of "Jewish-Christian Gospel" distort our understanding of the texts to which it refers?', *JSNT* 28 (2006), pp. 387–413.

Chapter 27

1. For a review of this evidence see Barbara E. Thiering, 'Qumran initiation and New Testament baptism', *NTS* 27 (1981), pp. 615–31. Her conclusions would not be accepted by all scholars, however. See further Adela Yarbro Collins, 'The origin of Christian baptism', *SL* 19 (1989), pp. 28–46.
2. ET London, 1999. This is reviewed by John Riches, *JTS* 55 (2004), pp. 208–16.
3. Pt. iii, pp. 121–60. See also pt. i, pp. 19–60.
4. Theissen, *Primitive Christian Religion*, p. 121.
5. *Primitive Christian Religion*, p. 125.
6. In addition to the literature mentioned in Chapter 12, see Paul W. Hollenbach, 'The conversion of Jesus: from Jesus the baptizer to Jesus the healer', in W. Haase (ed.), *ANRW* II.25.1 (Berlin, 1982), pp. 196–219; Martinus C. de Boer, 'Jesus the Baptizer: 1 John 5:5-8 and the Gospel of John', *JBL* 107 (1988), pp. 87–106; J. Ernst, 'Johannes der Taufer und Jesus from Nazareth in historischer Sicht', *NTS* 43 (1997), pp. 161–83; and Bruce D. Chilton, *Jesus' Baptism and Jesus' Healing: His Personal Practice of Spirituality* (Harrisburg, 1998).
7. See Chapter 12.
8. See the important collection of essays edited by Stanley E. Porter and Anthony R. Cross, *Baptism, the New Testament and the Church* (Sheffield, 1999); and Stanley E. Porter (ed.), *Dimensions of Baptism: Biblical and Theological Studies* (JSNTSup, 234; London, 2002).
9. C.F.D Moule, 'The nature and purpose of 1 Peter', *NTS* 3 (1956–7), pp. 1–11; and J.H. Neyrey, 'First Peter and converts', *TBT* 22 (1984), pp. 13–18.
10. See Nathan Mitchell, 'Baptism in the Didache', in Clayton N. Jefford (ed.), *The Didache in Context: Essays in its Text, History, and Transmission* (NovT-Sup, 77; Leiden, 1995), pp. 226–55; Willy Rordorf, trans. Jonathan Draper, 'Baptism according to the Didache', in Jonathan A. Draper (ed.), *The Didache in Modern Research* (AGJU, 39; Leiden, 1996), pp. 212–22; and Robert L. Williams, 'Baptism in two early church orders', *Southwestern Journal of Theology* 43 (2001), pp. 17–31.
11. 'Baptism in the first-century churches: a case for caution', in D.J.A. Clines, Stephen E. Fowl and Stanley E. Porter (eds), *The Bible in Three Dimensions: Essays in Celebration of Forty Years of Biblical Studies in the University of Sheffield* (SBT, 5; Sheffield, 1990), pp. 249–67. See also A.Y. Collins, 'The origin of Christian baptism', *Studia Liturgica* 19 (1989), pp. 28–46.
12. Hickling, 'Baptism', p. 250.
13. 'Baptism', p. 250.
14. See Joel B. Green, 'From "John's Baptism" to "baptism into the name of the Lord Jesus": the significance of baptism in Luke–Acts', in Porter and Cross (eds), *Baptism*, pp. 157–72.
15. *'In Namen Jesu'. Eine Sprach- und religionsgeschichtliche Untersuchung zum*

Neuen Testament, speziell zur altchristlichen Taufe (FRLANT, 1/2; Göttingen, 1903).

16. *Into the Name of the Lord Jesus: Baptism in the Early Church* (Edinburgh, 1997).

17. See Francis J. Moloney, *A Body Broken for a Broken People: Eucharist in the New Testament* (Peabody, 1997).

18. See J.M. van Congh, 'Evolution in the tradition of the Last Supper (Mk 14, 22-26 and par)', in B. Kollmann, W. Reinbold and A. Strodel (eds), *Antikes Judentum und frühes Christentum: Festschrift für Hartmut Stegemann zum 65 Geburtstag* (Berlin, 1999), pp. 364–88.

19. See Paul F. Bradshaw, 'The eucharistic sayings of Jesus', *SL* 35 (2005), pp. 1–11.

20. See Chapter 14.

21. See further Athalya Brenner and J.W. van Henten (eds), *Food and Drink in the Biblical World* (*Semeia* 86, 1999).

22. *Early Christian Worship* (ET London, 1953). See also Cullmann with F.J. Leenhardt, *Essays on the Lord's Supper* (ET London, 1958).

23. *Messe und Herrenmahl* (1926).

24. On this important text see Hub van de Sandt and David Flusser, 'The Didache: its Jewish sources and its place in early Judaism and Christianity', in M. de Jonge and S. Safrai (eds), *Compendia Rerum Iudaicarum et Novum Testamentum*, Section 3: *Jewish Tradition in Early Christian Literature*, vol. v (Assen and Minneapolis, 1974); C.N. Jefford (ed.), *The Didache in Context: Essays on its Text, History and Transmission* (NovTSup, 77; Leiden, 1995); Jonathan A. Draper (ed.), *The Didache in Modern Research* (AGJU, 39; Leiden, 1996); and Kurt Niederwimmer, trans. Linda M. Maloney and ed. Harold W. Attridge, *The Didache: A Commentary* (Hermeneia; Minneapolis, 1998).

25. See A. Vööbus, *Liturgical Tradition in the Didache* (Stockholm, 1968); Johannes Betz trans. Jonathan A. Draper, 'The eucharist in the Didache', in Draper (ed.), *Didache*, pp. 244–75; and Enrico Mazza trans. Lynda Palazzo, 'Didache 9–10: elements of a eucharistic interpretation', in Draper (ed.), *Didache*, pp. 276–99.

26. See Jospeh Ysebaert, 'The eucharist as a love-meal (agape) in *Didache* 9–10, and its development in the Pauline and in the Syrian tradition', in A. Hilhorst (ed.), *The Apostolic Age in Patristic Thought* (Leiden, 2004), pp. 11–27; and Paul F. Bradshaw, 'Yet another explanation of *Didache* 9–10', *Studia Liturgica* 36 (2006), pp. 124–8. There is interesting material also in Dennis E. Smith, *From Symposium to Eucharist: The Banquet in the Early Christian World* (Minneapolis, 2003).

27. Betz, 'Eucharist'.

28. For a statement of the issues see Paul F. Bradshaw, 'Anamnesis in modern eucharistic debate', in Michael A. Signer (ed.), *Memory and History in Christianity and Judaism* (Notre Dame, 2001), pp. 77–84.

Chapter 28

1. See K.H. Rengstorf, *Apostolate and Ministry: The New Testament Doctrine of the Office of the Ministry* (St Louis, 1969); C.K. Barrett, *Church, Ministry and Sacraments in the New Testament* (Grand Rapids, 1985); R. Schnackenburg,

The Church in the New Testament (ET New York, 1965); H. von Campen-hausen, *Ecclesiastical Authority and Spiritual Power in the Church of the First Three Centuries* (ET Peabody, 1997); and David A. DeSilva, *An Introduction to the New Testament: Contexts, Methods and Ministry Formation* (Downers Grove, 2004).

2. See H. Paulsen, *Studien zur Theologie des Ignatius von Antiochien* (Theopha-neia, 27; Göttingen, 1976); P. Meinhold, *Studien zu Ignatius von Antiochien* (VIEG, 97; Wiesbaden, 1979); W.R. Schoedel, *Ignatius of Antioch: A Commentary on the Letters of Ignatius* (Hermeneia; Philadelphia, 1985); and Mikael Isacson, *To Each their Own Letter: Structure, Themes, and Rhetorical Strategies in the Letters of Ignatius of Antioch* (CB, 42; Stockholm, 2004). There is fascinating material also in Paul Trebilco, *The Early Christians in Ephesus from Paul to Ignatius* (WUNT, 166; Tübingen, 2004).

3. See Schoedel, *Ignatius*, pp. 22–3.

4. See E. Lohse, 'Die Entstehung des Bischofsamtes in der frühen Christenheit', *ZNW* 71 (1980), pp. 58–73; Adam Hensley, 'Submission to bishop, presbytery and deacons in the letters of St. Ignatius of Antioch', *LTJ* 35 (2001), pp. 75–86; Harry O. Maier, 'The politics of the silent bishop: silence and persuasion in Ignatius of Antioch', *JTS* 55 (2004), pp. 503–19.

5. See Michael Slusser, 'Docetism: a historical perspective', *Second Century* 1/3 (1981), pp. 163–72; and I.S.A. Saliba, 'The bishop of Antioch and the heretics: a study of primitive Christology', *EQ* 54 (1982), pp. 65–76.

6. See Patrick Burke, 'Monarchical episcopate at the end of the first century', *JES* 7 (1970), pp. 499–518; and Eric G. Jay, 'From presbyter-bishops to bishops and presbyters', *Second Century* 1/3 (1982), pp. 125–62.

7. See Matthew W. Mitchell, 'In the footsteps of Paul: scriptural and apostolic authority in Ignatius of Antioch', *JECS* 14 (2006), pp. 27–45.

8. On which see Richard E. Boger, 'The historic episcopal succession', *Lutheran Forum* 34 (2000), pp. 21–5.

9. Schoedel, *Ignatius*, p. 49.

10. See Schoedel, *Ignatius*, p. 22.

11. See Part II; and Willi Marxsen, *Jesus and the Church: The Beginnings of Christianity* (Valley Forge, 1992).

12. See Chapters 13 and 14; and also J.C. O'Neill, *Who Did Jesus Think He Was?* (BIS, 11; Leiden, 1995).

13. See Chapter 11.

14. The classic study is Martin Hengel, *Between Jesus and Paul* (ET London, 1983). There is interesting material also in David Wenham, *Paul and Jesus: The True Story* (London, 2002).

15. See Chapter 16.

16. On whom see John Painter, *Just James: The Brother of Jesus in History and Tradition* (Edinburgh, 1999); Bruce D. Chilton and Craig A. Evans, *James the Just and Christian Origins* (NovTSup, 98; Leiden, 1999); Bruce Chilton and Jacob Neusner (eds), *The Brother of Jesus: James the Just and his Mission* (Louisville, 2001); and Bruce D. Chilton and Craig A. Evans (eds), *The Missions of James, Peter, and Paul: Tensions in Early Christianity* (Leiden, 2005).

17. See further Richard Bauckham, *Jude and the Relatives of Jesus in the Early Church* (Edinburgh, 1990). The source of the information about Symeon is

Eusebius, *Hist. Eccl.* 4.5. Eusebius states also that Symeon was crucified in the reign of Trajan (*Hist. Eccl.* 3.31).

18. In Luke's Gospel, however, the term 'apostle' is used synonymously with 'the twelve' (see esp. Lk. 6.13) as if Luke is restricting the usage to those figures to whom the historical Jesus had delegated eschatological responsibility.

19. See W. Schmithals, *The Office of the Apostle in the Early Church* (Nashville, 1969); K.H. Rengstorf, 'apostolos', in *TDNT*, vol. i, pp. 407–49; R. Schnackenburg, 'Apostles before and during Paul's time', in W.W. Gasque and R.P. Martin (eds), *Apostolic History and the Gospel* (Grand Rapids, 1970), pp. 287–303; and F.H. Agnew, 'The origin of the New Testament apostle-concept: a review of research', *JBL* 105 (1980), pp. 75–96.

20. Provocative is Eldon Jay Epp, *Junia: The First Woman Apostle* (Minneapolis, 2005).

21. There is a good explication of this Jewish background in Jan-A. Bühner, *Der Gesandte und sein weg im 4. Evangelium* (WUNT, 2.2; Tübingen, 1977).

22. See Robert P. Meye, *Jesus and the Twelve* (Grand Rapids, 1968); W. Trilling, 'Zur Entstehung des Zwölferkreises: eine geschichtskritische Überlegung', in R. Schnackenburg, J. Ernst and J. Wanke, *Die Kirche des Anfangs: Festschrift für Heinz Schürmann* (Leipzig, 1977), pp. 201–22; John P. Meier, 'The circle of the twelve: did it exist during Jesus' ministry?', *JBL* 116 (1997), pp. 635–72; and Scot McKnight, 'Jesus and the twelve', *BBR* 11 (2001), pp. 203–31.

23. An outstanding article is G. Friedrich, 'Prophetes', in *TDNT*, vol. vi, pp. 828–61. See also D. Hill, *New Testament Prophecy* (London, 1979); G. Dautzenberg, *Urchristliche Prophetie: Ihre Erforschung, ihre Voraussetzungen im Judentum und ihre Struktur im ersten Korintherbrief* (BWANT, 104; Stuttgart, 1975); U.B. Müller, *Prophetie und Predigt im Neuen Testament: Formgeschichtliche Untersuchungen zur urchristlichen Prophetie* (SNT, 10; Gütersloh, 1975); J. Panagopoulos (ed.), *Prophetic Vocation in the New Testament and Today* (NOVTSup, 45; Leiden, 1977); D.E. Aune, *Prophecy in Early Christianity and the Mediterranean World* (Grand Rapids, 1983); Christopher B. Forbes, *Prophecy and Inspired Speech in Early Christianity and its Hellenistic Environment* (WUNT, 75; Tübingen, 1995); Laura S. Nasrallah, *An Ecstasy of Folly: Prophecy and Authority in Early Christianity* (Cambridge MA, 2003); and Barbara R. Rossing, 'Prophets, prophetic movements and the voices of women', in Richard A. Horsley (ed.), *Christian Origins* (Minneapolis, 2005), pp. 261–80.

24. This charge appears related to the problem of docetism which we examined in Chapter 27.

25. See Aaron Milavec, 'Distinguishing true and false prophets: the protective wisdom of the *Didache*', *JECS* 2 (1994), pp. 117–36; Jonathan A. Draper, 'Weber, Theissen, and "wandering charismatics" in the *Didache*', *JECS* 6 (1998), pp. 541–76; and Kurt Niederwimmer, trans. Jonathan Draper, 'An examination of the development of itinerant radicalism in the environment and tradition of the *Didache*', in Draper (ed.), *The Didache in Modern Research* (AGJU, 39; Leiden, 1996), pp. 321–9.

26. See my explanation of this theme in *Disciples of the Beloved One: The Christology, Social Setting and Theological Context of the Ascension of Isaiah* (JSPSup, 18; Sheffield, 1996), ch. 3. I think that the *Ascension of Isaiah* comes from

the early second century CE, and thus that it is a close contemporary of Ignatius.

27. *The Acts of the Apostles* (ICC; 2 vols.; Edinburgh, 1994), vol. i, p. 304.

28. See Hengel, *Between Jesus and Paul*, pp. 1–29.

29. See J. Colson, *La Fonction diaconale aux origines de l'église* (Paris, 1960); J.G. Davies, 'Deacons, deaconesses and the minor orders in the patristic period', *JEH* 14 (1963), pp. 1–15; G.W.H. Lampe, 'Diakonia in the early church', in J.I. McCord and T.H.L. Parker (eds), *Service in Christ* (Grand Rapids, 1966), pp. 49–64; E.R. Hardy, 'Deacons in history and practice', in R.T. Nolan (ed.), *The Diaconate Now* (Washington, 1968); L.R. Hennessey, '*Diakonia* and *diakonoi* in the pre-Nicene church', in T. Halton and J.P. Williman (eds), *Diakonia: Studies in Honor of Robert T. Meyer* (Washington, 1986), pp. 60–86; J.N. Collins, *Diakonia: Re-Interpreting the Ancient Sources* (Oxford, 1990) and U. Falesiedi, *Le diaconie: I servizi assistanziali nella chiesa antica* (Rome, 1995).

30. See G. Bornkamm, '*Presbus, presbuteros*', in *TDNT*, vol. v, pp. 651–80; J.G. Sobosan, 'The role of the presbyter: an investigation into the *Adversus Haereses* of Saint Irenaeus', *SJT* 27 (1974), pp. 129–46; A.E. Harvey, 'Elders', *JTS* 26 (1975), pp. 403–5; R.A. Campbell, *The Elders: Seniority within Earliest Christianity* (Edinburgh, 1994); F.M. Young, 'On *episkopos* and *presbuteros*', *JTS* 45 (1994), pp. 142–8; Daniel Callam, 'Bishops and presbyters in the apostolic fathers', in Elizabeth A. Livingstone (ed.), *Studia Patristica* (Louvain, 1997), pp. 107–11; and by Clayton N. Jefford in the same volume, 'Presbyters in the community of the *Didache*', pp. 122–8.

31. See Sobosan, 'Role of the presbyter'.

32. See Gregory Dix, 'Ministry in the early church', in K.E. Kirk (ed.), *The Apostolic Ministry* (London, 1946), pp. 185–303; J. Colson, *L'Évêque dans les communautés primitives* (Paris, 1951); W. Telfer, *The Office of a Bishop* (London, 1962); idem, *L'épiscopat catholique: collegialité et primauté dans les trois premiers siècles de l'église* (Paris, 1963); E. Ferguson, 'Church order in the sub-apostolic period: a survey of interpretation', *RQ* 11 (1968), pp. 225–48; R.E. Brown, *Priest and Bishop: Biblical Reflections* (Paramus NJ, 1970); E. Dassmann, 'Zur Entstehung des Monepiskopats', *JAC* 17 (1974), pp. 74–90; H. Chadwick, E.C. Hobbs and W. Wuellner (eds), *The Role of the Christian Bishop in Ancient Society* (Berkeley, 1980); and A. Cunningham, *The Bishop in the Church: Patristic Texts on the Role of the Episkopos* (Wilmington, 1985).

33. See Markus Bockmuehl, *The Epistle to the Philippians* (London, 1997), pp. 53–5.

34. See Kenneth A. Strand, 'The rise of the monarchical episcopate', *Andrews University Seminary Studies* 4 (1966), pp. 65–88; and J. Burns Patout, *Cyprian the Bishop* (London, 2002).

35. A crucial study is John A.T. Robinson, *The Body* (SBT, 5; London, 1953). See also Ernest Best, *One Body in Christ* (London, 1955); and the examination of Michelle V. Lee, *Paul, the Stoics, and the Body of Christ* (SNTSMS, 137; Cambridge, 2006).

36. See the brief but suggestive comments of Alan Segal, *Paul the Convert* (New Haven and London, 1990), pp. 62–3.

37. See Chapter 16.

38. *The Body.*
39. Schweizer, in *TDNT*, vol. vii, pp. 1057–94.
40. See the summary in James D.G. Dunn, *The Theology of Paul the Apostle* (Grand Rapids and Edinburgh, 1988), pp. 548–52.

Chapter 29

1. There are many books on this topic. Among the most familiar see Wayne A. Meeks, *The First Urban Christians* (New Haven, 1983); Abraham J. Malherbe, *Social Aspects of Early Christianity* (Philadelphia, ²1983); Gerd Theissen, *The Social Setting of Pauline Christianity* (Philadelphia, 1982); Bruce J. Malina, *Christian Origins and Cultural Anthropology* (Atlanta, 1986); Richard A. Horsley, *Paul and Empire* (Harrisburg, 1997); Wolfgang Stegemann, Bruce J. Malina and Gerd Theissen, *The Social Setting of Jesus and the Gospels* (Minneapolis, 2002); Anthony J. Blasi, Jean Duhaime and Paul-André Turcotte, *Handbook of Early Christianity: Social Science Approaches* (Walnut Creek, CA, 2002); and J.G. van der Watt and F.S. Malan (eds), *Identity, Ethics, and Ethos in the New Testament* (Berlin, 2006).
2. See Chapter 18.
3. On the problems posed by Paul's death see Chapter 17. Peter's death in Rome is apparently mentioned by *Asc. Isa.* 4.3. See also E. Kirschbaum, *Die Gräber der Apostelfürsten* (Frankfurt, ³1974); Peter Oakes (ed.), *Rome in the Bible and the Early Church* (Grand Rapids, 2002); and Michael D. Goulder, 'Did Peter ever go to Rome?', *SJT* 57 (2004), pp. 377–96.
4. See Wayne A. Meeks and Robert L. Wilken, *Jews and Christians in Antioch in the First Four Centuries of the Common Era* (SBS, 13; Missouri, 1978); Robert L. Wilken, *The Christians as The Romans Saw Them* (New Haven, 1984); and Magnus Zetterholm, *The Formation of Christianity in Antioch: A Social-Scientific Approach to the Separation Between Judaism and Christianity* (London, 2003).
5. Wayne A. Meeks, *The Moral World of the First Christians* (LEC, 6; Philadelphia, 1986). By the same author see also *The Origins of Christian Morality* (New Haven, 1993); ' "To walk worthily of the Lord": moral formation in the Pauline school exemplified by the letter to Colossians', in Eleonore Stump and Thomas P. Flint (eds), *Hermes and Athena: Biblical Exegesis and Philosophical Theology* (Notre Dame, 1993), pp. 37–58; *In Search of the Early Christians* (New Haven, 2001); and *Christ is The Question* (Louisville, 2006).
6. Meeks, *Moral World*, pp. 102–4.
7. *Moral World*, p. 102. See also his 'Apocalyptic discourse and strategies of goodness', *Journal of Religion* 80 (2000), pp. 461–75.
8. On which see Wendell Lee Willis, *Idol Meat in Corinth: The Pauline Argument in 1 Corinthians 8 and 10* (SBLDS, 68; Chico, 1985).
9. See also David Horrell, *Solidarity and Difference: A Contemporary Reading of Paul's Ethics* (London, 2005).
10. *Moral World*, pp. 113–19.
11. See also Richard A. Horsley, 'Moral economy and renewal movement in Q', in Richard A. Horsley (ed.), *Oral Performance, Popular Tradition, and Hidden Transcript in Q* (Atlanta, 2006), pp. 143–57.

12. *Moral World*, p. 119.
13. 'The significance of the delay of the parousia for early Christianity', in Gerald F. Hawthorne (ed.), *Current Issues in Biblical and Patristic Interpretation* (Grand Rapids, 1975), pp. 82–107.
14. See Part II.
15. See Part III.
16. On this topic see J.L. Houlden, *Ethics and the New Testament* (Harmondsworth, 1973); Jack T. Sanders, *Ethics in the New Testament* (Philadelphia, 1975); W. Schrage, *The Ethics of the New Testament* (ET Edinburgh, 1988); Willi Marxsen, *New Testament Foundation for Christian Ethics* (ET Edinburgh, 1993); Gerd Theissen, *Social Reality and the Early Christians: Theology, Ethics and the World of the New Testament* (ET Edinburgh, 1983); and Frank J. Matera, *New Testament Ethics: The Legacies of Jesus and Paul* (Louisville, 1996).
17. A good discussion is that of C.E.B. Cranfield, *Romans*, vol. i (ICC; Edinburgh, 1975), pp. 413–14.
18. See Meeks, *Moral World*, ch. 5.
19. There is a good discussion in Schrage, *Ethics*, pp. 257–68.
20. Schrage, *Ethics*, p. 258.
21. On the issues raised here see Graham N. Stanton and Gedaliahu A.G. Stroumsa, *Tolerance and Intolerance in Early Judaism and Christianity* (New York, 1998).
22. Schrage, *Ethics*, p. 259. See also his p. 261.
23. *Ethics*, p. 263.
24. *Ecclesiastical Authority and Spiritual Power in the Church of the First Three Centuries* (Stanford, 1969), p. 113.
25. *Ethics*, p. 263.
26. A useful study is that of Richard Bauckham, *James: Wisdom of Jesus, Disciple of Jesus the Sage* (NTR; London, 1999). See also Schrage, *Ethics*, pp. 281–93.
27. Bauckham, *James*, p. 13.
28. His work is published as M. Dibelius and H. Greeven, *James* (Hermeneia; Philadelphia, 1976).
29. See Martin Hengel, 'Der Jakobusbrief als antipaulinische Polemiker', in G. Hawthorne and O. Betz (eds), *Tradition and Interpretation in the New Testament: Essays in Honor of E. Earle Ellis* (Grand Rapids and Tübingen, 1987), pp. 248–78.
30. See Patrick A. Tiller, 'The rich and poor in James: an apocalyptic ethic', in Benjamin G. Wright and Lawrence M. Wills (eds), *Conflicted Boundaries in Wisdom and Apocalypticism* (SBLSS, 35; Atlanta, 2005), pp. 169–79.
31. On this general issue see Alan Kirk and Tom Thatcher (eds), *Memory, Tradition, and Text: Uses of the Past in Early Christianity* (Atlanta, 2005).
32. Text edited by Willy Rordorf, *La doctrine des douze apôtres* (SC; Paris, [2]1998). Commentary by K. Niederwimmer, *The Didache* (Hermeneia; Minneapolis, 1998). See also Clayton N. Jefford (ed.), *The Didache in Context: Essays on its Text, History and Transmission* (NovTSup, 77; Leiden, 1994); Jonathan A. Draper (ed.), *The Didache in Modern Research* (AGJU, 37; Leiden, 1996); and Huub van der Sandt and David Flusser, *The Didache: Its Jewish Sources and its Place in Early Judaism and Christianity* (CRINT, 5; Assen and Minneapolis, 2002).

33. On which see Richard A. Freund, 'The Decalogue in early Judaism and Christianity', in Craig A. Evans and James A. Sanders (eds), *The Function of Scripture in Early Jewish and Christian Tradition* (JSNTSup, 54; Sheffield, 1998), pp. 124–41.
34. See Jonathan A. Draper, 'Weber, Theissen, and "wandering charismatics" in the Didache', *JECS* 6 (1998), pp. 541–76.
35. See further Vicky Balabanski, *Eschatology in the Making: Mark, Matthew and the Didache* (SNTSMS, 92; Cambridge, 1997).
36. See Hans R. Seeliger and Jonathan A. Draper, 'Consideration of the background and purpose of the apocalyptic conclusion of the *Didache*', in Draper (ed.), pp. 373–82.
37. See further Willi Rordorf, 'La Didaché en 1999', *Studia Patristica*, vol. xxxvi (Leuven, 2001), pp. 293–9.
38. P. Bettiolo, A. Giambelluca Kossova, C. Leonardi, E. Norelli and L. Perrone (eds), *Ascensio Isaiae: Textus* (CCSA, 7; Turnhout, 1995); E. Norelli (ed.), *Ascensio Isaiae: Commentarius* (CCSA, 8; Turnhout, 1995); E. Norelli, *L'Ascensione di Isaia: Studi su un apocrifo al crocevia dei cristianesimi* (Origini NS 1; Bologna, 1995); *idem, Ascension du prophète Isaïe* (Turnhout, 1993); M. Pesce (ed.), *Isaia, il Diletto e la Chiesa: Visione e esegesi profetica cristiano-primitive nell'Ascensione di Isaia* (TRSZ, 20; Brescia, 1983); A. Acerbi, *Serra Lignea: Studi sulla Fortuna della Ascensione di Isaia* (Rome, 1984); *idem, L'Ascensione di Isaia: Cristologia e profetismo in Siria nei primi decenni del II secolo* (SPM, 17; Milan, 1989). Robert G. Hall, 'The Ascension of Isaiah: community situation, date and place in early Christianity', *JBL* 109 (1990), pp. 289–306; *idem, Revealed Histories: Techniques for Ancient Jewish Historiography* (JSPSup, 6; Sheffield, 1991), pp. 137–47; Jonathan Knight, *The Ascension of Isaiah* (GAP, 2; Sheffield, 1995); *idem, Disciples of the Beloved One: The Christology, Social Setting and Theological Context of the Ascension of Isaiah* (JSPSup, 18; Sheffield, 1996); and Richard Bauckham, *The Fate of the Dead* (Leiden, 1998), pp. 363–90.
39. See Col. 3.1; and esp. Eph. 6.12.
40. See my *Disciples*, ch. 3.
41. For evidence of further conflict see Clayton N. Jefford, 'Conflict at Antioch: Ignatius and the Didache at odds', *Studia Patristica*, vol. xxxvi, pp. 262–89.
42. See Adam Hensley, 'Submission to bishop, presbytery and deacons in the letters of Saint Ignatius of Antioch', *LTJ* 35 (2001), pp. 75–86; and Harry O. Maier, 'The politics of the silent bishop: silence and persuasion in Ignatius of Antioch', *JTS* 55 (2004), pp. 503–19.
43. See especially Schrage, *Ethics*, pt. v.

Chapter 30

1. On which see K. Rudolph, *Gnosis: The Nature and History of an Ancient Religion* (ET Edinburgh, 1983); *idem, Gnosis und spätantike religionsgeschichte: gesammelte aufsätze* (NHMS, 42; Leiden, 1996); Charles Hedrick and Robert Hodgson (eds), *Nag Hammadi, Gnosticism and Early Christianity* (Peabody, 1986); Ithamar Gruenwald, *From Apocalypticism to Gnosticism: Studies in Apocalypticism, Merkavah Mysticism and Gnosticism* (BEATAJ, 14; Frankfurt, 1988); Simone Pétrement, *A Separate God: The Christian Origins*

of Gnosticism (ET London, 1991); Walter Wink, *Cracking the Gnostic Code: The Powers in Gnosticism* (Atlanta, 1993); Pheme Perkins, *Gnosticism and the New Testament* (Minneapolis, 1993); Alasdair H.B. Logan, *Gnostic Truth and Christian Heresy: A Study in the History of Gnosticism* (Edinburgh, 1996); and Birger A. Pearson, *Gnosticism, Judaism and Egyptian Christianity* (Minneapolis, 1990); *idem, Gnosticism and Christianity in Roman and Coptic Egypt* (New York, 2004).

2. See John D. Turner, 'Sethian Gnosticism and Johannine Christianity', in Gilbert van Belle, J.G. van der Watt and P.J. Maritz (eds), *Theology and Christology in the Fourth Gospel* (Leuven, 2005), pp. 399–433.
3. James M. Robinson (ed.), *The Nag Hammadi Library in English* (Leiden, 1977).
4. *ABD*, vol. iv, pp. 988–9.
5. F. Wisse, 'Gnosticism and early monasticism in Egypt', in B. Aland (ed.), *Gnosis. Festschrift für Hans Jonas* (Göttingen, 1978), pp. 431–40.
6. Translation in Robinson (ed.), *Nag Hammadi Library*, pp. 98–116.
7. 'The problem of "Jewish Gnostic" literature', in Hedrick and Hodgson (eds), *Nag Hammadi, Gnosticism and Early Christianity*, pp. 15–35.
8. See A.F.J. Klijn, *Seth in Jewish, Christian and Gnostic Literature* (NovTSup, 46; Leiden, 1977); and John D. Turner, *Sethian Gnosticism and the Platonic Tradition* (BCNHSE, 6; Quebec, 2001).
9. *Gnostic Revisions of Genesis Stories and Early Jesus Traditions* (NHMS, 58; Leiden, 2006).
10. Marvin W. Meyer, *The Letter of Peter to Philip* (SBLDS, 53; Chico, 1981).
11. See the description of the *Acts of John* in Luttikhuizen, *Gnostic Revisions*, ch. 12; and the teaching attributed to Basileides in Irenaeus, *Adv. Haer.* 1.24.3–7.

Chapter 31

1. John A.T. Robinson, *Honest to God* (London, 1963); John Hick (ed.), *The Myth of God Incarnate* (London, 1977).
2. J.V.M. Sturdy, edited by Jonathan Knight, *Redrawing the Boundaries: The Date of Early Christian Literature* (London, 2007).

Appendix

1. *Jesus: An Historical and Theological Investigation* (London, 2004).
2. *Theology* 108 (2005), pp. 442–3.
3. Good introductions are Robert H. Stein, *The Synoptic Problem: An Introduction* (Grand Rapids, 1987); *idem*, and E.P. Sanders and Margaret Davies, *Studying the Synoptic Gospels* (London, 1989). See also W.R. Farmer, *The Synoptic Problem: A Critical Analysis* (Dillsboro, 1976); David Laird Dungan, *A History of the Synoptic Problem: The Canon, the Text, the Composition and the Interpretation of the Gospels* (ABRL; New York, 1999); David Alan Black and David R. Beck (eds), *Rethinking the Synoptic Problem* (Grand Rapids, 2001); and Robert Allen Daerrenbacker, *Ancient Compositional Practices and the Synoptic Problem* (BETL, 186; Louvain, 2005).
4. The best is K. Aland, *Synopsis Quattuor Evangeliorum* (Stuttgart, ⁷1984).

5. These have long been recognized as significant in study of the Synoptic problem. See Frans Neirynck, T. Hanson and F. van Segbroek (eds), *Minor Agreements of Matthew and Luke against Mark with a Cumulative List* (BETL, 37;Louvain, 1974); Frans Neirynck, *Minor Agreements of Matthew and Luke against Mark* (Gembloux, 1974); Jarmo Kiilunen, ' "Minor agreements" und die Hypothese von Lukas' Kenntnis des Matthäusevangeliums', in Ismo Dunderberg, Christopher M. Tuckett and Kari Syreeni (eds), *Fair Play: Diversity and Conflicts in Early Christianity: Essays in Honor of Heikki Räisänen* (NorTSup; Leiden, 2001), pp. 165–202; Frank Wheeler, *Textual Criticism and the Synoptic Problem: A Textual Commentary on the Minor Agreements of Matthew and Luke against Mark* (Ann Arbor, 2002); and Michael D. Goulder, 'Two significant minor agreements (Mat. 4.13 par.; Mat. 26.62-68 par.', *NovT* 45 (2003), pp. 365–73.

6. See Christopher M. Tuckett, *The Revival of the Griesbach Hypothesis: An Analysis and Appraisal* (SNTSMS 44; Cambridge, 1983); and Sherman E. Johnson, *The Griesbach Hypothesis and Redaction Criticism* (SBLMS 41; Atlanta, 1991).

7. See Delbert Burkett, *Rethinking the Gospel Sources*, vol. i: *From Proto-Mark to Mark* (London, 2004). On the problematic ending, N. Clayton Croy, *The Mutilation of Mark's Gospel* (Nashville, 2003).

8. Geoffrey Styler 'The Priority of Mark', in C.F.D. Moule, *The Birth of the New Testament* (London, [3]1981), Excursus IV, pp. 285–316. See also Arthur J. Bellinzoni, Joseph B. Tyson, and William O. Walker (eds), *The Two-Source Hypothesis: A Critical Appraisal* (Macon, 1985); and Mark S. Goodacre, *The Case Against Q: Studies in Marcan Priority and the Synoptic Problem* (Harrisburg, 2002). The dissenting position is represented in British New Testament scholarship by Christopher Tuckett. See his *Q and the History of Early Christianity: Studies on Q* (Edinburgh, 1996).

9. 'Priority of Mark', p. 305.

10. See David R. Catchpole, *The Quest for Q* (Edinburgh, 1993); Burton L. Mack, *The Lost Gospel: The Book of Q and Christian Origins* (San Francisco, 1994); Tuckett, *Q and the History of Early Christianity*; Marcus Borg, *The Lost Gospel: The Original Sayings of Jesus* (Berkeley, 1996); and Dale C. Allison, *The Jesus Tradition in Q* (Harrisburg, 1997). In the opposite corner, Austin Farrer, 'On dispensing with Q', reprinted in Bellinzoni, Tyson and Walker (eds), *The Two-Source Hypothesis*, pp. 321–56; Goodacre, *The Case Against Q*; and also John S. Kloppenborg, 'On dispensing with Q? Goodacre on the relation of Luke to Matthew', *NTS* 49 (2003), pp. 210–36; and Paul Foster, 'Is it possible to dispense with Q?', *NovT* 45 (2003), pp. 313–37.

11. See James M. Robinson (ed.), *The Critical Edition of Q: Synopsis including the Gospels of Matthew and Luke, Mark and Thomas with English, German and French Translations of Q and Thomas* (Leuven, 2000); James M. Robinson, Paul Hoffmann and John S. Kloppenborg (eds), *The Sayings Gospel Q in Greek and English: With Parallels from the Gospels of Mark and Thomas* (CBET, 30; Leuven, 2001); Richard Valantasis, *The New Q: A Fresh Translation with Commentary* (London, 2005); and Harry T. Fleddermann, *Q: A Reconstruction and Commentary* (BTS, 1; Leuven, 2005).

12. Sanders and Davies, *Studying the Synoptic Gospels*, pp. 67–83. See also Goodacre, *The Case against Q*; idem, *The Synoptic Problem: A Way Through the*

Maze (Sheffield, 2001); and Mark S. Goodacre and Nicholas Perrin (eds), *Questioning Q: A Multidimensional Approach* (London, 2004).

13. 'St. Mark's knowledge and use of Q', in W. Sanday (ed.), *Oxford Studies in the Synoptic Problem* (Oxford, 1911), pp. 165–83.

14. *Studying the Synoptic Gospels*, pp. 84–92.

15. *Studying the Synoptic Gospels*, pp. 93–7.

16. *Studying the Synoptic Gospels*, p. 92. See also the literature mentioned at nn. 12, 13 above.

17. Commentaries include C.E.B. Cranfield, *The Gospel According to St. Mark* (CGTC; Cambridge, 1959); D.E. Nineham, *The Gospel of St. Mark* (Harmondsworth, 1963); V. Taylor, *The Gospel According to St. Mark* (London, [2]1966); E. Lohmeyer, *Das Evangelium des Markus* (KEK; Göttingen, 1967); E. Schweizer, *The Good News according to Mark* (London, 1971); M.D. Hooker, *The Gospel According to St. Mark* (London, 1991); J. Gnilka, *Das Evangelium nach Markus* (EKK, 5th edn; Zurich, 1978–9); Ben Witherington, *The Gospel of Mark: A Socio-rhetorical Commentary* (Grand Rapids, 2001); R.T. France, *The Gospel of Mark: A Commentary on the Greek Text* (NIGTC; Grand Rapids, 2002); and Francis J. Moloney, *The Gospel of Mark: A Commentary* (Peabody, 2002). Other literature includes John Painter, *Mark's Gospel: Worlds in Conflict* (NTR; London, 1997); Maurice Casey, *Aramaic Sources of Mark's Gospel* (SNTSMS, 102; Cambridge, 1998); David M. Rhoads, *Mark as Story: An Introduction to the Narrative of a Gospel* (Minneapolis, [2]1999); Elizabeth Struthers Malbon, *In the Company of Jesus: Characters in Mark's Gospel* (Louisville, 2000); Dwight L. Peterson, *The Origins of Mark: The Markan Community in Current Debate* (BIS, 48; Leiden, 2000); Richard A. Horsley, *Hearing the Whole Story: The Politics of Plot in Mark's Gospel* (Louisville, 2001); Michael E. Vines, *The Problem of Markan Genre: The Gospel of Mark and the Jewish Novel* (SBLAB, 3; Leiden, 2002); Susan E. Miller, *Women in Mark's Gospel* (JSNTSup, 259; London, 2004); and Suzanne Watts Henderson, *Christology and Discipleship in the Gospel of Mark* (SNTSMS, 135; Cambridge, 2006).

18. See the review of scholarship in James G. Crossley, *The Date of Mark's Gospel: Insight from the Law in Earliest Christianity* (JSNTSup, 260; London, 2004). There is a fully annotated discussion in J.V.M. Sturdy, edited by Jonathan Knight, *Redrawing the Boundaries: Further Thoughts on the Date of the New Testament Literature* (London, 2007), ch. 7.

19. John A.T. Robinson, *Redating the New Testament* (London, 1975); Sturdy, *Redrawing the Boundaries*.

20. This evidence is reviewed by Crossley, *Date*, ch. 1.

21. Notably, by Michael Goulder, 'Did Peter ever go to Rome?', *SJT* 57 (2004), pp. 377–96.

22. Commentaries include Ernst Lohmeyer, *Das Evangelium des Matthäus* (KEK; Göttingen, 1962); F.W. Beare, *The Gospel According to St Matthew* (Oxford, 1981); Robert H. Gundry, *Matthew: A Commentary on His Literary and Theological Art* (Grand Rapids, 1982); David Hill, *The Gospel of Matthew* (NCB; London, 1972); W.D. Davies and Dale C. Allison, *A Critical and Exegetical Commentary on the Gospel according to Saint Matthew* (3 vols.; Edinburgh, 1988, 1989, 1997); Ulrich Luz, *Matthew 1–7: A Commentary* (ET Minneapolis, 1989); *idem*, *Matthew 8–20* (ET Minneapolis, 1990);

D.R.F. Hare, *Matthew* (IBC; Louisville, 1993); Daniel J. Harrington, *The Gospel of Matthew* (SacPag; Collegeville, 1991); Rudolph Schnackenburg, *The Gospel of Matthew* (ET Grand Rapids, 2002); and Ben Witherington, *Matthew* (SHBC, 19; Macon, 2006). Studies include Margaret Davies, *Matthew* (Readings; Sheffield, 1993); Ulrich Luz, *Matthew in History: Interpretation, Influence, and Effects* (Minneapolis, 1994); *idem, The Theology of the Gospel of Matthew* (NTT; ET Cambridge, 1995); Paul Foster, *Community, Law and Mission in Matthew's Gospel* (WUNT, 177; Tübingen, 2004); John Riches and David C. Sim (eds), *The Gospel of Matthew in its Roman Imperial Context* (ECC, 276; London, 2005); and Robert Charles Branden, *Satanic Conflict and the Plot of Matthew* (SBL, 89; New York, 2006).

23. See Anthony J. Saldarini, *Matthew's Christian–Jewish Community* (CSHJ; Chicago, 1994); David C. Sim, *The Gospel of Matthew and Christian Judaism: The History and Social Setting of the Matthean Community* (SNTIW; Edinburgh, 1998); and Aaron M. Gale, *Redefining Ancient Borders: The Jewish Scribal Framework of Matthew's Gospel* (London, 2005).

24. Anne M. O'Leary, *Matthew's Judaization of Mark: Examined in the Context of the Use of Sources in Graeco-Roman Antiquity* (SNTSMS, 323; London, 2006).

25. Sturdy, *Redrawing the Boundaries*, chs. 8 and 10. See also J. Verheyden (ed.), *The Unity of Luke–Acts* (BETL, 142; Louvain, 1999); and C. Kavin Rowe, 'History, hermeneutics and the unity of Luke–Acts', *JSNT* 28 (2005), pp. 131–57.

26. Commentaries include I.H. Marshall, *The Gospel of Luke* (Exeter, 1978); J.A. Fitzmyer, *The Gospel of Luke* (AB; Garden City NY, 1981–5); E. Schweizer, *The Good News According to Luke* (ET Atlanta, 1984); M.D. Goulder, *Luke: A New Paradigm* (JSNTSup, 20; 2 vols.; Sheffield, 1989); C.F. Evans, *Saint Luke* (London, 1990); and John Nolland, *Luke* (WBC 35a–c; 3 vols.; Waco, 1989–93). Studies include Eric Franklin, *Luke: Interpreter of Paul, Critic of Matthew* (JSNTSup, 92; Sheffield, 1994); Jonathan Knight, *Luke's Gospel* (NTR; London, 1998); David P. Moessner, *Jesus and the Heritage of Israel: Luke's Narrative Claim upon Israel's Legacy* (Harrisburg, 1999); Christopher Mount, *Pauline Christianity: Luke–Acts and the Legacy of Paul* (NovTSup, 104; Leiden, 2002); Charles H. Talbert, *Reading Luke–Acts in its Mediterranean Milieu* (NovTSup, 107; Leiden, 2003); Andrew Gregory, *The Reception of Luke–Acts in the Period before Irenaeus* (WUNT, 169; Tübingen, 2003) Clare K. Rothschild, *Luke–Acts and the Rhetoric of History: An Investigation of Early Christian Historiography* (WUNT, 175; Tübingen, 2004); Todd Klutz, *The Exorcism Stories in Luke–Acts: A Sociostylistic Reading* (SNTSMS, 129; Cambridge, 2004); François Bovon, *Luke the Theologian* (ET Waco, [2]2006); C. Kavin Rowe, *Early Narrative Christology: The Lord in the Gospel of Luke* (BZNW, 139; Berlin, 2006); and John B.F. Miller, *Convinced that God Has Called Us: Dreams, Visions and the Perception of God's Will in Luke–Acts* (BIS, 85; Leiden, 2007).

27. Commentaries include Craig S. Keener, *The Gospel of John: A Commentary* (2 vols.; Peabody, 2003); John Marsh, *Saint John* (Harmondsworth, 1968); Bruce J. Malina and Richard L. Rohrbaugh, *Social-Science Commentary on the Gospel of John* (Minneapolis, 1998); Barnabas Lindars, *The Gospel of John* (NCB; London, 1972); Raymond E. Brown, *The Gospel According to John* (AB, 29, 29a; New York, 1966, 1970); and E. Haenchen, *John* (2 vols.;

Hermeneia; Minneapolis, 1980). Studies include D. Moody Smith, *Johannine Christianity: Essays on its Setting, Sources and Theology* (Columbia, 1984); *idem, John among the Gospels: The Relationship in Twentieth-Century Research* (Minneapolis, 1992); *idem, The Theology of the Gospel of John* (Cambridge, 1995); Raymond E. Brown, *The Community of the Beloved Disciple* (London, 1979); *idem, Introduction to the Gospel of John* (ABRL; New York, 2003); R. Alan Culpepper, *The Johannine School* (SBLDS, 26; Missoula, 1975); *idem, The Gospel and Letters of John* (IIBT; Nashville, 1998); Claus Westermann, *The Gospel of John in the Light of the Old Testament* (Peabody, 1998); and Raimo Hakola, *Identity Matters: John, the Jews, and Jewishness* (NovTSup, 118; Leiden, 2005).

28. According to Eusebius, *Hist. Eccl.* 6.14.7.
29. See Frans van Segbroeck and Christopher M. Tuckett (eds), *The Four Gospels 1992: Festschrift Frans Neirynck* (3 vols.; Louvain, 1992); and Ian D. Mackay, *John's Relationship with Mark: An Examination of John 6 in the Light of Mark 6–8* (WUNT, 182; Tübingen, 2004).
30. See the discussion of all these matters in W.G. Kümmel, *Introduction to the New Testament* (revised ET London, [17]1975), pp. 188–247.

INDEX OF ANCIENT SOURCES

INDEX OF NAMES